Myth, legend, dust

Myth, legend, dust

Critical responses to Cormac McCarthy

edited by
Rick Wallach

Manchester University Press

Copyright © Manchester University Press 2000

While copyright in the volume as a whole is vested in Manchester University Press, copyright in individual chapters belongs to their respective authors, and no chapter may be reproduced wholly or in part without the express permission in writing of both author and publisher.

Published by Manchester University Press
Altrincham Street, Manchester M1 7JA
www.manchesteruniversitypress.co.uk

British Library Cataloguing-in-Publication Data is available

ISBN 978 0 7190 5947 6 hardback
ISBN 978 0 7190 5948 3 paperback

First published 2000

The publisher has no responsibility for the persistence or accuracy of URLs for any external or third-party internet websites referred to in this book, and does not guarantee that any content on such websites is, or will remain, accurate or appropriate.

Typeset in Minion
by Best-set Typesetter Ltd, Hong Kong

Contents

Acknowledgements	*page* viii
List of contributors	x
Editor's introduction: Cormac McCarthy's canon as accidental artifact *Rick Wallach*	xiv
A writer's view of Cormac McCarthy *Madison Smartt Bell*	1
Part I The Appalachian works	**13**
Prefiguring Cormac McCarthy: the early short stories *Rick Wallach*	15
'They aint the thing': artifact and hallucinated recollection in Cormac McCarthy's early frame-works *Dianne C. Luce*	21
'Like something seen through bad glass': narrative strategies in *The Orchard Keeper* *William Prather*	37
Imposition and resistance in *The Orchard Keeper* *Barbara Brickman*	55
The evolution of the dead girlfriend motif in *Outer Dark* and *Child of God* *Nell Sullivan*	68
'He's hell when he's well': Cormac McCarthy's rhyming dictions *Terri Witek*	78
Detailing the wor(l)d in *Suttree* *Béatrice Trotignon*	89
The seventh direction, or Suttree's vision quest *William C. Spencer*	100

Ruder forms survive: Cormac McCarthy's atavistic vision 108
Matthew Guinn

Part II A detour into drama 117

Older professions: the fourth wall of *The Stonemason* 119
Peter Josyph

Cormac McCarthy's *The Stonemason*: the unmaking of a play 141
Edwin T. Arnold

Part III From east to west: shared elements in the Appalachian and Southwestern novels 155

McCarthy music 157
Jay Ellis

'I aint come back rich, that's for sure,' or the questioning of market economies in Cormac McCarthy's novels 171
Christine Chollier

The process of elimination: tracing the prodigal's irrevocable passage through Cormac McCarthy's southern and western Novels 177
John Vanderheide

Part IV The Border tetralogy 183

'A false book is no book at all': the ideology of representation in *Blood Meridian* and the Border Trilogy 185
David Holloway

De los herejes y huérfanos: the sound and sense of Cormac McCarthy's border fiction 201
Linda Townley Woodson

'A certain but fugitive testimony': witnessing the light of time in Cormac McCarthy's Southwestern fiction 209
John Beck

Liberty beyond its proper bounds: Cormac McCarthy's history of the West in *Blood Meridian* 217
Neil Campbell

Into the darkening land, the world to come: Cormac McCarthy's border crossings 227
Mark Busby

'Mexico para los Mexicanos': revolution, Mexico, and McCarthy's Border Trilogy 249
John Wegner

Female presence, male violence, and the art of artlessness in the Border Trilogy 256
Patrick W. Shaw

Contents

Games in the Border Trilogy *Marty Priola*	269
'The hands of yet other puppets': figuring freedom and reading repetition in *All the Pretty Horses* *James D. Lilley*	272
The trapper mystic: werewolves in *The Crossing* *S. K. Robisch*	288
The last stage of the hero's evolution: Cormac McCarthy's *Cities of the Plain* *Charles Bailey*	293
Appendixes Index of character names in the novels *Kyle Kirves*	303
Bibliography	386
Index	395

Acknowledgements

To everyone who has assisted or tolerated me for the two years I've taken to assemble this collection while juggling myriad other obligations, I must express my gratitude. First, of course, my wife Rowena, although wonderful, has had nothing to do with this anthology beyond keeping our house from falling in on my head while I paid attention to little else. I would, however, like to thank my insomnia, without which it might have taken months longer to complete this book. My friend and confidant of over fifteen years, Peter Josyph, was especially forthcoming with gratuitous criticism and suggestions; I wish I had a nickel for every nickel they have cost me.

I am also grateful to the venerable scholars of McCarthy's work, like Chip Arnold and Dianne Luce, and the correspondents to the Cormac McCarthy online forum for their insights and suggestions. I have for years gleefully stolen their ideas and taken credit for them, and fess up at last for the privilege. Although I know it is traditional for an editor to assume sole responsibility for the final product, I'm going to set a precedent for the new millennium by insisting that, since they claim to be my friends and accept a portion of the credit, they should share the blame as well if my work blows an occasional microchip. Moreover, it's high time that somebody besides Madison Bell bought *me* a drink.

Finally, I must acknowledge the enthusiastic support of the members of The Cormac McCarthy Society in North America, Europe and the Pacific Rim. Many, if not most, of the articles and essays anthologized here were originally written for, and presented at Society conferences in Texas, North Carolina and Germany, and at conference sessions sponsored by the Society at other venues such as the American Literature Association conferences. I have stalked the halls of the Academy in one guise or another for near on thirty years now and know of no other group of scholars so cheerfully prolific; this volume is dedicated to all of them. Anyone interested in the Society and its many worthy activities, not the least of which is a lively discussion forum, can access their home page on the World Wide Web at www.cormacmccarthy.com.

Miami, Florida

Several of the essays in this collection have appeared elsewhere, and appear here by the kind permission of their authors and/or publishers. 'Cormac McCarthy's *The Stonemason*: the unmaking of a play' by Edwin T. Arnold appeared in *Southern Quarterly* 33 (Winter–Spring 1995). 'Imposition and resistance in *The Orchard Keeper*' by Barbara Brickman appeared in *Southern Quarterly* 38 (Winter 2000). Parts of 'Liberty beyond its

Acknowledgements

proper bounds: Cormac McCarthy's history of the West in *Blood Meridian*' appeared in *Critique* 39:1 (Fall 1997). 'Ruder forms survive: Cormac McCarthy's atavistic vision' appears in slightly different form in *After Southern Modernism: Fiction of The Contemporary South* by Matthew Guinn, University of Mississippi Press (2000). Parts of 'Older professions: the fourth wall of *The Stonemason*' by Peter Josyph appeared in *Southern Quarterly* 36 (Fall 1997). 'Detailing the wor(l)d in *Suttree*' by Béatrice Trotignon was published in a slightly different form in *Proceedings of the First European Conference on Cormac McCarthy*, The Cormac McCarthy Society (1999). ' "He's hell when he's well": Cormac McCarthy's rhyming dictions' by Terri Witek appeared in *Shenandoah* 41:3 (1991).

A group of these chapters was published in slightly different form as proceedings of the 1998 Annual Conference of the Cormac McCarthy Society in the journal *Southwestern American Literature* 25:1 (Fall 1999): ' "I aint come back rich, that's for sure," or the questioning of market economies in Cormac McCarthy's novels' by Christine Chollier, 'The process of elimination: tracing the prodigal's irrevocable passage through Cormac McCarthy's southern and western Novels' by John Vanderheide, ' "A certain but fugitive testimony": witnessing the light of time in Cormac McCarthy's Southwestern fiction' by John Beck, ' "Mexico para los Mexicanos": revolution, Mexico, and McCarthy's Border Trilogy' by John Wegner, and 'Female presence, male violence, and the art of artlessness in the Border Trilogy' by Patrick W. Shaw.

Contributors

Edwin T. Arnold is a professor of English at Appalachian State University in Boone, NC. He is the coeditor (with Dianne C. Luce) of *Perspectives on Cormac McCarthy* (1993, rev. edn 1999). He has also published books on William Faulkner, Erskine Caldwell, film director Robert Aldrich, and nineteenth-century southwest humorist Henry Clay Lewis. He and Luce most recently coedited a special issue of the *Southern Quarterly* devoted to McCarthy's Border Trilogy (Spring 2000).

Charles Bailey is an essayist, short-story writer, and critic. He has taught English at East Texas State University (now Texas A&M at Commerce) and at Pierce College in Woodland Hills, California. Currently he lives in Houston and teaches at San Jacinto College in Pasadena, Texas.

John Beck is a postdoctoral research fellow at Darwin College, Cambridge, England. He is currently writing a book on representations of the Southwest in literature, photography, and art.

Madison Smartt Bell is the author of nine novels, including *The Washington Square Ensemble* (1983), *Waiting for the End of the World* (1985), *Straight Cut* (1986), *The Year of Silence* (1987), *Doctor Sleep* (1991), *Save Me, Joe Louis* (1993) and *Soldier's Joy*, which received the Lillian Smith Award in 1989. Bell has also published two collections of short stories: *Zero db* (1987) and *Barking Man* (1990). His eighth novel, *All Soul's Rising*, was a finalist for the 1995 National Book Award and the 1996 PEN/Faulkner Award. His ninth, *Ten Indians*, was published by Pantheon in November 1997. Born and raised in Tennessee, he has lived in New York and in London and now lives in Baltimore, Maryland. A graduate of Princeton University (A.B. 1979) and Hollins College (M.A. 1981), he has taught in various creative writing programs, including the Iowa Writers' Workshop and the Johns Hopkins University Writing Seminars. Since 1984 he has taught at Goucher College, along with his wife, the poet Elizabeth Spires. He currently directs the Kratz Center for Creative Writing at Goucher.

Barbara Jane Brickman is a Ph.D. candidate at the University of Rochester, New York. Her research interests include Film Studies, Twentieth-Century British Literature and popular culture.

Mark Busby is Director of the Center for the Study of the Southwest and Professor of English at Southwest Texas State University. He received his Ph.D. from the University of Colorado, Boulder, in 1977. His books include *Larry McMurtry and the West: An Ambivalent Relationship* (1995) and *Ralph Ellison* (1991). He is editor of *New Growth/2: Short Stories of Contemporary Texas* (1993) and coeditor (with Dick Heaberlin) of the journals

Contributors xi

Southwestern American Literature and *Texas Books in Review*. He has published in *Western American Literature*, *MELUS*, *New Mexico Humanities Review*, *A Literary History of the American West*, and elsewhere. His stories are in *Texas Short Stories* and *Texas Short Stories II*, and his novel is forthcoming from Texas Christian University Press. In 1996 he was inducted into the Texas Institute of Letters and currently serves as its secretary-treasurer.

Neil Campbell is Head of American Studies at the University of Derby, England. His published works include *American Cultural Studies* (Routledge, 1997), *The Cultures of the New West* (Edinburgh University Press, forthcoming) and, as editor, *The Radiant Hour: Youth and American Culture* (Exeter University Press, forthcoming).

Christine Chollier wrote the first Ph.D. thesis on Cormac McCarthy in France. She lectures at Reims University where she teaches American literature and continues to write about Cormac McCarthy.

Jay Ellis is a novelist, poet, and jazz musician. He teaches at New York University, where he is writing a dissertation on Cormac McCarthy.

Matthew Guinn received his Ph.D. at the University of South Carolina in 1998 and currently teaches at the University of Mississippi. His book on postmodern southern writing, *After Southern Modernism: Fiction of the Contemporary South*, is forthcoming from the University Press of Mississippi.

David Holloway received his Ph.D. from the University of Nottingham in 1995. He teaches in the Department of American Studies at the University of Derby in England, and is writing a book on Cormac McCarthy. He has previously taught for The Open University, and De Montfort University Leicester.

Peter Josyph works concurrently as a writer, painter, actor-director, and filmmaker. His books are *What One Man Said to Another: Talks With Richard Selzer*, and *The Wounded River*, which was a *New York Times* Notable Book of 1993. He cofounded Victory Rep in New York, where he wrote fifty plays. His series of paintings *Cormac McCarthy's House* exhibited at the Centennial Museum in El Paso, Texas. He is currently writing a series of novels about Matisse, and is making a documentary, *Acting McCarthy*, about the films *The Gardener's Son* and *All the Pretty Horses*.

Kyle Kirves works as a writer and journalist in Longmont, Colorado. He holds degrees in English from the Ohio University and the University of Dayton. He completed several research projects on Cormac McCarthy in conjunction with the completion of his Masters degree.

James D. Lilley's work on McCarthy has appeared in *ISLE* and *Southern Quarterly*. He is coeditor with Robert Brinkmeyer of *Writing (on) the Border: Essays on Cormac McCarthy's Fiction*, and coauthor of 'An Interview with Barry Hannah' (*Mississippi Review* 1997). Lilley is particularly interested in minority, postcolonial, and border literatures, and his essay, '"The Short Way of Saying Mexicano": Patrolling the Borders of Mario Suárez's Fiction,' is forthcoming in *MELUS*. He is coediting *The Future of Border Studies*, a collection of essays which examine the specificities of transnational border culture and contact, and is working on a dissertation at the University of Arizona that explores how Indian Removal was remembered, and forgotten, in early nineteenth-century American culture.

Dianne C. Luce is coeditor (with Edwin T. Arnold) of *Perspectives on Cormac McCarthy* (1993, rev. edn 1999). She has written on McCarthy, Faulkner, Simms, and other southern writers, and is compiler of the English-language Cormac McCarthy bibliography maintained on the Cormac McCarthy Society website. Dr. Luce chairs the English Department of Midlands Technical College in Columbia, SC.

William Prather is a doctoral candidate at the University of Georgia. He teaches literature at North Georgia College and State University in Dahlonega, Georgia.

Marty Priola earned his B.A. in English Language and Literature at Christian Brothers University and his *Juris Doctor* from the University of Memphis. In 1995, he started an internet site devoted to Cormac McCarthy and his work, which evolved into what is now *www.cormacmccarthy.com*. Marty continues to work with the Cormac McCarthy Society as its webmaster and assistant secretary. He has been a participant at most of the major McCarthy conferences since the Society's inception in 1996, and was awarded first prize in 1998 in the El Paso Public Library's 'Not Cormac' parody contest for his entry, 'All the Pretty Pebbles.'

S. K. Robisch currently teaches at Purdue University and lives in Battle Ground, Indiana with his wife, Patricia Henley, and their cat. He has written short stories and criticism for various publications.

Patrick W. Shaw is a professor of American literature at Texas Tech University. His essays have appeared in such journals as *American Literature, Literature and Psychology*, and *Southern Literary Journal*. He is the author of *Willa Cather and the Art of Conflict* (1992) and *The Modern American Novel of Violence* (1999).

William C. Spencer is a professor of English at Delta State University. His dissertation, entitled 'The Extremities of Cormac McCarthy,' was completed in 1993 at the University of Tennessee in Knoxville. He was the first editor of *The Cormac McCarthy Journal* and has published articles on McCarthy previously in *Sacred Violence, Southern Quarterly, POMPA*, and *Beacham's Encyclopedia of Popular Fiction*. Currently, he is vice-president of the Cormac McCarthy Society.

Nell Sullivan received a Ph.D. in American Literature from Rice University and is currently Assistant Professor of English at the University of Houston-Downtown. Her previous publications include articles on Eavan Boland, William Faulkner, Nella Larsen, and, of course, Cormac McCarthy.

Béatrice Trotignon is currently completing a Ph.D. on Cormac McCarthy at the Institut Charles V (Université Paris VII) and teaches English at the University of Tours.

John Vanderheide is currently working on his Ph.D. in English at the University of Western Ontario in London, Canada.

Rick Wallach teaches literature at the University of Miami. He is the editor, with Wade Hall, of *Sacred Violence: A Reader's Companion to Cormac McCarthy*, and has published numerous articles on Cormac McCarthy, William Faulkner, Patrick White, Charles Brockden Brown, critical theory, and other topics in modern fiction and American cultural studies. He is currently writing a book on jazz as representation and structural model in American fiction.

John Wegner is an Assistant Professor at Angelo State University in San Angelo, TX where he is also the editor of the *Cormac McCarthy Journal OnLine*. He has published on McCarthy, Hawthorne, and Ellen Glasgow.

Terri Witek received her doctorate from Vanderbilt University, where she studied with Vereen Bell, Donald Davie, and Mark Jarman. She has published a book of criticism, *Robert Lowell and Life Studies: Revising the Self* (University of Missouri Press, 1993) as well as poems which have appeared in *The New Republic, The Antioch Review, The Threepenny Review, Poetry, The Southern Review, The New England Review*, and other journals. She has been the recipient of a Florida Individual Artists Fellowship, and currently heads the Tim Sullivan Endowment for Writing Program at Stetson University, where she is an associate professor.

Linda Townley Woodson is Division Director of English, Classics, Philosophy, and Communication, and Professor of English at the University of Texas at San Antonio. Her research and interests include contemporary rhetorical theory, history of rhetoric, composition studies, and literature of Texas and the Southwest.

Rick Wallach

Editor's introduction: Cormac McCarthy's canon as accidental artifact

Seven years ago, following the first scholarly conference on Cormac McCarthy at Bellarmine College in Louisville, Kentucky, Texas Western Press asked Wade Hall and me to assemble from the conference presentations an anthology of essays which came to be titled *Sacred Violence* (1995). It was the third critical book about McCarthy's work published to that date. The second, Edwin Arnold and Dianne Luce's *Perspectives on Cormac McCarthy* (1993, rev. 1999), had been only recently issued. The first, Vereen Bell's groundbreaking *The Achievement of Cormac McCarthy* (1988), had been the sole critical resource for a small coterie of Cormackians (so called, one assumes, to avoid the pejorative allusiveness of 'McCarthyites') who were even then surely more numerous outside the academy than within it.

While his popularity has since inflated the ratio of his non-scholarly admirers, the last half-decade has also witnessed a burgeoning of academic McCarthy criticism. Arbiters of ye alabaster turret have introduced into pedagogy all of McCarthy's works, singly in genre-themed courses ('Modern American Fiction,' 'Literature of the American South/West') or collectively in dedicated courses. This is gratifying to those of us who encouraged study of his work through some or, as in Wade Hall's and Vereen Bell's cases, virtually all of the years before his 'discovery'.

With the conclusion of his epic Border Trilogy, begun with *All the Pretty Horses* (1992) and fleshed out by *The Crossing* (1994) and *Cities of the Plain* (1998), the McCarthy canon, though still in progress, has defaulted to us a neat symmetry. Onward from *The Orchard Keeper* (1965) he penned four more brilliant novels that rarely sold out their limited editions, working in an obscurity he did little to dispel except go on writing. As Madison Smartt Bell's prefatory essay demonstrates, though, he won the admiration of fellow writers while his reticence about his personal life and work became legendary. Then in 1992 he was, to invoke one of his most neatly turned phrases, spalded into the glare of bestsellerdom with *All the Pretty Horses*. Six years later, the antiphon of *Cities of the Plain* advised us that 'the story's told / turn the page,' suggesting a consummation had been achieved. In the wake of the Trilogy, then, the canon assumes the form of a temporary, if

Editor's introduction

not accidental, artifact whose shape is as much a product of what McCarthy has not yet written as of what he has published already. Ergo, the critical essays in this anthology take for their subject an artifice of time and textuality without disavowing the caveat of its formal impermanence.

Because several of these essays address the *unity* of McCarthy's canon, I want to stress the unique *division* of McCarthy's production (to date) into two geographic settings and sensibilities. The four Appalachian novels, *The Orchard Keeper* (1965), *Outer Dark* (1968), *Child of God* (1973) and *Suttree* (1979), and the two dramas, *The Gardener's Son* (1977) and *The Stonemason* (1994), demonstrate no structural coherence *as a set*. Nevertheless they are all in one way or another preoccupied with nostalgia for a receding paradise organically associated with lived youth and innocence. The movement towards expiation of this nostalgia, whose culmination is vividly depicted as the demolition of Knoxville's McAnally Flats neighborhood in the closing scene of *Suttree*, is a crucial thematic force in all the Appalachian works.

The Southwestern novels, *Blood Meridian* (1985) and the Border Trilogy, are built upon a very different foundation of mythic (or mythologized) national/cultural nostalgia – in particular, for a vanished pioneer lifestyle once galvanized by the individualism of the cowboy ethos. The conclusion of the Trilogy finally deposits Billy Parham, its sole surviving protagonist, in a family farmhouse early in the twenty-first century. McCarthy, likewise, has deposited his canon upon the cusp of the millennium facing backwards and forwards at once. Although the Southwestern adventures may share and amplify thematic concerns from the Appalachian works, they exhibit marked stylistic departures from their predecessors. Most important, the four Southwestern novels are unified by symmetries of chronology, geography, and diegetic overlapping. Any of these fundamental differences between the groups of texts would be defining generic qualifications even if the abrupt shift in geographical setting of the narratives were not alone a factor. Considering that McCarthy grew up in Appalachia and did not move to Texas until he was nearly fifty years old, we should not be surprised to discern such a pattern in the recent evolution of his work.

As the first anthology of critical essays to arrive post-Trilogy, the point of these readings is not to beta-test, refute or invoke iconographically the name or ideological signature of any critic or critical school. Although it is surely high time for ideologically unified or thematically specialized interrogations of McCarthy's work, I have here selected essays that display a range of critical methodologies because I believe that his canon still needs some exemplary treatments from perspectives not yet brought to bear in print. Marxist approaches like David Holloway's and feminist treatments like Nell Sullivan's have been especially wanting. I also include two personal essays by substantial artists in their own right, Madison Smartt Bell and Peter Josyph, to contradict the fallacious albeit widespread perception that authors of McCarthy's rank mainly stimulate academic responses if they stimulate anyone at all. So different in tone and scope, both essays stress the principle of personal influence in its most kaleidoscopic sense: culture as a sum of moments of inspiration and response transmitted from artist to artist via pathways that are anything but academic. Moreover, these essays also resonate with the pleasure of constructing that most personal creative artifice, the one that sustains all literature but which is never the same even unto itself nor ever lasts long enough to become an artifact: a *reading*. No anthology of McCarthy criticism could represent itself as a balanced account of his work lacking such expositions of readerly *jouissance*.

Another of my aims has been to remedy shortfalls in specific areas of McCarthy stylistics criticism. Three chapters follow having to do with McCarthy's euphonics. The pieces are different enough from each other – one treating the early works (Witek), one the later (Woodson), and one tracing the *evolution* of his technical mastery over the sound-sense of language (Ellis) – so that they give a well-textured overview of one of the most important aspects of his genius. I have also anthologized from prior publications essays which were pioneering discussions of their subjects, like Terri Witek's chapter on McCarthy's rhyming slang, or discussions of topics that are rarely considered but need to be, like Edwin Arnold's account of the human follies which doomed the production of McCarthy's only published play, *The Stonemason*. In her chapter Dianne Luce discusses McCarthy's television drama *The Gardener's Son* but, because the few extant copies of the film are confined to university and public film libraries, it is virtually impossible to view except at the annual Cormac McCarthy Society conferences, where it is a regular feature. Hence, I've concentrated on critiques of the most available texts.

I also meant this edition to be useful as a reference text. McCarthy has spun off a pantheon of major and minor characters, each one, even the most briefly introduced, deftly detailed and unique. But there are so many of them! The appendixes alphabetically list most of these figures, with the pages where they first occur. An indefatigable Kyle Kirves assembled them, and I feel sure not a few students of McCarthy's stories will be grateful for his industry.

Madison Smartt Bell

A writer's view of Cormac McCarthy

I was first introduced to Cormac McCarthy by George Garrett. I was a sophomore at Princeton University, and George was teaching his last semester before his departure from Princeton. I used to drop in and talk to him in the late afternoons. I forget how the subject of McCarthy came up, but maybe I had asked George what younger southern writers were worth paying attention to, besides Harry Crews, whose work I was very fond of at that time.

George said: *You know that old joke? There was an old hobo named Dave/ who kept a dead whore in a cave/&c &c &c. Well, Cormac McCarthy wrote a whole book on this premise and you ought to read it.*

I filed this information away for several years, during which time I moved to New York City and became, among other things, an habitué of the Strand Bookstore, a huge second-hand emporium, just a few blocks up lower Broadway from the New Wave Boutique/Army Surplus Store where I worked a security job. I didn't make a lot of money doing this, so when I saw something I wanted at the Strand I would sometimes have to climb a ladder and hide the item between rows of books on a high shelf until such time as I had the money to pay for it. Apparently that practice was fairly common because the Strand had signs up prohibiting it.

Anyway, I was walking through the Strand one day and saw a stack of somewhat battered copies of *Child of God*. The bell rang – this was the book George Garrett had told me about . . . the one about the dead whore in the cave. I picked it up. At $2.95 I didn't even have to stash it somewhere till payday. I had money in my pocket to buy it then and there and have the cashier drop it into a little red and white plastic bag for me. Besides, there was a big stack of them that went all the way down to the floor. This was in 1982 or 1983, and Cormac McCarthy was looking at a bare market then.

I took the book home and read it, fascinated and perplexed, and the next week sometime I went back into the Strand to see what else they had. Not *The Orchard Keeper*, not *Outer Dark*, but a big fat book called *Suttree*. On the back jacket was a full-cover picture of McCarthy himself, looking beefy enough to play football. He was standing on some kind of metal rigging, maybe a fire escape, above the

Knoxville riverfront, wearing a pair of bellbottom jeans with anchors on the cuffs of them (no kidding!) and firing a big toothy grin at the camera. The slightly tattered cover said that it was his fourth published novel but had begun as his first. I bought that one too and carried it home.

I think that for about the next two years, *Suttree* was never out of my hand's reach, whenever I was at my place in Brooklyn. If I was eating or typing, the book would be on the table somewhere. It went to bed with me at night and got up with me in the morning. It was a big sloppy novel and you didn't really have to approach it in an organized way. You could start reading it anywhere and there wasn't any good reason to stop.

At that stage of the literary game, the writers in vogue were sleek, slender, Twiggy-like minimalists. Raymond Carver, Jay McInerney. The first writers from the Gordon Lish fiction factory – Captain Fiction's Master Class – were beginning to come off the production line. Tama Janowitz was about fifteen minutes away from her regulation fifteen minutes of fame . . . and so on.

I wasn't much interested in these writers or their work. I read them without prejudice to begin with, because they came very highly recommended, but ended up unable to see what the excitement was supposed to be about. The work seemed bland, dull, empty . . . at least to me. It was good to have a big messy salivating hairy book to read in place of that. I kept rereading *Suttree* for twenty months or so. Just open it up anywhere.

In those days my first novel had either just come out or was about to. My friend Tom Alderson, who had just got out of the Army, was up at the Columbia MFA program, finishing his first collection of stories. We used to go around town together, and I told him where the McCarthy books could be found at the Strand. We used to get together and talk about them, often at a low-rent Welsh bar which was conveniently placed at the intersection of the West Side IRT with the Canarsie line and which, due to kismet no doubt, was actually called McCarthy's. These conversations weren't analytic or critical. They were more like that old gag where the prisoners in the penitentiary tell jokes by number. 3456, one con would say, and all the rest burst out laughing.

'"Do what," Ballard said,' Tom might quote, and we'd both grin and chuckle. He didn't have to go through the scene that led up to that line because we both had it memorized.

We had discovered something, but we didn't quite know what. The style was dense, demanding, sometimes downright difficult. The intentions were opaque and obscure. *No doubt the stuff has its limitations*, Tom would say to me a good many years later, *but when you once start reading it you just don't feel like reading anything else.*

At the time I am talking about, Cormac McCarthy was what you call a 'writers' writer,' which is, as my editor Cork Smith explained to me early on, a thing you don't want to be. The 'writer's writer' is read and admired and studied and heroized . . . but only by other writers, and as everyone knows there aren't enough of *them* to make the gears of a cash register turn very fast. There is nothing more flattering to your artistic ego than becoming a writer's writer, and nothing more deflating to your purse.

The early McCarthy admirers, clusters of devotees like me and Tom Alderson, had kind of an odd relationship to this situation. In one way you wanted to lift the bushel off the light of your discovery so as to let it illuminate more people. On the other hand you knew that if this ever happened, the books wouldn't be available for $2.95 any more, and your cherished secret would be lost to the world. Of course it's wonderful to see a writer's writer break out of that designation, but perhaps the delight of early McCarthy cult members at seeing their hero recognized by the awards and bestseller lists surrounding *All the Pretty Horses*, was tempered, maybe even soured, by the feeling that perhaps he had been sullied by so much sudden and popular attention. The idea of Cormac McCarthy as a celebrity writer, right up there with Tama Janowitz and everybody, was disheartening – though McCarthy, whose detestation of the celebrity game appears to be deeply rooted and sincere, managed to dodge that bullet. Almost. Even the obligatory interviews around the time of the National Book Award showed him with his guard held high. The *New York Times Magazine* profile ran a full color page and a half photograph of the back of his right ear.

Even before the bestseller lists, and the mostly deflected onslaught of the celebrity machine, there were people pulling for his wider recognition. That he was one of the first recipients of the famous MacArthur fellowship gave that operation instant credibility to a lot of his readers, including me. And two years before *All the Pretty Horses*, McCarthy drifted into the gunsight of *Esquire* magazine, with the result that Will Blythe (who'd been at Columbia around the same time as Tom) asked me to do a profile of him.

Now, I was thoroughly excited, thrilled as I could be. Just to meet the guy would be enough. Besides, it was *Esquire* magazine. You betcha, I said. But a complication developed. It seemed that McCarthy's agent, Amanda (Binky) Urban, preferred that they run the profile not now but in two years' time when the next McCarthy book would appear. I sensed unspoken irritation on the part of the magazine – who was she to be turning down an *Esquire* profile of her virtually unknown writer, or trying to set conditions for it? Anyway they had persuaded her to tell McCarthy neither yea or nay. Then they had put their heads together and decided that the initial approach should be made by me. Here was his address, a post office box in El Paso.

I wrote a fan letter expressing the seriousness of my interest and admiration, etc. The reply, while civil, was firmly negative. McCarthy hated publicity like poison, he wrote, and the only way he'd ever do it was if somebody told him he absolutely had to – which Ms. Urban must certainly have known when she conceded that she wouldn't tell him whether to do it or not. I thought this was pretty funny, despite my disappointment, and a nice little victory for her.

But while waiting for McCarthy's answer, I had been furnished with some background information, and I made one exploratory phone call, to Albert Erskine, recently retired from Random House, who'd been McCarthy's editor (as well as William Faulkner's). It took him a very long time to come to the phone. I like to think he was out fishing somewhere. When he finally picked up, I started in on the exposition of my project, but I didn't get very far before he burst out – *I don't see why you people can't leave a writer alone! Why don't you just read the damn books!*

BAMMM!

Good question, I thought, watching smoke curl out of the receiver. Why don't we?

In fact I had read the damn books many times over and would keep on reading them too. When one writer spends that long ruminating over another there will undoubtedly be influence – which is an interesting question concerning McCarthy – both the influence he has received and the influence he has transmitted.

As I see it McCarthy is one of the very few writers to walk through the shadow of Faulkner's high style and survive the experience. It has now been forgotten, maybe, that when Faulkner became critically popular, so late in his career and so very long after his much earlier spate of commercial popularity, he did spawn a good many stylistic imitators. But because Faulkner's high style is so very idiosyncratic, those imitators were all pretty rapidly recognized and dismissed as such.

Here the difference between Faulkner's and Hemingway's stylistic influence is glaring. Hemingway's style, apparently so simple and transparent, was so widely and easily imitated that it became the usual, typical voice for all American writers – from this plain-style evolved Raymond Carver and all *his* imitators who stood at the opposite end of the spectrum from McCarthy at the time when I first began reading him.

The Hemingway style was so nearly invisible that you could imitate it without getting caught (and wasn't everybody doing it anyhow?). But if you imitated Faulkner's densest, most elaborate rhetoric, what you were doing would be so painfully obvious that you would be sneered at for it. So a lot of writers just didn't go in that direction at all, and most of the ones who did ended up as blighted little acorns pushing up feeble sprouts under the vast shadow of Faulkner's huge, overshadowing achievement.

Not so with Cormac McCarthy. And yet, his style is hugely indebted to Faulkner's. Or to put it in more detail, McCarthy takes two very different styles, both of which were explored by Faulkner, and combines them in much the same way Faulkner did. The vernacular voice used mostly for dialogue or first person inserts, with its precisely rendered nuances of dialect and its strong southern accent, is embedded in a much denser voice pitched at a higher level of rhetoric – an oratorical, even vatic voice, reserved for pronouncements on the order of what Job heard from the whirlwind.

That vernacular voice is quite faithfully drawn from actual speech, and so Faulkner has no more special claim on it that anyone else with the ear and the skill to record it. But Faulkner's high style is much more idiosyncratically marked as his own, and McCarthy's high style uses the same devices: the long rolling run-on sentences, the repetition of conjunctions, the tendency to use linked independent clauses rather than subordinate clauses, the demanding vocabulary, the sonorous tone. Even the archaic diction of which McCarthy is so fond occurs (though to a lesser extent) in Faulkner. Moreover McCarthy's combination of this very, very literary language with passages in the vernacular voice seems directly derived from Faulkner.

And yet McCarthy's style does not *feel* derivative of Faulkner's. How, with so many similarities, can that be? I am reminded of that adage that while lesser artists borrow, truly great artists steal. Maybe McCarthy is simply big and strong enough to appropriate Faulkner's toolbag and use its contents to make artifacts entirely his own.

So we come to McCarthy's influence on others. I was very susceptible to this influence myself during those months I spent wallowing around with *Suttree* in my bed. I was in the doldrums then so far as writing was concerned. I was trying to start my second novel, which was supposed to be about a gang of terrorists blowing up New York City with a plutonium bomb, and which was partly set in a Brooklyn waterfront slum which I was having great difficulty expressing on paper. I tried my damnedest to imitate Cormac McCarthy's treatment of the McAnally Flats in *Suttree*, but somehow it didn't come out sounding like McCarthy. With luck, it came out sounding like me.

That was a deliberate effort to wrest McCarthy's high style into my own hands so that I could use it for my own purposes. During the same period, I also took a pass at his vernacular style. Like I said before, those dialects are out there to be listened to by them that's got ears to hear. I had been listening to the same sorts of voices as McCarthy, during my childhood in rural Tennessee, but still so far as rendering it on the page I was very consciously under McCarthy's influence when I wrote a little story called 'The Naked Lady.' I thought of the piece as a throwaway, not much count, but it ended up appearing in the inaugural issue of a little magazine called the *Crescent Review*, produced in the basement of the founding editor, Bob Shar, in Winston-Salem, North Carolina. From there it got picked up by the *Harper's* Readings section, and then made it into *Best American Short Stories*, and thanks to all that more people probably read that one story than read any of my first few novels.

I bring this up to show that, like any other bug, literary influence is virulently contagious. A few years later, when I was teaching at the Iowa Writers' Workshop, I met a young southern writer named Pinckney Benedict. According to the formalities of the situation he was supposed to be my student, but since he had already won the Nelson Algren Award and published a collection of stories I found very impressive, I tended to approach him as a colleague. Anyway in the course of some quasi-pedagogical encounter I mentioned that some of the stories in *Town Smokes* seemed to be much under the influence of Cormac McCarthy.

'Funny,' said Pinckney. 'People keep telling me that. But I've never read McCarthy. Maybe I should.'

Or maybe you shouldn't, I thought. What he said was plausible to me, because when my own first novel was going around, people kept telling me that it was excessively under the influence of Thomas Pynchon – this despite the fact that I had never managed to whip myself all the way through a Pynchon novel.

'You know where I really got the idea of writing that kind of dialect,' Pinckney said, 'is from that story of yours called "The Naked Lady."'

So, of course, I burst out laughing and told him right away that since that story was the most slavish McCarthy imitation I was capable of when I wrote it, he *was* in fact under the influence of McCarthy itself, even if it came through an intermediary. That's how transitive it can be, and who knows where it really started. McCarthy? Faulkner? the Book of Job?

Pinckney Benedict's excellent books, especially *Dogs of God*, have continued to have a McCarthyesque flavor, though I don't know if he ever got around to reading him or not. And McCarthy has continued to have an influence on me, and also (more noticeably since *All the Pretty Horses* enlarged his readership) on quite a few other people.

Among the examples I think the most interesting is Larry Brown's novel, *Father and Son*. Brown has gone on the record (in an independent short film called *In Search of Cormac McCarthy*) as saying that McCarthy is a more significant figure in the literary pantheon than Faulkner his own self. I think this pronouncement is particularly interesting since Larry Brown is sort of an auto-didact as a writer – or anyway, he never attended a Creative Writing Program and doesn't have an MFA. He taught himself to be a writer by studying books he was drawn to, and McCarthy's books seem to have drawn him hard.

I'll make two observations about Brown's most recent novel, *Father and Son*. First is that it captures the Cormac McCarthy style perfectly. It does not read like an imitation or something under the influence of. It reads like the real thing. You would think McCarthy had written it himself. Except (observation number two) for the content. The subject and the characters and the issues and concerns of Brown's novel belong one hundred percent to Larry Brown. They have nothing to do with what McCarthy writes *about*. Despite the stylistic resemblance, McCarthy would never have written such a book. Only Larry Brown could have conceived or executed it. It is tribute to the strength of Brown's own vision as a novelist that he could appropriate so much of McCarthy's technical and stylistic equipment without having any of McCarthy's attitudes toward the world rub off on him. Indeed Brown's relationship to McCarthy may be something like McCarthy's relationship to Faulkner.

Most writers are not this strong. Most writers, when they go out to steal style, end up with other baggage too.

The prize-winning, best-selling *Cold Mountain* is a case in point. Here again the author (in terms of the style of the work) appears to be channeling Cormac McCarthy. In the story line involving the wanderings of the wounded soldier Inman, not only the language but the content of the episodes is derived from McCarthy's work. Inman drifts around through a dark, inimical world, full of incomprehensible, unreasoning violence. He meets highwaymen and bushwhackers and other pilgrims with missions still more peculiar than his own and inscrutable but garrulous hermits who utter obscure but extensive discourses – in short he has all the adventures one would expect a Cormac McCarthy character to have. Except that those adventures do not have the same significance that they would have in a McCarthy novel. In fact they don't have any significance. These episodes constitute a series of ornamental layers draped over the sentimental love story at the heart of *Cold Mountain*. In this respect the novel resembles a marshmallow elaborately wrapped up in barbed wire, and so, no doubt, deserves its great success.

Then there is another I read not too long ago, whose title and author are unmemorable. This novel, about pioneers in the West, seems rather like a weak and fading echo of McCarthy's *Blood Meridian*. The author appears to have absorbed not only McCarthy's style but a superficial version of the substance. As so many writers used to do with Hemingway, he apes the gestures of the senior writer quite faithfully, but because the complex of ideas which motivates those gestures is not present in the derivative work, the imitated gestures are empty.

Unfortunately I think this is the best example of what happens to the average young writer falling under McCarthy's influence – and there will be more of those now that McCarthy is more widely read. The influencee is caught up, swept away, and obliterated. As Flannery O'Connor said of *her* attitude toward Faulkner, *you don't want your little old mule and wagon stalled on the track when the Dixie Limited comes roaring through.*

McCarthy's work may have its limitations, but when you once start reading it, you just don't want to read anything else.

Why is that?

It cannot be the style alone, though the beauty of the language, the sheer pleasure of washing around in McCarthy's sentences and paragraphs, is a large part of the attraction. That's why I have never managed to read any criticism of McCarthy's books. Sometimes I pick up a critical book, but I always get drawn off into the quotes, so then I put down the critical book and start reading the McCarthy novel all over again. McCarthy is infinitely rereadable, which most writers are not.

But the seduction of the work has as much to do with substance as with style. The substance, McCarthy's vision of the world, is magnetically attractive – though not because it is an especially pleasant vision.

I think McCarthy's opus so far can be divided into three phases. First is the sequence of *Suttree*, *The Orchard Keeper*, *Outer Dark*, *Child of God*, and *Suttree*. The three books in the middle are comparatively brief, perfectly crafted works. Not one hair is out of place in them. *Suttree*, the first novel eventually published as the fourth, brackets the series. *Suttree* is unlike the other books, being sloppy, baggy, shaggy and fundamentally unfinished, and yet it is a more ambitious work, not so much in terms of the issues raised as in the way they are addressed, than the three perfect little books it encloses.

Phase two consists of a single work, *Blood Meridian*, which marks a departure: McCarthy quits the Central South of his previous novels and becomes an historical novelist writing about the Old West. This novel is in my opinion McCarthy's masterpiece to date. In it the promise of *Suttree* is realized. That is, in *Blood Meridian*, McCarthy produces a book which seems to be rambling and disorganized and chaotic but which in fact expresses the occult formal order of the three short works which precede it.

The third phase is the Border Trilogy.

I revert to the early McCarthy cult which included me and a fair number of other people, a fair number of yourselves I would guess, but not enough people to put a novel on a best-seller list. A lot of people in the cult were disappointed in *All the Pretty Horses*, thought that it was a weak and superficial work, and in fact some considered it to be a sell-out, despite or indeed because of its skyrocketing critical and commercial success.

Now I am going to make some unsubstantiated inferences, based in part on circumstances I've had to deal with in my own career. McCarthy published his first novel in the sixties, when the publishing climate was much friendlier to difficult literary novels than it is now. *Blood Meridian*, published in 1985, was (I believe) his last book edited by Albert Erskine. Ecstatically received by McCarthy cult members, *Blood Meridian* sank, with scarcely a ripple, in the commercial marketplace.

It's easy to forget this now that McCarthy is a prizewinning, bestselling author, and in his own odd way a sort of inverse celebrity, but in the period immediately following *Blood Meridian*, his very survival as a published novelist would have been somewhat in doubt. I am guessing (I underline guessing) that in this situation he decided to make his new work somewhat more accessible by doing three things.

One: Introducing for the first time a truly sympathetic protagonist, with whom a reader could identify – first John Grady and then Billy Parham.

Two: Incorporating, again for the first time, a love story which in no way involved necrophilia.

Three: Dividing one long book into three more manageable units. The Border Trilogy has plenty enough unity of plot and theme to have been completed as a single novel, about the size of *Lonesome Dove* but a good deal less user-friendly. Breaking it into more easily digestible servings would have been a sane career move.

Do these three moves constitute a sell-out?

I don't think so. Mere survival for the literary novelist has become a very tricky business these days, and I think McCarthy negotiated his survival with less compromise than most. I also think that the content of the work is fundamentally uncompromised.

On my first reading of *All the Pretty Horses* I thought that McCarthy had sold all us faithful cult members down the river. Or at least that he had lowered himself to write an 'entertainment' like Graham Greene used to do. Six months later I read the book again and realized that the book contained all the same messages of the earlier work, though they were coated in a different way that made them easier to swallow. This too reminded me of something Flannery O'Connor said in a letter to a friend who was a playwright – *you have to figure out a way where they can see it on Monday but it won't make them sick until Wednesday.*

Despite the fact that *All the Pretty Horses* is the first Cormac McCarthy novel to feature a proper, conventional hero, the content is very much antiheroic. John Grady's heroic gestures and actions are completely futile and accomplish nothing except to win the respect of a few witnesses, like the judge who validates his ownership of his horses at the end of the story . . . like the reader. Even the love story, which offended apostate cult members more than anything else, is used to prove that same futility, most tellingly in the scene when the children who interview John Grady soon after his departure from the Mexican hacienda are obliged to admit the seamless impossibility of his ever winning his *novia*.

Not only are the gestures and actions futile but in the larger scheme of things they are insignificant. That point is presaged in this passage from the opening:

> In the evening he saddled his horse and rode out west from the house. The wind was much abated and it was very cold and the sun sat blood red and elliptic under the reefs of bloodred cloud before him. He rode where he would always choose to ride, out where the western fork of the old Comanche road coming down out of the Kiowa country to the north passed through the westernmost section of the ranch and you could see the faint trace of it bearing south over the low prairie that lay between the north and middle forks of the Concho River. At the hour he'd always choose when the shadows were long and the ancient road was shaped before him in the rose and canted light like a dream of the past where the painted ponies and the riders of that lost nation came down out of the north with their faces chalked and their long hair plaited and each armed for war which was their life and the women and children and women with children at their breasts all of them pledged in blood and redeemable in blood only. When the wind was in the north you could hear them, the horses and the breath of the horses and the horses' hooves that were shod in rawhide and the rattle of lances and the constant drag of travois poles in the sand like the passing of some enormous serpent and the young boys naked on wild horses jaunty as circus riders and hazing wild horses before them and the dogs trotting with their tongues aloll and foot-slaves following half naked and sorely burdened and above all the low chant of their traveling song which the riders sang as they rode, nation and ghost of a nation passing in a soft chorale across that mineral waste to darkness bearing lost to all history and all remembrance like a grail the sum of their secular and transitory and violent lives. (5)

And the same point is confirmed by the conclusion:

> In four days riding he crossed the Pecos . . . and rode up out of the river breaks where the pumpjacks in the Yates Field ranged against the skyline rose and dipped like mechanical birds. Like great primitive birds welded up out of iron by hearsay in a land perhaps where such birds once had been. At that time there were still indians

> camped on the western plains and late in the day he passed in his riding a scattered group of their wickiups propped upon that scoured and trembling waste. They were perhaps a quarter mile to the north, just huts made from poles and brush with a few goathides draped across them. The indians stood watching him. He could see that none of them spoke among themselves or commented on his riding there nor did they raise a hand in greeting or call out to him. They had no curiosity about him at all. As if they knew all that they needed to know. They stood and watched him pass and watched him vanish upon that landscape solely because he was passing. Solely because he would vanish. (301)

The message is the same as what is telegraphed by the title of *Child of God*, by the phrase Tom Alderson and I used to quote to each other, without context. *A child of god – much the same as you, perhaps.* It is the answer to the question first asked in Suttree's discussions about the nature of God with the hermit under the bridge in that novel. This answer is what differentiates McCarthy from Faulkner. Despite a very strong current of fatalism in his work, Faulkner is a humanist, first and last. He sees things on a human scale – envisions a world made to the measure of humankind.

McCarthy is not a humanist. Nor is he an anarchist, nor a nihilist, as I think he has sometimes been called. There is order in his universe but that order doesn't have anything much to do with us. We can give it a name and even pray to it if we wish. It won't make any difference. The only answer we will receive is the sort of answer Job got from the whirlwind – the world itself flung back in our faces. On the universal scale, we do not matter.

The power and intensity of this vision sets McCarthy free of Faulkner's influence and makes him altogether his own writer, never mind all the stylistic devices he appropriated from Faulkner's work. It is in no way a comforting vision, although I think it is probably an appropriate vision to emerge in our literature at the end of our century, the end of our millennium, at the time when we human beings have initiated so many different processes likely to wipe our species from the face of the earth once and for all. McCarthy's answer to this predicament is that we don't matter. The order of the universe does not require our survival. We are not so important as we like to think.

And if McCarthy's stylistic imitators (yes, there will be more of them) don't pick up this essential message, which gives his style its reason for being, well . . . I think you can see why. From the human perspective, the message is fairly bad news, and it's not going to pay anybody to pass it along, though that message, above all, is what gives McCarthy's work its numinous attraction.

To close, here's one of my favorite expressions, from an early scene of *Blood Meridian*: a conversation between 'the kid' and the expriest Tobin.

> At night, said Tobin, when the horses are grazing and the company is asleep, who hears them grazing?
> Don't nobody hear them if they're asleep.
> Aye. And if they cease their grazing who is it that wakes?
> Every man.

Then, from slightly earlier in the same conversation:

> For let it go how it will, he said, God speaks in the least of creatures.
> The kid thought him to mean birds or things that crawl but the expriest, watching, his head slightly cocked, said: No man is give leave of that voice.
> The kid spat into the fire and bent to his work.
> I ain't heard no voice, he said.
> When it stops, said Tobin, you'll know you've heard it all your life. (124)

Part I

The Appalachian works

Rick Wallach

Prefiguring Cormac McCarthy: the early short stories

Cormac McCarthy's earliest short stories appeared in the literary supplement of *The Phoenix*, the University of Tennessee at Knoxville's student magazine: 'Wake for Susan,' credited to C. J. McCarthy Jr. in the October 1959 issue, and the second, 'A Drowning Incident,' was published in March 1960.[1] Recently, McCarthy turned down a request from the *Virginia Quarterly* to republish them, saying he hoped to be long buried and mouldering before they ever were published again.[2] McCarthy's chagrin may be overstated, if humorously so, even though these stories are products of an immature art. 'Wake for Susan' blurs the line between nostalgia and sentimentality on several occasions; 'A Drowning Incident' suffers from lapses in the design of what otherwise appears to be a thoughtful deployment of multiple tropes. Nevertheless the latter story is economically told and features some strikingly intricate imagery, hardly as embarrassing an effort as McCarthy seems to think it is. Moreover, the stories display in embryonic form most of the major themes, and a variety of already well-formed stylistic signatures, which would characterize his mature work within just a few more years.

With 'A Drowning Incident', McCarthy shed the patronymic 'Junior.' By his next publication, *The Orchard Keeper* (1965), he had replaced his given name, Charles, with its old Celtic equivalent, Cormac. If this sounds vaguely Oedipal, perhaps it is because both stories indeed represent youthful disaffection. Wes, the central figure of 'Wake for Susan,' and the unnamed child protagonist of 'A Drowning Incident' display acute Oedipal anxieties; the theme of the thwarted prodigal would continue to dominate McCarthy's Appalachian works.

In 'Wake for Susan,' predications of McCarthy's mature style are few and, except for a scattering of characteristic tags, this story could have been written by just about any nearly competent young author with an eye for naturalistic detail. However, the images of decay that pervade 'Wake' expose that unmistakable McCarthy vision wherein man-made objects are drawn back into an organic world whose processes of reclamation operate indistinguishably from processes of fecundity: 'It was longer home this way and harder walking among the rotting ties and lecherous honeysuckle. The sagging rails were brown and rusty with disuse' (3).

The narrative, even at this early stage of McCarthy's craft, is layered with ironies both subtle and biting. Wes disengages himself from his squirrel-hunting reveries because 'he still had the yard to mow' (3), a life of ennui which he escapes by retreating into the woods and, finally, by using old hog rifle balls he finds in the forest and the dulled legends on gravestones to stimulate his anaesthetized imagination. He's in no hurry to go home to his chores, from which he distances himself spatially by detouring through the woods and a ruined cemetery hidden therein, and temporally, by first imagining himself in the company of ghosts of pioneer woodsmen and, finally, in a fantasy romance with the occupant of one of the graves. Yet as the compounded ironies of the tale begin to emerge, Wes becomes rather less the second coming of Hawkeye than he does the resurrection of Faulkner's hapless hunter Boone Hogganbeck in *The Bear.* Wes hasn't hit a squirrel all morning, even 'the one that came slithering down the tree directly in front of him,' and 'the old cemetery was not exactly where he remembered it being' (3). En route to the cemetery, he keeps running into spider webs, and his clothing is inappropriate to the increasing warmth of the day.

Wes' daydreams also contain a touch of ironic self-mockery; the antique rifle balls he picks up from the forest floor, and which he uses to conjure up his antique ghosts, are only there to be found because they didn't hit their targets either. We should bear in mind, too, that nothing so disenfranchises a southerner from his regional heritage as ineptitude at woodsmanship and the hunt.[3] Given his adolescent awkwardness, Wes' desire to rewrite the past is understandable. Unfortunately, his regeneration by imagination masquerading as memory is limited by the horizon of the hunt as he knows it; the muzzle-loaded hog rifle balls he finds are primitive, yet they might have been used 'only thirty or forty years ago' (3). McCarthy's forthcoming Appalachian and western novels alike engage the conundrum of the lost craft of the hunt; the Appalachian protagonists often ache to recover lost crafts. John Wesley Rattner of *The Orchard Keeper* attempts to master fur trapping, whereas Buddy Suttree learns mussel brailing. In the later books – the Border Trilogy novels especially – John Grady Cole is a master horsebreaker and Billy Parham undergoes a short, intensive apprenticeship in wolf trapping, and both seek to reconstitute the entire lifestyle within which those crafts are embedded.

This nostalgic element in McCarthy's mature work is prefigured by the progress of Wes' reveries, since 'It was probably the discovery of the rifle ball that prompted him to look for the burial plot' (3), whereupon he daydreams a rich albeit ultimately thwarted domestic scenario through his romance with Susan Ledbetter, the young girl in one of the graves. Susan's desire for him – 'O don't go just yet, it's not so late,' she implores him – seems calculated to alleviate an awareness of his own clumsiness that his day in the woods has engendered. Nevertheless, his daydream collapses against the irreducible fact of her mortality:

> She would see him again tomorrow night.
> The stars came back; if their luster paled, was because a part of beauty was no longer there to receive them. In his eyes they swam blurred and distorted in a salt sea. The year was 1834 and it was a very good year.
> How had she died? The mute stones left no testimony. There were so many ways. (6)

Metaphors of limitation abound, whether in the hard flattened surfaces of the rifle ball and the gravestone or the autumnal setting of the story, a suspicion that death intrudes into art just as an element of failure inheres in all creative acts. Wes' imagination fills in the blank spaces in Susan's history. Nonetheless, like his inability to improve his woodsmanship beyond the evidence of the limited hunting skills of the ghosts he conjures, his imagination lacks the puissance to rewrite the part of her history he *does* know, namely, that she died too young to have married. Dianne Luce believes, though, that Wes' imaginary foray into heartbreak allegorizes 'the artist's creative awakening' (see below, 21). Indeed, when he strides home 'towering even among the lean trees' (6) after the deliberate catharsis of his tears, smiling enigmatically to himself, he appears to have achieved the first requisite for distinguishing mere daydreams from the tough business of artistic creativity: a degree of detachment. Such is further evident in his repeated refrain, 'Long enough leaves.' Pursuing this line of interpretation, years later McCarthy would explore what happens when creativity functions beyond limits, as *Child of God*'s Lester Ballard, by constructing his family of rotting corpses, crosses the very line at which Wes' imagination halted.

McCarthy's amalgamation of the themes of prodigality, oedipal anxiety, craft, and inferences of *Bildungsroman* shortly achieves more disciplined shape in *The Orchard Keeper*. The boy John Wesley Rattner, with the avuncular Ather's encouragement, studies trapping only to run afoul of the deputy Legwater. This noxious opportunist represents an urban order built on regulations and licenses, which are structural substitutes for, rather than incarnations of, instinct and craft. At the other extreme, in *Suttree* Gene Harrogate's slingshot, baited for bats with poisoned meat, represents the *reductio ad absurdum* both of John Wesley's hunting skills and of the necessary failure of self-imposed apprenticeship. Severing the chain of master and apprentice amplifies the alienation of these characters' social circumstances, their frustrated nostalgia. *The Crossing*'s Billy Parham, on the other hand, is finally successful thanks to the arcane encouragement he receives from the old wolf trapper, but removed from the context of a living culture Billy's venture also fails. The ghostly woodsmen whose conjuration by Wes becomes an exercise in self-mockery are the earliest templates for this current in McCarthy's tales.

Furthermore, Wes' distaste for quotidian responsibility prefigures the restlessness of many of McCarthy's youthful protagonists from John Wesley Rattner to *Blood Meridian*'s kid, John Grady Cole and Billy Parham. However, the quality of the distancing effect in 'Wake for Susan' distinguishes McCarthy's Appalachian figures from the protagonists of his western novels, who exhibit more complex, less often disengaged relationships to their domestic and Oedipal circumstances.

Family or communal structure remains a significant element of the idealized and evanescing societies the Southwestern protagonists yearn to perpetuate and inhabit; John Grady dies while attempting to marry, and the aged Billy's saga concludes as he's tucked into bed like a child.

Unfortunately, however, when Wes breaks down and cries 'for all the lost Susans, for all the people so beautiful, so pathetic, so lost and wasted and ungrieved' he reaches for an epiphanous moment beyond his spiritual capabilities, and as yet beyond McCarthy's skills to illustrate convincingly. In an otherwise unremarkable seventeen year old, such a cosmic seizure reads like an irruption of sentimentalism. Wes' movement from frustration at his inability to kill squirrels to an outpouring of pathos for an imagined paramour, which expands into an encompassing empathy with the entire membership of the species' past, qualifies as an excessive emotional response to an inadequate stimulus. It is the most glaring flaw in the execution of the story. Instead of a climactic breakthrough of his visionary potential, the outburst foregrounds Wes' self-denigration. By insinuating himself into his fantasies, he reduces his brief list of mourned human archetypes to stereotypes. He assimilates his imaginary sweetheart's beauty to his own shortcomings and anticipated consumption by history, and weeps for them both. The spectacle of this young man weeping among the dying and decaying leaves of the autumnal forest reaches for, but does not achieve, the unsentimental pathos of, say, Gerard Manley Hopkins' meditation among the autumn leaf falls in his great poem 'Spring and Fall: To a Young Child,' 'It is the blight man was born for, / It is Margaret you mourn for.' A few years later, however, in the conclusion of *The Orchard Keeper*, McCarthy would redeem this callow moment by co-opting Wordsworth's unsparing vision of the dead 'sheathed in the earth's crust and turning the slow diurnal of the earth's wheel' (244).

Six months after 'Wake,' the darker, more economical 'A Drowning Incident' appeared in *The Phoenix*. During the intervening months McCarthy appears to have banished sentimentalism as well as any hint of casual narrative sprawl, and the voice of the mature author suddenly becomes audible. Susan, denied her dream of wifely domesticity, has dwindled into Suzy, the rather less romantic, dug-dragging yard dog whose puppies the protagonist's father drowns. Once again, the organic world reclaims the manmade objects recumbent upon it, yet the descriptions are now more detailed, more succulent. When the boy enters the backyard outhouse, he swings 'the rotted door back carefully; the planks were warped and soft and velveted with a pale green patina'; or again, he crosses a small bridge whose 'curling planks were cracked and weathered, bleached an almost metallic gray. The whole affair bellied dangerously in the middle, like a well used mule' (3). Yet in this story, these images are no longer ornamental, merely underfoot or even merely ambient. They are now woven into intricate synchronies of signs and portents, some of which McCarthy blanches to their very geometry. The black widow in the outhouse is announced by 'the two tiny red triangles touching at their vertices,' a pure synecdoche that presages the wills in collision within the fiction.

When the boy disobeys parental orders and leaves his baby sister in the house to cross to the outhouse, both sets of rotting planks, in the outhouse door and bridge alike, predicate scenarios of death. The door leads to the cricket the boy stomps and drops, guts extruded, into the black widow's web. His sojourn on the bridge occasions his discovery of the decomposing puppies his father had drowned, one of whose entrails, like the viscera of the cricket, tumbles out. The description of the bridge as a mule's belly recalls Suzy, dragging her own pregnant belly; the mule, a sterile equine crossbreed, adumbrates the pregnant bitch whose puppies are so quickly destroyed. Deepening and complicating the equation, both visions of protruding entrails are allied with arthropod images; the cricket with the spider and the decaying puppy with the crawfish that has burrowed into its intestines and which, like the spider, the boy routes. As the boy is about to drop the sack containing the dead puppy into his baby sister's crib to avenge their destruction, he notices 'through a feathered split in the bottom little black hairs protruded like spiderfeet' (4). It may also be worth noting, I think, that the squashed cricket, 'kicking one leg in slow lethargic rhythm' (3), anticipates one of the many memorable vignettes in *Suttree*, the dying wharfarined rat, 'moving one rear leg in slow circles as if to music' in tune with the 'bad news in its belly' (100).

This grim tale presages McCarthy's later barren domestic environments. The illness and prevarication which shape the boy's family life anticipate the delusional Mrs. Rattner, the lie behind which Rinthy Holmes' baby is discarded in *Outer Dark*, the motherless home of Lester Ballard and his subsequent construction of a family of corpses, *Blood Meridian*'s own nameless kid, the complex bitterness that sunders the families of both Cornelius Suttree and John Grady Cole, and the premature death of Mac's wife Margaret – which also foreshadows the never to be occupied cottage John Grady remodels for his bride – in *Cities of the Plain*. 'A Drowning Incident' also introduces the theme of sibling rivalry which finds its most virulent and problematic expression in *Outer Dark*, wherein Culla sets out to murder his son/brother and pays for his crime by becoming a hounded vagrant. Similarly, the boy's discovery in the stream of Suzy's decomposing puppies with their protruding entrails anticipates Culla's discovery of his mutilated and, shortly thereafter, murdered and cannibalized child, as well as Suttree's dream of strangling his twin brother at birth with his umbilical cord. Dead children appear numerous times in *Blood Meridian*, most vividly in the scene of the mesquite bush upon which the Comanche war party has impaled a constellation of decomposing babies.

No doubt about it; a Cormac McCarthy novel is the last place you would want to turn up if you were a child. The new baby in 'A Drowning Incident' doesn't fare very well either; it is neglected, chronically ill, and ultimately bedded down with a putrefied puppy. Left to mind the child, the boy escapes from the house and sojourns in the woods instead. In any event, the narrative first refrains from personalizing the family's new baby: 'The baby was taking *its* nap' (3), then briefly refers to the baby as 'her,' but only in an annoyed and contemptuous tone: 'Then he heard her cough – she was always coughing' (4); gender only emphasizes the difference, or the opposition, between the siblings. Otherwise, the sibling is merely referred to as 'the baby,' a calculated depersonalization that stands the reader within the hostile frame of mind of the young protagonist. The boy's retaliation against his father conflates with his virulent resentment of his sister, and takes the form of a calculated assault on her instead: 'What prompted his next action was the culmination of all the schemes half formed not only walking from the creek but from the moment the baby arrived. Countless rejected, revised or denied thoughts moiling somewhere in the inner recesses of his mind struggled and merged' (4). Wes' extensive interior monologue, by contast, is compressed here into an enigmatic, distanced description of the boy's *process* of thinking, but reveals very little of its *content*. This descriptive distance from the character's center of consciousness reaches its apogee in the mature works, whereupon it would become another key tenet of McCarthy's style.

The armory of techniques represented by this little story is all the more impressive when one considers that, given the lead times inherent in publishing schedules, only five years elapsed between its appearance and the publication of *The Orchard Keeper*. This means that McCarthy took only a few years – three and a half at most – to advance from this short fiction to the full deployment of his youthful powers in that confident and accomplished first novel, powers so impressive that no less a literary giant than Ralph Ellison proclaimed himself envious of them.

Notes

1 Currently, the only way to locate copies of the two stories is through the University of Tennessee at Knoxville student publication archives.
2 Ted Genoways, personal communication.
3 See Francis Lee Utley, 'Pride and Humility: The Cultural Roots of Ike McCaslin,' in *Bear, Man, and God*, Francis Lee Utley, Lynn Z. Bloom and Arthur F. Kinney, eds. New York: Random House, 1964. 234–5.

Dianne C. Luce

'They aint the thing': artifact and hallucinated recollection in Cormac McCarthy's early frame-works

From the outset of McCarthy's career, his work has embodied his meditation on the value and difficulty of recapturing the past. He repeatedly suggests the ambiguous function of the historical artifact in its capacity to evoke or to displace the thing of which it is a record, the primacy of memory and imagination over mere record, the paradoxical frailty of memory. His work also implies that the will to rewrite history may drive the imagining of the past.

This pattern is central to McCarthy's earliest known work, the short story 'Wake for Susan,' in which an old gravestone prompts Wes' act of creative imagination. It recurs in the graveyard scenes that frame *The Orchard Keeper*; and the similarities in the relationship of narrative framework to bracketed story suggest that the sketch is an early working out of some of the formal and thematic characteristics of the novel. With similar thematic weight, the frame appears again in the William Chaffee scenes opening and closing McCarthy's screenplay, *The Gardener's Son*. In all three, artifacts of the past – gravestones, ruins, photographs – both evoke the past and obscure memory, but the search to re-imagine the past is valorized.

'Wake for Susan' was published in October 1959 in *The Phoenix*, the literary supplement to the University of Tennessee student newspaper, *Orange and White*. 'Wake' is the story of a young man's coming to terms with human mortality and natural transitoriness through his act of creative imagination, an act triggered by his contact with the autumn woods and certain found or sought-after historical objects. 'Wake' is also a portrait of the artist's creative awakening. Wes has been hunting squirrels on a crisp October morning, and the story begins with his rising from the base of a 'towering shagbark hickory' (3), a muted Rip Van Winkle echo faintly hinting that in Wes' prior life he has been less fully awake than he is about to be. The allusion may also imply that what follows is as much dream as experience – a distinction that is of little significance to the unfolding of the story except that the suggestion of Wes' dreaming reinforces the emphasis on imagined experience.

As Wes makes his way slowly homeward, where his Saturday chores await, he notes the woods' autumnal decay together with artifacts of human culture from an earlier era: the 'dead leaves'; the 'damp leaf-carpeted woodland floor'; 'the remnants of an abandoned quarry' (an adumbration of the quarry visited by Lester Ballard in *Child of God* and, with its algae covering, of the old insecticide pit where Ather Ownby watches over the corpse of Kenneth Rattner in *The Orchard Keeper*); the old railbed with its 'rotting ties' and its 'sagging rails . . . rusty with disuse' (3).

Increasingly these artifacts impinge on Wes' attention, and when he finds 'a flattened hog-rifle ball', his progress home halts: 'He scraped the mud from the oxidized lead and examined it. Well. Wes wondered when it had been fired, who had fired it, and at what, or whom? Perhaps some early settler or explorer had aimed it at a menacing Indian. More likely it had been intended for game for a table of some later date, when the Indians were all gone' (3). Close observation, knowledge and wonder come together. In a Keatsian moment, the ball's reticence, the very incompleteness of its evocation of the past, elicits the act of imagination in the susceptible boy: 'As Wes examined the rifle-ball, the woods became populated with ghosts of lean, rangy frontiersmen with powder-horns and bullet pouches slung from their shoulders and carrying long-barreled, brass-trimmed rifles with brown and gold maple stocks' (3). Though it leads to no epiphany, Wes' imagining the ghosts of frontiersmen prefigures and causes his second, more extended and affecting act of recovery: 'It was probably the discovery of the rifle-ball that prompted him to look for the burial plot.' No longer heading home, Wes 'pocket[s] the relic and walk[s] quietly through time-haunted woods', now seeking out the old cemetery with its attendant 'rich and lonely haunted feeling' and inviting it to awaken his powers of imagination (3).

However, not only is the historical artifact provokingly 'mute' (6), but memory itself is elusive and incomplete: Wes finds that 'The cemetery was not exactly where he remembered it' (3). But while he recognizes that the burial plot is forgotten by most – 'especially forgotten', he thinks (3) – he perceives the life of Susan Ledbetter, buried there, as accessible to his memory because her gravestone is inscribed with the year 1834, and '1834 was a year one could remember; not like 1215, or 1066, but a real year' (4). Obviously, the memory Wes wishes to access is not personal recollection but historical construct: a 'memory' that imaginatively assimilates personal experience and knowledge with the evidence offered by tangible remnants of the past such as the rifle-ball or Susan's gravestone. The years of the Magna Carta and of the Norman Conquest, etched into schoolboys' memories, cannot truly be remembered because Wes knows directly too little of those eras: they are inaccessible to his historical imagination, and he thinks he can make no construction of these years. Less remote in time and space, the year 1834 has left behind more perceptible artifacts in the landscape, in his culture; so when Wes finds the burial plot, he perceives that 'The bearded stones themselves seemed arrested in that transitory state of decay which still recalls the familiar, which pauses in the descent into antiquities unrecognizable and barely guessable as to origin' (3).

The story of Susan that follows is precisely a constructed thing, a story constructed by Wes out of the familiar and inspired by the gravestone's laconic and therefore mysterious inscription: 'In this year . . . the Source of Life has reclaimed

His own.' What prompts Wes' imagination to wake for Susan rather than any other buried in the plot is her age at death. Pondering the engraved dates, Wes realizes, 'Susan had lived on the earth a full seventeen years.' The closeness of their ages awakens his subjective identification, and thus the grave marker elicits Wes' imagining of history: 'From a simple carved stone, the marble turned to a monument; from a gravestone, to the surviving integral tie to a once warm-blooded, live person. Wes pictured Susan' (4). He creates her story not as a record or document with claims to authority, but as an act of historical imagination that honors both the testimony of the artifact and the concerns of the artist (much as McCarthy himself would later create *The Gardener's Son* and *Blood Meridian*).

These concerns are hinted first in Wes' imagining Susan as an attractive and marriageable young woman, 'blue-eyed and yellow-haired, soft and bright in her homespun dress', capable and comfortable with her household chores, a nurturing girl who watches 'with womanly pride' as her brothers eat a plentiful and well-prepared country meal. Wes' subjective involvement is self-mockingly telegraphed when he thinks, 'Susan should have a lover, and the lover looked strangely like Wes' (4). (As in many of McCarthy's more mature works, the narrative voice of 'Wake for Susan' is ambiguous, the line between a removed authorial voice and an involved narrator often deliberately blurred. In this story, I would argue, Wes is to be read as a projection of the author's persona as Susan's lover is a projection of Wes'.) The story of their doomed courtship is the story of Susan's lover/Wes more than of Susan. She experiences death; Wes, participating as her imagined lover, confronts the transitory nature of life and is transformed by the experience.

Susan's story begins in the warmth of summer, but it soon partakes of the autumnal images Wes perceives in the woods around him on this October Saturday. As the youth and Susan fall in love and he experiences sexual urgency, Wes imagines the youth tutored by nature in the voice of 'wind-tortured trees that spoke in behalf of the silent stars':

> *You walk here, as so many others have walked. The ancient oaks have seen them. The lifesap courses through these twisted limbs as it flows hot through your veins – for awhile. . . . You walk here. Moonwarmed and wind-kissed, you walk here . . . for awhile.* (4)

The trees warn the youth to recognize mortality and seize the day: a lesson that Wes' historical perspective on Susan's fate allows him to absorb from nature perhaps for the first time, although his experience as a hunter has prepared him for it. As artist Wes communicates his new insight to his alter ego, Susan's lover, putting the warning back into the mouth of nature.

But as Wes shapes his story for dramatic irony, both Susan and her young man heedlessly enjoy the vigor of their lives, high-spirited with the 'seductive promises' of the 'tingling air' (5) and the sense of well-being evoked by a bountiful harvest. Although she too is urged on by her sexual feelings, Susan feels no larger urgency about their marriage: 'she was willing to permit him to take his time. The question of her future was settled quite agreeably and her youth told her all was well. Give him time; all will be well' (4). The young couple are like the cottonwood spoken of by the wind-tortured trees that '*cares not for the trees that sucked at this damp earth before its birth, but only for the earth, and the sunwarmth, and the seed*' (4). For both, as Wes repeatedly affirms, 'it was a very good time of year.'

However, Wes is less naive than the young pair, if only because the historical/authorial perspective carries the advantage of hindsight/foresight. Wes interrupts his story of Susan with a parable of fox and chipmunk, probably invented but perhaps a vignette he witnesses as he sits in the deserted cemetery. The paragraphs preceding this tale-within-a-tale oscillate between the present and 1834, suggesting that Wes is actively mediating the insights derived from the two sets of circumstances. He abruptly breaks away from his description of the young man's satisfaction with his daily life, recapping the lecture of the trees and foreshadowing the thematic resolution of his story of Susan:

> Diurnal forces carpeted the forest floor with thick layers of chunchy [*sic*] brown leaves, torn from the half-naked trees. Long enough these leaves had shaded the wooded ridges and slopes. Now they returned to the earth to decay and so provide life and sustenance for their unformed successors. Long enough, leaves. (5)

'Long enough, leaves' becomes a refrain as Wes assimilates his invented story of Susan with his recognition of the flow of time and natural cycles in his own life. This refrain is immediately followed and counterbalanced by the refrain Wes associates with Susan and her young man: 'The year was 1834, and a very fine year it was. It was fall, and that is a good time of year' (5).

The two refrains are succeeded by the story of the fox and the chipmunk, which, like the trees' warning, embodies naturalistic truth. The fox pursues the chipmunk because he needs a meal; the chipmunk tries to elude the fox. Trapped in a crevice where the fox cannot grasp him, the chipmunk dies from the clawing of the fox, and is left 'for the smaller carnivores.' Wes begins this subplot of his story with the assessment that it is a 'minor tragedy', suggesting that next to the tragedy of Susan's unfulfilled life with her suitor and her premature death, the tragedy of the chipmunk or the fox is insignificant. But the ending of the parable, with its emphasis on the continuity of life up and down the food chain, calls into question its very status as tragedy. Although the squeamish may flinch at the idea that the fox 'scraped and clawed at the chipmunk until it was bloody and lifeless', neither animal is granted tragic stature. Wes narrates the story more from the fox's perspective, stressing his missed opportunities and his whine of frustration, but against this he balances the chipmunk's victim status and the pathos of its death. The emotional impact of these creatures' wasted efforts and death finally is neutralized as the fox trots off to try for a meal elsewhere and the chipmunk feeds other life forms. Wes apparently comes to a new, naturalistic perspective on mortality even as he imagines this tale (5).

It is a perspective that prepares the reader for the end of 'Wake' and prepares Wes psychologically to resume his story of Susan, though it does not reduce his empathy for her and the young man. Indeed, he narrates this story too for pathos: his last image of Susan is of her undressing for sleep thinking, 'She would see him again tomorrow night.' Then, because the 'mute stone' gives Wes nothing more on which to hang the conclusion of his tale, he momentarily retreats into a romantic perspective, identifying fully with Susan's suitor and his loss: 'The stars came back; if their luster paled, it was because a part of beauty was no longer there to receive them. In his eyes they swam blurred and distorted in a salt sea. The year was 1834 and it was October' (6).

The gravestone, which has been a bridge to the past, brings Wes back to the present, and he breaks his identification with Susan's lover to wonder how she died, noticing that the marker 'left no testimony'. Now that his story of Susan is completed, though, he experiences catharsis: 'He threw his arms around the unyielding stone and wept for lost Susan, for all the lost Susans, for all the people; so beautiful, so pathetic, so lost and wasted and ungrieved.' As he heads home, 'drained and empty', he sees the dead leaves animated by the wind, dancing 'in a travesty of life'. But his story has done its work. He smiles, picking up the naturalistic refrain, 'Long enough, leaves', and walks home, 'towering even among the lean trees' (6).

Though it carries few hints of the master of style and tone that McCarthy was to become, 'Wake for Susan' is a rather intricate experiment in narrative strategy, and with hindsight we can say it is a remarkable introduction from the author of *The Gardener's Son*, *Blood Meridian*, and the Border Trilogy of McCarthy's concerns with history as both material and muse for works of the imagination. As character, Wes is a prototype for John Wesley Rattner in *The Orchard Keeper* and William Chaffee in the narrative frame of *The Gardener's Son* as these young men seek beyond the artifacts and records of history to come to imaginative apprehensions of the past. As an artist figure, Wes is McCarthy's prophetic self-portrait – a man whose intellect and wonder are engaged by the ambiguity of relics of the past and who seeks to bring the past to life through the narrative act while entertaining no illusion that his invention represents what actually happened. Recently Bernard Schopen has written of *Blood Meridian*'s 'shaping voice' as a subjective one that 'literally constructs as it speaks to us', a 'consciousness in search of meaning', a narrator who 'is not just recounting past events but also brooding over them, uncertainly searching for meaning within them' (179, 182).[1] The narrative voice of *Blood Meridian* is far more complex and sophisticated than that of 'Wake for Susan', and it remains cloaked in anonymity rather than presented as a character-narrator in any frame but for the one whispered in the opening invitation to 'See the child'; but surprisingly some of its defining characteristics are adumbrated in the persona of Wes in this early story.

The framing of a story of earlier days by scenes in a cemetery, where a young man contemplates the gravestone of a dead woman and attempts to remember/imagine the past, recurs in McCarthy's first published novel, *The Orchard Keeper* (1965). The young man is John Wesley Rattner (almost a namesake of the protagonist of 'Wake for Susan'), returned to Red Branch in the fall of the year to visit his abandoned childhood house. Like Billy Parham returned home to find his parents gone, murdered, in *The Crossing*, and Robert McEvoy returned to Graniteville to discover his mother has died in *The Gardener's Son*, John Wesley confronts evidence that in his absence the life and people he had known have slipped into the irretrievable past.² At the ancient, abandoned house, itself a relic, he observes that 'Old dry leaves rattled frail and withered as old voices, trailed stiffly down . . . like . . . curling ancient parchments on which no message at all appeared' (244). After sitting for a while under one of the trees in the yard, an echo of the beginning of 'Wake', he rouses himself and sets off to the graveyard to confirm what the deserted house has suggested, rather like Wes' seeking out the burial plot after finding the rifle-ball. John Wesley reaches the cemetery in late afternoon. There he finds his mother's gravestone, but only after some search, as the men who have been cutting a tree into lengths and who show him the fence '[g]*rowed all up in that tree*' (3) in the prologue have finished their work and departed in the evening hours of the closing chapter. Reading the inscription on the stone, John Wesley thinks, 'It was like having your name in the paper' (245) – this terse and public record of a human life and death.

Like Wes, John Wesley reads the stone for information that is of subjective importance, in this case that his mother has been dead for three years. Then 'He reached out and patted the stone softly, a gesture, as if perhaps to conjure up some image, evoke again some allegiance with a name, a place, hallucinated recollections in which faces merged inextricably, and yet true and fixed' (245). In 'Wake' Wes embraces Susan's gravestone after it has evoked his 'memory' or 'hallucinated recollection' of the year 1834 when she was courted by a young man like himself and died; but John Wesley's touch is more tentative 'as if perhaps' the stone could evoke image, allegiance, recollection. And when he touches it he finds it 'a carved stone less real than the smell of woodsmoke or the taste of an old man's wine' (245) – images he associates with his mentors Sylder and Ownby. As a defining influence on his character, his mother is less real to him than either of these men who have shaped his life and values, and thus her marker provokes no imaginative recovery of her story. The scene would seem to back away from the idea established in 'Wake for Susan', that an object from the past can speak to the memory and imagination. Yet John Wesley's thought affirms the possibility of hallucinated recollection that mingles and even mangles images, yet somehow remains 'true and fixed', suggesting at its very end that all of the narrative between the framing scenes in the cemetery has been John Wesley's partly remembered, partly imagined reconstruction of his past – and his father's, Sylder's, and Ownby's. As he walks in the cemetery looking for his mother's marker after speaking to the workers, John Wesley recollects and invents the story that is this novel. By the time he finds his mother's gravestone, the story has done its work and 'he no longer cared to tell which were things done and which dreamt' (245); he does not need the marker to evoke again the hallucinated recollection.

In some of the same ways in which Wes' presence is felt in the story of Susan, but much less obviously signalled, John Wesley's narrating presence can be detected in the story that disjointedly unfolds between the opening and closing frames of *The Orchard Keeper*. Especially in the early scenes – where John Wesley imagines the character of his father Kenneth, the youth of Marion Sylder, and the confrontation between them that explains his father's disappearance – details from his own frame-time experience inform the narrative, just as Wes' experience in the autumn woods becomes an integral part of his story of Susan. Like both Rattner and Sylder, John Wesley has just traveled back to Red Branch, quite likely by the Atlanta-to-Knoxville roads on which he imagines the two older men. Parallel images occur in the first moments of the story proper and in the end-frame's description of John Wesley's walk from his old house to the graveyard. In both the sun is setting, 'reddening the western sky' (7). John Wesley steps off the 'buckled asphalt' to watch wobble past 'slowly, laboriously' an old negro on a mule-drawn wagon that 'shimmered in waves of heat rising from the road' (244). Kenneth Rattner turns on 'the blazing strip of concrete' to watch a pickup truck 'struggling toward him' (7). Once past, the pickup appears to have been a 'fleeting mirage' (8); John Wesley's wagon dissolves 'in a pale and broken image' (244). The blown leaves that seem to John Wesley messageless parchments are transmuted in his revery into the 'dusty newsprint and candypapers pressed furtively into the brown wall of weeds' (8) edging the highway where Kenneth hitchhikes. Both John Wesley and Kenneth head toward forks in the road (8, 244).

As John Wesley imagines a past for his friend Marion Sylder, a time prior to their meeting, it is in one respect strangely like his own yet transformed with wishful thinking: for Marion, John Wesley invents a prodigal return, the men in the Green Fly Inn not recognizing him until he calls the bartender by name and Cabe studies him while 'the face of the lost boy grew in the features of the man standing at the bar' (14). John Wesley's own return to Red Branch is to a community incapable of recognizing its prodigal sons, and his salute to the man and woman in the car is not returned, an event that leads directly into the elegiac assertion of the last paragraph that the old people 'are gone now' (246).

If John Wesley is in this sense the narrator/inventor of the novel, then the relationship of the narrative strands focused on Rattner, Sylder, and Ownby, which readers often find only tenuously linked through the boy's association with each, is clearer. John Wesley as author of his 'hallucinated recollection' mediates the stories of his biological and chosen fathers, bringing them together in ways the three men themselves do not recognize and which may have only partial basis in historical reality. In doing so, John Wesley accommodates his past, especially the void that has been his father, known to him through his memory of being treated to a soda pop on the eve of his father's disappearance, the lionizing stories told by his mother, the old photo of Captain Rattner in his military uniform, 'soldier, father, ghost' (61), but mostly through his absence. With the construction of his story, John Wesley affirms the values he has learned from Sylder and Ownby and confirms their influence on his adult character. The hallucinated recollection fulfills his pledge to his mother that he will 'never forgit' (67) while it imaginatively frees him from her charge that he avenge his father. He reinterprets his meeting of Sylder and Ownby, the men whom he imagines respectively killed and hid his father, as fulfillment of her specific demand that he 'find the man that took away your daddy' (66) and of her prophecy that he will find a way. He does find a way.

Imaginatively reconstructing the past he has experienced and remembers, John Wesley exorcises the ghost of his father. He makes young Sylder his father's executioner, a psychologically true representation of Sylder's having replaced Rattner in the life of the boy as he neared adolescence, mentoring him as he mastered the masculine world of hunting and as he entered an adult world requiring ethical choices. By making Rattner an opportunist on a par with Gifford and Legwater, and worse, a highwayman and potential murderer, John Wesley refutes not only his mother's suspect history of his father, but also the historical testimony of the photo of Kenneth as an officer. He does so to absolve Sylder of the projected guilt of killing his father, and to absolve himself for his disloyalty to a father who has existed for him as little more than icon or artifact. In finding a way to question now the suspect versions of the past that he had not known how to reject as a child, John Wesley makes a necessary step toward self-reliant adulthood.

The role John Wesley imagines for Uncle Ather as guardian of Rattner's corpse is also psychologically healing. Watching over the corpse, the bones, the physical artifact of his dead father, Ownby performs for John Wesley the obligation placed on him by his unhealthy mother; and through this rite in some mysterious way Ownby anneals the Rattner family's loss. Ather's watch absolves John Wesley from meeting the gaze of the father who watches relentlessly from the photo on the mantel; by remembering the corpse, Ather frees John Wesley from having to remember a father who is mere ghost, from being haunted all his life by a task he can never complete. In John Wesley's imagination, his father's remains are respectfully guarded until they are dissolved, burned away, effaced. He even imagines his own innocent participation in the effacement, as the boys' tipsy experimentation with fire results in the burning of the cedar and the bones it hides. The detail of the corpse's entombment in the insecticide pit, concealed by vegetation, derives from young John Wesley's witnessing of the rabbit that fell down the well and died though he tried to feed it, remaining a vivid and moving image etched in his memory: 'He went away and he could see for a long time the rabbit down in the bottom of the well among the rocks with the lettuce over it' (64). That he 'remembers' Ather's performing the requisite death-watch rather than reporting the corpse to the authorities accords with Ather's other characteristics as challenger of impersonal civil law and institutions, champion of human values, and patient repository of the past in John Wesley's actual knowledge of him.

As suspect as Judge Holden's pronouncements always are, his claim in *Blood Meridian* that the death of the father is the son's birthright resonates nevertheless with this aspect of *The Orchard Keeper*. Whatever the judge's purpose and whatever the kid may derive from his statement, McCarthy's first novel suggests that before a boy can become a man, his father must be cut down to size. If the father's mortality masks his fallibility rather than revealing it, the child is doomed to remain a child in the shadow of an icon, never to inherit the mantle of manhood.

In reconstructing the history of his father, imaginatively filling the gaps so as to reject the suspect construction foisted on him by his mother, John Wesley transcends his own past.

The narrative voice of the frame itself reinforces and affirms the value of imagination as a supplement to the irretrievable past. The framing image of the fence grown into the tree that provokes such wonder and admiration from the workers is, from this perspective, an image of John Wesley's story: a blending of dead fact with living imagination so that the fence/material fact is seen to 'grow' and live with the tree/created story it informs. As the novel ends, the tree and fence are both down, and the tone is unabashedly elegiac as John Wesley heads 'out to the western road'. With his leaving, like those of his three fathers ('Fled, banished in death or exile, lost, undone'), no 'avatar, no scion, no vestige of that people remains.' *The Orchard Keeper* ends as 'Wake for Susan' does: both protagonists walk away from cemeteries into their futures, leaving behind the artifacts of the past that have attended their healing hallucinated recollections – the laconic monuments with their terse reminders of a past that was or might have been and out of which successive generations of the strange race to come will make what their imaginations can: 'myth, legend, dust' (246).

McCarthy was not done with this motif; he revisits it fully in his screenplay *The Gardener's Son*, his first historical work in the usual sense of the term.[3] Written in 1975–76 (Pearce, 'Foreword' v–vi) while McCarthy was also working on *Suttree*, and aired on television in January 1977,[4] the screenplay was not published until 1996 – and then in a version that differs both from the shooting script held by the South Caroliniana Library of the University of South Carolina and from the filmed version. (The widely available published version represents an earlier draft than the shooting script; in the discussion that follows, I will cite the published version except where the shooting script differs in ways relevant to the hallucinated recollection themes and image clusters.) Although cuts were made in the filmed version, many elements of the hallucinated recollection pattern appear in McCarthy's script as written: the frame structure, the monuments, cemeteries and ruins, the protagonist's return to a changed world, the autumnal imagery, the provoking silence of historical records, the musing on the act of recovery. Perhaps inevitably, the motif also shows up in the 'research newsletters' or progress reports director Richard Pearce submitted to the Alicia Patterson Foundation in New York in 1975, during the period of McCarthy's collaboration on the film. As a historical work, *The Gardener's Son* as McCarthy wrote it brings front and center the themes of the difficulty of recovering the past and the reticence of surviving artifacts; it develops in new ways the notions that histories and even contemporaneous records are suspect and that artifacts can efface the reality of which they are the traces; and it reaffirms in the face of this the validity of the search to recover the past through the human faculties of memory and imagination.

McCarthy's unfilmed opening frame of *The Gardener's Son* introduces the search for the past in a brief conversation between the Timekeeper, an old employee of the Graniteville mill, now a keeper of the old documents encrypting the mill's past, and a young man who like John Wesley in *The Orchard Keeper* remains unidentified until the end-frame. There it becomes clear that he is William Chaffee, grandson of Mrs. Gregg and nephew of the man Robert McEvoy has killed, and thus the subjectivity of his motive to recover history is revealed. But the opening frame just hints that the young man seeks information about a past event that may concern his family, and that he is somehow connected to the Greggs. Still, this prologue establishes far more directly than the opening of *The Orchard Keeper* that the enacted tale to follow is the story the young man has sought to re-collect. (Without it, the film itself relies on a frame of script informing the viewer that the dramatized events are historical, a clumsy device but crucial to the audience's understanding of the film.) Further, McCarthy's opening frame announces the idea that the documents kept by the mill will be of themselves insufficient tools in the recovery process: as spokesman of the Past and for the millworker class, the Timekeeper warns the young man that he will not find what he seeks in the mill archives: 'They're just boxes of records. There's some old pitcher albums here somewheres . . . They aint the thing. Old papers or pitchers. Once you copy something down you dont have it any more. You just have the record. Times past are fugitive. They caint be kept in no box' (5).

This notion, embodied in the script primarily in the frame which was not to be filmed, is a dominant theme in Pearce's newsletters chronicling his and McCarthy's research process. The first one, received by the foundation on April 7, 1975, describes the ceremony marking the return to Graniteville of the monument that had originally been the gravestone of William Gregg, founder of the Graniteville mill. (His wife, Marina, had moved the monument and the bodies of William and James to Charleston with her in 1876; see *The Gardener's Son* 87.) Pearce quotes from the speech of Dr. J. W. Speake, the black secretary of the South Carolina Methodist Conference, whom he ironically labels 'the Methodist Secretary of Industry' because on this occasion Speake appeared as apologist for Gregg and for the mill's treatment of its workers even while he articulated the principle of the subjectivity of historical accounts:

> The truth is, the history we know and read was made and written largely by those who do not share our point of view. We in all likelihood would have held with them but for the light of events that have for some of us flashed a spotlight of new understanding upon many of the pages of our history. Those of us making the history of our present order are in the presence, no doubt, of mistakes as tragic as those behind us, if indeed our mistakes are ever behind us. (3)

Speake continues: 'the ultimate end of all social relations must be that man may come to himself enriched, perfected, complete – thinking the true, willing the right, loving the good. This is and must be the key to judgement upon all social and economic institutions and the measurement of politicians and statesmen' (4). Undermining Speake's ceremonial account of William Gregg's industrial experiment, Pearce declares his intent to explore both sides of Graniteville's industrial revolution, that is, both her public mythology of monuments and ceremonial heroes, and at the same time her private underworld of ghost villains and legendary characters, family histories and photographs, each preserved and passed down through the generations family by family in solemn testimony to this extraordinary period in our economic history. (8)

We do not know the precise date on which McCarthy joined in the exploration, and he may have had no influence on this first newsletter in April – Pearce says that he contacted McCarthy in spring 1975 and received a response 'a few weeks' later ('Foreword' v) – but the statement makes it clear what their shared venture was to be, and the later newsletters and the screenplay as written are fully consistent with it.[5]

The sixth newsletter, dated October 8, 1975, when McCarthy was surely working on the project, demonstrates even more explicitly that the film was to break with the received interpretation of the Gregg murder recorded in contemporary documents and the celebratory 1928 biography of William Gregg by Broadus Mitchell. Pearce juxtaposes passages from the biography describing Robert McEvoy, 'the bad boy of the village', with the admonition of historian Jesse Lemisch that 'No contention about the people on the bottom of society ... even approaches being proved until we have in fact attempted a history of the inarticulate' (9–10) and with a fragment of the trial transcript that is used in the screenplay:

... AND IT BEING THUS SOLEMNLY DEMANDED OF THE PRISONER ROBERT MCEVOY IF HE HATH ANYTHING TO SAY WHY THE COURT SHOULD NOT PROCEED TO AWARD EXECUTION OF THE JUDGEMENT PRONOUNCED AGAINST HIM ...
HE SAITH NOTHING. (10; cf. *The Gardener's Son* 69)

Like the dead Susan Ledbetter in 'Wake', like the absent Kenneth Rattner in *The Orchard Keeper*, Robert McEvoy in his life as well as his death is one of the inarticulate. Both screenplay and film establish in the trial sequence that McEvoy cannot speak for himself and that no one in a position to control either his destiny or the public records that become his remains will speak for him. Thus the figure of William Chaffee, the young man of the frame, becomes another author-surrogate like Wes and John Wesley. The story told in the screenplay is Chaffee's attempt at a history of the inarticulate, as the screenplay itself is McCarthy's: a history that requires sympathetic identification and creative imagination to fill the gaps and compensate for distortion in the artifacts and monuments. That Pearce, and perhaps McCarthy too, felt the Chaffee frame could be eliminated from the film attests that, despite what was lost in the deletion, the story as imagined by the author and the story as imagined in Chaffee's framing perspective are essentially identical. As in *The Orchard Keeper*, the framing perspective as 'voice' is nearly imperceptible in the dramatic action, and no line is established between authorial stance and the meditations of McCarthy's 'narrators'. To borrow a phrase from McCarthy's play *The Stonemason*, the hallucinated recollection has its '*right autonomy*' (6) that transcends the subjectivity of its character-narrator.⁶ The 'voice' that communicates it in novel or screenplay is authorial, even omniscient, so that the construct carries an author-ity far beyond the historical evidence of document or artifact.

McCarthy's strategy in the screenplay and even Pearce's in his newsletters are similar to that of Herman Melville in such works as *Billy Budd* and 'Benito Cereno', where Melville's imagination is brought to bear on historical incidents and in which the conclusions juxtapose official legal depositions or newspaper accounts with the tales' 'inside narratives', more psychologically complex and sympathetic interpretations of the crimes of the characters and the natures of their victims: narratives that carry more authority than the appended documents they unmask. That McCarthy had *Billy Budd* specifically in mind as he wrote of McEvoy is suggested by the direct echo of Vere's response after Billy strikes and kills Claggart: ' "Fated boy," breathed Captain Vere in tone so low as to be almost a whisper, "what have you done!" ' (1405). In the screenplay, Mr. Giles, far less sympathetically than Vere, asks Robert McEvoy after he has shot James Gregg: 'You wretched boy, what have you done?' (57).

The difficulty of capturing a true story of the inarticulate is embedded in the shooting script and film's graveyard scenes in which Mrs. Gregg and her son James puzzle over the monument the Greggs have erected to an anonymous 'little boy' who came to Graniteville alone and soon after died unknown (shooting script 46–8).⁷ As in 'Wake for Susan', here is a monument without memory, provoking wonder but offering no answers other than those the strangers who witness it are able or willing to imagine. For Mrs. Gregg it is a monument to her family's bond to the community of millworkers: 'He must have had relatives somewhere... We tried to find out. Sent up to Columbia. It's hard to know what God would mean by such a thing. It seems a hard way to tell us to love one another' (48). James projects a different interpretation: 'He was probably run off from somewhere' (48); and to him the gravestone is a monument to his family's burden of responsibility for an unworthy class of millhands. The Greggs' interpretations are subjective, as are those of Wes and John Wesley, but they are more fleeting, less meditative than those of McCarthy's narrator-heroes. Rather like the tomb of the unknown soldier, the little boy's gravestone commemorates an abstraction to those who have erected it and maintain it, not a personal memory. It remains a mute icon, and for the Greggs it prompts no hallucinated recollection of the inarticulate. But the scene functions as so many of McCarthy's parables: the unknown child is an emblem of the anonymous and ungrieved millworkers in general and of Robert McEvoy in particular (whose grave is, if anything, more anonymous than the little boy's since it has no marker at all to prompt speculation (*The Gardener's Son* 91)); and the screenplay's frame, with its depiction of William Chaffee's search for an understanding of the past and a history of the inarticulate McEvoy, stands in direct opposition to this little vignette.

Along with the screenplay's many images of cemeteries, gravestones and corpses, photographs take on a special weight in the leitmotif of artifacts. In their research, Pearce and McCarthy found period photographs of the mill, the Greggs, and Graniteville residents, many of which are reproduced in the newsletters. However, these photos are not used in the film, which opens with a long cinematic shot of the mill through morning mist. Although the screenplay calls for a '*Series of old still shots of the town of Graniteville and of the people*' after the frame scene and the credits (5), the plan clearly was not to use the period photos but still shots from the film itself: '*These are to have the look of old sepia photographs and may look stiff or posed. They comprise an overture to the story to follow, being shots of the characters in the film in situations from the film itself, so that they sketch the story out in miniature to the last shot of an old wooden coffin being loaded into a mule-drawn wagon and a shot of the town*' (5). This overture extends the introductory frame, and the stills of the film's characters represent the visual artifacts from which William Chaffee partially constructs his new understanding of Robert McEvoy's murder of James Gregg.[8] Using historical photos would have undermined the film's 'right autonomy' by suggesting to the viewer that the film itself is mere construct with less authority than the historical documents. Instead the contrived stiffness of the film's photos, presented as authentic, suggests the suspect authority of photographs as documents of the lives they are meant to capture and validates Chaffee's imaginative construction that transcends the photos' limitations.

Like gravestones, photographs can be mementos, but as the old Timekeeper says, 'they aint the thing'. Like the court records and histories, they are – for all their illusion of objectivity – man-made and second-hand representations. The photographer who makes Robert's formal portrait and offers to share the proceeds with the McEvoy family if Robert will permit him to sell copies is an embodiment of the biased documentarian of the inarticulate (77–9); the cast of characters tellingly describes him as 'good-natured, perhaps clumsy with his equipment' and directs that 'He should not appear obsequious' in his relations with his subject (x). As the photographer thoughtlessly turns to personal profit the fate of his community's ghost villain, he contributes to the creation of a false myth, a false picture of Robert McEvoy – one that conceals his crippling but that fixes him for all time in his notoriety. This is a reversal of the effect of the formal photograph of Kenneth Rattner in his captain's uniform, a heroic picture of his father that John Wesley decides is a lie, noticing the fleshy face that the captain's bars and rakishly slanted cap cannot quite obscure.

The still photo, then, holds the status of mere artifact, and as a snapshot frozen in time it violates the truth of the living being it seems to capture. This failing of the frozen artifact is hinted again with the mysterious whittler silently and furtively at work in the hallway of the jail as Robert McEvoy is hanged and placed in his coffin. He works in wood, and if he whittles a likeness of McEvoy, it can be but a poor substitute for the living man – as the wooden leg Robert is shown whittling and carving for himself early in the shooting script (25) and film is a poor substitute for and reminder of the lost flesh and bone. In her conversation with William Chaffee in the closing frame, Martha McEvoy tells him that her father refused to have a photograph made of his dead wife: 'he didnt want to remember her dead' (92), and he erected no marker over Robert's grave for fear that it would be disturbed (91). Martha shows Chaffee a photo of her brother, probably the one taken at the end of his life by the photographer. It is clear she has wanted mementos of her family. But by the time Chaffee comes to see her in the state hospital, when Robert and her mother have been dead for many years, she has changed her mind about the artifact: 'Sometimes I wish I'd not even kept it. That lawyer said that the image of God was blotted out of his face. That's what he said about Bobby. I ort not even to of kept it. I think a person's memory serves better. Sometimes I can almost talk to him. I caint see him no more. In my mind. I just see this old pitcher' (93). Martha's affirmation of memory over artifact and William Chaffee's affirmation of sympathetic imagination together restate the value of hallucinated recollection that had informed McCarthy's framed works from the beginning. Chaffee tells her that before he had gone in search of the truth, 'It was just a family story. It was like something in a book. It didnt seem like real people' (90). And this is why he has come to see Martha. His gesture echoes Martha's earlier visit to his grandmother Mrs. Gregg to commiserate her loss, and it reflects his compassionate understanding of the McEvoy family achieved through contemplation of the records and artifacts thoughtfully and imaginatively enough to transcend their falsehoods.

The screenplay suggests that while records and artifacts may embody the distorted views of their creators, they are nonetheless the fragments out of which we may apprehend the past if we read them closely, sympathetically, and in context. The furtive and inarticulate whittler working in his poor medium may nonetheless create an icon to stand in opposition to the icon made by the clumsy and indifferent official photographer. Perhaps the whittler is to be compared with Melville's rude balladeer whose 'Billy in the Darbies' counterbalances the more literate received account of Billy Budd published in a naval chronicle and 'for the most part written in good faith' (1432–3). Certainly the film, with its moving pictures, counters the still photos and suspect accounts of the nineteenth-century custodians of history. The screenplay's frame calls attention to its story of Robert McEvoy as a construct like the stories 'hallucinated' by Wes and John Wesley – perhaps no more historically valid than theirs but, like theirs, given weight and authority by the 'narrating' persona. McCarthy once spoke of the film itself as an imaginative construct: 'The kid was a natural rebel, probably just a troublemaker in real life. But in our film he has a certain nobility. He stands up and says, "No, this is intolerable and I want to do something about it"' ('"Gardner's [sic] Son" on PBS This Week, Written by Louisvillian'). It did not concern McCarthy that the film might not be a 'true' representation of the historic Robert McEvoy. He and Pearce sought the nobility and humanity in the inarticulate boy who was hanged for murder, and sought it in precisely the artifacts and records that would deny McEvoy worth.

The concerns of these early works about imaginative acts of historical recovery do not receive as much focused attention in McCarthy's writings which abandon the frame structure, but they resurface in minor ways in Suttree's imaginative reconstruction of his family's past through the prompting of artifacts such as photographs or old houses, and in *Blood Meridian*, where the judge, who draws artifacts in his book and then destroys the originals, and who kills birds in order to draw them, demonstrates that the 'creative' act has the potential to efface history or life itself while inscribing it. However, in *The Crossing*, where the larger narrative frames several subordinate storytellers and their tales, McCarthy reshapes his earlier artifact material in the gypsy's brooding tales of the airplane he says he has been commissioned to recover. Billy meets the gypsy while he is journeying back to New Mexico with Boyd's bones. The gypsy implies a parallel between the bones and the wreckage of the airplane and admonishes Billy, 'La cascara no es la cosa' (The husk is not the thing) (411), an echo of the old Timekeeper's assertion to William Chaffee about old pictures and records. Uncomprehending, Billy asks him to go on with the third history of the plane as he has promised. And the gypsy replies:

> The past ... is always this argument between counterclaimants. Memories dim with age. There is no repository for our images. The loved ones who visit us in dreams are strangers. To even see aright is effort. We seek some witness but the world will not provide one. This is the third history. It is the history that each man makes alone out of what is left to him. (411)

What is perhaps most crucial to recognize in the narrator-heroes of the earlier frame-works is McCarthy's articulation of the kind of historical imagination to which he aspired from the beginning of his career. In all his work, his major characters are delineated as seekers after insight or non-seekers. Repeatedly, his works affirm the value of the search that demands man's inner resources – his compassion, his courage, his honesty, his spirit – even while many of them depict the lost or the non-seeking. McCarthy's narrator-heroes work through or circumvent the artifacts and records of the past to transcend obscurity, reject falsehood, and find insight. This insight is of another nature altogether from dead fact or the dry bones of history; though it gives these data their due, it insists that 'they aint the thing'.

Notes

1 I find Schopen's article cogently argued in all respects except one: arguing by historical fact, he takes Glanton to be the protagonist of the novel because he was the leader of the scalphunters. On the contrary, the focus and movement of the novel make the kid its protagonist, as most readers have seen.
2 It is tempting to speculate that this pattern is related to events in McCarthy's own life. While we know very little about his biography, we do know that his career as a writer began upon his return to Knoxville after a four-year term in the Air Force, spent largely in Alaska. We also know that his years of intensive writing on the Knoxville novels were punctuated with frequent travel and return to his home city. The nature of some of these road trips is indicated in the notes on contributors in the issue of *The Phoenix*

that published 'Wake for Susan': 'McCarthy spent this summer [1959] hitch-hiking across country to California and back' ('Contributors' 12). In 1969, he told a University of Tennessee interviewer, 'I've lived in Europe and in all 50 states' (Jordan 6). In December 1967, when he returned to Knoxville from his European tour with his new wife, Anne, it was just in time to see his parents move away from the city to relocate in Washington DC.

3 For a study of the circumstances that led to the writing of the screenplay, McCarthy's collaboration with the film's director Richard Pearce, and the play's treatment of the history which inspired it, see my article, 'Cormac McCarthy's First Screenplay: *The Gardener's Son*.'

4 Pearce indicates that the PBS airing was in January of 1976 (vi), but this is an error; it actually was televised and reviewed a year later.

5 In 'Cormac McCarthy's First Screenplay', I discuss the role of Tom Terrill, the film's historical advisor, in shaping Pearce's and the screenplay's revisionist view of William Gregg's industrial experiment, especially in the skepticism brought to bear on Broadus Mitchell's 1928 biography of Gregg. Terrill's association with Pearce dated from summer 1974.

6 The phrase is used quite differently in *The Stonemason* to refer to the staged action as an 'artifact of history' with greater authority than that of Ben Telfair speaking from the podium. Ben is the antithesis of the narrator-hero, and McCarthy's stage directions warn, '*Above all we must resist the temptation to see the drama as something being presented by the speaker at his lectern, for to do so is to defraud the drama of its right autonomy*' (6).

7 The shooting script's scene is adumbrated in the earlier draft, published in 1996, in Martha McEvoy's memory of the little boy's grave (92).

8 In the shooting script, the dumbshow of photos has been eliminated, replaced with a single photo over which the credits run: 'a still photograph of the period . . . showing the coffin of Robert McEvoy being brought from the ja[i]lhouse door carried by six men, with Mr. McEvoy waiting in the wagon' (4). It is likely that this photo too was to have been a still shot from the film rather than a period photo. No period photo of this description is included in the research newsletters.

William Prather

'Like something seen through bad glass': narrative strategies in *The Orchard Keeper*

Absurd reasoning, the aesthetic of the grotesque, and the novelistic universe created by Cormac McCarthy have much in common. They all concern the bias of anthropocentrism, the deterioration of conventional frameworks of meaning, and the process of life-world estrangement. In *The Myth of Sisyphus*, Albert Camus sketches the methodology of 'absurd reasoning' (9). The fundamental constituents of this process include the following: the existence of an unresponsive, sometimes hostile world; recognition of the existence of that world through the pressure of one or more triggering elements; and in reaction to that recognition, the election of one of three possible recourses: physical suicide, metaphysical suicide, or adoption of a posture of metaphysical revolt. Furthermore, Camus explains that the triggering elements may include a keen awareness of the passage of time; a conviction of the mathematical certainty of death through confrontation with its various forms; a realization of the denseness and malevolence of nature; a suspicion of the inhumanity of human beings; and a sense of weariness with the habitual aspects of daily life (13–15). According to Camus, consciousness of any one of these elements can fissure one's myths of human centeredness and provoke an apprehension of a primordial, existential world.

As analysts of the grotesque make clear, its sources are also rooted in the experience of estrangement. In *Fiction of the Modern Grotesque*, Bernard McElroy notes that apprehension of the grotesque may result from an event as metaphysically disruptive as recognition of 'the departure of religion and myth from the modern world and the inability of secular culture to supply any comparable conviction on which to base meaning or value' (x). In *The Gruesome Doorway: An Analysis of the American Grotesque,* Paula Uruburu observes that the experience may be grounded in an occurrence as minor as the sense of anxiety stemming from one's 'conscious awareness of existing distortions in everyday life' (1). In 1957, the year Albert Camus received the Nobel Prize and Cormac McCarthy returned to the University of Tennessee, Wolfgang Kayser published *The Grotesque in Art and Literature*. In this fascinating study, Kayser investigates manifestations of the grotesque from Roman times through the twentieth century; more importantly, he establishes the grotesque as an aesthetic category, 'a comprehensive structural principle of works of art' (180). According to his theory, the grotesque comprises three principal characteristics: 'the estranged world,' 'a play with the absurd,' and 'an attempt to invoke and subdue the demonic aspects of the world' (186–9).

It is crucial to remember that the grotesque and the absurd are not equivalent. As defined by Camus, the absurd is the feeling registered when one recognizes that a gap exists between the world as it is and the world as one desires it. For the sensation of absurdity to persist, both the existence of the existential world and, in opposition to it, a human desire for order and meaning are required. In contrast, as Kayser points out, the grotesque is the existential world itself, the universe suddenly revealed through the loss of anthropocentric illusions. It requires, first, a world perceived as normal and stable, and then a breakdown of the boundaries, categories, and myths constituting that world. Extending his theory, Kayser determines that the grotesque comprises 'a play with the absurd.' He means in part that it may be used to represent concrete aspects of the estranged world. These representations are achieved during the process of artistic creation by means of the selection and manipulation of detail, and through reliance on the techniques of distortion and exaggeration. Thus, though not equivalent, Camus' methodology of absurd reasoning and the aesthetic of the grotesque do overlap. Significantly, the dimensions of this intersection are embodied in Camus' instigative elements: the passage of time, death, the malevolence of nature, inhumanity, and habit. For a writer interested in articulating a framework of the grotesque and, as a narrative strategy, provoking intimations of the absurdity of existence, these elements constitute a virtually inexhaustible source. They may be used not only to represent the process of a character's estrangement and growing sense of meaninglessness, but also to nudge readers toward a similar metaphysical crisis.

In the case of *The Orchard Keeper*, it is important at the outset to establish the circumstances of narration. A case can be made that the narrative act largely occurs in a cemetery. It is the summer of 1948. In harmony with a pagan cycle described to him by Arthur Ownby (one of his boyhood mentors), exactly seven years after leaving Red Branch, John Wesley returns. The cryptic narrative style, itself suggestive of 'distortions in everyday life,' makes it difficult to reconstruct the events of the day of his return. However, it appears that John Wesley first visits the abandoned log cabin he and his mother shared on the outskirts of Red Branch. Then he walks into the town to visit her grave. Arriving at the cemetery, he spies two men, one black, one white, working on a section of the surrounding fence. Noting that the wrought-iron palings have been absorbed by the growth of an elm, he approaches and questions the men about the extent of the fusion. They explain, in a short but significant narrative of their own, that it is the fence which 'has growed all through the tree' (3). Subsequently, he seats himself on or immediately beside the grave of his mother. Thus, it is while visiting his childhood home, walking through the environs of Red Branch, and resting on a 'square of marble' (245) that John Wesley fashions his narrative. In his first full-length work, McCarthy attributes to a more mature John Wesley, now twenty-one years old, the power of creation contained in *The Orchard Keeper*. It is impossible to determine whether the young man actually voices a portion of the narrative. It is more likely that he simply thinks it through or rehearses it in his mind. In any event, his implied audience comprises himself, the two cemetery workers, and 'the strange race that now dwells' around and beyond Red Branch. Most importantly, it includes his mother – her spirit – Mildred Rattner. A lengthy recitation, it is evidently begun sometime in the afternoon and is only finished, toward evening, after the workers have left. Young Rattner touches his mother's gravestone and determines that no other images are forthcoming, no 'allegiances,' no 'hallucinated recollections.' The act is complete. His promise to his mother is kept. As he puts it, he 'no longer cared to tell which were things done and which dreamt' (245).

The discovery of John Wesley's status as narrator (or as co-narrator, along with the McCarthyean narrating intelligence) raises several questions. For example, Where has John Wesley been during the past seven years? Did he enter the military during World War II? Did the dimensions of the war affect his already damaged psyche and his prejudiced attitude toward government agents – the new generations of killing machines, for example, or the state-run programs of systematic genocide, or the atomic devastations of Hiroshima and Nagasaki? As he promised (and one of John Wesley's values is keeping his promises), has he returned in the interim to visit Arthur Ownby, and if so, what did they talk about? Did he visit Marion Sylder in Brushy Mountain? Moreover, regarding the day of the young man's return to Red Branch, much is left unsaid. Did his walk simply consist of a visit to his former house and the cemetery? Did he meet someone and talk about the days before the war? If so, what did he learn? Perhaps the most important questions, however, surround the disappearance of his father. How could he have known about the existence of a body in the pit, for example, or that it might have been that of his father, Kenneth Rattner? Interestingly, evidence in the text supplies answers to some of these questions and suggests responses for others. Nevertheless, as the 'revenant' himself acknowledges, much of the recitation is his own creation.

Based, then, not only on personal experience and knowledge, but also on dream, imagination and hallucination, his act of narration is – according to conventional criteria at least – gravely flawed. As imperfect as it is, however, his account serves several purposes. First, it is both elegy and eulogy. It recalls and pays tribute to the world of his boyhood, which is now only 'myth, legend, dust' (246). It memorializes men and women who inhabited this world, evaluates its traditional, agrarian values, and reveals how they were either esteemed or betrayed. In addition, the act of narration is dutiful; it fulfills a promise he made to his mother. At the time of his detention hearings, Arthur Ownby told a lawyer about the corpse in the pit and also that a man frequenting the orchard was the one who had dumped if there (228). Many in Red Branch learned about this, including Mildred Rattner. Before John Wesley left the hamlet, she told him about the discovery of the ashes in the Red Mountain orchard – and alleged that they were his father's (235). He had already sworn to her that he would 'find the man that took away [his] daddy' (66). 'He never forget' (67), the narrative of the older John Wesley reveals, and thus his monologue in the cemetery is, in a sense, a direct response to his mother.

Finally, the young man's account is restorative. It represents John Wesley's 'attempt to invoke and subdue the demonic aspects of the world.' It registers his emotional reaction to his return to Red Branch and to his apprehension of additional details about his past – for example, his discovery of the death of his mother and his understanding that the cabin he shared with her 'was never his house anyway' (244). The act of narration affords him an opportunity to reorder his past, a chance to recontextualize fragments of memory, an occasion to fill gaps in personal knowledge with passages of imagination and hallucination. Conceptualizing his intimations of the absurd and the implications of the existential world, he comes to terms with the psychological trauma resulting from his experience of estrangement, his loss of the world, and the emergence of the grotesque. Finally, in representing the chaos of detail, event, and horror he experienced before leaving Red Branch seven years earlier, he essays to constitute a more personal, provisional spectrum of values.

John Wesley was born into the innocence of everydayness. The process of his estrangement begins at the end of one summer when he moves his bed to the screened-in porch of the cabin he shares with his mother. This shift in perspective is metaphoric and rich with implication. Now he can see 'the acorns in the yard oaks' and on some nights a mysterious 'tall gaunt hound' comes to visit (64). The boy is full of energy and inquisitive. After his mother goes to sleep, he often slips out of the house to traverse 'the dark roads, passing by the shacks and houses, the people illumined yellowly behind the windowlights in gestures mute and enigmatic' (66). Even in these early days, however, he senses something disturbing in the surround of nature. In an exceptional passage, John Wesley violates his narrative protocol and enters into his text. After noting that the yard oaks speak in 'low admonitions,' he shifts from third to second person, and, as if to prolong his young self's sleep of innocence and peace, he shushes for silence (65). According to Kayser, the object of an artist employing grotesque strategies is to illustrate 'the gradual displacement of the individual, a continuous process without climax.' Furthermore, this process is manifested in a 'structural principle based on the continuous onslaught of exactly rendered details' (147). To represent his world, to engage the demonic and reshape his potentialities of being, John Wesley must awaken his young self; he must disturb the drowse of innocence and peace; he must reconstitute the history, the facticity, of his boyhood – including the principal elements of the 'continuous onslaught' that resulted in his trauma and estrangement.

A conviction of the certainty of death is one of the most forceful of Camus' instigative elements. 'From this inert body on which a slap makes no mark,' Camus writes, 'the soul has disappeared. This elementary and definitive aspect of the adventure constitutes the absurd feeling' (15). To gaze too often or too long at displays of death is provocative. It may result in recognition of the chasm separating desire and fulfillment. As narrator, John Wesley is aware of the existence of this unbridgeable gap. It is clear that his accumulated experience with the details of death is one of the factors catalyzing and maintaining the process of his alienation. He is careful to mention, for example, a dry well in the cabin yard containing 'the bones of rabbits, possums, cats, and other various and luckless quadrupeds' (63); he recalls a rabbit he found in the same well, and how, despite his efforts to feed it, it died (64); and he remembers how 'he dug up the flying squirrel he had buried in a jar and found only bones with bits of fur rolling around inside the glass like bed-lint' (206). In August 1940, when he is fourteen, he discovers a sparrowhawk, which he carries home and feeds 'meat and grasshoppers for three days and then it died' (77).

In *Nightmares and Visions: Flannery O'Connor and the Catholic Grotesque*, Gilbert H. Muller remarks that writers employing the grotesque often use violence 'to suggest the lack of any framework of order in the universe,' to suggest 'a world which is always on the verge of disintegration' (77–8). In November 1940, while running his traps, John Wesley has an experience that constitutes a crucial part of the structure of his recitation. Marion Sylder, a local whiskey-runner and eventual mentor to John Wesley, crashes into a mountain stream. The boy approaches, and what he sees 'burned such an image of death into his brain' that he ran mindlessly up out of the creek to a field where light shone 'on an unreal world' (101). This perception of an 'unreal world' under the stress of one of Camus' chief instigative elements is John Wesley's first clear sensation of the absurd, his first intimation of the presence of the existential universe. The first and least intense of three epiphanic moments (the other two being his visit to a government bounty office and his 1948 return to the cemetery), this insightful experience constitutes an important part of the grotesque composition of his narrative. Clearly, his confrontations with the horror and certainty of death cause psychological trauma and serve to augment the pressures of anxiety that lead to his metaphysical crises. 'A world,' Camus writes, 'that can be explained even with bad reasons is a familiar world. But, on the other hand, in a universe suddenly divested of illusions and lights, man feels an alien, a stranger . . . This divorce between man and his life, the actor and his setting, is properly the feeling of absurdity' (6).

The theme of childhood innocence confronted with violence and death is central to the cemetery narrative of John Wesley. Again and again, in what must be hallucinated compilations of personal experience, second-hand reports, and flights of imagination, he stages this extreme moment of existential crisis. He describes, for example, how Earl Legwater, the county humane officer, kills two dogs with a .22 rifle, adding that Legwater had to shoot one of the dogs 'seven times, it screaming and dragging itself along the fence in the field below the forks while a cluster of children stood watching until they too began screaming' (117). At another point, he depicts a boy and girl's discovery of the decaying corpse of his father, Kenneth Rattner, in an orchard insecticide pit. The narrator describes how Arthur Ownby, a lover of nature and self-appointed overseer of the orchard, discovers the dropped berry pails of the children and then the remains: 'The thing seemed to leap at him, the green face leering and coming up through the lucent rotting water with eyeless sockets and green fleshless grin, the hair dark and ebbing like seaweed' (54). 'Even the grinning skull and the moving skeleton,' Kayser writes, 'are motifs the macabre content of which structurally aligns them with the grotesque' (184).

Underscoring the significance of this especially aggressive image is the fact that John Wesley is describing his father. Although it is impossible in most cases to judge what parts of John Wesley's reconstruction of the past are based on personal knowledge and what parts are imagined, the fact remains that his construction of his father's existence, in life and in death, is horrific. The description of the body in the pit is representative. Repeatedly, in acts of narrative exorcism, John Wesley returns to the disturbing image of the decomposing corpse of his father, and with each representation he registers another grisly stage in its dissolution. Whatever the actions of Kenneth Rattner, it is apparent that he did neglect and finally abandon John Wesley and the boy's mother, Mildred Rattner. The neglect and the act of abandonment help to explain John Wesley's focus on and grotesque representation of his father's existence. It also helps to explain John Wesley's determination of his 'allegiances,' his homage not only to his surrogate fathers, Arthur Ownby and Marion Sylder, but also to others in and around the community who were kind to him. Exploiting triggering elements anticipated by Camus, John Wesley may be understood in part as striving to represent and thus to understand the process of his own abandonment, displacement, and alienation. His narration is simultaneously an act of revolt and an act of creation – a revolt against all that is irrational, unresponsive and estranging in life, and an attempt to create a provisional sense of his own history, self, values, and world.

Wounds, scars, and irregularities in the human form: as with death, representations of physical impairment are capable of sparking intimations of existentiality. Uruburu underscores this notion in observing that 'The violation of the human body, which is the core of human vulnerability, is a powerful weapon in the hands of those writers who wish to assault our senses and sensibilities' (11). Seated upon a square of gravestone in the light of the westering sun, John Wesley is haunted by images of human imperfection and violation. Much in the manner of Suttree, the eponymous protagonist of one of McCarthy's later works, John Wesley claims he made it a point to study 'blind men and amputees' in the Knoxville market (82). Furthermore, he asserts that Marion Sylder's favorites among the women of Knoxville were the 'ill-shapen,' including one with 'thighs the dimensions of oiltuns' (29). Sylder himself is depicted as having a 'big toe nailless and truncate' (28), and the fact that his damaged toe inexplicably shifts from one foot to another during the narration only makes its representation more macabre. Arthur Ownby has difficulty moving a leg which 'still had birdshot in it' (92), while Scout, his hound, has a 'hand-stitched belly and ribboned ears,' a testament to years of hunting incidents (92). A local, Ef Hobie, also has a 'hand-stitched belly,' the result of surgery after a car accident. After exhibiting 'the slick red scar that angled across his withered paunch' in Mr. Eller's store and boasting, 'They performed a autopsy on me and I lived,' he tumbles to his death, sudden and violent, 'in a cascade of cupcakes and moonpies' (95–6). The older John Wesley has clearly been wrenched from what Heidegger would term the world of 'average everydayness' into an ontological abyss. He has experienced neglect and abandonment by his father. He has been spectator to wounds, to death, and to violence. Though he apparently only alludes to it once – in describing Ownby and his dog Scout as 'maimed soldiers returning' (202) – he has lived through a brutal war of global dimensions. He has lost his sense of at-homeness in the world. He has been displaced from naturalized frameworks of meaning. As a result, his narration – in part creation, in part revolt, in part an act of exploration, evaluation, and assessment – is filled with representations of death and violation. These concrete images – 'like something seen through bad glass' (7) – are measures of the gap between the world as it is and the world as it is wished, the world of existentiality and that of anthropomorphism. Incorporated into John Wesley's structure of the grotesque, they are intended to account for the transformation in the alchemy of his perception and the trauma of his disworlding.

Other ways avail to represent the discontinuous texture of the existential. McElroy observes that writers of the grotesque often employ, as he puts it, 'humanised animals and animalised humans to reduce human relationships to an elemental state by stripping them of the rationalisations and illusions which are often the only things allowing them to exist' (49). John Wesley uses the same stratagem. In *The Orchard Keeper*, to cite only a few examples, shacks squat (11), gnats perform ballet (17), fenceposts resemble 'the soldiers of Pharaoh,' frogs sing in chorus (173), and wampus cats, hounds, and chicken hawks eye humans with strange intelligence. Marion Sylder and his friend June Tipton try to pick up two girls who, in the glare of their headlights, express 'the temporarily immobilized look of wildlife, deer perhaps' (17) and then 'group and sidle to the ditch as cows will' (18). It should come as no surprise that the narrator's father is described as ambulating 'like some squat ungainly bird' (7) and his lips, clamping on a beer glass, pictured as 'white and fat as leeches' (22). Mildred Rattner, the narrator's mother (and there is judgment and censure in this representation too), is described as composed of 'neckcords' and 'boneshapes,' and her eyes, 'lowered to her work, blink when she swallows like a toad's' (61). Humans tend to position themselves at the center of their universe, to elevate themselves above and hold themselves separate from the rest of nature. John Wesley's descriptions work to rupture these arbitrarily drawn boundaries and to undercut the categories on which such structures of transcendence are based. 'This discomfort in the face of man's own inhumanity,' Camus notes, 'this incalculable tumble before the image of what we are . . . is also the absurd' (15).

'It is conceivable (though just barely),' McElroy suggests, 'that some defense mechanism, developed who knows where on the evolutionary chain and passed on for who knows how long, remains vestigial in modern man and prompts an instinctive aversion from certain kinds of insects and animals' (9). Often described as 'animal phobia,' this aversion, whether it be rooted in instinct or cultural construction, is often exploited by writers, like Cormac McCarthy, as they strive to articulate structures of the grotesque. Gnats, wampus cats, leeches, chicken hawks, lizards, toads, bullfrogs, slugs, buzzards, skunks, muskrats, minks, coons, painters, possums, gars, fishcrows, vultures, crows, waterspiders, bobcats, woodhens, and bullbats crowd in amazing profusion among the hills and in the swamps around Red Branch. Their presence constitutes an integral part of his dramatization of the process of estrangement.

The malevolence of nature constitutes a powerful manifestation of the materiality of the existential. The world around Red Branch, at one moment seemingly familiar, at the next dreadfully strange, is always, to some extent, a savage, distorted, and menacing universe, a realm where '[t]he primitive hostility of the world rises up to face us across millennia' (Camus 14). As additional elements in his 'continuous onslaught of exactly rendered details,' John Wesley conjures storms of rain and snow so potent that they dominate significant portions of his narrative and influence human lives. The rainstorm, for example, nearly kills Ownby with a burst of lightning as he dances in the woods; moreover, its runoff contaminates Sylder's gas supply and is thus indirectly responsible for his breakdown and arrest on a bridge in Knoxville. Furthermore, John Wesley claims that the Appalachians have the power to 'contort the outgoing roads to their liking' (10), and he describes a river that 'seethed like the old disturbance of the earth erupting once again, black mist languid in the cuts and trenches as flowing lava' (201).

Finally, he mentions the 'Harrykin,' a mountain area struck years before by inlanding remnants of a great sea storm, an area that has not yet recovered from the fury of uprooted, scrambled, and flattened trees. Indeed, John Wesley recalls (or imagines) an incident in which Ownby is told, with some exaggeration perhaps, that 'they was places you could walk fer half a mile thout ever settin foot to the ground – jest over laurel hells and down timber, and a rattlesnake to the log' (194). So inaccessible is this massive area of blowdown that the reclusive Ownby, relentlessly hunted by government agents, decides to make it his provisional refuge. Plainly, the violence of nature can intrude at any time to destroy a person's life or even the world. The demonstrations of its power around Red Branch have had a significant effect on John Wesley. In seeking to represent the terrors of his past and to come to terms with his fears and anxiety, he announces the presence of massive tempests, mountains that shrug off roads, rivers that thunder like the area's originating lava flows, and impenetrable hurricane blowdowns. Considered in the context of absurd reasoning and the aesthetic of the grotesque, his intentions are clear: to represent the materiality of the 'unreal world'; to allow this strange universe to emerge, shaping itself in revelations of 'primitive hostility'; and thereby not only to exorcise the demons of his past but also to extend the limits of his consciousness to include a more accurate understanding of the phenomenal world.

The horror and certainty of death, ruptures in the boundaries of the human body, the violence of physical nature: in addition to these, recognition of the consequences of the passage of time is also powerfully instigative and may provoke a sentiment of the absurd and a vision of the grotesque. As McElroy explains, the grotesque is often employed to illustrate 'decline from a past state of health and excellence.' These illustrations may include 'an erosion of previously upheld personal and communal values; a dwindling of energy . . . a growing unconcern with the future . . . a spreading nihilism or cynicism' (97). In his rehearsal of hallucinated recollections, John Wesley includes many markers of erosion and decline. One of these, revealed through his nostalgia for a lost paradise, is the abandoned orchard.

Amid the rubble of 'grand' narratives and metanarratives cluttering the metaphysical terrain of Red Branch are remains of the enchanted garden. Macrocosmically, the idea of a garden or orchard suggests Edenic beauty, innocence, and plenitude, along with the presence of an omnipotent creator responsible for the maintenance of meaning and order. It thus invokes elements of Christian theology, a belief system that endured for centuries, affording its adherents an effective framework of meaning and the illusion of a less chaotic world. In his cemetery account, however, John Wesley depicts the Red Branch orchard in an advanced state of declension. Like him, it has been forsaken by its creator and cultivator. At the beginning of section II, for instance, he observes that 'the orchard went to ruin twenty years before when the fruit had come so thick and no one to pick it that at night the overborne branches cracking sounded in the valley like distant storms raging' (51).

Homologous, also, with the process of the elm absorbing the iron paling of the cemetery, this image of a lost paradise demonstrates both the power of nature and the result of human neglect: gradual decadence and dissolution, lost potential for meaning and richness in life, the ultimate failure of human responsibility. In a macrocosmic sense, John Wesley's description announces the absence of 'an omnipotent creator,' a failure of the Judeo-Christian framework of 'meaning and order,' and a loss of Edenic 'beauty, innocence, and plenitude.' On the mundane level, it signals a decay in 'health and excellence,' a deterioration of 'personal and communal values.' Humankind is pictured as fallen into patterns of diminishment, as estranged from its world and itself, as nostalgic for imperfectly remembered myths of former harmony and stability. Similar to images of a ravaged Tennessee river, windrows of buffalo bones, ruined churches, and derelict cathedrals described by the narrating intelligence in McCarthy's later works, the haunting, pervasive image of the forsaken orchard is a crucial component of the recitation's grotesque structure. It is meant to be provocative.

Other markers of the passage of time and the process of deterioration amplify the metaphysical significance of the abandoned orchard. Mountain cabins are an example. Still used by families around Red Branch (like the Rattners), these solidly built structures serve as reminders of fading agrarian values and suggest a 'decline from a past state of health and excellence.' Like the cabins, the coalescence of the

Green Fly Inn – which the revenant explains is 'there yet,' suggesting that his 1948 exploration of the Red Mountain area is more extensive than it appears – lying in a valley 'like some imponderable archeological phenomenon' (48), is a stark reminder of the forces of chance and change inherent in primordial temporality. But John Wesley goes further. Alluding to more distant eras and eons, he recalls pines bulking against the sunset like 'a mammoth cathedral gothically spired' (59). He studies 'Pompeian figures' in the architraves of buildings in Knoxville (81). He notes that he and Sylder resemble 'the last survivors of Armageddon' (104), and are 'druidical in their black solemnity' (120). He mentions 'a great stone tusk' and 'trilobites and fishbones, shells of ossified crustaceans from an ancient sea' (88). His flooded fields are invaded by gars with 'long beaks full of teeth, ancient fishes survived unchanged from mesozoic fens' (173). In John Wesley's imagination, Ownby takes note of 'blotches of moss and fungus on the pale concrete [of the insecticide pit] like land-shapes from some ancient atlas' (91). Furthermore, John Wesley terminates his narrative with a eulogy for rural highlanders whose remains he describes as 'celled marrow going to frail stone, turning, their fingers laced with roots, at one with Tut and Agamemnon' (245). Mountain cabins and the Green Fly Inn, Pompey and Egypt, ancient maps, fossils, and atavistic fish: along with his conviction of the vulnerability of frameworks of meaning and patterns of community, John Wesley clearly reveals his understanding of the malevolence of nature and the predations of time.

The literary equivalent of a union of collage technique and figural expressionism (similar to *l'art brut* of painters like Jean Dubuffet and Francis Bacon), John Wesley's verbal canvases represent the psychological trauma stemming from a realization of the finitude of human existence, the shock of human and natural violence, and the legacy of neglect and abandonment. His fears and anxiety, natural enough for someone his age, influence his perception, his sense of self, the way he shapes and assembles his narrative. They help to explain his elusive presence in the text, the flattening of his metaphysical perspective, the discontinuous passages disruptive of time and space, and his use of the third person to render a story in which his interests are passionately vested. Indeed, the fact that the views of the narrating intelligence and John Wesley appear to coincide may explain what appears to be a struggle over narrative perspective and the resulting ambiguity surrounding the identity of the narrative voice.

There is also the matter of his manipulation of point of view. As Vereen Bell points out in *The Achievement of Cormac McCarthy*:

> Huge stretches of narrative are ruled by no point of view whatever – long densely descriptive passages that seem to bring what there is of a narrative to a dead halt – descriptions of nature, a desperate cat. This high level of seemingly unassimilated raw material represents for us the ascendancy of the world-in-itself, the natural world, outside the jurisdiction of human forms. (13)

The Orchard Keeper is divided into four sections, each section further divided into several divisions. From division to division the point of view may shift, suddenly and radically, resulting in a composition rich in range of consciousness and polyvocality. Because young Rattner usually delays identification of the character to whom he has assigned the point of view, the opening of each division constitutes a separate mystery for the reader. That the point of view, as Bell later observes, may be ascribed to an animal only increases the confusion. For example, in the opening division of section IV, John Wesley imagines Arthur Ownby dancing in the rainstorm 'like some rain sprite' (172). A few lines later the world is partially rendered through the intelligence of a cat, which has been forced by rising water to seek new shelter. Next, Mildred Rattner is depicted entering her smoke house. She discovers a cat, perhaps it is the same cat, grasping at a piece of salt-cured pork. In a following division, the point of view is again shifted to the errant animal as it fends off the attack of four crows. Frequent, abrupt shifts in point of view combined with delays in identifying the person or creature in which the point of view is centered are strategies employed by a narrator of the grotesque. They lend additional force to the instigative structure. They work to explain the drama of estrangement, the sense of disorientation and bewilderment, the intimation of the absurd universe.

The ritualized, mechanical aspects of daily life: habit too is death. In the world of Red Branch between the wars, elements of the encroaching civilization embody this last aspect of the existential. Indeed, at one point, John Wesley conjures a narrative sequence in which Marion Sylder, while making one of his bootlegging runs, takes notice of the deadening effect of habit. Sylder uses a government installation to store his contraband; and one day, while exiting, he is depicted passing 'an olivecolored truck, the driver and the other man in the cab looking serious and official, but somewhat sleepy and not in any particular hurry.' Later, as Sylder motors toward Knoxville, John Wesley imagines him describing himself, in contrast, as 'Genial, unofficial, and awake' (98).

'Serious,' 'official,' and 'sleepy' are traits shared by many of the apparently less primitive characters in John Wesley's narrative. Jefferson Gifford, the constable, is one example. An agent of a system of institutions responsible for criminalizing the age-old activities of whiskey-making and whiskey-drinking, he is unquestioning and unrelenting in his efforts to fulfill his assigned duties. As a result, he sacrifices traditional human values. This is a system, after all, whose representatives have already disrupted and destroyed several of the mountain families around Red Branch. The family of Ef Hobie is a good example. Ef died from injuries received in a car accident while he was being pursued by government agents. His son Jack remains in Brushy Mountain state prison serving time for transporting 'contraband.' And Ef's seventy-eight-year-old wife, also incarcerated, was released only after it was discovered she had cancer. Moreover, Constable Gifford is so concerned with 'getting his man,' Marion Sylder, that he menaces John Wesley – unless he informs on his friend – with 'jail for trappin without license and bettin criminals' (159). Gifford's disregard for the worth of mountain families, especially for the lives of children and the elderly, amounts to a betrayal of older, more humane, agrarian values. In his cemetery narrative, John Wesley understandably pays him no tribute.

Earl Legwater, despite being the 'county humane officer,' is no exception. As portrayed by John Wesley, his unthinking demonstrations of perversion and cruelty are disconcerting to say the least, and furnish additional evidence that what we call 'human nature' may be as unplumbed, as dark, as unpredictable, and as potentially violent as 'physical nature.' For example, in addition to his specialty of maiming and killing dogs in front of small children, he is also part-time treasure hunter. After the cremated corpse of John Wesley's father is discovered in the spray pit, Legwater literally camps out in the orchard. 'Huntin platymum,' he spends days sifting through the flaking ashes in an effort to discover the plate of precious metal rumored to have been inserted in Rattner's head to repair a war injury. Described at one point as 'a feathery gray effigy – face, hair and clothing a single color' and as spitting 'gobs of streaky gray phlegm' (239), he constitutes an apt metaphor of death in life, the result of unconsciously accepting the encroaching society's hierarchy of values, including its appreciation of material wealth. It may come as no surprise then that it was, as Legwater reveals, the 'little bastard,' John Wesley, who told Legwater that the ashes in the pit were the boy's father's and that the 'platymum' plate was sure to be there (241). Thus, John Wesley knew of the existence of the body in the pit and was aware of hamlet speculation that it was his father's *before* he left Red Branch. Later, Legwater's action of shooting and killing Ownby's dog, Scout, when it returns to the orchard to find its caretaker, only confirms the depths of the 'humane officer's' depravity.

John Wesley evokes others who are serious, official, and sleepy: among them are the sheriff, his deputies, and the A. T. U. agent, all of whom literally 'hound' Ownby after he shotguns his 'x' in the side of the mysterious government installation near the orchard. Described by John Wesley as a 'barren spot' where 'not even a weed grew,' a 'great dome . . . coldly gleaming and capable of infinite contempt' (93), this object was determined by Ownby, self-appointed overseer of the mountain, to be unhealthy, and he counterposed himself in a significant act of revolt. As a result, though suffering the maladies expected of an octogenarian, he is mercilessly pursued by the sheriff, his deputies, and various others. Yet another institutional agent, this one unnamed, arrests him and brutally abandons his dog, leaving the animal 'standing there like some atavistic symbol or brute herald of all questions ever pressed upon humanity and beyond understanding' (205). Later, a Knox County social worker, who has apparently been educated not to recognize, much less respect, humanity, interviews and insults him. An organization with a single, calcified perspective, the state ultimately houses Ownby in a 'crazy house,' a sort of institutional *oubliette* for uncooperative citizens. A metaphor of the new order's possibilities of being, the institution for the criminally insane is described as 'a row of cages, a forest of sweating iron dowels, forms of men standing or huddled upon their pallets' (222).

David Paul Ragan was one of the first critics to recognize and respond to the importance and complexity of *The Orchard Keeper*. As he notes in 'Values and

Structure in *The Orchard Keeper*,' finding a 'center of value, a source of moral authority' (15) is one of the major preoccupations of the narration. As described by John Wesley, highlander values seem unquestionably positive and healthy. However, the people who esteem them are slowly being crushed or displaced. In their capacity as institutional agents, Constable Gifford, Humane Officer Earl Legwater, the sheriff and his deputies, the A. T. U. official, the employees of the local government installation, and the Knox County social worker represent the value and moral (and social) authority of the new order. However, as described by John Wesley, this contaminated center and source is patently unsatisfactory. Thus, the problem for the young narrator seems twofold. He must resist the dehumanizing forces of the spreading urbanization and industrialization, and at the same time, he must search for values that are positive and meaningful for him. The desire driving and shaping his narrative is figured in both acts of resistance and a quest for values.

Within the world of John Wesley's graveyard meditation, sources of alternative value are limited. Mildred Rattner's votive photograph of 'Captain Kenneth Rattner' must have been a constant reminder to John Wesley during his childhood of the man's failure to be a father, a traditional source of care and guidance. Portrayed by John Wesley as a panhandler, shoplifter, thief, and attempted murderer, Rattner's ineptly constructed facade of lies and half-truths suggests a Legwater sans portfolio. Indeed, the image of Legwater masked with Rattner's ashes corroborates this notion of affinity; at the same time it recalls John Wesley's describing himself as the unwitting cremator of his father's remains. Only great passion could produce such harsh narrative treatment of Kenneth Rattner. It suggests how deeply the boy was wounded by his father's neglect, repudiation, and abandonment.

Arthur Ownby, mountain recluse, and Marion Sylder, whiskey-runner, are represented as more promising sources of value and moral authority. As Ragan points out, 'These are the men whose values [John Wesley] has embraced as an adult' (17). According to Ragan, Ownby passes on his 'high premium on independence,' a sense of the importance of a 'vital connection with the natural world' (20), and a sense of 'personal responsibility and self-sacrifice' (23). Sylder's contribution seems less rich as Ragan suggests that Sylder, through his largely inconsistent behavior and even more confused explanations of it, teaches the boy the value of 'judging people's behavior' rather than 'accepting their pronouncements' (22).

Read in the light of absurd reasoning, however, their contributions seem more significant. Unlike John Wesley, Sylder and Ownby were apparently unable to fully conceptualize their feelings and to understand the forces that shaped and disrupted their lives. And yet, they are, as John Wesley himself becomes, men in revolt. This is the supreme measure of their importance for him. Like him, they were displaced from an agrarian way of life; they were trapped between the old and new dispensations; they endured a psychically damaging process of estrangement. Thus their examples, their consciousnesses, ways of being, and their perspectives on life are of primary value to him. They have responded to the brutalizing, nihilistic forces of the new order with ingenuity, courage, dignity, and defiance. Like him, in fashioning their lives, they also became creators of unique life-narratives. Each of them has sought, albeit imperfectly, to retain some sense of human worth. Each of them has long been in pursuit of his own source of values and center of moral authority. Their acts of revolt against degradation and dehumanization, their attempts to develop countervailing consciousnesses, as Camus suggests, are in and of themselves crucial values.

Ownby, as Ragan observes, is 'the primary avatar of traditional mountain values' (18). Yet, he seems strikingly untraditional in many respects. Piecing together fragments of memory and personal history attributed to him by John Wesley, it is apparent that when younger he had a job 'railroad blasting' and 'cutting sleepers for the KS&E' (145). This occupation suggests that early forms of technology were already invading, eroding – literally exploding – his agrarian way of life. He managed, however, to purchase a twenty-acre farm and married a woman named Ellen. Although details are sketchy, it is clear that one day Ellen ran away with a Bible salesman. Deeply traumatized, for nearly two weeks Ownby did nothing but sit, and wait, and wander around the house they had shared. Eventually, after the stock had died and 'an outrageous stench had settled over everything' (157), he buried her clothes, marked it with a cross, and began walking. When John Wesley first meets him, he is living a markedly different life. He has already experienced several stages of estrangement.

In addition to viewing him as an embodiment of traditional mountain values, it may be helpful to also consider him as having transformed himself into a strikingly different person, a state of being so innovative that it is difficult to categorize. He makes his own society, scant as it is, is able to survive through trade in roots and herbs, and lives in harmony with deep natural rhythms. He carries a 'chambered goat-horn' and negotiates the mountain paths with a staff of hickory; he has whittled 'it octagonal and graced the upper half with hex-carvings – nosed moons, stars, fish of strange and pleistocene aspect' (46). He even develops a mystical numerology, which he uses, among other things, to predict World War II, or as he puts it, 'a real calamity afore this year [1941] is out' (225). (The fact that John Wesley is 14, Sylder 28, and Ownby probably 84 – all even multiples of seven – when the crucial events of the story take place suggests that John Wesley may be relying on Ownby's 'rule of seven' to buttress his narrative composition.) Like John Wesley, he also has had his existential moments. He has been displaced, alienated, estranged. However, rather than surrendering, rather than opting for physical or metaphysical suicide, he has chosen to remain defiant. He is memorialized in the cemetery narrative because he took the time to care for John Wesley and to pass on specific values. Moreover, he demonstrates, not through words, but through his life choices, that the most important values are neither inherited nor imposed. They are personal. They are provisional. They are developed experientially.

Marion Sylder also lives defiantly. Again, because of John Wesley's disjunctive narrative, his history must be reconstructed. It is apparent, however, that he left school at the age of sixteen, worked a short time as a 'carpenter's apprentice,' and then disappeared for five years. During his absence from Red Branch, he worked off the Louisiana coast running whiskey, and thus acquired some proficiency in Spanish. In an incident involving the Coast Guard, he was nearly killed. Returning to Red Branch, he takes and then, because of a fist fight, loses a job in a fertilizer factory. He finally re-associates himself with several mountain families and begins running whiskey into Knoxville. Like Ownby, he elects to live largely outside, opposed to, and in revolt against the conceptions of value inherent in the new order. Not as contaminated with the lusts of commercialism, nor dulled by the monotony of a ritualized life, he quickly recognizes the vulnerable position of John Wesley. In a number of acts, which include gifting the boy a young coon hound and taking him hunting, Sylder makes it a point to take the time to get to know John Wesley, to help him, to offer him guidance.

In addition, after being jailed by Gifford, he instructs John Wesley on the futility of revenge and urges his perceived truth that 'they ain't no more heroes' (214). John Wesley clearly understands the crucial difference between revolt against unfair laws and the betrayal of one's friends and neighbors. It is also evident that he understands Sylder to mean that no hero can exist as part of a system whose values are fundamentally corrupted – which explains John Wesley's portrayal of both Sylder and Ownby (and himself) as (absurd) anti-heroes. Indeed, the fact that John Wesley views the corpse in the pit as his father's and Sylder as the one who killed and left him there does not hinder the young man from praising the former carpenter while he associates Kenneth Rattner with 'that being in the outer dark' (24). Clearly, John Wesley has learned to appraise others according to their values as revealed through life actions and not according to their assigned roles or positions. Marion Sylder, like Arthur Ownby, is recalled by John Wesley because of his generosity and compassion, and his courage in the face of estrangement. He is also recollected because he sets an example of choosing to live in revolt against the values of an order that he does not accept.

For the narrator of *The Orchard Keeper*, then, just as it was for his boyhood mentors, Sylder and Ownby, the illusion of centeredness, of being at home in the world, has been irrevocably shattered. While still a young man, he has been forced to acknowledge the existence of a forever unbridgeable abyss between his desire and what he can anticipate from the world. Caught up in a process similar to the one sketched by Camus, the scope and clarity of his consciousness have been amplified by his experience of a concussive onslaught of detail. As noted earlier, the stress of his life experience culminates in his first metaphysical crisis, his first clear moment of insight, when he witnesses Sylder's wreck.

A second, more intense, moment of epiphany occurs toward the end of the novel. At this point the implications of the 'unreal world' perceived in his initial epiphany become apparent. In a brief but powerful outburst, John Wesley conceptualizes what at first was only a sentiment. Having recently visited Marion Sylder in the Red Branch jail and Arthur Ownby in the Knoxville hospital for the insane, he decides to retrieve the remains of a chicken hawk he had turned over to the county government for a dollar bounty. However, when the official at the desk informs him that the chicken hawk has probably been incinerated, John Wesley, struck by yet another manifestation of the existential world, cannot restrain himself.

> Burn em? he said. They burn em?
> I believe so, she said.
> He looked about him vaguely, back to her, still not leaning on or touching the counter. And thow people in jail and beat up on em.
> What? she said, leaning forward.
> And old men in the crazy house.
> Son, I'm busy, now if there was anything else you wanted...
> He smoothed the dollar in his hand again, made a few tentative thrusts, pushed it finally across the counter to her. Here, he said. It's okay. I cain't take no dollar. I made a mistake, he wadn't for sale. (233)

Few moments in literature are more powerful. This fragment of dialogue embodies not only John Wesley's second moment of epiphany, but also his first distinct act of defiance. In Camus' words, he has experienced an 'incalculable tumble.' His father's neglect and abandonment, chance exposures to accident, mutilation, and death, recognition of the waste, ineptitude, and cruelty of government agents, the destructiveness of encroaching technology – the accumulated psychic shocks have worked to dislocate and forever alienate him from his potential position in the new order's frameworks of meaning. The process of estrangement has resulted in his perception of the existentiality of the world and his placing of himself, as his mentors have done, in opposition to it. Thus, the day he returns for the remains of the chicken hawk and finds they have been burned is the one of the most important days in his life. His recognition of the phenomenal world is the moment that effectively inaugurates the beginning of his movement toward an expanded scope and complexity of consciousness. From that moment on, it is possible for him to assume a stance of resistance, constantly aware of the depth of his desire and the opposing silence of the universe. Aware that the measure of the rift is in part the terrain of the grotesque, he will further understand that his consciousness is a dubious triumph.

This achievement – his discovery of consciousness, clarity, and revolt – only constitutes the beginning. As Camus observes, 'In this [existential] universe, the work of art is then the sole chance of keeping his [the absurd reasoner's] consciousness and of fixing its adventures' (94). John Wesley's attributed narration in the village cemetery may be characterized as an absurd creation, a work of art. Returning to Red Branch after seven years, his consciousness of what has changed and what has not must be particularly acute. This state of heightened awareness combined with the emotional impact of acquisitions of additional information about his past constitute an explosive catalyst. The old fears and anxieties, the psychic wounds and memories of betrayal – all that has long been avoided and repressed is expelled during that one summer afternoon. This moment of crisis constitutes the third and final moment of epiphany – the most extended, the most intense. Effectively estranged from the metaphysics underpinning conventional frameworks of meaning and their associated myths, and faced with numerous gaps in his personal knowledge, he is impelled to fashion parts 'done' and 'dreamt,' to manipulate portions of lived experience, second-hand accounts, intuition, imagination, and hallucination in order to reconstitute his own web, his own narrative, his own work of art. Thus he is able to live. Thus he 'retains his consciousness' and 'fixes its adventures.'

In *The Rebel*, as John Cruickshank points out, Camus goes on to elaborate an attitude of mind necessarily developing from absurd existence, an attitude that tends to emphasize 'individual human worth,' 'common human nature,' and the 'value of human solidarity' (xvii). John Wesley has recognized the chaos and potency of existentiality and in comparison the relative puniness of the artifacts of humankind. He knows that opposed to the forces of both external and internal nature, people's best hope is to recognize their 'human worth,' 'common nature,' and the 'value of human solidarity.' Evidence of John Wesley's realization of these fundamental values is incorporated into his absurd creation: his fulfillment of the promise he had made to his mother, his appreciation for the care and attention shown him by Sylder and Ownby, the underlying purposiveness of the narrative itself, his obvious love of the uncontaminated beauty of the world, his love for dogs, his dislike of technology that is disruptive and potentially cataclysmic, and his realization of the worth of all people, including the outcast and marginal.

His final acts are particularly significant. Recalling his visit to the hospital for the insane, where some of whose marginalized gestured 'hopefully to the passing cars of picnickers and bathers' (224), his wave to the couple who momentarily halt at the stoplight by the cemetery is emblematic of his act of narration: both gestures represent invitations, clear demonstrations of John Wesley's recognition of the value of human solidarity. Thus, it is significant that the couple fails to acknowledge him. Encased in their articulation of steel and plastic, they wait patiently for a 'box to click,' for a machine to signal them when they may motor away over a grid of roads that can only take them where they are meant to go.

Moments later, John Wesley stands and then walks 'through the gap in the cemetery fence, past the torn iron palings' (246). Viewed in the light of Camus' existential methodology, the cemetery paling may be interpreted as habit, as an unconscious life; it represents anthropocentricity, received frameworks of meaning or systems of belief, a grid of roads. The elm, on the other hand, through its absorption of the fence, suggests the powerfully fluxic forces of the existential world. Thus, John Wesley's act of exiting through the gap in the paling may be understood as a dramatization of his choice of perpetual revolt. It represents his decision not to leap, neither from the Knoxville bridge (mentioned by Ownby as a platform for suicides), nor into institutional agency, nor into a religious or secular faith. Instead, his act reveals his determination to take responsibility for his life and for the formulation of sane values. Like Arthur Ownby, John Wesley is becoming an orchard keeper.

Ragan sees him condemned 'to isolation in the modern world' (24), but the operative effect of the modern world's values, based as they are on an illusory belief in material wealth and not on a sense of individual human worth, guarantee John Wesley membership in the new order's lower social rank. This more populous stratum includes the displaced, the materially poor, the marginalized, the 'crazies,' and other artists like himself (a world marvelously depicted in *Suttree*, a novel on which McCarthy was working at the same time as he was writing *The Orchard Keeper*). As for the couple in the vanishing car and all other members of the 'strange race' addressed by John Wesley's view 'through bad glass,' his hallucinative recitation and gesture of hand, Ragan is right. This modern world, 'presided over by brutish constables, inept humane officers and governmental employees who follow nihilistic and futile polices they don't attempt to understand' (24), is assuredly the realm that McCarthy's readers must recognize as their own. This is so, unless, of course, through the wrenching effect of John Wesley's cemetery narrative, they are brought to a recognition of the existential; and thereby to a greater appreciation for the gloriously Sisyphean futility of this young man's quest. It is a quest, not for wealth, but for what he knows he can never find, a human world based on concern and care and accountability, one in which elderly eccentrics, and high school dropouts, and even sparrowhawks go unmolested – a world in which eighty-year-old men no longer have to forfeit their peace and health because, as Ownby so eloquently points out, 'they's things you have to do on account of nobody else wants to attend to em' (229).

Barbara Brickman

Imposition and resistance in *The Orchard Keeper*

Upon his first day of 'taking arms,' the young boy Cuchulain understands and accepts the prognostication of Cathbad the Druid, which denies him a long life but promises great fame: ' "It is little I would care," said Cuchulain, "if my life were to last one day and one night only, so long as my name and the story of what I had done would live after me" ' (Gregory, *Cuchulain of Muirthemne* 356). Cuchulain's wish for immortality, of course, is realized in the publication of *The Story of the Men of the Red Branch of Ulster* and in the re-emergence, at the beginning of the twentieth century, of Gaelic traditions and epic literature, which were used as political focal points for groups such as the Gaelic League in the struggle for Irish independence. Similarly, Cormac McCarthy's first novel, *The Orchard Keeper*, honors and relies upon Cuchulain's legacy or the continued influence of Gaelic culture. The novel's three main characters, John Wesley, Arthur Ownby, and Marion Sylder, adhere to an older code or system of values that shares much with Gaelic traditions in Ireland. This older set of values and its contention with a new order, represented by the city and the laws of centralized government, make up the central action of the novel. McCarthy, who borrowed his pen name from a nickname used by Irish aunts to refer to his father, Charles, Sr., ù Cormac being the Gaelic equivalent of Charles (Woodward 31), re-dramatizes, in the mountain community of Red Branch, Tennessee, the near destruction of Gaelic culture at the hands of English colonizers, and, in the process of mirroring that earlier conflict, he celebrates the older culture and demonstrates how no conquest is complete or absolute. By providing one survivor who has been indoctrinated into the old order, McCarthy allows for the preservation of that tradition and the resistance possible from such preservation, just as the few Gaelic pockets in conquered Ireland were able to preserve much of their own culture, including the heroic tales of Cuchulain.

The old way, the Gaelic tradition, which seemed doomed to many observers of sixteenth- and seventeenth-century Ireland, again in McCarthy's novel struggles to resist the destructive forces of colonization, urbanization, and centralization. 'Civilizing' weapons once wielded by English lords, bureaucrats, and lawmen are now employed by constables, social workers, and humane officers. This new order, imposed by representatives of 'the law' such as Jefferson Gifford and Earl Legwater, builds cities at the expense of community and destroys nature for profit or often for no reason at all. From the earliest reactions to the novel, critics have recognized, as the primary conflict of the work, this battle between an older, more 'primitive' set of values and the usurping new order. David Ragan, for instance, observes the 'deterioration' of 'traditional embodiments of value, religion, community relationships, agrarian connections with the earth' in the face of 'the increasing pressure of urban culture, commercial interests and governmental intrusions upon the lives of the novel's essentially rural characters' (10).[1] His summary echoes historical accounts of the struggles between the rural Irish population and their colonizers: 'Ireland was characterized by a fragmented policy: varieties of peoples defining their "Irishness" differently, many of whom denied the legitimacy of the official state apparatus and lived indifferently outside its writ' (Foster 3). McCarthy, by situating his novel in the neighborhood of Red Branch and by assigning to the community's traditional order certain central elements of Gaelic culture, uses the earlier conflict to inform the contemporary one and infuses his own tale with the pathos of the Gaelic oppression.

However, like the Irish model, the struggle in *The Orchard Keeper* does not follow a simple pattern of superior strength leading to absolute dominance. McCarthy's novel reveals that conquest depends upon laws and punishment as well as the imposition of culture, but it also allows one representative of the previous tradition to escape and therefore leaves the conquest incomplete. With even one vestige of a culture remaining, resistance is possible. Though the final scene laments that the older tradition has been 'banished in death or exile, lost, undone,' it does so *after* establishing that John Wesley has survived and his mentors have succeeded in passing on the old values to him (246). The significance of passing on that legacy can also be found in Irish history. Noting historian R. F. Foster's remark that the 'English colonial presence in Ireland remained superimposed upon an ancient identity' (3), one could contend that the British colonizers' inability to extinguish Gaelic culture (though many Gaelic traditions have been lost) contributed greatly to the rebellions that won Irish independence – that the identity below the colonizers' imposition or the one forced to move west to escape decimation caused the ruptures or troubles that made permanent conquest impossible. *The Orchard Keeper* carefully develops the principles that make the Gaelic-like community capable of resistance and then protects this capacity by providing one troubling survivor.

In the resisting figure of John Wesley, this chapter, contrary to much of McCarthy criticism, finds hope in the novel's defense of a tradition and a moral code threatened by modern 'civilization' and its corrupted, destructive, and self-serving new order. This reading diverges from a critical tradition influenced by Vereen Bell's early assertion of the author's 'nihilism,' in which he contends that 'ethical categories do not rule' and 'moral considerations seem not to affect outcomes' in McCarthy's novels and that the author himself is 'indifferent if not hostile to social order' ('The Ambiguous Nihilism of Cormac McCarthy' 31–2).

Besides articles more clearly indebted to Bell's assessment, such as Mark Royden Winchell's 'Inner Dark: Or, the Place of Cormac McCarthy,' even those which contend that *The Orchard Keeper* does possess a moral code, such as John Grammer's 'A Thing Against Which Time Will Not Prevail,' resist the notion of survival, seeing the novel as merely an *elegy* for a community 'nobly resisting but finally defeated by the gnostic will to deny history' (23). Though, in the novels immediately following *The Orchard Keeper*, the question of a moral standard becomes problematic, this paper contends that such a moral standard exists in the novel and, as mentioned above, wishes to extend David Ragan's discussion of 'values and structure' to propose that John Wesley's indoctrination and freedom at the novel's close suggest a continuation of the old values and a failure on the part of the new order to absolutely destroy Red Branch. Finally, not even Ragan's article, which seems most closely allied with this argument, has identified the 'old' system of values in McCarthy's Red Branch with the Gaelic tradition. However, before this comparison can be made, a background of the process of English conquest and Irish resistance must be established.

Although Anglo-Norman settlers began staking claim to Irish land as early as the twelfth century, the subduing of Gaelic culture became a reality only when, in the sixteenth and seventeenth centuries, a nascent empire regarded Ireland as a military threat. At this time, England was first imagining itself as an imperial power much like its own conquerors, the Romans, and would not allow a possible breeding ground for rebellion or a place from which enemies could launch attacks so close to its shores. Sir John Davies, initially a solicitor-general for Ireland and the Speaker of the Irish Parliament from 1613–15, wrote *A Discovery of the True Causes Why Ireland Was Never Entirely Subdued* from the perspective of England's growing sense of self-worth and imperial prowess (3). He questions why 'a barbarous country' such as Ireland, 'whereof our kings of England have bourne the title of "sovereign lords" for the space of four hundred and odd years' (or since Henry II's conquest), 'was not in all that space of time thoroughly subdued and reduced to obedience of the Crown of England' (70–1). Davies uses the Roman empire's methods in subjugating the Britons as an example of how the Crown of England might subdue the Irish. He specifically notes how the Romans gave 'their laws to the rude and barbarous people whom they had conquered' and how they brought these rude people to an 'absolute subjection' by teaching them 'to build temples, houses, and places of public resort,' instructing them in 'the liberal sciences,' and encouraging an appreciation for 'delicacies in buildings and furniture of household, in baths and exquisite banquets' (140–1). Davies clearly delineates two paths to sovereignty: the enforcement of legal and punitive powers along with the imposition of cultural dominance.

The culture that the English had to suppress in favor of their own was one never significantly touched by the Romans. Though archaeologists have found evidence of trade with Rome, as with other Gaelic strongholds in Scotland and the west of Wales, Ireland never bowed to Caesar or his successors. England, utterly changed by the Romans, predictably then viewed the Irish as alien and savage. Gaelic culture seemed in many ways the anarchical antithesis to the ordered and centralized tradition assumed by those within the Roman empire. Where the Romans would build unifying roads and aqueducts, the Irish preferred to keep the more natural routes of communication along rivers, and 'roads were not much attended to' well into the seventeenth century (Foster 7). Metropolitan centers, such as Rome or London, wherein one found the seat of government and the highest form of 'civilized' pursuits for the entire country, did not exist in the same manner in Ireland: 'The vast majority of this population was rurally based. Towns were not characteristic of Gaelic lordships' (16). However, the greatest obstacle to English conquest was not the infrastructure but the Gaelic social structure.

The Gaels, like other Celtic tribes, based their society on lineage, in which each individual belonged to a 'clan' stretching back four generations from the father (patriarch) to the great-grandnephew. Each clan occupied a certain amount of land which provided political and economic position; at the time of the patriarch's death, this territory was divided equally among all legitimate and what English law would call 'illegitimate' heirs (Nicholls 11). Encompassing the clan, Gaelic society followed the laws of the *tuath* or tribe, extended family groupings which occupied an even larger territory. Each *tuath* had a chieftain, and, beyond that, each province had a king. Finally, the ultimate authority belonged to the *Ard ri* or high king, who ruled over all provinces of Ireland from Tara. However, this structure was not quite as orderly as it appears. Each individual unit within this chain of order practiced a kind of autonomy. As a result, Jean Markdale finds that 'inter-tribal relations could become extremely complex,' approaching an 'almost built-in tendency to anarchy' (110). Judging solely from the basic hierarchical structure of the clan, *tuath*, and province, it would seem that the Gaels accepted the notion of a ruling authority; however, without the dependence on primogeniture, any member of the ruling family could stand for election as a chieftain or king and this created incredible rivalries. So, not only did each societal unit possess a kind of autonomy, but also each individual within the family had equal rights to ascendancy. One can understand, in light of this, how a king in Ireland would need to remain alert, diplomatic, and flexible. As Markdale warns, 'the Celts would never accept the dictates of one man' (110–11). With often tragic results, the English have spent eight hundred years battling that very mentality.

With a similar rebellious and decentralized nature, Cormac McCarthy's mountain community of 'Red Branch' mirrors the Gaelic model in its reverence for family ties and in its attention to certain bonds to community beyond those of blood. The difficulties experienced by Jefferson Gifford in his attempts to enforce 'the law' arise from the tribe-like community's resistance to unfamiliar forces, and this conflict evokes images of frustrated English lawmen and administrators who found that 'kinship links made the securing of impartial juries almost impossible' (Foster 25). To create an insular and aggressively autonomous tribal community, McCarthy weaves together several clans, in fact referring to Increase Tipton as the 'patriarch of a clan' at the opening of the novel (11). Attention to clan lineage appears throughout the novel, reinforcing the significance of the family line to the self-reliant *tuath*: Ef Hobie's story begins with a mention of his father and refers to the Hobie family history as 'mythical, preliterate, and legendary' (95); John Wesley is preceded by his father's reputation (61, 161, 235); and Uncle Ather identifies Warn Pulliam not with his given name but as 'Hiram Pulliam's grandson' (145). Perhaps significantly, Kenneth Rattner, on the other hand, chooses to give any name but his own as he hitchhikes at the beginning of the novel (10). These families protect their own members and look out for others within their tribe as well. Preserving the traditions and indeed the community itself depends on the alliances of family and extended family. McCarthy, while forming Red Branch from lineages, emphasizes in the relationships between the three main characters those bonds outside of blood relations which are equally as vital to holding the community together.

Gaelic society was of course based in kinship, but other cultural practices and ties also sustained the Irish way of life and contributed to the strength of the community as it faced oppositional forces. Through the action of his novel and in the lives of his three central characters, the author examines three of these extra-kinship connections: the practice of fosterage, shared religious beliefs, and the offering of hospitality. The first of these, fosterage, affects most deeply the only surviving disciple of the old order at the end of the novel, John Wesley Rattner. John Wesley's father has been killed (in the first section of the novel) in a confrontation with the man who will become the young boy's foster-father. Marion Sylder supplants the man he kills and perhaps acts more like a father than Kenneth Rattner ever would have; Rattner has selfishly fled his family and his community without explanation when he hitches his final ride with Sylder. With an evocation of 'council fires,' McCarthy highlights the major moments in the changing notion of fatherhood: the encounter between Sylder and Rattner, the first view of John Wesley, fatherless, and, finally, the realization of the foster-father-son relationship. As Sylder reaches over to light Rattner's cigarette, the two men face each other 'over the cup of light like enemy chieftains across a council fire' (36). Then, as John Wesley considers his obligation to revenge his father's death, he observes from the branches of a poplar tree his community, like an 'encampment settling for rest, council fires put out' (66). The transference of fatherly responsibility finally occurs when Sylder builds a fire to warm John Wesley after he has gone into the creek during a coon hunt and the boy stands 'naked, white as a slug in the cup of firelight' (125). Within the culture McCarthy uses as a model, this kind of transference of responsibility occurred often.

Though the origins of the practice of fosterage may predate the Gaels' arrival in Ireland, the Celtic people soon adopted it as one of their own most revered customs. The practice of fosterage involved the father's relinquishing of nearly all rights over his child and the giving over of the child's care to another family or relatives until he (the practice being almost always reserved for male children) grew to maturity. This new bond extended the child's family and created strong alliances within the larger community. An example taken from the story of Cuchulain illustrates the political import of such an affiliation. Dechtire, Cuchulain's mother, is also the sister of Conchubar, King of Ulster. As a young boy, Cuchulain goes to the palace at Emain Macha to live and receive guidance from his uncle, who has been named as his foster-father, as well as from 'all the chief men of Ulster' (353); he grows to maturity 'among chariot chiefs and heroes, among jesters and Druids, among poets and learned men' (369). In return for his education and upbringing, Cuchulain defends his uncle as if he were his own father. During the war for the Bull of Cuailgne, Cuchulain stands alone at the border and protects Ulster from attack by its enemies, who are led by Queen Maeve of Connaught. Though the example above does not depict it, the practice of fosterage could also benefit the child, who could rely on the protection of his foster-family throughout his life. Such a powerful cohesive force for the community resisted antagonists, and the Irish continued to practice fosterage into the eighteenth century (Markdale 109). The similar bond formed between Marion Sylder and John Wesley proves as problematic for Jefferson Gifford as it did for English administrators like Sir John Davies.

John Wesley Rattner, a boy of fourteen, cannot actually remember his own father. He recalls a man but is unsure whether he is 'his father or just some other man' (62). The thought of his father's disappearance and of his mother's insistence that he avenge the killing brings John Wesley to tears (66). At such a young age, he already feels 'weary' and sad (67); he sinks under the emotional weight of filial obligations, yet he has no father to guide him. Nonetheless, McCarthy indicates in early descriptions how John Wesley already belongs to the old tradition. He uses the weather and the seasons as 'his timepiece' (65), places his bed on the porch outside the kitchen because he cannot 'bear to be in the house,' and recognizes the 'council fires' of his community (66). Maturing without guidance, he wanders alone at night and once home finds that he cannot communicate with his mother, who lives in the past and sits knitting, 'fiercely sedate' (73). However, a simple act of fellowship changes all of this for John Wesley. Without a second thought, the boy enters the freezing water of the creek and pulls a stranger out of peril. Dragging Marion Sylder's body out of the wrecked car, he does not know that he is saving his father's killer. With a touch of irony as well as foreshadowing, McCarthy notes the way in which Sylder grasps John Wesley's shoulder, 'in an attitude of fatherly counsel,' as the boy supports his weight and they climb out of the creek (102). First in an effort to repay the favor and then from the emotional connection that quickly develops, Marion Sylder takes on the role of foster-father.

Mindful of his obligation after being pulled from the creek, Sylder invites John Wesley into his home and makes the first in a series of fatherly gestures toward the boy. Once inside the warm house, Sylder's wife demands that the boy change out of his wet clothes and insists that both of them sit down for breakfast. Wearing the older man's dry clothes, John Wesley looks like a child in his father's hand-me-downs, with the 'trousers turned up at the bottoms and gathered at the waist' (110). The boy tastes black coffee apparently for the first time, and before he leaves Sylder gives him a puppy from his prized hound Lady's litter. By keeping Sylder's illegal transportation of untaxed whiskey a secret, John Wesley earns the older man's trust and again reveals his devotion to the community and its values. Not long after the first encounter, Sylder expresses his appreciation and growing affection for the boy by taking him coon hunting. Guiding John Wesley through this rite of passage, the first hunt, firmly establishes Sylder as a surrogate father. Not only does the older man initiate the boy into an adult male tradition, but also he cares for John Wesley by building the fire along the creek bank, as mentioned above. While the boy's clothes are drying on a bush and he is warming himself by the fire, Sylder offers his first compliment to his foster-son; he indicates that the boy's 'got too much heart' in an unstated comparison between the boy and the loyal hound for whom he jumped in the creek (126). It was, after all, John Wesley's 'too much heart' that drove him into the creek the first time to save Sylder.

Once the relationship has been established, the older man assumes the role of guardian throughout the remainder of the novel. As with the Gaelic practice of fosterage, the foster-son in McCarthy's novel can depend on the protection of his adopted family. In an attempt to scare John Wesley and induce him to expose Sylder as the driver of the crashed car, the constable, Jefferson Gifford, threatens to arrest the boy for trapping without a license. Sylder comes to the boy's defense, expressing shame and disgust regarding Gifford's breach of traditional values: 'He knew you didn't have no daddy, nobody to take up for you in the first place is the reason he figured he could jump on you. He's a low life son of a bitch and caird to boot' (161). The constable was counting on John Wesley's weakness as individual without clan support. However, he clearly miscalculated, as he discovers that night when Sylder visits him in his bedroom with a 'shut fist rocketing down out of the darkness' (167). In a final gesture before the law catches up with him and he goes to jail, John Wesley's foster-father loans him the money to replace the traps confiscated by Gifford (207). The boy communicates his understanding of their foster-relationship when he visits Sylder in jail and promises to punish Gifford for his abuse of the other man. Never openly declaring it, John Wesley has chosen the old order by finding a foster-father in Sylder and has simultaneously rejected the new order represented by Gifford, who 'sells his own neighbors out for money' (215). In the act of returning the hawk bounty, the boy proclaims his allegiance.

In his relationship with Arthur Ownby, also called Uncle Ather, John Wesley makes another connection with the community and with the old system of values underlying that community. Arthur Ownby represents the second of those extrakinship bonds, the bond found in shared religious faith. He is the spiritual center of Red Branch. His reverence for nature, his prophetic ability, his storytelling or role as community memory, and his ritualized burial of Kenneth Rattner distinguish him as a holy man and as the preserver of tradition. However, Uncle Ather's particular faith predates Christianity and incorporates many more functions within the community. Druids, of whom Ownby is certainly an example, were more than 'priests' in Celtic societies like Gaelic Ireland. To the Gaels, a druid's words were to be understood as law, and even the king observed the druid's right to speak before him; as evidenced in the Irish literature, the druid 'encompasses all the power and every art protecting and promoting society' (Lonigan 84). The powers or arts used by druids for these ends include the following: astrology, prophecy, divination, sacrifices, knowledge of sencha (ancient tradition), knowledge of law and genealogy, shapechanging, divine pronouncements, pedagogy, tree-divination, consecration of land, philosophy, and medicine (Lonigan 89–112).[2] For the purpose of explicating Arthur Ownby's role as the protector and promoter of Red Branch, examination of only a few of these arts and powers will be necessary, along with identification of symbolic druid possessions and locales.

From McCarthy's first description, Uncle Ather is associated with practice of the druidic religion. He sits on his porch observing the affairs of the community and studies 'the movement of stars' (20). Emphasizing his connection to nature, he, like John Wesley, watches 'the seasons and their work' (90). David Ragan associates Ather, the orchard keeper to whom the title refers, with an 'almost mystical connection to the cycles of nature' (10) and later alludes to the older man's observance of 'pre-Christian religious traditions,' suggesting Merlin or Prospero (14). Without naming it, Ragan is recognizing the druidic religion, wherein mystical connections with nature, such as the practice of 'Astrology, in the proper sense of the word divination from the stars' or drawing auguries 'from the observation of clouds,' were fundamental (P. W. Joyce 48–9). Not coincidentally, Uncle Ather admits to being 'a lover of storms' (51) and carries a staff of hickory, having 'hewed it octagonal and graced the upper half with hex-carvings – nosed moons, stars, fish of strange and Pleistocene aspect' (46). The druid staff, used during divinations, was carved from a yew tree and had *ogham* marks cut into it, 'horizontal and diagonal strokes grouped together in numbers of one to five' (Markdale 108). The old man, who keeps watch over the orchard, gives the appropriate sacred import to trees, which the druids venerated and used in certain pagan ceremonies. He, in fact, lives surrounded by 'the silhouette of pines' that stretch upward like 'a mammoth cathedral gothically spired' (59) and incorporates the branches of cedars, described as 'rotund and druidical' (120), in an important religious ritual, the burial of Kenneth Rattner. Although Ather distinguishes himself further as the druid of Red Branch in his gift of 'vision' (59) and in his desire to live alone but remain 'neighborly' (55), his actions, such as the burial of Rattner, most define him as the protector and preserver of the community.

In three significant acts, Ownby defends his community and preserves its values. The first of these, the ritual burial, evokes sacrifices and burial rites performed by druids on consecrated occasions, including a king's initiation and the fertility ceremony. The body in the spray pit, which Ownby covers with cedars and guards for seven years, resembles those found in the bogs of Denmark and Ireland, identified by P. V. Glob as sacrifices for Celtic fertility ceremonies and preserved like Rattner by 'a tannic liquor' (90).[3] Often, in fertility ceremonies, the priest sacrificed himself for the assurance of the tribal land's fecundity in the coming spring, and Ownby almost does drown in the flood of rain in section four, hearing the 'mendicant-voiced' rain chant 'in that dark gramarye that summons the earth to bridehood' (184). Although McCarthy only gives one example of it, Uncle Ather also fulfills his druidic duties by protecting the *sencha* or the materials that make up the community tradition, such as history, local lore, law, and genealogies. In his recitation of the story of the wampus cat, Ather reveals his knowledge of local lore and performs the vital act of passing the lore on to another generation, Warn Pulliam and John Wesley (147–9). Druids not only protected the *sencha* but also educated 'the children of kings and chiefs – they were indeed the only educators' (P. W. Joyce 53). Finally, in a more openly violent manner (druids were present on battlefields), Ownby takes it upon himself to oppose the government's presence in the mountain community. He shoots a large 'x' into the government tank which looms over his property and the way in which he carefully creates the 'circumcised shotgun shells' intensifies the entire operation with the mode of ritual (94). Unfortunately, this protective act brings the law to his house and in that way decides his fate.

Long before Jefferson Gifford and the other deputies seek retribution for the marking of the tank, Uncle Ather has recognized the intrusion of and destruction caused by the new order. The orchard kept by Ather has been 'ruined' and allowed to go to waste twenty years before the present of the novel (51). He notices similar disregard and abuse of nature during his journey to collect ginseng roots: the quarry bares open 'monoliths of rock alienated up out of the earth,' turned into 'ruins' (189), and on his path back he finds the unused carcass of a rattlesnake, which has been killed only for its rattles (201). The lack of respect for life in the name of monetary gain extends to the bounty on hawks and even to 'bounty on findin dead bodies' by 'grapplehookin em when they jump off of the bridge' in the city (228). Whether consciously or not, Uncle Ather associates this change in traditional values with the new order of 'law' and commerce represented by the tank on the hill. After Ather has been taken away by the authorities and his staff is broken in the police car door (203), McCarthy stresses the new order's disregard for life again in 'humane officer' Legwater's final actions. Legwater not only desecrates Kenneth Rattner's grave, so carefully tended by Uncle Ather, in search of a non-existent piece of platinum but also kills the old man's intensely loyal hound, Scout (242). In a community named Red Branch, the killing of a hound, Cuchulain meaning 'the hound of Culain,' must signify an incredible betrayal.

A story from the Ulster cycle, which includes Cuchulain, provides an illustration of the importance of hospitality, the last of the extra-kinship ties depended upon in McCarthy's novel to strengthen the community. According to Jean Markdale, hospitality was 'sacrosanct among the Celts' and by that notion 'their king was to be a benefactor of the *tuath* and to serve others rather than profit by his influence' (111). One of the stories of the Ulster cycle involves King Conaire, who becomes high king of Ireland under the conditions of a *geasa* or bond; one of these conditions states that he cannot allow any woman or man into his house after sunset (430). However, once in the inn where he will meet his death, a woman comes to the door and asks for shelter. Knowing his bond, Conaire offers to send out food to her and she curses him, claiming that 'the king's hospitality is gone from him' (438). He breaks his *geasa* because he would rather do that than be thought inhospitable. The citizens of Red Branch in *The Orchard Keeper* who heed the old code also favor the offering of hospitality to their neighbors. Even outside of Red Branch, in other mountain communities, Uncle Ather finds the warmth of hospitality. In order for these communities to survive, there must be a respect for the land and for the history and traditions of the past, as well as a fellowship among neighbors. In fact, as mentioned above, the worst insult Marion Sylder can charge against Jefferson Gifford is that instead of looking out for his neighbors he sells them out for money and 'it's few lie that deep in the pit, that far beyond the pale' (215).

McCarthy's novel gives several examples of the hospitality and neighborly fellowship considered 'sacrosanct' in Gaelic culture. Perhaps not surprisingly, these acts of kindness and generosity occur often when a neighbor is most in need. For instance, after John Wesley has pulled Sylder out of the wreck (an incredible act of selflessness and generosity in its own right), the two men find shelter at June Tipton's house. Without asking any questions, Tipton and his wife take them in, offer food and drink, and finally drive them to Sylder's house (104–6). Similarly, on his long trek over the mountains to find ginseng roots to trade, Uncle Ather finds relief and comfort at the home of strangers. The old man has been traveling a long way, and, though he makes the appropriate gesture by at first refusing the two younger men's overtures, he eventually agrees to eat breakfast with them, soon beginning to 'feel right homey' (193). They offer tobacco and papers to Ather 'not ceremoniously but with that deprecatory gesture of humility which country people confer in a look' and pass a jar of 'good drinkin whiskey' around the table (193). The two hosts, though strangers and of a younger generation, understand the fundamentals of the old system of values, sharing what they have and showing respect for the older man. Finally, in a precursor to this scene, Uncle Ather performs his role as teacher of the old ways and shares his own jar of 'Muskydine wine,' while sheltering and entertaining Warn Pulliam and John Wesley; McCarthy attributes significance to their actions, describing them sipping 'their wine with the solemnity of communicants' (150). Advising John Wesley once again, Ather through his actions stresses the veneration for hospitality in the old order.

The Orchard Keeper, however, recognizes, in the midst of celebrating the old system of values, its tragic decline as it is confronted by the encroaching city and the modern values found there. As seen in the imprisonment of Marion Sylder and Arthur Ownby briefly mentioned above, the new order can rely upon 'the law' to further its values and eliminate the key representatives of the opposing tradition. As in the words of Sir John Davies, 'For to give laws unto a people; to institute magistrates and officers over them; to punish and pardon malefactors; to have the sole authority of making war and peace, and the like, are the true marks of sovereignty' (76). McCarthy carefully aligns a number of laws with oppression of the Red Branch community and often locates the origin of these codes in the city.

Many of these laws involve payments to the government: the unpaid property tax for John Wesley's house (63); the tax on whiskey (210); the license for trapping (159); and license plates (114). Also mentioned previously and more closely associated with the city, the new order will exchange money or 'bounty' for hawks and human bodies (79, 228). Respect for nature and community fellowship can hardly be expected in a place where human and animal lives amount to a bounty. McCarthy emphasizes the useless destruction caused by this mentality in the scene of the final siege of Arthur Ownby's house. In their effort to arrest Ownby, who has already fled, Gifford and other law enforcement officers open fire and destroy the old man's empty house, injuring one of their own in the process (188). Unfortunately, the ridiculous and deadly efforts of the new order possess enough strength to destroy most of the community.

In the final section of the novel, McCarthy dramatizes the nearly complete downfall of the old order and specifically ties its demise with the city and governmental or punitive institutions. As forewarned in the prologue by the mangled and soon-to-be-felled tree, the old system of values and Red Branch itself will first be infiltrated by the new and then consumed or driven away. Marion Sylder is caught with untaxed liquor and placed in jail, where he is vulnerable to attack from Gifford (211). Arthur Ownby is also arrested, on charges 'ranging from Destruction of Government Property to Assault with Intent to Kill' (218), and sentenced to spend the remainder of his life in an insane asylum. If he had not run away, John Wesley may have been arrested as well. The representatives of the new way of life, such as Gifford, Legwater, and the social worker who questions Uncle Ather in order to have an official 'record' for the Welfare Bureau (219), must find ways to control or debilitate those people who preserve and protect the old traditions. The social worker needs information in order to make sure he assigns the older man to the appropriate 'department or agency,' which will act as his ward (218), and Marion Sylder will certainly be locked away at Brushy Mountain with other moonshiners and 'criminal' members of the Red Branch community. Once the law has separated the families in the community and exiled its most vehement protectors, the new ways of life can change Red Branch in the name of 'progress.'

John Wesley proves in his act of returning the hawk bounty that he has finally and completely aligned himself with the old system of values. However, he and the code he follows must move west to avoid the crippling oppression of the new order. Upon returning, he finds that the new order occupies Red Branch. There is a road running along side the graveyard, wherein he find his mother's grave, and, as he attempts to connect with two members of the modern world, they do not respond to his neighborly wave. The time of hospitality, devotion to nature, and fosterage in the mountain community has 'Fled, banished in death or exile' (246). The Gaelic traditions kept now in John Wesley's memory must move west again as they did in the times of the English conquest. Beginning in Dublin and moving out to include the 'plantation' of other provinces, including Ulster, the Tudor state, 'preoccupied by the priority of uniformity, could not stomach this

[Gaelic Ireland's] complex, intuitive and protean way of life' and began creating massive estates and surrounding villages (Foster 32). For example, one wealthy Englishman, Richard Boyle, built a '"lordly mansion", surrounded by a stocked deer-park, selected fruit-orchards, fish-ponds, stud-farms, eyries, a meticulously constructed rabbit-warren,' which was to him as important 'as forest-clearing, castle- and town-building, iron-smelting and the foundation of almshouses' (7). Foster later summarizes the colonizers' building practices: 'the general English tendency was to equate urbanization with the advance of Anglicization and "civility"' (17). Indeed, McCarthy's version of 'plantation' only lacks the insertion of a government building, already foreseen by the presence of the government tank, where Uncle Ather's house once stood.

By using the Gaelic tradition and history to inform and impassion his Red Branch, McCarthy does more than remind his readers of the fall of older ways and express despair about the urbanization and centralization of modern life. In the midst of the overwhelming success of Anglicization, Romanization, and other civilizing forces in the United States, that other tradition still exists. Foster observes that in seventeenth-century Ireland 'as elsewhere, the intractable old identity remained beneath the English imposition: sometimes working with it, more often counteracting it' (25). McCarthy's work has been called nihilistic, most notably by Vereen Bell, and one early critic even declares that the work is 'not merely bereft of community and myth' but also that McCarthy 'has declared war against these ancient repositories of order and truth' (Sullivan 72). I believe that *The Orchard Keeper* belies these claims. Although the community of Red Branch may be 'banished in death or exile, lost, undone,' John Wesley survives to take his values west. And perhaps more importantly, McCarthy in the writing of the novel does not let those values become 'dust.' Cuchulain will accept an early death so long as his heroic life is remembered and McCarthy's novel serves that memory well. Finally, as Jean Markdale suggests, the Celts do never 'accept the dictates of one man' but remain hidden and present, constantly undermining his authority (111). As a famous member of the contemporary Ulster has said, 'Conquest is a lie' (Heaney 49). The English process of civilizing Ireland may have changed that country considerably, but, as twentieth-century history shows, the Gaelic tradition did not die. It moved to the west of Ireland and waited.

Notes

1 Many other critics identify this theme: John M. Grammer notes the resistance to 'civilizing' influences and the main characters' attempts to preserve 'their old-fashioned existence' in his article 'A Thing Against Which Time Will Not Prevail: Pastoral and History in Cormac McCarthy's South' (*Southern Quarterly* 30 (1992): 23); John Cawelti envisions mountaineers driven out of their home into 'the modern world' ('Cormac McCarthy: Restless Seekers,' *Southern Writers at Century's End*, ed. Jeffrey J. Folks and James A. Perkins (Lexington: University Press of Kentucky, 1997) 165); and Mark Royden Winchell again notes the 'rural setting' being 'besieged by the forces

of civilization' ('Inner Dark: Or, the Place of Cormac McCarthy,' *Southern Review* 26 (1990): 295).
2 I have included an incomplete list here and will not attempt to address all of those arts and powers listed. For a more detailed account of druidic history, I direct the reader to *The Druid Source Book*, ed. John Matthews (London: Blandford Press, 1997).
3 Seamus Heaney, in his collections *Wintering Out* (London: Faber, 1972) and *North* (London: Faber, 1975), drew attention to these bog bodies and to Glob's book, *The Bog People: Iron Age Man Preserved* (London: Faber, 1969), with a series of poems comparing the violent rituals of Iron Age Celts with the 'Troubles' in Northern Ireland. However, all three of these books were published after *The Orchard Keeper*.

Nell Sullivan

The evolution of the dead girlfriend motif in *Outer Dark* and *Child of God*

Forty years ago, C. J. McCarthy Jr. used the following lyric from Sir Walter Scott as the epigraph for his first published story, 'Wake for Susan' (1959):

> 'Who makes the bridal bed,
> Birdie, say truly?'
> 'The grey headed sexton
> That delves the grave duly.'

Although the story only hints at the artistic mastery Cormac McCarthy would eventually achieve, it does contain the germ of all his subsequent portrayals of women. Susan Ledbetter, its female romantic lead, is a long-dead woman onto whom a young man at her graveside projects his fantasies. With their conflation of the bridal bed and the grave, the lines from Scott's 'Proud Maisie' introduce a theme echoing throughout most of McCarthy's fiction: the theme of female sexuality inextricably bound up with death and, therefore, posed as a source of masculine dread. This insidious association leads inexorably to the narrative death sentence for young women in the McCarthy canon. Moving from its gentlest to most egregious articulation, the transition from *Outer Dark* (1968) to *Child of God* (1973) marks the crystallization of the 'dead girlfriend' motif in McCarthy's mature fiction.

Rinthy Holme of *Outer Dark* seems to be a rare exception among McCarthy's female romantic leads, for within the narrative itself, her corpse is not offered up as an aesthetic or erotic object, nor does McCarthy orchestrate her death within the narrative as a plot device, or literal *pretext*, for bringing male characters together. Instead, Rinthy accrues dignity and power in spite of overt narrative gestures that might otherwise trivialize her or make her ridiculous. She is not merely subject *to* male desire, but in the parlance of contemporary psychoanalytic theory, Rinthy is the subject *of* desire, the desiring subject, what Jacques Lacan, in a conscious revision of the Cartesian *cogito*, called the *desidero* (*Four Fundamental Concepts of Psycho-Analysis* 154).

Of course, Rinthy's characterization is sometimes vexed with misogynist details. She is frequently described in terms that would deny her agency or even any anima at all. The metaphor of choice for Rinthy seems to be the lifeless doll. She regards Culla at one point with 'doll's eyes of painted china' (24); at another point she moves like a 'crippled marionette' (32). When she prepares to leave home in search of her 'chap,' McCarthy uses the anachronistic image of the music-box ballerina: 'she pirouetted slowly in the center of the room like a doll unwinding for just a moment' (53). She then proceeds to 'rak[e] her dead yellow hair' with a broken comb (53) – the 'dead yellow hair' still today a prominent feature of many dolls. She is also described as a doll in the company of others besides Culla, so we cannot say that McCarthy is merely projecting or depicting Culla's point of view. For example, when she spends the night with the family, her face in the lamplight appears like a 'china mask' (59), while later, in the company of the unnamed man with whom she lives for a time, she moves about 'mute, shuffling, wooden' and when the man speaks to her, she strikes the music-box pose again, turning 'doll-like, one arm poised' (210).

At other times in the narrative when Rinthy *is* depicted as animate, the narrative suggests that she is not very bright. When she begins the search for her child, she sets out with 'a smile all bland and burdenless like a child's' (53). Elsewhere, there are intimations of catalepsy. At moments, her eyes 'held nothing at all' (14) and when she discovers the empty grave, Culla, the narrator, tells us, 'mistook for accusation' what was merely a blank expression, 'her own face still bland and impervious' (33). Much later in the narrative, she seems to sleepwalk, rising 'half tranced from the bed' (211). I once suggested that all McCarthy's male protagonists are versions of Twain's Huck Finn.[1] I could also argue that Poe's Madeline Usher is the model for all of McCarthy's major female characters. Like the Ushers', the Holmes' family tree is suspiciously denuded of branches, deficient in what Poe calls 'collateral issue' (Poe 140). With her doll-like movements, trances, and bland expression, Rinthy, like Lady Madeline, seemingly suffers from 'transient affections of a partially cataleptical character' (145). In describing Madeline's final decline, Poe's naive narrator says, 'she succumbed (as her brother told me at night with inexpressible agitation) to the prostrating power of the destroyer' (145). That is, like Rinthy, Madeline may have been raped or seduced by her brother, and in her cataleptical state that is mistaken by Poe's narrator for death, she wears 'a faint blush' and 'that suspiciously lingering smile' (151), much like Rinthy's witless smile. Rinthy's blandness – her version of catalepsy – seems at odds with Culla's constant agitation, which betokens a tortured mind like Roderick Usher's.

According to Gail Kern Paster, the female body is perceived in the Western canon as 'naturally grotesque – which is to say, open, permeable, effluent, leaky' (92). In another problematic aspect of Rinthy's characterization, these very conditions mark Rinthy as both maternal and abject. The fact that she is 'open' and 'permeable' – that is, pregnable – has rendered her an outcast in Johnson County and determined for her the life of misery that the novel details. After her water breaks, she leaks constantly for the rest of the novel – tears, blood and milk, the three often combined and conflated. Culla notices 'like dark tears two milkstains' on Rinthy's shift (30), and when he frightens her at the empty grave, 'the blood start[ed] again, warm on her leg' (32–3). As for milk, Rinthy says, 'I never needed none but I had too much all the time' (153). Felicia Pattison notes that the appellation 'mam' is actually a sly pun when applied to Rinthy, given the metonymic function of her leaky mammary glands. Indeed, lactation becomes her Pavlovian response to the cry of some other mother's child: 'already she could feel it begin warm and damp, sitting there holding her swollen breasts, feeling it runnel down her belly . . . thin blue milk welled from the rotting cloth' (99–100). The mere thought of her chap causes 'milk [to run] from the dark cloth' of her dress, as when she talks about him with the old woman (115). She seeks medical assistance only after she becomes like the weird Madonna of Richard Crashaw's poem 'Luke 11,' her 'paps' bleeding and lactating simultaneously (153).[2] The doctor himself further suggests Rinthy's abjection, as he confuses the human and the bovine: 'Are we talking about cow milk or people milk?' he asks her (152). To underscore Rinthy's similarity to a dairy cow, the narrator describes the sounds from the street below the doctor's window, where 'cattle were being driven through the rain and the mud' (156).[3]

Reading retrospectively from *Cities of the Plain*, we can also find problematic McCarthy's narration of Rinthy's labor, which is echoed strikingly in two of the depictions of Magdalena's seizures in the 1998 novel. The image of the female body prone and racked with pain is so powerful that it survived virtually unchanged through thirty years of McCarthy's vision and revision. During her first seizure Magdalena 'arched herself stiffly' so that the criada must 'climb into the bed' and '[hold] her' (72). During her second seizure, she is described as 'bowed and trembling . . . breathing harshly' (83). Similarly, Rinthy is shown 'coming tautly bowed,' her breath loud, and her body 'arched' (11). Like the criada, Culla must restrain her physically, kneeling 'in the bed with one knee, holding her' (14). Both the pregnancy and the epilepsy threaten to break the women's bodies as males (Culla, Tiburcio) look on impassively. One could say that McCarthy uses similar descriptions for different effects, but Culla's warning to the tinker, 'sickness here' (6), stresses the debased nature of Rinthy's pregnancy, which in normal (i.e. legitimate and non-incestuous) circumstances would confer sanctity; his warning is also reminiscent of the pimp Eduardo's claim that Magdalena's epilepsy is 'illness only,' not sacred, but something that could diminish John Grady's love for her (213). Both conditions, then, are coded by the men as reasons for shame and exile.[4]

In spite of these negative representations, Rinthy becomes a compelling character, a narrative force to be reckoned with. In conversation, Robert Jarrett has noted that Rinthy is unusual among McCarthy's women because she remains a narrative focus throughout the novel. This retention of focus makes her an equal partner with Culla; even Magdalena, whose presence in *Cities of the Plain* has been heralded by a few critics as some sort of feminist break-through for McCarthy, receives far less attention with fewer glimpses into her consciousness.[5] What then accounts for Rinthy's narrative dominion? In the Preface to the New York edition of *The Portrait of a Lady*, Henry James remarks on the organic nature of character development: 'These are the fascinations of the fabulist's art, these lurking forces of expansion, these necessities of upspringing in the seed, these beautiful determinations, on the part of the idea entertained, to grow as tall as possible, to push into the light and the air and thickly flower there' (James 4). In her gradual metamorphosis from grotesque outcast to willful and self-possessed subject, Rinthy becomes an example of 'the necessities of upspringing' within the novelistic process.

Rinthy's desires create a sense of personalization and particularity, but also a sense of agency at odds with the mechanical nature of her depiction. She is clearly the *desidero* from her first appearance in the narrative. According to Jacques Lacan, every articulation of the speaking subject is a demand, but demand always exceeds need, and that residuum is desire (*Four Fundamental Concepts* 154–65, 278). We see this excessive desire when Rinthy makes a request that seems outrageously extravagant, given her impoverished context: 'That pedlar have ary cocoa? . . . I sure would admire to have me a cup of cocoa' (9). There is no cocoa, so she asks instead for a fire: 'You reckon we could have us a fire tonight? . . . I sure do admire a good fire of the evenin' (9, *sic*). Later she will ask for 'more of that black candy' that Culla brought her earlier (29). These material requests are screens for more abstract desires, for when Rinthy asks for chocolate or candy, she is asking for love; when she asks for a spring-time fire, she is asking for emotional warmth. Tellingly, Rinthy identifies the tinker not only as someone who stole her child, but as someone who did not or could not fulfill her desire. He is 'that tinker' whom 'they said never had no cocoa' (55). When she finally confronts him face to face, he justifies his lack of cocoa by telling her, 'I don't get enough call for it to mess with totin it' (184, *sic*), a fact that underscores the singularity of Rinthy's desire.

In spite of McCarthy's use of doll metaphors for Rinthy, her erotic potential does not result in her sexual objectification. Rather, Rinthy has the power of *yes* and *no* throughout the novel. She is courted in a variety of ways by the men she encounters. In the midst of their great poverty, for example, Culla buys only the most basic staples, but somehow he adds to his shopping list the curious item, 'And candy for her' (6). The lawyer she meets tips his hat and smiles at her, ultimately ushering her into his own office and holding the door for her (147–9). The son of the family with whom Rinthy sojourns briefly goes to great, albeit comically ineffectual lengths to impress her, including his manly attempt to mount the wagon in one heroic leap, causing him to 'stove a hole in his kneecap' (70). Neither his mock heroics nor his 'histrionic anguish' impress Rinthy, as the narrator tells us, 'there had been no one looking to see him swing up . . . in one leap' (70). Merely annoying at first, he becomes insulting after Rinthy refuses a date:

> He coyly slid a sheaf of bills out and riffled them before her . . . He worked the money. It's a bunch of it ain't it? he said. Bet you ain't never . . .
> I got to go, she said. (74)

In order to possess Rinthy, the boy introduces cash into the equation of desire and thereby implies that she can be bought, that she is a whore, but Rinthy exerts her power of *no* by walking away: 'She kept on' (74). This kind of power is inconceivable for Magdalena in *Cities of the Plain*.

Moreover, because the novel begins *in medias res*, we do not know who instigated the sexual relationship that obviously once existed between Culla and Rinthy, and this narrative silence allows the possibility that Rinthy is not Culla's victim at all, that she exerted the power of *yes* as well as *no*. Rinthy's refusal to play the victim is evident when she tells the doctor, 'I wasn't ashamed' (156). Unlike Culla, she claims the child again and again, as when she tells the tinker simply, 'I'm the mother of that chap you got' (184). In fact, it is her desire for her child that drives her. 'He's mine,' she tells the tinker with her eyes 'huge and hungered' (192). Or as she tells the doctor, 'I just go around huntin my chap. That's about all I do any more' (156, *sic*).

While Rinthy quests single-mindedly for her child, Culla's quest is more ambiguous. Although it is unclear whether he is actively 'huntin' his sister, he seems to gravitate toward her, unable to escape her orbit any more than he can escape the three killers, McCarthy's 'Grim Triune.' The two siblings barely miss each other near Cheatham, Well's Station, the ferry, and the tinker's final encampment. Culla frequently claims to be 'huntin' Rinthy, or so he tells the beekeeper, the snakeman, and, on two occasions, the bearded one (81, 126, 177, 236). When he encounters the Triune a second time, he asks the bearded one, 'Where's she at?' – perhaps with a little anxiety about Rinthy's safety (233).

Besides the gravity that pulls Culla into her orbit, Rinthy also has *gravitas*, the sort of dignity that prevents her from becoming ridiculous even in the most humiliating circumstances. She nods to the German storekeeper 'gravely' (54) and dresses at one point 'with gravity' (211). When insulted by the young boy, she moves with an 'air of staid and canonical propriety' (64). 'They Lord,' she exclaims with mild indignation when the man near Cheatham accuses her of having illicit relations with the tinker. 'It ain't nothin like that' (102). Even when she is 'ragged, shoeless, deferential and half deranged,' she moves nonetheless in 'an almost palpable amnion of propriety' (151); McCarthy's use of the word *amnion* suggests that it is her dignity that sustains her and shelters her from the harshness of the world around her. Her final narrative appearance emphasizes this metaphor of Rinthy as infant *in utero* as we witness a sort of narrative kindness to Rinthy, a respect for her person remarkable in light of the horrors that happen to other bodies in the text. She enters the glade where the chap's bones lie and stands '*cradled* in a grail of jade and windy light,' eventually moving 'in a frail agony of grace' (237, emphasis added).[6] Perhaps yet another mercy is extended to Rinthy in the way in which her exit from the novel is narrated; we are told only that 'after a while little sister was sleeping' (238). Those who have read *Blood Meridian* may understand 'sleep' as McCarthy's ironic metaphor for death,[7] but here, the term *sleep* is fitting, for Rinthy has technically found her son and thus can finally rest.

However, in spite of Rinthy's relative strength and dignity, the final pages of *Outer Dark* predict the problematic direction in which McCarthy's fiction takes the 'dead girlfriend' motif. Rinthy's final appearance takes us back to Scott's Maisie and Poe's Madeline Usher at the same time as it points forward to Lester Ballard's necrophile harem in *Child of God*. She appears 'half wild and haggard in her shapeless sundrained *cerements*' (237, emphasis added) – that is, burial robes – and stands 'slender and trembling and pale with wandlike hands to speak the boneless shapes attending her' (237). At the end of 'The Fall of the House of Usher,' Lady Madeline is 'an enshrouded figure' with 'blood upon her white robes, and the evidence of some bitter struggle upon every portion of her emaciated frame . . . trembling and reeling to and fro upon the threshold' (157). Both Rinthy and Madeline represent the beloved arrayed for death, in that troubling confusion that will soon overtake McCarthy's women in *Child of God:* the lethal conflation of female sexuality with death. In the final pages of *Outer Dark* we discover yet another omen of these things to come. When the road Culla travels dead-ends at a swamp, he 'trie[s] his foot in the mire before him and it rose in a *vulvate* welt claggy and sucking' (242, emphasis added). Metaphor works reciprocally, so if the mire that threatens to swallow Culla and the blind man resembles female genitalia, then obviously female genitalia must resemble the deadly mire. The sexual woman's threat can be diminished only by avoidance or neutralized by annihilation. While Rinthy's mostly positive characterization in *Outer Dark* results from those Jamesian 'necessities of upspringing in the seed, these beautiful determinations . . . to push into the light and the air and thickly flower there' (4), the final image of the novel is yet another organic metaphor, the 'faintly smoking garden of the dead' surrounding the vulvate swamp (242). Rinthy grew toward the light, yes, but like those dead trees she, too, is blighted.

The image of Rinthy's slumber appears consonant with McCarthy's first heroine, Susan Ledbetter in 'Wake for Susan.' But while Rinthy's 'sleeping' follows the completion of her quest, Susan's 125-year interment seems merely a postmortem betrothal in anticipation of Wes's arrival. (With its missing article, McCarthy's title plays on both the funereal and arousal connotations of *wake*.) The mere sight of Susan's gravestone inspires romantic dreams in the story's young rifle-toting hero, who insinuates himself retroactively into her life: 'Susan should have a lover, and the lover looked strangely like Wes' (4). He readily imagines a life for Susan, but it is easy to script a life for someone who is already dead and has no will of her own. Unlike Rinthy Holme, she is completely subject to the desire of a man since she can offer no resistance in death. While Wes is an obvious forerunner of John Wesley Rattner of *The Orchard Keeper* (1965), he also prefigures *Child of God*'s Lester Ballard, another man with a rifle who dreams of love with dead girls after the first object of his affection, the dumpkeeper's 'long blonde flatshanked daughter' (28), runs off with another man.[8] Lester's victims are devoid of volition and desire, unable in death to exert the power of either *yes* or *no*, allowing Lester to function exclusively as *desidero*. The seeds of narrative misogyny lying dormant in *Outer Dark* come to fruition in *Child of God*, where Culla's command to Rinthy, 'Mend woman' (30), degenerates into Lester's edict to all of his women, 'Die, goddamn you' (119).

The misogynistic details that merely impinge upon Rinthy's characterization are entirely constituent for the women in *Child of God*. Shortly after discovering that his fair-haired beloved has decamped with some other 'jellybean' (38), Lester stumbles across 'a lady sleeping under the trees in a white gown,' whom he watches 'for a while to see if she were dead' (41). As long as the woman is sleeping and de-animated, she receives the approbative term *lady*, but waking, she becomes 'a goddamned whore,' in Lester's words, or 'the old whore,' in the narrator's (52). Lester and the narrator both seem disappointed that she is not really dead. One of the vigilantes who roust Lester from the hospital recalls the esteem that accrues to women with death when he refers to Lester's victims as 'them dead ladies' (182).

Just as Rinthy appears as an animate doll, McCarthy describes Lester's subsequent victims as puppets or giant dolls, implying that Lester prefers inanimate, 'sleeping' women – women whose movements he alone controls. His first dead girlfriend is in fact scavenged, a victim of carbon monoxide poisoning in the back seat of a car. When she is not in use, Lester hauls her up into the attic with a plowline, manipulating her as though she were a marionette:

> Then he went in and fitted rope about the waist of the pale cadaver and ascended the ladder with the other end. She rose slumpshouldered from the floor with her hair all down and began to bump slowly up the ladder. Half-way up she paused, dangling. Then she began to rise again. (95)

When Lester lowers her from the attic, he is chagrined to find her more mannequin than puppet, 'wooden,' 'nor would she fold' (102). These images resonate uncannily when the Sevier County Sheriff's Department removes Lester's harem from the cave later in the novel:

> The rope drew taut and the first of the dead sat up on the cave floor, the hands that hauled the rope above sorting the shadows like puppeteers. Gray soapy clots of matter fell from the cadaver's chin. She ascended dangling. She sloughed in the weem of the noose. (196)

Indeed, women are 'playpretties' in this novel, pretty toys that Lester dresses up, poses, undresses and penetrates. He undresses his first love to 'inspect her body carefully, as if he would see how she were made' and then goes outside to see how she looks 'through the window' (91–2). As if she were a giant Barbie doll, he buys her a pretty red outfit, 'dress[es] her in her new clothes,' 'brush[es] her hair with the dimestore brush he'd brought,' and 'paint[s] her lips' with the lipstick he buys for her (102). Once she is fully accessorized, he 'arrange[s] her in different positions' and then 'peer[s] in the window at her' (103); after these dress-up games end, Lester has intercourse with the woman, who cannot rebuff his advances.

Though Rinthy moves within an unlikely nimbus of physical safety, the women in *Child of God* suffer almost every indignity a body can. These ladies, like Rinthy, exhibit the grotesque, incontinent bodies often associated with women in Western art and literature, but whereas Rinthy's effluence stems from internal forces,

Lester's ladies leak only because they experience the violent rupture of bodily integrity at his hands. The Lane girl, for example, is 'slick with blood' after Lester shoots her; she bleeds in 'a thin stream' that seeps 'away darkly in the wood of the floor' (119). The most incontinent female in the novel, however, is the girl he shoots on Frog Mountain. Having been warned that she has to 'go to the bathroom,' he shoots her anyway: 'She dropped as if the bones in her body had been *liquified*. Ballard tried to catch her but she slumped into the mud ... Her head was lolling and blood ran down her neck' (151, emphasis added). Despite this forcible liquifaction and subsequent necrophile coitus, Lester is disgusted by her urine: 'Suddenly he stopped and raised up. He lifted her skirt and looked down at her. She had wet herself. He cursed and pulled down the panties and dabbed at the pale thighs with the hem of the girl's skirt' (151). Even years after death, the bodies of his victims exhibit this abject incontinence. 'The bodies were covered with adipocere,' the narrator tells us with scientific objectivity, 'a pale gray cheesy mold common to corpses in damp places' (196). The mausoleum contains 'a sour smell, a faint reek of ammonia' and the first body disinterred drips 'gray soapy clots' and a 'gray rheum' (196). The High Sheriff's introduction of 'muslin shrouds' to the crime scene suggests a bit of belated dignity in death, a respect for the dead, but the potential for such sanctity, nominally present in 'Wake for Susan' and in Rinthy's final appearance in *Outer Dark*, is undercut almost immediately. The shrouds are conspicuously stenciled 'Property of the State of Tennessee,' implying a simple transfer of title rather than liberation for the women. Further, the enshrouded women are completely objectified as 'enormous hams' on the novel's final page (197), denying the possibility of feminine *gravitas* such as Rinthy's.

The narrative misogyny that excludes live women from the text also allows the projection of guilt onto the victims themselves, a sort of blaming of the victim. Just as Rinthy has broken the incest taboo, the women whom Lester victimizes – including the 'old whore' whose nightgown Lester steals, the scavenged girl, the Lane girl, and the young girl whose urine-soaked panties disgust Lester – are all implicated in some sort of sexual guilt that could justify their victimization. The old whore is, after all, a whore, and the scavenged girl is caught (dead) having illicit intercourse on Frog Mountain. The deputy sheriff later implies that she was promiscuous, saying 'she was supposed to of been goin with that Blalock boy we talked to' (147, *sic*). Lester accuses the Lane girl of having given birth to the 'benastied' baby Billy, whom she passes off as her infant brother (77, 116). Even the narrator shows little remorse for her fate: 'But she let him in, more's the fool' (116). The young girl that Lester shoots on Frog Mountain is likewise promiscuous, for according to Lester, at least, she was 'fixin to screw' her date (150, *sic*). Moreover, Lester calls his first dead girlfriend 'Goddamn frozen bitch' (102), as if she were frigid rather than stiffened with rigor mortis. Similarly, the narrator reverses agency when describing Lester's removal of his last dead girlfriend from the crime scene: 'Scuttling down the mountain with the thing on his back he looked like a man beset by some ghast succubus, the dead girl riding him with legs akimbo like a monstrous frog' (153). A succubus is a female demon who 'screws' sleeping men, but the term can also mean 'strumpet.' Thus the dead girl appears the sexual predator, and Lester her victim.

As this image of the dead girl cum succubus suggests, women are objects of dread even in death, although death certainly renders them much less dangerous than they would otherwise be. Lester's desire cannot be safely assuaged by live women, as demonstrated by the aborted attachments to both his mother and Reubel's fair-haired daughter, both of whom desert him. Nor is possession of dead women adequate; he must also *be* the women. 'He'd long been wearing the underclothes of his female victims but now he took to appearing in their outerwear as well' (140). At one point he even sports a wig 'fashioned whole from a dried human scalp' (173). In this fashion Lester incarnates his victims' femininity, becoming at one point a 'gothic doll' (140), a bizarre version of his own victims.

Lester's desire for union with his dead girlfriends suggests an incomplete release from what Julia Kristeva calls 'the hold of *maternal* entity,' the separation from which is at best 'a violent, clumsy breaking away, with the constant risk of falling back under the sway of a power as securing as it is stifling' (*Powers of Horror* 13). Lester leads the vigilante mob through the 'narrow dripping corridors' of the caverns like an infant reversing the birth process (184), but later has 'cause to wish and he did wish for some brute midwife to spald him from his rocky keep' (189). The dread that forces Culla Holme to flee from the 'vulvate' swamp is also strong enough to force Lester Ballard to flee the caves that shelter him from the wrath of men, because like the swamp, the caves resemble the generative female body. He has used death to control women, but now the feminine threatens to control him. According to Kristeva, the narcissistic image of self is a fragile thing, requiring the subject's constant rejection and abjection of that powerfully attractive maternal entity (*Powers of Horror* 13). Before Lester escapes the cave, we see his narcissistic self-image compromised, as he becomes a 'drowsing captive,' 'inculpate in the fastness of his hollow stone,' and most tellingly, cognizant of himself as 'so grievous a case against the gods' (89). He even fantasizes his own dissolution as the caves incorporate his body, mice 'spawn[ing] their tiny bald and mewling whelps in the lobed caverns where his brains had been' (189). Spurred on by this terrifying fantasy, he digs faster. When he manages to escape the symbolic womb of the cave and presents himself at the hospital, he resembles a newborn suffering birth trauma, '*swaddled* up in outsized overalls and covered all over with *red* mud' (192, emphasis added). 'I'm supposed to be here,' he tells the night duty nurse; that is, he is supposed to be free from the figurative generative female body.

Significantly, both Culla Holme and Lester Ballard turn away from the feminine bodies that once enticed them. Culla leaves the bed he shares with Rinthy at the beginning of *Outer Dark* and turns away from the swamp at the end; Lester voluntarily leaves the caves that are at once mother and mausoleum. From young women arrayed for death to threatening landscapes personified as female, the vicissitudes of narrative misogyny are present in both *Outer Dark* and *Child of*

God, but the seven enormous hams that close the latter novel are not the end of the body count. Instead, this troubling image formalizes a narrative pattern already nascent in McCarthy's very first published work of fiction. Not even Rinthy is strong enough to withstand its force, which eventually claims Mrs. McEvoy in *The Gardener's Son* (1977), Wanda in *Suttree* (1979), the she-wolf in *The Crossing* (1994), and Magdalena in *Cities of the Plain* (1998).

Notes

1 I posited this analogy in 'All the Dead Fathers: Freedom and Fatherlessness in *Outer Dark* and *Child of God*.' The Cormac McCarthy Summer Colloquy, July 1997, Boone, North Carolina.

2 Richard Crashaw, 'Luke 11' *c*. 1646:

Blessed be the paps which Thou has sucked.

Suppose He had been tabled at thy teats,
　Thy hunger feels not what He eats;
He'll have his teat ere long (a bloody one),
　The mother then must suck the son.

3 The conflation of the feminine and the bovine is a frequent Faulknerian trick. See Lena's characterization in *Light in August* (to which Rinthy's characterization is partially indebted) and those of Flem Snope's daughters in 'Barn Burning.' The lowing cattle in this scene may also be present to inject an ironic reference to the Christ story; the carol 'Away in the Manger' particularly comes to mind in this scene, especially when above the 'lowing' of the cattle, Rinthy tells the doctor, 'I don't live nowheres no more...' (156).

4 Magdalena's name is a cognate of Madeline (French for Magdalene).

5 For example, in 1997, one male colleague attempted to quiet my fears about McCarthy's potential narrative misogyny with assurances that one of *Cities*' major characters was to be a woman. More convincing (and more comforting) is Jacqueline Scoones' eco-feminist treatment of Magdalena. Scoones argues that the women in the Border Trilogy, especially Magdalena, are aligned with nature in an ethical system at odds with the masculine order. See 'McCarthy's "Girls" and the Ethics of Dwelling in *The Border Trilogy*,' American Literature Association Conference. Baltimore, Maryland. May 28, 1999.

6 There are other instances of narrative kindness in the manifestations of the pathetic fallacy. For example, see *Outer Dark* (10, 97–8).

7 See the chapter header for *Blood Meridian*, Chapter XXIII, which suggests sleeping (*schlafen*) as a euphemism for dying: '... The jakes and what was encountered there – Sie müssen schlafen aber Ich muss tanzen' (316).

8 Dianne Luce notes Lester Ballard's genesis in both the character of Norman Bates in Alfred Hitchcock's *Psycho* (1960) and the historical person of James Blevins of North Georgia, who was accused of a number of murders in 1963 similar in nature to Ballard's. See 'The Murderers Behind *Child of God*,' Cormac McCarthy International Colloquy. El Paso, Texas. October 16, 1998. Wes' obsession with the dead beloved predates the Blevins murders, if not the murders that inspired *Psycho*.

Terri Witek

'He's hell when he's well':
Cormac McCarthy's rhyming dictions

When Samuel Coleridge takes William Wordsworth to task in *Biographia Literaria*, he pointedly disagrees with Wordsworth's espousal of 'rustic diction.' Rejecting Wordsworth's claim that such diction is inherently superior, the 'real language of men' for which poets often substitute 'arbitrary and capricious habits of expression,' Coleridge imposes an important distinction of his own:

> The rustic, from the more imperfect development of his faculties, and from the lower state of their cultivation, aims almost solely to convey *insulated facts,* either those of his scanty experience or his traditional belief, while the educated man chiefly seeks to discover and express those *connections* of things, or those relative *bearings of* fact to fact, from which some more or less general law is deducible. For facts are valuable to a wise man, chiefly as they lead to the discovery of the indwelling law, which is the true being of things, the sole solution of their mode of existence and in the knowledge of which consists our dignity and our power. (52–3)

This distinction, offered by the nineteenth-century's most famous literary theoretician, is audaciously tested and rewritten by twentieth-century novelist Cormac McCarthy who, at the service of a single narrative and using the same undifferentiated narrative voice, combines the furthest reaches of both educated and rustic dictions. In his first five novels – *The Orchard Keeper* (1965), *Outer Dark* (1968), *Child of God* (1973), *Suttree* (1979), and *Blood Meridian* (1985) – Cormac McCarthy moves effortlessly from the laconic dialogue of hill characters and street people, and from cleanedged, understated narration, to descriptive sections so dense with learned vocabulary and refined linguistic effects that the people who come so vividly to life in the former would quite patently neither read nor understand the latter. The following passages from *Suttree* illustrate the discrepancy. In the first, the protagonist discusses prison food with an appealingly guileless misfit who has just been sent up for debauching a field of watermelons:

> They wasn't no meat, said Harrogate.
> That's right, said Suttree.
> Do they ever have meat?
> I don't know.

> Have you ever eat any meat here?
> You mean other than breakfast bacon?
> Yeah. Other than breakfast bacon.
> No.
> Harrogate leaned against the bunk. After a while
> he said: How long you been here?
> About five months.
> They hell fire, said Harrogate. (43–4)

The comic tempo of this exchange is quite different from the rhythms of a descriptive passage offered by the narrative voice near the end of the book in which Suttree watches the destruction of McAnally Flats, the collection of dives and flophouses which had been his haunting ground:

> He watched the bland workman in the pilothouse of the crane shifting levers. The long tethered wreckingball swung through the side of a wall and small boys applauded. Brickwork of dried bloodcakes in flemish bond crumbling in a cloud of dust and mortar. Walls grim with scurf, a nameless crud. Pale spongoid growths that kept in clusters along the damper regions came to light and all day grime-caked salvagers with hatchets spalled dead mortar from the piled black brick. Gnostic workmen who would have down this shabby shapeshow that masks the higher world of form. And left at eventide these cutaway elevations, little cubicles giving onto space, an iron bedstead, a freestanding stairwell to nowhere. Old gothic soffits hung with tar and lapsing paintflakes. Ragged cats picked their way over the glass and nigger dogs in the door-yards beyond the railsiding twitched in their sleep. Until nothing stood save rows of doors, some bearing numbers, all nailed to. Beyond lay fields of rubble, twisted steel and pipes and old conduits reared out of the ground in clusters of agonized ganglia among the broken slabs of masonry. Where small black hominoids scurried over the waste and sheets of newsprint rose in the wind died again. (464)

Both of these passages are, in their separate ways, characteristic of McCarthy's prose style, and the first seems to fit Coleridge's classic description of rustic diction. The two men talk, in simplest terms, about food. Their conversation is a testimony to the minute negotiations which make up daily life: how much meat, what kind, how long Suttree has been in prison in order to know this. What they do not say, the generalization they do not make, is that prison is a place in which basic human needs are always thwarted, a bad place, where lack of meat is symptomatic of the lack of any kind of recognizable human comfort. But these connections are never made for us in the Coleridgian sense, and the passage ends not with an indwelling law, what Coleridge also called 'surview,' but with Gene's awed 'They hell fire,' a kind of verbal throwing-up-of-the-hands at the unverbalizable nature of the universe.

The second passage, on the other hand, is quite consciously literary, from the food of rich, often unexpectedly exact description ('lapsing paintflakes') to the archaic turn of 'eventide.' Each of the unusual word choices ('spalled') has a verifiable existence in the dictionary – although as more than one of McCarthy's reviewers has tartly observed it has to be a large dictionary – and some of the words seem even more pointedly particular because they connote specialized bodies of knowledge. More than one kind of education is required, for example, by words such as 'hominoid,' 'gnostic,' 'ganglia,' 'soffit,' and 'flemish bond', which have various professional meanings to zoologists, theologians, doctors, architects and bricklayers. Although we may recognize and understand them without help, such words carry connotations of their particular bodies of knowledge around with them like shadows, and literary as we may be, it is quite likely that 'flemish bond,' a technical term for a certain type of brickwork, will elude us precisely because we are educated in literature rather than masonry.

By allowing this language this type of educated particularity, McCarthy achieves a concreteness which differs from that of Suttree and Harrogate's discussion of meat. While the first passage deals with a most specific issue, it is notably reticent about the underlying dilemma. The passage describing the destruction of McAnally Flats, on the other hand, looks more obscure but is actually both exact in meaning and concrete in execution, as if the words themselves achieve a more than usual objective identity on the page. While the prison dialogue ends in a tacit acknowledgement of the inadequacy of human description, the more educated diction upholds the weight and worth of language itself, and the collection of individually weighted words helps give such passages their clotted, characteristic density.

In this very literary mode McCarthy manages to subvert Coleridge's description of the way educated diction operates. There is no effort to sweep the description into an indwelling law. At the same time, drawing attention to this narrative choice, McCarthy positions the scene's observer so that he is ideally placed to make such connections. Suttree is outside the scene he observes, and through his onlooking presence we get a panoramic, sky-high view of machines, buildings, and people. Strategically located in the physical sense, Suttree is one of the most educated of all McCarthy's protagonists: he's spent time in college as well as the workhouse. McCarthy could use Suttree to generalize for us and he quite consciously doesn't, so although the scene is sweepingly rendered from an optimal position, what is presented is a series of lush verbal cuts from detail to detail. As the words refuse to group consistently into sentences, neither does the passage connect in a forward pull toward some thematic statement. The closest thing to a generalization – and its elevated language gives it the look of an important point – occurs midway through the fragments: 'Gnostic workmen who would have down this shabby shapeshow that masks the higher world of form.'

By pulling away the shabby exteriors which separate the neighborhood into inside and outside space, the workmen reveal a 'higher world of form.' Yet, tellingly, this 'higher' world is a collection of mysterious particulars: blue mold, exposed cornice beams, open cubicles which used to be rooms.

The judgment that this scene of mysterious objects which have escaped human efforts at organization represents the higher world of form might be expected to occupy a prominent place in this passage as a statement of theme. But McCarthy is too skilled to let such a generalization do the work that form itself can accomplish to greater effect. Here 'the higher world of form' is a collection of tantalizing particulars, and the phrase that focuses this truth for us is a fragment buried in a long, richly detailed passage. As it is swept away by succeeding descriptions, we see that it too is a momentary connection, no more yielding to our desire for final knowledge than an iron bedstead. The point is made by position in the passage, fragmentary phrasing and even more subtly by the chime, soon after 'gnostic workmen,' of 'gothic soffits.' Both are the subject of their fragments, with the same adjective/noun structure and syllable count, and both also have something of the same sound, as if 'gnostic' said in a slightly different way could come out 'gothic.' Both match a word connoting theoretical knowledge with a word connoting knowledge of the practical world. Both, finally, are evenly weighted in the passage, so that what could be an important thematic statement is finally given no more than equal status with a building's discarded architecture, with remnants of ornamented wood which no longer have anything to support.

McCarthy is a master of such minute calculations, his word choice, not only particular in meaning but particular in sound as well, bringing our attention to the individual properties of words and then drawing them into a peculiar music. This type of organization requires a different logic than the forward narrative pull to connection and conclusion. As in the layering of 'gnostic workmen' and 'gothic soffits,' the organizing principle of McCarthy's style is a type of rhythmic repetition which resists indwelling law at the same time that it refuses to leave words and objects in rustic diction's limbo of 'insulated facts.'

In poetry, of course, rhythmic repetition is formally sanctioned in rhyme and meter. Donald Davie describes the memorable series of repetitions which open T. S. Eliot's 'Ash Wednesday' as 'syntax as rhyme,' and this phrase neatly sums up what happens over and over in different guises in McCarthy's prose style. Davie explains that while some lines in 'Ash Wednesday' are end-rhymed, others are 'tied together no less closely by similarity of grammar. What we have . . . is a sort of parity of esteem between rhyme and meter and grammar and syntax' (91).

Using syntax not only in a forward thrust toward meaning but also in the more vertical pattern of rhyme allows McCarthy's most intricate passages to be both exact and densely layered, to demonstrate a type of educated diction without surview, to remain suggestive of meaning without choosing between meaning's multiple possibilities. Importantly, McCarthy does not confine his prose rhyming to the dense crosswebbing of his descriptive passages, although that is where they work their most traceable magic. McCarthy uses paratactic rhyming not only in individual words and images, but in whole scenes and passages as well, so that a strategy of rhythmic repetition becomes an integral part of the larger narrative structure. Using syntax as rhyme on a larger scale means that the scenes which accrue are both memorable in themselves and full of echoes, and that plotline, the horizontal thrust of story which has more in common with Coleridge's connections between facts than with the depth-sounding of rhyme, will be, if not actually subverted, at least of no more than equal status with anything else.

Typically, McCarthy is so adept at this scene-rhyming we scarcely register it. When *Suttree*'s Gene Harrogate enters Knoxville, for example, the scene subtly calls up the way the protagonist moved through the same space some forty pages earlier. There is one straight verbal repetition in the scenes ('country commerce', 66, 102), but other echoes are more discreet, and more interesting. In both scenes the men pass farm trucks, beggars, and a fishmarket. There Suttree views, in a window, 'cold gray shapes dimly limned in troughs of powdered ice' (67). When Harrogate passes what seems to be the same window, he moves '[p]ast a long glass coffin where a few lean fish leered up with cold and golden eyes from their beds of salted ice' (102).

The image is similar yet different; aside from the fact that the 'few lean fish' in Harrogate's scene connote the end of a market day rather than its beginning, the difference is one of treatment, and relies on the observers' differing personalities. As Suttree sees it the image is dreamier, the fish barely registered as such: 'cold gray shapes.' The phrase which follows is a small, perfect example of sound/meaning overlay: 'dimly limned.' 'Limned' comes from the archaic word for illuminate, as in an illuminated manuscript, tracing back from the Middle English 'limnen' to 'lumen,' the Latin word for light. The whole image is extraordinarily delicate: the fish lie as if painted against powdered ice, and to be 'dimly limned' is also to be suffused in light. In Gene's scene, in contrast, the fish are almost malevolently animated, 'lean' and 'leer[ing]' with 'cold and golden eyes.' The ice here is 'salted' not 'powdered,' and the compounded 'cold and golden,' unlike 'dimly limned,' is almost painfully vivid, as if the dead fish eyes had become the center of both light and cold in the image.

The tonal difference in images holds true in the larger action as well. Suttree passes through early morning Knoxville easily, as if it were an interesting backdrop with which he is only half engaged: avoiding the clutch of a beggar woman, flicking a coin to a blind man, selling his fish. In the same milieu the always completely but wrong-endedly engaged Harrogate gets beaten for trying to hoist a peach, steals fifteen cents from maybe the same blind man, and gets bitten by a crippled beggar on a board. On the level of character development, the difference is between Suttree and Harrogate and the way in which both the educated and the rural characters are their own differing versions of outsiders in the world through which they move. What the difference in scenes finally illustrates is the way in which things can be both syntactically equal yet always relentlessly individual, no matter how tantalizing the echoes. We are reminded that the pleasure of rhyme is always exactly this, the simultaneous small shock of recognition and then the crucial variation, present here both in the near rhyming of 'cold and golden' or 'dimly limned' and in the larger way in which the scenes run parallel but not congruent, refusing to dissolve one into the other, equally weighted so we cannot choose between them.

McCarthy also employs principles of rhythmic repetition to order his plots. In *The Orchard Keeper*, McCarthy's first novel, the three protagonists are linked by an unprepossessing ne'er-do-well who appears in the flesh only in the book's beginning. Kenneth Rattner's brief but vivid appearance doesn't amount to much on the level of plot, but he acquires three separate and resonating existences in the character's lives: he is the fabled father of John Wesley, the thief killed by Marion Sylder, and the corpse tended by Arthur Ownby. The lives of the three protagonists touch and overlap at various points and then the concentric circles around Kenneth Rattner, which between them organize the book, disperse: Marion Sylder is consigned to jail, Arthur Ownby to the state mental hospital, and John Wesley Rattner to adulthood at the book's end.

The structure of *Outer Dark*, McCarthy's second novel, is even simpler. Using separate journeys by siblings Culla and Rinthy Holme (interjected with appearances by three evil Magi figures), McCarthy uses the plot to enact the careful series of missed connections which give the book both its poignancy and its pristine beauty. Culla and Rinthy Holme are propelled from their insulated existence (the rustic life which lies beneath rustic diction) into the world's outer dark by the birth and Culla's subsequent abandonment of their baby in the woods. The book chronicles their wanderings and, as we might expect, McCarthy does not lead his protagonists on geometrically opposite or linear routes but over virtually the same ground, crossing and recrossing each other's paths without ever once meeting. The district they travel, which could not be so very large, is in its particular details as familiar as the country stores at which they pause, yet as cumulatively strange as if the landscape were of another planet.

In *Outer Dark* Rinthy Holme's search for the lost child provides the principle forward thrust of plot: we wait, all along, for Rinthy to find her baby. And in the end she does; this is plot resolution, but strangely qualified. The child is by this time a tiny ribcage of whitened bones, and although Rinthy senses the importance of the place in which they lay, she falls asleep without understanding what the strange remnants signify: the most crucially missed connection of all. 'Little sister was sleeping' (238) as if she herself is the lost babe in the woods; in a culmination of the book's plot and structure, the resolution has been reached and then shown to be no resolution at all. The child has been transformed into something elusive and oddly beautiful: the delicate 'calcined ribcage' (237) is somehow not, in the end, Rinthy's baby. The connections which the author would not give us through his protagonist in *Suttree* are here provided by the plot only to be overthrown, and what we are left with is the poignant sense that all human connections to a world of form, even the most basic, are illusory.

In *Child of God* McCarthy orders a simple plot around a character who is himself a kind of off-rhyme for the community in which he lives. Lester Ballard enacts crazed rituals of courting, marriage, and housekeeping, and eventually makes his dwelling in caves beneath the seemingly ordered surface of the human community. McCarthy doesn't stop with a simple aberrant mirror of this community in his protagonist, but gives Lester a place in town myth, which re-imports him as a folk hero into the world from which he has been excluded. This multiple view of Lester as outcast from the community, as crazed patriarch of his underground world, and finally as mythic hero are, like Kenneth Rattner's multiple guises or like all of McCarthy's syntactic rhymes, deftly managed so that we see all three possibilities virtually at the same moment.

While McCarthy carefully does not choose among them, the community which offers the norm in *Child of God* is clearly the most impoverished version of reality through which Lester moves. The orderly townspeople can only defend themselves against Lester through their process of law, or savor his dangerousness vicariously through storytelling. Both strategies defuse the real threat of a gun-wielding necrophiliac, preserving the community in its myth of wholeness. McCarthy, even while suggesting that this norm is less interesting than its crucial variation in *Child of God*, refuses to let us rest with this seeming moral, but forces us to rhyme the whole thing backwards as well. If Lester is truly 'a child of Cod like yourself' (4), then the community is a group of potential Lesters and hard-won social order is as illusory as any other type of human bond. Lester becomes not only the aberration but the truest reflection of that community which is, for all its seeming harmony, always on the verge of becoming even more volatile than its lone outcast.

If Lester Ballard is an off-rhyme of the community which, in turn, mythologizes him, McCarthy's most recent novel, *Blood Meridian*, offers a large-scale example of the strategy in a plot which is a nightmare version of historical fact. Documented raids against Apaches conducted in the Southwest of 1849–50, complete with recognizable historic characters, are converted in McCarthy's text into a series of horrifically brutal encounters in which locations, incidents, and characters themselves begin to merge in an endlessly repeatable blood sacrifice. Traditional dichotomies become versions of the same principle: white men and Indians are equally murderous, and, in one pointed example, a white man and a black man bear identical names. If the effect of rhythmic repetition in McCarthy's novels is to make the plots something other than linear, then *Blood Meridian* suggests that history itself is not linear but a recurring nightmare ritual.

In *Blood Meridian* language itself is presented as multiple and subject to mysterious repetitions. McCarthy entwines Spanish and English in both the dialogue and the narration, for example, and in one notable scene, Indians listen raptly to English they clearly do not 'understand' in the usual linguistic sense of the term. Furthermore, this time around McCarthy offers two characters, 'the kid' and 'the judge,' as neatly dichotomized representatives of rustic and educated dictions. At the end of the novel, sole survivors of their adventures, they finally converse. The judge offers a final temptation to the boy who has resisted his persuasive rhetoric throughout the book:

> The world goes on. We have dancing nightly and this night is no exception. The straight and the winding way are one and now that you are here what do the years count since last we two met together? Man's memories are uncertain and the past that was differs little from the past that was not.
>
> He took up the tumbler the judge had poured and he drank and set it down again. He looked at the judge. I been everywhere, he said. This is just one more place. (330–1)

While the judge tries to collapse experience into indwelling law (dismissing distinctions between nights, paths, and versions of the past), the kid effortlessly cuts to the particular (this is 'one place' out of 'everywhere'). The kid seems to win each point back to the specificity of experience, but at the end of the novel he is killed by the judge, whom we last see in a crowded barroom, dancing gleefully and alone. We might take this as a triumph of indwelling law over isolated fact but for the suggestion that there will always be young men to take the kid's place: he too is a version of one place among everywhere. That the dancing judge suggests a trained animal performing for the pleasure of others also complicates his triumph, suggesting that a world of particulars has brought him to life and given him language, acting out a relation between words and world which is beyond history.

The rhythmic repetition which takes different forms in McCarthy's other novels receives its fullest thematic consideration in *Suttree,* in which the novelist channels both a life of concrete particulars and a sense of larger connections through the single figure of his protagonist. Cornelius Suttree, the educated son of well-to-do parents who elects to spend his time with the down-and-outs of downtown Knoxville, is haunted by the thought of the twin who preceded him into the world, dead at birth.

Suttree's malady is a 'subtle obsession with uniqueness,' and in the book which bears his name syntactic rhyming, the prose equivalent of twinning, forms the warp of every aspect of the storytelling. Each time we isolate a small incident, in *Suttree* it becomes surrounded by a multitude of echoes: once we learn of Suttree's twin, for instance, dead children begin to fill the book: Suttree's son, his child-lover Wanda, an unidentified corpse of a baby in the river and even hardened criminal Bill Ray Callahan, whose mother makes a single memorable appearance, taking her place with the novel's other grieving mothers. Once there is a talisman there are multiple talismans: the Indian's doll's eyes on a string, a strangely carved coin, the 'billiken' Suttree carved and hid as a child, a subway token, a mussel shell he gives his whore-lover Joyce, the lumpy Tennessee pearls Reese counts on to make his fortune, the mysterious objects Mother Gee the witch woman shakes out to conjure Suttree's fate. When Wanda dies we may suddenly recall a whore's tattoo early in the book: 'Wanda RIP 1945,' it reads, and Wanda's death beneath a moving wall of wet slate accrues other images around it as well: a dog stuck in a slop bucket, Gene caved in under Knoxville, the clotted density of the river where Suttree fishes, an announcement in the paper of a girl's body found buried in trash, an early description of death as 'sucking brown sewage', and perhaps even the homebrew everyone always seems to be drinking, bottles of mysterious liquid half-filled with sediment called simply by the detonating 'splo.'

The syntactic rhyming which does not permit a pull toward conclusion permits variations which are therefore not only endless, but endlessly daring, as McCarthy takes the same risks with plot that he takes with his dictions. But while unheard-of things seem to happen in McCarthy's novels (Culla and Rinthy's incest, Lester Ballard's necrophilia, the murder of children in *Blood Meridian*) the very strategy which allows them softens their shock. Or, more accurately, more and more things begin to acquire the same intensity so that the events themselves are finally no more shocking or even important than the context which surrounds them.

What McCarthy's characters do is shocking in the conventional sense but the more subtle and unexpected shock, one that is brought into equivalence by McCarthy's method, is the paradoxical innocence which makes these characters so defenseless in the larger world. Gene Harrogate may have burned down a house with its owner still inside and spent his manhood on a field of fruit, but isn't it equally shocking, although we aren't used to thinking of it this way, that he considers his hideout under the bridge luxurious uptown accommodations, or that he sails happily upriver in two soldered car hoods without, of course, knowing how to swim. Or that Culla and Rinthy, who have never lived anywhere else or been separated, should abruptly leave everything they know without any sense of where they're going, or any idea of coming back? Which, finally, is more disturbing: that Lester moves his dead consorts one by one from a flooded cave, or that he also moves, over and over, a set of stuffed animals, gaudy relics of what seems to be his life's only moment of triumph?

The end result is that McCarthy's characters, however wordless or at a loss they may seem in the course of their individual stories, are in the last analysis as complex and ultimately mysterious as every other object in McCarthy's world, as complex as people always seem to be outside the parameter of books. This is the parity of esteem which brings us back to a consideration of these characters' brand of rustic diction, which fits Coleridge's description but is clearly something else as well in the landscape of McCarthy's prose style. While McCarthy's most complex diction summons up a world of endlessly rearrangeable particulars, the rural diction takes what seems to be uncomplicated and particular and reveals it as stranger and more wonderful still. At the level of technique, a similar effect is achieved in less space. Instead of the reverberating compounds of McCarthy's most educated diction, McCarthy pares back even contractions still further, dropping the apostrophes ('I dont know. I didnt much blame him.'), leaves off the 'g' in the 'ing' words of certain speakers and uses colloquial, contracted forms: 'tater,' 'thisn,' 'yessir.' Of course this method is partly about sound, the way people actually sound when they talk, but because the words are written in unaccustomed fashion ('don't pint ye finger ye'll scare him') the rustic diction often seems as visually odd as some of McCarthy's more elaborate word choices. And when the characters speak they say so little, or rather they use so few words, the little layers of repetitive dialogue begin to have a funny rhythmic life of their own, like the tap of a code. In the simpler diction the underlying idea, tacitly accepted by the speakers, is that conversation is always somehow insufficient to the overwhelming flood of experience. 'Gene,' Suttree sighs after Harrogate has stirred up another jailhouse imbroglio:

What?
Nothing. Just Gene.

The country 'well,' other places, sums up the whole inconclusive nature of things. The words themselves display none of the minute exactness of the more literary passages. No dictionary documents the multiple possibilities of 'peart,' for example, the country expression which means feeling well and lively yet looks like both 'pearl' and 'heart' as well.

While other diction looks obscure but is actually painstakingly particular, made mysterious by dense patterning of sound and sense, the seemingly simple dialogue is finally, triumphantly elusive. After all the patterned foregrounding of Gene Harrogate's entrance into Knoxville, a 'lank black slattern's' come-on sounds like a line of jive music: 'Hey boydove, you gettin any gravel for yo goose?' (100), a sentence which treats description like nonsense rhyme, bypassing the carefully superseded particularity of McCarthy's more elaborate effects. The line is just as rhythmic, if not as dense, as what precedes it; and who can explain the charm of 'boydove,' lightly flicked back at the end of the sentence by 'yo goose.' People who are drunk (and obviously beyond worrisome particulars) often speak this way in *Suttree*: 'But J-bone had turned away with a whoop. Early Times he called. Make your liver quiver' (26).

In this diction the actual rhymes are clear and unimpeded as music, and the syntactic rhyming which allows us to see both tragic and comic associations as part of a single continuum in all of McCarthy's prose makes, in this mode, short work of any difference between them. Discussing whiskey, two characters collapse distinctions succinctly and not uncheerfully:

Early Times, Nig, cried J-Bone.
Early Tombs more like it. (24)

A tribute to the elusive nature of the world which is beyond our capacity of description is accomplished in different fashion by both dictions, and in a prose world which actively denies surview, the fact that both appear together over the course of five novels is significant and appropriate. In the technique of a novelist who structures words, scenes and plots around rhythmic repetition, the different dictions perform a verbal counterpart which is itself a kind of syntactic rhyme. Whether we are working our way through the clotted descriptive passages or are tossed along the brief rhythms of understated dialogue, we are forced to see each as a separate but equal version of a world we recognize.

As the most wordless of characters are made as rich and strange as every other object in McCarthy's world, and what they say becomes equally if not more suggestive than the most lavish diction, the narrator, or more precisely the narrative voice, is placed in a curious position. The careful weighing of syntactic rhymes on every level suggests that the narrative voice is himself unable to choose or, rather, refuses to choose; and this refusal which is another resistance to surview suggests that the narrative voice waives the privilege of narrational omniscience. What is finally rejected is any kind of willed distance between himself and the material he presents. That is why the world the narrative voice describes seems so full and unsorted and why the novelist allows so many different words, styles and voices to inhabit the verbal world of his prose style. In this verbal world there can be no privileged dictions, or rather all dictions are made privileged so that we are made aware that we are within a wholly fictional world, one which provides a mysteriously apt near rhyme of our own.

Béatrice Trotignon

Detailing the wor(l)d in *Suttree*

The dense verbal sequences favored by McCarthy create at one and the same time a feeling of intensely transparent concreteness and extremely opaque unreality exploring the metamorphosis of language. Details come to be the crux of this tension. By 'detail' I mean to invoke its poetic and rhetorical usages; that is to say that I primarily consider them as verbal arrangements and shifts, effects of perspective and style, based on as many conventions and artifices as any other type of verbal construction, rather than based on a mimetic link to a pre-set reality. Hence the title of my chapter, in which the 'world' appears to be in fact 'merely' made of 'words' (but as William Gass pointed out, words are never 'mere' (100)). There may also be sensed in my title two contradictory pulls, one that makes for the constructive drive of the text by which a stable referential frame and a fragmentary world are built through the additional procession of profuse details, and a disintegrating though dynamic pull, by which the sense of a world is slowly but surely replaced by a sense of foregrounded and echoing words.

The sheer amount of abject details, the very election of a tattered world and the thorough exploration of the lexical field of fragmentation make of *Suttree* the most representative work of McCarthy's in which the relation of details to the whole is seen as being problematic. Not only do the accumulated details all suggest wholeness might be a shattered illusion, but many of them belong to the category of the abject and the repulsive, that is to say to that which, by definition, cannot cohere, to that which is totally heterogeneous with any subjectivity (cf. Julia Kristeva) to that for which, in a Platonic representation of the world (*Parmenide*) there can be no transcendent form or idea, for fear of introducing negativity in the perfect world of noble ideas. Abject details, and details in general, become the redundant signs of a divided world, the signs of a crisis or a tension between accountable details and unaccountable ones.

The accountability of details and the access they provide to a united design may be linked not only to a Transcendentalist or Emersonian tradition[1] in which the close scrutiny of particulars, however mean or trivial, ranges them 'instantly on an eternal law' (Emerson 102), but also to a classical and idealist conception of aesthetics in which proliferating details are thought to be a menace to the hierarchical and organicist balance of meaning that is deemed necessary in a work of art, and by which peripheral, background or accessory elements must be subjected to central, foreground and essential ones (Schor 37). In the tradition of modernism, McCarthy's texts constantly stage shifting readings of details, from particularization to generalization and back again to particularization through various strategies, whether thematic, syntactical, symbolical, or poetical and, more specifically still to McCarthy's practice of writing, etymological. These constant shifts make for a tension that enhances the creation of a sense of the materiality of the world and the poetic circulation of words.

While keeping in the background philosophical and transcendentalist analyses, my purpose will be to focus myopically on microtextual shifts in the way details take on various functions, whether one of fragmentation in photographs (which in themselves are a means to detail the world), or one of dissemination in texts.

The process of detailing belongs to a double strategy, one by which a strong feeling of estrangement is conveyed (the whole falls to pieces), and one corresponding to an enhanced intimacy (we get a closer look). It has already been noticed that the activity of detailing, of scrutinizing, sampling and naming the world allows both for the mapping of the world and its inevitable loss or erasure. Examples such as the judge's eradications[2] in *Blood Meridian*, or the inconclusive dissection[3] of Ballard in *Child of God*, or the paradoxical activity of trapping in *The Crossing* are relevant enough.[4] For my part I will instead mention the way photographs and parataxis make for the same double feeling of intimacy and estrangement.

In *Suttree* and *The Crossing* photographs appear always to be coupled to death, fragmentation, loss of accountability and dissociation. Suttree, or Billy and the gypsy in *The Crossing*, come to discover that even though a photograph singles out from the world a piece of its reality, it is an illusion to believe it may work as a metonymy of the whole: on the contrary, it never strengthens links whether with the past or whether with the people and places photographed, but is always said to widen the gap and distance that already exist between men and their own selves, between men and the world. Instead of having integrating and salvaging powers, photographs dis-integrate. As objects, they are repeatedly described as being 'cracked', 'stained', undergoing a disintegrating process. Furthermore, the people and places represented not only lose form: 'In the old school photo he appeared childlike and puckish, *a composition of spots* in black and white and gray' (*Suttree* 403), but lose connection as the repeated use of 'redundant' and the idea of heterogeneity suggest in 'Old distaff kin coughed up out of the vortex, thin and cracked and macled and a bit *redundant*. The landscapes, old backdrops, *redundant* too, recurring unchanged *as if they inhabited another medium* than the dry pilgrims shored up on them' (129, emphases added). Photographic details which the gypsy in *The Crossing* imagines at one point to enclose the mystery and the intimacy of the world never offer access to the whole by means of a stilled, condensed form.

In this case parataxis and verbless clauses, as in both previous examples and in

> From the sepia-tinted buildings, the old shake roofs. The people on horseback. Men sitting among cardboard cactus in a photographer's studio in suits and ties with the legs of their breeches stogged into their boottops and rifles standing upright before them. The antique dresses of the women. The wary and haunted cast to their eyes. Like people *photographed at gunpoint* (*The Crossing* 345, emphasis added)

come to be efficient means of conveying a fragmented and dislocated world, in which objects and things stand 'upright and arrant' (*Suttree* 246), out of reach, thoroughly independent, outside synthesis.[5] Paratactically or tautologically accumulated as they are in all of McCarthy's texts, details which appear to be redundant and insignificant in terms of narrative function and structure may finally be interpreted as a way of simply signifying and designating the real, according to the workings of the Reality Effect and the referential illusion defined by Roland Barthes ('L'Effet de réel' 81–90). Hence all these signs of dislocation and fragmentation make for a sense of realist concreteness if not aesthetic wholeness.

Yet *Suttree* is an interesting case in point as parataxis is also used to represent a character's stream of consciousness, allowing for a modernist fragmented text unfolding both metonymically and metaphorically in enumerations of nominalized clauses under the direction of a totalizing, though fragmented, self, with the use sometimes of the first person pronoun. Yet, over and over again inner focalization is repeatedly broken or taken over by the first kind of paratax mentioned.

I believe McCarthy manages to indite within the symbolical construction stylistic and aesthetics shifts by which an idea of the non-human, non-symbolic world is given form. If many nominalized, paratactic descriptions in *Suttree* do represent the characters' symphonic perception of the world, many also suggest how passive contemplation gives way to the slow encroachment of the world's sheer materiality, by which objects are given eminence over the subject. The encroachment of nature over man may be felt in the way a lot of McCarthy's sentences conclude in landscape descriptions: 'They went up through the foothills among pine trees and barren rock and they went up through juniper and spruce and the rare great aloes and the rising stalks of the yuccas with their pale blooms silent and unearthly among the evergreens' (*Blood Meridian* 187). The first mentions of the environment appear in complements linked by the prepositions 'through', 'among' to the main verb and subject ('they went'), whose dominating role is further enhanced by the fact that those complements are defined in a minimal way (no articles, tautological or not really specific adjectives such as 'pine' and 'barren') and that the repetition of the 'They went up through' suggests how much the characters are wholly focused on their progression, not on the environment. However, the weight of the sentence then shifts onto the complements after the third 'and', with a slight pause provoked by the sudden use of definite articles and attributes ('and the rare great aloes and the rising stalks'). The unexpected occurrence of the definite article 'the' introduces a specificity and an intimacy that was lacking or which suddenly appears to have been lacking in the previous part of the clause. Yet this new feeling of intimacy appears just when one feels a new clause has started, breaking away from the enumeration that depended on 'they' as an organizing center of perception. But as no verb comes up in the rest of the clause, one realizes it merely stands as one further item in the previously started list. For a slight moment, one has had the illusion of a shift towards an autonomous nature with specifications that belong to it proper and are not dependent on the characters' perspective.

An example of this shift may also be read in the following extract at the very moment when Suttree as a child tries to pull himself away from death and its fascinating, petrifying summons:

> The dead would take the living with them if they could, I pulled away. Sat in an ivy garden that lizards kept with constant leathery slitherings. Hutched hares ghost pale in the shade of the carriagehouse wall. Flagstones in a rosegarden, the terraced slope of the lawn above the river, odor of boxwood and mossmold and old brick in the shadow of the springhouse. Under the watercress stones in the clear flowage cluttered with periwinkles. A salamander, troutspeckled. Leaning to suck the cold and mossy water. *A rimpled child's face watching back, a watery isomer agoggle in the rings.* (13, emphasis added)

Notice how the paratactic enumeration of stones, flowers and animals that corresponds to Suttree's metonymical perception of his surrounding world finally breaks away from the conscious 'I' that first ordered it: not only does the first person pronoun disappear, but it is replaced by the impersonal and distanced reflection of the child's face on the surface of the water.

The Gatlinburg retreat chapter stages the tension between these different functions of detailed notations, as they come to be either products of Suttree's solipsistic imagination or scientific observation which only gives illusory access to the world, or privileged means of access to a communing experience with some kind of oversoul, allowing communication, dissolution or identification with the world, or further still as a mute mass of unaccountable data. All of the details given seem at first to be part of the metonymical description of the forest, following Suttree's perceptions through the enumeration of paratactic nominal clauses. But the apparition of the first person pronoun in this passage coincides with the expression of a simultaneous loss, or the simultaneous apparition of something that yet remains inaccessible:

> Clouds lay remote and motionless across the sky like milt awash in some backwater of the planet's seas and a white woodcock rose from the ferns before him and dissolved in smoke.
> A curling bit of down cradled in this green light for the sake of my sanity. Unreal and silent bird albified between the sun and my broken mind godspeed. (291)

The bit of down is for Suttree a material proof that the bird is not a figment of his imagination, that is to say that he has actually seen it, captured it: yet the occurrence of 'dissolved', the two adjectives 'unreal' and 'silent' that follow, as well as the choice of a generic term with no article ('bird') in place of the specific clause 'a white woodcock', along with the expression of a dissociation of perception in the clause 'broken mind' all this suggests how problematic and elusive his capture of the world actually is. The tension between precise words and all englobing or highly generic ones (such as 'things', 'forms', 'something', or 'bird' in this case) as well as the extraordinary use McCarthy makes of the conjunction 'and',[6] 'a sword which cleaves things as it cleaves them' as Gass put it, also contribute to this tension between naming and the immediate loss it entails, between the converging and diverging forces at work in his texts.

I see in these constant shifts from one type of paratax to another, one of the strategies used by McCarthy to figure within the symbolical practice that writing is, the slow encroachment of the world's sheer materiality, as if outside human perception. Such a paradoxical quest is best expressed by somebody like Edward Abbey[7] whose book *Desert Solitaire* bears many links to McCarthy's work:

> The personification of the natural is exactly the tendency I wish to suppress in myself, to eliminate for good. I am here not only to evade for a while the clamor and filth and confusion of the cultural apparatus but also to confront, immediately and directly if it's possible, the barebones of existence, the elemental and fundamental, the bedrock which sustains us. I want to be able to look at and into a juniper tree, a piece of quartz, a vulture, a spider, and see it as it is in itself, devoid of all humanly ascribed qualities, antikantian, even the categories of scientific description. To meet God or Medusa face to face, even if it means risking everything human in myself. I dream of a hard and brutal mysticism in which the naked self merges with a non human world and yet somehow survive still intact, individual, separate. Paradox and bedrock. (6)

One of the most paradoxical strategies by which McCarthy manages to convey the impression of an enhanced perception of a concrete, bedrock reality outside the manacles of human perception and symbolical practices lies in the extremely sophisticated and detailed readings of some of the words he chooses. I am not referring so much to the particular use he makes of rare and technical words (even though they belong to a similar process of reduction, the analysis of which could be integrated here), as to the way he encourages the reader to scrutinize words and details not in view of integrating them in a narrative or symbolical structure but of dis-integrating them and their transient metaphorical meanings into literal statements, as though an in-depth reading of some words resulted in a dense surface perception[8] of the world.

Interest in surfaces constantly appears in *Suttree*. Indeed, the opening pages of the book enhance Suttree's preference for the observation of surface phenomena. In the following extract, one may read a relevant shift from 'face' to 'surface':

> He could hear the river talking softly *beneath* him, heavy old river with *wrinkled face*. *Beneath* the sliding water cannons and carriages, trunnions seized and rusting in the mud, keelboats rotted to the consistency of mucilage. Fabled sturgeons with their

horny pentagonal bodies, the cupreous and dacebright carp and catfish with their pale and sprueless underbellies, a thick muck shot with broken glass, with bones and rusted tins and bits of crockery reticulate with mudback crazings. Across the river the limestone cliffs reared gray and roughly *faceted* and strung with grass across their *face* in thin green faults. Where they overhung the water they made a cool shade and the *surface* lay calm and dark and *reflected* like a small white star the form of a plover hovering on the updrafts off the edge of the bluff. Under the seat of the skiff a catfish swam dry and *intransigent* with his broad *face* pressed to the bulkhead. (8, emphasis added)

The anthropomorphic 'face' is applied once to the river which is shown to cover depths. But it is then applied to the cliff, this time with a meaning closer to 'surface' thanks to the transition through the more strictly planar 'faceted'. The focus then shifts back to the projection of the shade of the cliff onto the 'surface' of the river which is then said to 'reflect the form of a plover'.

More interestingly, the tension between surface and depth is traceable not only in the string of transmuting words taking the reader from 'face', to 'facet' and 'surface', but also in the tension between the figurative and literal readings of the word 'intransigent'. The figurative and current reading of 'intransigent' (as 'uncompromising') is encouraged by the previously mentioned anthropomorphic use of 'face' (applied to the fish as well). However, this reading also immediately gives way to a literal reading when one notices there is a complete coincidence between the movement of the fish trying to swim through the bulkhead and the etymological root of the word intransigent (*in-*: not; *trans-*: through; *agere*: to drive, to do, to lead). Such a tension between those readings creates what Christopher Ricks, in an article on Robert Lowell, calls 'a war of words' in which only one of the two senses of the word called forth is finally admitted:

> The practice ... is that of inviting a word or a sense that is then fended off ... The practice is a variety of pun, but it is an anti-pun; whereas in a pun there are two senses which either get along or quarrel, in an anti-pun there is only one sense admitted but there is another sense denied admission. So the response is not 'this means x' (with the possibility even of its meaning y being no part of your response), but ('this-means-x-and doesn't-mean-y', all hyphenated). (265–6)

In McCarthy's case, I believe the tension remains balanced but that the undercurrent literal reading of words is powerful enough (as it comes as an afterthought, inverting as it were the more traditional shift from a literal to a more metaphorical reading of details or words) and is one of the instances by which is suggested the materiality of the world through the literality of words.

One can find further examples of similar literalizing processes in *Outer Dark*:

> He spat. His saliva bloomed palely on the water and wheeled and slid inexplicably upstream, back the way he had come. He turned and watched it in disbelief ... He spat again, and again the spittle flared and trembled and listed *perverse*. He surged from the water and began to run in the return direction ... As he lay there a far crack

of lightning went bluely down the sky and bequeathed him in an embryonic bird's first fissure vision of the world and transpiring instant and outrageous from dark to dark a final view of the grotto and the shapeless white plasm struggling upon the rich and *incunabular* moss like a lank swamp hare. (17, emphasis added)

Having abandoned his newborn son in the forest Culla loses his way as he goes back home in the night and he finally stumbles back to the very place he left the baby to die. Because of the incestuous context (made clear from the start of the novel), one immediately reads 'perverse' in its figurative, literary and most current meaning as though there were a transfer onto the spit of an adjective corresponding in fact to Culla. Yet, it is the literal and etymological sense of the word (*per-* thoroughly + *vertere* to turn) that finally comes through, all the more so as this very definition is given a few lines before the actual occurrence of the word: 'His saliva... *wheeled* and slid... upstream, *back the way he had come*.' This movement of return is also used just after to describe Culla not in moral terms but in purely spatial ones: '[he] began to run in the return direction'). Another process of literalization of what may at first seem to be a metaphorical word may be read in the occurrence of the word 'incunabular' at the end of this selfsame passage. Because of the biblical and archaic diction of the sentence ('from dark to dark') 'incunabular' is first read in its common figurative sense (corresponding to something that dates back to some early period; one is even tempted to read it metafictionally, McCarthy winking to his own archaic diction) and then read in a much more literal way, because of its Latin root (*incunabula*): swaddling clothes, cradle, infancy; *in* + *cunabula*: in + infancy, origin, cradle). The moss on which the baby has been laid is literally his swaddling clothes. At its highest point of artificiality, of poeticism, the text reveals its own way of being highly concrete: made of words. Words do not function so much as referential indexes of the world, or even as reality effects, as what Philippe Hamon (81)[9] calls a 'truth effect', in an inner-quotation and self-coinciding effect of word to word.

However, texts being texts, readers being readers, the desire to make sense of details, to figure them out and to integrate them in a stable and unified structure remains, and even rises in direct proportion to their apparent innocuousness. In *Suttree*, all of the characters are linked in some way to the tentative recycling of fragments, whether it be the ragpicker, Junkman Harvey, Harrogate settling under the viaduct (116), Reese sadly watching unattainable valuables rushing down the flooded river (357), or even Suttree, who, compared as he is to a 'dim paleontrope'[10] signals, through this relevant coinage, an undercurrent metaphor between paleontology and the act of digging up 'tropes' in a text.

And indeed, the reader is encouraged to lead his own private tropological dig, unburying links between distinct layers and distant moments of the text through the relentless work of collecting, connecting and assembling details, contextualizing them, fitting them back into a complete whole. One can only keep track of some of the characters, places and events in the novel if one pays close attention to their belongings or characteristics, such as for instance the cripple's pencils (68, 103), or Daddy Watson's watch at the asylum (434). These details have an identification function, which not only makes for a slick narrative but also for the transmutation of a primary feeling of estrangement into one of close intimacy. Sections 1, 4, 5, 6 and 7 are wholly built on the presentation of the same place on two different modes, one that corresponds to Suttree's intimate and familiar perception of McAnally Flats, and another one on an indefinite mode corresponding to Harrogate's unfamiliarity with the town. Ethel's tattoo (Wanda RIP 1945), as it has already been pointed out by Terri Witek, foreshadows Wanda's death, nearly 300 pages later, so that the tattoo that had first seemed part of the metonymical unfolding of a realist text with Ethel's description moving from one part of her body to the next one turns out to belong to a narrative or metaphorical chain of meaning, cluttering together death images.

Another example would be the way the very words used in the description of Suttree's ex-wife ('her *black* hair' (153) and 'she came down the steps slowly ... *Deep in the floor* of her *welling* eyes dead *leaves* scudding' (150, emphases added)) are recycled over a hundred pages later in the evocation of the drowned girl of the Gatlinburg Ballad:

> Yellow leaves were falling all through the forest and the river was filled with them, shuttling and winking, golden leaves that rushed like poured coins in the tailwater. A perishable currency, forever renewed. In an old grandfather time a ballad transpired here, some love gone wrong and a *sabletressed girl* drowned in an icegreen pool where she was found with her hair spread *like ink* on the cold and cobbled river floor. Ebbing in her bindings, languorous as a sea dream. *Looking up with eyes made huge by the water* at the bellies of trout and the well of the *rimpled* world beyond. (283, emphases added)

Not only do we notice the recycling of such words as 'leaves', 'eyes', 'floor', but also shifts made from 'welling' to 'well', or even in the way 'winking' not only twinkles but also winks, announcing the central importance of eyes in both passages. In later descriptions of Wanda,[11] one will find the same conjunction of water, black hair against a green backdrop and sea dreams.

But the strategy by which McCarthy integrates metonymical and realist details within all-enclosing symbolical networks disrupts a purely referential reading of his texts, while it paves the way for a play on language and rhythms, for a constant recycling and transmutation of words, and the redistribution of signifiers. In the process details and words come to be not so much subjected to a narrative or even a symbolical structure but come to be poetic matrices out of which the text unfolds.

A detailed look at the Gatlinburg extract (but it would be worth considering the chapter) reveals that the whole text seems to be a variation around the idea of loss, developing through the repetition and recycling of a limited number of words, sounds and rhythms, whether through the repetition of the word 'leaves', in which one reads its verbal homonym (to leave), or whether in the multiple occurrences of 'gone', and its mutations and dispersions in 'long', 'jargon', 'gone wrong', 'among', whose sonorities moreover evoke grief's woeful complaint. Added to this, the negativity and the sonorities of 'none still green' as well as the conjunction of the letters 'n' and 'o' in 'drowned', 'found', 'beyond' (bone), and more particularly 'stone', 'season' in which one finds Suttree's lost 'son' take part in the expression of loss and passage, along with 'old': 'sacking', 'old rusted trucks', 'cold gray light', 'clouds troweled', 'golden leaves', 'old grandfather time', 'cold and cobbled', 'rimpled world', 'cold gray stones':[12]

> He hiked up into the mountains. The season had *gone* before, some trees *gone* barren, *none* still green. He spent the night on a ledge above the river and all night he could hear the ghosts of lumber trains, a liquid clicking and *long* shunt and clatter and the *jargon* of old rusted trucks on rails *long gone*. The first few dawns half made him nauseous, he'd not seen one dead sober for so *long*. He sat in the cold gray light and watched mummied up in his blanket. A small wind blew. A rack of clouds troweled across the east grew mauve and yellow and the sun came boring up. He was moved by the utter silence of it. He turned his back to the warmth. Yellow leaves were falling all through the forest and the river was filled with them, shuttling and winking, golden leaves that rushed like poured coins in the tailwater. A perishable currency, forever renewed. In an old grandfather time a ballad transpired here, some love gone wrong and a *sabletressed girl* drowned in an icegreen pool where she was found with her hair spread *like ink* on the cold and cobbled river floor. Ebbing in her bindings, languorous as a sea dream. *Looking up with eyes made huge by the water* at the bellies of trout and the well of the *rimpled* world beyond. (283, emphases added)

In this perspective 'perishable' is worth considering in detail, not only as it evokes death and loss but also because the literal idea of leaving and movement appears in its Latin root (*per-*, away + *ire*, to go), which is further enhanced by its combination with another significant word, 'currency' (the Latin root of which also conveys movement: *currere*, to run). 'Perish' occurs twice again in this section, the first time in the children's cemetery ('the naked headboards all but perished in the weathers of seasons past' (286). The second time the term applies directly to Suttree himself: 'He saw with a madman's clarity the perishability of his flesh' (287).

It appears that the whole extract unfolds through the poetic circulation of a limited number of words, sonorities, all dealing with the idea of loss. All the denotative and referential details of the text seemingly corresponding to a metonymical description of Gatlinburg forest (the leaves, the jargon of the train, etc.) do help create the referential illusion of realist writing, but all these words find themselves at the crossroads of multiple readings, a paratactic one, a symbolical one and a semiotic one in which the signifiers, more powerfully than the signifieds, as details of the text (as something to be scrutinized, cut up), work as poetic matrices. The details of the text are not subjected to the narrative unfolding of the text; they seem rather to be that out of which the text proceeds. The process of detailing in McCarthy relentlessly moves the reader to slow down his pace and focus on the words themselves.

Notes

1 McCarthy is more akin to Thoreau than to Emerson.
2 Notice indeed that whenever he is described in the process of detailing the world, whether he is sampling it up or filling his ledgerbooks with sketches or drawing maps, a process of simultaneous erasure or loss is described as for instance on p. 140 or p. 173 with a telling anagram between 'scapple' and 'scalp'.
3 Notice how the divining powers attributed to the students is only so by means of a comparison and is furthermore imbued with indeterminacy by the adverb 'perhaps' (194).
4 Whenever the judge is described in the activity of detailing the world, a process of simultaneous erasure and loss is also described, as for example when he throws away the original piece in the fire (140), or when he 'scapples' away the designs he copies out (173). In the latter case, the anagrammatic link between 'scapple' and 'scalp' is rather telling. As for *Child of God*, the use of the adverb 'perhaps' in 'four young students who bent over him like those haruspices of old perhaps saw monsters worse to come in their configurations' sheds enough indeterminacy on the whole sentence to suggest Ballard's final elusiveness.
5 Interestingly enough, Mother She who seems to be immune to the test of time, and who is the one who restores Suttree and sets him back into motion, into life, does not come out on photographs: she cannot be stilled, she cannot be trapped into one of the 'dead places' of the picture: 'I was there. I never come out in the picture. I was there when it was took but I never come out./ Where were you in the picture?/ Right yonder in that dead place' (279).
6 A closer analysis of the use of 'and' in McCarthy's work would show its central role in the powerful creation of McCarthy's specific anonymous, a-semantic lyricism.
7 Interesting parallels may be seen between McCarthy's celebrated 'optical democracy' episode in *Blood Meridian* and Abbey's following descriptions: 'In the mixture of starlight and cloud-reflected sunlight in which the desert world is now illuminated, *each single object stands forth* in preternatural though transient brilliance, a final assertion of existence before the coming of night: each rock and shrub and tree, each flower, each stem of grass, diverse and separate, *vividly isolate*, yet joined each to every other in a unity which generously includes me and my solitude as well' (99). '*Each stone, each plant, each grain of sand exist in and for itself with a clarity* that is undimmed by any suggestion of a different realm. Claritas, integritas, veritas. Only the sunlight holds things together. Noon is the crucial hour: the desert reveals itself nakedly and cruelly, with no meaning but its own existence. Life has come to a standstill, at least for the hour. In this forgotten place the tree and I wait on the shore of time, temporarily free from the force of motion and the surge toward – what? Something called the future? I am free; I am compelled, to contemplate the world that underlies life, struggle, thought, ideas, the human labyrinth of hope and despair' (135). A detailed comparison of Abbey's and McCarthy's passages would show how both writers basically make the same observations, yet McCarthy does so through 'affirmative negations': 'no one thing nor stone nor . . .' (*Blood Meridian* 247).
8 This preference for surfaces is also present in Abbey's work: 'It will be objected that the book deals too much with mere appearances, with the surface of things and fails to engage and reveal the patterns of unifying relationships which form the true underly- ing reality of existence. Here I must confess I know nothing whatever about true under-

lying reality, having never met any . . . For my own part I am pleased enough with surfaces – in fact they alone seem to me to be of much importance' (xi).

9   ' "L'effet de réel", provoqué par la description, se double alors d'un "effet de vérité": en effet la seule manière qu'a un texte littéraire (qui, par ailleurs, ne relève ni du vrai ni du faux), d'être vrai, c'est-à-dire en fin de compte d'être "vérifiable" par un lecteur, c'est de se référer à la seule manifestation vérifiable, c'est de se citer, de se décrire soi-même.' (The 'reality effect', produced by description, then also has a 'truth effect.' Indeed, the only way a literary text (which, from another point of view, is not dependent on being true or false) can be true (that is, all things considered, to be 'verifiable' by a reader) is to refer to the only verifiable manifestation. And that is to quote itself and to describe itself.)

10 ' "he saw *upright and arrant* on the dead alluvial grimmer shapes, the city of his remembrance a ghost like him and he himself a shape among the ruins, prodding dried artifacts *like some dim paleontrope* among the bones of fallen settlements where no soul's left to utter voice at what has passed' (*Suttree* 246).

11 'She'd come pale and naked from the trees *into the water* like some dream old prisoners harbor or sailors at sea . . . he spread her *naked in the grass*, her grave and slightly smiling face *pooled in black hair*' (*Suttree* 353). 'These lovers lay crumpled in the dripping wood and listened to the fall of the rain heart on heart. Her wet hair lay across his face like *black seaweed*' (358, emphases added).

12 Notice in the rest of the chapter 'eaves of the world', 'coals . . . cracked . . . cooled', 'cold indifferent dark', 'old gray mist', 'cold day', 'sprawled', 'old rotted logs' (284), 'shoulders', 'kidneycolored', 'old logging road', 'cold green pool', 'old dry riverbeds' (285), 'arrowed', 'old distaff . . . blood', 'old and mascled', 'cold', 'followed', 'cobbled ways into an old stone town' (286), 'old spectral revenants', 'colliding', 'wortled bone' 'pauldron' (287), 'high cold ground' (288).

William C. Spencer

The seventh direction, or Suttree's vision quest

In late October he pulled his lines. Leaves were falling in the river and the days of windy rain and woodsmoke took him back to other times more than he would have liked. He made himself up a pack from old sacking and rolled his blanket and with some rice and dried fruit and a fishline he took a bus to Gatlinburg.
    He hiked up into the mountains. (*Suttree* 283)

So begins the chapter in which Suttree spends more than a month alone in the Smoky Mountains on an ascetic pastoral retreat, loafing and inviting his soul, courting a spiritual adventure. Little happens outwardly during Suttree's time in the mountains, but this idyll is crucial in revealing his character and his values, which have often been misinterpreted. John Aldridge, for example, in an *Atlantic Monthly* article claims, 'Suttree . . . does not enlarge his understanding of his experience. In spite of his intelligence, he remains almost to the end essentially what he was at the beginning – an oddly benumbed participant . . . seemingly without self-awareness' (93). Though Aldridge does soften his criticism with the qualifying phrase '*almost* to the end,' still his assessment is misleading. As I have already argued in a *Southern Quarterly* article, McCarthy indicates Suttree's spiritual and psychological progress through his protagonist's experience of a variety of altered states of consciousness. While Suttree may not find definite answers to all of his existential questions, McCarthy depicts him as too much of an active spiritual seeker for him to be described as 'benumbed' or 'without self-awareness.' In fact, Suttree's first trek into the Smokies evokes the tradition of the Native American vision quest. Suttree, like an American Indian, seeks insight and spiritual power by going alone and unprotected into the mountains, where he connects with nature and undergoes tests of courage and a mystical rite of passage.
    As described by Vinson Brown in his book *Voices of Earth and Sky: Vision Search of the Native Americans*, the vision quest, or *Hanblecheyapi*, typically was undertaken by young men of a tribe hoping to receive visions that would empower them and give direction and meaning to their lives. A youth would first be purified in an Inipi, or sweat lodge ceremony; then he would go alone with very little

clothing and a blanket to a high place for two to four days, during which time he would abstain from food and water. The fasting tested the youth's endurance, while the isolation and risk of a lightning strike tested the vision seeker's courage. Successful questers were rewarded with visions, sometimes of monsters but more frequently of animals, one of which might be revealed to be the seer's 'spirit animal' – an ally and symbol of the seeker's personality and proper path.

It is clear especially from McCarthy's Western novels that he has researched American Indian culture in some depth, and the importance of Native American wisdom to McCarthy is particularly indicated by the character Quijada in *The Crossing* and by Michael in *Suttree*. Quijada's description as a Yaqui Indian as well as Billy Parham's encounter with an old man considered a *brujo* (a shaman with magical powers) suggests McCarthy's familiarity with Carlos Castaneda's popular series of books on the brujo Don Juan, who taught a Yaqui way of knowledge, which for Castaneda involved ritualistic use of peyote and other mind-altering drugs. In *Suttree*, the Indian Michael, whom Suttree befriends, also seems cast in the role of Suttree's teacher. Suttree seeks him out after marveling at the 87-pound catfish Michael caught in the Tennessee River. Though they are both fishermen, Suttree learns that Michael lives a more primitive lifestyle in a cave, that Michael carries a talisman, and that he knows how to cook turtles. It is just five months and six chapters after Suttree meets his Indian friend that he begins his own experiment in the wilderness. Thomas D. Young, Jr. insightfully observes that 'Michael is a true avatar of the path Suttree is seeking to follow' and that through this experience Suttree 'consciously courts the more primitive realms of being he has sought also on the river' (103).

Suttree apparently enters the mountains with the appropriate attitude for one inviting supernatural guidance since he so carefully and minutely observes the life around him. Vinson Brown reports the following advice of a tribal elder to a boy departing for a vision search:

> When you are on the mountain ... watch the trees and birds and animals and even the insects with all your heart and mind and see within them the power of Wakan-Tanka [the lord of all], so you will be ever alert when voices speak to you or a vision comes ... All about you is the great mystery of the universe ... of every living thing, and among them is much sacredness and wisdom that is hidden from men, except those who seek with a pure and open heart. (123–4)

Suttree immediately puts this wisdom into practice. First, we are told that he 'lay on a warm rock above the river and watched the trout drift and quarter over the cold gray stones ... bulltrout with rutwarped snouts, pale trout with velvet fins' (283). Later while 'turning up the frostveined stones for bait he uncovered a snake. Soporific, sleek viper with flanged jawhinges ... [and] quartz goat's eyes' (283–4). Suttree also pays thoughtful attention to the flora:

> Suttree in the woods was surprised to find small flowers still. He fell into silent studies over the delicate loomwork in the moss. Annular forms of lichens fiery green that sprawled across the stones like tiny jade volcanoes. The scalloped fungus that ledged

old rotted logs, flangeous mammary growths . . . among the debris of humus and rich decay and mushrooms with serrate and membraneous soffits. (284)

As a culminating manifestation of his new, intimate relationship with nature, Suttree at one point is moved 'to discourse with the birches, with the oaks' (286). The fact that Suttree has achieved a more primitive, truer connection with nature in the mountains is also emphasized by a later contrasting scene when he gets to the restaurant in Bryson City just south of the Great Smoky Mountain National Park. Back in the city, the animals are dead, stuffed, artificial: 'A huge and blackened trout hung bowed on a board above the counter and knew not. Nor the naked leather squirrel with the vitreous eyebulbs' (292). When Suttree drinks from a mountain creek, he senses the 'taste of iron and moss and a silken weight on his tongue' (286), but later in the greasy spoon his glass of water is described as adulterated – as 'a long cold drink laced with chlorine' (291).

Besides developing an intensified awareness of nature, Suttree also experiences another parallel with the traditional vision quest – the test of his courage by lightning. The Teton Sioux spiritual leader Fools Crow has indicated the genuine threat to life that a vision seeker risks in his narration of his own quest at the top of Bear Butte in South Dakota. He asserts that to his knowledge only he and Crazy Horse sought visions at the very top of the Butte, that most stopped on the lower part of the promontory 'because of the danger from lightning' (Vinson Brown 167). Vinson Brown observes that in much Native American mythology, thunder would be interpreted as the voice of the Thunder Beings (127) and that lightning would be interpreted as a symbol of divine enlightenment. In this view, the sincere vision quester is actually inviting a storm – literal and figurative – and must in essence court the lightning. Thus, fear of lightning implies a fear of vision, a reluctance to truly open oneself up to the great power of supernatural guidance, a fear of being touched by God. (Significantly, Arthur Ownby of *The Orchard Keeper*, who is actually struck by lightning, is characterized as a wise man, while the imprudent, thoughtless Jimmy Blevins of *All the Pretty Horses* fears lightning above all else.) The vision quest chapter of *Suttree* mentions lightning five times, and McCarthy's protagonist survives two violent thunder storms. One afternoon he 'watched a storm close over the valley . . . ragged hot wires of lightning quaking in the dusk like voltage in some mad chemist's chambers' (284).

If lightning is to be so closely associated with insight, then one could expect that Suttree would experience visions coincident with a storm, and indeed when a second storm strikes, Suttree has a climax of chaotic hallucinations narrated in impressively difficult and exotic vocabulary:

That night he did not even make a fire. He crouched like an ape in the dark under the eaves of a slate bluff and watched the lightning. Down there in the wood the birchtrunks shone palely and troops of ghost cavalry clashed in an outraged sky, old spectral revenants armed with rusted tools of war colliding parallactically upon each other like figures from a mass grave shorn up and girdled and cast with dread import across the clanging night and down remoter slopes between the dark and darkness yet to come. A vision in lightning and smoke more palpable than wortled bone or plate or pauldron shelled with rot.

  The storm moved off to the north. Suttree heard laughter and sounds of carnival. He saw with a madman's clarity the perishability of his flesh. Illbedowered harlots were calling from small porches in the night, in their gaudy rags like dolls panoplied out of a dirty dream. And along the little ways in the rain and lightning came a troupe of squalid merrymakers bearing a caged wivern on shoulderpoles and other alchemical game, chimeras and cacodemons skewered up on boarspears and a pharmacopoeia of hellish condiments adorning a trestle and toted by trolls with an eldern gnome for guidon who shouted foul oaths from his mouthhole and a piper who piped a pipe of ploverbone and wore on his hip a glass flasket of some smoking fuel that yawed within viscid as quicksilver. A mesosaur followed above on a string like a fourlegged garfish heliumfilled. A tattered gonfalon embroidered with stars now extinct. Nemoral halfworld inhabitants, figures in buffoon's motley, a gross and blueblack foetus clopping along in brogues and toga. Attendants attend. Suttree watched these puckish revelers pass with a half grin of wry doubt. Dark closed about him. The lightning lapsed away and he could hear the grass kneeling in the wind. (287–8)

While the *value* of these visions to Suttree may be uncertain, there is no doubt that he has in fact been 'rewarded' with visions. At the very least, this parade of fantastic creatures constitutes another test of courage in which Suttree is forced to face death, among other fears. Vinson Brown reports that a spiritual leader named Sees-beyond-the-Lightning warned his charge that in visions 'great beasts might come and even strange evil powers' (126).

But the value of an earlier vision is undeniable since it helps to alleviate some of Suttree's psychological discomfort, including his sense of duality. In line with a traditional vision quest, Suttree has entered the mountains alone, vulnerable, and in the spirit of asceticism. He progressively relinquishes first his material possessions, then his reason, and, for a mystical moment, even his sense of self. We're told that 'his beard grew long and his clothes fell from him like the leaves' (285). In his near-starving condition, he can no longer trust his senses: 'He had begun to become accompanied. First in dreams and then in states half wakeful. One day in the full light of autumn noon he saw an elvish apparition come from the woods and go down the trail before him half ajog and worried of aspect' (285). The significance of this series of visions is much clearer than that of the fantastic hallucinations of the lightning storm, for Suttree's concern over his stillborn twin, which has led to his sense of a divided self, becomes manifest.

  In these silent sunless galleries he'd come to feel that another went before him and each glade he entered seemed just quit by a figure who'd been sitting there and risen and gone on. Some doublegoer, some othersuttree eluded him in these woods and he feared that should that figure fail to rise and steal away and were he therefore to come to himself in this obscure wood he'd be neither mended nor made whole but rather set mindless to dodder drooling with his ghosty clone . . . forever. (287)

Suttree's climactic mystical vision, appropriately triggered by his contemplation of his own reflection, momentarily moves him from an insistent feeling of duality to a sense of universal oneness.

> Lying on a gravel bar with the tips of his fingers in the icy water he could see his face above the sandy creek floor, a shifting visage hard by its own dark shadow ... Suttree felt a deep and chilling lassitude go by nape and shoulderblades. He slumped and crossed his wrists in his lap. He looked at a world of incredible loveliness ... Everything had fallen from him. He scarce could tell where his being ended or the world began nor did he care. He lay on his back in the gravel, the earth's core sucking his bones, a moment's giddy vertigo with this illusion of falling outward through blue and windy space, over the offside of the planet, hurtling through the high thin cirrus. (285–6)

By Indian standards, Suttree has been much blessed by this cosmic vision. In the words of Vinson Brown, 'The truly great visions of the Native Americans are those in which they appear to rise above all local and narrow views of their own tribe or even of their own race and see the future of the world as a whole and all its peoples' (139). Suttree's visions help him become more conscious of his fears and psychological problems and thus constitute an important first step in his spiritual development. As he experiences mystical unity, his sense of duality – though it does not permanently disappear – does lessen, and he seems to draw power from his contact with the natural and reassurance from his contact with the supernatural. Not only has Suttree been transformed, but it's clear he's aware of the change when he compares himself to a metamorphosed insect. Unable to swallow his food at the Bryson City diner, he mutters, 'The imago does not eat' (292). His change is further emphasized by two cathartic events: his own tears (294) and the cleansing rain back in Knoxville at the very end of the chapter (297).

McCarthy also exploits the vision quest tradition to more fully reveal Suttree's character through symbolic means – through hints of Suttree's 'spirit animals.' Often, vision seekers discover their spirit animals while fasting on the mountain; these animals reveal themselves as allies that can be counted upon to provide specific types of assistance and talent, and they furthermore reveal to the seeker his own personality and path in life. Sometimes these animals appear in a vision, perhaps even talking in the vision, and sometimes they offer a clear sign of their favor. For example, Brown notes that at the end of his four-day spirit ordeal, a Sioux youth named Dawn Boy awoke to find beside him 'one owl feather and a single feather of a crow' (129). Dawn Boy concluded that the feathers were magic, signifying that the crow was his 'helper in the daylight' while the owl was his ally at night (129).

Suttree likewise seems to be tapped by two winged spirit animals – in his case a white woodcock and the raven. On the last day of his running wild in the mountains, Suttree finally stumbles out of the woods and receives a tangible sign, a memento:

> At last he washed up in a little glade and fell to his knees gasping. Clouds lay remote and motionless across the evening sky like milt awash in some backwater of the

planet's seas and a white woodcock rose from the ferns before him and dissolved in smoke.
A curling bit of down cradled in this green light for the sake of my sanity. Unreal and silent bird albified between the sun and my broken mind godspeed. (290–1)

The dramatic gift of this feather additionally indicates the success of Suttree's vision quest. He has been blessed with a powerful sign. Though the symbolism of the woodcock is unclear, its whiteness connotes purity and verifies its spiritual significance. Like other albino animals, this woodcock, which is normally brown, is unique, an individual which doesn't fit in with the other members of its species, an outcast, yet because of its difference very powerful medicine. This white woodcock, like Moby Dick or like the albino falcon in Carlos Castaneda's *Journey to Ixtlan* (31–2), ultimately retains its mystery. Nevertheless, the feather serves as concrete evidence of the reality of this strange bird so that Suttree knows he's not hallucinating, thus restoring his faith in his own senses.

Suttree encounters several other animals during his wilderness episode – including trout, a mink, a snake, a newt, an owl, and horses – but there's only one animal that he sees three separate times – ravens. These repeated sightings may be McCarthy's insinuation of another characterizing spirit animal for Suttree, a line of investigation which does in fact prove rewarding. In Native American folklore the raven is a trickster figure (like the hare and the coyote). As Paul Lauter explains, 'The Trickster figure, stereotyped as alone and wandering on the margins of the social world, frequently engages in socially unacceptable acts to call attention to the arbitrary and tentative nature of established cultural patterns' (24). Suttree certainly matches this description: he lives alone; he's a wanderer; he's at times a lawbreaker; and he challenges the ingrained value system of his society through his deliberately chosen lifestyle of voluntary poverty. Admittedly, Suttree does not match *all* the characteristics of the typical trickster, who may engage in extremely scandalous, grotesque, stupid, even bestial behavior. (Gene Harrogate provides a much closer match for these traits.) But Suttree does appear to have been endowed with the gifts of a raven ally. According to Vinson Brown, raven people are noted for their wisdom and their ability to trick others. '[They] know where good hiding places are and how to use them' so they can't be found. The powers of the raven enable one to 'escape danger'; they grant insight into the ways of enemies and therefore help one fight against them (129). When Suttree late in the novel eludes the police who are chasing Ab Jones, launches the police cruiser into the Tennessee River, then apparently escapes the police for good thanks in part to an unrecognizable corpse in his bed – he quite clearly manifests the talents of a trickster. Perhaps what both the raven and the white woodcock intimate about Suttree is that it's not his path to fit in with his dominantly materialistic society; he is meant to be subversive, a holdout.

Reinforcing this conclusion is a later, contrasting scene which McCarthy offers as a foil to the vision quest chapter. For this second excursion into the Smoky Mountains, Suttree indulges in the extravagance of taking a cab, rather than the bus, from Knoxville into Gatlinburg. This second time, Suttree is not alone; he is with his lover Joyce, a prostitute, and this time Suttree forgoes hiking in favor of snuggling inside the cab while he drinks whiskey on ice and admires the wintry landscape through the taxi's windows: 'Suttree cozied up with his trollop and his toddy... It's fucking beautiful, she said' (399). This time Suttree forsakes the woods for a popular spot, Newfound Gap, where there's a big group of skiers. Once back in the car Suttree and Joyce 'made love under the blankets in the back seat like schoolchildren' (400). At one point they stop and get out into the snow for a break. Suttree, we're told, 'pissed a slushy yellow flower in the landscape, standing there with his drink in one hand... Just when he would have said that nothing lived in these frozen altitudes two small gray birds flew. They... crossed the slope in a loping flight like carnival birds on wires and vanished in the forest' (400). While drinking and whoring and being chauffeured around in a winter wonderland may not sound like such a bad deal on the face of it – the tone and the symbolism of this passage reveal the corruption that this episode represents in Suttree's life. He is intoxicated, indulgent, extravagant, promiscuous – wholeheartedly playing the role of the bourgeois tourist on holiday (but not holy day). This time, Suttree sees not a single white bird but rather two gray birds – fitting symbols for a corrupt couple – birds who seem as controlled, predictable, and domesticated as if they were circus birds on wires: Suttree and the woman the narrator describes as 'his soiled dove' (401).

Despite the fact that Suttree's visions in the wilderness do not solve all of his problems, McCarthy undeniably portrays his fisherman protagonist as an active spiritual seeker, one who has lost his childhood faith but who remains open to supernatural guidance. Suttree goes to great lengths of asceticism and becomes appropriately observant and meditative in order to invite a mystical experience, and he is rewarded with success as he partakes in the sacrament of the *Hanblecheyapi*. Native American belief illuminates Suttree's spiritual enterprise in yet one more way because of the direction that Suttree travels through the mountains. Native American philosophy endows each direction of the compass with significance: the path to the west signifies courage; the north signifies strength; the east, wisdom. Suttree, who enters the mountains from Gatlinburg and exits them somewhere between Cherokee and Bryson City, North Carolina, travels a line almost due south, the direction that Indian religion associates with spiritual growth. Suttree begins his journey in perhaps one of the most quintessential commercialized tourist traps imaginable, hikes over the highpoint of the Appalachian Trail ridge, traverses a wilderness, and comes out on the other side not many miles from the Cherokee Indian Reservation, thus completing a rite of passage and a spiritual crossing. Significantly, Suttree undertakes his vision quest alone, not seeking help from a minister, guru, mentor, or spiritual leader of any kind. He therefore practices what Vinson Brown calls 'the religion of the pure hunters... each individual hunter practically acting as his own medicine man and priest. Each individual in such a case sought for his own vision and medicine power' (24). When Brown undertook his own vision search in the company of Fools

Crow, he noted that Fools Crow took his pipe, 'filled the pipe bowl with tobacco, lit it, and smoked to the seven directions, west, north, east and south, up to Father Sky, down to Mother Earth' and then to the seventh direction – 'from the Great Spirit to his inner being' (166). Regardless of where he goes, Suttree is most interested in traveling the path of the seventh direction, into his 'own center,' where unmediated, he touches the divine (Vinson Brown 169). Thus as he leaves Knoxville for good, we are told that Suttree 'had divested himself of the little cloaked godlet and his other amulets in a place where they would not be found in his lifetime and he'd taken for talisman the simple human heart within him' (468).

Matthew Guinn

Ruder forms survive:
Cormac McCarthy's atavistic vision

I

Cormac McCarthy's vision is an unsettling one; the bleak and naturalistic landscapes of his novels are occupied by characters with primitive drives and simian shapes, more homunculi than human beings. McCarthy's world abounds with surrealistic, atavistic depictions of the human race, from the seven drovers of *Outer Dark* who make their way 'with no order rank or valence to anything in the shapen world' (227) to the eviscerated cadaver of Lester Ballard, the object of scrutiny for medical students who study his entrails 'like those haruspices of old' (*Child of God* 194). In all of McCarthy there is a relentless double focus on humanity's ignoble origins and the ineluctable presence of death; in his dark vision, human beings exist not at the pinnacle of teleological development but at some undefined point in a coarse evolutionary process.

Such a dark view has earned McCarthy a fair share of criticism, particularly among southern critics who maintain the importance of the modernist project to reclaim wholeness in the fragmented twentieth century, who cling to the values of the Southern Renascence. In the 1975 Lamar Lectures at Mercer University, Walter Sullivan berated McCarthy as a nemesis to the old order. Sullivan's comments are revealing, because they indicate McCarthy's important profile among postmodern writers who depart from the traditional style of the modern southern novel. Perhaps because of the Faulknerian prose and pastoral elements that characterize *The Orchard Keeper*, Sullivan initially welcomed McCarthy as a formidable new talent. So long as he worked within the tradition of earlier southern novels, McCarthy was laudable:

> His characters come immediately alive. He has a fine sense of dramatic scene and pacing and an ability to reproduce the countryside of east Tennessee where his fiction is set. In *The Orchard Keeper* he pursues a familiar theme: he charts the depredations of time and shows how old ways are doomed by the new. No southern novelist since William Styron has got off to a better start. (70)

Note the elements of the novel Sullivan praises; they are the traditional components of modern southern fiction – the familiar themes of regionalism and agrarianism one would expect to find in a novel by an author of the Vanderbilt school such as Allen Tate or Andrew Lytle. Initially McCarthy could be comfortably viewed as a gifted young novelist in a familiar vein.

But Sullivan's approval was short-lived. McCarthy's meditations on history proved to be far different from Styron's – and much more inimical to the tradition of the Renascence. Sullivan continues: 'But in his second book, McCarthy told a weird, almost gothic tale of incest and his third novel is clear evidence of the plane of madness to which our art has finally descended,' an 'affront to decency on every level' (70, 71). So much for the dark innovation of *Outer Dark* and *Child of God*. What is at work here in Sullivan's revulsion is the transition McCarthy represents from modernist to postmodern philosophy. Sullivan desires a southern fiction that reinforces 'moral certitude,' which seeks to redeem humanity from the atavism and primitivism represented by such characters as *Outer Dark*'s Culla and Rinthy Holme and Lester Ballard of *Child of God* (58). But McCarthy's use of atavistic portrayals is more postmodern in its objectives; he subverts the myths upon which culture rests, calling all certainty into question. As Sullivan puts it, 'McCarthy is the artist not merely bereft of community and myth; he has declared war against these ancient repositories of order and truth' (72). Perhaps John M. Grammer provides the most cogent image of McCarthy's break from the aesthetic Sullivan represents. Comparing McCarthy to Faulkner, he points out that 'it is hard to imagine McCarthy on some platform in Stockholm, assuring us that man will survive and prevail' (28).

This is McCarthy's atavistic strain, the vision that, as I have suggested, militates against a unified perception of humanity. While Sullivan calls this a 'destructive impulse in contemporary art' resulting in 'the impoverishment of southern fiction under a new dispensation,' I argue that it is McCarthy's unique version of southern fiction in the postmodern era (71–2, 66). If readers such as Sullivan insist on lamenting the passing of the Renascence, and refuse to accommodate McCarthy's intrepid aesthetic, they fail to come to terms with one of the most powerful forces in contemporary southern literature.

I cite Sullivan's response because it is indicative of the tensions at work in the larger shift from the modern to the postmodern – a conflict in which McCarthy's work is fully embroiled. Among the theories of postmodernism which most clearly speak to the evolution of the McCarthy canon, Brian McHale's schematic is particularly useful. Arguing that the literary modernists focused on epistemological concerns – how to interpret the world – McHale cites Faulkner's *Absalom, Absalom!* as a representative text. In Shreve and Quentin, McHale sees typical modernists piecing together a story of Thomas Sutpen, and, in a larger sense, concomitantly, a narrative means of interpreting the world. Yet by the postmodern era, according to McHale, the predominant concerns have become ontological. The question becomes not *How to interpret the world?* but *What is the world?* (McHale 9–11). McHale notes that many of the twentieth century's best novelists have followed this shift within the span of their careers, from their earliest, modernist works to later ones with postmodern features: in novelists such as Nabokov, Coover and Pynchon we see the transition from the epistemological to the ontological (19–25). We may also see this transition in McCarthy's work. Like any southern writer following the twentieth century's great output of renascence fiction, McCarthy does indeed muse upon the epistemological concerns of his predecessors in his first novel. Yet later he also imbues them with the ontological uncertainty that characterizes *Suttree*. While Cornelius Suttree is indeed concerned with the epistemological, his series of atavistic encounters becomes, most importantly, an ontological odyssey. This transition from modernist to postmodernist issues is what vexes Sullivan despite McCarthy's familiar east Tennessee setting. Yet it seems evident now, twenty years after Sullivan's lectures, that with the advent of his atavistic vision McCarthy truly came into his own as an artist; he moved from the traditional framework of *The Orchard Keeper* into the unique ontology of later masterpieces like *Suttree* and *Blood Meridian*. In this lies McCarthy's central importance to the southern fiction of this century.

II

Suttree is the author's most substantial meditation on these issues. Its protagonist, Cornelius Suttree, is a '[r]eprobate scion of doomed Saxon clans' (136) obsessed with death. Having abdicated his family connections, Suttree lives in McAnally Flats, a derelict section of Knoxville, while he searches (often indifferently) for a meaningful way to counter the inevitability of non-existence. Yet it is important to stress that, despite the existential strains in such a summary, *Suttree* is something more than a traditional existential novel.[1] McCarthy's atavistic view of humanity – in which depravity is depicted as essential to the human character – refutes the idea of existence preceding existence. Throughout his work, McCarthy takes pains to demonstrate that destructive patterns are inherent to human behavior. Thus while Suttree may determine his own fate, he lacks the sort of autonomy Sartre proclaimed; generations of racial ignominy haunt his actions. As Thomas Daniel Young has observed, 'after reading any of his books the certainty of man's depravity no longer seems anything less than fundamental truth' (*Tennessee Writers* 106).

The novel's enigmatic prologue presents futility not as a problem for the individual, but as the plight of the race. It depicts fifties-era Knoxville as a primitive, arcane landscape, a '*city constructed on no known paradigm, a mongrel architecture reading back through the works of man in a brief delineation of the aberrant disordered and mad*' (3). The city is pervaded by death and madness, its existence colored by the deceased pioneers who built it, '*old teutonic forbears with eyes incandesced by the visionary light of a massive rapacity*' (4). The passage culminates in a theater of the dead, an appropriate image for both the settlers' fate and the futility of Suttree's obsession:

> *A curtain is rising on the western world. A fine rain of soot, dead beetles, anonymous small bones. The audience sits webbed in dust. Within the gutted sockets of the inter-*

> locutor's skull a spider sleeps and the jointed ruins of the hanged fool dangle from the flies, bone pendulum in motley. Fourfooted shapes go to and fro over the boards. Ruder forms survive. (5)

This passage effectively summarizes McCarthy's vision. Beginning with a grandiose invocation of the drama of western civilization, it surveys a *dramatis personae* of the dead only to culminate in the flatly emphatic declaration that 'Ruder forms survive' – collocating beginnings (the curtain rising) with human death and the persistence of rudimentary life.

McCarthy's use of these ruder forms comprises the crux of evaluating him as either a modern or a postmodern writer. On one level, his use of racial history and literary allusion appears to resemble the modernists' use of archetypes and mythopoeia; he employs the past in order to establish continuous patterns of human behavior. But where the modernists used the stability of mythological patterns to inform and order the chaotic present (as Sullivan suggests), McCarthy subverts the dialectic, as the passage above demonstrates. His evocation of the past is anti-nostalgic; rather than presenting a lost stability, it emphasizes an elemental primitivism which humanity retains. Mythopoeia is replaced with atavism. Primeval comparisons continue in *Suttree* beyond the novel's prologue; Knoxville looks 'as must the ruins of many an older city seen by herders in the hills, by barbaric tribesmen shuffling along the roads' (179). Atavistic similes abound in the novel: poker players in an abandoned mansion 'like shades of older times or rude imposters on a stage set' (22); welts on Doll Jones's face 'like a sacerdotal brand on some stone age matriarch' (108); Gene Harrogate studying maps by lamplight in his 'little grotto' like a 'cherrycolored troll or demon cartographer' (116, 260); the 'filthy basilica' of the Knoxville sewers (262); Suttree and the Reeses crouching as if 'they could have been some band of stone age folk washed up out of an atavistic dream' (358); possumhunters squatting 'in the manner of apes' (359); Suttree sniffing the air 'in a gesture of some simpler antecedent' (447).

These passages hardly indicate a project of cultural reclamation such as the modernists undertook, for McCarthy moves farther back in time than the modernists, beyond the Fisher King and back to the caves. Instead of a mythological foundation to culture, these antecedents are remnants of the evolutionary past. In fact, they act counter to the modernists' use of myth and archetype. They do not lend meaning and stability to the disordered present, but underscore the perennially primitive nature of humanity – the past provides no refuge from the present. As Eudora Welty once said of Katherine Anne Porter's work, memory here is ironic. Racial memory is not a redemptive entity to be recovered (as in Yeats and Eliot) but an omnipresent handicap passed down to the present generation, whether from teutonic forbears or ancestors simpler still. The spiritual emptiness of the contemporary era, McCarthy indicates, is not a lapse from the organic past, but its legacy. For McCarthy, then, the modernist metanarrative – an idea of cultural coherence – is a chimera. The dilemmas of twentieth-century culture must be resolved in new terms.

However, unlike many postmodern writers, McCarthy stops short of mocking the quest for order. Even if the individual cannot depend upon the past for guidance – as Cornelius Suttree cannot – one is obligated to seek meaning without the benefit of precedent. Although transcendence is rigorously questioned in all of McCarthy's work, the individual's struggle to achieve form and order is not; the central conflict of *Suttree* is the protagonist's struggle with nihilism. Rather than celebrating the indeterminacy of his surroundings, McCarthy's protagonist seeks to integrate himself into a fallen world. His mission is reflected in his reaction to another derelict (the ragman) who has given in to despair and committed suicide. Addressing the ragman's body, Suttree reveals his own brand of stoicism: 'You have no right to represent people this way . . . A man is all men. You have no right to your wretchedness' (422). Suttree finds the ragman's desperate nihilism unacceptable. Even though he is himself lacking a meaningful paradigm, he perseveres in his search for order.

If Suttree's struggle appears to resemble that of the modernist hero seeking continuity and connection within the waste land, the manner in which it is resolved refutes the formalism of modernist practice. Until he reaches his epiphany, Suttree is obsessed with form; the image of his dead twin brother functions as a sort of archetype to him, an essentialist antecedent by which he may achieve connection. Suttree cannot accept the discontinuity of existing *sui generis*: 'His subtle obsession with uniqueness troubled all his dreams. He saw his brother in swaddling, hands outheld, a scent of myrrh and lilies' (113). He is keenly aware of the absence of his replicated form, and he seeks out his reflection throughout the novel. The fact that this 'othersuttree' (287) is dead compounds his nihilistic fixation with death, and spurs him into morbid reflections on mortality: 'What deity in the realms of dementia, what rabid god decocted out of the smoking lobes of hydrophobia could have devised a keeping place for souls so poor as is this flesh. This mawky wormbent tabernacle' (130). Thus his obsession with his twin brother – and the formalist paradigm he associates with it – hinders his ability to achieve any sort of transcendence. It is only by resolving his 'subtle obsession with uniqueness' that Suttree can produce meaning within his atavistic surroundings.

III

Two scenes from Knoxville depict the disparate ordering impulses between which Suttree ultimately charts his course. As polar opposites, these scenes provide Suttree (and the reader) with divergent responses to a daunting cosmos, two different approaches to imposing form on existence. Suttree's perambulations through the city present him with one mode of existence:

> and he saw an idiot in a yard in a leather harness chained to a clothesline and it leaned and swayed drooling and looked out upon the alley with eyes that fed the most rudimentary brain and yet seemed possessed of news in the universe denied right forms,

> like perhaps the eyes of a squid whose simian depths seem to harbor some horrible intelligence. All down past the hedges a gibbering and howling in a hoarse frog's voice, word perhaps of things known raw, unshaped by the constructions of a mind obsessed with form. (427)

Here is one alternative to the human drive for order – raw knowledge of the universe lacking the deduction and consequence of *a priori* interpretation, experience without logos. The idiot is McCarthy's supreme atavistic man: even more debased than hominoids like the possumhunters, he seems more animal (squid, frog) than human. Although he possesses perhaps the same 'news of the universe' as Suttree, his inchoate mind clashes with that of the protagonist, who struggles to establish a catechism of even the barest and most reductive beliefs (414). Suttree's discouraging compulsion is to order the same experience that the idiot knows raw and unshaped.

Yet the idiot represents some kind of alternative to the conventional life that Suttree has rejected to live in the derelict section of the city; at the very least, he proposes an alternative to the bourgeois values that Suttree's father represents. His father's letters urge Suttree to seek life 'In the law courts, in business, in government' (14) – at the obvious expense of conducting a true quest for meaning. The institutions endorsed by the elder Suttree reify meaning through a delusive ordering principle. As the ordering units of society, they operate with a reductive logos which seeks to make the transcendent tangible. The workmen who raze McAnally Flats serve the ordering vision of commerce and conventional progress:

> He watched the bland workman in the pilothouse of the crane shifting levers. The long tethered wreckingball swung through the side of a wall and small boys applauded ... Gnostic workmen who would have down this shabby shapeshow that masks the higher world of form. And left at eventide these cutaway elevations, little cubicles giving onto space, an iron bedstead, a freestanding stairwell to nowhere. (464)

In contrast to the idiot, these bland, gnostic workmen are obsessed with form. Clearing away the shabbiness of the tangible world, they make way for the abstract, the 'higher world of form.' Again, however, this approach to form is fruitless. At the end of the day, the workmen's efforts – their pursuit of the abstract – culminate in the surrealistic image of a staircase leading to nowhere. Their compulsion to refine the slums of McAnally is nearly as futile as the ravings of the tethered idiot. And beyond the site of their labors, the 'fields of rubble' remain, where 'black hominoids scurried over the waste' (464). The ruder forms of the shabby shapeshow and the black hominoids persist.

Suttree's deliverance results from abandoning both approaches to form. Coming out of typhoid fever he announces an epiphany: he has realized that 'there is one Suttree and one Suttree only' (461). By acknowledging his uniqueness, he relinquishes his fixation with the othersuttree. The gesture is vital; it is both realistic and life-affirming. It is a refutation of the abstract construct that Suttree has sustained like the gnostic workmen's formalism, an acknowledgment that his othersuttree, like their higher world of form, is an illusory abstraction. The vision makes it clear that teleology and ideal forms are as empty as their nominal opposites: the descent into subhuman oblivion the idiot represents, or the nihilistic self-destruction Suttree has practiced in McAnally Flats. As if to undermine the logocentrism of formal systems, Suttree's epiphany results from a naturalistic accident (his fever) and not from the ascetic journey he undertakes in the Smoky Mountains; the very teleological goal of the ascetic journey precludes real enlightenment. By accepting the solitude of being 'one and one only,' he comes to focus on the imminent instead of the abstract. Individual experience supersedes the imposition of ersatz paradigms upon the natural world.[2]

Suttree's declaration represents the abdication of an empty formalism that is ultimately, in McCarthy's larger vision, little more than anthropocentric self-delusion. McCarthy's atavism continuously pushes the reader toward the same conclusion. By emptying the past of transcendent significance, he stresses the contingency of existence – his primitive depictions adulterate the comfortable in order to force us to confront the present without artifice. The iconoclasm of this approach subverts all traditional means of ordering experience, calling into question the efficacy of societal institutions and even the early part of Suttree's quest. While conventional means of imposing form on existence are familiar and certainly understandable, McCarthy's atavistic vision constantly thwarts our compulsion to privilege such efforts. His focus isolates the individual in the present moment, forcing the one-and-one-only descendant of ruder forms to achieve a singular perception of the world.

IV

McCarthy's unique vision of the world effects the shape of his novels as well, as Vereen Bell notes: 'Reading a McCarthy novel for the first time and bringing conventional expectations of narrative to it will cause one to be misled – deliberately probably – and even mystified' (*The Achievement* of *Cormac McCarthy* 7). In this way, McCarthy's manipulation of traditional narrative structures complements the themes of his work. His subversive technique draws the reader into a struggle which parallels those of his characters; the reader's reliance on *a priori* interpretations of narrative comes to resemble Suttree's fixation with the othersuttree – both are vain impositions of the abstract. The ostensibly picaresque structure of *Suttree* ultimately follows few rules of the genre, encouraging the reader to break from familiar approaches to reading, and consequently, interpretation. *Outer Dark* also militates against formal structures. By all initial appearances, the novel is the dual *Bildungsroman* of Culla and Rinthy Holme. But it becomes a novel of devolution instead of development, and culminates (if that is the appropriate word) in the image of a blind man entering a swamp. The effect of such mutated narrative structures, as Bell and Young have observed, is to discourage the reader's urge to simplify an existence which is ultimately contingent and mysterious. McCarthy makes it clear that his fiction, like the vision of life it contains, resists reductive forms.

Clearly McCarthy's fiction partakes of postmodern approaches to fiction, augmenting modernist language akin to Faulkner's with the open narrative structures of postmodernism. Yet even within the postmodern period, he continues a search for whatever small ontology remains; in technique and vision he is unique among contemporary writers. In his work, closure and meaning are questioned more vigorously than in modernist fiction, but their pursuit remains central. While epiphanies like Suttree's are rare, their promise continues to be both appealing and attainable. Unlike many quintessentially postmodern writers, McCarthy remains aloof from a totally postmodern sensibility; he chronicles the decentering of his era without celebrating it. By combining the styles and approaches of both modernist and postmodern fiction, he has forged a form of his own that promises to transcend his own period, and to set a precedent for the southern fiction of the next century. In novels such as *Suttree*, he indicates a new direction in contemporary writing, intimating that while ruder forms survive, their revision may contain the seed of a new American fiction.

Notes

1 For existential readings of the novel, see William Prather's essay 'Absurd Reasoning in an Existential World: A Consideration of Cormac McCarthy's *Suttree*' in *Sacred Violence*, eds Hall and Wallach, 103–14, and Frank W. Shelton's '*Suttree* and Suicide', *Southern Quarterly* 29 (1990): 71–83.
2 Edwin T. Arnold reads this epiphany in more positive terms than I do. Regardless of our differences, however, Arnold does focus on the importance of Suttree's position in the tangible world, not in any teleological explanation for his survival. As he notes of the novel's concluding scene, 'Where [Suttree] goes is unimportant. The fact that the hound of the hunter Death comes to sniff his tracks is simply another indication that he is still alive' (Arnold and Luce, *Perspectives on Cormac McCarthy* 59).

Part II

A detour into drama

Peter Josyph

Older professions: the fourth wall of *The Stonemason*

I

That Cormac McCarthy's first published play, *The Stonemason*, is a failure places him even more securely in the tradition of great novelists. Although the art of the play is distinct from and, in some respects, opposed to that of the novel, rarely does a first-rate novelist resist the lure of the stage. And yet the yield is seldom successful. At one time novelists went to the theater to make a killing, as if that were all it was good for, and most of them found it a slippery business indeed. A few cheerful speculators, such as Mark Twain, have turned a theatrical profit, but most of these successes are adaptations or ephemera that have not enriched the dramatic literature. When novelists collaborate, blame is bifurcated but is seldom less deserved. Ten years have passed since I read *The Frozen Deep*, by Charles Dickens *and* Wilkie Collins, before the New York chapter of the Charles Dickens Fellowship and I am still living it down. Robert Louis Stevenson, while collaborating with W. E. Henley, wrote to his father: 'The theater is the gold-mine; and on that I must keep an eye' (Balfour 3), but when the several bad plays they wrote together were not hits, they returned to the less glittering rewards of literature, concerning which disparity Stevenson's first biographer, Graham Balfour, in a polite understatement, wrote: 'They had never affected to disregard the fact that in this country the prizes of the dramatist are out of all proportion to the payment of the man of letters' (3). With the lucrative lure of the screen providing ample distraction to novelists, the stage has been diminished as a solution for cash flow, but in the widening world of the workshop, which, by definition, calls for work that is flawed or incomplete, there is often more support to help a prose writer *develop* a first play than to commission a working playwright to create one. Unfortunately, the material hasn't improved because no one is more likely to develop a good play than to write one. Even works that are cast in dramatic form without the intention of performance, while they may prove interesting – Flaubert's *La Tentation de Saint Antoine*, Hardy's *The Dynasts*, Faulkner's *Requiem for A Nun* – seldom rank among an author's best.

This is to say nothing against novelists. Most plays are bad. 'Sir,' says Voltaire's Candide to an abbé, 'how many plays have you in France?' The abbé says: 'Five or six thousand.' 'That's a lot,' says Candide. 'And how many good ones are there?'

'Fifteen or sixteen,' the abbé replies, to which Candide's companion, Martin, says: 'That's a lot' (73). It is a lot. Few countries that do not have Shakespeare in them can boast that many for all their centuries combined. Even God, Faulkner said, 'dramatic though he be, has no sense for theater'.[1] The wonder is that authors of great novels are so blithe to enter a specialized forum in which they have no training at all.

This is partly because it appears to be a cinch to write for the stage, a view best stated by Alexandre Dumas *père*: 'If you locked me in my bedroom with five women, pens, paper, ink and a play to be written, by the end of an hour I'd have written the five acts and had the five women' (Goncourt 58). Assuming he puts the pen down, divides his duties in half, and portions himself equally, Dumas would have six minutes for each of the acts inferred. The novelist Henri Muger told the brothers Goncourt 'that it was just too stupid to slave away at writing books for which nobody thanked you and which brought nothing in, and that he was going to go on writing for the stage and make money the easy way' (57). Why not? Set people talking at cross-purposes, which *is* easy, and there you have the start of dramatic form. Talk, for most writers, perpetuates itself. Disencumbered of description, pens move swiftly. But writing theatrical dialogue can bring out the worst in even the best of writers. The more glib it is, even the more profound, the further it tends to stray from theatrical action. Gertrude Stein cautioned the young Hemingway that remarks are not literature. They are not theater either, but neither is literature. Theater attains to literature only by being uniquely itself. Plays determined to make a point – *The Stonemason* is one of these – increase the odds against them for, as James Thurber said, between a good cause and a good play are a thousand miles of desert few writers can cross alive (202). But the promise of the stage is a promise of blood to blood for which there is no substitute. Despite the proliferation of bombs and baubles to chasten us, our own dear century has not been able to stop James Joyce, Joseph Conrad, E. M. Forster, D. H. Lawrence, Ernest Hemingway, F. Scott Fitzgerald, John Dos Passos, Thomas Wolfe, Henry Miller, Somerset Maugham, Graham Greene, Vladimir Nabokov, William Styron, Saul Bellow, and other good novelists from proving that they, too, can write an unimpressive play. *The Stonemason* is a kind of *anti*-play, the *anti* deriving less from daring the rules of theater than from holding the play above them. This will not work. It never has.

Set in Louisville in 1971, it centers around Ben Telfair, one of a family of black stonemasons, who loses his granddad and mentor, Papaw, to old age; his father, Big Ben, to suicide; his nephew, Soldier, to heroin; and he is estranged from his sister, Carlotta, for lying to her in trying to keep her son from breaking her heart. Ben, who despises every hour spent away from his grandfather, is brought to see the need for greater charity to all and that a family, like a freestone house, can only be built on what is true. Because its theme of personal, familial, and professional integrity is so overtly, even ponderously *stated*, the play is a useful text for the schoolroom and an aid to McCarthy studies, for when a lecturer comments upon, and substitutes for, dramatic action, as in the case of Ben Telfair, there is no mistaking the message. After a work of such studied and relentless moralizing, with lines like 'The structure of the world is such as to favor the prosperity of men' (10), McCarthy can never again be charged with nihilism, although a case can be made, and probably will, for a schizoid variety that needs, now and then, to escape in the disguise of its opposite. Sadly, although it contains a couple of well-written scenes, some highfalutin language and an ethical idea, *The Stonemason* is, along with much of *The Crossing*, McCarthy's weakest offering to date. His one produced screenplay, *The Gardener's Son*, is not a great story and it is not great writing – its ambiguities, for instance, lead more to confusion than to mystery, and its class-consciousness sounds surprisingly amateur – but it is certainly sympathetic to the screen, enabling Richard Pearce, a first-feature director with a constrictive budget, to craft a film of intelligence and integrity. Dramatically disappointing, it is nonetheless compellingly photographed and remarkably well acted in all but one of its pivotal roles, and certainly there are levels on which the film can be said to work. The screen and the stage are, however, vastly different worlds. A look at *The Stonemason* chiefly in terms of its stagecraft can clarify, at least, the manner in which McCarthy has joined the long list of novelists who have tried the dramatic form and failed to meet its elusive demands. As for the why of this failure, I suggest it happened because McCarthy did not care to meet those demands.

It is instructive to look at McCarthy's stage directions. Pleading a longwinded case for twin Bens – one to interact or to sit in silence while the second addresses the audience – McCarthy cautions: 'Above all we must resist the temptation to see the drama as something being presented by the speaker at his lectern, for to do so is to defraud the drama of its right autonomy. One could say that the play is an artifact of history to which the audience is made privy, yet if the speaker at his podium apostrophizes the figures in that history it is only as they reside in his memory' (6). From this alone it will be obvious to any prospective players that McCarthy does not know, or care, where he is, for this is no way to speak to plain professionals of the theater, and it savors of the authorial bloat – portentous tones, pretentious syntax – that is ruinous to *The Crossing* and, as we shall see, to Ben's monologues. Presumably as a pepcall to the cast, McCarthy makes the bizarre mistake of quoting the German astronomer-mathematician Karl Friedrich Gauss (after whom the gauss, a magnetic unit, was named): 'Go forward and faith will come to you' (6). Now, who does McCarthy think he is talking to? It is certainly not Gauss's nor anyone else's exhortation to something called faith that I, as an actor, need to have in order to go before an audience. I need a relaxed body, burning objectives, refined character work, reliable personal parallels, energetic blocking, a talented cast tightly interconnected, a director who won't ruin me, and a very good play. Most of all it is the producer who needs more than faith to mount *The Stonemason*. He needs a bloody fortune, the world's widest stage, and a team of weightlifters.

Even more encumbered than stage-left, which contains only a podium, a telephone booth, the interior of a church, and the porch and the kitchen of a small frame house, or centerstage, which, for the first four acts, is freighted with only a frontroom, a livingroom, and a kitchen with a long table, a sink, a refrigerator, a working range and a woodburning stove, the stage-right of *The Stonemason* is one of the most oppressed in theatrical history, for it has to accommodate: 1) Ben's basement study, 2) a country farmhouse *with a real stone wall*, 3) a neighbor, Mrs. Raymond's house, 4) Carlotta's bedroom, 5) a parkbench and a streetlamp, 6) a backyard with picnic tables, chairs, lanterns and bunting, 7) Papaw's bedroom, 8) Big Ben's and Mama's bedroom and bathroom, 9) the family cemetery – with a stone farmhouse in the background! Offered a desert of empty stage with tracks of sun burning above it, this novelist who is known for his starkly beautiful landscapes has called for clutter. By Act Five even McCarthy seems to have wearied of moving around so much Louisville, for he forgets to tell us where to unload a cheap hotel and the diningroom and the kitchen of the farmhouse. A dog must be cast who can pick up his cuelines; an actor who can pass for a hundred has to be able – and willing – to do a nude scene; wind has to blow through the picnic and the cemetery; the kitchen stove needs a working fire; a breakfast is prepared – onstage – so swiftly that the Telfairs would have to digest raw sausages and eggs with unpercolated coffee; pigeons have to coo, streets must be busy, and there are footsteps, doorslams, and traffic noises throughout. There is no theatrical sound more false than that of automotive traffic: it is impossible to suggest a running car convincingly, as any production of *Death of A Salesman*, with its climactic 'There is the sound of a car starting and moving away at full speed' (Arthur Miller 129), will demonstrate. Or does McCarthy, who wants real stone walls to materialize and disappear, expect actual trucks to be driven around backstage, flocks of pigeons installed in the flies, and gusts of wind and snow to be tunneled into the theater?

Theatrical faith has not come to McCarthy. His persistent call for novelistic detail suggests a lack of trust in the enterprise of theater, which is – to borrow McCarthy's biblicanism – the word made flesh while *suggesting* a world around it. Many of Shakespeare's plays are busier with locations than five of *The Stonemason*, but, as stated by the Chorus in *The Life of King Henry the Fifth*, Shakespeare's plea is from the heart of the player's contract: 'And let us, ciphers to this great account/On your imaginary forces work' (17–18).

A closer look at McCarthy's fear of 'defrauding the drama of its right autonomy' shows a deeper fault of stagecraft. To distinguish between the drama and the lecturing Ben Telfair is to attempt to place him *outside* of the play, which is logically and practically impossible, and this misunderstanding drains the play of impact, for no measure of highblown caution – even if it were read, chorus-like, aloud – will keep the audience from integrating, or trying to integrate, the figure of Ben 1 with the action of Ben 2 or, alternately, from willing him off the stage. McCarthy's stated purpose in doubling Ben Telfair – to place the events 'in a completed past' (5) – misses the fundamental fact that in theater, no matter what you do, *everything* is happening in the present because the audience is sitting there in front of it. It also misses the fact that the goal of good performance is the illusion of *the first time*. Whatever else a scene is saying it must be saying *now*. In trying to place his drama in a completed past, McCarthy is a host who wants his dinner guests to not taste the food they are eating. In fact, from the outset McCarthy disobeys his own dictum. 'Above all,' he says, 'we must resist the temptation to see the drama as something being presented by the speaker at his lectern' (6), but no sooner has Ben 1 begun to speak than his double appears writing in a notebook. When Ben 1 introduces his grandfather, Ben 2 looks toward the kitchen and there is Papaw, who has entered to fix tea, after which Ben 1 says: 'He's come into the kitchen to fix his tea' (7). With Ben 1's mention of the house they are building together, there it is with the two of them chipping away. As Ben 1 speaks of reading in Papaw's Bible, his double does exactly that. This is puzzling from an author who wants his action not to be 'robbed of its right autonomy.' These and other instances of action mirroring word create the static sense of an illustrated lecture, worsened by the mistake of staging bits of funeral service after two of the deaths in the family. These stilted illustrations, far from vitalizing the play, suggest amateur docudrama. It is incorrect to call them cinematic: short, ineffective scenes are out of place anywhere.

The twin Bens, as managed by McCarthy, are infelicitous, but there is nothing unworkable in the notion of a monologist. If anything, though, Ben needs to be worked *into* the action. In his most defeating choice, McCarthy has set him squarely behind a podium or lectern, which, with Ben behind it, is tantamount to a pulpit. This is effectively the real stone wall of *The Stonemason*, and it prompts speculation that it cuts off Ben because it cuts off McCarthy the prose writer, the novelist, from the theatrical situation surrounding and threatening him. As long as he has that pulpit, McCarthy can, in a sense, novelize a little, and the novelist can sermonize a lot, a tendency apparent in McCarthy's recent work. Ben 1 has the cadence, the vocabulary, the tone, and the Hemingway *ands* of McCarthy's prose, but it is McCarthy at his worst, and the property I can best call bullying, which has increasingly hurt that prose, is largely what has shaped Ben's persona. The central character of a play should not resemble his author's pompous stage directions. McCarthy, like Faulkner, has striven for a style that is numinous, that is to say, an utterance of hallowed ground, inspiring us with wonder and with dread by association with deity. It works magnificently in *Blood Meridian*. Here and in the latter three sections of *The Crossing* it has put him into a bad way. Earthly entertainers such as playwrights and novelists ought to be leery of the numinous. One day an author is sitting behind his desk, next day he is standing behind a pulpit.

The fourth wall of a play is imaginary. If it is set up at all it is to help a cast to reach beyond the footlights by making its own world more tangible and compelling. Between the audience and the interpersonal conflicts of *The Stonemason* McCarthy has set a fourth wall of words. Ben the sermonizer so monopolizes the stage that he keeps the action off it; or, to put it another way, Ben's inactivity *is* the action. Rather than drawing us into the scenes of the play, he bullies us about them in order to sanctify his and his grandfather's participation. If Ben is a sourpuss, a blowhard, and a bore, he is so, I believe, because he is fashioned to be the mouthpiece of McCarthy's prose voice at its most misguided and misplaced.

In the drug-driven Soldier's defense, I am sure that if I, for one, were raised under a roof with an adult addicted to speaking, or even thinking, in these terms:

> I stood with my job-book beneath my arm in which were logged the hours and the days and the years and wherein was ledgered down each sack of mortar and each perch of stone and I stood alone in that whitened forecourt beyond which waited the God of all being and I stood in the full folly of my own righteousness and I took the book from under my arm and I thumbed through it a final time as if to reassure myself and when I did I saw that the pages were yellowed and crumbling and the ink faded and the accounts no longer clear and suddenly I thought to myself fool fool do you not see what will be asked of you? (112)

I should have been driven to shooting dope before I was five, and how could I blame Big Ben for putting a bullet through his head? Ben, who views professors and books as dangerous, refers to his own escape from teaching with palpable gratitude – 'Were it not for him [Papaw] I'd have become a teacher. I nearly did. I nearly did' (11) – messages that, along with his swipes at other professions, are not likely to lure his wayward nephew off the streets. If this is what Ben is like in the lecture hall, I would rather see him piling up stones.

To this activity Ben attaches a near psychotic measure of mystification, superstition, and exclusionism, in all of which he is proudly both belligerent and didactic. He is not the first man to make a religion out of his job but he is one of the most obnoxious. Ben's teleology for the profession – 'God has laid the stones in the earth for men to use and he has laid them in their bedding planes to show the mason how his own work must go' (10) – is positively medieval. Not content to puff it up with 'the warp of the world,' 'the thumb of God' (9–10), and the plumb bob 'pointing to a blackness unknown and unknowable both in truth and in principle where God and matter are locked in a collaboration that is silent nowhere in the universe' (67), Ben will have it the first and last of professions, the one that 'can teach you reverence of God and tolerance of your neighbor and love of your family' (64–5) but which itself cannot be learned. And since 'to a man who's never laid a stone there's nothing you can tell him. Even the truth would be wrong' (66), and since Ben is not likely to clam up, the audience is, of course, justified in walking out on McCarthy's play. Why waste our time or Ben's?

The simplistic Socialism that informs *The Gardener's Son* is here in full force. 'All trades have their origins in the domestic,' Ben says, 'and their corruption in the state' (65). In an absurd misreading of history and religion, Ben scorns hewn stone buildings as 'priestridden stonecraft' requiring 'nothing but time and slavery for their completion,' he praises the Semitic God as a God of the common man and the Old Testament as 'a handbook for revolutionaries' because it will have no slavery, and he believes the thought of a laborer is likelier to be tempered with humanity and tolerance (65). Standing at Speakers Corner in Hyde Park recently, assailed by the old gents of Labor on the one side, the zealous religionaries on the other – both sides equally sincere, equally off their rockers – I was reminded of Ben 1. The Marxist mission – consigning to a fabulous upper class everybody to whom you wish to feel superior – is fully realized in Ben, for whom it is not merely teachers, archeologists, historians, lawyers, psychologists, and priests who have known no honest work, but everyone else in the world who does not lay freestone. Ben tells us: 'When the last gimcrack has swallowed up its last pale creator [the mason] will be out there, preferring the sun, trying the temper of his trowel' (32), but Ben is in for a surprise when, after the last day, he discovers that it is not only masons, but gardeners, bathing-belles, sailors, poets, publishers, mountain-climbers, surfers, dictators, gigolos, and recipients of MacArthur grants who are out there tanning under the sun. That the Bible of which he and his grandfather are so enamored was proposed by a paleface Puritan, translated by forty-seven paleface scholars who stole its best lines from a paleface genius who went to the stake for his vocabulary, patronized by a paleface king who dissolved his paleface Parliament, and cranked out on one of the king's gimcracks called a printing press, does not trouble Ben's sanctimony.

Reading the play together with half a dozen do-it-yourselfers such as *The Art of The Stonemason* by Ian Cramb, *Practical Stonemasonry Made Easy* by Stephen Kennedy, and *The Forgotten Art of Building A Stone Wall* by Curtis Fields, one would expect that, in the light of Ben's philosophy, these down-to-earth guides would appear rather simplistic. In fact, they situate Ben even further over the mountain, their healthy, welcoming lack of pretension being a breath of fresh air. Of course they are not literature, but *The Stonemason* is literature that makes itself immensely unappealing when its author, despite the play's compassionate message, sends another message, equally plain, in the way that he cannot resist, through the autolithic Ben, looking down on the world of weakness, a curious strain which, although perceptible in *All the Pretty Horses* and, intentionally, the essence of *Blood Meridian*, seems here to have run out of control and to have wrecked his enterprise. This emerges most strangely when we are furnished with the detail that Ben's grandmother loved reading books. That is all we need to know, but that, in *The Stonemason*, could never be enough. She could recite, we are told, all hundred pages of Sir Walter Scott's *The Lady of the Lake*. So much the worse for her. As often as I have read this section of the play, my reaction is the same: *Come off it, Ben – come off it, McCarthy – can't you leave the old bird alone?*

It is a stretch, but an interesting one, to compare, in passing, the figure of Ben Telfair with Trollope's description of Roger Scatcherd, the stonemason in *Dr. Thorne*, bearing in mind that Scatcherd has little in common with Ben Telfair excepting his occupation, at which he is sensational, and the fact that he is a vigorous, if unselfconscious, democrat (in the anti-Tory sense), and has a sister engaged to be married to a man who, like Carlotta's ironically named Mason Ferguson, is sober, industrious, and respectable:

> He [Scatcherd] was known for the best stone-mason in the four counties, and as the man who could, on occasions, drink the most alcohol in a given time in the same

> localities. As a workman, indeed, he had higher repute even than this: he was not only a good and very quick stone-mason, but he had also a capacity of turning other men into good stone-masons: he had a gift of knowing what a man could and should do; and, by degrees, he taught himself what five, and ten, and twenty – latterly, what a thousand or two thousand men might accomplish among them: this, also, he did with very little aid from pen and paper, with which he was not, and never became, very conversant. He had also other gifts and other propensities. He could talk in a manner dangerous to himself and others; he could persuade without knowing that he did so; and being himself an extreme demagogue, in those noisy times just prior to the Reform Bill, he created a hubbub in Barchester of which he himself had had no previous conception. (*Dr. Thorne* 17)

The reader who knows Trollope can see, of course, that he is smiling, and expects us to smile, when he tells us that Scatcherd can do the work of thousands. The tone of *The Stonemason* invites no such play. When Scatcherd's sister Mary is seduced by Dr. Thorne's brother Henry, Scatcherd falls against him with his fists and a big stick, slaying Henry with such a blow that Scatcherd is accused of having attacked him with a stone or a mason's hammer, an accusation that could be brought against Ben – and McCarthy – when they fall against us. Scatcherd, with Dr. Thorne paying for his defense to save him 'from undue punishment' (19), is given six months for manslaughter. Ben, who, hopefully, will find his own defenders, has been put away for longer, for although he has been published he is not yet performed, the worst sentence for a character of the stage. But not, in McCarthy's case, a reformative one. After Scatcherd becomes a railway magnate and a baronet, he tells Dr. Thorne on his deathbed: 'I'm worth three hundred thousand pounds; and I'd give it all to be able to go to work tomorrow with a hod and mortar, and have a fellow clap his hand upon my shoulder, and say: "Well, Roger, shall us here have that 'ere other half-pint this morning?"'(112) Who could Ben have around him, clapping him warmly on the shoulder, excepting, perhaps, his own double? Trollope, in his genius, enables one to hear Scatcherd's gravelled heart beating: the mason's affection for his old life is palpable. Ben, by comparison, may as well despise his craft. It would be no shock to find him secretly ashamed of it. Michelangelo, they say, had the feel for stone in his blood because he suckled at the breast of a stonemason's wife. He certainly had it in his urinary tract, and Ben, who was nursed the same way, seems to have got it into his spleen. Ben is so sullen, so truculent over *the trade* that no joy of stone is communicated, nothing such as we find, for example, in Herman Hesse's *Siddhartha* when, in one of its finer passages, Siddhartha tells his old chum Govinda:

> This stone is stone; it is also animal, God and Buddha . . . I love it just because it is a stone . . . I see value and meaning in each one of its fine markings and cavities, in the yellow, in the gray, in the hardness and the sound of it when I knock it, in the dryness or dampness of its surface. There are stones that feel like oil or soap, that look like leaves or sand, and each one is different and worships Om in its own way; each one is Brahman. At the same time it is very much stone . . . and that is just what pleases me and seems wonderful and worthy of worship. (*Siddhartha* 117)

When, in Jacob Walter's *Diary of A Napoleonic Foot Soldier*, Walter, a mason and stonecutter, steals a moment away from the blood of battle to look at the fortifications at Torgau, his simple admiration of 'the beautiful jointing of the stones' (35), and of casements 'on the other side of the Elbe . . . which were all, even the roofwork, built of beautifully hewn stone' (36), is more moving in its appreciation of ashlar than anything that is said of freestone in *The Stonemason*. Ben cannot even refer to Papaw's affection for stone – 'He speaks of sap in the stone. And fire' (10) – without defensively adding: 'Of course he's right. You can smell it in the broken rock' (10). If this defensiveness is merely a character trait in Ben, then it is Ben who wrote the Border Trilogy. If McCarthy is master of writing about men at their tasks, he is either not good at, or not as concerned with, inspiring real love for them in the reader, for his descriptions of work are often *assertions* of work, and often they push too hard, savoring more of the dare than of the lure, as if he would rather pick a fight. When I am in Paris, I, who love cities of stone more than any man alive, and am made mad by a fever of stone, of which I cannot have my fill and am driven to walk amid the stone until I am flung down, senseless, in a terrible stone seizure, cannot, at such times, bear to think about Ben. Ben will make you want never to hear of stone again and could drive a man to write an ode in praise of Portland cement. One might even question his workmanship. At hewn stone he is, of course, an *obermensch*, laying seven hundred eighty-two at a time and, like John Grady in *All the Pretty Horses*, drawing galleries of adorers (as his grandmother must have done with *The Lady of the Lake*); but if Ben applies the rule of 'one over two, two over one' with characteristic constriction, his stonework could be as dull as he is. The lack of predictable order is part of the beauty of old stone. It is also part of the wonder of households. From all that I have observed, every kind of myth and mendacity contributes to the building and endurance of family structures, many of which hold together not like one-over-two, two-over-one stone, but like a windblasted spider's web, a thread here, a thread there, and yet, somehow, surviving.

Without Ben 1 *The Stonemason* is less a play than a series of conversations too short on conflictive tension to raise a spark. Plays need pressing objectives, hard obstacles, and willful resolutions being worked out between interesting characters. McCarthy, in whose novels men and women have the most tenacious wills in current fiction, has here not *played* out his themes but has *proclaimed* them, making them overly transparent and, at the same time, insufficiently bodied forth in dramatic event. We are told too much, shown too little. The fine first scene introducing the Telfairs shows McCarthy adroitly establishing situations with crisp crosstalk and humor, but the promise is unfulfilled. In a house full of flammable materials, nothing combusts. And it is almost the only time, prior to *Cities of the Plain*, that McCarthy lets a character be cute, or glib, such as when Maven asks Ben: 'Are you sicklied over with the pale cast?' (122) or when Carlotta says to Ben: 'You know, I don't think I could bring myself to actually shoot you. But poison's not out of the question' (88). The boy Soldier, whose lawless living precipitates the crisis of the play, is, along with his gang friend Jeffrey, that rare thing in McCarthy: a nonentity of a character, less important for being utterly out of place in Ben's house than for being utterly out of place in McCarthy's. One acknowledges Soldier's plight but one does not feel for it. Carlotta will never forgive Ben's lies, Ben will never forgive himself – but what is all the fuss about? Have we missed something? The *its* of the play don't happen. In an embarrassing exchange, Jeffrey, in sneakers and jeans, tells Ben: 'History done swallowed you up except you don't know it.' When Ben asks him: 'If history swallows everybody up who do you think is running the world?' Jeffrey answers: 'It look to you like somebody *runnin* it?' (74–5) Someone is certainly running them. Made to service a plot that is made to service a thesis, Soldier, Jeffrey, and most of the population are as stifled as the marionettes of G. B. Shaw, whose socio-political demonstrations would not permit even a rustic to cross the stage without making his contribution to the argument. The scene in which Papaw recounts the senseless murder of Uncle Selman while withholding the killer's name is effective use of monologue within dialogue, and it hints at one of the many powerful dramas that might have been. In fact this short scene alone is well worth the price of admission. It is especially tantalizing that in Ben's query to Papaw – 'What was the man's name?' (52) – there is the kernel of another kind of play, and in its repetition – 'What was his name?' – and Papaw's response – 'I guess I'd rather not say it' (53) – that play begins to generate itself to such a degree that if McCarthy, at his best, had proceeded from the focus of this scene in both directions, he could not have failed to bring off a winner. As it stands, all that is tangibly – and not compellingly – developed is Ben 1's relationship to himself. At play's end, taking the blame for the ills of his family, Ben says: 'I lost my way' (111). So has McCarthy. It is not too late for Ben. It is for the play. It is a mistake to equate the error of Ben with the error of Ben's ways and to excuse it as intentional. If McCarthy has lost his way it is because he has lost his balance. Less a character than a McCarthy sound-off, Ben is kept from being dramatically interesting, or interesting at all, because he is kept from being Ben.[2] At his worst, McCarthy, like Hemingway, wants to prove too much of what he knows and the burden of proof is on his characters. Right autonomy is the last thing McCarthy wishes to give them. But unless he can let his players play, a playwright does not have a drama.

Before the first stone walls rose up around caves such as those in the Aran Islands, one of McCarthy's ancestors acted out a scene in which was circumscribed the war of the rough winds against his people. It went poorly, so he set about refining it for a century or two before he formed it into something that would play. Ben is wrong in telling us that masonry is man's first gift and oldest craft. Theater is made of older professions whose secrets are just as long, as hard, and as necessary to master.

II

Ben has annoying views on many things, including evil, which he sees as 'not selective but only opportunistic' (97), and he is taken with a metaphysical construct,

God, which amounts to a kind of cosmological handiman and ineffectual Mister Clean of the soul: kindly, authoritative, unavailing – fatherly. This makes sense in a play full of fathers but it does not make much more than that.

Ben's God is a *he* until turning into an *it* when Ben says: 'I know nothing of God. But I know that something knows. Something knows or else that old man could not know. Something knows and will tell you. It will tell you when you stop pretending that you know' (97). For a man who knows nothing of God, Ben has certainly got God busy, collaborating with matter, putting to hand whatever a man can invent, laying stones in bedding planes, making laws to show the true mason how to build, shaping men in his own image, favoring the common man and disapproving hewn stones and slavery and presiding in a court of ultimate justice. Even God's thumb is occupied pressing keystones in place. God is nearly as busy as the stagehands needed for *The Stonemason*. Probably through a proofreader's lapse, the *he*-God becomes a *He*-God only when Ben dreams God.

In this self-styled 'cautionary' (112) dream Ben goes to see God. He brings the job-book of his life but it's a mess and Ben imagines old God stooping to ask him: 'Where are the others?' (112) There is no less bloat in the dream-Ben than in the waking, for he envisions God gazing into his soul 'beyond bone or flesh to its uttermost nativity in stone and star and in the unformed magma at the core of creation' (112), a passage suggesting that Ben should *not* be worried about his book, for if God is looking through him at the stones and the stars and the unformed magma he is not likely to notice the poor condition of Ben's assignment and if there is any blaming to do God will probably blame the magma and whatever is beyond that, presumably Himself. For Ben, however, this is a terrible question, as if he, not God, were responsible for 'the others,' despite the fact that 'He whom the firmament itself has not power to puzzle' (112) is put in charge of an awful lot. We aren't told whether the dream-God does, in fact, ask this question: this is only what the dream-Ben *imagines* he will be asked. We never go in to God at all. It is thus an anxiety dream about anxiety itself, a dream about a man who is standing around worrying; the ultimate, end-of-the-line *called into the office*. Ironically, we learn that the question is thought terrible by the Ben who dreamt the dream but we do not know the reaction of the Ben who is *in* the dream, the Ben who, in fact, has imagined God's question while he is waiting to be judged. Even in the dream Ben is *anticipating* a God and what he will say and do to him but he does not *see* this God and this God says nothing and the room next door, for all we know, could be empty. He sees God only as a figure of his anxiety, a function of his fear about the worth of his book. God does not come to Ben in a dream, *Ben* comes to Ben in a dream and this dream-Ben is worried into God. In his dream, as in his sermons, Ben's God is God *talk*.

Why is Ben's interpretation of this dream so literal? He is an educated man. Unlike Papaw, who knows nothing of psychology, Ben knows at least enough psychology to trash it and to say that it knows nothing of Papaw (whatever that means), and yet he appears to have taken the Ben in the dream to represent himself, the job-book in the dream to represent his job-book, the God in the dream to represent God, and the *others* in the dream to represent – others. In fact there *is* no symbolic representation in the dream: things are what they are and not other things. McCarthy, one of fiction's great searchers and researchers, appears not to have looked at his own dreams or anyone else's. He is not great with dreams. It is hard, for example, to say which is duller, the so-called dream with which the Border Trilogy drags toward conclusion, or the windbag deposing it. When Ben asserts that 'I had this dream but I did not heed it. And so I lost my way' (113), it is not because Ben has misinterpreted the dream – he has not really interpreted it at all – but because he did not do what it told him to do.

What should he have done?

We need to determine what he has lost. According to Ben, he has lost his way, although this business of the *lost way* is one of the flaws of the play, for the plaint is more imposed upon than rising out of the action. If Ben dreams a dream in which he worries that God will ask him about *the others* and then he *loses his way* for not heeding its message that 'we cannot save ourselves unless we save all ourselves' (113), Ben, then, is lost because he did not save *the others*.

Who *are* these others?

His father shoots himself. What could Ben have done to save him? Ben might have gotten closer to his father if, instead of submerging himself in the gravity of his work, he had submitted to 'that true bend of gravity which is the world's pain' (111), but the father–son relationship, even the lack of such a relationship, is sketched too sparsely to mean much at all and there is little to suggest that an improvement in relations might have spared Big Ben his suicide. The play in which Big Ben shoots himself is barely the same as the play in which his son mourns the loss, and even that regret is poorly managed. There can hardly be a clumsier, less evocative line than: 'Why could he not see the worth of that which he had put aside and the poverty of all he hungered for?' (111) Ben's nephew overdoses. So what? He is presented as a thoughtless punk. What could Ben have done, under the bend of the world's pain, to save *him*? When we discover that Soldier's name is also Ben, the boy's position as an *other*, one of Ben's selves to be saved, is underscored but not persuasively, for Soldier is doomed from the moment he enters the play. More than any McCarthy character prior to John Grady Cole, even more than Suttree, Ben has concerned himself with *the others*. Are we meant to believe that for all his praise of stone, praise of Papaw, praise of God, praise of spirit, praise of the Bible, praise of his grandmother, praise, in fact, of everything he loves, nothing and no one taught him, in advance of this wonderful dream, to love his neighbor as himself? He must have heard it. And if there is nobody and nothing in his life that could help him, either before or after the dream, to fasten to his *way* (however he may define it), why, then, are all these things, or any of them, praiseworthy? What good are they to him? What is the use of the message itself?

McCarthy has asked too much of Ben. He wants Ben to be a fundamentally good man and he wants us to feel for his imperfections. He also wants him to talk stone, mason, Bible, God, which is hard to listen to, and he tries to superimpose an appreciation of *lostness* that does not make sense, either in light of what he has told us (too much), or in light of what we have seen (too little). With regard to his family, Ben, for all his self-mortification, has not done a damn thing wrong, or very little. He may, for instance, have lied to his sister, may have paid off her son, but it does not *feel* wrong: what feels wrong is the manner in which he regrets it, telling us, in effect, *this is my tragedy*. What was he supposed to have done? Carlotta's break with Ben, meant to underscore Ben's Big Mistake, seems severe and works against the effect McCarthy is straining for. It is thus more puzzling than affecting for Ben to be lost of not saving all *the others*, and it is questionable to claim that philosophically the themes of *The Stonemason* are, at least, played out better than its action. *The Stonemason* shares a fault with *Cities of the Plain* in the divergence between McCarthy's bent for rendering his characters in (or at) their perfections, and his ability to put these men in trouble. If Ben's alleged downfall – 'I had this dream but I did not heed it. And so I lost my way' (115) – is simply not credible, it is even less credible that John Grady Cole, with all his boy's book abilities, imagines for one moment that his heart-of-gold whore can insert herself into a taxi, *a Mexican taxi in Mexico, alone*, and be driven, without accost, away from her Mexican pimp, her Mexican cathouse, and all her Mexican johns, over the Mexico border into his brilliant loving arms. With all that McCarthy has asked me to believe about John Grady Cole over the course of two novels (not to mention all the collective wisdom, skill, and strength of character at the ranch, including his friend Billy, another boy's book hero), he cannot also ask me to believe of John Grady *this is the best he can do*. I can only believe that this lame, *totally* halfassed scheme (non-scheme, really) for springing his little beloved is a lapse on McCarthy's part. The cause of trouble for John Grady, like the cause of trouble for Ben, is insufficiently imagined, with the result that it is wholly unconvincing.

As for Ben's dream, Ben has, in fact, misinterpreted it, but I believe he has done so because McCarthy has done so. As I have suggested, the message in the dream – 'Where are the others?' – does not derive from a dream-God, it derives from a dream-Ben's anxiety attack, an attack so upsetting to both the dreamed Ben and the dreamer that the dream is never concluded (or that is its conclusion). The message is judged as a glimpse into God's expectations. But to take its significations literally (and to maintain its cautionary status), the message of the dream is that to worry about justifying yourself through your work will make you fear even worse accusations. In other words, let your book speak for itself and do not go to answer questions about it. Regardless of who calls you in.

III

When I am in Paris . . . Now that I *am* in Paris, my apartment looks out on the quiet Passage des Abbesses. As this is Montmartre, which does not let you forget it is a mountain, the cobbled flagstone *passage* culminates in forty-eight steep stone steps. Half a minute up the street the Place Emile Gudeau – where young Picasso, in the shitstinking dump they called the Bateau Lavoir, stumbled through very bad French while inventing a new tongue only two men could speak – is made all of stone, as are most of the walks and ancient edifices of Montmartre. Nearby, the little Cimetière de St. Vincent encloses me in stone and reminds me that the mortals among us are fated to rest with stone over their heads. When I stumble in the streets because, carousing in circles daily, I have walked myself stupid, it is stone I am falling upon and breaking my back over. When I kneel to tie a lace I kneel on stone. When I lean against a wall to make a notation for my novel or to ink a small sketch, it is stone – as in the beautifully blackened northern fortifications – that supports me. Down at the Ile St. Louis or the Ile de la Cité, pausing against the parapets of the Pont au Change or the Pont Louis Philippe to scan the city with a monocular, I rest my case on stone. When I walk down stone steps to reconnoiter the Seine while forgetting, for an hour, Cocteau's remark (made in 1963) that 'Paris has become an automobile garage' (Plimpton 76), it is quais and bridges of freestone, burrstone, limestone, tombstone, Bastillesstone, *true*stone, over which I run my hungry hands and do whatever is legal to do with stone, including occasional yanks and turns of those big rusty rings, used for mooring the Seine barges, that look like remnants of antic creatures trapped and memorialized in stone whenever the quais were first laid. When, during his walks along these quais, the autobiographer-pornographer Restif de la Bretonne impulsively carved into *les pierres* perambulatory reflections and the date of his passage there, he was carving them into this Pierre as well. Crossing the oldest of Paris bridges, the Pont Neuf, from which entire sections of Paris-blacked *parapet, corniche, console, claveaux*, and *mascaron* are being removed for reconditioning, I reach over the barricades and swipe a few pebbles of crushed white stone from one of the huge blocks and I rub the powder into my scalp as a more direct form of influence. I would prefer the black stuff but that is rather silly because I, all of us in the city, are, in effect, the black stuff, for that is what we do to the stone we live by. In that old, popular scrapbook a devil who is renowned enough to be called *the* devil asks a very young rabbi to make the stones bread. This is because the devil is not a poet, at least he wasn't in those days, or he would have been out eating the stones without the aid of his enemy. Henry Thoreau, dear man, would embrace the shrub oak – 'a match found for me at last' (*The Journal of Henry David Thoreau* 146) – and thus his life was simplified. Stone complicates me and I am devoted to it.

For this it rewards me.

A few nights ago, leaning out the window with my dinner in hand, observing the Montmartoise in the *passage*, I saw, by the spill of a streetlamp, a slender man in a dark coat standing over a man in a beige jacket who was lying with his back on the pavingstones and who appeared to be in trouble. Short words passed, then a shining silver object appeared. *Don't let it be a revolver*, I thought. It was, and its barrel went up to the temple of the unfortunate on the ground. In the novel I was writing, the old Curé of St. Eustache importunes a loaded revolver against the head of an armless giant, prompting my narrator, Matisse, to say: 'Have you ever seen it? It will make your eyeballs fold over themselves.' I was wondering whether to cry bloody murder or to order the *gardien* to call the police but, writers being writers even in panic, I corrected the phrase to *coil around* themselves, which does not make any more sense but which is truer to the sensation. I was grateful to the stones of Paris for giving me the perception but I was sorry I had not seen this when I was writing of *Blood Meridian*. Well. It testifies as much against the world in which we live as it does for the achievement of that novel that it follows a reader everywhere. As for saving the man's life, I hesitated a moment because the gunman behaved strangely. The exchange of words continued and he fidgeted over the best way of raising his terrible weapon to its purpose, repeating the gesture of drawing it out of his coat with barely discernible variations. Incredibly, his antagonist appeared to be helping him out. And they call the French rude! I began to detect signs of my own profession. When a third party sprang out of the dark with further suggestions it was clear that the people of Paris, a city mad for film, were making one of their own on the cobbled *passages* of Montmartre.

This morning I mustered early. Having returned from my gallerist in Heidelberg, I was eager, as after any absence from Paris, to dive back deeply into the streets. Without taking the time either to shave or to shower off my journey, I somnambulated Montmartre to observe it about its morning ablutions, its incomparable bakery business, its runty little canine constitutionals... I genuflected before its conventual plainsong... and I descended into the heart of Paris, carrying *The Stonemason*.

I was a man with a mission.

But in Paris it is a mistake to go directly to one's object, for Paris is only knowable by diligent divagation, cunctation, circumambulation, and for me the first of any business in Paris is the business of Paris itself. Only the other day I digressed, in the heat of urgent business, in order to follow a man in the street. My mark was Michel Roethel, proprietor of the Librairie Jules Verne and a Jules Verne authority, but it was not out of tribute to one of the heroes of my youth that I tailed this man like a criminal across rue la Grange and down rue Favarre and rue Dante to number 63 in the cobbled rue Galande, a *brasserie* called The Navigator, where he sat in the last booth with a very well-dressed crony and joked heartily with his waitress... nor was it because he had thrown me out of his shop during my first encounter with Paris and had answered, when I asked him whether he spoke any English: 'Why should I?' so that I swore to return whenever I could say, in bad French: 'So you can thank my country for saving you from having to speak German'... no, I tailed Monsieur Roethel solely because he is the essence of a man who *needs* tailing, because Paris that day would be sadly incomplete without a tail on Monsieur Roethel and apparently I am the dick for the job... and so, without question, without rancor, even without interest, I follow him, consoling myself for lousing up my business with the reflection that if I decide to murder a man a la Roskolnikov or *Compulsion*, for the sake of the deed itself, this will be the beginning, and it is because such digressiveness is necessary in Paris that I have had to digress, and must continue to do so, here.

So in rue Montorguil I bought a cake for Père Bénéteau, the kind Curé of St. Eustache who was helping me to the Curé in my novel, some of which is set in his monster church in the *quartier* of Les Halles where Matisse, born the same year as Papaw, has one of his worst adventures . . . and I purchased exquisite *papier à la main* on which to paint Racine's house, which, since Paris plaques can lie as well as Paris men and the house that reads **ICI MOURUT [HERE DIED] RACINE** is not Racine's at all, can only be found in my pictures . . . and I wrote for a couple of hours on the Ile St. Louis while the sun settled slowly over the buttressed behind of Notre Dame. Finally, with McCarthy's play burning a hole in my hand and sinking a small stone in my heart, I sauntered along rue St. André des Arts to the Boulevard St. Germain where, at the intersection of rue Bonaparte, I sat on steps opposite the church of St. Germain des Prés, which is actually the ruins of an abbey whose mysterious faithful stone I have tried to suggest in hundreds of paintings, paintings that have always, thankfully, failed because its stone cannot be rendered in oil pastel. One would have to be painting in stone, with which I would end up building a St. Germain des Prés in New York, a contradiction in terms. After a dreamlike hour in which I papered the stone floor of one of the chapels of St. Germain with some of these paintings of that church, the Curé, shaking my hand warmly, told me he was moved to see someone else sharing his obsession with 'my tower.'

I have brought *The Stonemason* in order to read it directly in front of this great tower; to read it, so to speak, under the gaze of this glorious building and within its sphere of influence. As an approach to criticism this is tomfoolery, but I am not a critic, only a reader in the extreme and an irrational guilty American who is driven to inexplicable acts of worship and is hoping this dislocation will transform or, at least, temper his bilious view of a very great poet's play. It was only as I viewed *The Gardener's Son* in slow motion – literally one frame at a time – that it began to disclose some of its higher contrasts. This is a way, if you will, of slowing the play down. After reading the play in typescript in 1994 I endeavored, one could say, to slow the play for myself considerably by offering to direct it in the city in which it is set, but that production was not to be. To be friend to a man's work calls for constancy the way an Elizabethan understood it. Perhaps I am here in the Place St. Germain des Prés only to say: *I am constant.* If this evening only a few stone statues will hear me, that is sufficient. About rue Bonaparte, Henry Miller, during the days of *Black Spring*, wrote to his friend Alfred Perlès: 'Anything said away from this street is a lie' (77). If this is a fact, as I am certain it must be – any city that cruises its transvestites on a street called rue des Martyrs, and will tolerate, for window dressing, a string of stuffed rats, and can get away with publishing an unabridged cartoon of *As I Lay Dying*, must have a street of truth and if anybody can find it, Miller can – then everything I have said about *The Stonemason* must carry its weight here or it cannot be taken seriously. With any luck what I have written will fall to pieces and I can sweep out the wreckage before any of it is published.

Sitting on the steps of the hôtel at number 8, which houses the trunkmaker Louis Vuitton and is one door down from the Café des Deux Magots, whose expensive *terrace* is packed and buzzing, I read aloud, slowly, the part of Papaw, using my softest southern inflections, watching the words spirit off to the stone, savoring them as they home their way back down my throat. Not surprisingly, Papaw, even in the evening shadows of St. Germain des Prés, holds up beautifully. He is a sturdy old man. He is far from out of place. The streets do not disdain him. The Paris night protects him. The tower understands him. His *récit* moves me, not because of its anecdote: because of its nobility, *because of the way it is written*. Perhaps, too, despite the distances between us, because we are Americans together. Tears form. An American in Paris is sobbing over McCarthy. When I turn to the tiresome Ben Telfair, Ben proves as irksome a pest in Paris as he is in Louisville or Manhattan. What worse can be said of a man? When the prose of an author is so overindulged, it can hurt the rest of his work because it can poison the reader's ear. I do not want to be hearing the voice of Ben behind the novels. After less than half a page I am compelled to close the book.

I am beginning to feel the cold.

But as this is slow motion, I sit beneath the blue, red and white striped awning of the café Le Bonaparte, one of the many in which the addlepated Sartre, whose window on the *place* was five flights directly above my head, used to set up house at the height of his addlepated powers, and I order a *tea de la Menthe*. The last table on the left, adjacent the little booth of a *crêperie*, is very good for sketching one corner of the church and for catching the heat of a coalburning *brazier*, a fine French system which, without alleviating the cold, offers a countersensation with which the chill evening air coexists, an encouraging combination for a novelist in Paris. One sips the hot tea . . . one scribbles . . . one watches the promenade . . . one shivers . . . one calculates the tip . . . one appreciates the coal . . . one eavesdrops and misinterprets the gibberish . . . one wearies of being the foreigner forever . . . one regrets that half of Paris wants to become an American gangster . . . one shakes one's head over the myth of the Revolution . . . one is reduced to an imbecile by the entrancing columns of crêpe smoke rising in the booth . . . one is impressed by the beret above the blouse above the skirt above the stockings above the heels above the stone above the ruins of an outpost of old dying Rome . . . one postulates the sound of French love . . . one plots to steal Père Bénéteau from his monster church and into a quick matinee of *The Naked Spur* with Jimmy Stewart . . . one wishes McCarthy had let Billy Parham into the army, into the war, and into the city of Paris where he would marry a beautiful starcrossed Algerian with a brother who leads Billy into adventure until he dies in front of my table and escapes the demeaning subjugations of sequel and epilogue . . . one prays to Descartes' ashes, which reside across the street, for a sentence for one's novel or a thought about *The Stonemason* as good as anything in the *Méditations* . . . one calls for a *couteau* to cut the pages of an unread copy of *Corot* circa 1902 which, if one is lucky, ought to yield at least a sentence, not a bad return for a hundred francs given the high cost of sentences in Paris . . . one is fortified, welcomed home, exculpated, humiliated and put in one's place by the remains of St. Germain des Prés . . . and, with conversation for cover, again one voices *The Stonemason*. Here in Le Bonaparte, at the center of Miller's street, Papaw shines. 'A man that's killed by a fool that aint never had the first thought in his head it aint no different from if a rock fell on him' (50). Yes a failure of a play, but one in which McCarthy has planted a marvelous miniature. (Where is Miller for me to read it to him, damnit?) But this is far as I can go with *The Stonemason*. Ben is booted out of the café.

If old Sartre were over my head now instead of under my feet he would embrace Ben's blockheaded folderol, as would his Communist comrades reading *L'Humanité* and smoking over their second drinks in the fashionable cafés surrounding me. But I am forgetting about Ben's godtalk. Would that not ruin the romance? It ruins me. It ruins philosophy. It nevertheless puzzles me that critics who want to generate philosophy out of McCarthy character, landscape, image, and event have been slow to turn their attention to a philosophy – an attempt at it – delivered to them, *preached* at them, directly. With respect to *The Merchant of Venice*, James Shapiro, in his interesting book *Shakespeare and the Jews*, writes simply: 'Plays, unlike sermons, are not reducible to one lesson or another' (121). But McCarthy *has* brought a man into the pulpit to sermonize or something like it. For God's sake, McCarthyites – what are you waiting for? Perhaps we all prefer what is hidden to what is plain because it allows us to shape it into something we admire. But kneeling is not the only position in which to praise a writer.

A few tables down, two Polish men are talking international business. At least for them it is. In the course of this amazing conversation, which is conducted all in English, one of them – called Roman – says: 'I go for a walk and I establish a certain argumentation. Actually, it turn out to be worse than I thought. This was a nostalgia to argue.'

A nostalgia to argue... Yes, Roman, perhaps it was for me too... but... can we not at least concede that there are some works of art that do not know their own form or destiny? That a writer may believe, as Hemingway did, that he has fashioned a beautiful novel about loving and dying in Venice – 'If it isn't good,' he told Charles Scribner, 'you can hang me by the neck until dead' (667) – when he has, instead, rendered a superlative sportsman's sketch about duckhunting in Venice appended by forty-four chapters of flapdoodle? That there are first-rate characters who, because their authors cannot give them more than a page or two of adequate world to act in, are fated to exist only as fragments, and for a novel or a play to be attached to these fragments constitutes a case of mistaken identity? That some plays exist only for one small story to be told in them, told by a character who is lacking sufficient story of his own? That *The Stonemason* is not a failed play about a family, it is a good short story about a very old murder told from grandfather to grandson, flanked and oppressed by superfluities? That with writers of highest worth it is sometimes their abject failures that compel us to return to them and to give them another chance, a lifetime of chances, if for no other reason than a reluctance to be so sorely disappointed, a refusal to accept that they could fall so very far beneath the rules *they* created and the standard *they* have set... or a suspicion that the time was out of joint and that we must have been blind to something... or the hope, irrational but not unfounded, that the work, over time, will have rearranged and disgraced itself? That if a disaster does, in fact, drive us to a type of anserine desperation, that is something to thank it for, as I am thankful to *The Stonemason* for bringing me here tonight ... or for parking me under a tree along the Neckar River, on which a Heidelberger calypso boat is playing a slow 'Perfidia,' forcing me to ponder the play in the dark and to marvel, in drunkish dream-fatigue, how some strains of art, like some strains of music, come closer as they float away from us, up the river, and to capture a streak of light from one of those big yellow German phone booths the better to scratch out a couple of ideas ... or for leading me to the Campo San Vidal, the site of *The Stonemason's Yard*, Canaletto's masterpiece, by the Academia Bridge along the Venetian Grand Canal, where I sketch piledrivers, the original heroes of Venice, for a picture of my own, and where I contemplate McCarthy with my legs dangling over the *fundamenta*, and where I smooth one of my faces over the dark cool stone within the Church of San Vidal, stone you can see being cut for that structure when you look at the Canaletto, stone that would never have grazed my cheek were I not so disappointed in *The Stonemason* ... or for helping me to nose my way, with no map and no working knowledge of El Paso, to the house of which I have painted a hundred pictures, and to nudge me across the front yard, abandoned now to political handbills and soda bottles, to crouch under a low tree and to kneel in front of a few yards of freestone wall, a modest little wall that I had not noticed before, a wall with a rusty pipe and an open bag of trash behind it, a wall such as a man might make in his spare time just to keep his hand in, a wall McCarthy built while constructing one of the sturdiest reputations in America, and to put down my pen, my glasses and my paper and to lean my brow against it, not to tribute the man, the work, the wall, or this play that has led me to it, but to ask myself what the hell do I do now that I'm here, and to answer that by easing myself down from the pressures of life and to feel myself kneeling on McCarthy's old land and to realize *this is the point of reading*, to be brought to a place you wouldn't have thought mattered, to touch something you never expected to find, to kneel in dirt you are happy to have beneath you, to follow an indefensible impulse as if your life depended upon it, to dream the world back that insists on dreaming you, to make an ass of yourself and to get yourself arrested or chased off or shot in the head or healed for being a trespasser on property not your own.

Next morning in Montmartre, I find myself watching the City of Paris stonemasons who, in their bright red and white-striped outfits, are repaving the narrow blocklong rue St. Rustique, a street at least as old as Villon and the highest in Paris ... a street named for Rusticus, one of the priests who, executed with St. Denis by the Emperor Diocletian, gave Montmartre one of its several derivations, *Mons Martyrum* ... a street where Van Gogh took a studio ... a street you can find in Utrillo much the way it is this morning ... a street that offers a marvelously obscured and, because of that, the best view of Sacré Coeur ... a street where I have set one of the scenes in my novel. What was wrong with the old rue St. Rustique? What is a stone that is no longer streetworthy? Worn down? What am *I* if not that, and what am I doing here if not to replace myself? But an old Paris street is, of course, more important than a man. If it is worn by the Dutchman should we not leave it alone?

To defend a cobbled street it is helpful to have groveled or rejoiced in it, at least to have raised or have needed to raise a man from the dead in it, especially if that man is you. If you happen to be a mob a revolution is not necessary: an uprising will do. In the spring of 1968 the students of Paris defended and appreciated the streets around the Sorbonne by hurling, over barricades of burning Renaults, twelve thousand square yards of pavingstones to answer the *batons*, tear gas, and concussion grenades of President de Gaulle's CRS. Of course it ended in defeat and deportation, but it taught that spiteful son of a bitch de Gaulle that, when it came to the streets of Paris, for which the man cared nothing, heads could be broken in both directions. Alas it is too late for any apologist for the old stone of rue St. Rustique. As this is not a city of waste, doubtless it will reappear (already a small chunk has made its way into my pocket). Is it too late for me to be an apologist for *The Stonemason*?

I watch these masons for an hour, playing the part of a man who is not self-conscious about it, eventually *becoming* that man, for Paris permits the idler, the loiterer, even the loafer, the do-nothing – Paris permits *me*. One of these workers, a black man, barrows stones from a site in front of the oldest church in Paris, St. Pierre de Montmartre, whose arches knew a century when cement was made with the blood of a bull, and he dumps the stone, in rather a rude tumble, in front of a kneeling comrade who will select the stone with the most suitable shape, chisel off a chip or two, have a smoke, watch the girls, consult with one of his bosses, and pound it into place with that characteristic sharp stone-chink over dull thumping of earth. Because of its weight, its density, its powers of resistance, I am conscious of a rudeness inherent in the treatment of stone, as much as in my treatment of *The Stonemason*. These hardworking men, however skilled, are laborers to me, not artists. I prefer to preserve that term for something other, and I would begrudge it even to Papaw, despite all that Ben would have us believe about his work, which, in the world of stone, is doubtless in the higher altitudes. And this morning I would begrudge it to myself. When a man sails through the stone commotion with a large stretched canvas, I take it as a cue to return to work.

Passing the indefatigable schlock painters setting up their shitty little pictures in Place de Tertre, I can acknowledge that rocks, words, and masters of both are old things together, but I am unhappy with the notion, as applied to *The Stonemason*, that the art of laying stone is analogous to the art of literature. Nothing is analogous to literature; or, if it is, the analogy is less apt to enlighten than to confuse. 'Isn't as if we're talking about *journalism*,' I think . . . I am also thinking that while the work of the mason is, indeed, intended to last, often it is intended to be ignored. Stonework is not only for buildings: stone is a smoothness to walk upon, that is, *to be forgotten*, to be injured and insulted, to be wheeled, bounced, bled, drooled, pissed, puked, spat, shat, sleeted and spunked upon. The Phrygian hearth-gods that Aeneas carries away from Troy appear to him in a moonlit dream, saying: 'You must prepare great walls for a great race' (Virgil, *The Aeneid*

71), evidence for me that the gods are a pack of dolts, for the cities of all the greatest of races are built without walls. Even the beautiful fortifications with which I am so infatuated inspire only contempt in Rabelais' Panurge who, after telling Pantagruel 'an old cow with one fart could knock down more than a dozen yards of them' (300), proposes building them properly with the vaginas of Frenchwomen which, he claims, are cheaper than stone, more resistant to blows than metal, and perfectly disposed to rain pox upon the enemy. One of the Clowns digging graves in Elsinore asks his partner: 'What is he that builds stronger than either the mason, the shipwright, or the carpenter?' (Shakespeare, *The Tragedy of Hamlet* 5.1.41–2) He elicits the answer: 'The gallowsmaker, for that frame outlives a thousand tenants' (5.1.43–4), but the response he is fishing for is *gravemaker*, for 'the houses he makes lasts till doomsday' (5.1.59–60). In *Child of God* the fool of a smith who dresses Lester's rusty axhead imposes a lesson upon him, volunteering, flame-by-flame, the secrets of his trade without imagining that Lester is only there to get the ax, so that when, after three packed pages of instruction, Lester is asked whether he reckons he can do it, he cannot imagine what the smith is talking about and can only say: 'Do what' (74). For all Ben Telfair's talk of secrecy, I am afraid that he is fated for a premature dotage of such smith-like prattle, to which a Thoreauvian will say: 'I love better to see stones in place' (*Walden* 312), or: 'The world is but outdoors, – and we duck behind a panel' (*The Journal* 211), taking the wind out of Ben's view of building with stone, or building with anything.

But this morning what disturbs me is not the unbearable pride of Ben . . . this morning it is my own pride that irks me . . . as in the attempt at fine writing in my piece on *Blood Meridian* and its cautionary stance, as if a caution from me is worth half a damn to Cormac McCarthy or the world ('Up yours,' I say to the essay, *aloud*) . . . or in the way my 'Older Professions' has to go to such lengths to make a few simple points . . . as if the author of *Child of God* and *Suttree* does not deserve to have us lying, at least a little, or forgetting, perhaps a lot, about his play . . . as if we oughtn't to say that McCarthy had *gotten a little carried away*, or that Ben, who has lost a great deal, was having a bad day and, in that condition, ought not to have come to the theater . . . as if the one planned production of the play having been canceled after its author, who should have been black, had been accused of being white, were not reason enough to stage it, perhaps employing an all-white cast in blackface so that McCarthy, who went from being politically useful when he was black to being politically undesirable when he was not, will not be charged again with subjecting black performers to its racial stereotypes[3] . . . as if I oughtn't to play the part of Ben myself and in the transubstantiation by which Ben 1 and 2 become my own Ben 3, see him justified, for *as* Ben (as McCarthy), I, Ben (I, McCarthy), will make you, audience, believe, and I will leave you entertained, for that is the player's promise . . .

When, in Dublin's Talbut Place, Stephen Dedalus walked past Baird the stonecutter, 'the spirit of Ibsen would blow through him like a keen wind' (Joyce, *A Portrait of the Artist As A Young Man* 176). When I walk past *The Stonemason* this morning a spirit of shame blows through me. I come away from rue St. Rustique sick of myself, profoundly, and disgruntled with my work. For the remainder of the day I try to recover and redeem myself in fiction and in paint, where the fine French paper will admit of no notion, no argument or complaint.

Before day's end the City of Paris stonemasons have departed. Rue St. Rustique has been restored for another century of dogs to squat upon it, motorscooters to park in it, lovers to press in its darkness, geniuses to howl in its light, saxophones to swank down it, pilgrims to verify it, foreign exchange brats to laugh past it, long-aproned waiters to carry trays through it, veterans to limp across it, novels to be imagined in it, sisters of mercy to die on it, and, on it too, for unlisted, distempered, five-way fractured sons of bastards like myself to wonder about poets, about the uses and abuses of criticism, about lifelong failure, about trying to write one word truly, about stone and *The Stonemason*.

Notes

1 This quotation, which I have not been able to trace, is taken from *A Sound Portrait of William Faulkner*, part 8 of National Public Radio's *A Question of Place* series, 1980.
2 With few exceptions, most notably Judge Holden in *Blood Meridian*, McCarthy sound-offs represent his greatest weakness as a writer: the inability to resist putting the journal of his readings and ruminations into the mouths of his characters. His unpublished screenplay, *Whales and Men*, which contains numerous Ben-like passages that do to whales what *The Stonemason* does to stone, is so suffused with sounding off (and nothing better in between) that it is hard to imagine McCarthy could have envisioned it as a film.
3 See Edwin T. Arnold's 'Cormac McCarthy's *The Stonemason*: The Unmaking of a Play,' *Southern Quarterly* 33, 2–3, Winter–Spring 1995.

Edwin T. Arnold

Cormac McCarthy's
The Stonemason:
the unmaking of a play

Because Cormac McCarthy is recognized primarily as a novelist, it came as a surprise when Richard B. Woodward, in his April 19, 1992 *New York Times Magazine* article on the rarely interviewed author, revealed that McCarthy had a five-act drama in production. 'His play, "The Stonemason," written a few years ago and scheduled to be performed this fall at the Arena Stage in Washington, is based on a Southern black family he worked with for many months,' Woodward wrote. 'The breakdown of the family in the play mirrors the recent disappearance of stoneworking as a craft.' He then quoted McCarthy: 'Stacking up stone is the oldest profession there is . . . Not even prostitution can come close to its antiquity. It's older than anything, older than fire. And in the last 50 years, with hydraulic cement, it's vanishing. I find that rather interesting' (40).

This news excited longtime McCarthy readers, some of whom knew that the author had at least once before tried his hand at dramatic writing in his screenplay *The Gardener's Son*, directed by Richard Pearce and shown in 1977 on the Public Broadcasting System's *Visions* series. But prints of that film remain hard to find, and the possibility that a new work by McCarthy, an ambitious five-act stage play at that, would soon be made public set off a series of inquiries along the McCarthy grapevine. Calls to the Arena Stage revealed that *The Stonemason* was one of seven recipients of the 1991 American Express/John F. Kennedy Center Fund for New American Plays grants, announced in the summer of that year and presented at the New York Public Library in mid-autumn. The $50,000 award provided $25,000 up front to the Arena Stage for development of the play; the second half would be awarded at the time of actual performance. In addition, McCarthy, as playwright, received a $10,000 prize, which he had accepted in person at the New York ceremony. In March of 1992, the Arena Stage had done the play in 'workshop' format, directed by Laurence Maslon, assistant artistic director. McCarthy had participated in the workshop, and although there were remaining problems, the intention was to lead off the 1992–93 season with the premiere of *The Stonemason* in September. Indeed, in its renewal information to subscribers, the Arena Stage announced, 'Several new and exciting projects, currently under development, will come to fruition next season. THE STONEMA-

SON, a world premiere play, the first by the esteemed southern novelist Cormac McCarthy, garnered an award earlier this season . . . to support its development and production. Set in Kentucky, THE STONEMASON is a hauntingly poetic contemporary drama about the painful nature of truth and the mystical truth of nature for the family of a centenarian African-American stonecutter and his devoted grandson.'

In April of 1992, McCarthy's seventh novel, *All the Pretty Horses*, was published and became a surprise success; none of his earlier novels had sold more than several thousand copies each. *All the Pretty Horses*, however, remained on the *New York Times* bestseller list for twenty-one weeks and went on to win the National Book Award and the National Book Critics Circle Award and was a finalist for the Pulitzer Prize. *The Stonemason*, on the other hand, seemed to stall. Further calls to the Arena Stage indicated that production had been postponed on the play; then word came that the play was cancelled, the $25,000 Kennedy Center grant returned. At the 1993 first national Cormac McCarthy conference, held in October at Bellarmine College in Louisville, Kentucky, the fate of the play was a chief topic of between-sessions conversation. By the end of the year, Ecco Press (which had published some of McCarthy's earlier novels in paperback and thus kept them in print) announced upcoming publication of *The Stonemason*, described in a publicity release as 'a profoundly moving drama by one of this country's most important writers.' The book appeared in May 1994, shortly after publication of *The Crossing*, the sequel to *All the Pretty Horses* and the second volume of McCarthy's esteemed Border Trilogy. Although mostly overlooked among the reviews of *The Crossing*, *The Stonemason* quickly found its own audience. A limited signed edition sold out, at $125 a volume, within two hours; the initial printing of 10,000 copies had, by August of 1994, also sold out. A second printing is at this writing in process.

As the Ecco Press publicity release rightfully put it, '*The Stonemason* reveals afresh the mastery of character, plot, pathos, and the poetic facility for language which greatly distinguishes Cormac McCarthy's fiction.' So what, one might ask, happened to keep the drama off the stage? Interviews with some of those involved in the aborted production provide insight into the making and undoing of a remarkable but problematic work.

The Stonemason concerns four generations of the Telfair family, African-American laborers who live in one household in Louisville, Kentucky, in the early seventies. The title refers to the main character's 101-year-old grandfather, whom he calls 'Papaw' (pronounced 'Pap-paw'), a mason practiced in the old ways, who, in keeping with biblical admonition, uses only unhewn stone and eschews cement in his building. 'For true masonry is not held together by cement but by gravity. That is to say, by the warp of the world,' the main character explains. 'By the stuff of creation itself' (9–10). Papaw's son, Big Ben, also works in construction, but he has not followed in his father's ways. It is the grandson, Ben or Benny, the narrator of the play, who studies with the old man, having left graduate school and his intentions to become a teacher to learn the ancient and secret 'trade' of masonry.

'The old masons would quit work if you stopped to watch them, but I dont think you could learn by watching,' Ben explains. 'You couldnt learn it out of a book if there were any and there are not. Not one. We were taught. Generation by generation. For ten thousand years. Now in the memory of a single man it's been set aside as if it never existed' (26). Ben works for his father but spends his spare time learning from his grandfather as they rebuild an old stone farmhouse in which Papaw was raised.

Living also in the Telfair household are Ben's mother, his wife Maven and their baby, and his divorced sister Carlotta and her teenage son Soldier. Ben Telfair tries to hold his family together. Big Ben, his father, is constantly in debt; Carlotta has been devastated by her divorce; Soldier runs with a bad crowd. Near the beginning of the play, Soldier disappears; when he returns years later, he has become a gangster and a drug addict and his uncle Ben gives him money to stay away, to spare his mother further grief. In the course of the play, there are three deaths: Papaw by natural causes, Big Ben by suicide and Soldier by overdose. With each death, Ben takes on more responsibility, more moral authority. He finally discovers, however, that his honest work and good intentions and strong principles are not enough; that righteousness can become self-righteousness and intense vision a form of willful blindness; and that the gravity which holds together the truly made edifice must find its moral counterpart in the force which holds together those people who live within.

McCarthy apparently wrote *The Stonemason* in the late 1980s. He discussed the play with Richard Pearce, director of *The Gardener's Son*, as a stage presentation or possible film around 1988. Pearce was enthusiastic and tried to develop interest in the play in Los Angeles. With McCarthy present, Pearce directed a reading of the work at a small theater with a cast of black actors. 'It was not done before an audience,' Pearce recalled. 'There was just a group of us. I remember that the actors were very moved by it. But the reading did not work out. The play was too ambitious for this theater to handle, and they didn't pursue it.' Pearce, a graduate of Yale, then suggested contacting that university's theater. He and McCarthy met with the famed African American director Lloyd Richards, then the dean of the Yale School of Drama and artistic director of the Yale Repertory Theater, to discuss the play. 'I didn't know who McCarthy was at the time,' Richards remembered, 'but I thought he was a very strong playwright, a good writer. I met with him in New York and we discussed it. I made suggestions for changes, but I don't remember what they were. He didn't immediately respond, and I had the feeling he had other works he wanted to pursue. In any case, I didn't hear from him so I assumed he was no longer interested.' Pearce, on the other hand, did not recall Richards making suggestions but felt that McCarthy would have been open to his advice. Still, as Pearce saw it, they were offering the play to Yale, not to Richards himself, who seemed somewhat proprietary about the material.

In late summer or early fall of 1990, the play came to the attention of Wiley Hausam, at that time an agent specializing in dramatic works at International

Creative Management, Inc. (ICM) in New York. McCarthy had contacted ICM after the publication of *Blood Meridian* and the retirement of Albert Erskine, his longtime editor at Random House, explaining that he had never had an agent and asking if they would like to represent him. Since Amanda ('Binky') Urban had already read and admired *Suttree* (1979) and *Blood Meridian* (1985), she quickly agreed to serve as agent for his novels but passed the play on to Hausam, who could better judge it. 'Have you ever heard of Cormac McCarthy?' Hausam remembered Urban asking as she gave him the play. 'He's a living day Faulkner. Why don't you read it?'

Hausam found *The Stonemason* 'very poetic, unconventional in dramatic structure. An interesting hybrid, I thought.' After tracking McCarthy down by telephone and discussing the play with him, Hausam sent it to 'ten of the major regional theaters in America,' among them the 'ART in Cambridge, the Yale Rep., the Long Wharf Theatre, the Goodman in Chicago, the Taper in L.A., the Seattle Rep., the Actors Theater of Louisville, and the Arena Stage in Washington.' 'I didn't think it was the kind of play for New York,' Hausam, who is now artistic director of the Joseph Papp Public Theater, explained. 'I wouldn't have sent it to a New York theater.' Hausam immediately received five or six rejections – 'This is not unusual. You expect to get mostly rejections' – but Larry Maslon of the Arena Stage in Washington, DC, expressed interest.

The Stonemason was one of approximately eight hundred plays submitted to the Arena Stage that year, Maslon recalled. 'We got the script from ICM, with a letter that said McCarthy was considered to be the next Faulkner. This was in the Fall of 1990, I think. I called a friend in New York who's a fiction writer and asked, "Do you know Cormac McCarthy?" None of us here knew him. My friend said, "Yes, I'd do it if I were you." I read the play and thought it was terrific, but it frightened me in a way. The language was intimidating, although it had a central conceit which was interesting.' The Arena Stage was also attracted by the subject of the play, that of an African-American family struggling to hold itself together, to maintain its heritage, during a period of social upheaval and change. The company had recently committed itself to an awareness of cultural diversity in its presentations; *The Stonemason* offered them the opportunity to do a complex drama with an all-black cast. Moreover, they assumed they were dealing with an unproduced young black playwright. 'Based on the script, I assumed McCarthy was black. We all did,' Maslon said. He gave the play to Douglas Wager, the new artistic director of the Arena Stage, and he was 'really knocked out by it,' although he did feel on first reading that it was more literary than dramatic in its presentation and would need substantive structural work. Indeed, Wager, like Hausam, described the play as a 'hybrid,' a mixture of narrative fiction, cinema, and stage. 'There was a problem with length, with balance of scenes. In its present form, it lacked the theatrical momentum needed to sustain it as an audience event,' Wager remembered. Nevertheless, all involved were certain these problems could be solved through the normal revision process which any play undergoes in preproduction.

'Now, no one had spoken to McCarthy at this time,' Larry Maslon explained. 'He was not easily traceable. But we began to read his books and discovered we had the chance to work with a major talent.' They also discovered that McCarthy was not the young black dramatist they had imagined. 'I later learned that they assumed that Cormac was African-American because of the subject matter of the play,' Wiley Hausam said. 'I am associated with a number of black authors, and have worked with black directors ... so they probably just assumed that this unknown, to them, author was black. But when they discovered his race, it was not a big deal. I don't think it occurred to anyone that it would be a problem.'

In April of 1991, Maslon submitted *The Stonemason* for consideration to the Kennedy Center Fund for New American Plays, explaining in his letter that McCarthy's reclusion had delayed obtaining some of the information necessary for submission; that summer the play was named as one of seven chosen for funding. McCarthy came to Washington in the fall of 1991 and, accompanied by Douglas Wager, took the Amtrak Metroliner to New York to accept the award. Wager felt he and McCarthy quickly developed a good working relationship. 'Since I hadn't read his novels, didn't know his work, I didn't come to him with a paralyzing attitude. I had another agenda, to do his play. Therefore, I think he talked more freely,' Wager explained. 'We had a three-hour conversation on the way to New York on Hegel and the nature of narrative. It came out of nowhere. He talked about how narrative is basic to all human beings, how even people who are buried alive go over their life stories to stay sane. Verification of one's story to someone else is essential to living, he said; our reality comes out of the narrative we create, not out of the experiences themselves.' Wager found McCarthy to be an 'unforgettable conversationalist, but not at all extroverted or egomaniacal. His demeanor was very conservative; you would never pick him out of a crowd. He was immensely well read, especially in philosophy and the sciences. He has this tremendous ability to synthesize across disciplines.' Wager also remembered McCarthy's explaining that he was never interested in doing anything other than writing, that he tried to maintain a lifestyle of simplicity and clarity so that he could devote himself to that art. He told Wager that he never surrounded himself with possessions, and that when he had collected too many 'objects,' he knew it was time to move. He took jobs not for wealth but to accumulate life experiences, as he had done with the family of black laborers who inspired the Telfair family in his play. Wager saw many similarities between the trade of stonemasonry in the play and McCarthy's attitude toward his own writing. He was also struck when, in contrast to his openness on the train, McCarthy accepted his award at the New York Public Library ceremony with a simple 'thank you.'

In the spring of 1992, Arena Stage named *The Stonemason* as one of twelve plays being considered for presentation in the following season. Their most immediate problem, they felt, was finding a director suited to the subject. Wager, despite his great interest in the play and his desire to direct it, had already committed to another project. Moreover, he and Maslon also felt that the play should have an African-American director. Maslon discussed possible choices with Wiley Hausam. Hausam had, by this time, himself met McCarthy in New York. 'He's one of the most extraordinary people I've ever met, incredibly gentlemanly. I developed a strong connection with him almost immediately. I really wanted to help him get this play done,' Hausam explained. Hausam discussed Lloyd Richards as director and learned from McCarthy that Richards had already read the play. Hausam then suggested Richards to Maslon, who contacted Richards. Richards remembered McCarthy and the play, asked if the play had been revised and declined when he was told that the play had not been rewritten. Hausam next suggested Tazewell Thompson, artistic director of the Syracuse Stage Company. Hausam recalled that Thompson agreed to direct, but both Maslon and Wager said that Thompson, too, refused.

Wager and Maslon then decided to try the play initially in a workshop format, to be directed by Maslon. In workshop, new works or works in progress are performed informally, often on sets of other plays. Actors read through the script in the presence of the playwright and sometimes an audience, and all are encouraged to discuss the result. The play is constantly revised during the workshop based on these varied reactions and other problems which might arise. 'At the time we were doing a play called *Trinidad Sisters*, which had black actors in it,' Maslon said. 'So we used them and tried a workshop of ten days to two weeks for *The Stonemason*. McCarthy came down to take part; I think he stayed with his parents here in Washington.'

The workshop experience revealed a number of problems in the play. Foremost were those of structure and style. *The Stonemason* alternates between lengthy, densely worded monologues delivered by the lead character, Ben Telfair, directly to the audience, and scenes of naturalistic representation which carry forward the narrative plotline of the play. During the monologues, as Ben speaks from a podium at far stage left, his 'double,' played by another actor, performs the appropriate motions. McCarthy explained his intentions in the script through stage directions: 'It is important to note that the Ben we see *onstage* during the monologues is a double and to note that this double does not speak, but is only a figure designed to complete the scene which scenes will be described by Ben from his podium. The purpose, as we shall see, is to give distance to the events and place them in a completed past. The onstage double should nevertheless be as close to Ben in appearance as is practicable and the two should be dressed identically' (Script 1; essentially the same directions are given in the published version, 5). During the realistic 'action' scenes, the double becomes a full character, engages in dialogue and performance with the other actors in the play. Although intriguing as a literary device, the concept caused problems in rehearsals, and the director Maslon came to believe that the play was 'contextually dysfunctional. The audience could relate easily to the naturalistic scenes, but then it would jump to this dense material, these almost Joycean monologues. They were beautifully written, but they were at times almost impenetrable. McCarthy didn't make it easy for an audience, nor did he want to. You slam them up against this brick wall of monologues, yet you're confused as to how they are supposed to react.' Hausam, who remains a strong advocate of the play, also noted this contrast. 'You had these extraordinary readings at the lectern, but then you had scenes of everyday life that were actually kind of mundane . . . The realistic scenes were less effective than the spoken monologues.' Also, the last acts called for a growing number of short, abrupt scenes which resulted in a montage effect perhaps more appropriate to film than stage. 'A lot of the scenes in the second half, you have to move into them too rapidly,' Maslon said. 'Pacing on the stage is different, although cinematically it might work quite well. The play had this naturalistic-novelistic-cinematic framework. We began to realize that, in some ways, this was not a play meant for the professional theater.'

Further rehearsals showed that the 'splitting' of the main character raised other questions concerning staging and presentation. Would the 'double' Ben mime his actions while the 'narrator' Ben spoke? Would that action actually play on stage, or would it call too much attention to the contrast of styles employed in the drama? Moreover, the relationship between the two 'Bens' was simply unclear. From what perspective is the narrator Ben speaking? 'What does Ben know when he's narrating?' Maslon asked. 'What he's *saying* and what he *does* diverge to the final moment of the play. He's in the moment of experience at the end of the play, but what about before that? These were questions Cormac never adequately addressed.' (Hausam agreed there was a problem with the concept. 'You at least need to have the same actor play both roles so as not to confuse the audience,' he suggested.) Finally, in the reading some of the actors felt that there was 'not enough there' in their characters, that the roles were undelineated and the lines difficult to say or unconvincing. 'I don't know how to turn this into a character with these words,' as one actor put it.

Nevertheless, these problems were not considered insurmountable as the workshop began. Indeed, the whole point of the workshop format was to work through exactly these types of concerns, to discover what worked and what didn't and then to address the difficulties as they arose during the reading. Although McCarthy had already taken part in the Los Angeles reading directed by Richard Pearce, both Maslon and Wager thought he seemed unprepared for the experience. 'He had a lot of anxiety over the main role,' Maslon remembered. 'We had an actor in our company who was owed it but wasn't good enough to do it. It may be an unactable part, anyway. But Cormac wanted to know if we would have to use these actors in the actual performance. He didn't quite understand that this was a workshop, that if it went to production, then all bets were off. He took a liking to several actors, but it was more personal than otherwise.' There was also the question of revising the play. The rumor got around that McCarthy simply refused to rewrite, that he was 'very stubborn,' as one outside source put it, 'and they couldn't do much with him or the play.' But both Wager and Maslon explained it differently. 'McCarthy is not a fast writer,' Wager said. 'He is not glib about what he puts down on paper. He's a literary perfectionist, and he wants to take his time to get it right. But the kind of rhythm one gets into in a play workshop mode doesn't allow someone to go away and work on it. McCarthy wasn't able, or wasn't willing, to create lines on the spot. He was too much of a craftsman.'

Maslon added his own perspective:

> McCarthy made a few, but only a very few changes. He was always a real gentleman about it, but I don't think he enjoyed the process. He seemed grateful for any suggestions. The actress who played Maven [Ben's wife] was from Louisville, and she had a lot to offer from that background, and he listened to her. But we had some real problems with time sequences, especially in act 5, and we kept asking him to write something to explain what had happened, the time change, at this point in the play. 'It's coming, it's coming,' he would say. That's the infamous '85-A' page of the script, 85 A and B. One day he walked in with it, and it explained what was happening at the end, when the play speeds up, and it was wonderful. [This passage is Ben's monologue at the beginning of act 5, scene 3, 111–13 in the published book.] We had Arena Stage tee-shirts made up, with 'Page 85-A' on the back. Cormac didn't enjoy the workshop, but he was always game. Still, he played his cards close to his vest, very Faulkneresque. It was fascinating for the first few days, but then it became frustrating.

The *Stonemason* workshop was done on the set of Strindberg's *The Father*. The actors worked through it with scripts in hand and with some lighting and costumes. Maslon felt that the main scenes in the house worked 'terrifically well.' He was especially happy with the suicide scene (scene 9) at the end of act 4, and thought the actors playing Big Ben and Mama, the main character's parents, were very strong. Hausam came down from New York to watch the final reading. 'Right away I realized there was tension,' Hausam recalled. 'After the reading, Doug Wager gave Cormac a long list of suggestions. I knew Doug really wanted to direct the play, and he was trying to tell Cormac what didn't work about the play. Cormac was incredibly polite, but I could tell nothing was going in.' According to Wager, he and McCarthy did talk after the workshop, and McCarthy said that 'he would like to get into a real collaboration with the director' chosen for the actual production.

'But what happened next was beyond my imagination,' Maslon continued. During the workshop, a member of the Arena Stage literary staff, an African-American woman, had walked out of rehearsals during scene 4 in the final act. In this scene, Ben Telfair confronts and essentially denies his nephew Soldier, by now an experienced criminal. 'We talked to her about her concerns but had very inconclusive discussions,' Maslon recalled. Shortly thereafter, Wager received two letters (one dated March 24, the other March 25, 1992) from two staff members, both African-American women, objecting to the racial stereotypes they perceived in the play. Both felt that McCarthy, as a white writer, was unable to understand or dramatize the complexities of black family life. Although they found his language beautiful and sometimes moving, they felt it lacked authenticity. They questioned why both the father, Big Ben, and the young black male, Soldier, had to die violently, or to die at all, and why the women in the family were marginalized in the drama and denied an active role in the narrative. The *Stonemasons* (as both called it, missing the great significance that there is only *one* true stonemason in the play) simply reinforced prevailing racist views of dysfunctional black family life: the men angry and self-destructive; the women ignored, abandoned or abused. *Why were these characters black?* they asked. Did the play really reflect the Arena Stage's commitment to multiculturalism, or did it in fact show racial insensitivity and even insult? Each letter asked that, in light of these objections, the company reconsider its commitment to the play.

It is unclear how much McCarthy knew of this growing controversy, although he was certainly aware of the general protest. 'Cormac said that he had worked with the black family in the play. That was always his defense, that he knew them,' Maslon explained. 'He was not in the least bit interested in defending himself further against this. He had this novelist's integrity; it was almost a cliché. He was quite happy to work on it if there was a sense that it would be performed, but he would not make changes just to satisfy everyone.' Nevertheless, when he left Washington after the workshop to return to El Paso, McCarthy was still under the impression that the Arena Stage would perform the play during the fall season. His agent Hausam assumed the same.

> Several weeks went by and we didn't hear anything, and finally I called Maslon, who said that the play had problems, that it needed rewriting. At this time I also heard that there were protests in addition to the problems with the dramaturgy of the play. Then there were more months of silence, but I don't think Cormac worried about it. Finally Binky Urban called: 'What's happening with the play?' So I called Arena again, and they said they weren't doing it. They had given the money back to the Kennedy people, and this is something you *never* do. I was furious. I called Cormac and told him that what infuriated me most was that they were doing it to avoid a controversy. His reaction was very quiet, and I could tell he was upset. But he said very little.

An administrator with the Kennedy Center commented that while it was not unheard of for a grant to be returned for various reasons, in this case the decision seemed unusually political. 'The Arena Stage was quisling, you know. You can't do that to a writer. To listen to a small group of people who don't like a writer's work and make your decision on that basis just shouldn't happen,' she said. 'Unless you're a Nazi, I suppose.'

In all fairness, the matter of *The Stonemason* now seems a case of good intentions gone awry. Although McCarthy has long had an interest in the theater (and film: in addition to *The Gardener's Son*, he has written another screenplay entitled 'Cities of the Plain' on which the third volume of his Border Trilogy is based), it was not the medium he knew best. As Hausam noted, 'Very few novelists are good playwrights,' although he thought McCarthy's play showed tremendous promise. There was also the problem of McCarthy's reputation and demeanor.

> McCarthy's integrity was very intimidating to us mortals [Maslon joked]. There were times during rehearsals when you wanted to say, 'Cormac, cut the fucking speech

down.' But we wouldn't do that because we held McCarthy in such awe. It was very difficult working with him because he had his own set of rules. It's hard now to tell if he was right and we just weren't up to it, or if he was wrong and we couldn't get him to see it. He was right in not wanting to work on it until we got the right team, of course, and maybe we didn't give him the chance to work through it. On the other hand, drama has defeated many great novelists.

It also seems clear that the abbreviated workshop format was not the best approach to use for this play. 'The workshop exposed all of the flaws and celebrated few of the virtues of the play,' Wager felt. 'A full rehearsal would have revealed much more. The fun of it would have been to discover in a five-week rehearsal period how to animate it. In a production you could work through these problems, add dialogue, break up dialogue, establish clock-time.' Still, even under these conditions, Wager felt a production of *The Stonemason* would have made large demands which the Arena Stage had to consider. Wager viewed it as uneconomically written, with its large cast, number of scenes and probable running time of two-and-a-half hours. Maslon also felt that while the play would have attracted readers of McCarthy, its ultimate appeal would have been 'largely intellectual': 'There's a kind of play you go to for that experience – "Oh, my God, what language!" you know. But there was a fear that it never could be unlocked for an audience. That we didn't have the technology to do what he was after. And as much as we wanted it, we didn't know how to solve it. So we might have gotten several full houses of McCarthy fans, but could we play it for seven weeks, eight performances a week? That was a question we had to ask.'

Perhaps these kinds of considerations mitigate somewhat the question of 'political correctness' in the decision to cancel the play; nevertheless, the raising of racial and, to a lesser extent, gender objections clearly seems to have been the deciding motive. 'I would not hesitate to say that the play was, in one sense, a victim of political correctness,' Maslon said. Hausam also declared, 'I can honestly say that *The Stonemason* was caught up in multicultural politics. I believe that the theater is for everyone, and I don't believe in penalizing an artist for any racial reason. That's what happened to Cormac with this work, and it's a great injustice.' Although Wager argued that it 'ultimately had more to do with craft than with ideology. If PC were all that was wrong with it, it wouldn't have impeded its production,' Maslon observed, 'I've never seen anything go from the in-box to the out-box so quickly in my years of theater. And the irony is that a month later *All the Pretty Horses* comes out and McCarthy's in every magazine in the country. If we had committed, it would have been great publicity.'

Equally questionable was the Arena Stage's subsequent handling of their decision. McCarthy was notified, as Hausam related, in a second-hand manner, and the full reasons for the cancellation were never explained. Neither Wager nor Maslon felt able to discuss the matter with McCarthy, and McCarthy made no attempt to contact them for an explanation. 'It is the greatest disappointment of my seven years at Arena Stage,' Maslon admitted. 'We didn't handle it well at all.' Wager confirmed that they were less than forthright with McCarthy. 'I'm grateful to have had the experience of working with McCarthy, and I regret that we did the workshop and didn't just plunge in and do the play in the fall. It would have been great to have just gone and produced it and sailed with it. I haven't yet come to terms with the fact that I gave it up. It took me over a year to sit down and explain it all to him in a letter. I told him he didn't have to respond, and he hasn't. But it took me that year to work through it all.'

At the present time, the play has yet to be performed, although according to McCarthy's ICM representative, Brad Kalof, it is under active consideration at several regional theater companies. Most of the principals associated with the play agree that it will one day be staged. 'I have a feeling that this is a play that is going to have to be discovered by actors and directors in rehearsal,' as Hausam put it.

It is also evident that McCarthy did rethink and make some changes in the play based on the Arena Stage workshop, most obviously to clarify his conception of the 'double' Bens and in Ben's examination of his own motivations in the '85 A and B' pages of the revised script. The following explanatory passage, for example, was added to the stage directions at the beginning of act 1, scene 1:

> *What must be kept in mind is that the performance consists of separate presentations. One is the staged drama. The other is the monologue or Chautauqua which Ben delivers from the podium. And while it is true that Ben at his podium is at times speaking for or through his silent double on stage, it is nevertheless a crucial feature of the play that there be no suggestion of communication between these worlds. In this sense it would not even be incorrect to assume that Ben is unaware of the staged drama. Above all we must resist the temptation to see the drama as something being presented by the speaker at his lectern for to do so is to defraud the drama of its right autonomy.*
>
> *One could say that the play is an artifact of history to which the audience is made privy. Yet if the speaker at his podium apostrophizes the figures in that history it is only as they reside in his memory. It is this which dictates the use of the podium. It locates Ben in a separate space and isolates that space from the world of the drama on stage. The speaker has an agenda which centers upon his own exoneration, his own salvation. The events which unfold upon the stage will not at all times support him. The audience may perhaps be also a jury.*
>
> *And now we can begin. As the mathematician Gauss said to his contemporaries: Go forward and faith will come to you.* (5–6)

This is, of course, a significant addition, for it causes the *reader*, if not the viewing audience, to question Ben's reasons from the beginning, to act as 'jury' during the play. As Maslon had put it, 'In terms of character, Ben is in a major state of delusion and denial about himself; his motives and his actions are at odds. His blindness and self-righteousness have resulted in all this tragedy, and he finally comes to understand that.' This is also the point made in the revised act 5, scene 3 monologue, in which Ben acknowledges, 'I lost my way. I'd thought by my labors to stand outside that true bend of gravity which is the world's pain. I lost my way and if I could tell you the hour of it or the day or how it came about I should not have lost it at all' (111–12). The other significant addition is found at the end of the play, in scene 11 as Ben stands in the cemetery and shows evidence of his self-realization. The script has him speak of grace and charity and courage, but the book adds the last passage: 'For we are all the elect, each one of us, and we are embarked upon a journey to something unimaginable. We do not know what will be required of us, and we have nothing to sustain us but the counsel of our fathers' (132). There are other, less significant changes involving Soldier's age, problems in chronology, a character's name and dialogue polishing; but the major revisions show that McCarthy recognized the validity of some of the objections raised during the workshop and sought to address them.

And finally there is the relative importance of the play within McCarthy's overall body of work. Thematically it addresses the questions of moral choice, familial responsibility, dedication to craft and the workings of fate found in most of McCarthy's writings. It is, in fact, tempting to read the play as a gloss on McCarthy as writer. Certainly it is a celebration of art and the artist. Craftsmanship, working in 'the trade,' is an essential motif in the play. The grandfather, 'Papaw,' practices the old-time, traditional form of stonemasonry at which he excels. 'People believe that the stonemasons of his time were all like him but that was never so. Anything excellent is rare,' Ben tells the audience (8). True masonry, and by extension, true art, is holy, ultimately derived from the spiritual. As Ben says:

> The keystone that locks the arch is pressed in place by the thumb of God . . . According to the gospel of the true mason God has laid the stones in the earth for men to use and he has laid them in their bedding planes to show the mason how his own work must go. A wall is made the same way the world is made. A house, a temple. This gospel must accommodate every inquiry. The structure of the world is such as to favor the prosperity of men. Without this belief nothing is possible. What we are at arms against are those philosophies that claim the fortuitous in mens' [sic] inventions. For we invent nothing but what God has put to hand. (10)

Narrative, obviously, is a form of construction, of order imposed, of meaning derived. McCarthy's discussion of Hegel and the fundamental importance of narrative in our lives surely illuminates the seriousness in which he holds his own craftsmanship in writing.

At the same time, the play indicts the self-assured artist absorbed in the 'trade' to the tragic exclusion of those closest to him. As his father and his sister and his nephew and his wife all tell him, Ben thinks he can 'fix' everything, but his need to 'fix' is fueled by his need to judge, to 'get to say' (125), and results ultimately in tragedy and violence in the family. It is appropriate that the minister who delivers Soldier's funeral quotes David's lament against false friends in Psalms 55:12, 'For it was not an enemy that reproached me. Then I could have borne it' (128). The biblical passage continues, 'Neither was it he that hated me that did magnify himself against me; then I would have hidden myself from him; But it was thou, a man mine equal, my guide, and mine acquaintance.' Ben's father's suicide forces Ben to face the fact that he never knew him other than as an indifferent craftsman, one who had not followed the 'trade' practiced by his own father, Papaw. When he visits his father's mistress after the death, she tells him, 'Did you want to know that he was kind and sweet and generous? And a real man too. Because he was. Or did you come here to find out about yourself' (109). 'That's why you here aint it?' she continues. 'Cause you caint get around that daddy? Caint get around that daddy' (110). Fathers and sons play an essential role in almost every McCarthy work, but nowhere is this sad conflict and misunderstanding so clearly delineated as in this drama. 'Because I thought of my father in death more than I ever did in life. And think of him yet. The weight of the dead makes a great burden in this world,' Ben tells us (111), but it doesn't prevent him from rejecting his nephew, his surrogate son Soldier, with as much alacrity as he did his father.

The Stonemason is, in sum, McCarthy's most clearly religious work. The whole framework is built on biblical references, from the old Abraham Papaw to the lost great-grandchild Soldier, whose name is finally revealed to be, like his uncle and grandfather's, Benjamin. The mystery of masonry, of the order of journeyman artists, is essentially an order based on spiritual mystery, arcane lore passed to the chosen by shared experience rather than by random preaching. 'There aint nothin triflin about God,' Papaw tells Ben (47), and by the end of the play Ben has learned this of the Holy: 'Grace I know is much like love and you cannot deserve it. It is freely given, without reason or equity. What could you do to deserve it? What?' And he then concludes, 'What I need most is to learn charity. That most of all' (131).

I would argue that these are all essential themes found throughout McCarthy's work, although in tone *The Stonemason* philosophically and theologically comes closer to *All the Pretty Horses* and *The Crossing* than the earlier books. As drama, the work is flawed, but the accusation of racial insensitivity seems essentially unwarranted (although McCarthy's characterization of Soldier is by the far the weakest element in the play. One participant described the Soldier subplot as 'straight out of "Kojak,"' but at times Soldier himself seems straight out of Faulkner by way of Luster and Benjy in *The Sound and the Fury*). Nevertheless, the question leveled at the play – 'Why are these characters black?' – is both its chief accusation and defense, for in a larger sense the Telfairs' race is far less important than their humanity; and although certain situations evolve from their social status as African-Americans in the South, it is finally their roles as members of a troubled family that determine their fates.

Despite these concerns, however, *The Stonemason* deserves to be read and studied and performed. In Ben's monologues, especially, McCarthy writes with great beauty and profound accomplishment. Indeed, this play may someday be seen as the moral touchstone to his work.

Acknowledgement

I would like to express my appreciation to Sophia Burnam, Wiley Hausam, Brad Kalof, Larry Maslon, Richard Pearce, Lloyd Richards, Amanda Urban, Douglas Wager, and Lisa-Ann Weisbrod for sharing their information, thoughts and observations on *The Stonemason*. Obviously, this article could not have been written without their help.

Part III

From east to west: shared elements in the Appalachian and Southwestern novels

Jay Ellis

McCarthy music

> *Words are things. The words he is in possession of he cannot be deprived of. Their authority transcends his ignorance of their meaning.* (The judge in *Blood Meridian* 85)

Discussions of McCarthy's art often tend to *talk about what he's talking about*. To be sure, this is an author important for the landscapes he provides us with, the spaces in which lay readers and scholars engage in lively contests over *what it all means* (or, for postmodernists, *doesn't*). We even, as Bakhtin said of Dostoyevsky, talk about his characters as if they were alive. To write about McCarthy is therefore to grapple after the 'eternal verities' (or 'always already undecideabilities,' as a good postmodernist might put it) implicit in his narrative and sometimes – in the form of the direct speeches of his characters – hung just above our heads, grapes of wisdom.

Such matters, however, are not my concern here. Rather, I intend to explore the music of McCarthy's language through stylistic shifts most easily seen in three novels. I will argue that from *The Orchard Keeper*, through the historical *Blood Meridian*, to the heavily symbolic *The Crossing*, McCarthy has developed a style that depends heavily upon the *sound* of language. Following Walter Pater's claim that all art constantly aspires towards the condition of music, I'd like to examine a few passages of McCarthy prose insofar as they are more or less about words for their own sake, particularly to musical effect.

Not everyone loves a parade

By my implicit comparison of McCarthy's style to music I do not mean to suggest that music itself is highly regarded in his work. Quite the opposite. Music, along with any other form of culture beyond oral tradition, is highly suspect in the McCarthy worldview. In particular, a passage from *The Orchard Keeper* uses sound turned against the production of sound for meaning. A marching band moving down the street is parodied using techniques of language that are, ironically, musical in their effect – discordantly musical.

> *When he got to the corner he could see them coming, eight and ten abreast, a solemn phalanx of worn maroon, the drill-cloth seedy and polished even at that distance, and*

their instruments glinting dully in the sun. In a little knot to the fore marched the leader, tall-hatted and batoned, and the four guidons bracing up their masts, the colors furling listlessly. A pair of tubas in the mass behind them bobbed and rode like balloons, leaped ludicrously above the marchers' heads and belched their frog-notes in off-counterpoint to the gasping rattle of the other instruments. (80)

The bulk of initial description is visual; prior to this we have *heard* only that '[a] band was playing, wavering on the heat of the city strains of old hymns martial and distantly strident' (80). The phallic phalanx is impotent, though 'seedy and polished.' Knotted, the leaders carry impotent flags. But the tubas[1] are described almost onomatopoeically, before they 'leaped ludicrously' in 'off-counterpoint' to the rest of the band. Not everyone loves a parade. Here sound is no more enticing than the deliberately dead visuals that take up most of McCarthy's descriptive passages. Our pleasure at his 'style' is in his deft usage of the right word and – in his first books – punctuation to achieve the right effect while adding to the idea. We are to imagine the band as cacophonous; his writing makes that easy.

Distinctions

So it is important to make several distinctions between different noticeable uses of sound in McCarthy's style. First, we must distinguish between sound that is pleasing in and of itself – words and phrases that flow to a pleasing aesthetic effect – and sound that reinforces meaning. Then of those instances where McCarthy could be said to indulge in sound for sound's sake, we should distinguish between instances where this is effective in and of itself and does not unduly distract from the surrounding material; and instances where sound techniques seem self-indulgent. Last but not least, of instances where sound reinforces (or arguably seems meant to reinforce) meaning, there are certainly some passages that work better than others. The worst remind the reader too much of Faulkner – and usually bad Faulkner. The best place him among all, if not above most, of the strongest stylists working in the American novel.

I will also draw attention to a particular stylistic feature of McCarthy's writing as it has developed from *The Orchard Keeper* to *The Crossing*: punctuation. In general, there is an easily discernible movement away from close punctuation (already rare in *The Orchard Keeper*) to a near total absence of anything but periods in *The Crossing*. In particular the loss of commas in all but standard distinctions between speech and attribution is relevant to discussions of meaning in McCarthy. Without going as far here as I would elsewhere on that subject, I will eventually cheat my initial semantic limitations enough to suggest something about this shift.

First, back to Pater's normative claim. What is the condition of music in McCarthy? There are many passages, particularly in the novels, remarkable for the pure beauty of their language.[2] An early example stands out in *The Orchard Keeper*: 'He looked as one peering from vast heights, the sky seeming to lie below him in a measureless spread, flickering like foil by half-light and gleaming lamely into shadow where it folded to the trees' (89). This starts out normally enough, then after the first comma the situation is conveyed in a translation of a common trope from the paintings of German romanticism, but after that third comma it hardly matters what we are to puzzle out from the words. Of course, one *can* puzzle them out: the sky is described as 'flickering like' a piece of 'foil' that is dimly lit. I could stop at this and find similar passages in all the novels where metal and other man-made objects are referred to in descriptions of nature, go on to investigate the philosophical implications of a descriptive mode that denatures nature from the usually assumed living part of our environment by substituting for its organicism and temporal mutability an artificial atemporal lifeless substance. Fine. But what does 'gleaming lamely into shadow where it folded into trees' mean? With a little more difficulty, one can see that the piece of foil standing in for the sky is of course a flat thing become a curved surface 'folded into' the trees – but why does it gleam 'lamely?' *Because 'lamely' follows 'gleaming' beautifully.*

The Orchard Keeper is arguably a formative novel in many ways. The characters are not as compelling as those in later McCarthy novels; Uncle Ather, in particular, and everything he does is so set apart from the rest of the characters by the novel's laboriously fractured structure that the effect is more of a dated early sixties' refusal to employ effective mainstream narrative technique than it is a revelatory prism of juxtaposition.[3] The structure is also weak in the jumps in and out of italicized material, some of which would have been better left in McCarthy's notebooks for the novel, where it presumably helped in character development but now distracts the reader with information out of context and elsewhere ignored, such as the scene (161–2) that is apparently a flashback to a smuggling skirmish. Other italicized passages tell us more than we need to know, or tell it late – in such a way as creates a false 'oh yeah, that's why' meaning to explain a character's actions: Uncle Ather's shotgun courtship, for instance (153–4). Worse, McCarthy's refusal to use names where the reader needs them is needlessly confusing. The point is well taken: names only exist in relation. I don't use my own name when I'm alone – I'm simply me; therefore, whenever a character is out and about alone (as most of the characters are much of the time in this novel) they are simply 'he.'[4] The plot bites its own tail only to spit it out when the reader's understandable expectation of revelation – at least of the boy's deeper relationship to Sylder – is deliberately passed up (220); disappointing the reader's reasonable expectation for resolution of a tension developed by the author is cheating to make a modernist point. Of course readers decide for themselves whether they are ready to trade once again for meaning or formal beauty for more modernist (these days read 'postmodernist') meaninglessness. Finally, the Tennessee existentialism of Sylder's jail cell speech to the boy (213) is already undermined by a lapse of the authorial stance into sentimentality when the boy is 'perched delicately on the edge of the metal pallet [in the cell] as if loath to sit too easily where so many had lain in such hard rest' (213).

But if we read *The Orchard Keeper* as a formative work, it stands up well enough alongside the novels that followed precisely because it is a mixed bag of what will be good and bad in McCarthy's work as a whole. Judging its use of sound, McCarthy *a de beaux moments, mais de mauvais quart d'heures*. Sound for sound's sake is one place where the writing goes wrong. Not always, but in some passages a reach beyond the immediate meaning for an otherwise desirable effect if sometimes distracting. 'Sylder heard the skirling tin sound of the lid being unscrewed and he reached out his hand for June to pass the jar' (17). This sentence makes no sense because of the first verb: it is highly doubtful that Sylder's ears would have thought the sound of a tin lid being unscrewed at all remarkable; it *is* a beautiful and distinctive sound, but one that is more remarkable to the weekend visitor to country folk who store their whiskey and iced tea in mason jars, than to a bootlegger for whom the sound is as common as the sound of a sheriff's siren.

McCarthy's word choice in *The Orchard Keeper* is sometimes beautiful in moments, but distracting in the absence of a sure hand at what has come to be called 'the free indirect style.' The next sentence after the 'lid being unscrewed' is all vision and sound: 'Moths loomed whitely before the windshield, incandesced, dusted the glass with mica.' Worth reading and then reading again, if it were not followed by 'A ballet of gnats rioted in the path of the headlights.' This cannot be intended as a visual effect. It begins with an idea (always dangerous) and before one can believe in – yet alone imagine – a 'ballet' of bugs, they've 'rioted.' Strong verbs are *usually* a good idea; not when they unduly distract. Two sentences later, however, we get 'Under the black hood the motor hummed its throaty combustions' (17). This is an awful lot to be alive in a McCarthy novel, even if it is about to die. But again, it *sounds* good, and this time we are not expected to notice a commonplace sound beautifully described from within Sylder's ears.

Better still for the larger success of a novel are sentences that reinforce meaning with sound. In the same scene, Sylder's car flies down a hollow with a friend, then stops to pick up three hitchhikers – including two prospects for quick sex. 'The little one between him and Tipton squealed once and then hushed with her hand clapped over her mouth as they swerved across the pike and shot out into darkness, the lights slapping across the upper reaches of trees standing sharply up the side of the hollow' (19). These are the perfect words to hear but also to think about, suggesting, rather than telling, what is to come. In addition to the alliteration, the rhythm is strong and one feels the acceleration in the sentence as much as in the car with 'shot out into darkness.'[5]

The prologue to *The Orchard Keeper* is also reinforced by rhythm. Three men are working to cut down a tree that has grown around a fence – except that in the men's judgment the fence has 'growed all through the tree' (3). Not only the idea (of what a fence does and how it is made and makes itself) but the technique prefigures the epilogue to *Blood Meridian*. The phrases in this passage begin and stop, and begin again with the work, after it is interrupted by the anomaly they discover.

Many words in *The Orchard Keeper* seem to have been chosen as much for their sound as for their meaning. There are many ways to describe a meal replete with fat, but McCarthy does it in such a way both as to convey the meal, its effect, and even an underlying condition requiring such food. The reader gets it all. 'Beans and fatmeat oozing grease into the greasy gravy that leaked down from the potatoes, a beaded scum of grease on the coffee, everything in fact lubricated as if all who ate there suffered from some atrophy of the deglutitive muscles which precluded swallowing' (29). Say 'deglutitive' out loud and do *not* think of swallowing. Then swallow.

'Once a bobcat stood highlegged and lanterneyed in the road, bunched, floated away over the roadbank on invisible wires' (31). Once again we have a bit of metal in an otherwise 'natural' setting. But this is at once dreamlike and realistic (particularly to anyone, I suspect, who has nearly hit a bobcat on a lonely road). But 'lanterneyed' is especially typical of McCarthy in that his compound word is not hyphenated, and accomplishes several descriptive tasks at once, even suggesting the odd way in which the 'highlegged' cat will '[float] away.'

Later a deliberate dangling modifier allows one word to serve as an interesting dual function.[6] 'In the summer wasps nested over the boards, using the augerholes where dowels had shrunk in some old dry weather and fallen to the floor to emerge out into the hot loft and drone past his bed to the window where a corner of glass was gone and so out into the sunlight' (62). Again the effect is strikingly realistic; here it does not at all distract one from the sense nor unduly slow the eye through the description of the boy's house. Yet what 'had shrunk' and 'fallen' only to 'drone past' is simultaneously wooden dowel and wasp; ultimately it is a curious unity of both – many wasps do bore through wood, and the dowel is also a nice way of suggesting the compactness of a wasp not in flight, while a flying dowel is as unusual to the reader as a real wasp would be alarming.

The bad Faulkner appears early in *The Orchard Keeper*, but not too often in the beginning of the book. We get through page 12, however, with a bad feeling for what can happen before McCarthy has sufficiently dealt with his anxiety over Faulkner. McCarthy tells us of houses:

> They were rented to families of gaunt hollow-eyed and darkskinned people, not Mellungeons and not exactly anything else, who reproduced with such frightening prolificness that their entire lives appeared devoted to the production of the ragged line of scions which shoeless and tattered sat for hours at a time on the porch edges, themselves not unlike the victims of some terrible disaster, and stared out across the blighted land with expressions of neither hope nor wonder nor despair. (12)

I'd be worn out and hopeless too if I had to carry all that ponderous descriptive weight.[7] This is like bad Faulkner in its egregious use of prepositional transitions that run-on into gross faulty generalizations about people grouped by class and race, and ultimately, made to exemplify a philosophical importance overwhelming to their validity as characters. It is too much. Thankfully, the homage to Faulkner's 'The Bear' that comes midway through *The Orchard Keeper* (121) substitutes a raccoon that is not much less ferocious, and is written with admirable economy.

Effective use of language becomes less frequent toward the end of the novel.[8] Having been structurally handicapped by the self-conscious irony of fictive technique in the American *Zeitgeist* of the early 1960s, having argued, here and there, a lifeless landscape that avails no man of anything but a sort of bootlegger's existentialistic pursuit by a redneck Javert, the novel grasps for more significance in the form of high-flown Faulknerian rhetoric: 'and the old man felt the circle of years closing, the final increment of the curve returning him again to the inchoate, the prismatic flux of sound and color wherein he had drifted once before and now beyond the world of men' (222). Whether or not any novel can successfully use the word 'inchoate,' this one's sudden descent into a miasma of quasi-spirituality is confusing. Sound, here, does not save. Later, the least interesting, most stereotypical character in *The Orchard Keeper*, the dumb deputy Legwater, wakes up on the mountain in the dark, accompanied by 'an astral quiet where planets collide soundlessly, beyond the auricular dimension altogether' (238).

To be fair, however, *The Orchard Keeper* is especially valuable as an example of how McCarthy used punctuation before honing a style that seems hardly to need more than periods. In many modes, sound and others, McCarthy's language is already working on a level unapproachable by most novelists; the bad bits are arguably all the more interesting because they almost seem, in retrospect, parody of better passages in the better novels to follow. His development of techniques of sound in *The Orchard Keeper* is key to his progression to *Blood Meridian*, and interesting in contrast with *The Crossing*. Sound is as important to understanding McCarthy's style as is attention to his more visual passages; and *The Orchard Keeper* offers sounds other novelists would be happy, and lucky, to achieve. The following passage could certainly be taken apart and examined for its meter, the larger rhythms of its structure, the use of another dual-function dangling modifier, the alliteration, the hard 'c's rolling the mouth to a 'q,' the shifts through vowels, and the repetitions of sounds – even the pun in the second word. It is so good in all of these, however, that it seems better simply to present the passage and let it stand whole:

> Light pale as milk guided the old man's steps over the field to the creek and then to the mountain, stepping into the black wall of pine-shadows and climbing up the lower slopes out into the hardwoods, bearded hickories trailing grapevines, oaks and crooked waterless cottonwoods, a quarter mile from the creek now, past the white chopped butt of a bee tree lately felled, past the little hooked Indian tree and passing silent and catlike up the mountain in the darkness under latticed leaves scudding against the sky in some small wind. (88)

The bridge and two Englishes

Denis Donoghue relates a talk given by Hugh Kenner in 1958, speculating that American English had developed differently than its 'parent' in England. Specifically, Kenner's idea was that Elizabethan drama made requirements on the language of its writers that were not made on English as it branched off in the new colony. Kenner suggested that the English of the English theater did not grow from Chaucer as much as it did from the desire that an actor sound good speaking his lines. American English was rather, to Kenner, the greater inheritor of Chaucer's daring with words, including those borrowed already from the continent.

Of course, American literature began with insecurity and is still sometimes plagued by it. Kenner therefore sees the American imagists, and some other American poets (not Stevens and not Eliot), as poets returning to a mode of language 'lost' by the Elizabethan theatrical preoccupation with sound. If for a moment we take Kenner's as a reasonable premise, then a reader may understand some American poets as more or less American than others insofar as they partake more or less of the visual, rather than the aural, possibilities of language. Eliot, for example (in print, apart from in life), is especially English (as it were) in his refusal to admit anything before sound to his development of poetry. Pound and the other imagists, by contrast, are distinctly visual, as was elsewhere argued by Kenner – one of the few critics in the fifties who read William Carlos Williams and Marianne Moore *as poets*. One can write poetry without it having to *sound* to the reader the way the English have thought poetry *ought to sound*.

Without a reliable linguistic history to back up the premise of Kenner's argument,[9] it is impossible to judge it as historically accurate. But experientially one does not have to work hard to agree with it. What better way to make sense of the impossible-to-speak portions of some imagist poetry but through a tradition that does not place sound at the forefront of normative standards? It does not matter to Eliot or to the more insightful of his admirers *whom* the women are talking about in the room, as long as it rhymes with 'come and go.' In the Kennerian American alternative tradition, it matters mostly what they look like – both on the page and in what Pater would have called one's impression. This is not to say that sound is unimportant in that tradition, but that it is not sought by the imagists at the expense of visual effects or mental impressions.

Novels, of course, require entirely different things than poetry; in general, novelists have (or at least had, and perhaps ought to have now but don't) far fewer restrictions and greater possibilities word by word, than poets. Yet I submit that it is no stretch to understand some novelists as more concerned with image and others with sound; still others, more clumsy in their clauses, with meaning (I am thinking of all those who make of an avoidance of discernible 'style' their normative conditions for style). The form is certainly elastic enough – big enough already – however, to allow the better writer to work in one mode in one moment and in another mode later on. Given a spectrum of possibilities along which a writer may work, I would claim that McCarthy is most successful in those novels where he is working on every level with every available technique. *Blood Meridian*, in particular, is the novel so far most obviously based on 'historical' material; it is also the most complex and ambiguous – if not ambivalent – in philosophy; while the varieties of style in the book allow McCarthy in one moment to write a sentence of pure sound – an Englishy English sentence (if we reserve language particularly directed toward effective sound for the English[10]) – in another moment to write one of his stark flat images, and in yet another moment to run an idea out on the page with as little intrusiveness of technique as possible.

Words as things, and more

As the judge in *Blood Meridian* makes clear, style is a tricky thing. The judge's attempts to seduce the kid are not unlike the whispering of Satan in Eve's ear – he's as slick as a Miltonic snake. And it is not only in what he says but how he says it that he stands out so much among McCarthy characters. The judge allowed McCarthy to be as grandiose as Faulkner without pretension, without corn, because we can never be sure he *means* what he says. The judge says things – terrible things – so beautifully that his own contradictions are likely to slide in one ear and out the other. The judge tells us that '[w]ords are things. The words he is in possession of he cannot be deprived of. Their authority transcends his ignorance of their meaning' (85). But the same man tricks the men later with a phony distinction.

> Books lie, he said.
> God dont lie.
> No, said the judge. He does not. And these are his words.
> He held up a chunk of rock.
> He speaks in stones and trees, the bones of things.
> The squatters in their rags nodded among themselves and were soon reckoning him correct, this man of learning, in all his speculations, and this the judge encouraged until they were right proselytes of the new order whereupon he laughed at them for fools. (116)

Not only the judge's bulk, the respect he has earned by this point in the novel with his mysterious appearance and salvation of the gang from a band of indians, but his own *words,* convince. 'He speaks in stones and trees' paints a pretty picture, and the 'bones' add to it in meaning; but the cadence of the phrase 'the bones of things,' following that comma, is incantatory. It does what it says, drops in the ears the thinginess of the world along with a nice idea.

Blood Meridian also makes excellent use of a punctuation technique already used in *The Orchard Keeper*. Fragments. In *The Orchard Keeper* fragments are likely given as poetic lists in a description: 'A night for meteors tonight. They cannonaded the towering hump of Red Mountain. Rain falling now from a faultless sky. A girl's laugh on the road' (20–1). This is not so unusual a technique. In this usage it accomplishes the free indirect style by moving into Arthur Ownby's consciousness. But another type of fragment is used by McCarthy to achieve a large effect within a paragraph. Specifically, McCarthy regularly breaks long complex sentences into separate entities, each made distinct by the substitution of periods for commas. In *The Orchard Keeper* this technique is used in Boog's dialogue to tell us how slow he is:

> It's a old Indian trick, said Boog.
> What's that?
> Puttin bark down like that. To lay your fire on. (137)

But by *Blood Meridian*, McCarthy has more marvelous things to do with this technique. First, the novel begins with the most simple sentences, with the biblical (and Nietzschean) 'See the child.' After this imperative, two noun-verb-modifiers. Then, a preposition and description outside. The sentences grow as if the world is first awakening in language.

The second paragraph jumps to a daring stance not taken up again after its single appearance: 'Night of your birth. Thirty-three. The Leonids they were called. God how the stars did fall. I looked for blackness, holes in the heavens. The Dipper stove' (3). This is remarkable in its voice – the voice of a parent or a god who will not speak again in this dark novel. It looks to meteors, after a similar look at them in *The Orchard Keeper*. And it ends with another dual function, with stove as both noun and verb.

The sentences of *Blood Meridian* grow increasingly complex as McCarthy moves us from the early childhood quick to the kid's violent coming of age. Then, when the kid and Sproule are astray in the desert, McCarthy substitutes periods for commas and makes connection, time itself, hard.

> With the dawn they were climbing among shale and whinstone under the wall of a dark monocline where turrets stood like basalt prophets and they passed by the side of the road little wooden crosses propped in cairns of stone where travelers had met with death. The road winding up among the hills and the castaways laboring upon the switchbacks, blackening under the sun, their eyeballs inflamed and the painted spectra racing out at the corners. Climbing up through ocotillo and pricklypear where the rocks trembled and sleared in the sun, rock and no water and the sandy trace and they kept watch for any green thing that might tell of water but there was no water. The[y][11] ate piñole from a bag with their fingers and went on. Through the noon heat and into the dusk where lizards lay with their leather chins flat to the cooling rocks and fended off the world with thin smiles and eyes like cracked stone plates. (61–2)

This is McCarthy's first of the so-called Southwestern novels, and is arguably the high-point of his work, in terms of its aesthetic qualities and in its unity of meaning and expression. Its landscape is very different from the lush mountain hollows of that part of Tennessee where the Appalachian mountains make the border between that state and North Carolina natural. The desert, its heat, its lack, is paradoxically wide open to the eyes, even along switchbacks – there the vegetation does not make a newer, closer, horizon. And so the sentences tie one to another and go on and become exhausted and stop. What would be the next phrase in the wide compound construction has to continue on its own, the 'ing' verb taking for granted a memory of the subject left behind on the march. You know yourself through your thirst and fatigue and do not need reminding of that or your incidental companion when the 'noon heat' is more pressing.

Blood Meridian eventually ends with power on every level. Limiting, momentarily, our appreciation of the last paragraph to a consideration of McCarthy's language, one is no less amazed by the techniques dared but earned at this point. 'And they are dancing, the board floor slamming under the jackboots and the fiddlers grinning hideously over their canted pieces.' As with the rare passage in *The Orchard Keeper*, this last paragraph exploits repetition ('dancing' occurs five times, along with 'dance' once; 'He never sleeps' three times, and 'He says ['he'll' or 'that he will'] never die' three times as well – all within 180 words). McCarthy is deft with surprises in vowel sounds and independent clauses enjambed with the conjunction 'and.' Yet it is all standard grammar. Most remarkable is the way the end torques around to the beginning in an increasing shortness of sentence. Along the way, however, the language dances as impressively as the judge. Sentences spool out and lead into one another. Then 'He never sleeps, he says. He says he'll never die.' And to put the paragraph in perspective, it is important to remind readers without the book at hand that all 334 preceding pages are mostly in the past tense. Suddenly we are in the continual present of a dangerous immortal, who 'dances in light and in shadow and he is a great favorite. He never sleeps, the judge. He is dancing, dancing. He says that he will never die' (335).

Commas and time

Reading *The Crossing*, it is possible to regret that McCarthy seems to have lost the variety of techniques, so much at their zenith in *Blood Meridian*, in the desert. Commas are especially interesting in McCarthy's work for their gradual disappearance. There are, to be sure, plenty of compound sentences without them in the first novel: 'He was pushing time now and he could feel it give' (*The Orchard Keeper* 65). But passages in both *The Orchard Keeper* and *Blood Meridian* still use commas in ways that develop a complexity hard to find in *The Crossing*. A reinforcement of meaning is accomplished with a blink of punctuation in 'Eyes lowered to her work, blink when she swallows like a toad's' (61). The dual function of 'lowered' and the odd possessive toad (is it her blink or her swallow – or both – that is toad-like?) make the sentence otherwise beautiful and effective enough to earn what would otherwise be a glib tail after 'work.'

In *Blood Meridian*, commas sometimes provide sound for sound's sake, where the deft word choice is reinforced by the rhythm afforded by punctuation. The fourth paragraph, building in complexity from that simple beginning, lists two items alone in a fragment: 'The firewood, the washpots.' Then continues:

> He wanders west as far as Memphis, a solitary migrant upon that flat and pastoral landscape. Blacks in the fields, lank and stooped, their fingers spiderlike among the bolls of cotton. A shadowed agony in the garden. Against the sun's declining figures moving in the slower dusk across a paper skyline. A lone dark husbandman pursuing mule and harrow down the rainblown bottomland toward night. (4)

If only more contemporary poetry could be scanned with such interesting results, or offered half as many delights in the manipulation of a rhyme passed from 'flat' to 'pastoral' to 'landscape' and then to the connection daring in its honesty 'Blacks,' then followed 'lank,' which stoops into 'o's from the labor of bending work over rows of cotton. Here McCarthy is using as many techniques, including commas, as in the final paragraph and more; this novel is a masterpiece of language as much as of difficult, perhaps ultimately ambiguous, philosophical themes. If *The Orchard Keeper* suffers from a surfeit of story and theme to support with the developing skills of McCarthy's particular writing techniques, *The Crossing* is arguably short on formal support for the heavy load of less ambiguous (and therefore perhaps less interesting) philosophy.

What is particularly crippling for *The Crossing* is its deep dependence on story, when McCarthy for some reason seems to have needed to shed himself of a regular and sure usage of the variety of techniques working to the level of mastery in *Blood Meridian*. Rereading *Blood Meridian*'s indian attack on the desert (52–4), with its long sentence (over half a page) piled up with details after commas, but with the suspension in time such that it seems so clearly a translation of slow motion in a Peckinpah film, one sees what a suspension in time through commas can do to accomplish suspense. After this complex, timeless, description of the 'fabled horde' (and here McCarthy is justified in his otherwise questionable habit of mythologizing hyperbole), the response of the officer is our own: 'Oh my god,' he says. The massacre to follow is *then* written in a breathless paragraph longer than a page and a half: and there are in those terrifying sentences only seven commas, six of them following each one a body part, five of these as the indians proceed 'chopping,' 'ripping,' 'gutting,' and 'holding' them up from their hapless owners. Even when McCarthy uses, as he does more often in *Blood Meridian* than in *The Orchard Keeper*, the type of compound sentence that governs *The Crossing*, he knows when to use a comma to maximum effect: 'They did not noon nor did they siesta and the cotton eye of the moon squatted at broad day in the throat of the mountains to the east and they were still riding when it overtook them at its midnight meridian, sketching on the plain below a blue cameo of such dread pilgrims clanking north' (88).

By stark contrast, *The Crossing* is almost entirely bereft of all punctuation save periods. Commas are used almost purely (and are used regularly) to separate McCarthy's usual un-quote-marked dialogue from its attribution. One reads page after page of the singular technique of compounds joined by 'and' and where the only variety comes in some variety of sentence length. The exceptions are rare before the back stretch,[12] and are usually welcome, even beautiful: section II begins well enough with its third paragraph's 'The hawk turned and skated off down the wind and vanished beyond the cape of the mountain, a single feather fell' (129). But the vast majority of the prose is simply one thing after another, *without* commas, 'for all and without distinction' (426).

My quote from the provocative last sentence is intentional, despite the fact that it reads in full 'He sat there for a long time and after a while the east did gray and after a while the right and godmade sun did rise, once again, for all and without distinction' (426). For what are we to make of this stylistic shift?

Cities of the Plain recalls variety, joining the styles *and* characters from the trilogy's first two books. Luckily there will be (one hopes) many more McCarthy novels, perhaps one approaching *Blood Meridian*. But provisionally I find *The*

Crossing harder to value without looking beyond the philosophy plopped into my lap by its many stories. After the wolf is dead, the novel moves on one thing after another. This can be an effective technique. But what it does, I will suggest as tentatively as one should when looking for trends in the work of a living author, is flatten out time.

> He got the fire going and lifted the wolf from the sheet and took the sheet to the creek and crouched in the dark and washed the blood out of it and brought it back and he cut forked sticks from a mountain hackleberry and drove them into the ground with a rock and hung the sheet on a trestlepole where it steamed in the firelight like a burning scrim standing in a wilderness where celebrants of some sacred passion had been carried off by rival sects or perhaps had simply fled in the night at the fear of their own doing. (126)

This is beautiful and moving in that its description of what Billy – who must, one assumes (and with the emotions of McCarthy characters one does have to make assumptions), be grieving over the death of a wolf he has travelled hundreds of miles to return to its wild Mexico – does around the dead body of the wolf is underwritten. By the time we get to the theatrical analogy of the 'scrim' and then the usual mythologizing speculations, it almost does not matter that the hand is unsure. But it does. That 'perhaps,' along with its descent into overwritten hyperbolic imaginings, is typical of McCarthy's Joycean mode.

By this I mean that he is trying to accomplish what Eliot so lauded in Joyce's *Ulysses*: that is, it juxtaposes the breadth and grandeur of classical epic with the tedious normality of an average man's life. Bloom put through an apparently banal day against the reader's understanding of a simultaneous correspondence of the travels and travails of Ulysses enables us to see – without dishonesty or desperation on the part of the narrative voice – the heroic in the everyday. McCarthy similarly wants to place his normal country folk, fools, children, old mountain men, orphans, and the like, as mythically great. The most ridiculous of them, as ridiculous even as *The Orchard Keeper*'s Legwater, is likely to bear witness to universal grandeurs no less than a sky 'where planets collide soundlessly, beyond the auricular dimension altogether' (238).

This is as noble an aspiration for a contemporary writer as it was for Joyce, and McCarthy is working in territory where it has not yet been successfully accomplished. McMurtry comes closer on screen than off, where he has forgotten all the sounds and smells – indeed, the many beauties possible in the words on their own and not only in the imaginative effects they may stimulate in the reader's mind – that are possible in novels and not possible in movies. Norris tried out West in California; but in many ways I suspect Norris will not be mentioned alongside McCarthy once posterity has sorted them both out.

When I say that this particular stylistic shift flattens time, I do not mean that it stops it. I mean that it relativizes one moment against another because they all take place along a hard linear line. It is as if, in the terminology of J. T. Fraser, we have lost the complexity of time. 'Nootemporality, or noetic time . . . the temporal reality of the mature human mind,' gives way to a temporality lower in the subsumptive hierarchy of time: 'Biotemporality, or biological time ... the temporal reality of living organisms including man, as far as his biological functions are concerned' (367). The relentlessness of the technique of phrase and phrase and phrase sometimes even descends to what Fraser calls 'Eotemporality,'

> or the time of 'the physicist's *t.*' So named after Eos, the Greek goddess of dawn, this is the simplest form of continuous time. It is the temporal reality of the astronomical universe of massive matter. It has also been described as the time of pure succession. It is a continuous but nondirected, nonflowing time to which our ideas of a present, future, or past cannot be applied. (368)

Billy Parham takes a wolf to Mexico, it dies, he takes his brother Boyd to Mexico, Boyd nearly dies, Billy leaves, Billy tries to join the army, Billy returns to Mexico, Boyd is dead, Billy tries to take him back across the border, Billy witnesses the first nuclear explosion.[13] There are of course elements to *The Crossing* that suggest more than a simple linearity (indeed, linearity as a problematic aspect of narrative has not been argued into existence against the persistent complexity of real novels as they exist outside theoretical discourse). The novel begins with Billy trapping and then trying to 'save' a wolf and ends after he has chased away a lonely stray dog.

But the effect on time of this stylistically stark novel is persistent; perhaps it is why the preponderance of 'storytelling' does not ring true against its simple action. But even if one reads around the 'stories,' as it were, McCarthy's intrusive grandiosity undermines the bleak temporality created by the style. Perhaps the best way to understand the style is through an investigation of that explosion – a very odd thing to conclude such a late 'western.' That explosion distant and enigmatic hangs in the imagination like a sun at midnight – oddly soundless.

Notes

1 McCarthy must have been thinking of sousaphones, whose bells are turned forward on twisted necks, presenting the open mouth of the horn to an audience and thus creating a round shape. Tubas, shorter and pointed up, would not be so visible over the rest of the band and in any case would present more the shape of large spittoons than of balloons.

2 This chapter of course requires a willing suspension of disbelief on the part of readers unaccustomed *ever* to reading for aesthetic valuation apart from ideological pressure. My attention to the aesthetic in McCarthy here is no more an argument against other readings in other essays attending to ideology than McCarthy's demonstrable indulgence in language for sound's sake is a refusal to treat weighty matters of philosophy – if not politics. Rather, this essay assumes the possibility that a novel is a large enough artifact to be seen through more than one lens (even if one of the lenses is commonly understood as the impossible – or where possible politically or ethically untenable – reserve created by a liberal bourgeoisie circumscribed by history and judged politically unconscionable). So too this writing avows the genre label of 'essay' in a similar move to suggest rather than proscribe critical possibilities.

3 It is impossible not to imagine *The Sound and the Fury* as an influence here, but also the refusal of contemporary novelists in the sixties to tie characters together, as a less desirable model.
4 As I said, there are other places and times to go into ideology, including the paucity of 'she' in McCarthy's work – which *might* and might *not* be defensible within an allowable reserve of masculinist literature.
5 Another interesting incident that will be repeated in *Blood Meridian* – with horrifying differences in the particulars – is sex in an outhouse. The violence in *The Orchard Keeper*, as well as the sex, is mild in comparison with what follows up to McCarthy's fifth novel two decades later.
6 In harmonic theory this is a note (or chord) which is heard first one way because of the note (or chord) it follows, but then immediately in a second way because of the note (or chord) which follows it. The common term for harmonic theory actually does not do justice to the effect, as there is often a curious 'third' function of such a note (or chord), especially if the listener hears the two functions closely enough to experience a harmonic effect otherwise impossible in either of the two contexts.
7 Barry Hannah's *Ray* is much more fair to its poor 'white trash' tenants of a country house, while giving the reader more evidence than judgment to convince her of the paucity of their existence.
8 Another area of investigation for McCarthy scholars not dealt with here is the apparent difficulty getting to the endings – even in *Blood Meridian*.
9 Most linguists, such as Richard Bailey, would be suspicious of such a generalizing theory. But Kenner's idea is persuasive within the context of a careful criticism of 'high' literature up to and including his modern era.
10 I would not.
11 The Vintage edition gives 'The,' but this must be a misprint for 'They.'
12 At which point, I have to say in all subjective honesty, the novel seems to tire before the remarkable ending – again, an interesting formal phenomenon even detectable in *Blood Meridian*.
13 This is arguably a strong interpretation given attention to the presumed date and time of Billy's sleep at the end of the novel and his geographical position relative to the Trinity site.

Christine Chollier

'I aint come back rich, that's for sure,' or the questioning of market economies in Cormac McCarthy's novels

So far the issue of economics has hardly ever been addressed in McCarthy studies because his novels have been examined as reconfigurations of pre-existent literary myths, themes or characters. Apart from Robert L. Jarrett's extensive study, which was concerned with cultural exchange, no book or article has scrutinized economic exchange. However, McCarthy is undoubtedly interested in the interaction between different modes of exchange. The comment by Billy Parham in *The Crossing* which serves as a title to this chapter, illustrates McCarthy's sensitiveness to economic relations including values associated with the American Dream, such as work, exchange, value and property. In *The Orchard Keeper* his narrator ironically substitutes the image of the mafioso-whiskey-runner for that of the Prodigal Son (13–14): 'this affluent son returned upon them bearing no olive branch but hard coin and greenbacks and ushering in an era of prosperity, a Utopia of paid drinks' (29). As Marion admits when trying to warn John Wesley against taking revenge on Gifford for the imprisonment of his adult friend, he not only broke the law but made a living at doing so (213), and in this he has to be opposed to Arthur Ownby who never did anything 'to benefit [him]self' (228–9). A lot has already been said and written on the legacy both men left to the young boy but it must be noted that after visiting his two interned mentors he returns the hawk bounty – or what is left of it – because he believes that hawks 'must have some value or use commensurate with a dollar other than the fact of their demise' (233). Reality teaches him that the extermination of hawks has been commodified, and that their death is deemed to have more value than their life, and he bluntly rejects this fact by giving back the money.

However, the words 'use' and 'value' used by the omniscient narrator to convey the boy's thoughts are strongly connoted. They refer to the economic concepts of 'exchange value' and 'use value', which must be distinguished. 'Use value' is the intrinsic quality that makes a given commodity useful for man, whereas '(exchange) value' is acquired only when goods are traded; as such the latter is a fiction that appears only in the act or process of exchange. The term 'value' is thus directly linked to economies based on exchange, that is market economies. So what John Wesley has realized is that the economic system he lives in sets a higher value on death and annihilation than on life and nature.

A market economy is an economy in which goods are traded or exchanged – according to the traders' agreement that they have equal value. One commodity can be money, of course, but not necessarily so, as barter is considered as one instance of exchange. The non-market-directed economies of the past were based on gifts, which could be mandatory if, for example, you were threatened into giving something, and which did not necessarily require reciprocation. Gifts did not depend on the rules of exchange but were certainly highly dependent on the status and position of the individuals concerned. *Potlatch* belonged to that kind of economy because, although it required reciprocation, the gifts did not have to have the same value: they were appreciated for their intrinsic value.

It is obvious to McCarthy's readers that not only his outcasts are excluded from the dominant social body but that they do not take part in the market economy system. Those excluded from the monetary exchange system nevertheless survive by practicing simpler modes of exchange. By intruding on the auction sale of his father's house, *Child of God's* Lester Ballard is resented as someone who stalled the bids and consequently undermined the exchange. He is unaware of this as his relation to money is a very simple one: indeed, as a child he planted fenceposts to buy the rifle he coveted; as soon as he had made the sum of money required – which amounted to 700 posts – he quit. Lester did not aim at the accumulation of money but merely at the purchase of the object for immediate consumption.[1]

The same remark applies to Suttree. The fact that he sells his fish to a market, of all places, may be significant. Indeed, the fisherman is well aware of and dependent on the laws of supply and demand, for once the Whites' market has been supplied either by himself (67–8) or somebody else, he trades his fish on the Blacks' market. However, the money he has earned he spends immediately, more often than not on a big dinner or drink (69). In other words, Suttree stands for a simple mode of production for two reasons: first, he does not sell his labor, unlike some of his friends who end up 'Tennessee wetbacks drifting north in bent and smoking autos in search of wages. The rumors sifted down from Detroit, Chicago. Jobs paying two twenty an hour' (398); what Suttree sells is the product of his labor – his fish. Second, whatever he has earned from his work is not used to accumulate capital but to meet his need for consumer goods. Seen from a contradictory point of view, he has to catch fish – the product of his labor – if he wants to eat and drink, although he first of all refuses salaried work, that is, he refuses to trade his labor. The novel shows that he barely lives from hand to mouth, on the fringes of that capitalist society otherwise described as 'interstitial wastes' (4), which usually allow the outcasts of capitalism to survive. He has opted for a simple mode of production, which gives him some leeway – some scope for generosity – as when he gives fish to people who are as badly off as he is. Another category of people can be identified and that is the people with whom he barters fish; the goatman being a new character he does not want to offend ('We can trade it out if you like', 205), Suttree trades his fish for half a dozen postcards which are completely useless to him. At the opposite end of the spectrum to Suttree's system stands Harrogate's. The young outcast is a prey to the American Dream of success which takes the form of easy money – primarily obtained by cunning or robbery – yielding all the trappings of the rich, cool businessman:

> He saw himself ascending the stairs at Comer's in pressed gabardines and zipper shoes, a slender cigar in his mouth, an Italian switchblade knife silver bound with ebony handles in one pocket, a gold watchchain draped across the pleats of his slacks. Greeted by all. Pulling the roll of bills from his pocket. He went back down the stairs and came up again in different attire, a pullover shirt like Feezel's. Dark blue. With pale gray trousers and blue suede shoes. Belt to match. (217)

One of Harrogate's functions in the novel is to distance Suttree from the temptations conjured up by Reese's pearls (312–13) and optimistic tales (317). The musselfishing episode is set against a backdrop of disasters, and the only possessions Reese finally manages to obtain, in an ironic emulation of capitalistic accumulation, are 'a strange collection of goods' drifting down the waters while the valuables hurtle past 'with the speed of a train'; his confidence that things 'of value' should come down is betrayed by the waters which 'grew too treacherous for this commerce' (357). Suttree's second attempt to escape his simple mode of production is represented by Joyce, the prostitute with whose money he buys the car she hysterically destroys.

Among these simple modes of production is barter, which is still based on exchange, although an outmoded form of it. In McCarthy, it is the Indians who practice barter more than occasionally, as both *The Crossing* (133) and *Suttree* point out. When barter is not considered as being reliable enough to meet the characters' needs, contraband ensures income, as *The Orchard Keeper*, *Child of God* and *Suttree* imply. But bootlegging means running a commodity whose exchange value is no longer part of the convention underlying the market system. It is a perversion of the system, which is relentlessly fought by the Authorities.

It is in *Suttree* that the tradition of gift and counter-gift is best illustrated. Suttree may sell his fish on the market for the wealthy to buy it but he also gives it to his McAnally friends. In return, he will be given food and drink (232) without the question of reciprocal value even being raised. His relationship with Michael is also based on gifts: first, Michael gives him bait; then, Suttree offers to take his boat to look for Michael's skiff; the Indian returns the offer by proposing to pay for the favor (223–5); Suttree turns the proposal down but is invited to a turtle dinner. The gifts just mentioned may not have the same value but are appreciated for their own sake.

Then, when even barter or giving is impossible because there is no longer anything to trade, or give, predation is the next step, which is the lesson Ballard is taught. Hunting and fishing he extends to include the capture of women. After all human sex did not seem to him very much different from hawk mating (*Child of God* 169).

The above definition of market economies specifies that the so-called peace of the market must be ensured so that transactions can be freely carried out, contracts agreed upon and mutual obligations honored. For such an economy to prosper, economists say, arms must be laid down before entering the market-place and potential conflicts solved by the justice of the peace. Furthermore, the fact that the traded goods are assumed to be of equal value implies the traders' equality in the exchange. Thus exchange supposedly assures the equality of the participants. In *All the Pretty Horses* the prison acts as a microcosm of the world at large, and this microcosm in turn acts as a magnifying glass for social and economic relationships:

> The prison was no more than a small walled village and within it occurred a constant seethe of barter and exchange in everything from radios and blankets down to matches and buttons and shoenails and within this bartering ran a constant struggle for status and position. Underpinning all of it like the fiscal standard in commercial societies lay a bedrock of depravity and violence where in an egalitarian absolute every man was judged by a single standard and that was his readiness to kill. (182)

Not only is the presumed equality introduced by the act of exchange constantly jeopardized by 'a constant struggle for status and position' but, it is implied, force is the underlying element of relationships based on barter, and even more so, of relationships based on gifts, the latter being made mandatory if need be. Furthermore 'the egalitarian absolute' established by man's 'readiness to kill' means that violence puts an end to that equality, which thus remains a fiction forever. The unleashing of force cancels the basis of equality and exposes exchange as mandatory gift. The prison teaches romantic John Grady a hard lesson – that, refuse as he might to negotiate the price of his release ('Some people don't have a price', 193), the *cuchillero* has been paid to kill him and his final release is the result of a transaction between Alfonsa and Alejandra.

Blood Meridian is, of course, the novel that best exemplifies the substitution of violence for exchange. 'The disposition to exchange was foreign to them' (121), the narrator observes when the Company comes across people with whom they might have traded meat. The others are perceived as potential scalps, or people to rob and massacre, but never as partners with whom exchange is made possible on a basis of equality, however fictitious that equality may be. Robert Jarrett has observed that '[i]n this novel, the dynamics of cultural exchange are primarily controlled not by language but by violence' (88). Already in *Outer Dark* the outlaws exchanged clothes, or boots, with those whom they murdered, in a grotesque parodic emulation of socio-economic exchange. What is also interesting in *Blood Meridian* is that White's greed for gold and silver, which is hardly concealed by his mystic and religious arguments, is replaced, as White leaves the stage, by a company which is first interested in financial reward but eventually loses sight of that former motivation. Murder generates murder, the novel shows, and general massacre replaces trade. However, the judge argues that war is '[t]he ultimate trade awaiting its ultimate practitioner' (248). So violence, which first appeared as complete annihilation of trade, is reestablished as the ultimate form of trade – its quintessence: as Patricia Nelson Limerick put it, '[c]onquest was a literal, territorial form of economic growth' (27). In this gang, Robert L. Jarrett has very effectively shown, Glanton is the cold-blooded executioner-technician, whereas Holden is the ideologue and scientist, who remains the judge of what should or should not be, including trade and exchange.

Actually the issue of exchange based on equal value is problematized in the dream of the wounded, delirious kid. In this strange dream about the judge's visiting appears a very interesting figure, that of the coldforger. This 'false moneyer' is said to be fixing 'an image that will render this residual specie current in the markets where men barter' (310). He is thus trying to establish a system where exchange would no longer depend on barter but on currency, which might perhaps limit some of that violence. However, we are told that '[o]f this is the judge judge and the night does not end' (310); the ideologue of the gang will not permit a trade other than war to dominate the market of predation.

In *Cities of the Plain* John Grady's love for Magdalena comes up against the economy of prostitution which Eduardo practices. This economy stands in stark contrast with that of capitalism. Indeed, a prostitute belongs to a master, and, like a slave, she can be sweated to death. In a capitalist economy the individual offers to rent his labor force for an undetermined period of time to which he can put an end by simply giving notice. Thus, when John Grady offers $2,000, he believes the pimp will part with a labor force that belongs to him indefinitely and ensures regular income, which is highly unlikely. The economy of prostitution is consequently similar to the economy of slavery, and it may also be significant, in the American context, that the one seeking to free the slave happens to be the Northerner, while the slave-owner is the Southerner from Mexico. In such a situation with two conflicting systems, only violence can erupt. The first one to die is the slave-prostitute, the second one is the procurer – the one holding on to an archaic system, and the weaker fighter. But in McCarthy's story, even the liberator dies of his mortal wound, and nobody wins.

That John Grady stands for a form of capitalistic exchange, albeit a decadent one, is obvious in his pawning of the inherited family gun. Pawning consisting in depositing an object as security for the payment of money borrowed, it is linked with exchange. John Grady's attempt to buy up Magdalena is pitted against the economy of prostitution-slavery, although one is first made to understand that in Mexico everything can be bought, including a job, as the bartender in The White Lake explains to Billy (128). Conversely, in Northern America, everything can be sold, as Mr. Johnson implies when he explains that violence has nothing to do with the West itself but with Sam Colt's invention (185). What is alluded to, here, is an economy of violence in which weapons create a violence which is not linked to a given geographical area.

So market economies in McCarthy largely bypass the main characters who find themselves in a position where they have to resort to a lower form of market economy – barter, or any other simple mode – or where they operate through gifts, like Suttree and Michael, or where they are the instigators or the victims of mandatory 'gifts', which means predation, theft, pillage, and so on. McCarthy is sensitive to the fact that History's progress is not linear but alternates periods when market economies dominate and periods when non-market economies prevail.[2] His works deconstruct exchange as violent projections of the masculine will onto the cultural and natural chaos of both the Appalachian South and the Southwest. They expose theoretical exchange as being basically a non-existent fiction. It would be wrong to assume that McCarthy calls for a romantic return to barter or even gifts; but he nevertheless creates a society which is supposed to have reached a more sophisticated stage of capitalism than the previous ones and yet is marked by the reintroduction of attitudes foreign to or established prior to, or antagonistic to the foregrounding of market economies. It is that contradiction which I hope to have highlighted in this chapter because it questions both progress and conservatism. It shows that the progress of capitalism is neither universal – because it bypasses some individuals – nor linear – because it is characterized by alternating periods of rapid advance and eras of stagnation or regression. The issue thus raises the question of progress, which is obliquely addressed in *The Crossing*, for when Billy visits old Mr. Sanders, he notices an ashtray from the Chicago World Fair bearing the inscription '1833–1933. A Century of Progress'. Does it mean that Progress stopped after that date, that is, 1933, which incidentally – or maybe not – is McCarthy's birth date? Billy's acquired distance at the end of *The Crossing* sheds an ironic light on the American Dream: 'I aint come back rich, that's for sure' (410).

Notes

1 Similarly, when he sells his victims' watches, he merely mimics a vendor's attitude but is eventually superseded by the man who buys the objects and immediately sells them off with a profit margin (*Child of God* 129–32).
2 The history of mankind is marked by alternating market and non-market economies: primitive, archaic societies did not rely on exchange but gifts. Antiquity established exchange. The economy of the European Middle Ages was not predominantly based on exchange. The underlying force of modern capitalism is exchange. Transitional periods include mixed situations. What is more, evolution is not linear as periods of non-market economies are recurrent. However, the development of the market has reached a point-of-no-return insofar as latter-day capitalism is much more dependent on the market than it was in Antiquity, for example. Interestingly, according to some economists, contemporary capitalism is characterized by an increasing number of non-market-related elements.

John Vanderheide

The process of elimination: tracing the prodigal's irrevocable passage through Cormac McCarthy's southern and western novels

The border between Cormac McCarthy's southern and western novels has many different crossing points. As Edwin T. Arnold asserted, all the novels somehow 'speak one to another whatever their setting' ('The Mosaic of McCarthy's Fiction' 17). Certain themes, imagery, narrative elements and modes of discourse recur continually through McCarthy's body of work. Among these, Arnold detects the persistent theme of what he calls 'the search for the father' (22). Strangely, the novels that most vividly dramatize the search for the father are the two that seem least to resemble each other, *Suttree* and *Blood Meridian*. Although Arnold suggests the search for the father may refer to a theological 'quest for God' (22), threads common to both novels suggest other referential possibilities as well. These threads invoke versions of the search for the father deployed by some of McCarthy's modernist precursors, such as Rilke, Mann and Joyce, who treated this theme not as a religious allegory, but as an allegory of writing and authorship.

The inscription of the search for the father in *Suttree* and *Blood Meridian* results, on the structural level, in allegorical modes. On the thematic level the protagonist figures as an earlier, but now discarded, self of the narrator. The protagonist is thus an ontological phase the narrator passed through in the stream of becoming. The narrator himself is at some other indeterminable point in the stream, and at that point discursively begets in the act of narrative his earlier self as protagonist. Seen in this way, the novels trace the winding but ineluctable passage of a discursive son to an 'ontological' father who reproduces him in discourse.

In both *Suttree* and *Blood Meridian*, McCarthy situates the searching son in squalid or abject conditions that recall the circumstances of the archetypal prodigal. This intertextual invocation is perhaps most evident in *Suttree*. Suttree bears a strong resemblance to the truant second son of the biblical parable. A second son (14), Suttree often adopts the role of the prodigal to ironic effect, as when he excuses himself for a recent spell in prison by claiming that he 'fell in with a bad crowd' (87). As a derelict fisherman from a respectable white-collar home, Suttree acts 'contrary to conduct befitting a person of [his] station' (457). The station befitting him is, as his father writes him, '[in] the law courts, in business, in government' (14) – in other words, somewhere in the middle class. However, the abandoned family mansion that Suttree visits suggests his forefathers once had an even higher position in the social formation. Placing Suttree at the end of an exhausted lineage is one of the ways that McCarthy affiliates his protagonist with such characters as Joyce's Stephen Dedalus and Rilke's Malte Brigge.

Rilke devotes the last chapter of his novel *The Notebooks of Malte Laurids Brigge* to a reinterpretation of the parable of the prodigal son. His narrator and protagonist, Brigge, interprets the parable as 'the legend of a man who didn't want to be loved' (251). He imagines the prodigal spending his boyhood in solitude, engaging in such purposefully meaningless activities as '[peeling] himself a willow flute' (252). McCarthy invokes this passage when the narrator reports Suttree waiting for Reese and his family to return from church, 'sitting on a log carving a whistle from willow wood' (328). Brigge's account of the prodigal's flight from home could also clarify the somewhat obscure reasons for Suttree's self-exile. The prodigal leaves his family, Brigge suggests, because staying would mean coming 'to resemble them all in every feature of his face' (254). Suttree also has 'a subtle obsession with uniqueness' (113). 'But I'm not like you,' he tells his uncle, 'I'm not like him. I'm not like Carl. I'm like me. Don't tell me who I'm like' (18). When Suttree's mother visits him in prison, 'the son she addressed was hardly there at all' (61). The mother addresses the child she remembers, not the person the child has become. Suttree leaves his father's letters unanswered, perhaps thinking like Brigge that 'If I'm changing, I am no longer who I was; and if I am something else, it's obvious that I have no acquaintances. And I can't possibly write to strangers' (Rilke 6). Suttree's exile thus seems instigated by an overpowering sense of otherness brought on by a succession of self-transformations. By becoming himself, Suttree has become someone else.

Possibly the most condensed treatment of self-transformation in the novel is Suttree's third visit to Mother She. Moments after he swallows the witch's hallucinogenic restorative, Suttree feels 'a door [close] on all that he had been' (426). However, this foreclosure is not a single event; it is a continuous unstoppable process: 'Suddenly he realized that this scene was past and he was looking at its fading reality like a watcher from another room. Then he was watching the watcher' (426). Suttree can do nothing but observe a succession of selves fade in an endless relay of death and rebirth. The hallucinogenic experience concludes with a dramatic juxtaposition that is yet another metaphor of this perpetual process: 'He lay with his feet together and his arms at his sides like a dead king on an altar. He rocked in the swells, floating like the first germ of life adrift on the earth's cooling seas, formless macule of plasm trapped in a vapor drop and all creation yet to come' (430).

Many other images in the novel suggest this theme of life redeemed from an extinguished past, from 'the gray flaky ashes' that '[break] open to an orange heart of burning wood' (237), to the junkman's garden that exists 'by whatever miracle renders grease and cinders arable' (208). The 'odor of violated graves' (282) that

Suttree detects about Mother She, coupled with the scars 'where she'd survived some murder' (429), suggest the graves that she has violated were none other than her own. 'Only where there are graves are there resurrections,' as Zarathustra writes (Nietzsche, *Thus Spoke Zarathustra* 136). Yet what kind of resurrection is possible in a world where nothing stops moving and where what is past is inaccessible? When Suttree asks Mother She what he should do while her elixir takes its course, she answers 'You dont do nothin. You will be told' (425). He then asks her if *she* will tell him and she says no. But Suttree is never told anything by anyone, real or hallucinated. Does this mean Mother She's prediction failed to come true? Not necessarily. Perhaps she did not mean to say that someone would be telling Suttree something; rather, she meant that Suttree would literally be told, that is, transformed from a material subject into a discursive one. Therein lies the manner of his resurrection and redemption, as in this passage from Rilke's novel:

> But the day will come when my hand is distant, and if I tell it to write, it will write words that are not mine . . . In spite of my fear, I am still like someone standing in the presence of something great, and I remember that I often used to feel this happening inside me when I was about to write. But this time, I will be written. I am the impression that will transform itself. It would take so little for me to understand all this and assent to it. Just one step and my misery would turn into bliss. (52–3)

By telling Suttree that he will be told, Mother She divines a future in which he, as he is now, will be redeemed discursively. In his disquisition on Hamlet in *Ulysses*, Stephen Dedalus speaks precisely to the same effect. 'In the intense instant of imagination . . . that which I was is that which I am and that which in possibility I may come to be. So in the future . . . I may see myself as I sit here now but by reflection from that which then I shall be' (160). Thus, the future Dedalus would resurrect, redeem, or re-produce this present incarnation of himself – that time will have by then eliminated – in discourse, becoming, in a strict sense, his own father.

Dedalus and Brigge are perhaps more obviously inchoate artists than Suttree, but the narrator does bestow many authorial qualities on Suttree, not least his solitary musings that the narrator simply transcribes 'verbatim.' For what purpose is Suttree constantly trying to remember things that he has seen? 'Beyond in a yellowlit housewindow two faces fixed aspectant and forever in some domestic vagary. Rapid his progress who petrifies these innocents into stony history' (178). The 'stony history' is the text itself, a text that exists by recuperating the memories of its protagonist. Suttree seems aware of the possibility that a narrative will eventually appear out of his transient experiences of the present. For example, when Rufus tells him that he 'got a old dog stobbed up in [his] slopbarrel,' Suttree's 'lips moved as if he were repeating this to himself' (271). He seems to be saving this impression for the future, for a time when it will be transformed into discourse. A motif that recurs over and over again throughout the novel is the phrase 'Come back' (12, 29, 68). This innocent gesture of farewell expresses a desire for recurrence, for what has passed to come to pass again. McCarthy's use of this phrase invokes the Nietzsche of *Thus Spoke Zarathustra*, who claimed the desire for recurrence is the hallmark of a true creator. In many respects, *Suttree* records a stage in the process of becoming just such a creator. 'I will be hard and hard,' Suttree vows. 'My face will turn rain like the stones' (29). One must be hard, Zarathustra says, if one is 'to compose into one and bring together what is fragment and riddle and dreadful chance in man – as poet, reader of riddles, and redeemer of chance, I taught them to create the future, and to redeem by creating – all that *was past*' (Nietzsche 216). Suttree, as the narrator predicts, lives 'to see the city of [his] youth pulled down to the last stone' (188). As it breaks off, the narrative points ahead to the time when that city itself will be redeemed discursively, and thus the narrative retrospectively predicts its own incipience. Suttree's transformation into the discursive son of the father he will himself become takes place in the silent gap between the end of the narrative and its self-divined recurrence.

Blood Meridian, however, dramatizes the very transformation that *Suttree* defers. It accomplishes this dramatization in the culminating moment of the antagonistic relationship between Judge Holden and the nameless protagonist known for most of the novel as the kid.

One of the central mysteries in *Blood Meridian* is the kid's (that is to say, the man's) fate after the judge ambushes him in the jakes. The conversation between the three men who subsequently attempt to use the outhouse supports the assumption that something horrific has happened. 'Good God Almighty,' one of them says upon opening the door (334). We find it hard to resist concluding that the man's cry of disgust means he *sees* a terrible sight, and that what he sees is the mutilated corpse of the judge's victim. But if there is a body in the jakes, why is the third man so calm? Why does he refuse to answer the question if someone is in there or not, only laconically warning the other man not to go in (334)? Perhaps Griffin is so lively a place for murder that it renders its inhabitants completely desensitized to the most brutal manifestations of death. However, the man who opens the door is anything but calm. So what does he see?

Upon closer examination, the interaction of these minor characters bears a disquieting resemblance to the discovery scenes of Christ's resurrection in the gospels (for example, Mark 16:1–6). The two men may replace the Marys, the outhouse the tomb, and the tightlipped man the revelatory angel, but the structural resemblance between the two scenes is too striking to ignore. The third man, like the angel, possesses some kind of knowledge about what is inside the structure, but the two men, like the two Marys, feel compelled to look inside for themselves. Reading the scene of the jakes in this way thus suggests that what the man saw when he opened the door was what Mary saw when she peered into the tomb of Jesus: nothing. If it was therefore not a terrible sight that provoked the man's cry of disgust, then what else could it have been, given that it was, after all, an outhouse, but a terrible odor?

The resemblance between what occurs outside the jakes and what occurs outside Christ's tomb predetermines the extension of the analogy *into* the jakes as well. According to the gospel narratives, what occurred inside the tomb was of course Christ's victory over death, his resurrection, and, subsequently, the sundering of the mortality he had assumed since the Incarnation. This suggests that one can read the judge and the man as representative of the two aspects, divine and mortal, of a single, Christ-like entity. As the mortal aspect of the equation, the man is thus literally *eliminated* in the apotheosis, and what is left, of course, is the judge, the vacant closet, and the odor heretofore mentioned. The very fact that this whole scene takes place in Fort Griffin underscores the suggestion that the jakes can be read as the site of a kind of resurrection, as the mythological creature by the same name was an emblem of the victorious Christ.

Once the scene in the jakes has been rewritten as the site of the man's transformation into the judge, the reader must decide what to make of such a thing. One could argue that this transformation is a terrible defeat, as Orc's transformation into Urizen is a defeat in Blake. This is undoubtedly a justifiable line of reasoning, but I would like to focus on other textual moments that suggest this resurrection scene is another allegory of writing and authorship. John Sepich briefly notes that the last subheading of the final chapter – *Sie mussen schlafen aber ich muss tanzen* – is a line of poetry that Thomas Mann quotes in his novella *Tonio Kröger*. 'The sentence is appropriate to the scene with which it is positionally associated,' Sepich asserts, 'as it refers to the final scene of the novel, the dancing of the judge after the death of the kid' (171). Unfortunately, Sepich fails to note the significance of 'sleeping' and 'dancing,' as Mann particularly applies them in his novella. For Tonio Kröger, the line expressed a particular 'melancholy northern mood': 'To sleep ... To long to be able to live simply for one's feelings alone, to rest idly in sweet self-sufficient emotion, uncompelled to translate it into activity, unconstrained to dance – and to have to dance nevertheless, to have to be alert and nimble and perform the difficult, difficult and perilous sword-dance of art, and never to be able quite to forget the humiliating paradox of having to dance when one's heart is heavy with love' (Mann 188). Thus, the juxtaposition of this line in the chapter subheading links the judge's dancing to the act of artistic creation. Moreover, Kröger's own metaphor of artistic activity as a *sword*-dance fits perfectly within *Blood Meridian*'s overarching theme of war, and compels us to read Holden's others actions and statements in the same allegorical vein. Interestingly, a main feature of the ritual of the sword-dance 'is the symbolic death of one of the characters and his revival' (Cuddon).

Rick Wallach notes that 'Holden's journal inscriptions elide their subjects, from the birds he kills in order to sketch them ... to the mesoamerican petroglyph he copies and then scrapes away' (132). Reading this activity allegorically, McCarthy's description of Holden's elisions suddenly resemble certain brutally ironic conceptions of the writer. 'Apply to a writer,' Tonio Kröger tells his friend, 'the whole thing will be settled in a trice. He will analyze it all for you, formulate it, name it, express it and make it articulate, and so far as you are concerned the entire affair will be *eliminated* once and for all ... Anything that has been expressed has thereby been eliminated – that is his creed' (Mann 160). The judge's intention 'to expunge [the subsects of his notes] from the memory of man' is thus in perfect accord with Kröger's manifesto. Furthermore, Holden's fascistic prescription for putting a child into a pit of wild dogs as part of his or her upbringing (146) could be a slyly humorous reference to a passage from *Zarathustra*: 'Once you had fierce dogs in your cellar: but they changed at last into birds and sweet singers' (64).

The judge is not the only one we can allegorically revaluate. The coldforger of the kid's dream seems another avatar of the artist: 'this other man . . . seemed an artisan or worker in metal. The judge enshadowed him where he crouched at his trade but he was a coldforger who worked with hammer and die, perhaps under some indictment and an exile from men's fires, hammering out like his own conjectural destiny all through the night of his becoming some coinage for a dawn that would not be' (310). As an artisan, the coldforger makes things; and what he makes, of course, is counterfeit. His job description is thus indistinguishable from the poet's, according to the standard Renaissance formulation that sees the poet as 'both a maker and a counterfeitor, and poesy an art not only of making but also of imitation' (Puttenham 640). McCarthy specifically links this forger with the man, when the latter, during the final bar scene, looks up to see the judge 'enshadow him from all beyond' (327). This verb is used so seldom in *Blood Meridian* that its application in these two cases suggests that the coldforger is none other than the man himself. The dream can thus be thought of as prophetic, and the kid as a kind of passive *vates* receiving visions of the future. The *vates* was seen as the complementary feature to the *poeta*, the active maker and craftsman, a function fulfilled by the judge.

'[Living] and working are incompatible,' Tonio Kröger says, 'one must have died if one is to be wholly a creator' (Mann 152). For Nietzsche, 'there must be much bitter dying in your life, you creators! For the creator himself to be the child newborn he must also be willing to be the mother and endure the mother's pain' (111). Thus, the novel's conclusion recapitulates the manner in which it began. The narrative begins with a disclosure that the kid's mother died in the process of delivering him into the world; it ends with the man himself being eliminated while metaphorically giving birth to his own enormous infant, his father.

As Stephen Dedalus wanders off from the library where he has just finished producing his disquisition on Hamlet, he recalls the conclusion from *Cymbeline*: 'Laud we the gods/And let our crooked smokes climb to their nostrils/From our bless'd altars' (Joyce, *Ulysses* 179). With the subtle humor of a true satirist, McCarthy at once invokes and literalizes this passage in the excremental setting of the culmination of his novel.

Part IV

The Border tetralogy

David Holloway

'A false book is no book at all': the ideology of representation in *Blood Meridian* and the Border Trilogy

Reading literary fiction and writing literary criticism has never been so complicated or so dialectical as it is today. In the case of Cormac McCarthy, a commercially successful writer who is also positioned on the cusp of canonical status within the academy, these complications are magnified severalfold. Since *All the Pretty Horses*, interest in McCarthy has risen at such a rate that discussion of the novels themselves has become almost indivisible from debate about the substantial body of critical opinion that has risen up around them: How useful are the southern/western axes of McCarthy scholarship in any assessment of McCarthy's oeuvre as a whole? What contribution might a biographical criticism make to the critical canon? Is it still necessary to acknowledge the debt to Faulkner, and if so what does it mean, in the twenty-first century, to describe McCarthy as a modernist? This dialectical 'problem' – of criticism's relation to text, and one kind of critical text's relation to another – points us toward a wider set of objective historical issues.

For some, questions like these might seem remote indeed from an appreciation of *Blood Meridian* or the Border Trilogy. Objections might rest upon the bourgeois assumption that criticism is essentially parasitic, that the world is a transparent place, that the literary 'work' has some magical capacity to speak for itself, projecting to its audience a world of meaning sealed tightly in the artistic vacuum of the printed page. But this act of abstraction, this letting the work speak for itself is, in a very political way, part of that wider process of historical forgetting, the repressing of history and its objective contents which has become the rule of successive periods lived under specific historical and ideological conditions. The positing of 'art' as a transcendent experience engineered by a numinous 'artist' is in any case a largely nineteenth- and twentieth-century – that is, a historically relative – notion.

Why this set of assumptions about art or culture should have arisen when it did is of course a significant issue in its own right. For the moment, however, we might simply reiterate the self-evident fact that a desire to avoid politics or critique and let the work of art speak in its 'own' voice is itself a critical and political act. In forcing the work to stand alone, we make an active and an ideological decision to bury, obscure, or mystify the connection between artistic and historical activity. As well as repressing the historical processes involved in the thinking and writing of a novel, to define the printed page as an artistic vacuum is also to deny the embeddedness of bestselling fiction within a process of worldwide economic exchange, all the way from the felling of the tree that makes the page, to the labour that fells the tree, to the labour that builds the chainsaw that fells the tree, to the final consumption of the book in commodity form. These are scattered and somewhat random examples, but the point is that literature and literary criticism are both in one way or another inescapably products of the particular historical circumstances and conjunctures in which they get written (although the relatively recent longing that this should not be so may be a revealing historical symptom in its own right).

It is also an issue with which Cormac McCarthy seems very much concerned. So before we go any further we must agree with Matisse that if all art necessarily tells us something about the historical moment in which it is produced, then the very greatest art, far from being the most abstract or rarified, is that in which history is most visibly marked (Eagleton 3). Like it or not, literary fiction is inextricably part of a wider social and historical totality. McCarthy is often compared to Faulkner, Hemingway, Melville. But such comparisons only become living analytical tools if we ask how and why these voices of the past should be speaking now, through the words of a writer living in a very different world, or a different phase of the same world. There is a structural and a political limit on the significance with which we might read any recrudescence of modernism in McCarthy if we confine the process to mere stylistic cross-reference, just as we can learn very little from Hemingway, or Faulkner, without some consideration of the world, the time, the objective historical conditions, to which their own writing responds. Again, these are issues which seem important to Cormac McCarthy. His characters remind us that 'the story of the world, which is all the world we know, does not exist outside of the instruments of its execution. Nor can those instruments exist outside of their own history' (*Cities of the Plain* 287); that 'existence has its own order and that no man's mind can compass, that mind itself being but a fact among others' (*Blood Meridian* 245); that 'the phantoms formed in the human brain are also, necessarily, sublimates of ... material life process ... Life is not determined by consciousness, but consciousness by life' (Marx and Engels, *The German Ideology* 47). And if we concede a historical basis for that most privileged of abstract activity – authorship, art, the free play of imagination itself – it then follows that the experience of reading must also be seen as an operation conducted within, as well as upon, the raw materials of history. Just as any literary work is a historical symptom (and agent), so too any response to literary fiction is always overdetermined by the specific historical limitations of the reading or reading-strategy. The way in which we read McCarthy's words, the act of consuming his language, is one more material transaction, one more material text, alongside the thinking, writing, and mass production, of the words themselves.

With this in mind, and with the burgeoning industry of McCarthy criticism now taking canonical shape around a set of foundational texts and political-theoretical positions, the time seems right to ask whether the novels can be read in another way, and reinscribed within a broader critical polemic whose adherents have so far seemed untroubled by this most troubling of writers. Methodologically this will be a threefold process. In the first instance it means working with the hermeneutic potential inherent in our acknowledgement that McCarthy's writing and McCarthy criticism inhabit the same historico-material realm (a strategy that has particular value in a case like McCarthy's where the literature is itself in any case a kind of self-reflexive literary criticism). This will mean reading the criticism on the same 'level' as the fiction, reading the writer through the writings of other readers who have read the writer in a particular way, and who have thus in some sense helped to re/write the 'original' novels in a historical domain which is shared by writers and readers alike. In particular, it means asking whether we can create a fusion or synthesis between certain seemingly irreconcilable claims that have become established positions within McCarthy criticism.

For example, Leo Daugherty connects *Blood Meridian* with the Gnostic story of a fall from grace, 'a condition of perfection and thus of literal plenitude, in the divine realm' (158). How might we test this against Steven Shaviro's reading of the novel, where exile, deprivation and loss become primordial and positive facts of human existence, where 'there can be no alienation when there is no originary state for us to be alienated from' (145)? Shaviro argues persuasively that the judge 'kills out of will and conviction and a deep commitment to the cause and the canons of Western rationality' (147). What does this mean when set against Rick Wallach's equally persuasive suggestion that Holden 'invokes the intertextual in its disseminative boundlessness' (131), his embodiment of Derridean textuality standing as a 'satire of deconstructive criticism' (132)? One way of resolving questions such as these might be to focus on the space between the arguments, acknowledging and privileging the contradictory ways in which critics have approached the problem of representation in McCarthy's fiction.[1] By accepting the plausibility of each position we might test their truth value in a rather different way, measuring the rich contradictions of McCarthy's writing against the broader contexts in which they are shaped. Words, as the judge tells us, are 'things', language is material stuff, and the matter from which words are formed is historical stuff (*Blood Meridian* 85). In the final instance, therefore, this will mean drawing connections between an aesthetic/literary-critical 'level' of enquiry and the sublime materiality which circumscribes the political and aesthetic imagination of these millennial days. Ultimately, it will mean a contextualizing of 'McCarthy's' contradictions within a world where the inner laws of capital take their most developed form, a world in which – as foretold by Marx – the global market, a truly millennial eclipse of alternative economic and ideological structures, has become a reality.[2] Already implicit within these two operations is a third issue, which is what these novels tell us about the fate of writing, or the endgame of culture in general, its motor forces, its limitations and its possible futures, during that phase of human history which has become known as late capitalism.³

We begin mediating among these three levels of inquiry by turning to the epilogue from *Cities of the Plain*, where the storyteller who confronts Billy Parham continues a debate about language that McCarthy has conducted with gathering momentum in his recent fiction. For Wallach the judge may be McCarthy's intertextual avatar, but the resistance of the world to concrete interpretation, its refusal to be altered by having meaning inscribed within itself from without, is the same lesson learned by Billy Parham in *The Crossing*. It is also a lesson that Billy is unable to communicate to John Grady Cole, a character who in this regard has more in common with Ahab than does Judge Holden in his Enlightenment guise. As we shall see, the culmination of this debate in the epilogue to *Cities of the Plain* arrives in the leap which McCarthy makes between a shattering of the Real into so many acts of mere representation, and the pain of historical closure. In a move characteristic of the late twentieth-century moment in which it is produced, the epilogue might be read as a self-reflexive inquiry into the act of writing itself, and an assessment of the failing potential for a critical effectivity or agency in the realm of culture, a realm which in earlier social formations had retained a certain privileged status in terms of its notional autonomy from the world at large: a transcendence of the world postulated in modernism's emphasis on the unique personal aesthetic, the epiphany, and other subjectivist formal strategies which claimed to penetrate the raw, unmediated nature of existence. In this respect, indeed, I would take the failure of modernism to sustain the illusion of a cultural autonomy to be at the very heart of McCarthy's project in the Border Trilogy, for in the epilogue to *Cities of the Plain* the very possibility of individual or collective autonomy from the structures of the world as we find it, is relentlessly problematized. 'You think men have power to call forth what they will?', Billy is asked.

> 'Evoke a world, awake or sleeping? Make it breathe and then set out upon it figures which a glass gives back or which the sun acknowledges? . . . You call forth the world which God has formed and that world only. Nor is this life of yours by which you set such store your doing, however you may choose to tell it. Its shape was forced in the void at the onset and all talk of what might otherwise have been is senseless for there is no otherwise. Of what could it be made? Where be hid? Or how make its appearance? The probability of the actual is absolute'. (285)

Despite John Grady's strenuous attempts to locate it, at the very end of the Trilogy there is no outside, no beyond – 'no otherwise' as McCarthy puts it – to the world as given.

What is the 'otherwise' that John Grady is seeking, and what is the 'actual' that he wishes to escape? Throughout the Trilogy John Grady's quest is characterized by a quixotic resistance to the very materiality of his – or rather McCarthy's and our – world. The initial flight into Mexico in *All the Pretty Horses* is governed on the one hand by the failing laws of primogeniture, a disappointment in the legal regulation of private property (7), and on the other by a search for unfenced, uncommodified landscape which might be ridden with a freedom 'lost to all history and remembrance' (5). Its eventual undoing is wrapped up within the defensive class-relations of la Purísma and the intricacies of Mexican revolutionary history.[4] *Cities of the Plain* intensifies John Grady's struggle with the commodity form. The skill with which McCarthy renders the horse auction scene (106–15) not only depicts the violent struggle of competition and the act of consumption as products of a new unconscious whose eruptions are driven by the instinctual pursuit of pleasure.[5] It also reiterates the extent to which John Grady's professional knowledge – or its exchange value in the division of labour – makes him complicit in the commodification of that same wish-object, the horse, which in *All the Pretty Horses* had seemed to offer him a route out of 'the actual'.[6] It is no surprise that his quest for the whore Magdalena, a quest whose object is a reversal in the commodifying of human flesh itself, should end ironically in death at the hands of a pimp. As McCarthy's new sobriquet for John Grady – 'the all-American cowboy' – suggests, this Don Quixote for the commodity age eventually becomes little more than a hollow pastiche of the character he so much wants to be. A pastiche, because the kind of world and the kind of selfhood which he pursues – character as such, in the humanist sense of a self which has agency and depth beyond a superficial exchange value – is no longer accessible.[7] As Billy Parham already suspects at the end of *The Crossing*, in *Cities of the Plain* there will be this world, or there will be no world. In the end the best that John Grady can do is absent himself in the kind of death he always wanted. How could it be otherwise, when there is 'no otherwise'?

As the epilogue to *Cities of the Plain* then suggests, the stories of John Grady and Billy Parham form an analogue for the deeper historical story of the Trilogy, which is what has happened to culture, what has happened to language in our time; or rather, what has happened to the way we and McCarthy think about language or culture, its limits and its potentialities. The conclusion of the Border Trilogy is framed explicitly within the terms of a deconstructive problematic which addresses the act of writing, and the philosophical limitations of that act. When the storyteller/dreamer suggests to Billy that 'those stories which speak to us with the greatest resonance have a way of turning upon the teller and erasing him' (277), he is simply following the moral of his own story to its logical conclusion. In the epilogue's central trope – a definitive trope for the Trilogy as a whole – we are given the story of two dreams, where the character that is dreamed in the initial dream then acquires his own dream life. The second of these two dreams is thus dreamed by a man 'whose own reality remains conjectural' (272), this whole receding line of signification being stitched together for Billy by an unnamed character whose own corporeal reality he initially appears to question, and whose structural function in the novel is to tell a story within a story (a McCarthy staple in recent years). In a scene such as this any one moment of the storyteller's and McCarthy's narrative always points beyond itself into a web of signification whose textual spread – whose expropriation of concrete meaning – is potentially without limit. 'In such a case', as the storyteller suggests, 'one can come upon no footing where even to begin' (278). It then follows that the tool of the storyteller, language itself, is a flawed mechanism, the words used to articulate his story's meaning referring always to other meanings and other contexts beyond those which are intended. Where language is conceived thus, as a virus which fatally undermines the doctrine of human intentionality, then the very act of utterance in storytelling might indeed turn upon the teller and erase him.

It might then be that the storyteller from the epilogue – in simultaneously positing the disappearance of McCarthy's own narrative – is offered us as something like a figure for authorship itself. Or, more specifically, the figure of authorship as conceived within the limitations of our own historical moment: self-cancelling, denuded of hermeneutic agency or effectivity, always on the point of reinscription within whatever structures it might seek to understand or oppose. As Billy Parham has long since accepted, the ramifications of this are political as well as aesthetic. One cannot stand outside a text or a world order and grasp it intellectually or aesthetically, and one certainly cannot transcend or overcome it politically, when the meaning of that text or world order, and the truth-value of the language by which one might interpret or resist it, is always deferred or absent.[8] And so this abandonment of objective interpretive distance which characterizes contemporary hermeneutics must necessarily proceed to its logical concomitant, a position from which the storyteller insists that 'there is no otherwise', no thinkable alternative space beyond the world as we find it (the text with no outside being the equivalent of a world order, or a mode of production, which itself has no imaginable otherwise). Here we might reverse the poles of an idealist equation by which recent trends in literary and cultural criticism are supposed to have led our reconceiving of history.[9] If we take a step back and consider these developments in literary and critical theory as historical symptoms, then it would not seem too far-fetched to suggest that the collapse of literary narrative conceived of as linear and diachronic might have something to do with the collapse of history itself, or at least the collapse of history conceived of as diachronic narrative movement through and beyond existing social conditions. It is in this sense that a marxian criticism like Fredric Jameson's can designate postmodernism as an ideological strategy of containment, a blocking agent which sets limits around what is thinkable in any particular historical moment. As Jameson puts it, 'insofar as the refusal of narratives is viewed as the place of the permanent present . . . [t]he whole point about the loss in postmodernism of the sense of the future is that it also involves a sense that nothing will change and there is no hope' (Stephanson 65, 72).

Grasped in this marxian way, the ultimate function of ideology would be to repress from view those deeply rooted contradictions of material life which might reveal a movement beyond capitalism to be desirable, necessary, or inevitable. *Cities of the Plain* is a remarkable book in part because of the skill with which McCarthy reproduces this mediation between the aesthetic, the political and the economic, in the different textual levels of the novel itself. For the Trilogy is not *about* the failure of language, any more than John Grady's eventual death is caused by his inability to represent the world more accurately or pragmatically to himself.

It is the world itself, the objective social relations within which his story unfolds, which kills John Grady Cole.

Most particularly in *Cities of the Plain*, it is the erasing of horseflesh and female flesh as a workable 'otherwise' that might stand in space beyond the commodity-form. It is McCarthy's marketizing of a Mexico which had in earlier volumes appeared to the characters – in varying degree – as an atavistic, salvational other. In *Cities of the Plain* there is a vendor on every street and corner, exchange value in almost every act we are shown in Juárez, from bars to cafes to taxis to the White Lake itself. A collapse in language, the inability cognitively and aesthetically to stand outside the world as given, is not the cause of historical closure or death. Rather, in the relationship between different textual levels of the Trilogy, a notional failure of language is exposed as the ideological form of more concrete material realities. The failure confirms the absolute probability of the actual, the 'ultimate authority' as Holden would have it, 'of the extant' (84).[10]

This melting down of language to its base properties sourced in material and ideological life continues a project which McCarthy first initiates with real force in *Blood Meridian*. There are any number of reasons why McCarthy's first 'western' novel is a difficult book, not the least of which is its restless self-consciousness. *Blood Meridian* might be read as a critique of how we think about language. But it is also a novel which thinks hard about the language with which its own critique is formed, and which reflects upon the difficulty of rewriting the past when critical programmes such as poststructuralism and new historicism have dismantled any notion that some unifying causal energy might be glimpsed behind the surface effects of historical change. As in the epilogue to *Cities of the Plain*, McCarthy's self-critique in *Blood Meridian* represents something more interesting than mere self-reflexive irony or postmodern conceit, standing instead for a kind of straining at the limits of contemporary aesthetic practice, a pushing against the barriers of the mode of intellectual production in which McCarthy finds himself situated. Taking centre ground in this self-reflexive procedure is the figure of Judge Holden, Shaviro's embodiment of enlightenment grand narrative who is simultaneously for Wallach a grotesque configuring of anti-enlightenment critical theory.

How might we account for – and find a way through – this contradiction? One way is to return to what Holden himself tells us about the thingness of language, where words are objects whose meanings are to be owned or 'possessed' (85). If the epilogue to *Cities of the Plain* suggests that meaning cannot ever legitimately *be* possessed, the judge gets around this problem by simply stealing it wholesale wherever he sees fit. The ledgers that Holden uses to store the copies he makes of natural and human artifacts are ideological scripts, where the representations of the Real which he makes in sketches or in words supercede the originals which he destroys or expropriates (116, 127, 139, 140, 173, 243, 251). 'Whatever in creation exists without my knowledge exists without my consent', for 'only nature can enslave man and only when the existence of each last entity is routed out and made to stand naked before him will he be properly suzerain of the earth' (198).

This notorious speech suggests the judge has already absorbed the lessons of the epilogue to *Cities of the Plain*. A capacity for representation, he argues, gives political power over the material world. In whatever semiotic form – speech, ledger, story, parable – it is Holden's ownership of language and meaning, his control over the act of representation, which underpins his agency and guarantees his suzerainty. Just as surely it is Billy Parham's exclusion from such ownership which imprisons him within an order of things that has no visible – or permissible – otherwise in the epilogue to *Cities of the Plain*.[11]

A part of what McCarthy is attempting in *Blood Meridian* is a revisionist account of western American history, and as any revisionist historian or novelist understands it is the expropriation and redistribution of meaning – the ownership of language – that structures the form in which histories appear and vanish before us. It is therefore entirely appropriate that language should become the motor force of Holden's totalizing energy from the first significant intervention he makes in the narrative, the rhetoric in which his spurious charges against the Reverend Green are couched when he persuades a mob to drive the unfortunate preacher from Nacogdoches (5–8). Particularly in the later stages of the novel, the control which Holden exerts over Glanton and the others is channeled primarily through his deployment of the spoken word. He twice speaks as Glanton's legal representative to Lieutenant Couts after the shooting of Owens, on the first of these occasions announcing 'I represent Captain Glanton in all legal matters', before protesting his leader's innocence in such terms that Couts, 'stunned at the baldness of these disclaimers . . . turned and pushed past the men and quit the place' (237). When Couts returns for a second attempt, 'the judge translated for him latin terms of jurisprudence. He cited cases civil and martial. He quoted Coke and Blackstone, Anaximander, Thales' (239). Nothing more is heard of the lieutenant, nor of the charges he seeks to bring against the Glanton Gang. Glanton's dawning realization that Holden has led the gang to ruination (243) is accompanied by a series of vignettes in which the judge repeatedly speaks on Glanton's behalf, intervening in scenes or in dialogue which are initiated by his putative leader. As well as the scenes with Lieutenant Couts, Holden usurps Glanton during the recruitment of Cloyce Bell in Tucson (233), and speaks for him again during the altercation with Mangas, the fragile properties of a truce between the gang and the Apache being 'abused to the utmost of their enduring when the judge stood slightly in the saddle and raised his arm and spoke' (229). Though it is Glanton who first approaches the doctor at the ferry, 'soon the doctor and the judge were deep in discourse to the exclusion of anyone else' (254), and when Glanton attempts unsuccessfully to dupe the doctor into arming himself against a non-existent threat from the Yumas, 'the judge intervened . . . spoke reasonably and with concern and when Glanton and his detail returned down the hill to cross to their camp they had the doctor's permission to fortify the hill and charge the howitzer' (260–1). The extent to which Glanton is usurped – or effectively silenced – as leader of the gang by Holden's voice, and the extent to which Holden's control of language eventually assumes control of the narrative itself, is illustrated in the precis for chapter XIX, where the impending slaughter of Glanton does not merit a mention (260). To all intents and purposes he has ceased to exist, at least as the voice of authority within the gang, a long time before his actual death. Throughout, Holden's rhetoric is a weapon turned discriminately upon those he seeks to subsume within his own will, a point that is well understood by the expriest Tobin as he and the kid are hailed by the judge in the desert of bones after the Yuma massacre. 'Don't listen', Tobin says to the kid. 'Stop your ears' (293). It is the best advice given in the whole book.

The control which Holden has over others is thus sourced in the act of representation, the expropriation and exclusion of meaning. How does McCarthy respond to this, and what might this tell us about the ideology of representation in *Blood Meridian* and the Border Trilogy? Specifically, how does this square with what we are told about the essential lack in language, in the epilogue to *Cities of the Plain*?

Though he eventually proves an irresistible force in *Blood Meridian*, the judge is not entirely unopposed. Jarrett notes the roles played in this respect by Tobin, the kid and Davy Brown (Jarrett 83–6). To this we might add the various strategies that McCarthy uses in order to problematize the notions of totality, grand narrative and determinate meaning upon which the judge draws in his 'forcing of the unity of existence' (*Blood Meridian* 249). Whilst Holden's words and actions are structured around a set of rigidly defined metaphysical pairings – nature/culture, truth/falsity, will/fate, the collective 'inside' space of the Glanton Gang as against the individualistic 'outside' space of the kid and various deserters – *Blood Meridian* is simultaneously saturated in an epistemology which undermines the life of such doctrine. There is the sustained assault on the notion of manifest destiny, a critique conducted in large part through McCarthy's deconstruction of the Turner thesis, where frontier space is defined in a binary collision of savagery and civilization (Turner, 'The Significance of the Frontier' 3). Less obviously there are formal issues like 'optical democracy', a phenomenological prose style which picks apart the distinction between nature and culture, dispersing into textuality and *jouissance* the metaphysical notions upon which such distinctions are grounded.[12] There are the deconstructive properties of some of Holden's own statements – 'every man is tabernacled in every other and he in exchange and so on in an endless complexity of being and witness to the uttermost edge of the world' (141) – and there is the steady accumulation of detail which drips a logic of *differance* relentlessly into the very fabric of the text: the black Jackson and the white Jackson whose fates are 'tabernacled' in the way that Holden suggests (81–107); Tobin's descriptions of Holden as a 'saviour' who is simultaneously the embodiment of some primal satanic 'evil' (122–35); the rendering of the sun which, in rising metaphorically 'out of nothing like the head of a great red phallus' (44), recasts the penis as a nothingness, a lack or an absence requiring completion by its now masculinized vaginal other. If Holden aims to totalize all existence within himself by controlling the act of representation, that control is cumulatively undone by the deconstructive rhetoric of the text itself.

Putting this differently, we might say that the epilogue to *Cities of the Plain* bears witness to a fault line in the totalizing rhetoric of Judge Holden, just as much as it reflects upon the quixotic tragedy of John Grady Cole or the stoic resignation of Billy Parham.

Blood Meridian's self-reflexive structure here raises real difficulties for both reader and writer, for – crucially – the oppositional voice which the text raises against Judge Holden is never more than provisional. The deconstructive method of that voice is itself placed under erasure. Again, the problem can be viewed retrospectively, through the point of exhaustion and closure to which McCarthy winds the Border Trilogy. The paralysis of cognitive and political agency which underwrites the epilogue to *Cities of the Plain* is foreshadowed in several coded warnings during *The Crossing*, notably in the advice of another McCarthy storyteller – again to Billy Parham – that 'narrative is itself... the category of all categories for there is nothing which falls outside its purview. All is telling. Do not doubt it' (155). McCarthy anticipates the conclusion to the Trilogy here, but he also reflects back once more upon the judge, disturbing the metaphysic of binary pairings – the structure of freestanding and mutually opposed meanings – through which Holden guarantees his agency. Earlier in the same sequence, however, *The Crossing* has advised us that we abandon the binary at our peril, that we *rightly* 'long for something of substance to oppose us. Something to contain us or to stay our hand. Otherwise there are no boundaries to our own being and we too must extend our claims until we lose all definition. Until we must be swallowed up at last by the very void to which we wished to stand opposed' (153). This cautionary notice is flagged up elsewhere in the same sequence, where the madman in the broken church sees 'the world pass into nothing in the very multiplicity of its instancing' (154). When instancing is multiple and multiplicity is nothingness, where all is telling and the Real is just one representation tabernacled in another, there is no such thing as truth-value: by definition, as Holden suggests, 'books lie' (116). And yet, as he also informs us, 'a false book is no book at all' (141): things, as the storyteller tells Billy Parham in *Cities of the Plain*, 'need a ground to stand upon' (272).

One of the textual voices which *Blood Meridian* raises in opposition to Judge Holden works by deconstructing the idea of a fixed metaphysical ground upon which meaning might stand, thereby eroding at its foundations a totalitarian agency which seeks to force the unity of existence. In its demolition of certain binary pairings *Blood Meridian* can certainly be seen as a text that works along deconstructionist lines, just as the conclusion of the Border Trilogy appears to stress a generally poststructuralist epistemology. The question then arises, how can *Blood Meridian* avoid the dangers identified in *The Crossing*, where McCarthy warns against the pull of the 'void', and the perils of being subsumed by that which one opposes? How can McCarthy's book avoid the falsity which Holden tells us is the fate of all books? How is it possible for *Blood Meridian* to circumvent the historical closure and the paralysis of dialectical – that is, oppositional – language with which McCarthy will go on to conclude the Border Trilogy?

One answer to this is that *Blood Meridian* perhaps cannot avoid such a fate. For all its quite stunning deconstructions of Holden's claim to force the unity of existence, there is little doubt as to who or what remains as a dominant force at the end of *Blood Meridian*. By virtue of the hold which he has upon language, Holden manifestly outlasts the textual challenge to his suzerainty. Since the judge is an agency who expropriates and totalizes all meaning – who owns, we might say, the ideological capital – in the text, and since it is the judge who eventually thus bestows meaning upon the narrative, we are left with little choice but to accept at face value the world as revealed to us through the words that he uses. And so the refrain which closes the main body of the text – 'He says that he will never die' (335), repeated three times in the concluding paragraph – guarantees his permanence. If Judge Holden says that he will never die, if Holden uses his control of language to claim a status which is both primordial and monolithic, then his words come before us as propositions which guarantee their own truthfulness simply by being spoken. One point about deconstruction which then emerges in *Blood Meridian* is not the familiar – and misplaced – truism that the method works nihilistically, approaching all meaning and value as metaphysical abstractions to be derided and dispensed with. McCarthy's writing and thinking seems too supple – and indeed too dialectical – for that.

Rather, as writing which is made in the closing decades of the twentieth century, *Blood Meridian* seems to raise broad questions about the difficulty in thinking and articulating an oppositional voice under the historical conditions of late capitalism. *Blood Meridian* may 'oppose' a part of itself to the totalizing meta-force of the judge, and it may present the reader with a deconstructive voice as an agent of that opposition within the text. But this act of 'opposing' implies a conceptual distancing of the critique from its object, a demarcation of the two which deconstruction would repudiate as the worst kind of binary thinking, insisting instead that any oppositional voice necessarily inhabits the structures of what it opposes. And so, in the act of opposing one succeeds only in confirming the intractable presence of what one might hope to remove. The enduring of the judge, in other words, is a proposition which McCarthy's deconstructive approach to meaning and to language seems powerless to resist.

We might say that in the end *Blood Meridian* surrenders even a provisional control of meaning to the totalizing force of the judge precisely *because* McCarthy's critique is informed by a deconstructive methodology. In surrendering this, the text also gives up the critical – and the political – agency which it needs to bring witness against him. Here again Tobin's is an instructive voice, for as the expriest well knows it is Holden's very *textuality*, his unfathomable origins, the absence – to paraphrase *Cities of the Plain* – of any ground upon which to stand him, that lends him his totalitarian impregnability. The mystery of being, Holden tells the Glanton Gang, is that there is no mystery. 'As if he were no mystery himself', Tobin responds, 'the bloody old hoodwinker' (252).[13]

In this respect, it is not just the revisionism of *Blood Meridian* which marks it out as the symptomatic product of a late capitalism which some continue to hail as the end of history. Admittedly, the anxieties which lie behind McCarthy's revising of how history works tap into the unconscious of our own time in striking ways. The novel's suspicion that anarchic destruction is not simply an economic accident but an inner historical necessity, the very life blood of capitalist accumulation, remains sublimated but acute; whilst history's *appearance* before human beings as 'an alien force existing outside them . . . the origin and goal of which they are ignorant, which they thus cannot control', is in certain respects the key trope of the novel (Marx and Engels, *The German Ideology* 54).[14] The demolition of Frederick Jackson Turner's frontier ideology – where a heroic, self-propelling individualism miraculously transforms the fetters of bourgeois unfreedom into liberty itself – is also savagely rendered.[15] The way in which *Blood Meridian* revises the nineteenth century certainly tells us something quite profound about how the novel also conceives the present in which it is written (late capitalism in general and specifically, in *Blood Meridian*'s case, the Reagan/Thatcher axis of the eighties).

But as in the Border Trilogy it is the fatalistic conclusion that one can never really transcend or overcome that which one opposes which might tell us most about *Blood Meridian*'s rootedness in the broad historical and economic discourses which help produce it.[16] It is not simply that the novel's deconstructive method forces it to accept the loss of a critical language which might position it outside of Holden's totalizing energy. By accepting the relativism of all truths, including its own, the oppositional voice within the text must leave itself open to expropriation by other textual agencies, in this instance by that of the judge. In *Blood Meridian*, as in the tragedy of John Grady Cole, it is the capacity *for* representation, the ability to forge concrete meaning, which constructs agency and which empowers human activism in the world. If the epilogue to *Cities of the Plain* provides us with an ideological template for this, the hold which Eduardo has over Magdalena – the means by which the pimp continually reinscribes flesh with exchange value – gives us the hard, material corollary:

> He spoke in reasoned tones the words of a reasonable man. The more reasonably he spoke the colder the wind in the hollow of her heart. At each juncture in her case he paused to give her space in which to speak but she did not speak and her silence only led inexorably to the next succeeding charge until that structure which was composed of nothing but the spoken word and which *should* have passed on in its very utterance and left no trace or residue or shadow in the living world, that bodiless structure stood in the room a ponderable being and within its phantom corpus was contained her life. (212, emphasis added)

She does not speak. Eduardo controls Magdalena by violence, but also by policing the use of language, even though the words which he speaks are explicitly characterized as a lack or failure in meaning. At the White Lake language acquires meaning and becomes determinate in the hands of he who has the economic power to expropriate it, and vice versa: he who controls the production of meaning determines the process of commodification. Similarly, at the close of

Blood Meridian Judge Holden can be quite sure that he will never die because the novel lacks the ownership of language – the epistemological confidence, the agency within ideology – needed to kill him off.

In these respects *Blood Meridian* and the Border Trilogy read less like a critique of metaphysics – the linguistic sign, metanarrative, manifest destiny, bourgeois ideology, whatever – and more like a series of questions about how to go about formulating that critique. In *Blood Meridian*, where the oppositional voice is converted suddenly and violently into its own negation, one core feature of McCarthy's aesthetic might then be summarized as a testing of ideological limits, an exercise in what Jameson terms 'transcoding': a speaking of theoretical codes experimentally, a determining of 'what can and cannot be said in each of those theoretical private languages', where what is 'blurred, left out, what does not compute or is inexpressible in this or that theoretical language may then be a more damaging indictment of the theory in question than traditional ontological or metaphysical critiques' (*Ideologies of Theory* Volume 2, ix). This transcoding or testing of limits may be one reason why Holden – as in Wallach and Shaviro – comes before us as a 'character' so rich in conflicting and contradictory meanings. For he embodies McCarthy's modernist attempt to retrieve a sense of relatively fixed meaning in the world, just as surely as he stands for a decidedly postmodern warning against where such a search might eventually lead. But it is the mode of intellectual production in which they are sited, and the contradictions which bourgeois history can never fully conceal, which give McCarthy his self-reflexive edge, and which turn Holden into a riddle, a living paradox, a bloody old hoodwinker.

It is also abundantly clear that McCarthy is a superbly accomplished technician, that his 'own' use of language in *Blood Meridian* at times attains a density and a rhetorical complexity that is beyond even Judge Holden. *Blood Meridian*, as Bell puts it, 'is haunted by the mystery that its own language challenges the very nihilistic logic that it gives representation to. The language is itself a presence' (Bell 1988, 128). This suggests there are strategies at work in McCarthy's writing which are designed precisely to bulwark the novels against the kind of expropriation that Holden practises. And – although there is not time for this here – it is therefore to form and once again to modernism that we must turn, if we are to assess more fully the ideology of representation in McCarthy's fiction.[17]

Notes

1 Vereen Bell does something like this in his undervalued reading of *Blood Meridian*. 'The judge is a worshipper of truth. Truth is what can be known, not what can be supposed or dreamed up. He therefore absolutizes history because history is the repository of all that can be known' (1988, 120). 'What the judge says and he and his confederates act out eventually seems like an only slightly demented revival of Enlightenment philosophy, and the judge's intellectual imperialism may be read finally as an instance of what happens if Enlightenment doctrine is pressed to its logical conclusion' (124). But, as

Bell argues, Holden's determination to absolutize Truth is at times self-deconstructing: 'It is the very cornerstone of his own argument that the judge himself discloses to be fundamentally insecure' (126). 'Judge Holden is such an imposing conception and such a bizarrre intellectual, as well as physical, presence partly because he is both Marlow *and* Kurtz' (119, emphasis added). 'If the judge is a failed priest, he may as well be Satan; but if he is Satan, he may as well be God also, for in this context the two are not conceived as inversions of one another' (122). Though here we are leaving aside the possibility that deconstruction's accounting for the world is itself a hermeneutic strategy, which merely substitutes one grand narrative (*differance*) for another (the *logos*). See Fredric Jameson, *Postmodernism, or The Cultural Logic of Late Capitalism* (217–59).

2 'The tendency to create the world market is directly given in the concept of capital itself' (Marx, *Grundrisse* 408). 'A precondition of production based on capital is ... the production of a constantly widening sphere of circulation, whether the sphere itself is directly expanded or whether more points within it are created as points of production' (407). Capital is 'the constant movement to create more of the same. The quantitative boundary of the surplus value appears to it as a mere natural barrier, as a necessity which it constantly tries to violate and beyond which it constantly seeks to go' (334–5). Capital is 'the endless and limitless drive to go beyond its limiting barrier. Every boundary is and has to be a barrier for it. Else it would cease to be capital – money as self-reproductive. If ever it perceived a certain boundary not as a barrier, but became comfortable within it as a boundary, it would itself have declined from exchange value to use value' (334). The world market is therefore 'the very basis and living atmosphere of the capitalist mode of production' (*Capital* 205).

3 The most immediate sources for the methodology used here are taken from Louis Althusser, 'Contradiction and Overdetermination', in *For Marx* (89–116), and the writing of Fredric Jameson, particularly 'Metacommentary' in *The Ideologies of Theory Volume 1* (3–16), and *The Political Unconscious: Narrative as a Socially Symbolic Act*.

4 An ideological dimension to John Grady's initial trip into Mexico – a perceptual distance between the idealism that he claims and the material agenda which these claims disguise – is discussed in Dianne C. Luce, '"When You Wake": John Grady Cole's Heroism in *All the Pretty Horses*'.

5 The old Freudian 'pleasure-principle', the *id* itself, is thus transfigured by commodity relations. See Herbert Marcuse, *Eros and Civilization: A Philosophical Inquiry into Freud*, and Fredric Jameson, 'Pleasure: A Political Issue', in *Ideologies of Theory* Volume 2 (61–74).

6 As intimated by Luce. 'Such horses are pretty wishes; were they flesh and blood, all men would ride' (Luce, 'When You Wake' 156).

7 Jarrett is good on these and related issues (*Cormac McCarthy* 97–107) but underestimates, I think, McCarthy's own self-reflexive critique of the categories – pastiche, the postmodern quest, a postmodern loss of self – that he uses. Edwin T. Arnold has repeatedly implied that McCarthy is trying to rescue the kind of humanism which is absent in Jarrett's reading. See Arnold on McCarthy's repudiation of nihilism, in 'The Mosaic of McCarthy's Fiction', and 'Naming, Knowing and Nothingness: McCarthy's Moral Parables'.

8 '[A]s the power to speak of the world recedes from us so also must the story of the world lose its thread and therefore its authority' (*Cities of the Plain* 286). Shaviro's reading of *Blood Meridian* – where the problem, as we shall see, is if anything more complex – reaches a similar conclusion: in *Blood Meridian*, 'just as we can never possess

the world (since we cannot even possess ourselves), by the same logic we can never transgress the order of the world or estrange ourselves from it – no matter how hard we try' (148).

9. Keith Jenkins, 'Introduction: On Being Open About Our Closures', outlines the benefits and the problems of this approach.

10. See Jameson's chapter on theory in *Postmodernism, or The Cultural Logic of Late Capitalism* (181–259), and Bryan D. Palmer, *Descent into Discourse: The Reification of Language and the Writing of Social History*.

11. The judge, as Wallach notes (129), is a master linguist. 'Him and the governor they sat up till breakfast and it was Paris this and London that in five languages, you'd have given something to of heard them' (123). He is 'as eitherhanded as a spider, he can write with both hands at a time' (134).

12. On 'optical democracy' see Dana Phillips, 'History and the Ugly Facts of Cormac McCarthy's *Blood Meridian*'. For a Barthesian reading of *jouissance* in *Blood Meridian* and *Suttree*, see Nell Sullivan, 'Cormac McCarthy and the Text of *Jouissance*'. See also Shaviro on McCarthy's 'erotics of landscape' (152).

13. As Wallach argues, 'the judge's eeriness finally derives from how, like the Satan of CG Jung's *Answer to Job*, who hides within the very bosom of Yahweh, he does seem to stand, or perhaps hide would be a better word, within the very narrative, guarding the secret of inscription as ferociously as a *dharmapala*' (129).

14. 'Crossing those barren gravel reefs in the night they seemed remote and without substance. Like a patrol condemned to ride out some ancient curse' (*Blood Meridian* 151): 'They rode like men invested with a purpose whose origins were antecedent to them, like blood legatees of an order both imperative and remote' (152); 'these elect' (48); 'trammeled to chords of rawest destiny' (154). The essential anarchy of this rawest destiny is summarized in a famous passage from *The Communist Manifesto*: 'The bourgeoisie cannot exist without constantly revolutionizing the instruments of production, and thereby the relations of production, and with them the whole relations of society. Conservation of the old modes of production in unaltered form, was, on the contrary, the first condition of existence for all earlier industrial classes. All fixed, fast-frozen relations, with their train of ancient and venerable prejudices and opinions are swept away, all new-formed ones become antiquated before they can ossify. All that is solid melts into air, all that is holy is profaned' (24). The movement of history is here conceived by Marx and Engels as a series of different modes of economic production, the structural contradictions of which – rooted in the systemic contradictions of capital itself, its contradictory laws of motion – force each existing mode to destroy and then reinvent itself during phases of periodic crisis or rapid expansion.

15. Turner's 'qualification' of this insists that liberty is compromised by evil individuals or accidents of environment, rather than by systemic historical laws. 'But the democracy born of free land, strong in selfishness and individualism, intolerant of administrative experience and education, and pressing individual liberty beyond its proper bounds, has its dangers as well as its benefits. Individualism in America has allowed a laxity in regard to governmental affairs which has rendered possible the spoils system, and all the manifest evils that follow from the lack of a highly developed civic spirit. In this connection may be noted also the influence of frontier conditions in permitting lax business honor, inflated paper currency and wild-cat banking. The colonial and revolutionary frontier was the region whence emanated many of the worst forms of an evil currency' ('The Significance of the Frontier' 18).

16 The suspension of historical time in *Blood Meridian*, the absence of telos, the permanence of the present in which the action takes place, have become critical commonplaces in various different approaches to the novel. See, for example: Bell, *The Achievement of Cormac McCarthy*; Shaviro; Brian Evenson, 'McCarthy's Wanderers: Nomadology, Violence, and Open Country'; Schopen, ' "They Rode On": *Blood Meridian* and the Art of Narrative'; Thomas Pughe, 'Revision and Vision: Cormac McCarthy's *Blood Meridian*'.
17 On the importance of form in *Blood Meridian* see Schopen. See also Nancy Kreml, 'Stylistic Variation and Cognitive Constraint in *All the Pretty Horses*'.

Linda Townley Woodson

De los herejes y huérfanos: the sound and sense of Cormac McCarthy's border fiction

One of the threads that may be unraveled from the web of Cormac McCarthy's border fiction, beginning with *Blood Meridian* and extending through the Border Trilogy, is his concern with the relationship between language and reality. Like the Anna Livia Plurabelle episode of Joyce's *Finnegans Wake* (cf. Lechte 216–19), the border fiction taken as a whole becomes a 'polylogue' (Kristeva, *Desire in Language* 158), that is, a number of voices, modes, and genres, particularly narration and dialogue, about how language can become real and reality become language. McCarthy's use of the multiple voices and genres reinforces the very point that is being made: language becomes reality for us as we exist in a world of many voices that assimilate to form meaning. The genius of his fiction is that through its multiple genres of narration and of dialogue framed by narration, the works leave the reader in a position of autonomy with assurances only of the continuation of the telling and of the sanctity of witnessing in both its senses: by acts of observing others and, later, by testifying to their existence. Through poetic sentences reflecting the ruptures and rhythms of presymbolic language (that which McCarthy indicates is the language of the heart) and through its other characteristics of oral language – for example, the lack of punctuation such as the absence of apostrophes in contractions and the omission of quotation marks and speaker tags, which would call attention to the written language itself – McCarthy's fiction creates a place between the real and the word while the relationship between the two is interrogated continuously through the insinuation of contemporary language philosophy into the words of the characters themselves.

Just as Joyce presents us with 'a tree, a stone, a river, and a new story' (Lechte 218), McCarthy begins the creation of his semiotic landscape in *Blood Meridian* where 'death seem[s] the most prevalent feature of the landscape' (48). Death becomes the 'agency' (329) of non-meaning as, in Freudian theory, it is the strongest of the drives – and this the judge asserts with candor. His is the candor required by 'honest' semiotic systems because, like language, the judge is beyond good and evil most starkly when he insists that '[w]ords are things,' that '[b]ooks lie' (116), but that God speaks 'in stones and trees, the bones of things' (116). Rick Wallach ('Judge Holden') has demonstrated convincingly that the judge represents writing or inscription, the socio-cultural record of collective memory. Much that is found in *Blood Meridian* establishes a basis for exploring the relationship between language and reality, language and truth, that is found throughout the Border Trilogy. That socio-cultural record makes possible the atrocities exhibited in the novel resulting from the corrupt cause-consequence reasoning known as 'manifest destiny'. In the midst of these acts of horror are deposited Nietzschean concepts about language and truth that appear so directly in *The Crossing*.

In particular, two episodes in *Blood Meridian* demonstrate the attitudes about language that are explored more directly in *All the Pretty Horses* and in *The Crossing*. The first such episode begins with the judge's story of the traveler and the harnessmaker (*Blood Meridian* 142–7), a remarkably candid performance which vividly represents the judge as the embodiment of language. In particular, the judge is candid with his listeners about semiotic systems; his story illustrates how little humans are ultimately guided by the concepts of language. In the judge's tale, a traveler delivers a lecture to the harnessmaker's family to which the harnessmaker responds by *repenting*, one of the performative words identified by J. L. Austin as a word that is the act itself (79). In addition, the harnessmaker's son appropriates the traveler's language into an oration of his own. Finally, both harnessmaker and son become killers, demonstrating the power of the drives of the heart to overcome the action of the word and demonstrating also that, as Austin says, it is appropriate that the person speaking 'should have a certain intention, viz. Here to keep his word' (11). Only the woman in the story attempts to keep alive the memory of the traveler by placing his bones in a grave, thereby acknowledging the sanctity of his former existence. In her old age, she tells others that the bones in the grave are those of her son, emphasizing the similarity of all journeys toward death. And, just as the traveler's lecture is appropriated, so also the judge's tale is appropriated immediately by its hearers: 'all began to shout at once with every kind of disclaimer' (145). The dead traveler is frozen in historical language, trapping his son in adolescence, in a Freudian sense, unable ever to see the 'follies' (145) of the father that would allow the son to break free of the burden of the Father (as symbolized by History, Language, Law):

> Now this son whose father's existence in this world is historical and speculative even before the son has entered it is in a bad way. All his life he carries before him the idol of a perfection to which he can never attain. The father dead has euchered the son out of his patrimony. For it is the death of the father to which the son is entitled and to which he is heir, more so than his goods. (145)

In the final encounter of the kid with the judge, a foundation is further established for the Border Trilogy's explorations of the relationship between language and reality. The kid has studied the judge throughout the novel, but cannot kill him in the desert; if language *is* the human activity, a human cannot destroy completely Language/Law/the Father without destroying the self. As the kid begins to understand this truth about the judge, a truth the expriest already knows, 'they spoke less and less between them' (303). But the kid is unable to read, that ability that presents humans full entrance into the operation of words as things. After surviving the hardships of a desert crossing afoot, the kid tries to use his oral language to convey the horror he has witnessed, and 'he began to speak with a strange urgency of things few men have seen in a lifetime" (305), but he is not understood. Consequently he attempts to achieve silence, carrying a Bible 'no word of which he can read' (312) and traveling with 'no news at all' (312). In dreams he has seen the judge joined by a 'false moneyer with his gravers and burins who seeks favor with the judge' (310), like Nietzsche's coiner of illusional language ('On Truth and Lies in a Nonmoral Sense' 84). Ultimately, the judge exposes the kid's attempt at silence: 'Was it always your idea that if you did not speak you would not be recognized?' (328). And just as the historical record of the father was the undoing of the traveler's son in the judge's story, here, too, the judge (in the role of the Father) kills the kid, after telling him that he could have loved him like a son (306). The 'flawed place in the fabric' (299) of the kid's heart, his building skepticism, has been his heresy; we shall see that in the Border Trilogy those who speak about the inability of the word to speak reality are heretical in their questioning of the power of the Word.

I have explored elsewhere the Nietzschean/Foucaultian concepts about the relationship between the word and the real that appear in *All the Pretty Horses* ('Deceiving the Will to Truth'). John Grady Cole begins his journey in search of power, yet naive about this relationship between word and real. When his girlfriend asks if everything isn't talk, he replies, 'Not everything' (28). When the police captain tries to make him understand how words work as things in the world, John Grady argues, 'The truth is what happened. It aint what come out of somebody's mouth' (168). Like the candid semiotic system mentioned earlier, like the revelations of the judge, each participant in creating the 'truth' of the land, the prison, and the hacienda is straightforward about how words become things. The captain tells John Grady, 'We can make the truth here' (168), the hacendado warns, 'There is no greater monster than reason' (146), and more than all the others, the Dueña Alfonsa tries to make John Grady see from the history of the Madero brothers how profoundly language, laws, customs, and rituals of a place, in short its history, are entrenched and are made to operate as truth in service of the drive for power. She urges him to the recognition of 'what is' (240), even as she uses the power of the word against him: 'I was pleased to be in a bargaining position at all' (229).

In *The Crossing*, McCarthy continues the polylogue about the relationship between the word and the real, but more directly as he becomes Nietzsche's 'philosopher/artist.' McCarthy places the words of Nietzsche ('On Truth and Lies in a Nonmoral Sense') into the words of the heretics of the novel: those of the aged man whom Billy consults about trapping wolves and those of the old man who comes to the church in Caborca as his words are created by the expriest who remains there. Here, because of the directness of the presentation of this philosophy, we may be seeing the writer himself being candid concerning his doubts about the ability of the word to capture the real.

The first section of the novel, a traditional tragic tale, illustrates (like the history of the Madero brothers in *All the Pretty Horses*) that good intention (Billy's desire to save the pregnant wolf by returning her to the mountains of Mexico) has little to do with consequences in a world where the drive of human nature, the drive to power gained by exerting one's will over the other, holds sway. Billy is powerless to prevent gamblers from staging a pit fight between the wolf and their dogs, a bloody game that is played for the ultimate stakes. As the judge says in *Blood Meridian*, 'But trial of chance or trial of worth all games aspire to the condition of war for here that which is wagered swallows up game, player, all' (249). And later, 'War is the ultimate game because war is at last a forcing of the unity of existence. War is god' (249). The men play the game with the lives of other living, but non-human beings, forcing the recognition of their separation and power over those others.

In the mock scholastic dialogue that forms the revelation of Nietzschean concepts in the church at Caborca, the dialogue is actually a monologue dialogical in nature. The reader is placed in an autonomous position regarding Nietzsche's concepts, and the responses of conventional religion to those concepts, by this odd rhetorical form. Kristeva would suggest, however, that this dialogue is no parody because it involves a challenge of God and social law ('Word Dialogue and Novel' 49), a challenge to the core of our human activity, language. The fact that the expriest may actually be creating the story of the old man can be attested to in the way that the story moves from past to present tense throughout, for example, from 'He believed that in the world was another agenda, another order, and with this power lay whatever brief he may have held' (*The Crossing* 147), to 'By now he is a pensioner in Mexico. He has no friends' (148), and so on. This movement among tenses suggests the literary tense of the created story that has the power to transport us into another time and space. Finally, then, the encounter between Billy and the expriest becomes an episode of witnessing to the existence of the old man, as the priest concludes, 'The story on the other hand can never be lost from its place in the world for it is that place. And that is what was to be found there. The corrido. The tale. And like all corridos it ultimately told one story only, for there is only one to tell' (142) – the common journey of all toward death. To affirm the value of this witnessing, the expriest tells Billy, 'the lesson of a life can never be its own. Only the witness has power to take its measure. It is lived for the other only' (158) and again, 'There is another who will hear what you never spoke' (158). The judge also speaks of the value of this witnessing when he asks the kid whether or not he has left witnesses to his existence (*Blood Meridian* 331). Both instances inflect the Nietzschean concept that humans have created language as a stay against the brevity of human existence in a 'minute of "world history"' (*Thus Spoke Zarathustra* 79) beyond which nothing will have been changed by their existence, but McCarthy adds a rider: we can learn from the tales of others.

In yet another example of witnessing and interrogation of the relationship of the word and the real, Billy encounters the blind man whose eyes have been sucked from his head in a bizarre act of retribution. Following the man's blinding, the intervention of three others – a man, a woman, and a child – contributes to his salvation. These three are described as travelers that everyone encounters along the road of life: 'Como en todos los cuentos hay tres viajeros con quienes no encontramos en el camino' (*The Crossing* 284). The man helps him from the river where he is attempting to drown himself, the woman feeds him, and the child becomes his caretaker. This progression of the blind man's salvation is a reversal of the Freudian stages of the child's growth into language: the child's separation from the Mother and its loss of connectedness with all things through identification with and mastery of language, symbolized by the Father. In his blindness, with sight the most intellectual of all our senses, the man has come to see the world as described by Nietzsche, the world whose light is 'in men's eyes only for the world itself move[s] in eternal darkness and darkness [is] its true nature and true condition.' The blind man has learned that 'in this darkness it turn[s] with perfect cohesion in all its parts but there [is] naught there to see' (*The Crossing* 283). In his gradual loss of memory of the known and seen world, in that loss of 'un mundo fragil' (291), he realizes that 'in the deepest dark of that loss that there also [is] a ground and there one must begin' (291). Although Nietzsche posits that '[o]nly by forgetting this primitive world of metaphor can one live with any repose, security, and consistency' (293), nevertheless, as we have already seen, we can never completely abandon language. As the blind man insists, 'En este viaje el mundo visible es no mas que un distraimiento. Para los ciegos y para todos los hombres. Ultimamente sabemos que no podemos ver el buen Dios. Vamos escuchando. Me entiendes, jove? Debemos escuchar' (292) ('In this journey, the seen world is but a distraction. For the blind and for all men. Ultimately we know that we cannot *see* the good God, but we ought to listen'). The reader of *Blood Meridian* has heard the words of the judge that 'el buen Dios' is in the trees and stones. The words 'Debemos escuchar' suggest another language, the kinetic rhythms and ruptures of presymbolic language called by Plato the *chora*, what Joyce called the sound sense of language which is the artist's proper concern.

A final interrogation of the relationship of the word and the real comes toward the end of *The Crossing* with another tale within the narration. This rhetorical form once again creates a frame that places the reader in a position of autonomy, but this time in close proximity to Billy as he hears the story of the airplane, a story that has three possible versions. Although he requests the one that is 'true,' the finished story begins again in yet another version with the coming of Quijada, similar to the way darkness brings another telling in Joyce's Anna Livia Plurabelle episode, thus creating a work in progress:

> A 'warping process' evokes a 'work in progress,' the title Joyce gave to *Finnegans Wake* before it was published. This warping process produced, in part, by punning and agglutination, would bring about a deformation of the symbolic that at one and

the same time pluralizes meaning and gives rise to the echo of the real: language returning to its origin in the semiotic, poetic dimension of the signifying process. (Lechte 218)

Through these multiple investigations into the relationship of the word and the real, the reader finally stands alongside Billy when he declares that it has *not* been his experience that most of what one hears is right (418). We are reminded of the words of the hermit that the kid encounters at the beginning of *Blood Meridian*: 'A man's at odds to know his mind cause his mind is aught he has to know it with. He can know his heart, but he dont want to' (18).

In the epilogue of the final book of the Border Trilogy, *Cities of the Plain*, some resolution of the conundrum posed between language and reality takes place. The epilogue serves for all three works as it concludes the exploration of attitudes toward language and the role of the storyteller, the role of telling tales, in light of those attitudes. This odd coda follows a stereotypical story of John Grady Cole, Billy Parham, and the prostitute Magdalena, a story of ill-fated and youthful love – the power of the heart over reason, revenge that knows no bounds, and the bittersweet taste of early death – all the substance of fiction-making throughout time. Yet as stereotypical as it may be, this story, *because* it has been told so many times, illustrates the power of language as used by the storyteller to create a reality that enfolds us and sustains us over time, the power to enlist the emotions of readers and to transport them to another dimension of imaginative being. The fact that McCarthy can take the same episodes, the same stories, and accomplish this demonstrates not only his skill with language, but also the very point that he seems to be making: language *is* the human activity. Our witnessing of the existence of others through attending to the stories they weave is the consecration of our being and worth.

As the aging Billy leaves El Paso and travels toward what is perhaps his final destination, the home of the family just outside of Portales, New Mexico (a scene reminiscent of Frost's poem 'Death of the Hired Man'), he encounters under an overpass a fellow traveler (266). This fellow traveler, significantly first confused by Billy with Death, becomes established as an allegorical figure, the Storyteller. The similarity of Death to God is explored in the passage (268), and as we have already seen Death is often described as the ultimate destination of all our journeys, Death is the nature of the landscape in *Blood Meridian*, and Death is that against which we create a stay, as described by Nietzsche, in our 'minute of history.' Identifying the issue about the relationship of language to the real which has been consistently addressed by the trilogy, Billy asks the storyteller the controlling question, 'You sure you aint makin all this up' (277). The storyteller describes the use of language and the making of narratives about the world as responses to questions about the world, wherein questioning is inherent in being and can have no answers, no end:

> It is senseless to claim that things exist in their instancing only. The template for the world and all in it was drawn long ago. Yet the story of the world, which is all the

world we know, does not exist outside of the instruments of its execution. Nor can those instruments exist outside of their own history. And so on. This life of yours is not a picture of the world. It is the world itself and it is composed not of bone or dream or time but of worship. Nothing else can contain it. Nothing else be by it contained. (287)

Once again, language *is* the human activity. Then, addressing directly the postmodern contention of Barthes and Foucault that the author is 'dead,' the storyteller asserts, 'And those stories which speak to us with the greatest resonance have a way of turning upon the teller and erasing him and his motives from all memory. So the question of who is telling the story is very consiguiente (consequential)' (278). This statement refers to the appropriation of the storyteller's story, as we saw illustrated in the judge's harnessmaker tale in *Blood Meridian* and in the story of the airplane in *The Crossing*. The storyteller suggests that because a story does have the power to transport us into a created reality that is the reality of our only known existence, but where we lose sight of the story's creator, the author's motives are indeed significant. According to Barthes, 'literature is always unrealistic, but its very unreality permits it to question the world – though these questions can never be direct' ('Authors and Writers' 187). As to the author's responsibility, Barthes goes further:

> What we can ask of an author is that he be responsible; again, let there be no mistake: whether or not an author is responsible for his opinions is unimportant; whether or not an author assumes, more or less intelligently, the ideological implications of his work is also secondary; an author's true responsibility is to support literature as a failed commitment, as a Mosaic glance at the Promised Land of the real. (188)

Regarding how we can go forward, given postmodern understandings of the power of language to distort truth and to create deception, and the urge, given those understandings to distrust Language/ Law/ History/ the Father, the storyteller's words point out that we have little choice concerning our dependence on history and the unfolding story of humankind: 'What has no past can have no future' (281). But the storyteller describes a greater form of knowing, outside of language. This form, according to the storyteller, is at the core of our lives and 'in that core are no idioms but only the act of knowing and it is this we share in dreams and out. Before the first man spoke and after the last is silenced forever. Yet in the end he did speak, as we shall see' (281). The storyteller tells his dream about the pilgrims to Billy and then, in turn, the dream has the power to alter what Billy sees in his world: the dome of the radar tracking station becomes an ancient Spanish mission, and rags of plastic wrapping blowing in the wind appear as passing pilgrims (289). As Billy sits in the mouth of the concrete pillar 'like a man in a bell' and sees the world before him transformed through the dream story, he becomes a symbol for the human in a natural world whose 'template . . . and all in it was drawn long ago' (287), but which can only be known through its story. Billy, his world transformed by language, is Everyman.

At one level, McCarthy's border fiction can be seen as the writer exploring his own search into language's ability to convey the real, the writer's task to try to achieve that goal, and the reason for the teller of tales to continue in a world informed by postmodernism: 'He appears to be required to choose his tale from among the many that are possible. But of course that is not the case. The case is rather to make many of the one' (*The Crossing* 88). Beyond that, the many rhetorical forms that create the polylogue place the reader in a position that invites analysis. Set as the first two books of the Border Trilogy are on either side of the first atomic explosion – depicted as a mysterious false sun in *The Crossing* (425) – we are reminded of the precariousness of human existence. As we increasingly question the reality created by language – the Father, the Law – we understand that we are all *herejes*, heretics twofold in our separation through our use of language from the Mother – the interconnectedness of all – and in our separation from the Father through our questioning of the power of language to give us the ability to know truth, making us also *huérfanos*, orphans, like the kid, John Grady Cole, and Billy Parham. The potential for abjection exists. If a theme may be tentatively drawn from the border fiction, it may be that we are urged to understand that our storytelling is perhaps our greatest achievement because it is there, in our telling of and listening to the stories, that we learn from others' experiences, that we hear the echoes of the rhythms of existence, the *chora*, that verify our common bond with all, both animate and inanimate, and that we validate and consecrate in our memories the identity of the Other, the *you* implicit in the *I*. We are urged to listen to the sounds of the human heart, the same rhythms of all, the sound that the expriest Tobin suggests we have heard all our lives but will only recognize when it stops (*Blood Meridian* 123). Our ability to hear that 'soundsense' has been blackened by the 'sensesound' of language, our ears shriveled like those on the scapular of ears worn about the neck of the kid and others in *Blood Meridian*. Finally, we are urged to the posture of John Grady Cole as he stands over the grave of Abuelita:

> for a moment he held out his hands as if to steady himself or as if to bless the ground there or perhaps as if to slow the world that was rushing away and seemed to care nothing for the old or the young or rich or poor or dark or pale or he or she. Nothing for their struggles, nothing for their names. Nothing for the living or the dead. (*All the Pretty Horses* 301)

We are urged to listen and to witness.

John Beck

'A certain but fugitive testimony': witnessing the light of time in Cormac McCarthy's Southwestern fiction

> With the Photograph, we enter into flat Death ... I shudder ... over a catastrophe which has already occurred. Whether or not the subject is already dead, every photograph is this catastrophe. [This is] vividly legible in historical photographs: there is always a defeat of Time in them: that is dead and that is going to die. (Barthes, *Camera Lucida* 96)
>
> All past and all future and all stillborn dreams cauterized in that brief encapture of light within the camera's closet ... Every representation was an idol. Every likeness a heresy. In their images they had thought to find some small immortality but oblivion cannot be appeased. (McCarthy, *The Crossing* 2)

There is a famous image by Timothy O'Sullivan of a mule-drawn wagon parked incongruously among the sand dunes near Sand Springs, Nevada. Positioned to the right of the photograph, the wagon sits uneasily within a landscape otherwise smooth and unmarked by human presence. The picture was taken during Clarence King's Survey of the Fortieth Parallel (1867–69), for which O'Sullivan was the official photographer, and the wagon is in fact the converted ambulance which served as a portable darkroom (Naef 3).[1] What had only a few years before carried the wounded, broken and dead bodies from the battlefields of the Civil War now functions as a vehicle for the exposure and preservation of images of 'all the work of nature in that wild and unknown region' of the West, work that has been 'scanned by shrewd and highly-educated observers.'[2]

Photography was as essential a component in the transmission of information about the West as it was for documenting the Civil War. Many photographers, including O'Sullivan, participated in both enterprises not as outside observers but as integral parts of, respectively, the army and survey team. Just as the war, for most non-combatants, especially in the North, was more an image than a fact, the West, as Rebecca Solnit suggests, 'became the first region that a culture got to know largely through images – an authentic born utterly mediated' (40). The way of perceiving the landscape and its inhabitants, the beginning of mythic construction, is mediated at the outset by the camera and the aesthetic preoccupations of those first Western photographers, the first official witnesses. O'Sullivan's picture notably places the dark form of the wagon before the bleached-out backdrop of a swollen sand dune. The hold that the deserts of the Southwest have had on photographers from O'Sullivan to the present is immense and not reducible to the plain facts of spectacular scenery and excellent light. There is, I suggest, a matrix of concerns which bonds the nature of the photograph and the trope of the desert, and it is this matrix that I want to explore in relation to Cormac McCarthy's Southwestern fiction.[3]

The use of the desert as a site for political and spiritual testing and self-scrutiny has ancient roots, and this tradition of deprivation and revelation powerfully shapes McCarthy's fiction. McCarthy's desert is an actual and a metaphysical space which provides a testing ground for the moral positions assumed by his protagonists in the face of a universe apparently bent on destruction, and for his own narrative and formal concerns. The desert is in the text as a fictional site and as a historical place; furthermore, the desert is, in part, the stuff of the text itself, a linguistic desert of dry and shifting particles. 'One walks with some caution,' warns Western historian Patricia Nelson Limerick, 'in these historic regions; land that appears solid may be honeycombed, and one would not like to plunge unexpectedly into the legacy of Western history' (18). McCarthy and his characters do indeed plunge into the legacy of their place, a honeycomb of fact, myth, and mystery.

The desert reveals the beginning and the end, pre- and post-history, 'fear in a handful of dust.' Its granules expose the entropic movement of time toward a slow obliteration through erosion. Desert space is not literally empty but it is not lived in so much as it is lived upon. To this extent it can be said to be depthless, and those who go there scud across its surface. Deserts are disastrous places. They suggest an apocalypse that has already happened and which remains unredeemed. Deserts also seem to prefigure some future catastrophe that might befall places of habitation. In the scale of this pulverization they are both expansive and reductive, everything and nothing. One way or another, deserts signal and invite annihilation. The desert is evidence of cosmic indifference or, worse, of an actual hostility toward human life, a mineral disdain for the vulnerability of the organic.

Desert places are sites where any trace of human presence is easily voided, where space is literally deranged. Without the existence of visible markers, three-dimensional vision is collapsed into a flat, depthless surface. The relationship between perception and knowledge is vividly revealed in the desert, where objects are severely exposed to the glare of the sun; so severely exposed, in fact, that the sharp edges defining things – usually enabled by the casting of shadow – are annihilated and the reading of spatial depth becomes difficult, if not impossible. In *The Crossing*, 'The country itself was changeless,' making travel some kind of optical effect: 'He rode on and the high mountains to the southwest seemed no nearer at the day's end than had they been some image in the eye itself' (88). A celebrated passage in *Blood Meridian* also reveals the uncanny way the desert levels distinctions and troubles the eye's ability to read what is before it:

> In the neuter austerity of that terrain all phenomena were bequeathed a strange equality ... The very clarity of these articles belied their familiarity, for the eye predicates

the whole on some feature or part and here was nothing more luminous than another and nothing more enshadowed and in the optical democracy of such landscapes all preference is made whimsical and a man and a rock become endowed with unguessed kinships. (247)

Here, McCarthy deliberately yokes landscape, perception, and politics in a way that enables him to develop a disturbing discourse of power and knowledge that runs through the Southwestern novels. Descriptions of terrain are never without cosmic inflection, nor are they ever separate from issues of ownership, exploitation, and domination. The land is only neutral in the sense that anything is possible there, it is host to all human depravity and, perhaps, any human kindness. What is clear from this passage, however, is that conventional relationships between observation and cognition do not apply.

Analogous to the flattening of space in the desert is the foreshortening of time evident in the practice of storytelling by many incidental characters within the novels, where history does not unfold in temporal succession but is always already here, a surface rather than a line. The past is, of course, made present in the words of the storyteller, but the past is also concretely present in the unchanging patterns of life, in the material life of the country, in the obstinate stasis of the terrain. The stories, given the curious repetition of the same forms of existence, are themselves all concerned with the same thing. In the desert, then, are we faced with the materiality of the eternal?

McCarthy places in his deserts numerous outcasts, loners, infidels, and remnants of dead or dispersed communities. Through the parables and reminiscences of these incidental characters, he is able to fold the past into the present of his fictions in the form of supplementary fictions. In this way he can develop an ongoing examination, or internal critique, of the function and forms of storytelling – of representation – from within ostensibly realist texts that are themselves self-consciously replaying mythic themes. McCarthy's texts, like his strange, abandoned, or lost commentators, are perpetually troubling their own ability to testify; that is, to tell what has happened. What makes these parables still more confusing for the reader is that the auditor – invariably one of McCarthy's heroic youths – is seemingly oblivious or indifferent to the import of the tales, usually showing little or no interest in them. There appears to be precious little communication between the storyteller and his or her listener, which leaves the tale hovering uneasily within the text, blown away by more pressing plot development. If McCarthy's desert wanderers are seekers in the wilderness, they do not acknowledge whatever they are looking for in the testimony offered by the desert dwellers.

The reader cannot be indifferent to this testimony, however, for the counterpoint between the kind of existential praxis enacted by the protagonists and the ahistorical folk wisdom of the taletellers constructs a discursive tissue through which serious political and aesthetic issues can be followed through. The protagonists' acceptance of action over thought, of the present over the past, of the empirical over the theorized, is the bedrock of America's mythic pragmatism. Under the burden of this myth the Western novel labours, and without McCarthy's meditative interruptions, placed in the mouths of outsiders, his books might tilt toward a vicarious celebration of blood and soil. McCarthy is too much of a revisionist for that, and too much aware of the terrible legacy of Western history. Through his desert prophets, the violent exercise of ideologically legitimated state power manifested at the level of plot is revealed and broken. We learn from these rambling philosophers not a coherent metaphysics but the art of questioning; in particular, we learn that scrutiny of given information is crucial, that representation drives history through its construction of time passing into present fact.

I want to consider this issue with reference to two instances towards the end of *The Crossing* where Billy contemplates photographic images from the past. As I mentioned above, the history of photography in America is intimately bound up with the exploration of the far West. Furthermore, the photograph is, or used to be seen as, representation offered up as presentation, a form of image-production separated from interference by the objective gaze of technology. As such, it is the acme of verisimilitude and thus a useful paradigm for the ambitions of a 'straight', documentary aesthetic and the concomitant discourse of verifiable and unquestionable truth that underwrites it as a representational practice. We might say that photography, like the desert, has a 'neuter austerity'; nothing the camera sees is 'more luminous' than any other; man and rock may become endowed with 'unguessed kinships'.

From the peculiarities of photography as a medium – that is, literally, as a transmitter or channel through which the light of the past travels into the present – the space between history and representation is revealed as the space of death, the unrepresentable yet ever-present subject of all human tales. Through the photograph the past impacts on the present, not as metaphor but as a physical trace. Roland Barthes suggests that:

> The photograph is literally an emanation of the referent. From a real body, which was there, proceeds radiations which ultimately touch me, who am here . . . the photograph of the missing being, as [Susan] Sontag says, will touch me like the delayed rays of a star. A sort of umbilical cord links the body of the photographed thing to my gaze: light, though impalpable, is here a carnal medium, a skin I share with anyone who has been photographed. (*Camera Lucida* 80–1)

As the imprint of the past, the photograph offers an immanent history which is both separate from the past – since the imprint is the trace of a previous presence – and also coterminous with the present as artifact. Epistemological issues are sidelined by the ontological certitude of the fact of the image as thing. In photography, suggests Barthes, 'I can never deny that the thing has been there. There is a superimposition here: of reality and of the past.' He goes on to consider that 'Perhaps we have an invincible resistance to believing in the past, in History, except in the form of myth' (76).

The photograph, for the first time, puts an end to this resistance: 'Henceforth the past is as certain as the present, what we see on paper is as certain as what we touch. It is the advent of the Photograph... which divides the history of the world' (*Camera Lucida* 88). When Billy looks at photographs, this division between history accessed by myth and history as the light of the past shining in the present is partly what he sees, and certainly what the reader is asked to contemplate. Whether the second phase of history provides a more meaningful engagement with the past than the first, however, is questionable.

The first episode concerning photographs is fleeting and takes place at Sanders' house where old photographs and portraits commemorate long dead and forgotten friends and relatives. These images 'seemed like artifacts salvaged from some ancient removal' (*The Crossing* 344), archeological curiosities as severed from their context as the ashtray from the Chicago World's Fair which celebrates 'A Century of Progress' (345). Like the ashtray, the photographs are icons of a long dissipated optimism for a future, which, in fact, saw the collapse of the notion of history as progress. A similar view of the alienness and savage severing of past from present achieved by the photograph is presented near the end of *All The Pretty Horses* as John Grady Cole watches the clumsy posing of newlyweds who 'already had the look of old photographs. In the sepia monochrome of a rainy day in that lost village they'd grown old instantly' (284).

The image of this forlorn couple could easily be among the pictures Billy sees in his second encounter with photographs, which also seems to confirm a sense of atrophied, worthless testimony to the past, a past divorced from any living thing. This is at the gypsy's cart, where a collection of old prints hang like scalps on clothespins above the wagon: 'These likenesses had value only to the living who had known them and with the passage of years of such there were none' (*The Crossing* 412). As a boy, the gypsy 'took them for a cautionary tale and he would search those sepia faces for some secret thing they might divulge to him from the days of their mortality' (412). For the gypsy's father, the pictures are cryptic messages from the anglo world, which was, for him, inscrutable. The photographs 'became for him a form of query to the world. He sensed in them a certain power and he guessed that the gorgios considered them bad luck for they would scarcely look at them but the truth was darker yet as truth is wont to be' (413).

The gypsy's father is suspicious of the photographs because they promise an unmediated testimony, a history without witness, and thus without responsibility. Earlier in *The Crossing* the hermit living in the old church provides a perspective on the issue of witnessing which is crucial to McCarthy's understanding of history. The hermit claims that 'Acts have their being in the witness. Without him who can speak of it? In the end one could even say that the act is nothing, the witness all' (154). Without the witness, the world must 'pass into nothing in the very multiplicity of its instancing.' This is what photography does, eliminates the witness, or at least voids any trace of the witness, and in doing so it eliminates the responsibility of the witness to take a measure of the world:

> A false authority clung to what persisted, as if those artifacts of the past which had endured had done so by some act of their own will. Yet the witness could not survive the witnessing. In the world that came to be that which prevailed could never speak for that which perished but could only parade its own arrogance. It pretended symbol and summation of the vanished world but was neither. (*The Crossing* 410–11)

This is what troubles the gypsy's father, that, unlike a tale transmitted by word of mouth, a photograph is not infused with the life of the witness, and can therefore never hold past and present together as a living, moving process. Instead, what he senses is the presence of death in every photograph.

> What he came to see was that as the kinfolk in their fading stills could have no value save in another's heart so it was with that heart also in another's a terrible and endless attrition and of any other value there was none. Every representation was an idol. Every likeness a heresy. In their images they had thought to find some small immortality but oblivion cannot be appeased... He said that what men do not understand is that what the dead have quit is itself no world but is also only the picture of the world in men's hearts... In those faces that shall now be forever nameless among their outworn chattels there is writ a message that can never be spoken because time would always slay the messenger before he could ever arrive. (413)

All photographs, claims Barthes, 'are agents of Death... Death must be somewhere in a society; if it is no longer (or less intensely) in religion, it must be elsewhere; perhaps in this image which produces Death while trying to preserve life.' With the elimination of rites in modern society, photography 'may correspond to the intrusion... of an asymbolic Death, outside of religion, outside of ritual, a kind of abrupt dive into literal Death. Life/Death: the paradigm is reduced to a simple click... With the Photograph, we enter into flat Death' (*Camera Lucida* 92). In earlier times, Barthes suggests, memory, 'the substitute for life, was eternal,' and the monument, 'the thing which spoke Death,' was immortal.

> But by making the (mortal) Photograph into the general and somehow natural witness to 'what has been,' modern society has renounced the Monument. A paradox: the same century invented History and Photography. But History is a memory fabricated according to positive formulas, a pure intellectual discourse which abolishes mythic Time; and the Photograph is a certain but fugitive testimony; so that everything, today, prepares our race for this impotence: to be no longer able to conceive duration, affectively or symbolically: the age of the Photograph is also the age of revolutions, contestations, assassinations, explosions, in short, of impatience, of everything which denies ripening. (93–4)

What is suggested by McCarthy's gypsy is that the technological attempt to preserve the life of the past through the photograph fails and confirms only the inevitability of death. While the photograph, as synecdoche for Euro-American rationality, seeks to abolish mythic time, it displays only its inadequacy in the face of an enduring tradition of skeptical testimonials. 'The Photograph is violent,' says Barthes, 'not because it shows violent things, but because on each occasion it fills the sight by force, and because in it nothing can be refused or transformed' (91).

Against the pristine reification of the photograph, McCarthy's witnesses offer flawed testimonials from cultural positions outlawed and all but destroyed by the history Glanton and his ilk have enforced upon the land. In *Blood Meridian*, the judge documents artifacts and then throws them into the fire. Asked what he plans to do with the notes and drawings, he says it is his intention 'to expunge them from the memory of man' (140). Webster reckons that 'them pictures is like enough the things themselves. But no man can put all the world in a book. No more than everything drawed in a book is so' (140–1). Despite his skepticism, Webster won't have the judge draw him: 'save my crusted mug from out your ledger there for I'd not have it shown about perhaps to strangers.' Smiling, the judge replies that 'Whether in my book or not, every man is tabernacled in every other and he in exchange and so on in an endless complexity of being and witness to the uttermost edge of the world' (141).

In the Border Trilogy, Billy and John Grady are constantly advised to weigh carefully the information they are given and to open themselves to the power of a living knowledge. Arguing over the accuracy of maps, one man suggests to another that 'it was not so much a question of a correct map but of any map at all. He said that ... one needed to know the country itself and not simply the landmarks therein' (*The Crossing* 184–5). To follow a false map was to invite disaster. To believe in false maps, like subscribing to the fake presence of the photographs, is to cave in to the duplicity of a representational landscape designed to dispossess us of communications emanating from a living body. One form of this kind of counter-imperialist practice is the corrido:

> Listen to the corridos of the country. They will tell you. Then you will see in your own life what is the cost of things. Perhaps it is true that nothing is hidden. Yet many do not wish to see what lies before them in plain sight. You will see. The shape of the road is the road. (230)

The corrido offers a form of representational knowledge which cannot be burned in the judge's fire. It is 'the poor man's history. It does not owe its allegiance to the truths of history but to the truths of men' (386).

The corrido, the tale, 'has no abode or place of being except in the telling only and there it lives and makes its home and therefore we can never be done with the telling. Of the telling there is no end' (143). While a photograph reveals the death of time, the tale lives in time and in the telling. The epilogue of *Cities of the Plain* makes the same point. 'A picture ain't your life,' says Billy, 'It's just a picture.' 'Well said,' replies the Mexican:

> But what is your life? Can you see it? It vanishes at its own appearance. Moment by moment. Until it vanishes to appear no more. When you look at the world is there a point in time when the seen becomes the remembered? How are they separate? It is that which we have no way to show. It is that which is missing from our map and from the picture that it makes. And yet it is all we have ... The picture seeks to seize

and immobilize within its own configurations what it never owned. Our map knows nothing of time. It has no power to speak even of the hours implicit in its own existence. Not of those that have passed, not of those to come. Yet in its final shape the map and the life it traces must converge for there time ends. (273–4)

McCarthy's desert of representation is a place where all markers are inadequate, where traces of the past cannot long endure. Knowledge and memory must be carried as part of the necessary survival kit. With such a suspicion of representation, the novels as texts themselves are precariously placed, testaments to their own inadequacy. They occupy the space between the trace of dead light emanating from the photograph (history as notionally authentic truth) and the mythic circularity of the corrido (history as organic myth), wandering between modes of telling and knowing, persistent in attempting to show 'that which we have no way to show.' McCarthy's skepticism toward the capture of the light of time demands the diligent posting of witnesses to report 'on the continuing existence of those places once you'd quit them' (*Blood Meridian* 331). For he is clear that vision itself is a trickster and must be accompanied by another, more sanguine knowledge which passes through the blood of generations. As with the fire which shifts and misleads like 'some ignis fatuus belated upon the road behind them which all could see and of which none spoke,' the photograph, as the mark of 'things luminous,' has the 'will to deceive' which 'may manifest itself likewise in retrospect and so by sleight of some fixed part of a journey already accomplished may also post men to fraudulent destinies' (120). Faced with this ambivalence, McCarthy leaves us to wonder whether, as Emily Dickinson suggested, it is 'Better an ignis fatuus / Than no illume at all.'

Notes

1 See Naef 125–36 on O'Sullivan and the King Survey. The title of the image of the wagon is 'Desert Sand Hills Near Sink of Carson (Nevada). 1868.'
2 *New York Times*, May 8, 1867. Quoted in Naef 127.
3 I use the term desert to signify a conceptual as much as an actual space. The deserts of the Southwest are, of course, topographically incredibly different. They are also far from empty, and never have been, neither of flora and fauna nor of human settlement. As a trope, however, the desert has, at least in Western culture, operated as a term for vacancy, barrenness, and often the site of evil and death.

Neil Campbell

Liberty beyond its proper bounds: Cormac McCarthy's history of the West in *Blood Meridian*

> Depend upon it, there is mythology now as there was in the time of Homer, only we do not perceive it, because we ourselves live in the very shadow of it, and because we all shrink from the full meridian light of truth. The truth about the world, he said, is that anything is possible. (*Blood Meridian* 245)
>
> ... A false book is no book at all. (141)

Blood Meridian is an excessive, revisionist and contradictory narrative of the American West which both rewrites the myths and histories of the West inherited from Frederick Jackson Turner and maintains and utilizes many of the Western archetypes familiar in this genre of writing. Its poetics are those of transgression and the text plays with contradictions, unsettling the reader in a number of ways, in terms of both form and content. How do we read a novel that begins with epigraphs from Valéry, Boehme and *The Yuma Daily Sun* of 1982? How do we read a novel whose opening chapter is a series of shifting narrative styles and modes of address echoing the Bible, fairy tale, myth and the Western? These questions begin the process of destabilization and ambivalence that surges through the novel as McCarthy lays siege to conventional ideas about the West and its history in order to rupture expectations and beliefs. I would agree with Jarrett's assessment of *Blood Meridian* as a 'revisionary western' but feel that his comments about the novel as 'postmodern' are too narrowly fixated upon the 'discursive tension between fictional and historical narrative' (69), when in fact McCarthy's novel is exciting precisely because it traverses new territory that is continually blurring those kinds of distinctions. Part of what is being revised in McCarthy is a whole tradition of historiography, like Frederick Jackson Turner's, predicated upon a narrative told by the victor in which the dominant story is represented as a triumphal procession. McCarthy knows what Walter Benjamin meant when he wrote, 'There is no document of civilization which is not at the same time a document of barbarism' and examines just such an idea in *Blood Meridian*, whose central concern is the duality of westering and colonization of the West. Behind the images and rhetoric of Turner's historical narrative of the West lies a 'barbarism' in need of telling, and the imaginative scope of fiction allows

McCarthy, as Benjamin would put it, 'to brush history against the grain' (*Illuminations* 248).

McCarthy's work has a good deal in common with the so-called New Western History, which began as a challenge to the mythicized view of the West Frederick Jackson Turner helped to create in his 1893 essay, 'The Significance of the Frontier in American History.' As leading New Western Historian Patricia Nelson Limerick has argued, 'Reorganized, the history of the West is a study of a place undergoing conquest and never fully escaping its consequences' (26). McCarthy's novel reorganizes the received histories of the West, is concerned with the notion of conquest, and is obsessed by the continued consequence of this process. Engaging in a dialogue with the myths of the West, McCarthy follows their strange logic to dark conclusions, to the point where the myths turn in on themselves, implode and begin to deconstruct. McCarthy's work therefore creates the sense of reading simultaneously a Western and an anti-Western, employing many aspects of the genre in order not to perpetuate unquestioningly that form and its values, but to analyse the hidden history of the West and its generic styles. 'One has to push one's work as far as one can go: to the borderlines,' notes Trinh T. Minh-Ha, 'where one never stops walking on the edges, incurring consistently the risk of falling off one side or the other of the limit while undoing, redoing, modifying this limit' (218).

At this vertiginous point on the borderlines, where identities and communities fragment and where any claims on absolute, authoritative truth are challenged, one locates McCarthy's writing as 'postmodern.' His Southwestern novels peer into the abyss of Western American history and bear fictional witness to its terrifying and spectacular events. Set on and around the border of the USA and Mexico, his fiction walks the edges of a liminal territory. In *Blood Meridian*, McCarthy uses the figure of Judge Holden as a vehicle for an extreme refocusing of history, and through him we are given an ambivalent, contradictory version which cannot be easily or comfortably accommodated into the simple mythic sense of the West. Instead, the judge challenges and interrogates received rules, values and myths, allowing McCarthy to comment on the way in which recorded history is a process of selection and control, whilst providing a fictional landscape for acts of imperialism and conquest so often omitted from these historical stories. To borrow the title from a television exploration of nationalism, McCarthy is concerned with the stories his country tells him and how these stories can be exposed and retold.

Frederick Jackson Turner claimed that 'The United States lies like a huge page in the history of society. Line by line as we read this continental page from West to East we find the record of social evolution' ('The Significance of the Frontier' 6–7). Onto this page Turner inscribed his version of history, marking out his concept of the West as the key to American development. He believed that 'The nation needed ... a coherent, integrated story of its beginnings and its development. Connectedness, wholeness, unity,' Trachtenberg observes, and 'these narrative virtues, with their implied telos of closure, of a justifying meaning at the end of the tale, Turner would now embody in the language of historical interpretation' (13). Turner translated the text of the American West for us and reproduced for our consumption a grand-narrative of America in which social evolution was spelt out in the very development of the frontier itself. America, he argued, grew from its movement West, its character forged in the challenges presented by this adventure. What Turner established was indeed a creation myth for America, a story of its very origins as a democratic nation. But as Slotkin has shown, this myth has specific ideological underpinnings, 'those same "laws" of capitalist competition, of supply and demand, of Social Darwinism's "survival of the fittest" as a rationale for social order, and "Manifest Destiny" that have been the building blocks of [America's] domestic historiographical tradition and political ideology' (*The Fatal Environment* 15). Thus Turner's blank page filled up with the tenets of an American nationalism forged by the notions of Western expansion and frontier values. However, such myths have to be examined closely because they 'distort' by naturalizing history, hollowing it out into a neat, closed, unambiguous process, just as the myth of the Frontier West did. 'Above all,' writes Slotkin, 'the restorative and regenerative power of the land was emphasized: its ability to redeem the fortunes of those fallen from high estate ... the New World's capacity to fulfil even the most extravagant expectations' (40). Roland Barthes extends this point, noting how myth 'abolishes the complexity of human acts ... it does away with dialectics ... organizes a world which is without contradictions because it is without depth, a world wide open and wallowing in the evident' (*Mythologies* 143). Reading Turner's work on the West from this perspective reveals that it does, indeed, carefully avoid contradictions and complexities.

McCarthy produces something akin to Slotkin's 'productive revision of myth' which challenges the given narratives and permits the myth of culture 'to adjust its beliefs [and the fictions that carry them] to changing realities,' because, if not, the alternative is 'the rigid defense of existing systems, the refusal of change, which bind us to dead or destructive patterns of action and belief that are out of phase with social and environmental reality' (*Gunfighter Nation* 654–5). *Blood Meridian* intervenes against the neatness of Turner's ideas such as Manifest Destiny and progress, and rejects the 'ordained sequence of events' through which 'the world is rendered pure,' recognizing that 'myth ... can be understood as an abstract shelter restricting debate' (Truettner 40). Turner's assertions are like a corral constructed to hold a view of America and exclude a number of other voices (women, Native Americans etc.) and other interpretations which did not fit the particular story he wanted to tell. As he wrote in 1889, four years before delivering his frontier thesis, 'American history needs a connected and unified account of the progress of civilization across the continent' (quoted in Trachtenberg 13), and the notion of a frontier provided the opportunity for him to produce a coherent, integrated story, a creation story for America.

So when Turner writes of America formed 'in crossing a continent, in winning a wilderness, and in developing at each area of this progress out of the primitive economic and political conditions of the frontier into the complexity of city life' ('The Significance of the Frontier' 8), the language signifies precise ideological readings of the West: winning wilderness, progress vs. primitivism – which McCarthy's novel interrogates by extreme analysis. For example, the assumption of 'winning a wilderness' is exposed as a brutal wrangle over power where only the strong and ruthless survive, and in Turner, where there is a belief that 'a return to primitive conditions' (2) is a necessary point in achieving a 'higher stage' (7) of evolution, in McCarthy there is only endless violent struggle. If there is an American character being formed on this frontier, McCarthy's version is dark, destructive and without mercy.

Expansionism, however, was for Turner as natural and inevitable as glaciation on the landscape; indeed, it was destined and anything that obstructed the natural movement would be swept aside. Turner's natural westward flow, in a particularly memorable section, is described with all the ideological assumptions at work to present a reductive, closed and racist view: 'Thus civilization in America has followed the arteries made by geology, pouring an ever richer tide through them, until at last the slender paths of aboriginal intercourse have been broadened and interwoven into the complex mazes of modern commercial lines . . . It is like the steady growth of a complex nervous system for the originally simple, inert continent' (7). In contrast, McCarthy's view of history is a non-progressive, brutal 'repeated circle of estrangement and displacement . . . whose only patterns are of darkness and death' (Messent 92). *All the Pretty Horses*, the novel with which McCarthy followed *Blood Meridian*, makes this dark view plain: 'What is constant in history is greed and foolishness and a love of blood and this is a thing that even God – who knows all that can be known – seems powerless to change' (239). The silences and gaps in Turner's work are central to McCarthy's fiction, showing the West not as a corral, but an open range of contesting forces in a landscape of changing meanings. *Blood Meridian* unfolds an ambivalent, contradictory, contested West through the double journeys of the judge and the kid.

To understand McCarthy's sense of the West one must return to much earlier interests in the significance of it in the American psyche. The West is a region of the unknowable, uncharted darkness, a place 'beyond reckoning,' like that drawn in *Blood Meridian*. Judge Holden, *Blood Meridian*'s antagonist, sees the West as a testing-ground for his self, a place 'beyond men's judgements [where] all covenants were brittle' (106). Death is the only law and what counts is feeling life asserted against the risk of being at the very edge of existence itself, at the point of true West. The challenge is to know and experience that which lies beyond or behind the sun even at the risk of destruction, for that moment makes you almost God-like. As Leslie Fiedler wrote, the voyage West is fraught with danger, 'left-handed, ill omened, sinister . . . A turning away from the direction out of which the sun rises, signifying salvation, to the direction into which it sets, signifying death; a flight compared by implication to the fatal course of Phaeton . . . it is mad, since to enter the West is to try to live in a dream, ie to go insane' (32–3). McCarthy recognizes this paradox of the West as a place that lures with its promise of freedom, inhibition and all the expectations invested in the American dream, only to deliver a kind of madness, a fatal course. Indeed, at one point, Judge Holden is described as 'a lunatic and then not' (127), aligning him with this doubling of the West. McCarthy's *Blood Meridian* is the point at which one reaches the climax of life and simultaneously recognizes the proximity, even the inevitability of its end. The blood is both life-giving and life-destroying, hence the qualification of the novel's title by 'or the evening redness in the west', reminding us of a larger mythic fear about the West as a place where even the sun dies. 'The western hole into which the sun descends is the archetypal womb of death destroying what has been born,' writes Neumann; 'before the earth and human consciousness existed, everything was contained in the realm of the dead in the West . . . thus the West is the place of the world before the world' (184).

McCarthy's West is a space of contradictions which is both womb and death, where 'this world must touch the other' (*Blood Meridian* 130). The geographical frontier is the feint line between the two, a line crossed and recrossed by the characters in the novel who struggle in a 'terra damnata' (61) and 'purgatorial waste' (63) full of 'itinerant degenerates bleeding westward like some heliotropic plague' (78). McCarthy strips the urge West of Turner's mythic glamour and equates it with a baser human need 'both imperative and remote' (152) which pushes men to a terrible confrontation with their mortality. He ironically calls the would-be pioneers 'argonauts,' but the quest for the golden fleece has become a hunt for scalps in a brutal economics of death where a scalp is a 'receipt' (98) and 'the trail of the argonauts terminated in ashes' (153).

Manifest Destiny has been reinterpreted as a surreal compulsion, a test of survival, that invokes Turner's concept of the heroic pioneer in Judge Holden, whose will to succeed through all the trials of the desert resembles Eric Mottram's definition of the true Western man who 'lives close to death and maiming in that region of pornographic thrill at the body's vulnerability to breakage and extinction. The villain and hero edge into each other at the point where stoicism and endurance demonstrate how a man can take it, live beyond the worst, and anticipate the inevitable by mocking its approach' (Mottram 19). Judge Holden is the hero-villain who straddles the border between life and death filling the void of the desert with his huge form, at turns mad and magical, murderous and maternal. He hovers beyond the worst, mocking and denying the presence of death like a desert Ahab chasing life-in-death embodying the terrifying, but often ignored, contradictions of the West. In 'reading' the judge, we can see the multifaceted nature of the West, for he is like Melville's Ahab, 'a man of elements not of sins' who would say 'I own thy speechless, placeless power, but to the last gasp of my earthquake life will dispute its unconditional, unintegral mastery in me. I am darkness leaping out of life' (*Moby Dick* 616). Both men are extreme versions of Turner's frontier character traits, exhibiting 'That coarseness and strength . . . that practical turn of mind . . . that masterful grip of material things . . . that restless, nervous energy; that dominant individualism, working for good and evil, and with all that buoyancy and exuberance which comes with freedom – these are the traits of the Frontier' (Turner, 'The Significance of the Frontier' 8).

In extremis, these become not the traits of decent, democratic society – as Turner had claimed – but the trappings of imperialist conquest and individual greed through which McCarthy creates his vision of an archetypal West(ern) man in Judge Holden; part Faust, Ahab, Lear and Macbeth whose 'predacious' (*Blood Meridian* 146) nature acts out a dark version of American history. Turner himself recognized this duality, writing of the frontier as 'anti-social,' with an 'antipathy to control' which could encourage 'selfishness' by 'pressing individual liberty beyond its proper bounds,' and yet for him individualism of this kind is essential to the development of democracy ('The Significance of the Frontier' 17–18). For McCarthy, the judge embodies this dualism: he is Satanic and Godly, equipped to exist in the land 'whose true geology was not of stone but fear' (*Blood Meridian* 47). In the demon kingdom of McCarthy's West, the judge is a suzerain of the new golden land transformed by predation and commerce into a 'shoreless void' (50) where survival is about control, mastery and conquest, and where the promised land of the West has become 'like some ignis fatuus [that] . . . may also post men to fraudulent destinies' (120). Turner's guarded warnings of 'manifest evils' ('The Significance of the Frontier' 18) are played out to their full in McCarthy's West where the only equality is in death and the only democracy is 'optical' (see *Blood Meridian* 146, 227, 284, 247). In a world outside of the myth of Eden, there is not even the comfort of religion, only the stark presence of 'a dead Christ . . . broken in the chancel floor' (60). Yet amid this the judge, resembling D. H. Lawrence's 'essential American soul' at its most extreme – 'hard, isolate, stoic and a killer . . . who lives by death, by killing' (68–9) – is obsessed by a desire to control his own fate. At the beginning of the novel McCarthy spells out the quandary: 'whether the stuff of creation may be shaped to man's will or whether his own heart is not another kind of clay' (5). The judge's journey, if it means anything, is his extreme resistance to passivity, powerlessness and being shaped by others. His desire is to define the terms of his own existence, author himself because there is, ultimately, no Manifest Destiny, no God-given right to the West in McCarthy's work, but rather a terrible struggle of individuals to try and impose their own destiny upon the world.

Just as Turner inscribed his version of history so too does the judge, who keeps a notebook in which he rewrites his interpretation of what was (past) into what could be and thereby wrests control of the past by authoring it. As readers we witness his ruthless efforts to alter the past as a parallel to the means by which the West has been written into history as mythology. The judge says, 'men's memories are uncertain and the past that was differs little from the past that was not' (330). He is unprepared to accept the limits of life in any way, believing that 'a man seeks his own destiny and no other' (330) and although he knows that 'the truth about the world' (245) is that it is framed by the certainty of death, he seeks a 'largeness of heart' (330) despite the 'ultimate destination' of life, which is 'calamitous and beyond reckoning' (245). The judge asserts that 'each man's destiny is as large as the world he inhabits' (330), and it is man's job to create that world, not expect it to emerge divinely. In this respect, as in so many, the judge is the logical hero of Turner's thesis of development, defying all in his determination to succeed in crossing frontiers and to forestall death's 'reckoning.' Judge Holden seeks to control and erase time, both the past in the fossilized rocks he destroys (173), and the future through his acts of infanticide. Thus his heroic struggle to achieve 'mastery and activity' over his own fate is bound up with his brutal denial of others' rights. It is a personal imperialism, like Ahab (as described by Edward Said): 'obsessed, compelling, unstoppable, completely wrapped up in his own rhetorical justification and cosmic symbolism' (*Culture and Imperialism* 349).

Such is the judge's way, consuming those around him and drawing out their strength as he plunders the world for knowledge. He devours the earth because in the minerals 'he purported to read news of the earth's origins' as if they were God's words, for God 'speaks in stones and trees, the bones of things' (116). The land becomes the judge's stage and a reminder of his quest for immortality. His lust for knowledge justifies his violence towards the earth and people, as he literally hacks his way to the 'bones of things' in order to know them. In the spirit of the imperialist collector, the judge craves knowledge as he does power. By reducing life to its constituents, its bones, he can 'read' it, engulf it and ultimately control it. The judge's complex assault on time and destiny, involves a challenge to the past, represented by the dead fathers of history – the ancient Anasazi Indians – whose historical mark is scratched into the land. The judge must remove their record and replace it with his own narrative ledger, just as he would challenge the will of God to write his words in 'the bones of things.' Dead fathers occur throughout the novel, representing the past and the process of time which must be usurped by the judge: 'For it is the death of the father to which the son is entitled and to which he is heir, more so than his goods' (145). Thus he challenges the law of the Father by claiming authority for himself.

Yet the judge also inverts this dictum with his vampirical destruction of children, and his infanticides abound in the novel. He literally enacts the myth of the West which Slotkin calls 'regeneration through violence' whilst parodying Turner's sense of the frontier as the space of 'perennial rebirth' ('The Significance of the Frontier' 3). As McCarthy's version of the essential American soul, Judge Holden feeds upon the lives of the young in a gruesome ritual of renewal that appears to defeat time and keep the judge at once 'child-like' (6), 'like an enormous infant' (335) and powerful. He has stepped outside time by being both father and son, and killing both to steal their power and prolong himself. At the end of the novel the judge says he will never die (335), believing he has taken charge of the world and is therefore able to dictate the terms of his own fate. This Faustian urge represents a totalitarian wish for omnipotence and to permanently recapture a lost moment of perfection and power. The judge seeks a pre-Oedipal harmony beyond time, and his violent erasure of time and human life is an ironic and contradictory desire for a mythic American innocence. The judge wants to be both child-like and 'suzerain of the earth' (199), son and father, God and Satan and able to declare, 'in order for it to be mine nothing must be permitted to occur upon [earth] save by my dispensation' (199). He is America in extremis, challenging the Gods, nature, time itself on a blasted heath, now a desert, 'like some egregious saltland bard' (219) or, like Lear, 'some scurrilous king stripped of his vestiture and driven together with his fool into the wilderness to die' (282). As the judge says to the kid, his challenging 'son' and shadow throughout the novel:

> We are not speaking in mysteries. You of all men are no stranger to that feeling, the emptiness and the despair. It is that which we take arms against, is it not? Is not blood the tempering agent in the mortar which bonds? (329)

This special bond that the judge feels for the kid is important. As a shadow the kid reminds the judge of himself, the rebel-son, born to violence and sent out to wander the West. But the kid also represents time, being born in 1833 with the Leonid meteors[1] and being continually related to the movement of stars in the novel as if 'tethered to the polestar' (46). As a son without a father he presents a challenge to his substitute father, the judge, who has taught him so much on their journey through the West. The kid has 'all history present in [his] visage, the child the father of the man' (3), but he cannot kill the judge when the opportunity arises (299) and so allows Holden to usurp time again.

Both the kid and the judge know about the darkness that awaits them 'beyond reckoning,' but it is only one of them who has the courage to seek it out and face it. Their lives are like the stars that lead them through the desert: 'He [kid] stood in the yard. Stars were falling across the sky myriad and random, speeding along brief vectors from their origins in night to their destinies in dust and nothingness' (333). But, as we have seen, the judge refuses to pass into dust and nothingness and will kill the kid in order to further deny the powers of time. At the end the kid says to the judge, 'You ain't nothin,' and Holden replies,' You speak truer than you know' (331). To be more than nothing is exactly the judge's aim. He wishes to be empowered by dominance and authority in all its forms so that he feels there is 'only room for one – one desire, one will, one power, one "imperial self"' (Bleikaster 142), whereas 'All others are destined for a night that is eternal and without name. One by one they will step down into the darkness before the footlamps' (*Blood Meridian* 331). He wants to remain the one and delay his move into the darkness. To become that one means to have 'been to the floor of the pit and seen horror . . . and learned . . . that it speaks to his inmost heart' (331). This is Turner's dominant individualism at its most extreme, wherein the survival of the fittest is uppermost and any moral law is irrelevant since, as the judge notes, 'moral law is an invention of mankind for the disenfranchisement of the powerful in favour of the weak' (250). The West permits these traits to flourish because, like war, it reduces life to its basics. The judge says war is God because it sanctions no mystery, no ambiguity and validates a man's worth in the simple battle of life against death. The cost of such self-validation is immense and bloody, as McCarthy's novel shows, and the judge's actions suggest the true brutality behind the myths of American regeneration in the West.

When Frederick Jackson Turner wrote 'The Problem of the West' he believed that 'the individual has been given an open field, unchecked by restraints of an old social order, or of scientific administration of government [and] the self-made man was the Western man's ideal' (*The Frontier in American History* 213). The judge literally acts out the ideologies of the frontier. The American dream of escape from time and the past is central to his desire for total power and control, and the unrestraint of the West justifies his authoritarian relations with people and nature. Even Turner recognized the potential for such behavior, but he characteristically chose to ignore the implications in his writing. 'What the Mediterranean Sea was to the Greeks, breaking the bond of custom, offering new experiences... the ever retreating frontier has been to the United States' (38). This is exactly where *Blood Meridian* goes, taking the myths to their natural conclusion, 'to the west... toward the evening lands and the distant pandemonium of the sun' (185). McCarthy sees that the pursuit of the American dream in the West contains within itself the horrific inevitability of its own failure. Just as life is eternally reaching upwards but constantly shadowed by death, and just as the stars, however bright, are condemned to dust and nothingness, so too is man 'to bloom and to flower and die... His meridian is at once his darkening and the evening of his day' (146–7). A similar vision is described by the Dueña Alfonsa in *All the Pretty Horses*: 'For me the world has always been more of a puppet show. But when one looks behind the curtain and traces the strings upward he finds they terminate in the hands of yet other puppets, themselves with their own strings which trace upward in turn, and so on' (231). The West is part of the puppet show of power, an unattainable dream that cannot be possessed, only edged towards in a movement which is ruthless and violent and driven by a kind of madness to succeed which pushes aside all moral law.

The Western lands, as William Burroughs has written, are always ahead of you. 'All the filth and horror, fear, hate, disease and death of human history flows between you and the Western Lands' (257). The push West can only ever be a movement towards death. There is no great design or Manifest Destiny, and there can be no total, national history or metanarrative but just the individual struggles of people against the starkness of life and the inevitability of death. The vision of the judge dancing naked on the stage at the end of *Blood Meridian* is a terrifying image of a man regenerated through the violence of death and possession. His authority is unmatched and his power unstoppable. This is, however, McCarthy's ambiguous hero in whom there is a prophetic play of antitheses. He rages against totalizing authorities like the Church, Government, and History, only to replace them with his own regime of power and control. Having just killed the kid, the judge assumes the description of the kid that opens the novel: 'All history present in that visage, the child the father of the man' (3). In this surreal mixture McCarthy provides a dark signification of the complex histories of the West, a vision that, ultimately, might come closest to McCarthy's vision of America itself and substantiate Turner's sense of 'liberty beyond its proper bounds' ('The Significance of the Frontier' 18).

Note

An earlier version of this chapter appeared in *Critique* (Fall 1997). I acknowledge the permission of Critique and Heldref Publications for allowing me to reprint it here.

1 In 1833 the Leonid meteors fell on America giving rise to the song 'Stars Fell on Alabama'. The events tie the novel to a specific starting point in historical time, around November 12, making the kid a Scorpio, ruled by the planet Mars, a violent planet (see Sepich, *Notes on Blood Meridian*).

Mark Busby

Into the darkening land, the world to come: Cormac McCarthy's border crossings

Cormac McCarthy's Southwestern novels are tied together by the repetition of the powerful metaphor of border crossings. In the three novels of the Border Trilogy – *All the Pretty Horses*, *The Crossing*, and *Cities of the Plain* – McCarthy uses the border as a metaphor for a complex and oxymoronic melding of nihilism and optimism, good and evil, illusion and reality, and several similar contrasts. He also employs similar structural patterns to examine the complex intertwining of positive and negative forces to present ultimately a worldview that suggests a nihilistic optimism. While all three novels dramatize a dialectic struggle between hope and despair, each has a different perspective and emphasis, moving from *All the Pretty Horses*' stress on human responsibility to *The Crossing*'s focus on responsibility to nature, whereupon the third novel, *Cities of the Plain*, combines the styles, themes, and characters of the first two novels.[1] In *The Crossing* McCarthy particularly stresses storytelling's power to provide synthesis, but the entire trilogy demonstrates the power of stories.

McCarthy therefore draws from a powerful tradition – from Dostoyevsky, to Melville, to Twain, to Crane, to Faulkner and southern literature, to American Westerns – for his powerful works that at the center are about ontology and epistemology – being and knowing. He uses the border metaphor to create a complicated way of knowing the world that is not simply black or white, good or evil, life or death, but is an oxymoronic melding, an ongoing dialectic between the forces of death and life, end and beginning, and other apparent dualities. Metaphors of play acting and dream are seemingly opposed by the 'real' of trees, rocks, rivers and emphasize the liminal state of humankind, the border living in a world of between: the Dueña Alfonsa tells John Grady Cole: 'the world is quite ruthless in selecting between the dream and the reality, even where we will not. Between the wish and the thing the world lies waiting' (*All the Pretty Horses* 238). And yet at the center is paradox. As the judge in *Blood Meridian* asserts, 'Your heart's desire is to be told some mystery. The mystery is that there is no mystery' (252).

McCarthy's world yields violence, struggle, and despair; but there are also powerful moments that enhance living: John Grady Cole riding on a flatbed truck with *campesinos* as he escapes his hellish experience in prison, understanding that 'after and for a long time to come he'd have reason to evoke the recollection of those smiles and to reflect upon the good will which provoked them for it had power to protect and to confer honor and to strengthen resolve and it had power to heal men and to bring them to safety long after all other resources were exhausted' (219); Billy Parham attempting to take the wolf home, a gypsy treating a stabbed horse in *The Crossing*, moments of intense friendship as between John Grady Cole and Rawlins in *Horses* or between John Grady and Billy Parham in *Cities of the Plain*. These are the moments that mesh with the violence, sadness and despair and that are part of the fabric of life.

McCarthy's genius is that he melds the most significant concerns of southern literature, the dominant American fiction of the first half of the century, with Western fiction with its roots deep in the traditional frontier myth and its emphasis on the border between the east/west frontier. McCarthy then swivels north/south and uses several of the major elements of the east/west frontier myth in a new way – creating a Southwestern fiction that synthesizes these concerns.

As Lewis Simpson makes clear in *Dispossessed Garden*, the twentieth-century southern literary consciousness has struggled with two opposing forces, the force of memory and history – the presentness of the past in southern life – and the historyless post-World War II alienated self. The first force necessarily concentrates on the redemptive (or corrosive) power of memory to merge (or subsume) the individual into the communal force of time. The South is a region of memory, forever wedded to the tragic history of slavery, where, as Faulkner said, the past is not passed. The second alienated consciousness focuses on the power of the individual to wrest the future from time and to forge its own future. This individualistic emphasis is also the traditional land of the Western writer who draws from frontier mythology.

In his survey of 'Southern Fiction' in *The Harvard Guide to Contemporary American Writing*, Simpson elaborated on his analysis of southern literature in *Dispossessed Garden*, and drawing from Allen Tate's 'The Profession of Letters in the South' as his source, Simpson mentioned the metaphor McCarthy turned to for his title in the second novel of the Border Trilogy:

> Bringing into focus the history, and the historical aftermath, of a slave society at once novel and anachronistic – a society which had attempted at the same time to become a modern nation-state and a replication of a patriarchical community, a major supplier of raw materials to the world industrial machine and a pastoral retreat from it – southern novelists of the 1920s and 1930s realized the possibilities of the South as a representation of the crossing of the ways. They created in the southern novel a compelling drama of self and history. (155)

Perhaps McCarthy realized that as long as he wrote about the South, he would seem a pale reflection of Faulkner. As Flannery O'Connor once said about Faulkner's overpowering image in southern literature, 'Nobody wants his mule and wagon stalled on the same track the Dixie Limited is roaring down.' So when

McCarthy left the South for Texas in 1976, he switched to the Tex-Mex Express and turned to another territory with a fertile history of crossing[2] and one with a rich frontier history.

Traditional American frontier mythology refers to a cluster of images, values, and archetypes that grew out of the confrontation between the uncivilized and the civilized world, what Frederick Jackson Turner called the 'meeting point between savagery and civilization.' Civilization is associated with the East, with the past and Europe, with society – its institutions, laws, its demands for compromise and restriction, its cultural refinement and emphasis on manners, its industrial development, and its class distinctions. The wilderness that civilization confronts offers the possibility of individual freedom, where single individuals can test themselves against nature without the demands for social responsibility and compromise inherent in being part of a community.

McCarthy draws from these frontier dichotomies, particularly the emphasis on the Southwest as a land of freedom and opportunity, where individuals can demonstrate those values that the Southwestern Anglo myth reveres – courage, determination, ingenuity, loyalty, and others. But Southwestern frontier history and geography produce deep feelings of ambivalence. On one hand, the vastness of its area seems to negate borders; on the other, the region's location on the edge of Southern and Western culture and along the long Rio Grande border with Mexico reinforces an awareness of borders. As Tom Pilkington pointed out in *My Blood's Country*, the Southwest is a land of borders: 'Men have always been fascinated by rims and borders, ends and beginnings, areas of transition where the known and the unknown merge. In the Southwest one feels something of this fascination, because one of the central, never-changing facts about the region, I believe, is that it is a borderland' (3).

The border, therefore, represents a line between such opposing forces as civilization/wilderness, individual/community, fate/free will, past/present, aggression/passivity, and numerous others central to the Southwestern legend. This awareness of borders grows in intensity in the contemporary Southwest as the schism between old and new tears more strongly at the human heart. Increasingly, contemporary Southwestern writers such as McCarthy examine the sharp division between the frontier myth that lives inside and the diminished outside natural world fraught with complexity, suffering, and violence but leavened with humor, compassion, and love. What McCarthy adds to the older frontier formula is his use of 'la frontera,' the North/South border between the American Southwest and Northern Mexico, as the boundary line between warring forces.

As Alan Riding makes clear in his important book *Distant Neighbors* (published in 1984 when McCarthy was writing his first novel to use Mexico), the country provides the perfect setting for books that use complex and troubling opposition as a basic part of their structure:

> Probably nowhere in the world do two countries as different as Mexico and the United States live side by side. As one crosses the border into Mexico from, say El

Paso [McCarthy's home], the contrast is shocking – from wealth to poverty, from organization to improvisation, from artificial flavoring to pungent spices. But the physical differences are least important. Probably nowhere in the world do two neighbors understand each other so little. More than by levels of development, the two countries are separated by language, religion, race, philosophy and history. The United States is a nation barely two hundred years old and is lunging for the twenty-first century. Mexico is several thousand years old and is still held back by its past. (ix)

If the American frontier hero pushes west into a historyless land, then when that figure turns south and crosses the border, he encounters a land with a strong and troubling past, for Mexico represents a country with a lengthy and distressing history, part of which involves a complicated story of dispossession of land first from the Aztecs and Mayans, then from the remaining *Indios*, and later from the church. Aztec history may have been especially important to draw McCarthy to Mexico because of the Aztecs' violent emphasis on human sacrifice, on the importance of blood in Aztec ritual sacrifices, and on the Aztec belief in the repetition of history. Believing that the sun needed blood to be reborn every morning, the Aztecs performed human sacrifices that allowed the victim's blood to seep into the earth to satisfy the sun. This history connects with and highlights the violence in McCarthy's border novels and may account for the repeated blood imagery and expressions such as 'the bloodred sun.' Human sacrifice returns forcefully in the epilogue of *Cities of the Plain* as the deathlike traveler tells Billy Parham a dream about a rock with 'the stains of blood from those who'd been slaughtered upon it to appease the gods' (270).

Aztec mythology may have provided other images and ideas. The canine imagery may have been suggested by the Aztec deity Xolotl, who was usually pictured with a human body, clawed hands and feet, and a large canine head. He combined the human and the wild and was pictured with both human and animal sets of ears. Another story that relates to McCarthy's novel concerns how Xolotl was charged by the gods to journey to the underworld to retrieve the bones from an earlier race of humans to use to begin a new one. On his way back, Xolotl dropped and fragmented the bones into many pieces. The gods then sprinkled the fragments with their blood to produce first a male then a female child. Billy Parham, of course, journeys south to retrieve the bones of his brother Boyd, whose twin sister supposedly died when Boyd was young. McCarthy is known for his wide and varied reading. Perhaps these aspects of Aztec myth helped suggest some of the canine (dog, wolf), journey, bone, twin imagery in a book that uses contrasts and Mexican history.

Another possible result of Aztec history concerns Mexico's emphasis on repetition. The Aztecs adapted a complicated Mayan calendar based on a fifty-two-year cycle, and the belief in the returning god Quetzalcoatl led them to accept Cortes as the reappearing god. As a result Mexican time is circular, quite in contrast with Anglo-European linear concepts of time. Riding explains:

> For Mexicans, neither birth nor death is seen to interrupt the continuity of life and neither is considered overly important. In songs, paintings and popular art, death is even mocked. On the Day of the Dead each November, Mexicans crowd the country's cemeteries, carrying flowers and even food and drink to the graves of their ancestors, much as the Aztecs did. Belief in communion with the dead is widespread, not in a psychic or spiritualist sense or as a function of a Christian faith in the afterlife, but simply as an outgrowth of the knowledge that the past is not dead. (7)

Just as the Civil War in the southern American writer's most important historical touchstone, the single historical event that reverberates throughout Mexican history and in McCarthy's border novels is the Mexican revolution, which began in 1910 when Francisco Indalecio Madero, then thirty-seven, led opposition to President Porfirio Díaz who had controlled the country since 1876 and had allowed white landowners to seize the lands of its six million Indians and eight million mestizos. Through the revolution the exploited peons wanted to retake the large land holdings and distribute farmland among the *campesinos*. Madero, in fact, becomes a character in *All the Pretty Horses*, as the Dueña Alfonsa recalls her attraction to Gustavo Madero.

McCarthy, therefore, combines Southern, Southwestern, and Mexican history into a rich fiction that uses older American elements such as the story of the young boy's initiation as the basis. Each McCarthy novel takes a representative young boy's initiatory experience through a border crossing and turns the experience upside down so that the expected initiation is thwarted and seemingly denied. But ironically, it is through the denied experience that a young man is initiated into a more profound understanding than the expected initiation could have offered. Each novel focuses on a complex series of opposing forces, but each novel provides a different emphasis. While all three deal with reality/illusion, individual/community, linearity/circularity, home/not home, dispossession/possession, life/death, and father/son, *All the Pretty Horses* highlights the opposing forces of fate/free will, cowardice/courage, restriction/freedom, class/classlessness, time/timelessness, reason/imagination, order/chaos, master/slave, home/not home, and justice/injustice. *The Crossing* focuses more on wild/tame, reality/illusion, good/evil, kindness/malice, restriction/freedom, change/stability, time/timelessness, god/godlessness. Although the Trilogy suggests that the world is an amalgam of forces, all three novels in different ways suggest that the resulting mixture – the world – is mediated by the power of storytelling to bring order to the chaos of forces in the world. The final novel in the Trilogy also emphasizes valuing the natural world.

All the Pretty Horses

McCarthy's sixth novel won the 1992 National Book Award and the 1992 National Book Critics Circle Award for fiction. Like his fifth novel, *Blood Meridian*, *All the Pretty Horses* uses the history, geography, and landscape of the Southwest and the border as setting for the story, which leads to a profound examination of a series of oppositions, particularly the theme of the individual and the community and the theme of the opposition of illusion and reality sounded in the novel's opening paragraph. Repeated images of illusion occur as John Grady Cole walks in to view his grandfather's dead body and sees reflections in the pierglass, portraits on the wall, and a wax imprint of his thumb:

> The candleflame and the image of the candleflame caught in the pierglass twisted and righted when he entered the hall and again when he shut the door. He took off his hat and came slowly forward. The floorboards creaked under his boots. In his black suit he stood in the dark glass where the lilies leaned so palely from their waisted cut-glass vase. Along the cold hallway behind him hung the portraits of forebears only dimly known to him all framed in glass and dimly lit above the narrow wainscotting. He looked down at the guttered candlestub. He pressed his thumbprint in the warm wax pooled on the oak veneer. (3)

As he looks at the lifeless body of his grandfather, he considers the finality of death – an unambiguous reality that will continue to impinge upon his consciousness throughout the novel, as the life/death opposition returns though the deaths of Jimmy Blevins, the cuchillero whom John Grady kills in self-defense in the prisión Castelar, John Grady's father, and then the last death, the death of Abuela, John Grady's substitute mother, at the novel's close.

The grandfather's death sets in motion another important opposition for possession/dispossession recurs throughout the novel, from the beginning section's emphasis on how the grandfather's death signals John Grady's dispossession and loss of land. As Gail Moore Morrison in '*All the Pretty Horses*: John Grady Cole's Expulsion from Paradise' makes clear, the grandfather's death

> portends the loss of the family ranch. And, although [John Grady] is technically a boy, only sixteen, he recognizes that he is 'like a man come to the end of something' (5). The last of his grandfather's line with its generations-deep commitment to the land, he is certainly as powerless to protect it against foreign encroachment – twentieth century technology and the oil interests to which his often absent actress mother sells it – as was the Comanche nation he envisions as he rides out along their ancient war trail under a 'bloodred and elliptic' sun 'under the reefs of bloodred cloud' after his grandfather's funeral, 'with the sun coppering his face and the red wind blowing out of the west.' He hears 'the low chant of their traveling song which the riders sang as they rode, nation and ghost of nation passing in a soft chorale across that mineral waste to darkness bearing lost to all history and all remembrance like a grail the sum of their secular and transitory and violent lives' (5). The comparison to the defeated and eradicated Comanche is made explicit by John Grady's divorced, dying father during their last horseback ride together. (176)

Connections with the past become even stronger once John Grady crosses into Mexico with its lengthy and troubling history as I have said, part of which involves a complicated story of dispossession of land first from the Aztecs and Mayans, then from the remaining *Indios* and the church. The character most fully representing the past is the Dueña Alfonsa, the grandaunt of Alejandra, the daughter of the hacendado for whom John Grady goes to work in Mexico: 'The Dueña Alfonsa was both grandaunt and godmother to the girl and her life at the hacienda invested it with oldworld ties and with antiquity and tradition' (132). It is she who invests human scars with an existential reality connected to the power of the past: 'Scars have the strange power to remind us that our past is real. The events that cause them can never be forgotten, can they?' (135).

The power of forces outside the individual's control becomes one of the most important aspects of Mexico and suggests to Tom Pilkington that the novel's major focus is on the contrast between free will and fate:

> Which is the dominant agent – free will or fate? Perhaps there is no either-or answer. In her final – rather improbable – conversation with John Grady, Alfonsa argues for a kind of modified predestination. The conditions of the physical universe impose certain conditions on the individual, including total unpredictability. But life is a shimmering web, and every time a strand is struck by the assertion of will, the web vibrates with consequences for all. Actually Alfonsa uses the metaphor of puppets. If one looks behind the curtain at the puppet show, she says one finds puppets who control puppets who control puppets and on to infinity. There is, in other words, a vast interconnectedness of things, so that clear causal relationships are impossible to isolate. (*State of Mind* 133)

As Pilkington makes clear, when John Grady and Rawlins ride into Mexico they reenact a clearly recognizable Western story: 'A wandering cowboy and his sidekick ride innocently into hostile territory. There ensue fights against insurmountable odds, the hero's romance with a lovely young senorita, chases on horseback through a harsh but beautiful landscape' (133). And John Grady is the distinctly recognizable American: 'He believes in individualism, free will, volition. He thinks that every man born on this planet is an Adam, free of memory and external constraint, able to shape his illimitable "self" in any way he chooses. He is shocked when Alejandra refuses to break all ties to go with him.'

Two other important elements from the Western American literary tradition are the captivity narrative and the youthful Adam who becomes a messianic figure following an initiation. John Grady's initiation through captivity and imprisonment recalls numerous other American heroes from Mary Rowlandson through James Fenimore Cooper's Natty Bumppo and captured females to Ralph Ellison's Invisible Man to Joseph Heller's Yossarian. After or during initiation many of these archetypal youthful heroes become Christlike figures, either messianic like Faulkner's Ike McCaslin, Ellison's nameless narrator, and Yossarian or martyred like Joe Christmas, Stephen Crane's Jim Conklin, or Steinbeck's Jim Casy. These last three figures' initials signal their symbolic status, and it is interesting to point out John Grady Cole's initials put him in their company. These Christlike figures in American literature, along with others such as Melville's Billy Budd and Ken Kesey's Randall Patrick McMurphy, introduce the theme of communal responsibility.

Certainly, John Grady's ultimate recognition of the limitation of self is one important aspect of the novel. Indeed the sharp contrast between the individual and community, between concern for self and concern for the other, is another one of the central conflicts. Faced with his grandfather's death, rejected by his girlfriend and his mother, supported weakly by an ineffectual father, John Grady replaces his broken family community with the comradeship of Lacey Rawlins, and this small community is broadened by chance when the irrepressible Jimmy Blevins joins them. Blevins forces John Grady to consider his responsibility for another, much to the pragmatic Rawlins' dismay. John Grady is initially led to these concerns when Blevins (pointing to another contrast – rationality/irrationality) crazily shucks his gun, horse, boots, and clothes out of his fear that he is fated to be struck by lightning ('I'm double bred for death by fire', 68). John Grady tells Rawlins: 'I dont believe I can leave him out there afoot' (71).

John Grady strong feelings of responsibility for Blevins continue and expand after Blevins is executed in the woods by the captain. Haunted by his failure to act and only vaguely understanding his motives, John Grady makes a choice to pursue the captain in language that recalls probably the most famous moral decision in American literature, Huck Finn's famous conclusion, 'All right then, I'll go to hell', when he decides not to return Jim to slavery. Rejected by Alejandra, John Grady rides aimlessly until he reaches a crossroads. Sitting on his horse, he reads road signs and seeing the arrow to La Encantada, he 'looked toward the darkness in west. The hell with it, he said. I aint leavin my horse down there' (257). Unlike Huck's clear decision, John Grady's is murky and unformed, and he only vaguely understands why he sets off to repossess his horse from the captain.

Later he feels compelled to tell his story to the judge, saying 'The reason I wanted to kill him was because I stood there and let him walk that boy out in the trees and shoot him and I never said nothin' (293). But in McCarthy's world good and evil are often intertwined, and John Grady must seek out the judge after the hearing to tell him, 'I guess what I wanted to say first of all was that it kindly bothered me in the court what you said. It was like I was in the right about everthing and I dont feel that way.' Instead, he says, 'I dont feel justified' (290). Ultimately, then, John Grady Cole's border crossing has taken him into a world of complexity, ambiguity, and ambivalence – a mixture of good and evil, rationality and irrationality, fate and free will in a mestizo culture that is itself an amalgam. Nowhere is the complex mixture more apparent than in John Grady's dealings with the Dueña Alfonsa, whose statements and personal history are belied by her actions. Gail Morrison points out the mixture:

> Alfonsa is both a radical and a reactionary. On the one hand she rebels against the suppression of women and paternal authority, refusing marriage and rejecting a conventional marriage for her great-niece. She has espoused the reformist causes of the Maderos, in her seventeen-year-old idealism, although they run counter to the traditional interests of the landed aristocracy of which she and the Maderos are members

and which seems to have managed to preserve its way of life. But she is sent safely out of the line of revolutionary fire to Europe where she is checkmated by being not only unable to rebel against her father but also unable to forgive him for her deportation. Her frustration is reflected in her vision of the world as a 'puppet show' (231). And if she has been in her youth a puppet, so now in her old age she becomes the puppeteer who pulls the strings of her great-niece's life. What is left her is to live vicariously through Alejandra, who 'is the only future' (239) she contemplates, whose name echoes her own. Without scruple, she bends the girl to her will and changes her destiny by taking advantage of the opportunity to save John Grady's life. (188–9)

Ironically, it is Alfonsa, the former idealist, who most fully challenges John Grady's idealism, telling him: 'In the end we all come to be cured of our sentiments. Those whom life does not cure death will. The world is quite ruthless in selecting between the dream and the reality, even where we will not. Between the wish and the thing the world lies waiting' (238).

For John Grady, the idealistic dream is represented by the world of horses, an ideal world of peace achieved in dreams:

> That night he dreamt of horses... and in the dream he was among the horses running and in the dream he himself could run with the horses... and they ran he and the horses out along the high mesas where the ground resounded under their running hooves and they flowed and changed and ran and their manes and tails blew off of them like spume and there was nothing else at all in that high world and they moved all of them in a resonance that was like a music among them and they were none of them afraid horse nor colt nor mare and they ran in that resonance which is the world itself and which cannot be spoken but only praised. (161–2)

After the experiences in prison and with Alejandra and Alfonsa, John Grady still dreams of horses, but the early dream's idealism is tempered by the disorder, death, and sadness now part of John Grady's knowledge:

> In his sleep he could hear the horses stepping among the rocks and he could hear them drink from the shallow pools in the dark where the rocks lay smooth and rectilinear as the stones of ancient ruins and the water from their muzzles dripped and rang like water dripping in a well and in his sleep he dreamt of horses and the horses in his dream moved gravely among the tilted stones like horses come upon an antique site where some ordering of the world had failed and if anything had been written on the stones the weathers had taken it away again and the horses were wary and moved with great circumspection carrying in their blood as they did the recollection of this and other places where horses once had been and would be again. Finally what he saw in his dream was that the order in the horse's heart was more durable for it was written in a place where no rain could erase it. (280)

Although John Grady's idealism is challenged and he now understands the sadness in the world,

> He remembered Alejandra and the sadness he'd first seen in the slope of her shoulders which he'd presumed to understand and of which he knew nothing and he felt

a loneliness he'd not known since he was a child and he felt wholly alien to the world although he loved it still. He thought that in the beauty of the world were hid a secret. He thought the world's heart beat at some terrible cost and that the world's pain and its beauty moved in a relationship of diverging equity and that in this headlong deficit the blood of multitudes might ultimately be exacted for the vision of a single flower. (282)

This mixture of sadness and beauty is now part of John Grady's more intricate understanding of the world of responsibility to both humans and animals. On the way back to Texas he sees a wedding, a celebratory beginning that is tempered by the 'pale rider' as he passes (284). Very shortly after seeing the wedding, traditional ceremonial beginning, he attends the funeral of the woman who had worked for his family for fifty years:

> he said goodbye to her in Spanish and then turned and put on his hat and turned his wet face to the wind and for a moment he held out his hands as if to steady himself or as if to bless the ground there or perhaps as if to slow the world that was rushing away and seemed to care nothing for the old or the young or rich or poor or dark or pale or he or she. Nothing for their struggles, nothing for their names. Nothing for the living or the dead. (301)

When John Grady rides off into the sunset at the end of this novel, it is not the optimistic triumph of the traditional Western. It is instead a complex image of how the 'rider and horse passed on and their long shadows passed in tandem like the shadow of a single being. Passed and paled into the darkening land, the world to come' (302).

The Crossing

Crossing the border, of course, is the central image that connects the three novels of the Border Trilogy. Indeed, in *The Crossing* McCarthy tells the same story he told previously in *All the Pretty Horses*, and in the second novel of the Trilogy, he tells the same story three different times. It is the story of Billy Parham's crossing from his New Mexico home into northern Mexico and his travels around the state of Chihuahua. The first time he takes a she-wolf he had trapped; the second he goes with his younger brother, Boyd, who meets and stays with an enigmatic Mexican girl; and the third time Billy returns in search of Boyd.

As Charles Bailey notes, these crossings are presented in a carefully structured novel: 'The novel's three crossings are divided into four artistic parts, each presenting a storyteller, an Ancient Mariner whom Billy serves as wedding guest.' Bailey explains: 'Each narrates a different story, but each has the same message. And the message of the four storytellers (from McCarthy's perspective, the message of all storytellers) is, not incidentally, about time' ('"Doomed Enterprises" and Faith' 58).

As in *All the Pretty Horses* McCarthy continues to explore contrasts such as diverging approaches to time symbolized by the cultures north and south of the border. In *Horses* McCarthy concentrates on more earth-bound concerns, particularly the individual's freedom to counter the demands of class, circumstance, the past, and particularly, human responsibility to others. *The Crossing* shifts the focus from the human to the natural world in the first part and to more metaphysical questions, especially the existence and purpose of God in a violent and inhumane world. Billy Parham's crossings into Mexico and encounters with numerous characters in quest for God recall Mexican dictator Porfirio Díaz's famous statement: 'Poor Mexico, so far from God, so close to the United States.'

As before though, the novel is concerned with the relationship between self and other, beginning initially when Boyd looks into the eyes of the Indian he and Billy discover lurking nearby:

> The indian squatting under a thin stand of carrizo cane and not even hidden and yet Boyd had not seen him. He was holding across his knees an old singleshot 32 rimfire rifle and he had been waiting in the dusk for something to come to water for him to kill. He looked into the eyes of the boy. The boy into his. Eyes so dark they seemed all pupil. Eyes in which the sun was setting. In which the child stood beside the sun. He had not known that you could see yourself in others' eyes nor see therein such things as suns. He stood twinned in those dark wells with hair so pale, so thin and strange, the selfsame child. As if it were some cognate child to him that had been lost who now stood windowed away in another world where the red sun sank eternally. As if it were a maze where these orphans of his heart had miswandered in their journey in life and so arrived at last beyond the wall of that antique gaze from whence there could be no way back forever. (5–6)

In the Indian's eyes, Boyd finds himself twinned and intimations of worlds beyond, worlds of red suns and wandering orphans, in short the world of the novel to follow.

Similarly, when Billy looks into the eyes of the she-wolf he has made it his mission to befriend and care for, he also sees worlds beyond:

> When the flames came up her eyes burned out there like gatelamps to another world. A world burning on the shore of an unknowable void. A world construed out of blood and blood's alcahest and blood in its core and in its integument because it was that nothing save blood had power to resonate against that void which threatened hourly to devour it. He wrapped himself in the blanket and watched her. When those eyes and the nation to which stood witness were gone at last with their dignity back into their origins there would perhaps be other fires and other witnesses and other worlds otherwise beheld. But they would not be this one. (74–5)

The emphasis on the connections between the wild creatures of the world and the innocent, growing youth recalls the night John Grady Cole lies considering the stars, sensing that

> In that false blue dawn the Pleiades seemed to be rising up into the darkness of the world and dragging all the stars away, the great diamond of Orion and Cepella and the signature of Cassiopeia all rising up through the phosphorous dark like a sea-net. He lay a long time listening to the others breathing in their

sleep while he contemplated the wildness about him, the wildness within. (*All the Pretty Horses* 60)

These are the kinds of questions that return throughout *The Crossing*. What is the relationship between the self and the 'other,' particularly the wild and violent other such as the Indian, the wolf, and the numerous violent human beings Billy and Boyd encounter on their border crossings? Often the questions are answered by the many wandering *filósofos* the two meet. Along the roads they travel, Billy and Boyd meet numerous characters – an Indian shaman, old man in the ruined church, a blind revolutionary, a gypsy – men and women who feel compelled to tell their stories to the innocent *güeritos*, the blond Americans whose youth inspires the telling of stories meant to guide them through the violence and suffering, the kindness and comfort in the world.

On the first crossing, after the death of the wolf, Billy is heading north and after stopping among Indians in the mountains, an old man, perhaps a shaman 'dressed in odd and garish fashion,' speaks to him earnestly:

> He told the boy that although he was huerfano still he must cease his wanderings and make for himself some place in the world because to wander in this way would become for him a passion and by this passion he would become estranged from men and so ultimately from himself. He said that the world could only be known as it existed in men's hearts. For while it seemed a place which contained men it was in reality a place contained within them and therefore to know it one must look there and come to know those hearts and to do this one must live with men and not simply pass among them. He said that while the huerfano might feel that he no longer belonged among men he must set this feeling aside for he contained within him a largeness of spirit which men could see and that men would wish to know him and that the world would need him even as he needed the world for they were one. Lastly he said that while this itself was a good thing like all good things it was also a danger. (134)

The old Indian is one of several mentors the wandering Billy meets, each providing similar instructions about understanding a world of seemingly irreconcilable forces, forever separate.[3] Shortly after leaving the old shaman, Billy chances upon an old man living in the ruins of an adobe church destroyed by an earthquake. As happens throughout this novel, the old man tells Billy his story, explaining the terrors and joys of his life and his reasons for his existence, as best as he understands them. He says that he had come because of the devastation from the *terremoto*:

> I was seeking evidence of the hand of God in the world. I had come to believe that hand a wrathful one and I thought that men had not inquired sufficiently into miracles of destruction. Into disasters of a certain magnitude. I thought there might be evidence that had been overlooked. I thought He would not trouble himself to wipe away every handprint. My desire to know was very strong. I thought it might even amuse Him to leave some clue . . . Something unforeseen. Something out of place. Something untrue or out of round. A track in the dirt. A fallen bauble. Not some

cause. I can tell you that. Not some cause. Causes only multiply themselves. They lead to chaos. What I wanted was to know his mind. I could not believe He would destroy his own church without reason. (142)

Ultimately the old man tells Billy that what he had learned was the 'corrido. The tale. And like all corridos it ultimately told one story only, for there is only one to tell.' He continues:

> For this world also which seems to us a thing of stone and flower and blood is not a thing at all but is a tale. And all in it is a tale and each tale the sum of all lesser tales and yet these also are the selfsame tale and contain as well all else within them. So everything is necessary. Every least thing. This is the hard lesson. Nothing can be dispensed with. Nothing despised. Because the seams are hid from us, you see. The joinery. The way in which the world is made. We have no way to know what could be taken away. What omitted. We have no way to tell what might stand and what might fall. And those seams that are hid from us are of course in the tale itself and the tale has no abode or place of being except in the telling only and there it live and makes its home and therefore we can never be done with the telling. Of the telling there is no end. And whether in Caborca or in Huisiachepic or in whatever other place by whatever other name or by no name at all I say again all tales are one. Rightly heard all tales are one. (143)

The old man's belief in the power of storytelling seems the closest statement of McCarthy's own aesthetics in all of his works,[4] a defense of the charges against his tales of violence and blood, of his repetition. The old storyteller suggests why McCarthy headed for new territory when the old man remarks that the difficulty in stories is not creating unity out of diversity but of making 'many of the one' (155), since all stories are the same story. And the old man's emphasis on the power of stories to unify disparate elements suggests the reconciliation or amalgamation of contrasting forces that seems to be at work in these border novels. In fact the story is one of borders and contrasts. He tells of the man he calls 'the old anchorite,' a man doubly damned, having lost his parents and his child in the 1887 earthquake. After wandering the earth, he returns to the church of La Purísma Concepción de Nuestra Señora de Caborca where his parents had died and begins to challenge God and in turn test the beliefs of the local priest (who turns out to be the old storyteller himself). In his attempt to understand God, the old anchorite wants to '[a]ssess boundaries and metes. See that lines were drawn and respected' (151). Ultimately, he decided that God could only be known through those who witness his works and that God could have no witness:

> And he began to see in God a terrible tragedy. That the existence of the Deity lay imperiled for want of this simple thing. That for God there could be no witness. Nothing against which He terminated. Nothing by way of which his being could be announced to Him. Nothing to stand apart from and to say I am this and that is other. Where that is I am not. He could create everthing save that which would say him no. (154)

This conclusion challenges the priest, who 'believed in a boundless God without center or circumference. By this very formlessness he'd sought to make God manageable. This was his colindancia. In his grandness he had ceded all terrain. And in this colindancia God had no say at all' (152–3).

The storyteller's tale is a paradox, for the old anchorite's firm brief against God, even unto his deathbed where he drives the priest away with stones, challenges the priest's faith in a boundless God. His faith shaken by the heretic's unbending opposition to God, the priest becomes a wanderer, searching, and, he suggests, finding God. For his final statement to Billy confirms the paradox of his tale: 'In the end we shall all of us be only what we have made of God' (158), and, of course, the stories about God such as the one he has just told Billy (and by extension the one McCarthy tells his readers).

Billy then returns to the United States to find that he is indeed, as the Indian shaman had told him, an orphan, his parents having been killed while he was gone. With his brother Boyd he then sets out on the second crossing, another possession/dispossession story, as he and Boyd cross determined to regain the family's horses, which they soon find and recover, only to be set upon and Boyd shot. Trying to escape in the night, Billy encounters the third major storyteller, whose tale continues the emphasis on the illusion/reality contrast along with the other contrasts of past/present, dark/light, chaos/order, and evil/good. The past returns through the story of an old revolutionary, violently blinded in his youth when the federales took him prisoner and a German captain with enormous hands named Wirtz bent as if to kiss him and suddenly leaned 'to suck each in turn the man's eyes from his head and spit them out again and leave them dangling by their cords wet and strange and wobbling on his cheeks' (276). This radically evil, grotesque act recalls Flannery O'Connor's statement about extremes:

> The novelist with Christian concerns will find in modern life distortions which are repugnant to him, and his problem will be to make these appear as distortions to an audience which is used to seeing them as natural; and he may well be forced to take ever more violent means to get his vision across to this hostile audience. When you can assume that your audience holds the same beliefs you do, you can relax a little and use more normal means of talking to it; when you have to assume that it does not, then you have to make your vision apparent by shock – to the hard of hearing you shout and for the almost blind you draw large and startling figures.[5] (33–4)

The blind man eventually draws a similar conclusion about the existence of such excessive evil:

> He said that even the sepulturero would understand that every tale was a tale of dark and light and would perhaps not have it otherwise. Yet there was still a further order to the narrative and it was a thing of which men do not speak. He said the wicked know that if the ill they do be of sufficient horror men will not speak against it. That men have just enough stomach for small evils and only these will they oppose. He

said that true evil has power to sober the smalldoer against his own deeds and in the contemplation of that evil he may even find the path of righteousness which has been foreign to his feet and may have no power but to go upon it. Even this man may be appalled at what is revealed to him and seek some order to stand against it. (*The Crossing* 292–3)

The existence of violent evil calls forth the opposite, the desire for forces to oppose it. In his one public interview McCarthy told Woodward:

There's no such thing as life without bloodshed . . . I think the notion that the species can be improved in some way, that everyone could live in harmony, is a really dangerous idea. Those who are afflicted with this notion are the first ones to give up their souls, their freedom. Our desire that it be that way will enslave you and make your life vacuous. (31)

Ultimately, the blindman goes beyond his conclusion about the power of evil and explains to Billy his conclusion about justice in the world when he tells Billy in Spanish:

Lo que debemos entender, said the blind man, es que ultimamente todo es polvo. Todo lo que podemos tocar. Todo lo que podemos ver. En este tenemos las evidencia más profunda de la justicia, de la misericordia. En este vemos la bendición mas grande de Dios. [What we must understand, said the blind man, is that ultimately all is dust. All that we can touch. All that we can see. In this we have the most profound evidence of justice, of mercy. In this we see the greatest blessing of God.] (*The Crossing* 293)

This is another of many statements about the nature of reality – all is dust. But that the world is ultimately dust and to be interpreted by humans – and that is all he can know.[6]

Several critics such as Edwin T. Arnold and Sven Birkirts have pointed out the combination of good and evil in McCarthy. Arnold labels him a 'mystic in the way his favorite writer Melville is a mystic, acknowledging and in fact honoring the majesty of the astounding and awful as well as of the simple and beautiful' ('The Mosaic of McCarthy's Fiction' 23); and Birkirts calls him a Gnostic:

McCarthy has been, from the start, a writer with strong spiritual leanings. His orientation is Gnostic: he seems to view our endeavors here below as a violation of some original purity. But a sensibility so attuned to earthly beauty cannot be oblivious to the higher promptings of the soul. His intuitions are of the most primary sort, never even remotely doctrinaire. In the early books we heed his exacerbated awareness of violence and cruelty, of evil, without finding much place for the good. But now, in these most recent works, we meet up quite often with decency. There are venal killers, yes, but they are outnumbered by the poor who emerge from their dwellings to offer succor. (38)

Indeed as Billy leaves the blindman, a woman rushes up and drops into his hand a small silver heart, saying it is 'Un milagro' (298), a good heath and healing charm for his wounded brother. When he answers that Boyd was not wounded in the heart, she waves him on. Ironically, when Billy returns to the States, discovers that World War II has begun, and tries to enlist, he is rejected because of a 'heart murmur' (339). After wandering, Billy with perhaps his heart aching for a reconnection with his brother, makes his final crossing into Mexico to search for Boyd, only to discover that Boyd has died, fighting against the establishment, and become a hero with corridos sung about his fame.[7]

After Billy decides to dig up Boyd's bones and return them home (in a scene recalling Larry McMurtry's *Lonesome Dove* where Woodrow Call returns Gus McCrea's dead body to Texas for burial), Billy encounters his final major mentor/philosopher, a gypsy hauling the remains of an old airplane. McCarthy's description of the airplane suggests the connection between the plane and Boyd's bones:

> The airplane was little more than a skeleton with sunbleached shreds of linen the color of stewed rhubarb clinging to the steambent ashwood ribs and stays and inside you could see the wires and cables that ran aft to the rudder and elevators and the cracked and curled and sunblacked leather of the seats and in their tarnished nickel bezels the glass of instrument dials glaucous and clouded from the pumicing of the desert sands. (401)

The connection between the plane and Boyd becomes clear when the gypsy tells the plane's story(ies). Like Boyd the plane has a twin, but the most important connection refers to storytelling: 'Con respecto al aeroplano, [the gypsy] said, hay tres historias.' (With respect to the airplane, he said, there are three histories.) (403). He then tells how he and his band had been recruited by a grieving father to recover the plane and return it and how they worked in brutal conditions to bring it home. The truth of this story is challenged later when Billy encounters a horseman from Texas who tells that he had engaged the gypsies to recover the plane. It is the stories that have life, as Billy has learned about Boyd. Although Billy believes he knows the truth about Boyd's life and death, now that Boyd has entered history, his story has a life and truth of its own in the corridos, just as the plane has three histories. Charles Bailey explains:

> There are the 'real' story (the rider's story) and the 'true' story (the gypsy's fiction); and the third story is 'la historia de las historias [the story of the stories]' (411), the 'really true or the truly real' story, 'the one story,' God's story, at which the other two can only hint. For McCarthy, the 'real' story does not matter, for it has no witness; the 'true' story matters, the fiction, the one shaped by the witness/artist; and the 'true' story matters desperately because it implies the 'really true' story, which must always lie beyond human power to know or to tell. ('"Doomed Enterprises" and Faith' 64)

The only human history available, the gypsy says in Spanish, is the telling: 'Es que ultimadamente la verdad no puede quedar en ningun otro lugar sino en el habla [It is ultimately that the truth of it cannot be placed in any other place but in the speaking of it]' (411). He explains:

The past, he said, is always this argument between counterclaimants. Memories dim with age. There is no repository for our images. The loved ones who visit us in dreams are strangers. To even see aright is effort. We seek some witness but the world will not provide one. This is the third history. It is the history that each man makes alone out of what is left to him. Bits of wreckage. Some bones. The words of the dead. How make a world of this? How live in that world once made? (*The Crossing* 410–11)

Not only is the past an argument among counterclaimants, but in McCarthy's world life itself is. Even Billy's encounter with the gypsies suggests the intertwining of good and evil in the world, for they come upon Billy shortly after he was attacked by bandits who spilled Boyd's shrouded bones and stabbed Billy's horse. In another counter act, the gypsies treat the horse's wound and help Billy return where he encounters an old, grotesque dog. In one of McCarthy's most affecting scenes of ambivalence, when Billy sees the 'arthritic and illjoined thing . . . wet and wretched and so scarred and broken that it might have been patched up out of parts of dogs by demented vivisectionists' (423), he first throws rocks and chases it off with a pipe, the dog howling '[a]s if some awful composite of grief had broke through from the preterite world' (424). But when Billy awakens the next day, he calls out for the dog, and when it does not come, he 'bowed his head and held his face in his hands and wept' (426). This powerfully compassionate scene ends the novel, and the last line denies differences as 'the godmade sun' rises 'for all and without distinction.'

As Alex Hunt demonstrates in 'Right and False Suns', when Billy is awakened by a flash of 'white light of desert noon' that is 'no sun . . . and no dawn' (425), he is probably witnessing the Trinity Test that occurred in Alamogordo, New Mexico, July 16, 1945. For both McCarthy and Leslie Silko, who uses the test at the climax of *Ceremony*, the dawning of the atomic age is the ultimate symbol for human alienation from nature. The novel begins with Billy Parham's compulsion to reintegrate with the natural world that the pregnant wolf represents and ends with the nuclear test. In between, the old man's emphasis on stories that connect all things carries much of McCarthy's argument.

All of this is told in high literary style, with lilting Faulknerian prose and memorable descriptions such as this one referring to the eyes of a drunk who challenges Billy in a bar: 'Like lead slag poured into borings to seal away something virulent or predacious' (357). Some readers may find the style heavy-handed, but every page of McCarthy reveals a careful stylist, a writer who refuses to yield to the cliché, and whose language, characters, and plot simultaneously seem as new as afterbirth and as old as dust. *The Crossing*'s language steps constantly across the border as well, merging Spanish and English seamlessly. Throughout *The Crossing*, McCarthy returns to the complex intertwining of good and evil that appeared in the earlier border novel. These repeated stories continue to tell stories of good and evil, reinforcing McCarthy's acute awareness of the inextricable mixture of forces with the border as the overriding metaphor and storytelling as the intermediary.

Cities of the Plain

Cities of the Plain combines many of the varied elements of the first two books in a powerful end of the millennium examination of human responsibility, desire, chance, folly, the changing natural world, and of the ineluctable human desire to make sense of things.

On the surface, the first two books in the Trilogy seem quite similar: both are about youthful Southwestern boys who travel south of the border and undergo initiatory experiences involving horses, cattle, senoritas, and vaqueros. Despite these surface similarities, the two books are quite different. *All the Pretty Horses* is a spare, more traditional story of romance, imprisonment, and revenge, while *The Crossing* is a dense, philosophical, often violent book filled with long stories that seem like parables, particularly the long opening section in which Billy Parham captures a wolf and then tries to return her and free her in Mexico.

For the first half, the concluding novel seems more like *All the Pretty Horses*, even though both John Grady Cole from *Horses* and Billy Parham from *The Crossing* appear, at first in a whorehouse in Juárez, where the older Billy takes John Grady Cole and introduces him to a beautiful sixteen-year-old prostitute significantly named Magdalena. It is three years after the end of *All the Pretty Horses*, the early 1950s, and Billy and John Grady work near El Paso for an aging West Texas/New Mexican rancher named Mac. The first half is filled with a crisp West Texas dialog that is so right in nuance and sound no one would know the writer spent his first forty-five years outside of Texas, much of it in his home state, Tennessee. But when McCarthy moved to El Paso in 1976, he began to listen and to capture the language and dialect so completely that the dialog resounds with authenticity (rendered, like McCarthy's major influence Faulkner, without quotation marks). Here, for example, McCarthy dramatizes a horse auction as John Grady and his boss Mac examine a horse:

> A Fool and his money, said Mac. John Grady what's wrong with that horse?
> Not a thing that I know of.
> I thought you said it was some kind of a mongrel outcross. A Martian horse or somethin.
> Horse might be a little coldblooded . . .
> I got five got five got five got five now, called the auctioneer . . .
> The horse was sold at seven hundred. Wolfenbarger never bid. Oren glanced at Mac.
> Cute sumbuck, aint he? Mac said. (*Cities of the Plain* 169)

McCarthy's stylistic debt to William Faulkner has long been clear, and he echoes the Faulknerian language with the long sentences and heightened vocabulary in much of the last section of the novel, particularly in the epilogue. The stylistic debt in the first part is clearly to Ernest Hemingway with this almost pure Hemingway paragraph with its straightforward description and 'there is/there are' statements:

> Eduardo stood at the rear door smoking one of his thin cigars and looking out at the rain. There was a sheetiron warehouse behind the building and there was nothing much there to see except the rain and the black pools of water standing in the alley where the rain fell and the soft light from the yellow bulb screwed into the fixture over the back door. The air was cool. The smoke drifted in the light. A young girl who limped on a withered leg passed carrying a great armload of soiled linen down the hall. After a while he closed the door and walked back up the hallway to his office. (78)

And Hemingway may have influenced McCarthy's use of the contrasting elements suggested by the title: the plains versus the mountains. As Carlos Baker made clear in his seminal study of *A Farewell to Arms*, Hemingway used the mountains to represent the high, appealing country far from the war below on the plains. Similarly, McCarthy's high country here is the refuge from much of the corruption of the cities of the plain. In the mountain John Grady renovates the Cedar Springs cabin that he hopes will be the wedding grotto to which he can escape. But as in much of McCarthy, the dichotomies are often set up and collapsed. It is in the mountains where the feral dogs are slaughtered and the pups saved.

The realistic often humorous dialog lulls the reader into a seeming light-toned book, another initiatory story with Billy playing the realistic foil to the romantic John Grady as he purses Magdalena. But as she walks down the street with the foreshadowing name of *Calle de Noche Triste*, the street of the sad night, it soon becomes clear that the last novel in the trilogy is, like the other ones, a tragicomic examination of the twists and turns along life's journey.

In several ways, *Cities of the Plain* returns to, and, in some cases, comes closer to resolving themes and issues that appeared in the previous novels. Like *All the Pretty Horses*, it presents the conflict between realism and romance, but where the previous novel left the issue in limbo after John Grady Cole loses his Alejandra but recovers his horse, *Cities of the Plain* offers several characters and events who come down squarely on the side of romance. Again and again, characters endorse the notion that one should follow his or her heart. 'I think you ought to follow your heart, the old man said. That's all I ever thought about anything' (186). And later: 'I only know that every act which has no heart will be found out in the end. Every gesture' (194). 'A man is always right to pursue the thing he loves' (197). Later John Grady catches a ride with a man who has been married for sixty years. And hovering behind the novel is the story of the love affair between Mr. Johnson's daughter and the current story of John Grady's relentless and tragic pursuit of the epileptic whore Magdalena.

Her biblical name connects with John Grady Cole's initials. Like numerous previous characters in American literature, his initials signify the youthful Adams who become messianic figures following an initiation. In *All the Pretty Horses*, John Grady Cole's awareness of responsibility for others is played out in his relationship with Blevins, for whom he demonstrates concern throughout. In *Cities of the Plain* the theme of human responsibility takes several forms, through Billy's concern for John Grady, and primarily through Cole's almost inexplicable connection with Magdalena. John Grady seems drawn to her simplicity and helplessness, never acknowledging either her life as a whore or her epilepsy.

Ultimately, then, John Grady Cole's border crossings take him into a world of complexity, ambiguity, and ambivalence – a mixture of good and evil, rationality and irrationality, fate and free will in a mestizo culture that is itself an amalgam. Ambiguity prevails at the end of *All the Pretty Horses*, continues in *The Crossing*, but *Cities of the Plain*, except for the inchoate epilog, leaves the indeterminate and takes stands on such issues as human responsibility for others, for the value of love, and for the landscape.

The powerful theme of responsibility is doubled in *Cities of the Plain*, for John Grady shoulders the responsibility for Magdalena's welfare and sacrifices himself to his vision. Billy Parham's strong feelings of responsibility for John Grady mirror Cole's. And these two figures bring together the various themes of the earlier books.

Cities of the Plain continues McCarthy's emphasis on the changing landscape of the Southwest. Again McCarthy dramatizes the negative results that are the effect of human alienation from the natural world. In *Cities of the Plain* a subtle background motif concerns the end of things, especially the changing natural landscape. The title, for example, is an allusion to Sodom and Gomorrah, which was the title of one of Marcel Proust's volumes of *Remembrance of Things Past*. McCarthy presents the following dialogue between John Grady Cole and an aging cowboy. With gentle nostalgia, the old cowboy recalls the older natural world:

> Mr. Johnson . . . flipped the butt of his cigarette out across the yard in a slow red arc.
> Aint nothin to burn out there. I remember when you could have grassfires in this country.
> . . . There's hard lessons in this world.
> What's the hardest?
> I dont know. Maybe it's just that when things are gone they're gone. They aint comin back.
> Yessir.
> They sat. After a while the old man said: The day after my fiftieth birthday in March of nineteen and seventeen I rode into the old headquarters at the Wilde well and there was six dead wolves hangin on the fence. I rode along the fence and ran my hand along em. I looked at their eyes. A government trapper had brought em in the night before. They'd been killed with poison baits. Strychnine. Whatever. Up in the Sacramentos. A week later he brought in four more. I aint heard a wolf in this country since. I suppose that's a good thing. They can be hell on stock. But I guess I was always what you might call superstitious. I know I damn sure wasnt religious. And it had always seemed to me that somethin can live and die but that the kind of thing that they were was always there. I didnt know you could poison that. I aint heard a wolf howl in thirty odd years. I dont know where you'd go to hear one. There may not be any such a place. (*Cities of the Plain* 125–6)

Like other Texas writers, McCarthy approaches the natural world through an ironic double vision. He suggests that humans derive value from working the harsh landscape but adds the notion that the disappearance of that harsh landscape is being accomplished by the acts of the same people who begin to understand the value of the disappearing world – the cattlemen who destroy the wolves, the people who cause the overgrazing that diminishes the grass. It was a good old world, the one that is disappearing, and it was good because it allowed us to work in it, and that work led us to destroy it. This emphasis on caring for wolves, of course, ties the last novel to the long beginning story in *The Crossing*. Similarly, the episode concerning the killing of the feral dogs that ironically leads to John Grady's concern for the pups points to this double nature of the human relationship with the natural world that must lead to caring for that world lest it disappear.

And in the Epilogue and Dedication to *Cities of the Plain*, McCarthy draws together the various themes of the Trilogy. With John Grady's death, Billy decides to return to his home territory of De Baca County, New Mexico. The Epilogue begins: 'He left three days later, he and the dog' (263), again returning to the theme of responsibility to the natural world that the Trilogy's emphasis on horses, wolves, and dogs has stressed throughout. Billy responds to the 'pup shivering and whining until he took it up in the bow of the saddle with him.' Then he and Mac make their goodbyes, and Billy says, 'I should of looked after him better' to which Mac responds, 'We all should of' (263). Thus the Epilogue begins by combining the themes of the responsibility to the natural and human worlds that McCarthy stressed in various ways throughout the Trilogy with crossing borders as its central metaphor.

The Epilogue then returns to the power of storyteller, one of the dominant themes in *The Crossing*, when the aging Billy in 2002 encounters the deathlike traveler under the highway bridge and shares his meager food with him. As before in McCarthy's telling of another story of human journeys, it becomes clear that we are all actually on the same journey told again and again in different but always similar ways in which deep questions about the process and the telling are often explored. As before, those questions are traced by this strange minor figure who becomes an interlocutor for Billy and by extension for the readers. This figure ushers in the millennium and recounts a dream about a dream within a dream. As Edwin Arnold notes, the Epilogue is about 'the role of the artist, or the dreamer, or the creator, and his responsibilities to the subjects of his dreams' ('First Thoughts' 242).

McCarthy reemphasizes the theme of human responsibility again at the end when the old Billy lives with a family near Portales and helps their children care for a colt. When Billy awakes from an uneasy dream about Boyd, the mother, named Betty, sits comforting him with her hand on his shoulder. When Billy tries to tell her that he is unworthy of her concern and that he is not who she thinks, she tells him emphatically, 'I know who you are' (292). She also states clearly that she also knows why she cares for him. Such is the stuff that dreams and the novels of Cormac McCarthy are made of, and *Cities of the Plain* is the product of the vision of perhaps America's most important writer at century's end.

It is a world that grows warm and cold, a world with both love for children and the old and heathens who rage, as the concluding Dedication stresses. The seeming oppositions exist in the stories told in the Border Trilogy, stories of raging love and other oxymoronic border crossings. And as we turn the final page, we wait for the next story to give shape to the world to come.

Notes

1 Charles Bailey in 'The Last Stage of the Hero's Evolution: Cormac McCarthy's *Cities of the Plain*' finds a different pattern for the three novels: 'The heroic character of the knight from the courtly love romances of the Middle Ages inspires *All the Pretty Horses*. The tragic hero of ancient Greek and Renaissance drama inspires *The Crossing*. Proceeding naturally from the courtly hero through the tragic hero, the anti-hero, developed by Byron in such works as *Lara, Childe Harold's Pilgrimage*, and even the comic *Don Juan*, provides the inspiration for *Cities of the Plain*. And as the first two novels deconstruct the models on which their heroes are based, so the third deconstructs the most recent heroic model, the anti-hero, to prepare the way for the emergence of a new hero' (below, p. 5).

2 In one of the few interviews McCarthy has done, he told Richard B. Woodward: 'I've always been interested in the Southwest . . . There isn't a place in the world you can go where they don't know about cowboys and Indians and the myth of the West' (29).

3 McCarthy perhaps drew from Aztec and Mayan history here as well. Enrique Florescano points out in *Memory, Myth, and Time in Mexico: From the Aztecs to Independence* that both the Mayans and Aztecs placed heightened emphasis on the scribe who recorded historical stories: 'The Nahua texts that describe the scribe, or *tlacuilo*, sometimes elevate him to the category of sage, or they represent him as an individual possessing specialized techniques and knowledge' (31).

4 McCarthy told Woodward that the novel can 'encompass all the various disciplines and interests of humanity' (30). He also told Woodward: 'The ugly fact is books are made out of books. The novel depends for its life on the novels that have been written' (31), and he identified Melville, Dostoyevsky, and Faulkner as his most important influences.

5 For a discussion of similarities between O'Connor and McCarthy, see Tim Parrish's 'The Killer Wears the Halo: Cormac McCarthy, Flannery O'Connor, and the American Religion.'

6 Dianne C. Luce in 'The Road and the Matrix: The World as Tale in *The Crossing*' writes that 'McCarthy is concerned with the role or function of story in human experience of life, not only our own stories, our autobiographies, but our biographies of others, our witnessing' (195).

7 On two separate occasions Billy is described as standing 'with his pistol in his hand,' perhaps alluding to the most famous study of the Tex-Mex folkloric tradition of the corrido, Américo Paredes' *With His Pistol in His Hand* (University of Texas Press, 1958).

John Wegner

'Mexico para los Mexicanos': revolution, Mexico, and McCarthy's Border Trilogy

What's a plebiscite? said Oren. (*Cities of the Plain* 51)

'Mexico para los Mexicanos!' (*El Hijo del Ahuizote*, banner headline of an intellectual magazine/newspaper during the Porfirio Díaz regime)

Each act in this world from which there can be no turning back has before it another, and it another yet. In a vast and endless net. Men imagine that the choices before them are theirs to make. But we are free to act only upon what is given. Choice is lost in the maze of generations and each act in that maze is itself an enslavement for it voids every alternative and binds one ever more tightly into the constraints that make a life. (The maestro, *Cities of the Plain* 195)

Just as John Grady Cole and his companions and Billy and Boyd Parham can cross back and forth into Mexico with relative ease throughout the novels of Cormac McCarthy's Border Trilogy, so history can seep northward across the border to affect the lives of Americans. The Mexican revolution helps shape the ideas and actions of the Trilogy's protagonists and antagonists alike. Because the revolution and its corollary effects symbolize the historical complexities of the two countries McCarthy writes about, the history of each person and place is intricately tied to the history of another, 'And in it is a tale and each tale the sum of all lesser tales within them' (*The Crossing* 143). '[A]ll tales are one' because each story has as its central tale one larger tale. In McCarthy's Border Trilogy the story that contains all other stories is the Mexican revolution. '[T]he seams ... hid from us ... The joinery' are those corollary stories that 'separate from their stories have no meaning,' and it is precisely these seams that we must search for in order to give the larger story meaning (*The Crossing* 143, 142). The shared histories of John Grady Cole and Billy Parham, El Paso and Juárez, and the United States and Mexico are the same relationships. The history that connects these people and places is a complex web of stories; yet each story contains within it the story of the Mexican revolution.

At virtually every encounter, the boys who are the protagonists of the Border Trilogy learn that 'the soul of Mexico is very old' (*The Crossing* 385), and they learn that they cannot simply ignore the influence of that history. As the maestro in *Cities of the Plain* claims, the actions of Cole and Parham as well as the actions and responses of the Mexicans they meet are a by-product of the historical tapestry woven well before the boys cross the border. Mexico is a foil to these youths who grow up in a country where one's choices are advertised as one's own, freely made, in a country of plebiscites. By contrast, John Grady Cole and his companions and Billy and Boyd Parham cross into a country that, until recently, had only one free election – that of Francisco I. Madero as President after a hard-fought revolution that began in 1910. Madero and his supporters had fought for economic equality, redistribution of land, free elections, and humane treatment for all; however, references to the revolution serve primarily to illuminate the violence of the Border Trilogy. Cole's eventual death is not predestined so much as it is the logical extension of choices limited by the labyrinth of history, and the historical paradigms behind the Trilogy condition both the possibilities and restrictions the past presents to these characters. 'Each man is the bard of his own existence' (*Cities* 283), but in the Southwest of McCarthy's Border Trilogy, the bard is bounded by a certain historical legacy within which he must work. McCarthy's precise incorporation of historical artifact into his fictional world makes the revolution a virtual character who must also be discussed and interpreted, and our knowledge of Mexico's revolution is essential to understanding the common history shared by the Trilogy's protagonists and antagonists alike.

Madero's presence in the first novel remains fairly overt. Both Don Héctor and Dueña Alfonsa discuss Madero's politics, and they both recognize that in telling Madero's story they can 'tell [Cole] how Mexico was. How it was and how it will be again' (*All the Pretty Horses* 231). Madero's failure is seminal to understanding Mexico and understanding the Mexico that Cole and Parham enter in the early to mid 1900s. Antonio's and Luis' servitude, Orlando's false imprisonment, and the corrupt *cacique*'s power to 'make the truth here' are all products of Madero and the revolution's inability to empower the Mexican people. Midway through *All the Pretty Horses*, Cole and Rawlins are in the mountains herding wild horses with a *mozo* 'named Luis who had fought at Torreón and San Pedro and Zacatecas ... and he and his father had fought in the cavalry and his father and his brothers had died in the cavalry but they'd all despised Victoriana Huerta above all other men and the deeds of Huerta above all other visited evils. He said that compared to Huerta Judas was himself but another Christ' (110). In 1913 Huerta helped overthrow the Madero government, and his eventual arrest and order for the murder of Francisco and Gustavo Madero and Piño Suárez ended *La Decena Tragica* (February 9–19, 1913). Madero's inability to hold the presidency and enact the reforms he promised leaves Luis, former cavalry rebel, working as an aged *mozo* (a conscript or servant) to two young Americans: Luis does not have his own ranch and horses to work and he is subservient to both Americans and the wealthy landowner for whom they work in turn.

However, the resonance of the revolution is most apparent in *The Crossing*, the novel whose main action takes place chronologically closest to the revolution itself. Billy's foray into Mexico begins in 1939 during the presidency of Lazaro Cardenas, the first Mexican executive following the revolution to serve six consecutive years. He was, in many respects, the first post-revolutionary president to represent stability in Mexico, but in a country that has endured seven years of revolution and civil war, the fighting is foremost in people's minds. After Billy crosses into Mexico with the wolf, he meets an old woman who 'said that the revolution had killed off all the real men in the country and left only tontos [idiots]' (84, 86). Hers is the first of at least five direct references to the revolution in the novel. The blind revolutionary tells the most graphic story directly after Boyd has 'fired' his shot for the common man. The old man 'asked for news of the revolution but the boy had no news to give. Then the blind man said that although the countryside was tranquil this was not necessarily a good sign' (275). Later, as Billy carries Boyd's bones back to Lordsburg, the gypsies tell him of an airplane 'lost in the mountains in the calamitous summer of nineteen fifteen' (404). Coupled with Mr. Sanders' story 'about Villa's raid on Columbus New Mexico in nineteen sixteen,' the revolution is never far below the narrative surface of the novel. The blind revolutionary's warning that the revolution lurks quietly in the background is apt.

Boyd's immediate acceptance as an *hombre de la gente* derives from the story 'abroad in the country... all the world knew that the güerito had killed the gerente from Las Varitas. The man who had betrayed Socorro Rivera and sold out his own people to the Guardia Blanca of La Babícora' (322). *La Guardia Blanca of La Babícora* (the White Guard) is exactly what it sounds like: a mercenary group hired to protect Babícora, land owned by W. R. Hearst, from rustlers and squatters, including those families Hearst's ownership of the ranch has displaced. The revolution, McCarthy's Trilogy constantly reminds us, has done little to thwart foreign investment and the concentration of power. In fact,

> None of it done anybody any good, Travis said. Or if it did I never heard of it.
> I been all over that country down there... They didn't have nothin. Never had and never would... You could see that the revolution hadnt done them no good. A lot of em had lost boys out of the family. Fathers or sons or both. Nearly all of em, I expect. They didnt have no reason to be hospitable to anybody. Least of all a gringo kid. (*Cities* 90)

Porfirio Díaz, dictator from 1877 to 1911, had courted American investment and capital in Mexico to the disdain of Mexican intellectuals who feared a growing dependence on American money. Their fears were well grounded. By 1910, American real estate holdings totaled over 100 million acres and encompassed much of the nations most valuable mining, agricultural, and timber properties. In 1902 a consortium of U.S. capitalists controlled 80 percent of Mexico's railroad stock; and Americans owned 22 percent of Mexico's land surface (Hart 6, 134, 158). In 1925 American and British investors controlled 91.5 percent of all Mexican oil wealth (Swanberg 394). Of the foreign investors, the Hearst family was one of the largest. *La Babícora* covered fourteen hundred square miles, about one million acres, of prime Mexico real estate. George Hearst purchased the land in 1887 for between twenty-three and forty cents an acre after 'receiving through his friends in the Mexican government early information of Geronimo's capture' (Carlson and Bates 13). Hearst then offered the land to his son, William Randolph, who rejected the ranch, asking instead for the *San Francisco Examiner*. The ranch expanded and 'many Mexican peons were forced from the ranch, in some cases from small farms and rancheros they had worked for three generations. Hearst hired American cowboys and gunmen to protect his cattle lands from Mexican "squatters" and paid local officials to further discourage trespassing' (Hanrahan 134). W. R. was not afraid to use his newspapers to call for intervention in Mexico, and 'as early as 1913 Hearst had not scrupled to fake news and photographs in the effort to involve the American people in conflict with the republic below the Rio Grande' (Lundberg 220). Hearst, then, represents the greatest transgressor in Mexico. His ownership and control of a one million acre ranch helps fuel the Mexican revolutionary spirit, Mexican nationalism, and anti-American sentiment. Hence, Boyd's rapid assumption into folklore for his rumored killing of the *Guardia Blanca* collaborator echoes Mexican popular resentment against American imperialism.

Indeed, despite the generosity of the Mexican laborers Cole and Billy meet, Anti-American sentiment runs deep. Much like the blind revolutionary's warning that the peaceful countryside is deceptive, the Mexican laborers' altruism masks a lurking hatred for American imperialism.

Madero's popularity with the masses stemmed from his promise of agrarian reforms, and the essence of these reforms promised a repatriation of lands sold by absentee owners and foreigners. Billy's journey to *La Babícora* is both convenient (the ranch is 240 miles south of New Mexico and Texas) and politically charged. Hearst 'is not so popular in this country. There is a prejudice I think is how you would say it,' Señor Soto tells Billy (*The Crossing* 200). This prejudice is apparent when Billy returns to Mexico in search of Boyd. He enters a cantina, orders a Waterfills y Frazier (good Kentucky sipping whiskey), and eventually joins a group of men drinking mescal. Alfonso

> drank not . . . The younger man said that the drunk man had been a soldier in the revolution and that he had fought at Torreón and at Zacatecas and that he had been wounded many times . . . The younger man said that he had received three bullets in the chest at Zacatecas and lain in the dirt of the streets in darkness and cold while the dogs drank his blood . . . When all the glasses were filled the younger man raised his glass and offered a toast to the revolution. (358–9)

Alfonso protests 'that he objected to the seal which was the seal of an oppressive government. He said that he would not drink from such a bottle. That it was a matter of honor' (360). He refuses to capitulate and compromise the bullet holes he earned fighting an oppressive United States government by drinking with Billy and sharing in this barroom communion of sorts 'For the sharing of bread [or liquor] is not such a simple thing nor is its acknowledgment' (161). Billy's mere presence reminds 'the patriot' of Mexico's lack of self-rule and its economic dependence on America and its capitalists.

The patriot fought in the war, rallying around 'Mexico para los Mexicanos.' Several years later, in *Cities of the Plain*, Eduardo's claim during his knifefight with John Grady Cole that 'We will devour you, my friend. You and your pale empire' elevates this fight to something beyond simply a battle over a whore. The death of the Mexican pimp and the American john is a microcosm of the history of bad blood that lies between Sodom and Gomorrah, El Paso and Juárez, America and Mexico. Eduardo's condemnation of the American 'empire' to the north seems well supported. After Pancho Villa 'come back in nineteen and nineteen . . . We'd slip over there and hunt for souvenirs. Empty shellcases and what not' (*Cities* 90). Archer's innocent comment portrays the Americans as vultures picking the bones of Juárez clean after the battle. Billy, in the tense moment in the bar, sees 'the only manifest artifact of the history of this negligible republic . . . that ha[s] the least authority or meaning or claim to substance . . . seated here before him in the sallow light . . . all else from men's lips or from men's pens would require that it be beat out hot all over again upon the anvil of its own enactment before it could even qualify as a lie' (363). The patriot, steadfastly loyal to his country and his mescal, represents Mexico. Concomitantly, Billy, John Grady Cole, and Hearst represent American oppression. Boyd's ability to adapt to the countryside not only endears him to the people, it dooms him to share their fate.

One of the Maderos' stated goals was economic independence; yet, as the third novel opens, John Grady, the 'all american cowboy' and his friends are in Mexico to buy a cheap piece of Mexican flesh. These cowboys have come to Mexico to 'pick out' a woman much the same way they cut out cattle on the ranch. Juárez, once a city representing independence, has become a city of cheap whores, whiskey, and tourists 'drunk laboring up the sidewalk carrying a full suit of armor' (*Cities* 37). The decline of Juárez begins during the revolution. Long a separate city in name only, 'The *laissez-faire* attitude toward the U.S.-Mexico border region underwent a dramatic change in the fall of 1910 with the outbreak of the Mexican Revolution' (Meyer, Introduction 2). The dramatic change in Juárez was, in large part, caused by American soldiers stationed at Ft. Bliss with nothing to do during their free time. Exasperating already racist feelings about Mexico, the *Boston Herald* in a 1915 news article, named Juárez 'the most wickedest city' on earth (quoted in Vanderwood and Samponaro 47). Juárez becomes, for all intents and purposes, less El Paso's sister city than her wicked step-sister. In spite of the degradation of Juárez, its population 'was all on the side of the rebels' (*Cities* 89). Federal officials 'estimated that the majority of the Anglo population and 90% of the Mexican-Americans supported the revolutionists' (Carman 24). Even Archer's story about his 'Mama's Uncle Pless' turning new firing pins recalls I. Thord Gray's personal account of taking a breech firing pin into El Paso for a replacement (Gray 25).

The thematic centrality of the whorehouses of Juárez to the conclusion of the Border Trilogy inflects the economic and nationalistic foci of the revolution. In light of the revolution's influence on Mexico and the Border Trilogy, Eduardo's character becomes much more complex. He tells Cole he has 'seen your kind before. Many and many. You think I dont know America? I know America' (*Cities* 248). America is a 'leprous paradise' full of farmboys (249), a 'pale empire' tottering 'upon an unspoken labyrinth of questions' (253). Eduardo is the creation of American farmboys coming to Mexico – the product of American intervention in Mexico's affairs. Cole might be a sympathetic character because of his love for a Mexican whore, but the fact remains that he goes to a whorehouse with friends prepared to buy Mexican flesh. His attempt to buy Magdalena from Eduardo does more than warn him that she considers leaving. Cole's actions, no matter how noble they appear, involve buying and selling a woman for two thousand dollars. In the larger scheme of things, El Paso buys and Juárez sells; their relationship continues Mexico's economic independence on America. Eduardo is simply the new *gerente* selling Mexico to the highest bidder, and Magdalena's story is the story of Mexico. An abused child from Chiapas, abandoned and abused by the church and the state, she 'owes [Eduardo] a certain amount. Money that was advanced to her for her costumes. Her jewelry' (134). Her debt to the company store traps her in Mexico, which in any case she would not be allowed to leave without the 'documents necessary for her to cross' (205). Eduardo might not be a 'whiteslaver,' but he is a reincarnation of Huerta. Admittedly, Eduardo is an odious character, but the actions of the men from America warrant as much condemnation. They take advantage of the Mexican people's economic weakness, a weakness caused, in part, by Americans who have controlled Mexican capital, and this control, in turn, may be attributed to the revolution's failure. Madero and the other revolutionaries' inability to achieve independence from America creates the necessary climate for men like Eduardo and his customers.

The history and politics of the Mexican revolution thus subtly dominate the narrative. Both Cole and Parham learn, among other things, that Mexico is not some borderland region, simplistic and attic, where 'warriors would ride on in that darkness they'd become, rattling past with their stone-age tools of war' (*Horses* 6). The continual revolutions, the constant revolving, of history signifies the constant retelling and re-creation of history. The tale never ends; the thread of the story runs from character to character. The map of Billy's life is contained in his 'hand. Gnarled, ropescarred, speckled from the sun and the years of it. The ropy veins that bound them to his heart. There was map enough for men to read. There God's plenty of signs and wonders to make a landscape. To make a world' (*Cities* 291). These two boys are the bards of their own existence, but the shape of their hands is determined by the larger common history we share. The map of existence McCarthy creates within this Border Trilogy fuses history and fiction and reminds us that our choices are limited by all choices made before us, whether with our consent or not. History, like the wolf, knows 'nothing of boundaries' but,

McCarthy reminds us, 'the boundary [stands] without regard' (*The Crossing* 119). Cole's attempt to transcend the boundary of history and country fails and only Billy, who recognizes that it is our response to our shared history, survives to tell tales 'about horses and cattle and the old days. Sometimes he'd tell them about Mexico' (*Cities* 290).

Patrick W. Shaw

Female presence, male violence, and the art of artlessness in the Border Trilogy

Let us begin with a plot summary of a Cormac McCarthy narrative.

Two teenage brothers from Southwest ranches try to return a trapped wolf to her native mountains in Mexico. Unsuccessful, they return home to find that their parents have been murdered and their horses stolen. Joined by a runaway boy riding a magnificent horse, they again cross the border. In Mexico the younger brother falls in love with a peasant girl they have rescued from desperadoes, the runaway's horse is stolen, and the runaway himself is murdered. Later, while working as cowboys, the older brother begins a torrid sexual relationship with the rich hacendado's young daughter. The angry father has the older brother imprisoned, while the vengeful desperadoes track down and shoot the younger brother. Though he survives and returns to the girl he rescued, he is soon murdered and becomes a martyr to the peasants. Released from prison, the older brother sets off to revenge the death of his brother and to retrieve the stolen horses. Though ultimately successful, he returns to Texas, depressed over the loss of his brother and the girl he loves.

The most casual reader of McCarthy's novels immediately realizes that this plot summary is a garbled amalgamation of *All the Pretty Horses* and *The Crossing*.

The plots are so easy to (con)fuse, however, because the situations and actions of each novel are so strikingly similar. Inasmuch as the novels are two-thirds of a trilogy, the shared particulars and similar historical-philosophical backgrounds are expected. However, even for trilogies, the reiterated plots are anomalous. Unlike most trilogies (such as John Dos Passos' *U.S.A.* or Faulkner's Snopes trilogy) the first two novels of McCarthy's trilogy share none of the same characters, are set a decade apart, and occur in reverse chronological order. What they do emphatically share is the one element that C. Hugh Holman defines as 'merely a mechanical means' by which more significant narrative elements are arranged (336). In other words, *All the Pretty Horses* and *The Crossing* duplicate the one element an author of McCarthy's capabilities would seem least eager to exaggerate: plot. The third novel of the Trilogy serves further to highlight this exaggeration. *Cities of the Plain* unites John Grady Cole and Billy Parham in a summary conclusion that emphasizes their biographical similarities and modes of action in the anterior novels. Considering the differences in their ages, the historical environment of the two eras they represent, and the vastness of the U.S.-Mexican borderland, it remains improbable that John Grady Cole and Billy Parham would have met as they drifted about. McCarthy implicitly acknowledges this improbability, for though the two men do indeed meet and become fast friends, McCarthy in *Cities of the Plain* chooses not to clarify the circumstances of their union. What is clear is that McCarthy is less concerned with feasibility and more concerned with having John Grady Cole and Billy Parham paired so that he may reassert the exceptional correspondence of their personalities and actions – concerned, that is again, with plot.

The obvious question, therefore, is why does McCarthy offer a trilogy in which plot is so repetitive and so emphatic that it risks detracting from other, more important artistic elements? The simplest answer, perhaps, is that McCarthy is fascinated by travelogues and the *Bildungsroman*. Few plots are more serviceable than to set an adolescent on the road, let him experience life's difficulties, and have him (or at least the reader) emerge as a wiser individual. If American novelists recognized the potential of the journey-*Bildungsroman* genre, they just as quickly recognized its limitations. Mark Twain, for example, attempted to replicate Huck Finn's journey down the Mississippi by setting him loose on the Western frontier. Twain soon recognized the limitations of the genre and abandoned the tale. Yet, despite such precedents as this, McCarthy employs the combination twice in succession and reemphasizes it in the third novel.

We may dismiss forthwith the possibility that McCarthy simply errs in overplaying a time-tested apparatus. From the publication of *The Orchard Keeper* (1965) onward, McCarthy has proved to be an eloquent rhetorician, an astute intellect, and a meticulous craftsman. *Blood Meridian*, the novel immediately preceding the Border Trilogy, affirms McCarthy's creative genius and immense narrative skills. Vereen M. Bell is correct in concluding that *Blood Meridian* is so complex that 'what it may be said to mean in conventional discourse is beyond claiming' (*The Achievement of Cormac McCarthy* 128). While neither as philosophically intricate nor as historically far ranging as *Blood Meridian* (still McCarthy's masterpiece), the first two novels of the Trilogy equal it in authorial control and text management – in every particular except plot.

The most feasible explanation of McCarthy's reiterating the plot of *All the Pretty Horses* in *The Crossing* is that the act was intentional and purposeful. It is too flagrant to have been incidental, and McCarthy is too masterful a craftsman for it to have been accidental. That the simplest of narrative devices was spotlighted in such a way may only be construed as an instance of premeditated artlessness. The essential question facing the critic, therefore, is how does this exaggerated simplicity relate to the profound issues otherwise raised by the texts and subtexts of the three narratives? The answer is that the obvious technique of doubling the plot acts as a matrix for a complex technique that in another context Gilles Deleuze defines as 'a self-differentiating difference that generates divergent series and structures them across a dispersional field' (quoted in Bogue 167). It is this subtle technique camouflaged by the obvious that I want to clarify.

We can begin to discover the objective of such intentional artlessness by noting a metaphor common to the first two novels of the Trilogy. It appears first at the conclusion of *All the Pretty Horses* when the anachronistic Indians 'stood and watched [John Grady Cole] pass and watched him vanish upon that landscape solely because he was passing. Solely because he would vanish' (301). It is then rephrased in the interpolated story told by the old heretic in *The Crossing*. After having contemplated the universal 'matrix' for many years, the ex-Mormon concludes that creation 'flowed out of nothing' and 'vanished into nothing once again' and that 'Not chaos itself lay outside of that matrix' (149). At first, the plotlessness of this rambling parable seems to mar the precision of the matrix text. This mad theodicy, however, is actually a metafictional statement that clarifies McCarthy's intent. Because McCarthy has already called attention to the art of fiction making with his exaggerated similar plots and by having the ex-Mormon admonish us that 'Rightly heard all tales are one' (*The Crossing* 143), we may feasibly interpret this 'vanishing' or 'from nothing to nothing' metaphor as a metafictional key to the texts at hand. Fiction is created out of nothing and ultimately vanishes into nothing again. What it may mean is revealed only by the traces left in that vanishing.

The most promising traces in *All the Pretty Horses* and *The Crossing* appear in the form of numerous motifs that are extended through but less pronounced in *Cities of the Plain*. Of these motifs, two will suffice for analysis here: the feminine presence and masculine violence. Others may be subsumed within those classifications.

Feminine presence

One hesitates to use the term 'female characters' because McCarthy paints no portrait of a lady. The girls and women do not emerge from the androcentric narratives with attributes enough to define them as distinct personae. The characterizations are implied by a favorite McCarthy image: birds' shadows passing over a divergent landscape, their essence out of sight as soon as their presence is realized. Often the females are not granted names, thus losing conventional and convenient nominal tags and traveling through the text with pronominal anonymity. At other times they are granted very specific names meant to exaggerate the minimal narrative consequence afforded them – as Mary Catherine Barnett, the girl who rejects John Grady Cole for a boy with a car (*All the Pretty Horses* 10). The length of her name is disproportionate to the space committed to her actual appearance in the text. However, when seen as examples of differential relationships, the collective feminine presence causes the three narratives to resonate at frequencies no one of the females could cause individually. This resonance is both an inter- and intratextual phenomenon.

In *All the Pretty Horses* the feminine presence is composed of John Grady Cole's mother, the Dueña Alfonsa, and Alejandra Rocha y Villareal. A theatrical quality ultimately accrues to all these females and hints at the nebulous role McCarthy has assigned them. Although John Grady Cole's dying father scolds him for alluding to his 'Mama' as 'she' (8), the reprimand only emphasizes that Mrs. Cole is never identified except by the pronominal label. The 'She' villainess abandons John Grady Cole when he is a baby, rejects her war-damaged husband, and callously expels Grady from the ranch he loves – all to indulge her amateur acting and adultery in San Antonio. At the risk of sounding too Freudian, we might even accuse 'Mama' of being the reason John Grady is so desirous of and vulnerable to Alejandra and Magdalena, the Mexican whore who causes his death in *Cities of the Plain*. After page 22 of *All the Pretty Horses*, John Grady's mother vanishes from the text, neither having spoken in her own defense nor having acted in any scenario that encourages us to transcend the moral disapproval mandated by her exaggerated selfishness. Unlike the Dueña Alfonsa, Mrs. Cole is granted no manic declamation in defense of her being.

Dueña Alfonsa, though of a generation and culture different from Mrs. Cole, reflects the same vagueness of character. She magnificently plays her part as rancorous grande dame and spoiler of romance. Sadly, however, she overestimates her influence. Her 10-page monologue recounting the history of Francisco Madero and the Mexican revolution (230–40) summarizes the social divisions that have racked Mexico and that overshadow her own eventful life. While her tale reveals much about the nuances of civil war, it tells comparatively little about its messenger. She says that she has suffered severely and loved passionately, yet we witness no dramatic on-stage proofs of such emotions. Like John Grady Cole, whose suffering we have convincingly witnessed, we are a captive audience to the Dueña's nondramatic monologue. Like him, we are not disappointed when it ends. Thus, in this her most substantial scene, the Dueña is reduced to an unheeded spokeswoman for the industrial-agrarian class struggle that has determined her own unhappy life and that in turn dictates the fate of Alejandra and John Grady. Moreover, though she appears to command Alejandra's destiny, the relationship between Alejandra and John Grady is doomed by social and traditional forces that even the authoritative Dueña can not alter. Her missing finger symbolizes how little control she has over her puppets. Though she claims to be an early-day feminist and revolutionary, everything we hear about and from the 'grandaunt' indicates that she is subservient to the masculine forces of war and revolution and to the text itself in her role as a subplot narrator.

Ironically, though Alejandra is conspicuously identified by a distinct name that is frequently repeated, her identity relies primarily on traits stereotypically associated with the passionate Latin female. Her hair is black and 'loose.' She is arrogant, flirtatious, and temperamental. From the moment she prances into the narrative on her black Arabian horse and smiles demurely from beneath her 'flat-crowned hat of black felt' (94), we know first that John Grady Cole will succumb to her sexual allure (she soon visits his bed nine nights running) and, second, that her jealousy of family prerogatives will preclude anything other than a temporary association. Alejandra is imaged by her fancy clothing and high-bred horse but attains no memorable psychological distinction. She and her relationships approach clichés. Her only significant role is that of plot facilitator. Because of her, John Grady and Lacey are arrested, reunited with Blevins, imprisoned, and nearly killed. Her story and fate subsequent to this facilitation are unrecorded and unimportant. John Grady himself reflects the lack of definition in the girl's persona. Even after encountering Alejandra for the third time, his thoughts at night are not of her directly but of 'horses and of the open country and of horses' (117–18). In short, the horses in the novel emerge with more narrative distinction than the girl and motivate the males more profoundly.

None of these females appears in the second third of the Trilogy. In *The Crossing*, the feminine presence is epitomized by a female who does not appear in the text at all: Margarita Evelyn Parham, Boyd Parham's twin sister. Dead since infancy, she haunts the narrative and subsumes all other females. Only two corporeal females gain enough narrative space to command attention. Appropriately, both are nameless: the Mexican 'girl' who controls Boyd Parham's short life and the 'wife' who narrates the convoluted story of the blind revolutionary. The association with the ghostly sister is especially pronounced in the young girl that Billy and Boyd overtake on the road in Mexico (203). The brothers' efforts to be heroes by saving the barefoot girl from rapists lead to Boyd's being shot and to his ultimate martyrdom. Though Billy is the first to be attracted to the girl, she soon directs her own attention to the younger Boyd. Their apparently sexless relationship – contrapuntal to John Grady Cole's carnal liaisons with Alejandra – suits a girl whose skin is 'so perfect it appeared oddly false. As if it had been painted on' (321). As a manifestation of the dead twin sister, she is distanced from Boyd by subconscious taboos he cannot understand. At once sensual and yet painted like a tin retablo of the Virgin, she enthralls Boyd. She tacitly admits to Billy that she 'fears all men' sexually (321), thereby substantiating the contention that her interest in the adolescent Boyd stems from motivations other than lust. The only other female of note is the wife (or at least long-term companion) of the revolutionary whose eyes have been sucked out by the German Wirtz. Like Dueña Alfonsa, the wife acts as narrative facilitator. Actually, there seems little reason to have her narrate the husband's tale other than to emphasize her narrative (and domestic) subservience. As he later demonstrates, the blind man is quite articulate, yet he remains speechless while the wife patiently and fluently conveys most of his dark tale to Billy Parham. Such verbal adroitness suggests that wanderers before Billy have had to play audience to the tale and that the wife has embellished it in the retelling.

Several parallel elements connect the blind man's wife to the girl who enthralls Boyd Parham. The wife was once the 'girl' who aids the blind revolutionary and who ultimately becomes his wife and spokesperson. She is both a victim and an advocate of insurrection. The role she plays in shaping and disseminating the tale of the 1913 revolution parallels the role that the girl plays for Boyd Parham a generation later in another segment of the same rebellion. Like the blind man's wife, the girl accompanies Boyd in the class struggle and then instigates and broadcasts the ballads that transform him from gullible boy to folk hero. The blind husband, however, survives to witness against such bloodshed and the mythologizing that perpetuates it. He killed no one in the glorious struggles, did not die valiantly, and changed nothing. His only distinguishing act was to put himself into a situation where a proto-Nazi madman could suck out his eyes. He concludes, after twenty-eight years of darkness, that 'Somos dolientes en la oscuridad. Todos nosotros. Me entiendes? Los que pueden ver, los que no pueden' (293). (We are mourning in the darkness. All of us. Do you understand? Those that can see, those that cannot.)* His plight personifies the absurdity of the massacres and fratricides that pass into history as glorious revolutions. The wife's exaggerated tale and the husband's debunking of romantic mythicizing foreshadow the events that dictate Boyd Parham's short, bloody life.

These intratextual collations extend to intertextual cognates. The female characters in *All the Pretty Horses* are paired, albeit in different guise, with the women of *The Crossing*. We see this cross-textual duplication both in textual specifics and subtle thematic resonance. The innocent 'girl' who enthralls Boyd in *The Crossing* parallels the sophisticated Alejandra who captivates John Grady Cole in *All the Pretty Horses*. Both ultimately merge into the demure, 'schoolgirl' whore Magdalena in *Cities of the Plain*. For example, one scene in which Billy comes across the girl after Boyd has been shot coincides with the scene in which John Grady first sees Alejandra. Like Alejandra, the girl is riding a horse, wears a hat, and fixes Billy 'with her dark eyes' (*The Crossing* 320). The comparison expands when the usually taciturn girl relates a tale with conspicuous similarities to the long tale that Dueña Alfonsa relates to John Grady in *All the Pretty Horses*. Echoing the Dueña's own life, the girl's story concerns her grandmother's being thrice widowed before the age of twenty by the revolution (321). Both are doleful tales of how women are wounded, mangled, and scarred by men who soon die 'on that senseless plain' of the revolutions (322). As the girl's grandmother warns her, 'rash men were a great temptation to women' (322) – the same conclusion that the Dueña reaches. The girl-Dueña cognate reconfigures again when we recall that the blind man's wife also tells a story that carries the same message as those tales of the girl and the grandaunt. In short, the plots of these three interpolated stories merge and blur much the same way as the matrix plots of *All the Pretty Horses* and *The Crossing*. In so doing, the subplots fuse the individuality of the various females into an amorphous presence that assumes an identity separate from and larger than its components.

Moreover, the fusion is continued rather than distinguished in the vague persona of the virginal whore Magdalena in *Cities of the Plain*. About *Cities* we must first reiterate how improbable it would be for John Grady Cole and Billy Parham to so quickly find each other and become compadres. McCarthy, as he has shown in *Blood Meridian* and the first two novels of the Border Trilogy, is acutely aware of the immense dominance of landscape over the human individual. No matter how much we as reader and McCarthy as fictive creator might desire such a satisfying union of two like souls, it is unlikely that the two would ever have met and more unlikely still that they would have become close friends as they drifted about the vast borderland region, no matter how much they both tended toward horses and ranch work. In this context, therefore, we realize that the final novel of the Trilogy stretches credulity and risks artifice to explain the various story lines of the first two novels. In this concluding narrative, we once again see McCarthy consciously manipulating plot in order to attain what he perceives as a more important artistic goal: to develop further the perplexing amorphous quality of the female characters.

The resultant irony of this narrative technique of manipulating plots and subplots resonates in numerous ways. Perhaps the most consequential way is that this collective feminine presence proves more subtle of intellect and manifestly more clever than the males who are distinctly characterized by traditional narrative techniques. Whereas the male characters are literally the actors – fighting, riding, killing, dying – the passive women regulate those actions through a keen sensitivity to the male ego and to the female's covert powers in an overtly patriarchal society. We have already noted how John Grady Cole's mother dictates his life by refusing to assume the roles of stereotypical motherhood. Billy and Boyd Parham's mother is nurturing, but she clearly runs the home and decrees her children's actions within the circle of her domestic influence. When the boys are surreptitiously feeding the renegade Indian, they worry not about their father's wrath but about their mother's disapproval (*The Crossing* 12f). Alejandra easily seduces John Grady, thereby not only satisfying her own sexual passions but also punishing a distant mother whom she admittedly dislikes and a grandaunt who dominates her life. She makes a point of telling her father about her affair with the Texas cowboy, thus guaranteeing that her revenge works and that the affair terminates. Her pledge not to see John Grady to get him freed from prison may seem altruistic, but the motivation underlying the agreement is ancillary more than primary. Then too, the Dueña arranges to have John Grady ransomed out of prison not because she has any 'sympathy with people to whom things happen' (*All the Pretty Horses* 240) but so that she might continue her modicum of control over Alejandra and to celebrate that power in the long audience she inflicts upon John Grady. In some convoluted way, her domination of Alejandra and John Grady partially compensates for her mangled hand and the young men who would not court her when she too was a girl. On a more fundamental level, the blind man's wife controls him by literally being his eyes and his voice. Even Magdalena, though abused and eventually brutally murdered, has her posthumous revenge when John Grady and her pimp kill each other in a bloody knifefight that eventuates because of her subtle manipulation of both men and that ironically duplicates plot and action from *All the Pretty Horses*.

In contrast to the women's intelligent maximizing of the prerogatives allowed them, the males evince a troublesome lack of right reason. The male is often likable and stoically heroic, but almost fatally flawed by this intellectual obtuseness. For example, despite Lacey Rawlins' prophetic warnings against such thoughtless actions, John Grady Cole persists in courting Alejandra and accommodating the psychopathic Blevins. Such lack of reason, as we see in *Cities of the Plain*, leads to John Grady's death. Billy Parham's lament over the horribly wounded body of his dying friend emphasizes the illogic of John Grady's actions: 'Aint that pitiful, he said. Aint that the most goddam pitiful thing ... Goddam whores, he said' (261). Billy himself has learned from the disastrous consequence of wrong reason. Years before, ignoring his brother Boyd's warnings, Billy leads the mean-tempered Indian to his parents' ranch, carries the wolf to Mexico, and then returns for a second losing battle. As a result, the wolf is dead and his parents and brother are murdered. Don Héctor Rocha postures in his opulent hacienda, flaunts his airplanes and fine horses, but remains insensitive to how much his life is manipulated by an absent wife, a spoiled adolescent daughter, and an embittered aunt. The obvious question is what is McCarthy's purpose in juxtaposing this intellectual obtuseness with the subtlety and cleverness of the collective feminine intelligence? To propose feasible answers to the question, we need to move our analysis to the violence that marks the masculine personality and that is thematic in all three novels.

Violence

Definitions of violence and theories explaining it abound in the literature of aggression. In one of the best texts on violence theory, Leonard D. Eron states that 'The factors involved in [violent human behavior] range from genetics, neuroanatomy, endocrinology, and physiology through exogenous substances and firearms to gangs and community influences. No one of these factors by itself can explain much of the variance in the extent and intensity of violent behavior in the population' (9). Writing in *Aggression and Peacefulness in Humans and Other Primates*, Marc H. Ross recognizes these diverse factors and defines violence as any conflict 'in which physical force is used' (272–3). To that commonsensical and manageable definition, Hans Toch adds that violence '*is* injurious, is rarely planned, and almost invariably is affect-laden' (1). These definitions combine to form the working definition that informs my discussion: violence is physical force that erupts from a cause-effect series of actions, results in injury, and has meaningful consequences.

Measured against the absolute violence of *Blood Meridian*, the violence of the Border Trilogy is understated. Yet, as in *Blood Meridian*, violence remains pervasive in the Trilogy. Two instances will serve to make the point. In *All the Pretty Horses*, the defining occurrence of violence is the Saltillo prison episode, exemplified by the bloody knifefight between John Grady and the hired assassin:

> [The cuchillero] leaned and took hold of John Grady by the hair and forced his head back to cut his throat. As he did so John Grady brought his knife up from the floor and sank it into the cuchillero's heart. He sank it into his heart and snapped the handle sideways and broke the blade off in him. (201)

This scene is duplicated in greater detail to form the violent denouement of *Cities of the Plain* when John Grady and the pimp mortally slash each other.

Violence in *The Crossing* is exemplified by the protracted battle the Mexicans stage between the pregnant wolf and the fighting dogs:

> [The wolf] was a sorry sight to see. She'd returned to the stake and crouched by it but her head lay in the dirt and her tongue lolled in the dirt and her fur was matted with dirt and blood and the yellow eyes looked at nothing at all. She had been fighting for almost two hours and she had fought in casts of two the better part of all the dogs brought to the feria. (122)

Such violence is disquieting because it places the reader in an unfamiliar zone of emotional involvement. That is, all three scenes depict the ordinary in conflict with the bizarre; or, put another way, the scenes put the domestic into conflict with the savage. Good, free youths are suddenly enclosed with vicious criminals; trained killer dogs battle a wild wolf; and a compassionate, polite young man is pitted against the personification of evil in a losing battle. That our sympathies shift allegiance from one scene to the next emphasizes the ambiguity of our emotional response to violence. Comforted by our own domesticity, we unequivocally side with John Grady and Lacey against the prison savages and John Grady against the Mexican pimp. Yet we can easily change our allegiance and root for a wild beast whose only hope for survival is its savagery. We are as much savage as civilized, and realizing that truth creates a discomforting moral dilemma. Yet the one emotion that is unambiguous is that we quit each brutal scene wanting to see someone punished – most probably the Mexican authorities who either manage or tacitly condone such unsettling encounters. What we forget in our impulsive need to mete out vicarious retribution is that the violence emanates not from some exotic villain but from the irrational actions of the male protagonists. In short, if we anticipate the circumstances of action (as the protagonists themselves seldom do) we must place blame for the violence on someone very much like ourselves – someone from our country, who speaks our language, who is recognizably 'good.' Subconsciously we realize the fault is our own. Once we analyze the violence and become conscious of who truly is at fault, however, we are little less absolved from blame. Knowing the cause does not significantly lessen the disquietude. At some level we rationalize that had the protagonists made themselves conscious of outcomes before acting so rashly, they might have saved us the pain of realization. Then the rationalization itself becomes unsettling. Our culpability becomes cyclic, growing more undeniable and inescapable.

More perplexing than the thoughtless acts themselves is that they do not induce behavior modification in the protagonists. Cognitive thinking does not seem to be part of masculine psychology. Even after the most traumatic experiences, John Grady Cole resorts to Western movie stereotypes and clichés. 'But it aint my country,' he laments to Rawlins as he saddles up to depart his home range for the final time. 'I'll see you old pardner,' he drawls in farewell (299). He seems unaware that his own actions may have contributed to Rawlins no longer being his compañero and to his having to leave his homeland. This blindness later contributes to his own death in *Cities of the Plain*. Similarly, at the end of *The Crossing*, Billy Parham demonstrates how little he has learned in his borderland journey from adolescence to adulthood. For no apparent reason he brutalizes the 'arthritic and illjoined' old dog that seeks shelter with him in the dilapidated waystation (423). He does not merely shoo it away, but pursues it down the road with a water pipe and rocks, as it staggers 'brokenly on its twisted legs' (424). Next morning, repentant, he tries to find the dog. Unable to do so, he sits and weeps in self pity. It is a scene reflected years later when, as a derelict in the twenty-first century, Billy sits under a concrete overpass eating dry crackers and pondering the difference between reality and illusions. As he later tells his caretaker Betty 'I aint nothin' (292). He dies personifying the disturbing trait of letting rash action precede thought. Considering such persistent wrong-headedness, and given McCarthy's parodic tone in closure of all three novels, the reader is left with little cause to sympathize with the male protagonist who has placed us in uncomfortable proximity with violence and who learns little that is salutary from his experiences. Such failure to respond reasonably to experience contradicts the empiricism by which most Americans define themselves.

Seen from another perspective, the male's psyche seems more instinctual than rational. Since the majority of his actions are violent, we can safely postulate that his instinct is energized by violence. This is hardly a new revelation, since many studies support the psychobiological origins of aggression. One of the most informative is Luigi Valzelli's *Psychobiology of Aggression and Violence*. The point that needs attention, however, is that McCarthy's violence is neither goal oriented nor self-serving. It promotes few of the male's basic needs. Instead, it leaves him hungry, poorly clothed, unsheltered, wounded, and without a mate. Nakedness, hunger, inadequate clothing, exposure to all sorts of weather, and ultimate alienation are thematic in the novels. We can only conclude, therefore, that instinctive violence is not in the best interest of the male. Since we have already noted that women are often victimized by such reckless male behavior, we can therefore conclude that it is detrimental to the entire species.

Because every character in McCarthy's harsh literal and figurative landscape is controlled by the universal randomness expressed in economics, environment, and heredity, we might conclude that Naturalism is the philosophical matrix that encompasses the violence of the Trilogy. The connectors and links in the chain of events leading to Boyd's death certainly epitomize the Naturalistic matrix. Given the self-destructive traits seen in the male behavior, however, we could argue that Naturalism itself lacks identity and equilibrium, gaining name and shape only when we impose referents and terminology from outside the texts. Moreover, characters in the novels make choices that could be termed free will and that are not defined solely or even principally by the deterministic impulse to self-preservation. As the pragmatic Lacey Rawlins says, 'Ever dumb thing I ever done in my life there was a decision I made before that got me into it. It was never the dumb thing. It was always some choice I'd made before it' (*All the Pretty Horses*

79). On the one hand, the female perceives, reflects, then acts. Her decisions emanate from what Art Berman terms 'the suppositions of a philosophical empiricism, which within the Anglo-American setting simultaneously define the grounds of objective knowledge and the limitations of such knowledge' (1). Contradictions mark such empiricism, but the process is nonetheless logically structured and self-preserving. On the other hand, the males' actions stem from what seem to be simple behavioristic motives. The males encounter stimuli and they respond, with limited regard to self-preservation or, in Rawlins' words, to the 'dumb thing' that might result. The cerebellum, not the cerebrum dominates. Consequences of such responses go unrecorded, and experiential cognition does not eventuate. From a purely textual perspective, therefore, Naturalism is not the fundamental principle of McCarthy's design. It is the matrix within which other epistemological forces are generated but not the forces per se. It neither explains nor accounts for the culpable actions of the male personae.

The second ramification of the male-female contrast argues less negatively for the male and for humankind generally than the epistemological scenario just presented. Adequate textual evidence exists to suggest that the alienation that overtakes John Grady Cole and Billy Parham implies the existence of an empathy that has somehow been distorted into severity. Appropriately, given the narrative settings, the clearest signs of this frustrated compassion appear in the protagonists' relationship with animals. John Grady is a local hero because of his loving concern for the horses on the Rocha ranch (book II). Billy Parham's mystical affiliation with wolves generally and his especial love of the she-wolf motivate all of *The Crossing*. Both of these relationships are marked by cajoling, patience, and caressing. Secondary manifestations of this compassion for animals do surface in a few of the human relationships. The textual pairings suggest that John Grady Cole and Lacey Rawlins, Billy and Boyd Parham, and John Grady and Billy do value each other above their typical level of concern for others. One hesitates to term these emotions 'love,' yet they do surpass mere camaraderie. Equally clear, however, is that the youths must camouflage these emotions – from each other and from those around them. In contrast to the animal relationships, these human relationships are permitted comforting words and physical contact only under circumstances most often pertaining to violence. In prison, John Grady and Lacey 'fought back to back and picked each other up and fought again' (*All the Pretty Horses* 182). When Boyd is shot, Billy 'knelt and turned his brother over where he lay in the bloodstained dirt . . . He lifted his head out of the dust' (*The Crossing* 271). Not until the doctor demands that he help treat Boyd's gunshot wound is Billy seen touching his brother again. Finally, only after John Grady is dead does Billy permit himself to gather his friend 'in his arms' (*Cities of the Plain* 261) and carry him away. Other than these rare moments born of trauma, the youths' conversations are circumspect (sometimes harsh) and physical contact is incidental. A clarifying antithesis to the emotional and physical chasms that separate best friends and brothers is the prolonged and detailed account of the doctor's professionally detached examination of the critically wounded Boyd (*The Crossing* 303–14).

We cannot extrapolate too much critical material from this inchoate compassion. Insofar as character development and motivations are concerned, it tantalizes more than explains. However, it does seem to alleviate the harsh conclusion that the masculine personae are unmitigatedly obtuse and violence prone. As we will soon discuss, the signs of underdeveloped compassion are another manifestation of the divergent technique that McCarthy uses throughout the two novels.

We argued earlier that the narrative flows out of nothing and ultimately vanishes into nothing and that thus the meaning of the narrative lies only in the traces left in that vanishing. The considerations of our two indicator topics (feminine presence and masculine violence) lead us back to this peculiar textual 'vanishing.' Every conclusion we might draw from McCarthy's distinct narrative techniques disintegrates into additional questions, each generating yet another entropic process. In so short a chapter we cannot exhaust the potential of these endlessly intersecting entropic relationships, but we can briefly exemplify the problematic domain in which they leave us. We have deduced, for example, that the males of the two novels act on instinct and that they abjure compassion and brotherly love. Are we also to conclude, therefore, that compassion and brotherly love are not native to the male instinct? Refusing that syllogistic gamut, are we to turn elsewhere and blame the paucity of reason and logical actions on culture? Is lifelong submersion in a violent, androcentric society the culprit? If so, the males (as cultural masters) must be blamed for fathering an endless chain of intellectual obtuseness that no female could ever breach. Such thinking in turn leads to the supposition that males and females are so essentially dissimilar that despite biological compatibility, they remain psychologically antagonistic. This sobering dichotomy in turn leads to questions about most of our cultural icons. Why do we marry; why do we choose to have children; why do we glorify the American family that Albert Ellis long ago recognized as a 'neurotic tangle' (182)? To explain how these cruel uncertainties came about, we must either embrace evolutionary absurdity or yield control to some Jester God not unlike the one who has driven the Caborca anchorite mad.

Such interrelationships are hardly unique to McCarthy (Thomas Pynchon comes to mind), but more than in any other modern writer the interrelationships are central and intentional rather than subsequent and subordinate. By evoking Pynchon, I do not want to imply undue parallels. Pynchon's is a different narrative form altogether. McCarthy's complexity is not Pynchonian obscurantism and his ethic is not apocalyptic paranoia. Molly Hite eloquently praises Pynchon's 'trope of the unavailable insight' (25); but no such insightless tropes typify McCarthy. Richard Poirier claims that 'sentence by sentence he can do more than any other novelist of this century with the resources of the English-American language and with the various media by which it is made available to us' (18). Though Poirier is speaking of Pynchon, the evaluation is equally apropos to McCarthy.

Despite the absence of quotation marks and a vocabulary that is occasionally daunting, McCarthy's prose is lucid. From text to text, his style is notably (and reassuringly) traditional. We find no self-conscious verbal pyrotechnics, no misaligned sentences, no multilateral dialogues, no extended Joycean/Faulknerian stream of consciousness. In fact, the immense irony that dominates McCarthy's narratives is born in the contrast between his traditional prose style and his postmodernist refusal to espouse ultimate causes and effects.

The maddening facet of McCarthy's texts is how they epitomize the immensely complex interrelationships that Gilles Deleuze elaborates in his analysis of *Alice in Wonderland*. Ronald Bogue elucidates Deleuze's idea: 'Like the object in the Looking-Glass shop that is always on the shelf above the one Alice is looking at, the aleatory point "lacks its own place": "it lacks its own identity, it lacks its own resemblance, it lacks its own equilibrium, it lacks it own origin." A mobile element or empty slot, the aleatory point is a self-differentiating difference that generates divergent series and structures them across a dispersional field' (Bogue 166–7). Like Alice's elusive object in the Looking-Glass shop, meaning in McCarthy seems always on a plane above the one we are looking at – or below, or beside, or beyond. The issue finally, however, is not whether McCarthy's complexity is unique, but that it is so profoundly anticipated in the simplest of traditional narrative components: plot.

* For this and all other translations of Spanish language passages in the novels, I thank Leighanne Thornton of Texas Tech University.

Marty Priola

Games in the Border Trilogy

Games play an important part in the worldview of Cormac McCarthy. What limited biographical information we have of him suggests that he is a great devotee of at least two games: pool and golf. And games appear throughout his novels, though they are more prominently featured in the Western works than the southern ones. As John Sepich and others have illustrated, the tarot cards in *Blood Meridian* may provide a door to the symbolic meaning of the book. The judge ascribes metaphysical stature to games in *Blood Meridian*:

> Men are born for games. Nothing else. Every child knows that play is nobler than work. He knows too that the worth or merit of a game is not inherent in the game itself but rather in the value of that which is put at hazard. Games of chance require a wager to have meaning at all. Games of sport involve the skill and strength of the opponents and the humiliation of defeat and the pride of victory are in themselves sufficient stake because they inhere in the worth of the principals and define them. But trial of chance or trial of worth all games aspire to the condition of war for here that which is wagered swallows up game, player, all. (249)

McCarthy's notion of games, then, is closely linked to his notion of fate and chance, fortune and misfortune, order and disorder. John Sepich's *Notes on Blood Meridian* lists references to game-playing in his concordance under the broader category of 'Chance, Fortune, and Deception' (164). It appears that the judge believes that games played for stakes prove that there must be order in the universe, because war, the ultimate game, is a 'forcing at last of the unity of existence' (249).

So what then do we make of John Grady Cole's chess-playing skills, and why are scenes of chess playing depicted so prominently in the Border Trilogy? The fact that chess appears at all in the Border Trilogy is odd; the fact that McCarthy is able to get away with it in a genre whose characters are not traditionally well-educated men of leisure is proof of his genius as a writer. But the references are not at first obvious. John Grady Cole is undeniably mythic in a way that transcends the hardbitten, instinctual image of the cowboy. He excels at everything, including chess. But the mind of a chess player is one that is different: Grady thinks carefully and analyzes everything about the board. These characteristics conflict with his seemingly impetuous actions involving other aspects of his life, such as horsebreaking and romance, and make him a more complex character than might be supposed. He can see several moves ahead, and he is able to anticipate the moves of his opponents. He is clearly not a rash young man. Chess requires too much patience.

Chess seems to be merely incidental to the scene where it first appears in *All the Pretty Horses*. McCarthy brings it up casually during his introduction of the Dueña Alfonsa; the game is the ostensible purpose for the meeting between her and John Grady Cole: 'he was invited to come to the house in the evening to play chess' (133). During the three games of chess that follow, the Dueña and John Grady discuss Alejandra and her reputation and how 'a woman's reputation is all she has.' John Grady wins the first two, and McCarthy is fairly specific in recounting the games:

> Like him she was lefthanded or she played chess with her left hand... Finally when he took her queen she conceded and smiled her compliments and gestured at the board with a certain impatience. They were well into the second game and he had taken both knights and a bishop when she made two moves in succession which gave him pause. He studied the board. It occurred to him that she might be curious to know if he would throw the game and he realized that he had in fact already considered it and he knew she'd thought of it before he had. He sat back and looked at the board. She watched him. He leaned forward and moved his bishop and mated her in four moves.
> That was foolish of me, she said. The queen's knight. That was a blunder. You play very well. (133)

In the third game, the Dueña 'used an opening he'd not seen before. In the end he lost his queen and conceded' (134). This scene offers several readings, each one equally problematic: it may, for example, be read to suggest that Cole is accomplished; the Dueña herself remarks upon his apparent gift: 'I could not use that opening again with such effect, she said' (134). But one may also read the scene as implying the greater skill of the Dueña, who toys with her victim before destroying him. Once she sees that he will not throw a game and that he will not make stupid moves, she has to play to win.

Though we will see more of John Grady's skill at chess in *Cities of the Plain*, several things are notable about its appearance in *All the Pretty Horses*. First, it demonstrates how closely linked the books of the Border Trilogy are. Almost nothing that happens in the last volume is not foreshadowed by something that happened in the first two. John Grady Cole's mastery of chess is not a new facet of his character in *Cities of the Plain*; rather, it is a refinement of his character in *All the Pretty Horses*. Second, the fact that John Grady beats the Dueña Alfonsa, herself no fool, demonstrates that Cole is at the very least a talented amateur player. When asked by the Dueña where he learned to play, his response is: 'My father taught me... He was about the best I ever saw' (134–5). John Grady Cole's passion for chess ties him to his father in a positive way, which is a rarity in

McCarthy's books prior to the Border Trilogy. Though John Grady Cole has already left his family, he will not abandon his memory of it. While the chess scene in *All the Pretty Horses* may be merely a representation of the struggle between John Grady Cole and the Dueña Alfonsa, the chess scenes in *Cities of the Plain* also emphasize paternal influence; Mac serves as a father figure to the young cowboy. However, chess represents only one aspect of their relationship. The games further imply that John Grady Cole has found a home at the ranch, and that Mac and the others are family to him. In broader terms of continuity, the games of chess in the Border Trilogy emphasize tradition; chess provides all of the characters a link to the past as well as something in the way of tradition to hang on to. While the world around these people is changing, the ancient game remains.

The chess games also serve as a reminder that Grady is a man of integrity and honesty. He will not lose a game to make Mac feel better. His skill is remarked upon, and he is teased for it: 'Son, you better cut the old man some slack. You might could be replaced with somebody that cowboys better and plays chess worse' (39). The last two chess games in the series between the rancher and his employee anticipate the endgame of the novel as well; Mac unexpectedly wins the antepenultimate game against the more skillful John Grady, but perhaps most interestingly, the final game of chess in the Trilogy, which Grady wins, is one where he sacrifices his bishop in order to win. Sacrifice is one of the essential metaphors of the Trilogy, and here, the sacrifice of the chesspiece foreshadows that John Grady will later give his life in avenging the death of the woman he loves.

Indeed, in the Border Trilogy chess also, if ironically, serves to remind us of the judge's pronouncements in *Blood Meridian* that life is *not* a game to be played lightly. In the conduct of his short, passionate life, John Grady does not always allow for the same dispassionate deliberation he invests in his chess playing; rather, in a game played for stakes, he demonstrates the true traits of a hero: he is unafraid to make sacrifices for those he loves, and he accepts his fate knowing full well what it will be. Nevertheless, like the various outcomes of the games, John Grady's destiny is not fated. He chooses it. His conflict with the posturing pimp Eduardo is much like a chess game: moves are made after deliberation. Though John Grady seems compelled by a force larger than himself, he walks willingly and with no little premeditation into his own death. Their contest of wills reveals that though Eduardo can set him up, his moves are not always the expected ones; the sudden thrust of John Grady's knife through the pimp's throat was a move that Eduardo had not anticipated. At the last, we see John Grady rising above his abilities, and winning against the much more skillful *cuchillero* – even as he loses everything. Sometimes the bishop must be sacrificed in order to win the game.

James D. Lilley

'The hands of yet other puppets': figuring freedom and reading repetition in *All the Pretty Horses*

A self that has no possibility is in despair, and likewise a self that has no necessity.
(Søren Kierkegaard, *The Sickness Unto Death*)

To what extent are we free to influence and control the patterns of our lives? From the feral Appalachian wilderness of his first four novels to the austere Southwestern borderlands of his most recent fiction, Cormac McCarthy's work investigates the extent to which we can ever claim to be 'at home' in our environment. The McCarthy canon is patterned by a network of fables and tales, but there is one story that is told time and time again. This story involves a youth whose childhood is permeated with pain and absence. Born into an existence that is always already inscribed with the most profound of losses, the child escapes in a futile attempt to restore some sense of worth – of wholeness – to his life. And yet this quest for novelty, for freedom, takes place within a landscape that has already determined and doomed its outcome: McCarthy's texts form the same narrative shapes time and time again, mapping the repetitive movements of pawn-like protagonists[1] who are dragged around an uncompromising landscape by forces completely outside of their own control.[2]

However, despite the familiar terrain, the common cast of characters, and the overarching determinism of McCarthy's landscape, there is something about what happens within the repetitive pages of his novels – the dynamic spaces between and inside his texts – that continually delights, disgusts, and mesmerizes. As readers we mirror his characters' progression through the landscape, carried along by a plot in which the seeds of denouement are planted in the opening lines of the text, yet totally absorbed in the process of watching the patterns develop and grow. When we attempt to articulate the kind of freedom John Grady Cole achieves in *All the Pretty Horses*, we may be well advised to keep the ambivalence and complexity of our responses as readers absorbed in McCarthy's fiction close at hand since, as I will argue, the freedom John Grady achieves seems, paradoxically, to operate within the confines of necessity. As Tom Pilkington says of *All the Pretty Horses*, 'The inextricability of fate and free will has never been more vividly dramatized' ('Fate and Free Will on the American Frontier' 318).

'How it was with the old waddies': repeating and reliving the frontier West

It is hard not to read *All the Pretty Horses* without McCarthy's previous novel, *Blood Meridian*, in mind. As Edwin T. Arnold comments, 'McCarthy loves the idea of dark twinship . . . and it seems clear to me that John Grady Cole and [*Blood Meridian's*] the kid are such twins, a century apart . . . but brothers nonetheless' ('The Mosaic of McCarthy's Fiction' 19). In more ways than one, *All the Pretty Horses* begins where *Blood Meridian* ends. The novel opens as our protagonist, John Grady Cole, confronts a lifeless body. However, whereas *Blood Meridian* closes with the implicit murder and mutilation of 'the kid,' we begin *All the Pretty Horses* with John Grady gazing at the embalmed, candle lit remains of his maternal grandfather: 'Along the cold hallway behind him hung the portraits of forebears only dimly known to him all framed in glass and dimly lit . . . He pressed his thumbprint in the warm wax pooled on the oak veneer. Lastly he looked down at the face so caved and drawn among the folds of funeral cloth . . . That was not sleeping. That was not sleeping' (3). The ranch that John Grady's grandfather established in the Old West has now disappeared into the reluctant hands of a divorce lawyer, and from the disintegration of his father's relationship with his mother to the inexorable cancer-driven deterioration of his father's body, a sense of loss and decay pervades John Grady's Texas from the outset of *All the Pretty Horses*. Compared with the murderous Southwestern borderlands of *Blood Meridian*, however, the first two chapters of *All the Pretty Horses* present a surprisingly benign landscape – as if *Blood Meridian* has exhausted and incinerated all the available blood:[3]

> Back in the old days, said Blevins, this'd be just the place where Comanches'd lay for you and bushwhack you.
> I hope they had some cards or a checkerboard with em while they was waiting, said Rawlins. It dont look to me like there's been nobody down this road in a year . . . What in the putrified dogshit would you know about the old days? (57)

Perhaps the most disturbing loss of all for John Grady is the destruction of the Old West's chivalric code. Whereas John Grady's grandfather was always prepared to fight for the honor of his mother, his own father is even reluctant to put up a legal fight for the ranch that was to be his inheritance.[4] John Grady's relationship to both his family's history and the history of the West is one of distance and separation; in the same way that he watches his mother performing on the San Antonio theater stage, desperately looking for a connection with his own past, his father also seems to share his son's sense of loss and control: 'People dont feel safe no more, he said. We're like the Comanches was two hundred years ago. We dont know what's goin to show up here come daylight. We dont even know what color they'll be' (26). John Grady has become an outsider in the Twentieth-Century West, the object of awkward glances from surrounding theater audiences as he disposes of his cigarette ash in the turned-up bottoms of his jeans, and the dutiful but estranged son, musing over the body of his dead grandfather – the last male

Grady – as the unfamiliar eyes of his 'dimly known' forebears watch over him and the funeral collapses around his feet, racing 'away [and] tumbling among the tombstones' (5). The patterns and liturgies of the present (burials, plays, courting rituals) no longer speak to him, and he drifts among empty signifiers in a West where even the decomposed carcass of a horse skeleton has been replaced by the hollow, rusted shell of a broken automobile, a world in which his mother no longer uses her real name and acts out a role on a distant stage.[5] The codes and the code words of the Old West have lost their authority and currency, and the gradual dissolution of his own name – from Grady into Grady Cole – is simply part of a larger and more pervasive disintegration: from the airy words that the preacher, Jimmy Blevins, transmits over the radio, to the timeworn language that his old girlfriend clings to ('What if it is just talk? Everything's talk isn't it?', 28), John Grady's Texas is as empty and devoid of ground as the name 'Blevins' or 'Cole':

> There's any number of Jimmy Blevinses out there in the world but its Jimmy Blevins Smith and Jimmy Blevins Jones. There aint a week passes we dont get one or two letters tellin us about a new Jimmy Blevins this or Jimmy Blevins that . . . We get em from overseas you know. Jimmy Blevins Chang . . . What was your name?
> Cole. John Grady Cole. (295)

Gail Moore Morrison notes that *All the Pretty Horses* 'is fundamentally a *Bildungsroman*, a coming of age story in the great tradition of Hawthorne, Twain, Melville and James, that archetypal American genre in which a youthful protagonist turns his back on civilization and heads out . . . into the wilderness' (176). In this respect, it is not hard to see why the open space of the West and the symbolic resonance of the American frontier are appealing to McCarthy; for, as Jane Tompkins notes, 'life on the frontier is a way of imagining the self in a boundary situation – a place that will put you to some kind of test' (14). However, *All the Pretty Horses* is a Western, not a *Bildungsroman*, and although there are obvious similarities between these two genres, their differences are significant. Hawthorne and Twain were writing *Bildungsroman* when the frontier was still a living reality and America was looking to establish its own geographical boundaries; however, *All the Pretty Horses* takes place at the time of Heisenberg, *Invisible Man*, and John Wayne. John Grady does not want to *extricate* himself from the past – establishing a new beginning, divorced of all precedent, on the frontier; rather, his journey down into Mexico becomes an elegy to the Old West, an attempt to move backwards in time to a place where the codes of the Old West are still valorized. Whereas the *Bildungsroman* is driven forward by a quest for novelty, Westerns are necessarily retrospective, repetitive and elegiac, driven by a desire to repeat and relive the established patterns and plots of the past: 'Within a terribly strict set of thematic and formal codes, the same maneuvers are performed over and over . . . Half the pleasure of Westerns comes from this sense of familiarity' (Tompkins 25). Afloat in a time that has lost its grounding in the solid, unwavering codes of the past, John Grady looks in the only direction he has ever known, determined to live his own Western, complete with strict chivalric codes, daring rescues, and, much to the chagrin of many critics, love at first sight.[6] Repeating the motion of 'the painted ponies and the riders of that lost nation [that] came down out of the north,' John Grady, his sidekick, Lacey Rawlins, and the young outlaw, Blevins, move down into Mexico from the north 'across that mineral waste to darkness ... lost to all history and all remembrance' (5).

Whereas Blevins and his stolen horse move through the landscape in an attempt to escape from the law, to *avoid* returning to the grounded confines of a prison cell (and sometimes to flee literal grounding – death by lightning), John Grady looks to the Mexican landscape to provide him with a ground that reunites him with the codes of the Old West. In particular, John Grady wants to anchor his journey in the Western's traditional locus of meaning, the natural world: 'he put his hands on the ground at either side of him and pressed them against the earth and in that coldly burning canopy of black he slowly turned dead center to the world, all of it taut and trembling and moving enormous and alive under his hands' (119). Of all the nineteenth-century American writers, McCarthy shares most in common with Melville and Thoreau; his characters are often forced into a confrontation with the awesome, transcendent, power of the natural world (especially the centrality of death within its processes), and although their successes are limited, they seem to be motivated by the same quest that drives Thoreau's *Walden*:

> Let us settle ourselves, and wedge our feet downward through the mud and slush of opinion, and prejudice ... and appearance, that alluvion which covers the globe, through Paris and London ... till we come to a hard bottom and rocks in place, which we can call *reality*, and say, This is, and no mistake; having a *point d'appui*, below freshet and frost and fire, a place where you might find a wall or state, or set a lamp-post safely, or perhaps a gauge. (779)

In this sense then, John Grady is not simply repeating his grandfather, he is also repeating the American project itself, looking for a new beginning that reestablishes itself with a forgotten past. When Rawlins is about to cross the river into Mexico, he asks Blevins why 'the hell would we want you with us for?'; Blevins replies, 'Cause I'm an American' (45).[7]

The journey through Mexico and back into time soon uncovers an ostensible Eden, the origin and *point d'appui* of all time and history: 'In the lakes and in the streams were species of fish not known elsewhere on earth and birds and lizards and other forms of life as well all long relict here for the desert stretched away on every side' (97). For John Grady, the Hacienda de Nuestra Señora de la Purísma Concepción represents everything that his grandfather's ranch in San Angelo was in the halcyon days of the frontier; or, as Rawlins comments, 'This is how it was with the old waddies, aint it?' (96). La Purísma is even complete with its own grandfather-figure, Don Héctor Rocha y Villareal, who, like John Grady's grandfather, is the first male heir to carry the name beyond the ravages of time (7, 97). However, unlike Eden or the Immaculate Conception after which La Purisma is named, the hacienda was not created out of nothing. Under the God-like gaze of Don Héctor, La Purísma is the site of a breeding program that attempts to fuse the best stallions America has to offer with the horses that run wild around the ranch. We sense in Don Héctor's design something of the frontier attitude that neurotically sought to control and shape the West, at any cost, according to the will of America.[8] Indeed, when Don Héctor lands at La Purísma in his personal airplane from the industrial center of his homeland, we cast our mind back to the myth of the frontier which, as Richard Slotkin comments, 'represented the redemption of the American spirit or fortune as something to be achieved by playing through a scenario of separation, temporary regression to a more primitive or "natural" state, and "regeneration through violence"' (*Gunfighter Nation* 12). With La Purísma, McCarthy brings together several 'New Beginnings' – the American frontier, the Mexican revolution, John Grady's journey into Mexico – and frames each within a rigid structure originating in, and driven by, loss.

Negotiating the symbolic: language and loss

Given the centrality of loss within Jacques Lacan's work, it should not be surprising that his theories help to cast some light on the dark patterns of McCarthy's work. Lacan's familiarity with linguistics and philosophy are fused into a radical revision and extension of Freud's work, locating the Oedipus complex at the center of both psychological development and language acquisition. At the heart of the Oedipal drama is a profound sense of detachment: like the kid's birth in *Blood Meridian* ('The mother dead ... did incubate in her own bosom the creature who would carry her off', 3), life is a gift that implicitly carries with it the loss of the Mother – specifically, the loss of fusion with the Mother inside the womb. The Lacanian subject is always seeking to reinstate the wholeness that is lost at birth. Within the Oedipal conflict, the child becomes aware of its separation from the Mother and, unable to become the sole object of the Mother's desire, is forced to look for union with the Mother on an Other, symbolic, level: language. In short, the child identifies with the position of the Father, the symbolic source of language, in the Oedipal triangle, directing its speech toward that Other – Lacan's Name of the Father (*nom-du-père*).

When John Grady leaves Texas, he leaves, essentially, an orphan.[9] Although his mother and father are still alive (at least for the moment), we have seen the extent of his alienation from his heritage, the distance he feels from his birth. In order to reestablish the relationship with his lost past (the blood and motion of the horses and the landscape of the Old West) he enters into Don Héctor's Symbolic Order, identifying with his position as master. As sovereign of the signifying chain, Don Héctor controls words and their meanings: within his own house, complete with its own chapel for worship, even a priest's words lose their power to signify

('The powers of the priest are more limited than people assume', 144). The greatest worry that Don Héctor has for his daughter is that she will become a free-thinker; for, as he cautions John Grady, 'Beware gentle knight. There is no greater monster than reason' (146): no transgressions of his Law, no deviations from his Word, will be tolerated. John Grady's identification with Don Héctor baptizes him into the realm of the Symbolic. He is given the authority to ride the central phallic signifier of La Purísma, the black stallion, and his power soon goes to his head, riding it without permission and even bareback as it copulates with a recently tamed mare, 'swinging up while Antonio still stood holding the trembling mare by the twitch, the mare standing with her legs spread and her head down and the breath rifling in and out of her . . . and him leaning low along the horse's neck talking to him softly and obscenely' (129).

Given John Grady's earlier oath to the 'ardenthearted' blood of the horse, it is hard not to sense the corruption of that wildness in the pliant splendor of the stallion, set out to stud, that he loves to ride on the hacienda: 'What he loved in horses was what he loved in men, the blood and the heat of the blood that ran them. All his reverence and all his fondness of his life were for the ardenthearted and they would always be so and never be otherwise' (6). In La Purísma, union with the 'ardenthearted' blood of the horse is inseparable from a ruthless mastery:

> [H]e spoke constantly to it in spanish in phrases almost biblical repeating again and again the strictures of a yet untabled law. Soy comandante de las yeguas, he would say, yo y yo sólo. Sin la caridad de estas manos no tengas nada. Ni comida ni agua ni hijos. Soy yo que traigo las yeguas de las montañas, las yegyas jóvenes, las yeugas salvajes y ardientes.[10] (128)

His relationship with Alejandra is similarly narcissistic, enjoying the stallion not for its inherent beauty and blood, but rather for what it signifies to her, for the reaction it will produce from her: 'Because John Grady loved to ride the horse. In truth he loved to be seen riding it. In truth he loved for her to see him riding it' (127). He revels in the new-found power of his language, shaping and playing with Alejandra's words and searching 'for the meanings he wished to hear, repeating them silently to himself and then questioning them anew' (123). John Grady creates his own narrative, his own Western, using the power of the Symbolic Order to erect patterns and mold experiences according to his own demands. Alejandra is an undeveloped character because for John Grady she becomes, like the broken mares, a mirror in which he can watch his own Symbolic power growing. Subsequently, the most erotic image for John Grady at La Purísma is his own reflection; Alejandra is never more sexual than when she is mirroring his own actions and words – perhaps in the 'dark' and 'silky' reflective waters of the lake where he watches her 'across the still black surface to where she stood on the shore,' undressing with him and descending into the water, merging her naked reflection with his (141), or when her words become a perfect echo of his, creating an almost masturbatory moment of pleasure: 'Tell me what to do. I'll do anything you say. The selfsame words he'd said to her' (146).[11]

At La Purísima, John Grady is witness to the intricacies of life inside Don Héctor's 'discourse community' (Woodson 151), and he begins his own metaphorical process of language acquisition as he starts to realize the Symbolic power of words. For Lacan, speech enables us to vocalize our desire for the Mother, to establish an artificial linguistic order in the empty middle ground between ourselves and the absent Mother's womb. However, the acquisition of language, achieved through an identification with the Symbolic (specifically the 'Name of the Father'), is always a double-edged sword. On the one hand, it is the medium through which the son, unable to merge with the Mother from its prelinguistic position, substitutes discourse for intercourse; however, as Lacan's mirror stage suggests, a linguistic union with the Mother is no real union at all: language, the mirror surface, can only bring together 'specular,' shadowed, reflected egos. In Lacan's words, language is 'frustration in its essence'; 'I identify myself in language, but only by losing myself in it like an object' (*Écrits* 42, 86). So, as Malcolm Bowie comments, in identifying with the Symbolic Father, the child is confronted by

> the original Other ... [who] introduces a gap between desire and its object[s] which the subject is bounded by, and bound to, throughout his life and at all levels of his experience. This primordial estrangement is by its very nature destined to recur ... ubiquitously. It is the origin of language and the subject alike, and provides an essential precondition for the humanity of man. (119)

In the same way that language must always miss the mark in its attempt to force a union with the Mother, there is a sense at La Purísima that Don Héctor's 'breeding program' is attempting to transport Mother nature into the realm of the Symbolic, controlling the shape of her future by breaking her into manageable parts. So although the action within La Purísima is reminiscent of Eden, the text begins to juxtapose life on the hacienda with another order – an order more powerful even than Don Héctor or his horse-breaking surrogate son.

As John Grady begins to break the wild horses he notices that 'The wild and frantic band of mustangs that had circled the potrero that morning' soon cease to exist when he has tamed them: the tamed horses quietly cry to each other 'as if some one among their number were missing, or some thing' and now look like 'animals trussed up by children for fun' (107, 105). When John Grady and Luis are out in the mountains, surrounded by wild horses, Luis suggests that the horse transcends even the power of God or his earthly surrogates: 'among men there was no such communion as among horses ... Rawlins asked him ... if there was a heaven for horses but he shook his head and said that a horse had no need of heaven' (111). In Lacanian terms, horses and their fluid, ardenthearted blood constitute the realm of the Real in *All the Pretty Horses*. For Lacan, the Real represents the underlying, inarticulable nature of reality figured by the Mother's position in the Oedipal triangle. Given the limitations of the human situation, we can only approximate an encounter with the Real, bouncing our ineffectual language off of its surface (like John Grady breaking a horse) in a vain attempt to establish a connection with, and domination over, our surroundings. However, as Luis reflects in the mountains, horses have their own heaven, their own community that, like Lacan's Real and the Mother's womb, can never authentically be penetrated. In the same way that there is a narcissistic flavor to the Symbolic's mastery of the Real, there is also something sadomasochistic, as if its domination is annihilating the very source of its original desire. In other words, although the child's identification with the Symbolic Father is motivated by its incestuous desire to possess the Mother, the acquisition of language and control also contains within itself the seeds of distance, nostalgia, and castration. As the child moves closer toward the Mother, it is confronted by the very distance of language: the Name of the Father represents the possibility of separation and castration as well as identification and incest. Indeed, as John Grady moves closer toward the objects of his desire, attempting to control and master the equinal 'Real'ity of nature and perhaps even the realty of La Purísma (Alejandra is, like John Grady's mother, the only sibling of the last male heir of her family), his relationship with Alejandra causes division and separation rather then unity and possession. In the same way that his own mother leaves him alone and without a home, so too Alejandra effects his castration from the Symbolic Order of La Purísma when she tells her father of their relationship; and she will later leave John Grady alone in Zacatecas feeling 'a loneliness he'd not known since he was a child . . . wholly alien to the world' (282). So, like the drama of Eden, transgression of the Law of the Father results in expulsion; the relationship between John Grady's Eve, Alejandra, and the Adamitic protagonist is forbidden, and violation of this Law propels John Grady toward his prison cell in Saltillo, his body confined like the mares he has tamed.[12] He is turned over to the captain, another figurehead of the Symbolic Order, who further perpetuates the repetitive cycle of loss that patterns the novel.[13]

'Within the walls of a prison': history as revenge, repetition as freedom

In the same way that the judge inhabits the center of *Blood Meridian*, directing the dance of the kid toward his ultimate fate, Dueña Alfonsa stands at the heart of *All the Pretty Horses*, moving John Grady around like a pawn at her chessboard. Like the judge, she speaks in parables and her skill with language is reminiscent of the judge's omniscient garrulity. The dueña helps John Grady to contextualize the losses he suffers in the novel by sharing the lessons of her own life history. In his first meeting with the dueña, John Grady is witness to Alfonsa's appetite for revenge; she apparently throws the first game of chess she plays with him in order to set the scene for her intricate revenge ('the King's Own opening', 134). However, Alfonsa has a much more significant revenge in mind. Like John Grady, the dueña has been scarred as a youth – both literally and figuratively – and in the same way that our protagonist is victimized and cast out by his lover's father, so too Alfonsa's love for the young revolutionary, Gustavo Madero, has been forbidden by her own father, leaving her, like John Grady in San Angelo, exiled 'in her own country'

(239). In an echo of our protagonist's fall from grace – from heir to the Symbolic throne, to pawn of the signifying chain – so too Alfonsa's impressive schooling in language allied her with 'free-thinking' revolutionaries such as the Maderos and, like John Grady's transgressive romance with Alejandra, these alliances inevitably led to censure and castration by the Law of the Father.[14]

The dueña's reading of the Spanish Civil War becomes a model for all history, repeating the familiar patterns of her own life and the Mexican revolution:

> The political tragedy in Spain was rehearsed in full dress twenty years earlier on Mexican soil . . . Nothing was the same and yet everything. In the Spaniard's heart is a great yearning for freedom, but only his own. A great love of truth and honor in all its forms, but not in its substance. And a deep conviction that nothing can be proven except that it be made to bleed. Virgins, bulls, men. Ultimately God himself.[15] (230)

For Dueña Alfonsa, John Grady represents an opportunity for revenge. Driven by a desire to reverse the patterns of history that have left her a pawn to Symbolic circumstance, the dueña uses her grandniece, Alejandra, to effect a vicarious revenge on history;[16] in the matter of her niece's fate at least, the dueña will finally be 'the one who gets to say' (137). Alfonsa is dedicated to preventing Alejandra from bending to the power of her father and her society; she wants her grandniece 'to have a very different marriage from the one which her society is bent upon demanding of her. I wont accept a conventional marriage for her' (240). Ironically, it seems as if John Grady could have been the perfect suitor for Alejandra, for the dueña 'has long been willing to entertain the notion of [Alejandra's] rescue arriving in whatever garb it chose' (240). However, our protagonist is never able to make his 'case' to the dueña since his fate is sealed before he even sets foot in La Purísma: 'the affair of the stolen horses was known here even before you arrived' (228). The dueña rejects John Grady's 'case' essentially because his luck is bad, because 'certain circumstances . . . conspired against' him (228), and although Alfonsa is prepared to believe that John Grady's involvement with Blevins and the stolen horse is unfortunate, her uncompromisingly fatalistic ethical code will not allow this fact to mitigate his guilt: 'I know your case. Your case is that certain things happened over which you had no control . . . But it's no case. I've no sympathy with people to whom things happen. It may be that their luck is bad, but is that to count in their favor?' (240).

At the heart of the dueña's worldview is a radical determinism that views the present as inextricably tied to the puppet strings of the past, and she tells John Grady the parable of the coiner in order to explain 'those very things which led me to decide against you in the end':

> My father had a great sense of the connectedness of things. I'm not sure I share it. He claimed that the responsibility for a decision could never be abandoned to blind agency but could only be relegated to human decisions more and more remote from their consequences. The example he gave was of a tossed coin that was at one time a slug in a mint and of the coiner who took that slug from the tray and placed it in the die in one of two ways and from whose act all else followed . . . It's a foolish argu-

ment. But that anonymous small person at his workbench has remained with me...
My father must have seen in this parable the accessibility of the origins of things, but
I see nothing of the kind. For me the world has always been more of a puppet show.
But when one looks behind the curtain and traces the strings upward he finds they
terminate in the hands of yet other puppets, themselves with their own strings which
trace upward in turn, and so on. (231)

Framed by the parable of the coiner and the image of life's puppet strings is a view of history in which the present is driven by an endless process of repetition. The only constants within such an existence are the blood and pain of those subjected to the inexorable and illimitable unfolding of history: 'It is supposed to be true that those who do not know history are condemned to repeat it. I dont believe knowing can save us. What is constant in history is greed and foolishness and a love of blood and this is a thing that even God... seems powerless to change' (239). Indeed, as Gail Moore Morrison notes, Dueña Alfonsa's meeting with John Grady is reminiscent of Faulkner's *Absalom, Absalom!*, itself a novel about reading history: 'In her monologue, as in Miss Rosa's, Alfonsa reveals her outrage at her own sense of her powerlessness, inferiority and missed opportunities' (186). However, unlike Miss Rosa, the dueña does not see her puppet strings terminating in the hands of an omnipotent and unknowable God; her picture of history is more akin with Mr. Compson's, the ultimate fatalist, for whom all history disappoints and frustrates as it reaches back into an infinite, unknowable, and Godless past:

We have a few old mouth to mouth tales... we see dimly people, the people in whose living blood and seed we ourselves lay dormant and waiting, in this shadowy attenuation of time... They are there, yet something is missing; they are like a chemical formula exhumed along with the letters from that forgotten chest, carefully, the paper old and faded and falling to pieces... you bring them together again and again nothing happens; just the words, the symbols, the shapes themselves, shadowy inscrutable and serene, against that turgid background of a horrible and bloody mischancing of human affairs. (*Absalom, Absalom!* 80)

And yet there is an important difference between Mr. Compson's and Dueña Alfonsa's reading of history that accounts for her decision to reject John Grady's 'case': for, unlike the passive fatalism of Compson, the dueña does not use the overarching determinism of the present as an excuse for a drunken retreat to the attic:

It's not so much that I dont believe in [fate]. I dont subscribe to its nomination. If fate is the law then is fate also subject to that law? At some point we cannot escape naming responsibility. It's in our nature. Sometimes I think we are like that myopic coiner at his press, taking the blind slugs one by one from the tray, all of us bent so jealously at our work, determined that not even chaos be outside of our own making. (*All the Pretty Horses* 241)

Alfonsa's somewhat paradoxical position is that freedom is a rebellious choice that we make when we realize 'That there is nothing left to lose,' that we are pawns played according to the ruthless rules of history. Whereas John Grady takes the more passive approach to fate, rejecting Rawlins' adamant request to leave Blevins behind since life could have just as easily pushed either one of them into his awkward position, Dueña Alfonsa rejects John Grady precisely because he is guided by unfortunate and unlucky puppet strings. Her position combines John Grady's tacit fatalism with Rawlins' dedication to freedom of choice ('Ever dumb thing I ever done in my life there was a decision I made before that got me into it. It was never the dumb thing. It was always some choice I'd made before it', 79). Because of the radical fatalism of her worldview, Alfonsa recognizes the importance of the puppet strings that drag people through the present (regardless of whether 'certain circumstances... conspired against' them, 228); however, in order to escape the deterministic wheel of history that has ruined the women in her family, she refuses to accept John Grady's excuse that he had nothing to do with his fellow traveler's crimes: responsibility and meaning must be erected at some point to make a stand against fate.

The dueña refers us back to the central question of McCarthy's texts. Her parable of the coiner, shaping destiny as he places the slugs in the die, reflects the very first image of the novel, the candle wax that John Grady shapes with his finger before confronting the body of his dead grandfather, and the description of the kid's movement West in *Blood Meridian*: 'Only now is the child finally divested of all that he has been. His origins are become remote as is his destiny and not again in all the world's turning will there be terrains so wild and barbarous to try whether the stuff of creation may be shaped to man's will or whether his own heart is not another kind of clay' (*Blood Meridian* 5). As John Grady rides back to America, he hears 'a steady distant hammering of metal as of someone at a forge' (*All the Pretty Horses* 279). In the same way that the parable of the coiner continues to haunt the dueña, so too it appears as if John Grady has inherited the figure of 'that anonymous small person at his workbench.' He immediately takes Alfonsa's advice when he reaches the crossroads after leaving La Purísma for the last time, declaring 'The hell with it... I aint leavin my horse down there' in an echo of the dueña's realization that within the determinism of life 'there is nothing to lose' (257, 239). His return to La Encantada echoes Alfonsa's desire to avenge her past, to rebel against the powers of the Symbolic by repeating and reversing history. Indeed, the text ceases to expand at this point as if, like John Grady, its 'life led only to this moment' and all that remains is to rewind the novel back to the point when the horses were joined together, before fate threw them into dislocation and disarray. We witness John Grady reverse the roles of his own recent history, dragging the body of the manacled captain through the center of the same town that he had been taken to with Rawlins, and forcing his prisoner to repeat his words in the same way that the captain coerced Rawlins to 'Tell em whatever they wanted to hear':

John Grady stepped behind the captain. Tenemos un preso, he said.
Tenemos un preso, called the captain.
Un ladrón, whispered John Grady.
Un ladrón. (262)

John Grady even manages to repeat the single shot with which the captain disposes of Blevins – this time, however, using the captain's pistol to aid his own escape by using the same 'dead flat pop' that killed Blevins to gauge the distance of his enemies: 'Captain, he said. You just fired a shot for the common man' (271).

Both the dueña and John Grady exact revenge on their past, attaining a paradoxical and problematic freedom *within* the deterministic patterns of history. Aware that there is nothing left to lose, they do not so much perform free and original acts but, rather, repeat the same acts in reverse, thereby changing the qualitative essence of the patterns of history. The dueña's gift to John Grady is, like the acquisition of language, a double-edged sword. On the one hand she forces him to realize that his life will always miss the mark, will never ground itself in a stable past. However, she also helps him to see the world more clearly and truly, enabling him to articulate his loss and desire in language:

> He thought that in the beauty of the world were hid a secret. He thought the world's heart beat at some terrible cost and that the world's pain and its beauty moved in a relationship of diverging equity and that in this headlong deficit the blood of multitudes might be exacted for the vision of a single flower. (282)

Although John Grady loses much and gains little over the course of the novel, his bloody progression through the text culminates in this vision. He immediately realizes that his father has died, that his life will take place in a future divorced from all precedent, shaped by puppet strings that regress toward an asymptotic past, and situates himself within an existence that finds its only grounding in death.

For Lacan, the goal of analysis is to attain a freedom *within* the ultimately empty and determined symbols of language. Influenced by a strand of philosophy that runs from Kierkegaard through Nietzsche and up to Heidegger, Lacan sees the human subject, like the dueña and John Grady, placed at the center of a drama fueled by loss, and situated among surroundings that determine their destinies and the shape of their language. However, although language is as powerless to map Reality as the newborn child is to return to the womb, Lacan, like the dueña, appreciates the necessity of making a stand: to not speak, to refuse to erect necessarily empty meanings and responsibilities, is to become, like the blind man who cannot sign his way out of the captain's jail, a pawn to the Symbolic and a victim of fate. As Mikkel Borch-Jacobsen comments, 'the subject of desire must unveil himself (decipher himself) outside, openly, *even as the nothing (the gaping hole) that he is*. Hence the inextricable double-bind where Lacan is caught ... "Present your absence," "Announce your desire," "Manifest your nothingness," "Speak your death"' (134).

The difference between the John Grady that leaves San Angelo to recover the lost past of the Old West and the John Grady that returns at the end of the novel is not that one has broken free from the determinism of his past (the traditional denouement of the *Bildungsroman*); rather, the protagonist that returns is fully aware that life, like the Western, is driven by repetition, that the strings of the present are pulled by the hands of 'yet other puppets.' Yet both the dueña and John Grady represent the possibility of another kind of paradoxical freedom that, like Pérez inside the Saltillo jail, exists within the inescapable confines and patterns of history – a freedom, to use Lacan's words, 'never more authentic than when it is within the walls of a prison' (6). Within the deterministic landscape of McCarthy's work, this is the most authentic human existence possible, fully aware of its destiny as, to use Heideggerian language, a being-towards-death, yet at the same time refusing to subscribe to fate's 'nomination,' waging an unending and futile war to assert the only rebellious freedom that exists: the freedom to will the repetition of the past toward the future.[17] Heidegger describes this position as 'an impassioned *freedom towards death* – a freedom which has been released from the Illusions of the "they," and which is . . . certain of itself, and anxious' (311), and Lacan reminds us that this kind of paradoxical authenticity, aware of the inevitability of absence and emptiness, is precisely the goal of the speaking individual.[18] What is of utmost significance is not *what* is spoken because, as John Grady finds out, all speech takes place on the inauthentic and reflective mirror surface of language; rather, at issue in McCarthy's work is *how* to speak, how to use language freely while remaining fully conscious – like the judge, the dueña, and John Grady – of the limitations of life as a speaking, and dying, subject.

This is why the subjective experience of reading a McCarthy novel is so central to the interpretive process. In the same way that his characters realize a paradoxical freedom within the determinism of their landscape, so too we as readers – similarly subjected to the determinism of plot and language – find an impressive, qualitative 'dynamic space' within the confines of the text. And like John Grady's inherently frustrating struggle to break horses and to use language, our interpretations that attempt to apportion meaning – to 'break' the text – within this space are also destined to miss the mark by rationalizing what is essentially a subjective, qualitative, and irrational experience of freedom. Yet like John Grady we must move on, repeating, reordering, and reinterpreting the given, Symbolic patterns of the text, asserting our responsibility like a coiner 'hammering out like his own conjectural destiny all through the night of his becoming some coinage for a dawn that would not be' (*Blood Meridian* 310). The challenge that McCarthy seems to issue the interpreter is to carry the shadows of his text forward into the future, 'the world to come' (*All the Pretty Horses* 302).

Notes

1 If we must compare McCarthy with Faulkner, as many critics seem to insist, perhaps it is here that the grounds for a more interesting comparison can be established; for, as Donald Kartiganer has noted, Faulkner, like McCarthy, employs repetition as a narrative strategy: 'Faulkner's craft of fiction is to tell stories, and then to tell them again. This is the strategy that animates each of the novels, and is implicit to the stories; moreover, it describes the dynamic space between the texts, the relation from one text to another' (21).

2 As D. S. Butterworth avers, McCarthy's characters 'are always already doomed ... [as] inert and passive objects with little or no control' (96).
3 Indeed, much seems to have changed in the hundred years that separates the borderlands of *Blood Meridian* from *All the Pretty Horses*; the foundation-stones placed in the first surveys of the West, detailed in the Epilogue to *Blood Meridian*, have now become fences and telegraph poles, 'yoked across the constellations passing east to west' (11), that in conjunction with the meager remains of American Indian culture strictly delineate the boundaries of John Grady's existence: 'He rode where he would always choose to ride, out where the western fork of the old Comanche road coming down out of the Kiowa country to the north passed through the westernmost section of the ranch and you could see the faint trace of it bearing south' (5). Indeed, the text seems to hint that there is something about the very nature of definition and division that is anathema to the West: 'In eighteen-eighty-three they ran the first barbed wire. By eighty-six the buffalo were gone. That same winter a bad die-up. In eighty-nine Fort Concho was disbanded' (7).
4 Gail Moore Morrison comments that '*All the Pretty Horses* is permeated with a sense of loss, alienation, deracination and fragmentation' (173); it seems as if both our protagonist and the West itself have 'come to the end of something' (*Horses* 5).
5 Linda Woodson comments that 'At the beginning of *All the Pretty Horses*, the physical and metaphorical country which John Grady Cole knows has come to an end with the death of his grandfather and the selling of the ranch ... His world is gone and cannot be replaced' (150).
6 Perhaps we should not be surprised that McCarthy's description of the love affair with Alejandra is so remarkably flat and unoriginal; John Grady must see her in this way for his own narrative, his Western, to work.
7 McCarthy complicates matters in *Blood Meridian* by showing this project to be an unending one; for, as the fence posts and telegraph poles that end *Blood Meridian* and begin *All the Pretty Horses* suggest, the very movement West brought about the seeds of its civilization and therefore destruction as a mythic, untouched Eden. This is precisely the repetitive pattern of loss-mastery-loss that drives John Grady out of Texas, and it will be the overarching, inexorable pattern of the rest of his life.
8 Patricia Nelson Limerick comments that 'A belief in progress has been a driving force in the modern world; as a depository of enormous hopes for progress, the American West may well be the best place in which to observe the complex and contradictory outcome of that faith' (29–30).
9 From *The Orchard Keeper* (1965) to his latest work, *Cities of the Plain*, McCarthy's landscape is littered with orphans. All of his protagonists, and many of his secondary characters, are either literally or figuratively orphaned.
10 'I am commandant of the mares, he would say, I and I alone. Without the charity of these hands you have nothing. Neither food nor water nor children. It is I who bring the mares from the mountain, the young mares, the wild and ardent mares' (quoted in Morrison 191).
11 For further discussion of Alejandra, see Dianne C. Luce's 'When You Wake' and Terri Witek's 'Reeds and Hides: Cormac McCarthy's Domestic Spaces.'
12 The Symbolic Order of the prison is governed by another master who, like Don Héctor, represents a figure of wealth and, surprisingly, freedom: 'All agreed that Pérez was a man whose power could only be guessed at. Some said he was not confined to the prison at all but went abroad at night. That he kept a woman and family in town. A mistress' (190).

And like John Grady in La Purísma, Pérez enjoys hearing, speaking, and practicing words, creating an environment in which there are more signifiers than signified objects ('How many damn names have they got for a cigarette butt?', 185) and in which gossip becomes the most valuable commodity that John Grady can offer to Pérez: 'tell me stories of your life of crime.... I like to practice my english' (191). But John Grady is not careful enough with language; he does not heed the words of Pérez's advice – 'Take care with whom you break bread' – and almost meets his death when he sits down to dine with his assassin. Life outside of the prison's Symbolic Order is extremely treacherous: those not affiliated with its Law and Master are 'simply outside. They live in a world of possibility that has no end' (188). Rawlins and John Grady barely survive their ordeal in the prison; they emerge violated and marked by the Symbolic Order, carrying blood foreign to their bodies and resembling the cattle they worked with 'in the holdingpens branding and earmarking and castrating and dehorning and inoculating' (98).

13 The captain has his own form of 'breeding program'; this time Rawlins and Blevins become the wild American mares as the captain rapes and abuses them – Blevins the virginal 'mare' with 'no feathers' and Rawlins the victim of the 'shower room': 'He keeps a white coat back there on a hook. He takes it down and puts it on and ties it around his waist' (169). Like Don Héctor the captain controls words, shaping their meanings according to his desire, and looking for their reflection in the responses of the Americans: 'Tell em whatever they want to hear, bud, whispered Rawlins. It dont make a damn' (165). Yet John Grady's quest is for ground, for a stable 'truth' rooted in the uncompromising codes of the Old West; the captain's words, *empty* of signified ground, are precisely what led him to flee 1940s' Texas, and so his position is not negotiable: 'There aint but one truth, said John Grady. The truth is what happened. It aint what come out of somebody's mouth' (168). It is not so much that John Grady believes words are powerless (his whole experience at La Purísma is testament to their power) but, rather, that he believes them to be grounded in a fixed, foundational truth; indeed, he tries to save his relationship with Alejandra by insisting that his words do represent something other than 'just talk': 'I told you things I've never told anybody. I told you all there was to tell' (251). By refusing to acknowledge to the captain that all Symbolic language is empty and ungrounded, constructed according to the desires of whoever is master, John Grady both preserves the illusion that his *true* love is grounded forever in reality and necessitates, once again, his symbolic castration, expelled along the signifying chain toward the prison at Saltillo where even his name – the most important word of all – has been lost from memory.

14 Alfonsa describes the accident that caused the amputation of some of her fingers as a kind of Symbolic castration, losing the most important signifier she possesses – her wedding ring finger – when she is alone with her 'father and uncle' (234).

15 Of course, Alfonsa's reading of history also paraphrases John Grady's movement through the text – his experience with the Symbolic Order of Don Héctor's La Purísma, the captain's La Encantada, and Pérez's Saltillo – and also obtains as a reading of the American project, allying John Grady with the fate of the Indians that haunt and propel him at the beginning of the novel and that watch him fade into the sunset at its denouement: 'They had no curiosity about him at all. As if they knew all they needed to know. They stood and watched him pass and watched him vanish upon that landscape solely because he was passing. Solely because he was vanishing' (301).

16 Indeed, as Morrison notes, 'Alejandra is precisely the same age Alfonsa was when Francisco and Gustavo returned from Europe and her "life changed forever"' (187).

17 In a phrase that reminds us of John Grady's fate, John D. Caputo comments that 'Being-toward-death . . . means staying in motion' (199).
18 See also Gilles Deleuze's *Difference and Repetition* and J. Hillis Miller's *Fiction and Repetition: Seven English Novels* for insightful and thorough discussions of repetition theory.

S. K. Robisch

The trapper mystic: werewolves in *The Crossing*

The wolf and the trapper play a game in which the trapper tries to predict the wolf's behavior and the wolf tries to scrape up a meal without being killed. The trapper employs a 'set' of signs to lure the wolf, which must decode the signs properly in order to escape the trap. During the turn-of-the-century campaign against wolves in America, the game developed such sophistication that trappers had to become amateur chemists and ethologists. As the number of wolves dropped off, both the government and the popular press mystified trappers as crusaders against demonic cattle killers. By the thirties, the decade in which *The Crossing* opens, the Southwestern United States was all but rid of its wolves, and a 'great trapper' might catch three or four in a season. When the few wolves left escaped the most carefully planned efforts to catch them, their infamy achieved legendary proportions. The Snowdrift Wolf, The Custer Wolf, Las Margaritas, Lobo the King of the Currumpaw, Old Three Toes, and dozens more became ghosts who merely inhabited the bodies of wolves.

The mystification of the wolf has certainly continued, from its malevolent persona in children's stories to its benevolent one on wildlife calendars. No wonder, then, that the first published excerpt of *The Crossing* was called 'The Wolf Trapper' when it appeared in the July 1993 *Esquire*. An editorial comment on the first page assigns McCarthy a part in the drama as well, calling him 'a literary lone wolf who is rarely seen beyond his natural habitat of El Paso' (96).

McCarthy's wolf-westerns did not begin with *The Crossing*, but with *Blood Meridian*. As John Sepich explains in the concordance to his *Notes on Blood Meridian*, the outlaw wolf 'may be emblematic' of both a 'kind of man' and of 'a non-moral rapacity' (145). In *Blood Meridian*, the kind of man equated with the wolf is the outlaw; in *The Crossing*, the wolf is less emblematic, but still connected to an archetype – the trapper. A 1941 movie audience attending *The Wolf-Man* laughs at the supporting cast on screen playing characters who can't see that Harry Talbot, sweating and filthy, clothed in rags, bearing a pentagram on his hand and wearing the obvious pallor of guilt after having just mauled someone in the forest, is the werewolf. They leave the theater, go to a bar, and raise their glasses to a man in boots, a ducking jacket, and a cowboy hat, who reeks of lupine menstrual blood, week-old urine, skunk hide, and rotten meat, and who mere hours earlier was thinking like a wolf in order to commit a murder.

A man's man (until recently all recognized trappers were male) who champions the proliferation of humanity and its claims of ownership, the trapper is himself trapped – in the body of a man with a limited olfactory capacity, slow locomotion, and susceptibility to the elements. Therefore, he must learn to think like a wolf in order to catch one – to have a mind like a steel trap. And while most wolfers have been working men who felt some remorse after earning their blood money from government agencies and stock-growers associations, others have tortured wolves before killing them, stringing them up and peppering them with small-caliber fire, wiring their mouths shut and turning them out to starve, committing the acts of monsters.

If the she-wolf in *The Crossing* is of the subspecies *Canis lupus monstrabalis*, then her kind would have been wiped out by 1935; if *Canis lupus mogollensis*, then by 1942. Either is likely, though both have recently been folded into *Canis lupus baileyi*, a subspecies brought back from near extinction in the 1970s with the help of trapper Roy McBride. The dates of demise for *monstrabalis* and *mogollensis* straddle the story's time frame in the late 1930s, at both the apex of early monster movie popularity and the end of the Bureau of Biological Survey (the principal agency of animal 'control'). The passing of the cowboy, a leitmotif throughout the Border Trilogy, is connected with the passing of the she-wolf in *The Crossing* as well, and anticipates Billy's final condition in *Cities of the Plain* as an out-of-work movie extra sleeping under a bridge in the year 2002.

He is part of a long tradition of trappers. William Penn established possibly the first governmental wolf bounty in the 1600s; in 1739, before gaining some fame as a Major-General in the Revolution, Israel Putnam was recognized for crawling into a wolf den in Pomfret, Connecticut and killing its resident she-wolf (McIntyre 41); in 1820, seventeen-year-old Sewell Newhouse invented the famous 4½ trap, which he soon would be producing by the thousands (Bateman 59–60); at the turn of the century, Jack London, Ernest Thompson Seton, and Teddy Roosevelt were embroiled in the 'Nature Fakers' controversy, at the heart of which were several wolf and trapper tales. And in the late 1920s, J. Stokely Ligon, who oversaw the New Mexico district of the Bureau of Biological Survey, made heroes of the trappers on his payroll.

Ligon was a better public relations agent than a scientist, and occasionally dressed up the accomplishments of his bounty hunters in order to justify federal funding increases. When he found a successful trapper like W. C. Echols, he made it a point to mythologize the man. Not that the legend went very far – Echols never became the historic figure Ligon might have hoped – but McCarthy has made his own contribution (David E. Brown 67, 76, 83, and telephone interview). In *The Crossing*, one werewolf is the master trapper Echols, doubted by another werewolf, Don Arnulfo, who questions the theory that 'Echols es medio lobo el mismo,' (Echols is half wolf himself) and that 'conoce lo que sabe el lobo antes de que lo sepa el lobo' (he tells me that he knows what the wolf knows before the wolf knows it) (45).

In addition to identifying the Newhouse 4½ as the wolftrap of Billy's era, McCarthy authenticates his story by referring to the trapper's practice of reading up on other methods and engaging in the tradesman's art of cataloging the wolf's tricks. He includes the cowhide horse-hoof slipper and the buckskin dismounting cloth and describes in detail the preparation, scenting, setting, and anchoring of traps. Echols and another man, named Oliver, are invoked as wizards of the trade; Billy's father tells him that Oliver could set traps from horseback, though he doesn't know how the man accomplished the feat (23). McCarthy even personifies the traps 'with their jaws agape like steel trolls silent and mindless and blind' (36) just as the cannons in Stephen Crane's *The Red Badge of Courage* are personified as participants in a chaos transcending human design. McCarthy has given us opportunities to romanticize and mystify the wolf, but he has also loaded his narrative with the blood and darkness that ensue when we seize those opportunities – that is, when we trap the wolf.

Four particular moments in the novel assure us that McCarthy is spiritualizing the trapper's occupation. The first occurs in Echols's cabin (actually located at the OK Bar Ranch in Cloverdale, New Mexico (David E. Brown 87)), a war room made to look like a friar's apothecary 'with its chemic glass a strange basilica dedicated to a practice as soon to be extinct among the trades of men as the beast to whom it owed its being' (17). The vials contain matrices, scents of wolf and prey brewed to draw the wolf to its death, 'dark liquids. Dried viscera. Liver, gall, kidneys' which are to the trapper sacred material. But the god of human beings, who have taken as their mission the destruction of the wolf, is depicted as 'insatiable,' unable to be appeased by 'any measure of blood' (17), so the success of the trapper results in his own extinction as well as his prey's.

The second moment is when Billy's father teaches him how to dig and set a trap. We are witness to the process until Will Parham finishes and backs away, at which point he is transformed:

> Crouched in the broken shadow with the sun at his back and holding the trap at eye-level against the morning sky he looked to be truing some older, some subtler instrument. Astrolabe or sextant. Like a man bent on fixing himself someway in the world. Bent on trying by arc or cord the space between his being and the world that was. If there be such a space. If it be knowable. (22)

Here is Ahab hunting the white whale; Will Parham's effort to fix himself in the cosmos, tying an arc or cord to, possibly around, space, is consistent with a motif common to many wolf stories – the wide open region, whether tundra, desert, or sky, and by whom that space is given a boundary or fitted with an anchor.

The third mystical scene is the most powerful. Billy is led to Don Arnulfo, who knows the wolf better than anyone and who in fact bears its name. Billy tells the don that he holds two of Echols' matrices from the old cabin and is trying to trap a wolf, to which the don responds 'that the matrix was not so easily defined. Each hunter must have his own formula,' and that 'only shewolves in their season were a proper source' (45). This is a contradictory response – a coyote method of teaching. The don violates his premise that each matrix must belong to the hunter who mixes it by then dictating an ingredient. When Billy tells the don that he is after a she-wolf, Arnulfo replies that the wolves have all been trapped by Echols, as though the conversation to this point has been irrelevant. Eventually, the don gives the cryptic advice that leads Billy to set the trap in the dead campfire – 'that place where the acts of God and those of men are a piece,' where earth and fire are one- and the more important advice, that

> El lobo es una cosa incogniscible, he said. Lo que se tiene en la trampa no es mas que dientes y forro. El lobo propio no se puede conocer. Lobo o lo que sabe el lobo. Tan como preguntar lo que saben las piedras. Los arboles. El mundo. [The wolf is an unknowable thing, that which one has in the trap is no more than teath and fur. One cannot know the true wolf. Wolf or what the wolf knows. It's like asking what the stones know. The trees. The world.] (47)

Billy learns, as an Arthur from a Merlin, that in the trap the wolf begins the transformation toward incorporeality, a monster existing only in the imagination. 'Not even God can bring it back,' says Don Arnulfo, whom the other villagers think is a *brujo*, the Mexican equivalent of a Navajo skinwalker and a Euro-American werewolf.

Following the old oracle's clues, Billy sets the trap beneath the warm ash of the vaqueros' fire, the technique used by Roy T. McBride to catch the outlaw wolf Las Margaritas before McBride went into the business of trapping the progenitors of the Blue Range population, which was governmentally reintroduced in 1998 (McBride 59–60). Billy encrypts the trap twice, first under the cover of fire, to fool the wolf's sharp senses, then with a note to the vaqueros, written in Spanish and in sand – an on-site revelation of the trap that the wolf will not be able to understand. Ironically, Billy's father tells him to go back to the set and dig it up because the vaqueros might be illiterate.

Unlike the easy domestication of White Fang in Jack London's novel, or Ernest Thompson Seton's kitsch pathos in his story of Lobo and Blanca, McCarthy devotes one hundred pages to the meticulous formation of Billy and the she-wolf's uneasy alliance. Billy comments following his setting of the trap in the ashes of the vaqueros' campfire, 'you read my sign . . . if you can' (50), which implies that he knows he will catch the wolf this time, and that he isn't sure he wants to. After the catch, the negotiations between the two characters follow a slow and expertly crafted course leading to Billy standing by the wolf in the bottom of the fighting pit. It is the first scene since her capture in which she is finally free of any muzzle – and now they are both trapped. When the hacendado's son steps into the pit and up to the bargaining table, he uses two techniques to establish the new rules of negotiation. First, he lies. He claims that the wolf 'had been caught in a trap in the Pilares Terras,' and encountered 'crossing the river at the Colonia de Oaxaca,' and refers to the wolf as 'him' (118). The lie carries some historical interest, Oaxaca being the southernmost point of Gray wolf territory on the continent (Link and Crowley 135). Second, he equates Billy with the wolf, thus denying them both the power to bargain. When Billy explains that the wolf 'knew nothing of boundaries' the young man agrees, but he declares that 'whatever the wolf knew or did not know was irrelevant and . . . the boundary stood without regard' (119). He also reminds Billy of the *portazgo*, for which the town has decided to accept the wolf in lieu of cash. 'When the boy said that he had not known that he would be required to pay in order to pass through the country the hacendado said that then he was in much the same situation as the wolf' (119).

Earlier in the novel, just after he has seen wolves pack hunting antelope, Billy wonders about the tastes of his blood, the blood of the wolf's prey, and 'the world it smelled or what it tasted.' Later, while riding out to bury the wolf, he learns the answer: 'He could feel the blood of the wolf against his thigh . . . and he put his hand to his leg and tasted the blood which tasted no different than his own' (125). At the burial site, he places his hand on the wolf's head and closes his eyes, and in so doing steps from a merely sympathetic position to one like John of Patmos', in a beautiful passage of what he thinks the world might imagine the wolf to be: 'What we may well believe has power to cut and shape and hollow out the dark form of the world surely if wind can, if rain can. But which cannot be held never be held and is no flower but is swift and a huntress and the wind itself is in terror of it and the world cannot lose it' (127). This is the end of both the last wolf and the last wolfer, who have been chased into oblivion by the border law they learned in the fighting pit. And, having been at some time both a trapper and an outlaw, Billy has learned, in the tradition of trappers, outlaws, and readers, to become a wolf in his imagination.

The final mystification of the hunt is found in McCarthy's indication that the she-wolf is caught in Billy's trap on the day his parents are killed (52–3). On McCarthy's desert, just as on Melville's ocean, there is no mechanical trap without its astral counterpart, no trapper without dark insight, no body without either a soul or the argument over a soul, no world of blood without a matrix for blood behind it, and no Wolf without a Ghost Wolf.

Charles Bailey

The last stage of the hero's evolution: Cormac McCarthy's *Cities of the Plain*

I want a hero: an uncommon want,
   When every year and month sends forth a new one,
Till, after cloying the gazettes with cant,
   The age discovers he is not the true one.
                         (Byron, *Don Juan, Canto the First* lines 1–4)

In my youth's summer I did sing of One,
The wandering outlaw of his own dark mind.
        (Byron, *Childe Harold's Pilgrimage. A Romaunt, Canto the Third* lines 19–20)

Where's the all-american cowboy at? (McCarthy, *Cities of the Plain* 3)

Lord Byron and Cormac McCarthy: a curious yoking. Certainly critics have remarked the echoes of Homer, Shakespeare, Melville, and Faulkner in the novels of Cormac McCarthy, but none, insofar as I know, cites Byron. *Cities of the Plain*, however, makes the connection to Byron unavoidable and, considering its position as the last of the Border Trilogy, also inevitable. The heroic character of the knight from the courtly love romances of the Middle Ages inspires *All the Pretty Horses*. The tragic hero of ancient Greek and Renaissance drama inspires *The Crossing*. Proceeding naturally from the courtly hero through the tragic hero, the anti-hero, developed by Byron in such works as *Lara, Childe Harold's Pilgrimage*, and even the comic *Don Juan*, provides the inspiration for *Cities of the Plain*. And as the first two novels deconstruct the models on which their heroes are based, so the third deconstructs the most recent heroic model, the anti-hero, to prepare the way for the emergence of a new hero.

Harold Bloom and Lionel Trilling, editors of Romantic poetry and prose for *The Oxford Anthology of English Literature*, claim that Byron provided in his hero's persona 'a thoroughgoing transvaluation of values,' the hopelessness of which was 'precisely prophetic of... recent literature' (Kermode and Hollander 315). In fact, the self-satirical *Don Juan*, though it was on the surface a comic take-off on Byron's other darker works, only masked Byron's loss of belief in a conventional heroic attack upon life. Responding to the social, economic, and scientific developments of his age, Byron sensed the irrelevance of the romantic and optimistic heroes of previous times, and produced instead the High Romantic hero. Reserving some discomfort for the seeming selfishness and cruelty of the character, he nevertheless followed his own instincts to what critics have come to call the anti-hero. Thus, when I use the term 'anti-hero,' I do not mean the clumsy, often inept character of the picaresque novel that started the tradition, nor do I mean the tortured, raging, mysterious, Satanic Byronic hero of Byron's own serious work, so popular later in nineteenth-century fiction. You will find no Tom Jones or Heathcliff in the Border Trilogy. Instead, I mean the character of highly developed sensitivities, the 'wandering outlaw' intent on self-realization and personal salvation, capable of great courageous moral action in the cause of human freedom, whose unconventional impulses rise from some inherent spiritual core, one (in Byron's words) whose 'madness [is] not of the head, but heart' (*Lara* line 358). This description might easily apply to John Grady Cole and to Billy Parham in *Cities of the Plain*. And just as Byron became disillusioned and, in lament, debunked the previous heroes as incompatible with a world that is too much with us, so does McCarthy lament even the anti-hero, made finally irrelevant in a world corrupted and degraded by advancing science and nuclear technology. Moreover, McCarthy's work clearly views this anti-hero sifted through the tradition of the American novels of the late nineteenth and twentieth centuries. Hence, it is only natural – evolutionary – that Byron's desire for a 'hero: an uncommon want/When every year and month sends forth a new one' should transvalue to the question of McCarthy's last novel: 'Where's the all-american cowboy at?'

Let me begin with the first layer of this argument, which, because of time and space, must at best comprise only some brief comments. *All the Pretty Horses* is a courtly romance. John Grady Cole, the knight-errant, wanders into the wilderness and falls in love with an unattainable lady of a distinctly higher aristocratic class. He performs for her as a knight should, displaying a God-given talent for martial skills – in this case, taming horses. When he comes to dinner at the hacienda after the first day of breaking horses, the vaqueros treat him with the reverence due a saint. In the Saltillo prison, he even engages in direct tournament combat, in which homemade knives become swords and metal cafeteria trays become shields. In his futile attempt to win Alejandra's hand, John Grady plays chess, in all its medieval imagery of knights and bishops and kings and queens, with her great aunt Doña Alfonsa, who at one point addresses him directly: 'Beware gentle knight' (457).

The lady Alejandra is the epitome of the courtly lady who inspires John Grady's heroism. Not only do her looks and social position establish her as the idealized embodiment of perfect beauty, but the religious imagery with which McCarthy presents her associates her clearly with the Virgin, just as the lady of the courtly romance is a version of the Madonna. Her home is the Hacienda de Nuestra Señora de la Purísima Concepción (the Estate of Our Lady of the Immaculate Conception). In a contest to prove his worth, one that echoes the chess game with

Doña Alfonsa, John Grady plays pool with her father, Don Héctor, the hacendado (a sort of landed baron). The poolroom, once the hacienda's chapel, has never been desanctuarized. As Don Héctor says, 'What is sacred is sacred' (144). They play on holy ground. The ritual of the lovers' secret affair is to ride into the mountains by moonlight and stop on the shores of a lake. On one occasion, she literally becomes Our Lady of the Lake (evoking both the Arthurian legend and the Virgin Mary), emitting the celestial light of the Madonna:

> The water was black and warm and he turned in the lake and spread his arms in the water and the water was so dark and so silky and he watched across the still black surface to where she stood on the shore with the horse and he watched where she stepped from her pooled clothing so pale, so pale, like a chrysalis emerging, and walked into the water . . . She was so pale in the lake she seemed to be burning. Like foxfire in a darkened wood. That burned cold. Like the moon that burned cold. (141)

Finally, when John Grady parts with his friend Rawlins to return to make one final bid for Alejandra, Rawlins asks him why: 'On account of the girl?' John Grady's reply unites the spiritual and physical aims of the cowboy as romantic knight: 'The girl and the horses' (211).

Likewise, *The Crossing* takes classical tragedy as its model. The works of literature it self-consciously echoes are *Hamlet* and *Oedipus the King*. In terms of the novel's plot structure, the opening initiation tale concerning Billy Parham and the wolf (though it seems complete in itself) actually sets up the Oedipal and Hamletesque nature of the story of the next two crossings. After the burial of the wolf, Billy returns to New Mexico to find his family's ranch abandoned. During his absence, an itinerant Mexican Indian, whom he had unfortunately directed to his home for a secret meal, has murdered his parents and looted the ranch. Without reflection, Billy collects his fourteen-year-old brother Boyd, and the two of them cross the border to retrieve the horses, their only inheritance and their dead father's property. From this point on, even through the third crossing, the *Hamlet* parallels become undeniable. For one thing, like Hamlet, Billy is a dispossessed son whose father's murder took place while he was away. Second, out of moral responsibility and guilt, he must reclaim what the dead father, in the son's absence, has been robbed of. Other details support this same view. Namely, along the way, he encounters a troupe of traveling actors. And the core event of the third crossing is a gravedigger's scene when, discovering that Boyd has died in a gunfight, Billy personally digs up his brother's bones.

As McCarthy knows, if *Hamlet* is present, then *Oedipus* is present. McCarthy has set this connection up in Billy's first crossing, accompanied by the pregnant she-wolf. In this section Billy not only discovers himself (the initiation), he also asserts himself Oedipally against his father. Billy follows his father's orders as he sets traps for the wolf, knowing that, to protect the cattle, his father will kill her. But no sooner does Billy set the traps than he contrives to check them alone. Acting from an Oedipal impulse, he replaces his father, and when he captures the wolf, instead of bringing her back to the ranch as his father has instructed, Billy steals his father's wolf (a female and a mother) and pursues his own course. Moreover, the Oedipal significance of his father's death, Billy's fault because he led the Indian to the ranch, seems again unmistakable. In the second crossing, having 'killed' his father and stolen his 'mother,' Billy goes after the horses – like Oedipus and Hamlet, to claim what remains of his father's kingdom, the primogeniture he has been denied. Although he loses the other horses, he does hold onto his father's personal horse, Niño, which he rides until the book's end. Can one imagine a more Freudian, Oedipal image? Further details corroborate this reading. The book is a veritable mine of blind soothsayers, all of whom warn Billy that truth is 'seen' only in blindness and that the greatest temptation is *orgullo*: pride, hubris.

So *All the Pretty Horses* presents the courtly knight as hero. *The Crossing* presents the tragic man as hero. In sequence, *Cities of the Plain* presents the antihero, introduced by Byron and developed in the American novel. The first clear indication of the heroic nature of the action lies in the enterprise that is the focus of the plot. As in *All the Pretty Horses*, the enterprise is to save a lady and enshrine her in a kind of chapel. This time, the lady is Magdalena, held in the cruel and degraded life of a prostitute by the dark pimp Eduardo. John Grady falls in love with her, but her Mexican nationality and the life that traps her make her as unattainable to him, really, as Alejandra in *All the Pretty Horses*. He means, however, to marry her and bring her to a little house on Mac McGovern's land, a cottage that he paints blue, the color of the Virgin, and that he decorates with nothing but a crude *santo*. This time everyone in the novel knows the enterprise is doomed, even Billy, who becomes his cohort, but John Grady continues despite the obstacles because he is driven by his sense of heroic mission. This dedication to his mission is that kind of madness that Byron identifies in his assessment of Lara – the 'madness . . . not of the head, but heart' (line 358). The idea that this mission amounts to madness, though presented comically, suffuses Billy's reactions to John Grady's request that Billy help and act as courier to buy Magdalena from Eduardo. Variously he says: 'Shit . . . Smile or something, will you? Goddamn. Tell me you aint gone completely crazy . . . Do you know what they're goin to do with you? They're goin to hook up your head to one of them machines and throw a big switch and fry your brains to where you wont be a menace to yourself no more . . . You're in a dangerous frame of mind, son. Did you know that?' (*Cities* 118–20). But, as I said, it is a madness of heart, the driven quality of the hero. In his own defense, John Grady says, 'I feel some way like I didnt have nothin to do with it. Like it's just the way it is. Like it always was this way . . . There's some things you dont decide. Decidin had nothin to do with it' (121). Even Eduardo, the enemy pimp, says of John Grady that he is 'in the grip of an irrational passion' (134). Both of the figures of aged wisdom in the book – Mr. Johnson and the blind maestro – advise John Grady to follow his heart, no matter the consequences. According to Mr. Johnson, 'I think you ought to follow your heart, the old man said. That's all I ever thought about anything' (188). In the next scene, juxtaposed as if for emphasis, when John Grady asks the maestro if he is a fool to try to marry Magdalena, the old man replies:

> A man is always right to pursue the thing he loves.
> No matter even if it kills him?
> I think so. Yes. No matter even that. (199)

This driven quality makes John Grady a hero from another sphere, a spiritual world where the values of good prevail. Like the references to his madness, the assessment of his 'other worldliness' fully informs the book. One of his fellow cowboys, Troy, defines that quality prophetically early in the story when he talks about his brother, another cowboy of John Grady's ilk, who fell in love with a whore: 'There's a kind of man that when he cant have what he wants he wont take the next best thing . . . I think he [Troy's brother] loved that girl. I think he knew what she was and he didnt care . . . I think he was just lost. This world was never made for him. He outlived it before he could walk' (28).

Moreover, as in *All the Pretty Horses*, the action of the story is knightly. If anything, John Grady is the more fully developed knight. His martial powers with horses become unsurpassed and unsurpassable, a mystical association with the horses' souls. He has also become the undefeatable chess player, moving the knights and bishops of the board about with the strategy of the schooled and experienced master. And, of course, the knifefight, the duel, of *All the Pretty Horses* is repeated in the climactic, bloody confrontation with Eduardo, in which John Grady rises to become a filero, a cuchillero – for which I can find no exact English equivalent. But he becomes the 'expert wielder of the knife blade.' Metaphorically, he becomes the swordsman, the fencer, the knight.

Furthermore, he exercises this martial, if irrationally driven expertise, again as in *All the Pretty Horses*, in the cause of the lady, the Madonna. Magdalena is another version of the courtly lady, her cause made more desperate by the horrors of the world that entraps her. Her physical description, her pale skin and lush black hair, suggest Alejandra from the previous novel. She is also Our Lady of the Lake, only this time from the whorehouse named the White Lake. She has the beauty of the courtly lady, but the world has made her a whore. In a neat exchange, while her criada dresses her, the old woman whispers, 'Como una princesa [Like a princess] . . . Como una puta [Like a whore], said the girl' (101). McCarthy provides an interesting touch in the one-eyed criada who attends Magdalena. She corresponds to Doña Alfonsa, the imperious dueña of *All the Pretty Horses*. But what a degradation! She also suggests the nurse/servant figure of traditional courtly romances, like Angela the Old of Keats' 'Eve of St. Agnes' or Juliet's nurse. The Madonna/Magdalene dichotomy that McCarthy chooses to characterize Magdalena should not be confused with the archetypal attitudes toward women expressed in Jung's universal symbols or the dialectic poles of Levi-Strauss's structuralism. Magdalena is clearly the innocent Virgin stained and degraded by the modern world. She tells her own story: at thirteen sold into prostitution to pay a gambling debt, resold by the church where she sought protection, resold another time by the police after they abused her. She is Magdalena, the holy whore, victimized by the church and state. Even her epilepsy, which seems at first a blot on her perfection, McCarthy offers up in the biblical sense as part of her spiritual mysticism, what he calls 'the dormant sorcerer' (225), finally prophetic and visionary. Just prior to her murder, barely warding off an attack, Magdalena cups her palms before her eyes and, in the darkness, sees 'herself on a cold white table in a cold white room' (225). When she dies, she dies clutching a *santo*, the only relic she has brought from her earthly life. Her name also associates her with the other female, saint-like figure of the novel. Mr. Johnson's dead daughter, Mac McGovern's dead wife, whose spiritual presence hangs over the ranch like a guardian angel, was named Margaret, a derivative of the name Mary, and shortened, of course, to Maggie. Margaret, Maggie, Magdalena, Mary Magdalene, Saint Mary – they all become one in the spiritual fusion of the novel.

For all its nobility, what dooms the enterprise and, finally, what dooms John Grady himself is a completely degraded world. Both the physical and spiritual worlds in which the hero must act make true, successful heroism impossible. The urban world encroaches on the wilderness, and the urban world is rotten – El Paso and Juárez, the cities of the plain, Sodom and Gomorrah. The arena for the cowboy/knight's heroism quickly and irreversibly diminishes. Some of these degradations I have already mentioned. The Madonna is forced into prostitution. The aristocratic dueña has descended to the cowardly one-eyed criada. The lake has become a whorehouse. But not only that, the cowboy's way of life is reduced and disappearing in the face of advancing, destructive technology. The American government has commandeered the wilderness for nuclear testing. The romantic wilderness has changed, losing both its romance and its spirituality. McCarthy briefly comments on what the West was and what it has become in recalling the history of old man Johnson: 'He'd been born in east Texas in eighteen sixty-seven and come out to this country as a young man. In his time the country had gone from the oil lamp and the horse and buggy to jet planes and the atomic bomb but that wasnt what confused him. It was the fact that his daughter was dead that he couldnt get the hang of' (107). Mr. Johnson's daughter was, of course, Margaret, the spiritual ideal (perhaps the actual spirit) of the ranch country, and she is dead. The warrior spirit of the wilderness has also passed. At another point in the novel, Mr. Johnson discusses the poisoning of wolves, the animals presented somehow as fit opponents for the cowboy in his struggle against nature. The wolves, spoken of with respect and dignity, of course, hark back to the associations of the wolf's nobility as a natural creature in Part I of *The Crossing*. Mr. Johnson mourns because the passing of the wolves has stolen the noble character of both the country and the cowboy's work. He says, 'when things are gone they're gone. They aint coming back . . . it had always seemed to me that somethin can live and die but the kind of thing that [the wolves] were was always there. I didn't know you could poison that. I aint heard a wolf howl in thirty odd years. I dont know where you'd go to hear one. There may not be any such a place' (126). The story plays this judgment out. When the cowboys face predators that threaten their cattle, they face not wolves, but scavenging wild dogs that, like the puppy John Grady retrieves from their den, can be easily domesticated, unlike a wolf, to a pet.

What is the upshot of this degradation of civilization, and the spirit and character of nature? It makes the heroic attack upon life impossible. As anticipated in Byron's presentation of the anti-hero, the enterprise of the modern hero – chivalric or tragic – makes him a 'wandering outlaw' (*Childe Harold's Pilgrimage. A Romaunt, Canto the Third* line 20). This is, in fact, the very language McCarthy uses. Billy says to John Grady:

> I just wonder if you even know what a outlaw you are.
> Why?
> Why do I wonder it?
> Why am I a outlaw.
> I dont know. You just got a outlaw heart. (219)

On top of that, the hero's wandering shrinks to retreat, not a search for new heroic adventures, but an escape from the horrors of a corrupt and repulsive world. After Magdalena's murder, John Grady says to another cowboy he encounters on the range: 'I wish I could ride . . . I wish I could . . . I'd ride and I'd never look back. I'd ride to where I couldn't find a single day I ever knew. Even if I was to turn back and ride ever foot of that ground. Then I'd ride some more.' It is the state of mind of the modern hero: 'I've been thataway, said the rider' (231). The point is that all heroes – courtly or tragic or 'anti' – now wander in alienation from the modern world. But where?

Let me insert a qualification at this point. I do not mean to imply that the Border Trilogy, *Cities of the Plain* included, is simplistically a Byronic dirge for the passing of the hero. For one thing, *Cities of the Plain* is distinctly an American novel, not Byron's High Romanticism. It belongs to that literary genre called the Western, after all. But the truest homage to its American ancestors it pays in the fact that it is a buddy novel in the truest sense of its American ancestors. The symbiotic relationship between its two protagonists makes it such. The previous novels anticipate that characteristic – the fusion of the two buddies into one hero – in the relationships between John Grady and Lacey Rawlins, between Billy and Boyd. And surely the closeness of the friends and the brothers lends psychological credence to the bond between Billy and John Grady. But the first two books function merely as feelers toward the fully realized union of the heroes of *Cities of the Plain*. In both of the earlier books, the pals, Rawlins and Boyd, disappear well before the novels end, leaving the heroes alone in their adventures. Not so in *Cities of the Plain*. The heroes are together, at least in spirit, until John Grady dies. Their familiar address to each other is the single word 'bud.' Less than halfway through the novel, Billy, who in his older wisdom has advised the younger man, ceases to play the skeptic about John Grady's mission and agrees to approach Eduardo about buying Magdalena. He enters the enterprise. Here McCarthy begins a stylistic convention of the novel that prevails up to John Grady's death.

He begins each new scene solely with the pronoun 'he.' The reader must read well into the scene to discover whether 'he' refers to John Grady or Billy; in each section, initially it could refer to either. The ambiguity begins to merge the two characters. Then, they begin to share duties both to Magdalena and to the tasks of the cowboy. For instance, they paint the little house together. They ride the range together. When they go after the wild dogs that have ravaged the herd, they almost become the same person. First, pursuing the last of the dogs, they trade horses as they execute the difficult climb to the mesa, thus blurring their separate identities. And when they rope the leader of the pack, the repugnant yellow dog, they do it in simultaneous, unspoken concert. They are the same cowboy:

> John Grady came riding up behind Billy and swung his rope and heeled the yellow dog and quirted the horse on with the doubled rope and then dallied. The slack of Billy's catchrope hissed along the ground and stopped and the big yellow dog rose suddenly from the ground in headlong flight taut between the two ropes and the ropes resonated a single brief dull note and then the dog exploded...
> Damn, said Billy. I didn't know you was goin to do that.
> I didnt either. (167–8)

Moreover, acting from the impulse of his sympathetic heart again, the next day John Grady awakens Billy to retrieve the dead dogs' pups, and despite Billy's protests that this samaritan's action is madness, they rescue the pups together. What McCarthy says of John Grady and his heroism he also says of Billy. What is true of the courtly hero is true of the tragic hero. And they both become the anti-hero, futilely acting in a degraded world – not only a world beneath them, but a world indifferent to them. Therein lies the deconstruction of the entire trilogy. Heroism, no matter its form, is irrelevant in a world consumed in materialism and the instruments of its own destruction. The two heroes say it best themselves in a quiet conversation alone on the range. John Grady says about his own impossible desires:

> You cant tell anybody anything, bud. Hell, it's really just a way of tellin yourself. And you cant even do that. You just try and use your best judgment and that's about it.
> Yeah. Well. The world dont know nothin about your judgment.
> I know it. It's worse than that, even. It dont care. (219)

Then, toward the end, as Billy carries John Grady's lifeless body in a mock pieta through the streets, he passes a group of children, halted by a traffic guard, on their way to school. McCarthy says:

> This man and his burden passed on forever out of that nameless crossroads and the woman stepped into the street and the children followed and all continued on to their appointed places which as some believe were chosen long ago even to the beginning of the world. (262)

So what is the answer to the question of this narrative, the question McCarthy's characteristic philosopher recalls to mind in the epilogue of the story: 'Where's the all-american cowboy at?'? He is dead. Or he has played, at best, an extra's role in the drama of American life. The romantic hero has passed. The tragic hero has become pathetic. In the twenty-first century, the anti-hero has regressed into a second childhood. Who is the new hero, now that these are all relegated to irrelevance? Who knows? *Cities of the Plain* and the Border Trilogy end with 'an uncommon want': 'I want a hero' (Byron, *Don Juan, Canto the First* line 1). That is, I think, the curious meaning of the Dedication and its curious placement at the book's closing:

The world grows cold
The heathen rage
The story's told
Turn the page. (293)

Appendixes

Index of character names in the novels

Kyle Kirves

Appendix 1

The Orchard Keeper

List of characters

Character	Notes	First appearance or mention (page)
Aaron Conaster	Gets in the fight with MARION SYLDER at the fertilizer factory that costs Sylder his job.	30
Arthur Ownby *also* 'Uncle Ather' and the 'old man'	The man who keeps watch over the orchard, the Orchard Keeper. A kind of druid in the hills around Red Branch, a mystical figure. A keeper also of the 'old ways.' 'He . . . rose stiffly, fingering a chambered goat-horn slung from his neck by a thong . . . He raised his horn. His call went among the slopes echoing and re-echoing stilling the nightbirds, rattling the frogs in the creek to silence, and on out over the valley where it faded thin and clear as a bell for one hovering breath before the night went clamorous with hounds howling in rondelays, pained wailings as of phantom dogs lamenting their own demise . . . He had cut a pole of hickory, hewed it octagonal and graced the upper half with hex-carvings – nosed moons, stars, fish of strange and pleistocene aspect.' (46)	20
Berrypickers (boy and girl)	Discover the corpse in the spray pit and lead ARTHUR OWNBY to it.	52
Bibledrummer	Steals ARTHUR OWNBY's wife ELLEN from Ownby. Possibly the one who shoots Ownby with a shotgun (230–1).	156
Bill	Hunting friend of MARION SYLDER. On the scene when JOHN WESLEY RATTNER rescues LADY.	122

Continued

Character	Notes	First appearance or mention (page)
Bill Munroe	Works with ARTHUR OWNBY on the road crew. Captures a baby panther.	151
Blind man	One who knows things before they happen. A figure from ARTHUR OWNBY's past.	225
Blue boy	A policeman taunted by MARION SYLDER on one of the latter's booze runs.	164
Bob Kirby	Taunts ARTHUR OWNBY about 'painters' (panthers) and 'wampus cats' in MR. ELLER's store.	148
Boog	Friend of JOHN WESLEY RATTNER. Not as bright as the others, perhaps.	133 (by name 135)
Buster	Dog owned by ARTHUR OWNBY.	44
Cabe	Proprietor/bartender of the Green Fly Inn.	13 (by name 14)
Cas	Hunting friend of MARION SYLDER. On the scene when JOHN WESLEY RATTNER rescues LADY.	122
Cat	A she-cat who harries MILDRED RATTNER in her smokehouse and makes off with JOHN WESLEY RATTNER's trapped mink.	172
Cat girl	Girl who rescues the blind cats from MR. ELLER's store.	182
Cat owner	One who owns a cat that could talk. A figure from ARTHUR OWNBY's past.	227
Coast Guard	Chases the younger MARION SYLDER in a recalled episode. Responsible for shooting his toe off.	161
Colored woman	A kind of witch woman who advises the child ARTHUR OWNBY about wampus cats. 'Ain't no sign with the wampus cats, she told him, but if you has the vision you can read where common folks ain't able.' (60)	59
County worker	Woman who receives JOHN WESLEY RATTNER on his second trip to the courthouse. Denies John Wesley the chance to buy his hawk back.	232
Coy Tipton	Finder of the lost pants in the ravine behind the Green Fly Inn.	26
Delozier also 'Uncle Whitney'	Sells ARTHUR OWNBY his first house. Ownby's uncle.	152

Appendixes

Character	Notes	First appearance or mention (page)
Deputy (Jefferson) Gifford *also* 'Gif'	Deputy sheriff. Leads the investigation into the car accident on the creek.	112
Dock Foreman	Brings MARION SYLDER his pay and explains that he tried to intervene on Sylder's behalf after the fight with AARON CONASTER.	30
Driver	First man to give KENNETH RATTNER a ride. Possibly killed by Rattner for his wallet.	9
Earl Legwater	The Knox (perhaps Sevier) county humane officer. Known throughout the county for cruelty to animals. 'Most of the old men had been there the day he shot two dogs behind the store with a 0.22 rifle, one of them seven times, it screaming and dragging itself along the fence.' (117)	113
Ef Hobie	Object of celebration at the Green Fly Inn for his release from Brushy Mountain correctional facility. Originally charged with illegal possesion of liquor and sentenced to eighteen months. Dies in MR. ELLER's store three weeks after a car wreck.	23
Ef Hobie's father	Patriarch of the whiskey-making Hobies. Dead.	95
Ellen (Arthur Ownby's wife)	A memory. Appears in ARTHUR OWNBY's dreams. Ran off with a BIBLEDRUMMER.	21 (by name 152)
Ellen's father	Disapproves of the marriage between ARTHUR OWNBY and ELLEN. Threatens to kill Ownby. Possibly the one who shoots Ownby with a shotgun (230–1).	154
Exhorter	Religious figure in Knoxville who brandishes a tattered bible at the crowd of spectators and screams.	82
Fisherman	Fishes early in the morning from trot lines in the same waterways JOHN WESLEY RATTNER traps in.	67
Garland Hobie	Brother (son?) of EF HOBIE. Last remaining male Hobie.	95
Grandaddy Pulliam *also* 'Hiram'	WARN PULLIAM's grandfather. Contemporary of ARTHUR OWNBY, with whom he worked on the K S & E railroad.	145

Continued

Character	Notes	First appearance or mention (page)
Grandmaw Pulliam	Grandmother to WARN PULLIAM.	227
Grappler	Earns living fishing for dead bodies in the Tennessee river with a grappling hook.	228
Grayhaired man	Attendant at the hardware store who sells JOHN WESLEY RATTNER his traps. Draws up a contract between the store and John Wesley so he might buy his traps at the lot price. A good-natured soul who speeds John Wesley on his way well-wished with a smile.	83
Increase Tipton (and clan)	Influential landlord of the 'jerrybuilt shacks' (11) in and around Red Branch. The hills and valleys surrounding are populated with the branches of his family tree.	11
Intern	Orderly who examines ARTHUR OWNBY and finds the shotshell pellets in his leg.	230
Jack the Runner	Whiskey runner who 'drops' whiskey for convoy by MARION SYLDER.	16
Jimmy *also* 'Jimenez'	Pilots the craft that MARION SYLDER works as a bootlegger on.	162
John (Law)	The police who give chase to MARION SYLDER. Avoided by means of a store-wreck evasion tactic.	76
John Wesley Rattner *also* 'the boy'	Son of KENNETH and MILDRED RATTNER. Traps and fishes in the woods in and around Red Branch. Spiritual heir of ARTHUR OWNBY. Is 'adopted' by MARION SYLDER.	23 (appears on 62, by name 68)
Johnny Romines	Friend of JOHN WESLEY RATTNER. Descended from prolific racists.	133 (by name 135)
Johnny Romines' uncle	One of JOHNNY ROMINES' racist forebears. A white-cap.	140
June Tipton	MARION SYLDER's partner on whiskey runs. Rides shotgun. Screws a girl in a backhouse. 'Shithouse then.' (21) Aids Sylder and JOHN WESLEY RATTNER after the car crash in the creek.	17
Kenneth Rattner	Loquacious criminal. Husband of MILDRED RATTNER. Father of JOHN WESLEY RATTNER. Shoplifter, pickpocket, hitchhiker, probable murderer.	7 (by name 10)

Appendixes

Character	Notes	First appearance or mention (page)
Lady	MARION SYLDER's hunting dog and mother to JOHN WESLEY RATTNER's pup.	112
Lawyer	Advises ARTHUR OWNBY of the statute of limitations on crimes.	228
Marion (Paris) Sylder *also* 'the man'	Charismatic bootlegger, fighter, hunter. Admired by all in Red Branch for his freeness with his money (during prohibition), 'this affluent son returned upon them bearing no olive branch but hard coin and greenbacks and ushering in an era of prosperity, a Utopia of paid drinks.' (29) After prohibition, works in a fertilizer plant. Kills hitchhiker in self-defense. Becomes 'adoptive' or spiritual father of JOHN WESLEY RATTNER.	11
Marion Sylder's mother	Evoked by the wife to scold MARION SYLDER. Not dead.	108
McCrary	Finances the purchase of the new car MARION SYLDER uses to convoy whiskey from Red Branch to Knoxville. The car could possibly be the wrecked Plymouth.	165
Mildred Rattner	Faithful wife of KENNETH RATTNER. Mother of JOHN WESLEY RATTNER. A devout Christian. Seamstress, launderer.	23 (by name 26)
Mr. Eller	Works in a store he probably owns. Sells MARION SYLDER new socks weekly for a quarter. Hosts all manner of men in his store.	28
Mr. Huffaker	Storeowner who begrudingly hosts the man in pressed clothes. Answers questions about Arthur Ownby's shopping habits. Tries (probably) to warn Arthur Ownby away from the store, but is seen by the man in pressed clothes.	196
Mr. Petree	Watches MARION SYLDER fight AARON CONASTER and initiates Sylder's dismissal.	30
Mrs. Eller	Works in a store probably owned by her husband. Relates the story of the demise of the Green Fly Inn and the pickpocketing.	26
Mrs. Fenner	Woman who receives EF HOBIE's soupbone on loan.	23

Continued

Character	Notes	First appearance or mention (page)
Mrs. Hobie	EF HOBIE's mother. Loans out Hobie's soupbone to MRS. FENNER. Turned in on liquor-related charges by her other son, GARLAND HOBIE.	23
Mrs. June Tipton	Wife of JUNE TIPTON. Breakfasts MARION SYLDER and JOHN WESLEY RATTNER after the car accident in the creek.	105
Mrs. Marion Sylder	Wife of MARION SYLDER. Gives JOHN WESLEY RATTNER a change of clothes.	107
Mrs. Pulliam	WARN PULLIAM's mother.	134
Mrs. Walker	Milk maker.	199
Oliver Henderson	The milk man who brings water to the Rattners thrice weekly. Discovers MARION SYLDER's car in the creek.	63
Ownby's mother	Prays over the child ARTHUR OWNBY when he relates the story of the COLORED WOMAN (witch) and her advice.	60
Preacher	Warns his congregation not to mess with themselves.	69
R. L.	Speculates on ARTHUR OWNBY's return to his homestead after ELLEN leaves. Possibly Uncle Whitney's son and Ownby's cousin.	156
Scout	Dog owned by ARTHUR OWNBY.	44
Sheriff	Man in charge of the expeditions to arrest ARTHUR OWNBY.	185
Stiefel	Owns a yard in which a poplar stands. JOHN WESLEY RATTNER uses the tree for shelter on his trap runs.	66
Stocky Man	Man in charge of cutting down a tree. Has three fingers bound up in a dirty bandage and a splint.	Prologue
Storekeep	Person of dubious intelligence. Quizzes KENNETH RATTNER on what kind of tire pump he requires.	8
Three deputies and the county officer (including 'Luther Boyd')	Those who accompany the SHERIFF on his second attempt to arrest ARTHUR OWNBY. One deputy, Luther Boyd (222), is shot in the leg by Arthur Ownby.	185
Wanita Tipton	A girl who performs a childish seduction on JOHN WESLEY RATTNER. Versed, perhaps,	68

Character	Notes	First appearance or mention (page)
	in the ways of sex, she tells John Wesley he shouldn't be 'messin with himself.' Later, John Wesley takes a leech off of her.	
Warn Pulliam	Friend and trapping companion of JOHN WESLEY RATTNER. Owns Rock and a turkey buzzard. Probably slightly older in years than John Wesley.	133
Young man	Pipes into the debate on wampus cats between ARTHUR OWNBY and BOB KIRBY in MR. ELLER's store.	149

Appendix 2

Outer Dark

List of characters

Character	Notes	First appearance or mention (page)
Afflicted man	Man whose unknown or undefined affliction makes the PREACHER (2) go away.	241
'Anthropoid'	An old woman who offers hospitality to RINTHY HOLME. Rightly identifies Rinthy as a recent mother.	108
Baby Holme	CULLA and RINTHY HOLME's child. Rescued from the woods by the TINKER, 'a gross eldritch doll with ricketsrung legs and one eye opening and closing softly like a naked owl's.' (235) Killed by the THREE STRANGERS.	14
Barn owner	Hires CULLA HOLME to paint the roof of his barn at a dollar a day wages.	90
Beehiver	Fellow traveler with CULLA HOLME on the way to Cheatham. Offers to trade for Culla's boots. Gives Culla whiskey that he won on a bet for hiving bees without a smoker or a mask.	82
Bill	Informs CULLA HOLME and the CHEATHAM MERCANTILE CLERK that the graves were robbed.	87
Billy	Hog drover. VERNON's younger brother. Demands justice for Vernon's death.	216
Blind man	The last of CULLA HOLME's fellow travelers. Advises him on the Lord's work and the ways of the blind. Provides Culla with a certain amount of insight regarding all men, not just the blind.	239

Appendixes

Character	Notes	First appearance or mention (page)
Bossman	Foreman for the turpentine camp work crew. Directs CULLA HOLME to CLARK for work.	132
Bud (boy)	LUTHER's son. Tries to attract the attention of RINTHY HOLME. Shows her his money and tries to get her to go to a show.	59 (by name 61)
Bud (turnip planter)	Man whose turnips RINTHY HOLME steals. Offers supper to Rinthy. Debates with CLARK whose duty it is to take down the hanged MILLHANDS. Uses profanity prolifically.	100 (by name 140)
Bud's wife (buttermaker)	Professional buttermaker. Fights with BUD (turnip planter), possibly over her morality.	102
Buddy Sizemore	Man who purchases CULLA and RINTHY HOLME's father's shotgun.	56
Cecil	Hog drover who works the wagon. In possession of the rope with which the drovers intend to hang CULLA HOLME.	224
Cheatham Mercantile clerk	Works in a general store and is sleeping when CULLA HOLME enters. Directs Culla to the waterjug and explains that the townfolk are at the church for a 'commotion.' (84)	83
Clark	Wealthy and influential man who debates with BUD (turnip planter) whose duty it is to remove the hanged MILLHANDS. CULLA HOLME is directed to him for work. Probably the sheriff. 'a man dressed in a filthy white suit and so huge that the mule and the wagon which carried him looked absurd, like a toy rig.' (139) Hanged before he can pay Culla for digging the two graves for the hanged MILLHANDS.	132 (appears on 139)
Clerk	Store clerk who sells Culla crackers, cheese, and a dope.	38
Coroner	Man who breaks every bone in the MINK TRAPPER's body in order to bury him.	120
Creech girls	Unseen women of dubious reputation, but unliked by the GARDENING WOMAN.	99
Culla Holme	Brother of RINTHY HOLME. Father of Rinthy's child. Abandons the child in the woods where it is rescued by the TINKER. Seemingly remorseless, but at least	5 (by first name 9; by last name 38)

Continued

Character	Notes	First appearance or mention (page)
	embarrassed, by his sins. Follows after Rinthy when she leaves to find the baby. Also a petty criminal.	
Daddy Holme	Father to CULLA and RINTHY HOLME. Dead; 'the unluckiest man in the world.' (192)	30
Deitch	Name of a tinker that stocks at Belkner's. Possibly the TINKER who rescues the baby.	75
Deputy	CLARK's deputy. First man off a wagonload of bean-pickers.	143
Doctor *also* 'John' (151)	Diagnoses RINTHY HOLME with disbelief. Gives her salve for her breasts.	147 (by name 151)
Driver 1	Drives the dead cart.	86
Driver 2	A wagon driver who directs CULLA HOLME to a mill and, later, on to THE SQUIRE's house when Culla inquires about work.	38
Earl	ANTHROPOID's husband.	110
Earl's daddy	A squire.	110
Essary	Person whose property is hosting an auction.	135
Ethel	Woman in the SQUIRE (lawman)'s house where CULLA HOLME is taken after his arrest for trespass. Possibly the SQUIRE's wife or servant.	199 (by name 202)
Ferrymaker (Ferryman's father)	Builds, although does not design, the ingenious ferry for crossing the river on the road to Morgan.	161
Ferryman	Runs the ferry on the road to Morgan. Somewhat surly. Hurled off of the ferry when it tears its cable. Probably drowns.	157
Gardening woman	Woman who offers hospitality to RINTHY HOLME.	98
Gardening woman's granddaughter	Infant whose crying incites RINTHY HOLME to lactation.	99
Geechee nigger	A midwife who lives near CULLA and RINTHY HOLME. Culla had promised to send for her when Rinthy's birthing time came, but does not. 'She's been a midnight woman caught them babies lots of times. You said your own self.' (10)	10

Appendixes

Character	Notes	First appearance or mention (page)
Greene	Unseen interest in the hog drive. Probably the owner of the hogs, or part-owner.	223
Harold	Clerk in CLARK's store.	137 (by name 143)
High sheriff	Comes into Cheatham and goes into a building.	87
Hog drovers	Men responsible for driving GREENE's hogs to market.	213
Horseman	Taunts the FERRYMAN to one side of the river with the promise of a horse fare.	158
Hunter	Provides CULLA HOLME with a drink of water from his pump. Relates anecdotes from his life and the surrounding landscape to Culla.	117
Hunter's granddaddy	Could play a fiddle without even seeing one.	123
Hunter's wife	Woman who runs off from the HUNTER several times.	126
John	THE SQUIRE's mute stablehand. Sharpens CULLA HOLME's axe.	42
John's daddy	Owner of the cabin CULLA HOLME trespasses in. Father to the OLD MAN WITH SHOTGUN.	200
Leroy	Unseen man sought by both BUD (turnip planter) and CLARK. Possibly the DEPUTY.	139
Luther (man with lantern)	Hosts RINTHY HOLME at a stop on her search for the TINKER. Father of two girls and a boy.	57 (by name 60)
Mama	VERNON and BILLY's mother. Weeps when Billy leaves to drive the hogs to market.	216
Man (Lawyer)	Escorts RINTHY HOLME to his office to wait on the DOCTOR. Has a brief conversation with her.	147
Man at Belkner's	Answers RINTHY's questions about the TINKER. Identifies the Tinker as possibly being named 'Deitch.'	75
Man with sheriff	Comes into Cheatham and goes into a building with the sheriff.	87
Millhands	Those employed by the mill. Referenced by the DRIVER 1 as possible coworkers for CULLA HOLME. Two of their number are hanged by the crowd at the probable provocation of 'the bearded one' of the THREE STRANGERS.	40

Continued

Character	Notes	First appearance or mention (page)
Mink trapper	Anecdotal figure. 'he got snakebit and died. Been snakebit afore and thowed it off. This'n got him in the neck. When they found him he was kneelin down like somebody fixin to pray. Stiff as a locust post.' (120)	120
Mrs. Laird	Recent mother to whom the TINKER is directed by the WOMAN for nursing.	22
Old cripple	Old man who is ministered to by the PREACHER (2) and who is apparently healed. Possibly a shill.	241
Old lady	Related to the HORSEMAN. Probably his mother or wife.	159
Old man with shotgun *also* 'John' (199)	Arrests CULLA HOLME in his father's abandoned cabin and conducts him to the SQUIRE (lawman) for sentence.	197 (by name 199)
Old rifleshooter	Man who advises the HUNTER: 'Study long and ye study wrong.' (125)	125
Old woman	Passes on in the road as RINTHY HOLME watches for CULLA HOLME's return from the store.	54
Parson	Mad preacher who judges and condemns CULLA HOLME for the death of VERNON. 'He was dressed in a dusty frock coat and carried a walking stick and he wore a pair of octagonal glasses on the one pane of which the late sun shone while a watery eye peered from the naked wire aperture of the other.' (221)	221
Preacher 1	Man who first instructs VERNON on the Jews and the cloven hoof.	215
Preacher 2	Faith healer who once ministered to the BLIND MAN.	241
Rider on ferry	Rider whose fare allows CULLA HOLME to cross the river to Morgan. Hurled off of the ferry when it tears its cable. Probably drowns.	162
Rinthy Holme	Sister of CULLA HOLME. Mother who gives birth to her brother's child. Seeks the abandoned and rescued baby. Continues to lactate for the child long after the birth.	5 (by name 14)
Salter	A corpse in the road. Probably THE SQUIRE.	95

Appendixes

Character	Notes	First appearance or mention (page)
Sermon blind man	Subject of one of the PARSON's sermons. Wants to renounce God for his affliction and is saved by the parson.	226
Squire (lawman)	Sentences CULLA HOLME to ten days labor for trespassing. Works it off on the squire's property. Not the same person as THE SQUIRE.	199
Squire's daddy	Advises the SQUIRE (lawman) that 'a man made his own luck.' (207)	206–7
Squire's wife	Unseen wife of THE SQUIRE. born in the same place as CULLA HOLME, 'Chicken River.' (46)	46
Storekeeper	Answers RINTHY HOLME's inquiries as to the TINKER. Tells Rinthy that CULLA HOLME sold their daddy's shotgun to BUDDY SIZEMORE. Possibly same as the CLERK.	56
Storeman 1	Christian who will not open his store nor sell his goods to CULLA HOLME on a Sunday.	26
Storeman 2	Answers RINTHY HOLME's inquiries as to the TINKER. Tells her he may shop at Belkner's.	72
Sun prophet	One of CULLA HOLME's dream visions. Promises to heal the sick and forgive the sins of all once the eclipsed sun returns.	5
Teamster	Man fixing a wagon wheel on the street. Directs CULLA HOLME to CLARK for work.	135
The Squire	Hires and advises CULLA HOLME on the advantages of work and the wages of sin. Although harsh, the Squire does give Culla a half-dollar more than his agreed upon day wages of 'supper.' Culla steals his boots. Killed by the THREE STRANGERS with a brush-hook, possibly his own. Probably identified as 'old man SALTER' later.	40 (appears on 41)
Three Strangers	Three men who wreak havoc and perform atrocities throughout the landscape. The three always appear together within the confines of the story. • The Bearded One: 'wore a shapeless and dusty suit of black linen that was small on him and his beard and hair were long and	*Prologue (by name: 'the bearded one' (prologue) 'Harmon' (50) 'the nameless one' (180))*

Continued

Character	Notes	First appearance or mention (page)
	black and tangled. He wore neither shirt nor collar and his bare feet were out at the toes of a pair of handmade brogans' and 'nothing of his face visible but the eyes like black agates, nothing of his beard or the suit he wore gloss enough to catch the light and nothing about his hulking dusty figure other than its size to offer why these townsmen should follow him along the road this night.' (95) Incites the crowd to lynch two millhands for killing Old Man Salter. • Harmon: 'holding a rifle and picking nervously at his teeth' (168) and 'a lean and dirty cat.' (175) • The Nameless One: 'stood with his arms dangling at his sides, slightly stooped, his jaw hanging and mouth agape in a slaverous smile' (169) and 'the mute one seemed to sleep, crouched at the man's right with his arms dangling between his knees like something waiting to be wakened and fed.' (234)	
Tinker	Rescues the baby from the woods where CULLA HOLME had left it to die. 'a small gnomic creature wreathed in a morass of grizzled hair, watching him with bland gray eyes.' (6) Killed by the THREE STRANGERS.	6
Vernon	First of the HOG DROVERS to stop and speak with CULLA HOLME. Explains the mulefoot hog and the biblical importance of hogs and the cloven hoof. Dies when shoved off of the bluff by the stampeding hogs.	213 (by name 220)
Woman	Woman who advises the TINKER on where to take the rescued baby for a nursing.	21

Appendix 3

Child of God

List of characters

Character	Notes	First appearance or mention (page)
Ape attendants	Lead the ape into the ring in a story told by one of the unidentified speakers.	59
Ape man	Promotes the ape side show challenging men to get in a ring with an ape for three minutes for a fifty dollar prize.	58
Arthur Ogle	Man whose mule team and plow are sucked into the earth when the roof of a cave collapses.	195
Ballard's father	Hangs himself after LESTER BALLARD's mother leaves (Lester nine or ten years of age at the time).	21
Bill Parsons	COTTON's hunting partner. Has reputation for breeding dogs of dubious hunting skills.	49
Bill Scruggs	Anecdotal figure. COTTON jokes that he gave Scruggs a ticket for speeding down Bruce Street in a motor boat.	161
Billy	Idiot child who lames the robin by chewing its legs off. 'A hugeheaded bald and slobbering primate that inhabited the lower reaches of the house, familiar of the warped floorboards and the holes tacked up with foodtins hammered flat, a consort of roaches and great hairy spiders in their season, perenially benastied and afflicted with a nameless crud.' (77) Son of the THOMAS BOY and the LANE GIRL.	77
Blalock boy	One whose girlfriend was a member of the couple whose disappearance Sheriff FATE TURNER is investigating.	147

Continued

Character	Notes	First appearance or mention (page)
Bob Wade	Implicated in the murder of the WHALEYS. No relation to MR. WADE.	167
Bobby	One of the copulators in the car LESTER BALLARD discovers in the mountains. A black man.	19
Boy (shot in neck)	Defies LESTER BALLARD when he is confronted by him. Is shot in the neck, yet manages to start and get away in his truck.	149
Boy 1	Copulates with one of REUBEL's daughters.	27
Boy 2	Copulator discovered by FATE TURNER.	44
Boy's mother	One who initiates the search for the couple whose car Sheriff FATE TURNER finds on Frog Mountain.	147
Buster	Man who hits LESTER BALLARD in the head with an axe. 'Lester never could hold his head right after that.' (9)	9
C B (Auctioneer)	The auctioneer who gives to the auction a celebratory atmosphere. Confronted by LESTER BALLARD.	4
C B's uncle	Anecdotal figure who profits from real estate.	6
Catlett Tipton	Man arrested and hanged (with PLEAS WYNN) for murdering the WHALEYS in front of their daughter. His death marks the end of 'White cappin in Sevier county.' (167–8)	166
Cecil Edwards	Helps one of the unidentified speakers cut down LESTER BALLARD's father from where he hangs.	21
Cotton	Sheriff FATE TURNER's driver and deputy.	49
Darfuzzle	Visitor to LESTER BALLARD's cabin. Warns him about Sheriff FATE TURNER's investigation into the LADY IN WHITE. 'He sounded like a man with a mouthful of marbles, articulating his goatbone underjaw laboriously, the original one having been shot away.' (46)	46
Deputy	Deputy who accompanies Sheriff FATE TURNER as he tries to reconstruct a crime scene on Frog Mountain.	145
Deputy also 'Earl'	Guards LESTER BALLARD's room at the hospital to prevent his escape.	176 (by name 178)

Appendixes

Character	Notes	First appearance or mention (page)
Deputy Walker	One of Sheriff FATE TURNER's deputies. Possibly COTTON.	122
Ed	Man with the flashlight during the cave exploration. One of the cave explorers.	184
Ernest	Asks LESTER BALLARD what he wanted with the dead women.	183
Eustis (likely Mr. Parker)	Owner of a store that stocked guns. Robbed during the flood. Papers which identify the guns are locked in his basement.	162
Fate Turner	The High Sheriff of Sevier county.	44
Finney boy	Boy who refuses to rescue LESTER BALLARD's softball from the weeds. Is punched in the nose by Lester.	17
Floyd	Referenced by one of the unidentified speakers for validation of the story of LESTER BALLARD, the cow, and the tractor.	35
Four students	Students who dissect LESTER BALLARD.	194
Fox	A storekeeper to whom LESTER BALLARD owes a substantial debt.	99
Fred (vigilante)	Man with the cable, presumably to hang LESTER BALLARD with.	182
Fred (watch buyer)	One of the watch buyers.	131
Fred Kirby	Whiskey maker/seller.	10
Girl (at the fair)	Object of LESTER BALLARD's attention at the fireworks. 'a young girl with candyapple on her lips and her eyes wide. Her pale hair smelled of soap, womanchild from beyond the years, rapt below the sulphur glow.' And 'she saw the man with the bears watching her and she edged closer to the girl by her side.' (65)	65
Girl (shot in head)	Killed by LESTER BALLARD. To Lester's profound disappointment, she wets herself before Lester has a chance to couple with her.	149
Girl 1	One of the copulators in the car discovered by LESTER BALLARD on the mountain.	19
Girl 2	Copulator discovered by FATE TURNER.	44
Girl 3	Goes to the ape show with one of the unidentified speakers.	58

Continued

Character	Notes	First appearance or mention (page)
Gresham	Man who loses his mind when his wife dies. Sings the chickenshit blues at her funeral.	22
High Sheriff	Sheriff who investigates the disappearance of ARTHUR OGLE's mule team. Probably, but not necessarily, Sheriff FATE TURNER.	196
Husband	Marries (supposedly) one of REUBEL's nine daughters. Leaves shortly thereafter.	27
Jerry	Man who takes out a jar (presumably of whiskey) during LESTER BALLARD's abduction.	181
Jessie	One of the ladies working the auction. Responsible for taking bidders around the property.	5
Jimmy	A yardstick for telling how tall the ape is. Possibly one of the unidentified speakers.	58
Jimmy (vigilante)	A small member of the VIGILANTES.	185
John	Narrates the story of FATE TURNER and Fate's discovery of copulators on the roadside.	44
John Greer	Man who purchases LESTER BALLARD's property at auction. From Grainger county.	9
Lady in white	An old whore set out into the road (probably by DARFUZZLE and PLESS) and discovered by LESTER BALLARD. Throws a stone at Lester. Lester tears her dress off and leaves her naked in retaliation.	41
Lane girl	At home when LESTER BALLARD goes to visit RALPH. Ralph's daughter. Warns against giving BILLY the robin to play with. Shot by Lester.	76 (by name 177)
Leader (of VIGILANTES)	First of the VIGILANTES to speak to LESTER BALLARD. 'A heavyset man.' (177) The evidence of 'Then the man said' on 178 suggests that dialogue following is his (through at least line 6, page 178).	177
Leland Ballard	Grandfather to LESTER BALLARD. Registers for the Union army pension, even though all he did in the Civil War was 'scout the bushes.' (80) Also a White Cap.	80
Leland Ballard's brother	Younger brother of LELAND BALLARD. Fellow White Cap. Hanged in Hattiesburg, Mississippi.	81

Appendixes

Character	Notes	First appearance or mention (page)
Lester Ballard	Man who lives in the hill country around Sevier county. 'small, unclean, unshaven.' And 'A child of God much like yourself perhaps.' (4) His property is auctioned off, probably for inability to pay property taxes. Takes up residence in an abandoned cabin owned by WALDROP, later caves. A sharpshooter. Falsely accused of rape. Through a series of strange events and choices, degenerates into necrophilia, homicide, and transvestism.	(by name 7; by full name 9)
Lester Ballard's mother	Leaves LESTER BALLARD and Lester's father before Lester is ten.	21
Man 1	Present with one of REUBEL's daughters when she hangs laundry. Concurs with LESTER BALLARD on her desirability.	28
Man 2	Found dead in the act of copulation by LESTER BALLARD. Probably asphixiated by carbon monoxide.	86
Man in white shirt	Dismisses LESTER BALLARD's case. Probably the district attorney.	55
Man who figures out the pigeon killing scheme	Pulls down the PIGEON SHOOTER's gun and watches as the bird still explodes. Exposes the pigeon shooter's scam.	58
Mr. Wade	One of the town elders. Relates stories of community history regarding the White Caps, the Bluebills, and TOM DAVIS. Present at PLEAS WYNN and CATLETT TIPTON's hanging when he was fourteen.	164 (by name 166)
Mr. Wade's daddy	Man who describes the White Caps and Bluebills as 'sorry people all the way around, ever man jack a three hundred and sixty degree son of a bitch, which . . . meant they was a son of a bitch no matter which way you looked at em.' (165)	165
Mrs. Walker	Postal worker.	163
Nigger John	Sole cellmate interred with LESTER BALLARD. Arrested for cutting 'a motherfucker's head off with a pocketknife." (53)	53
Nightduty nurse	On-duty nurse when LESTER BALLARD arrives back at the county hospital after being abducted by the VIGILANTES.	192

Continued

Character	Notes	First appearance or mention (page)
Nurse	Feeds LESTER BALLARD his food at the hospital. Informs him of JOHN GREER's health.	175
Old hermit	Another of MR. WADE's anecdotal figures. 'a ragged gnome with kneelength hair who dressed in leaves and how people were used to going his hole in the rocks and throwing stones on a dare and calling to him to come out.' (168)	168
Old lady Bright	Arrested by the liquor agents. Locked up in the Cocke county jail.	114
Old man Cameron	First to report on LELAND BALLARD's involvement in the Civil War. Recognized as a reliable source.	80
Old man Whaley	Hires LESTER BALLARD on to set fenceposts at eight cents a post. Lester Ballard sets approximately seven hundred posts and uses his earnings to buy his rifle.	57
Old woman	Decides the flood is a plague or judgment on the people of Sevier county. 'Wages of sin and all that.' (164)	164
Orvis *also* 'fat boy'	Man who first expresses interest in buying a watch from LESTER BALLARD.	130
Otis	Probable guard of LESTER BALLARD.	180
Parton	Old man who burns to death in his bed when his house catches fire.	112
Pigeon boy	Shoves firecrackers into the pigeons so they explode and look to be shot by the PIGEON SHOOTER.	58
Pigeon shooter	Scams the locals with his supposed skill at arms. Nearly tarred and feathered by the fair crowd.	58
Pleas Wynn	Man arrested and hanged (with CATLETT TIPTON) for murdering the WHALEYS in front of their daughter. His death marks the end of 'White cappin in Sevier county.' (167–8)	166
Pless	Arrested by the Sheriff in connection with the LADY IN WHITE.	47
Prather	Man whose property is bought by C B'S UNCLE.	6
Ralph (Lane)	Unseen friend of LESTER BALLARD.	78

Appendixes

Character	Notes	First appearance or mention (page)
Reubel *also* 'the dumpkeeper'	Man whose dump, home are frequently visited by LESTER BALLARD. Sire of nine daughters. Commits incest with one daughter.	26 (by name 37)
Reubel's mother	Mother of the dumpkeeper. A churchgoer.	38
Reubel's nine daughters	REUBEL's progeny. Named from a discarded medical dictionary. They include: 'Urethra, Cerebella, Hernia Sue' (26). '12 year-old' (27). 'Long blond' (28). 'Half-naked girl' (37). The 'least 'un' (110).	As noted
Reubel's three grandkids	Progeny of REUBEL's children and their courters.	27 (another mentioned 110)
Reubel's wife *also* 'the dam'	REUBEL's wife and mother of nine girls.	26
Reubel's wife's sister	A churchgoing woman. REUBEL's WIFE is visiting her when LESTER BALLARD pays a visit to the dump.	111
Shooting gallery pitchman	Attendant at the shooting gallery booth. Points out to LESTER BALLARD that he has not shot out all of the red on the card. Denies Lester Ballard the chance to win more than three large prizes.	63
Smith	Grinds LESTER BALLARD's axe and gives him a lesson in blacksmithing that does not take.	70
Squire Helton	Man who loans LESTER BALLARD a tractor.	35
Susie	One of BILL PARSON's hunting dogs.	49
Thomas boy	Probable father of the idiot boy, BILLY.	117
Tom Davis	Deputy under Millard Maples who was responsible for bringing in the White Caps and Bluebills and effecting their demise.	165
Tommy	Asks ED to hold his light while he tries to follow LESTER BALLARD. First to discover that Lester has escaped. Asks: 'Hand me that light up here.' Proclaims: 'Shit.' Then yells: 'Ballard!' Calls Ballard 'That little son of a bitch.' States: 'He's by god gone.'	184–5
Tratham boy	Starts fire under his oxen to get them to move. Oxen move and put the fire under his wagon. He almost has his legs broken trying to put the fire out.	36

Continued

Character	Notes	First appearance or mention (page)
Two hunters	Those whose boar hunting exploits LESTER BALLARD watches from a tree.	69
Vigilantes ('some hunters' 177)	Members of the party of men who accost LESTER BALLARD from the hospital and demand he lead them to the bodies. • **NOTE:** In the episode that appears on pages 177–86, there are at least ten men present, probably many more. McCarthy offers a clue when he writes: 'Ballard entered the hollow rock that used to be his home attended by eight or ten men with lanterns and lights. The rest of them built a fire at the mouth of the cave and set about to wait.' (183) Consequently there are at least eight who accompany him, and 'the rest' quantifies at least two (hence the minimum of ten). Not all have names or spoken dialogue, and those with spoken dialogue may be the same character as another, unidentified speaker (for example, the leader may speak an unidentified line of dialogue). There are a few contextual clues, but for the most part, the context is ambiguous. However, the episode does not suffer for its ambiguity. The reader is left to make his or her own connections.	177–86
Waldrop (possibly first name 'Charles')	Owner of a cow LESTER BALLARD shoots and kills. Owner of the cabin Lester occupies after his eviction.	34
Watch buyers	Contemplate purchasing watches from LESTER BALLARD. Some are named, others not. • **NOTE:** In the episode that appears on pages 130–2 there are at least three watch buyers, although possibly more people speaking. The context is ambiguous. McCarthy offers some clues when he writes: 'the other man who had been looking at the watches', indicating three actual interested customers: two men and Orvis. This does not, however, preclude other men 'looking over their shoulders.' The episode does not suffer for its ambiguity.	130
Whaley daughter	Watches while PLEAS WYNN and CATLETT TIPTON kill her parents.	167

Appendixes

Character	Notes	First appearance or mention (page)
Whaleys	Shot and killed by PLEAS WYNN and CATLETT TIPTON while the former's daughter looks on. BOB WADE may have been involved.	166
Willy Gibson	Proprietor of a gun shop from which Sheriff FATE TURNER is dispatched to go and retrieve the corpses of LESTER BALLARD's victims.	196
Woman (corpse)	Found dead in the act of copulation by LESTER BALLARD. Probably asphixiated by carbon monoxide. Becomes the first necrophiliac experience for Lester. Later, consumed in fire at the Waldrop cabin.	86

Appendix 4

Suttree

List of characters

Character	Notes	First appearance or mention (page)
Ab Franklin	A whiskeymaker.	131
Abednego Jones	A gypsy king. A man of influence in McAnally. A voodoo well-wisher.	29 (appears on 108)
Allen	Probably ALICE's husband. Died of cancer.	433
Aunt Alice McKellar	De facto historian for the Suttree family.	432
Aunt Liz (Elizabeth)	SUTTREE's maternal aunt (possibly great-aunt, or even great-great-aunt). Unseen save for a photo of 'an ancient woman, spreadeagled in bed, dried hands at her sides, a cured looking face . . . hair on either side of her head . . . opposed and extended like pale horns.'	126
Aunt Martha	SUTTREE's maternal aunt (possibly great-aunt). A soft-spoken woman with a catalog of the dead.	125
Bert Vincent	A fish expert.	220
Big Frig	One of SUTTREE's greeters on Central Street when Sut gets out of the hospital.	192
Black butcher	A black fishmonger.	69
Blackburn	Workhouse guard. Sergeant or better, perhaps. Guard at Jordonia (same workhouse SUTTREE was in?).	25 (appears on 53)
Black-haired girl	A pick-up. 'her grimestreaked legs fullthighed under the thin dress, she moved with a kind of lyrical obscenity. She had a tooth out in the front and when she smiled she'd poke the tip of her tongue in the gap.'	246

Appendixes 329

Character	Notes	First appearance or mention (page)
Blind musician	Victim of GENE HARROGATE's first success as the city rat.	103
Blind Richard	A blind lackey of SUTTREE's cronies.	72
Bobbyjohn	Probable workhouse companion.	23
Bondsman	Man having the ill-luck to be called in to bail out SUTTREE with J-BONE LONG's signature.	84
Boneyard	A compatriot of SUTTREE's. A drunk.	70
Bromo	A legendary workhouse inmate.	48
Brothers Clancy	More of SUTTREE's greeters on Central Street when Sut gets out of the hospital. JOHN CLANCY possibly among them.	192
Byrd Slusser	A fellow inmate with SUTTREE. Fights Suttree and CALLAHAN. Loses miserably. Has a pickax welded around his ankle.	51
Cabbage	A compatriot of SUTTREE's. A drunk.	73
Callahan (Billy also Ray); called Red	Inmate with SUTTREE in the workhouse. Prone to fighting. If Suttree is Harrogate's spiritual (brother? father?) then Callahan is his spiritual (father? grandfather?).	23 (appears on 47)
Carl	SUTTREE's other brother.	16
Chemist	An apothecary who will not sell strychnine to GENE HARROGATE. An old fart.	212
Clayton (Uncle?)	Witness at the unnamed child's burial.	429
Clifford	Old drunk HARVEY's nephew. Son of W. D.	267
Clockshop goer	Witness for the prosecution in SUTTREE's hallucinatory trial.	454
Coalcolored woman (probably Doll)	Directs GENE HARROGATE to Hell for directions to SUTTREE.	106
Cook (Rufus's wife, sister, daughter?)	Resides with RUFUS WILEY. Talks down to GENE HARROGATE.	143
Cornelius Suttree 'Buddy' 'Sut' 'Jerome Johnson'	Protagonist, main character. Narrative waxes into Suttree's thoughts infrequently. Sometimes dreams, thoughts, etc. Educated, son of wealthy family. Father assumed to have married beneath him. Abandoned family – at every chance.	3, 6
Crossbow hunter	A real figure.	288

Continued

Character	Notes	First appearance or mention (page)
Crumbliss	An anecdotal figure. A drunk driver.	27
Daddy Watson	An ancient railroader with an immense gold watch. Perhaps lives in a delusionary world where the railroad still runs.	87
Deputies (at workhouse)	Tormentors and ridiculers of GENE HARROGATE. Skeptical (but not for long) of his ignorance. Include George, Ed, Coatney, Mr. Williams and Wilson. Wilson gets a shoeshine from Harrogate.	36
Doctor at hospital	Comes the nurse's aid when GENE HARROGATE arrives at the hospital with his bushel of bats.	216
Doll	ABEDNEGO JONES' wife.	108
Dr. Hauser	Speculative man. Interviews GENE HARROGATE about his bat enterprise. Offers one dollar for the knowledge; pays one twenty-five.	217
Dr. Neal	A ghost from SUTTREE's past whom he sees on the streets of Knoxville.	366
Dream son	A knifer in the dark. A phantom. A conjuration and a condemnation.	28
Ethel	A tattooed whore with a brash attitude. 'She hiked her skirt up around her waist with one hand and cocked her leg forward. A hound was chasing a rabbit down her belly toward her crotch. She said: When you get your eyes full, open your mouth.'	75
Farmers ('Two pairs of brogans')	The two who deduce the melon mounter M. O. and apprehend him. Bring him ice cream in the hospital.	33
Female evangelist	An unheeded siren. A liar.	50
Fishbutchers	Two marine ghouls covered in blood and frightening on the riverside.	92
Fred Cash	The poet of AB JONES. Recites the 'Signifyin Monkey' and the ballad of Jack-off Jake 'the poolroom snake who . . .'	113
Funeral home woman	Provides SUTTREE with directions to McAmon cemetery.	152
Gatemouth	A frequenter of HOWARD CLEVINGER's store on Front Street.	110

Appendixes

Character	Notes	First appearance or mention (page)
Gene Harrogate	The moonlight melon mounter. Ward, of sorts, to SUTTREE in the workhouse and after. Entrepreneurial. Criminal. The smallest prisoner. The country mouse, the city rat.	30
General	The coalseller. SUTTREE is literally indebted to him during the cold winter.	162
George Holmes	A criminal. 'a tall boy who used to like to shoot people.' CALLAHAN whips him.	374
Goatman	An old preacher who abides by the scripture. Trades SUTTREE some worthless postcards for a catfish.	195
Grandma Cameron	An ancient relative of SUTTREE's. Probably his great-grandmother (or great-great-grandmother). Unseen save for a photo.	127
Gravediggers	Employees of McAmon cemetery.	152
Harvey (The Junkman)	Employs GENE HARROGATE – briefly – to clean out a crumpled auto. A drunk.	93
Helen	A relative of unknown type. Possibly a cousin or aunt (daughter of AUNT MARTHA and UNCLE CLAYTON?). Unseen save for a photo.	127
Hitchhiker	A big meanlooking kid who fights with SUTTREE over what he doesn't have.	160
Hoghead (Henry)	A compatriot of SUTTREE's. A drunk.	70
Holt	Works at Miller's Department store with J-BONE LONG.	69
Housedweller	A bellower. Shouts at the WASHERWOMAN and demands. GENE HARROGATE's mother?	31
Howard Clevinger	A storeowner. Probably caters to blacks.	109
Hudson driver	Picks up the hitchhiking SUTTREE.	132
Huntsman	An image of death.	471
Invector	A deity. A demigod. A former minister. A eunuch. A shouter of profanity and blasphemy. A prophet.	66
Irish Long	Father of JUNIOR and J-BONE LONG. Known for his generosity in extending credit from his store. Mean fighter. 'he would mortally whip your ass if you messed with him' and 'they wasnt nobody in McAnally no betterhearted. He give away everything he had.'	25

Continued

Character	Notes	First appearance or mention (page)
J Basil	A radio personality.	134
Jabbo	A frequenter of HOWARD CLEVINGER's store on Front Street. Eats red devils.	110
Jake the rack	A poolhall manager.	70
J-Bone (Jim) Long	Sometimes called 'Brother.' Older brother of JUNIOR LONG; son of IRISH LONG. Friend of SUTTREE since childhood.	22
Jeffrey	AUNT ALICE's father.	433
Jeffrey Junior	AUNT ALICE's brother. Hanged for a homicide in Rockcastle County Kentucky July 18, 1884.	433
Jimmy Smith	(Owner? Bouncer?) of a local (flophouse? bar? brothel?) (possibly called the 'Corner').	21
Jimmy the Greek	A proprietor of a cafe/deli sandwich shop.	70
Joe (probably Junior Long)	Bankwalker on the Tennessee River.	10
John (Suttree's Uncle, maternal)	Alcoholic. Provides crucial insight into SUTTREE's background. Unloved by his nephew's family. 'my father is contemptuous of me because I'm related to you.'	15
John Clancy	A citydweller. Informant for Uncle John at the Eagles. 'I like old Suttree.'	15 (appears on 78)
Josie Harrogate	GENE HARROGATE's sister. Comes looking for him for unknown reasons. SUTTREE tells her he's in the penitentiary.	465
Judge	Presides over SUTTREE's hallucinatory trial.	454
Judge Kelly	Releases SUTTREE from the workhouse days after Sut's mother visits.	62
Junior (possibly Joe) Long	Sometimes called 'Brother.' Friend to SUTTREE since childhood. Brother of J-BONE LONG, son of IRISH LONG.	22
Katherine	Woman companion of KENNETH HAZELWOOD. Sister?	26
Kenneth Hazelwood (Worm)	Friend of SUTTREE, a drinking man who gives up drinking Early Times.	26
Leithal King	Innocent bystander and victim of BLACKBURN's baton.	52
Leonard	Small weird Leonard. A petty criminal. A fraud artist. Perhaps a spiritual twin to GENE HARROGATE.	235

Appendixes

Character	Notes	First appearance or mention (page)
Leonard's father	A corpse and cash cow.	242
Leonard's mother	Collects welfare on her dead husband.	242
Loftis, Lonnie, and ?	Three boys, brothers, who come to the Goatkeeper like children at a petting zoo.	197
Lorina	Probably LEONARD's sister. She's six or seven years old.	244
Mad preacher	A street preaching, turnip eating madman. Proclaims that 'This aint going to get it.'	382
Maggeson	A fellow fisher. Akin to Charon, perhaps.	65
Mary Lou	Waitress at the Walgreen's who feeds SUTTREE and GENE HARROGATE on Thanksgiving Day.	171
May Maude	An 'oldtimey note' singer appearing at the tent revival SUTTREE does not attend.	124
Michael	Indian fisherman and connoisseur of turtles.	220, 221
Miss Aldrich	The nurse who takes care of SUTTREE while he is in the hospital.	190
Mother She	A geechee priestess. A crippled gnome. A seductress and confidante. 'a female dwarf coalblack in widow's weeds who wore little goldwire spectacles on a chain about her neck. Scarce four feet tall she was, her hand on the doorknob at her ear like a child.' (228)	65
Mother She's grandma	A corpse in a photo.	279
Mr. Hatmaker	A bartender at The Huddle.	72
Mr. Turner	A white fishmonger.	67
Mrs. Long	J-BONE's (wife? sister? mother probably).	82
Nurse	Another who works on SUTTREE at the hospital where he recuperates.	458
Nurse and Wanita	Two nurses who speculate on the relative merits of SUTTREE's organs.	458
Nurses	Desk worker at the hospital when GENE HARROGATE arrives with his bushel of bats; and attendees on the waiting Harrogate.	216, 217
Oceanfrog Frazer	A frequenter of HOWARD CLEVINGER's store on Front Street.	110
Old Hooper	A reference to a man obsessed with death. Possibly the RAGPICKER.	193

Continued

Character	Notes	First appearance or mention (page)
Old merchant lady	Bludgeons GENE HARROGATE with a ladle.	103
Old negress	A cripple and beggar on the streets of Knoxville town. Invokes God against SUTTREE.	245
Old Orville	A farmer. Possibly the owner of a melon patch. Shoots GENE HARROGATE in the backside for raping his melons?	30
Orville	Driver of the McAmon Cemetery truck.	155
Pinky	Deputy who rides with the SHERIFF.	156
Possumhunters	The twins. Brothers with an uncanny ability to read the other's mind.	358
Priest	A catatonic shaman and teacher of 'christian witchcraft.'	304
Priest in hospital	Gives SUTTREE last rites.	460
Priest in hospital (perhaps same as above)	Offers SUTTREE sacraments.	461
Priest in Immaculate Conception Church	Finds the sleeping SUTTREE in the church of the Immaculate Conception. 'The virtues of a stainless birth were not lost upon [Suttree], no not on him.'	254
Ragpicker (the old man)	A troll. Lives under the bridge. 'The old man used to go from door to door and he could make the dolls and bears to talk.'	11
Reese	Patriarch of the Musselin Mascot family.	309
Reese's daughters	Unnamed progeny of the Musselin Mascot family.	309
Reese's wife	Matriarch of the Musselin Mascot family.	307
Robert	Probably Alice's son. Killed in the war. See earlier episode for clues.	433
Roy	A relative of unknown type. Possibly a cousin (son of AUNT MARTHA and UNCLE CLAYTON).	127
Rufus Wiley	'a black of contemplative nature.' Pig farmer. Catches GENE HARROGATE butchering one of his hogs.	140
Sam Slusser	A criminal who has a reputation for beating up cops. Probably BYRD SLUSSER's brother.	226
Sheriff	Exiles SUTTREE from the area where his son is buried and his former in-laws live. Gives Suttree $5.	156

Appendixes

Character	Notes	First appearance or mention (page)
Sisters	SUTTREE's sisters, one of whom he sees in a vision lifting his dead infant brother from its coffin and carrying it like a doll.	429
Smokehouse (Tom)	A sometime, onetime employee of AB JONES who doesn't like working for him.	200
Sue	Probably LEONARD's sister. Shares home with his mother.	242
Suttree	See CORNELIUS SUTTREE.	
Suttree's father	An enemy. 'he said that the world is run by those willing to take responsibility for the running of it . . . There is nothing occurring in the streets but a dumbshow composed of the helpless and the impotent.'	13
Suttree's father-in-law (Leon)	Goes for the shotgun.	150
Suttree's grandfather	A wraith. 'The dead would take the living with them if they could.'	13
Suttree's mother 'Grace'	Married above herself. Forever beneath her husband; her children the same.	16 (appears on 61)
Suttree's mother-in-law	Brawls with SUTTREE and chews up his hand.	150
Suttree's twin	Dead at birth.	14
Suttree's wife	Abandoned.	150
'Tarzan' Quinn	A cop. AB JONES' nemesis.	226
Trippin Through the Dew (John) The queen of Front Street	Local transvestite, 'a black and ageless androgyne in fool's silks. A purple shirt with bloused sleeves, striped fuchsia trousers and matching homedyed tennis shoes. A gold leather motorcycle belt about a vespine waist.' (Referred to by both singular pronouns he and she.)	110
Turtlehunter	A memory from SUTTREE's childhood.	119
Tweetiepie	Victim in SUTTREE's hallucinatory trial.	454
Uncle Carter	SUTTREE's uncle (possibly great-uncle or great-great-uncle). Unseen save for a photograph. 'a goodlookin something.'	127
Uncle Clayton	SUTTREE's maternal uncle (possibly great-uncle) and husband to AUNT MARTHA. A drinker and harsh man. Obvious heir to a legacy of drunks and hard-livers.	125 (appears on 130)

Continued

Character	Notes	First appearance or mention (page)
Uncle Milo	'Lost under Capricorn all hands aboard a bargeload of birdshit one foggy night off the limeslaked coast of Chile.' Probably SUTTREE's uncle (or great-uncle). Unseen save for a photo.	127
Uncle Will	SUTTREE's uncle (possibly great-uncle). A blacksmith. A drunk. A grifter.	130
W. D. 'Dubyedee'	Brother of old drunk HARVEY the junkman. A junkman himself.	265
Wallace Humphrey	'In an oldfashioned suit he looked like one of those western badmen photographed hanging from barndoors or propped up in shopwindows shot full of holes.'	384
Walter	A musician.	68
Wanda	REESE's daughter.	309
Washerwoman	A washer of clothes and a keeper of an old woman. GENE HARROGATE's sister?	30
Willard	REESE's son	310

Appendix 5

Blood Meridian or the Evening Redness in the West

List of characters

Character	Notes	First appearance or mention (page)
Aborigines (Yuma) *also* 'Yumas' (278) 'savages' (279) 'painted horde' (279) 'indians' (279) 'the enemy' (281)	YUMAS who pursue the KID and TOADVINE across the desert after their attack on the ferry crossing, which has wiped out all the remaining members of the Glanton Gang except the judge.	278
Alcalde (San Diego)	Mayor of San Diego. Visited first by DAVID BROWN to demand release of Long Webster and TOADVINE. Later visited and abused by JOHN GLANTON and other members of the GLANTON GANG demanding release of David Brown. Left tied in a hut by the ocean.	265
Alcalde's wife	Wife of the San Diego ALCALDE. At his house when JOHN GLANTON arrives with his five men. Left tied in a hut by the ocean.	270
Anchorite	An old hermit with whom the KID stays. 'Solitary, half mad, his eyes redrimmed as if locked in their cages with hot wires.' (16) Once a slaver. Paid two hundred dollars for the heart of a 'black son of a bitch.' (18)	16
Apache *also* 'Apaches' (226)	Members of the Apache encampment ridden upon and slaughtered by the Mexican soldiers. 'women and children, the bones and skulls scattered along the bench for half a mile and the tiny limbs and toothless paper skulls of infants like the ossature of small apes.' (90)	90

Continued

Character	Notes	First appearance or mention (page)
Apache archers *also* 'warriors' (109)	The first band of warriors encountered by the GLANTON GANG after leaving Janos: 'a thin frieze of mounted archers that trembled and veered in the rising heat. They crossed before the sun and vanished one by one and reappeared again and they were black in the sun and they rode out of that vanished sea like burnt phantoms with the legs of the animals kicking up the spume that was not real and they were lost in the sun and lost in the lake and they shimmered and slurred together and separated again and they augmented by planes in lurid avatars and began to coalesce and there began to appear above them in the dawn-broached sky a hellish likeness of their ranks riding huge and inverted and . . . the howling antiwarriors pendant from their mounts immense and chimeric and the high wild cries carrying that flat and barren pan like the cries of soulds broke through some misweave in the weft of things into the world below.' (109)	102
Apaches *also* 'the savages' (125) 'niggers' (125) 'half of Apacheria' (126) 'redskins' (132)	The Native Americans who pursue the powderless GLANTON GANG across the desert in TOBIN's story. Slain wholesale at the rim of a volcano. They number at least a hundred, according to Tobin.	125
Argonauts (goldseekers)	Men travelling west in search of gold. 'patched argonauts from the states driving mules through the streets on their way south through the mountains to the coast. Goldseekers. Itinerant degenerates bleeding westward like some heliotropic plague. They nodded or spoke to the prisoners and dropped tobacco and coins in the street beside them.' (78)	78
Arrieros *also* 'drivers' (194) 'drivers below' (195) 'muleteers' (195)	Muleteers leading a conducta of quicksilver to the mines.	194
Artisan (coldforger)	Minter who produces coins in a coldforge in the KID's hallucinations. 'he was a coldforger	310

Appendixes

Character	Notes	First appearance or mention (page)
	who worked with hammer and die, perhaps under some indictment and an exile from men's fires, hammering out his own conjectural destiny all through the night of his becoming some coinage for a dawn that would not be. It is this false moneyer with his gravers and burins who seeks favor with the judge and he is at contriving from cold slag brute in the crucible a face that will pass, an image that will render this residual specie current in the markets where men barter.' (310)	
Barman (Bexar)	Saloon keeper who cannot speak American. Insults the KID and pays for it with two bottles to the head, and a bottleneck to the eye.	23
Barman (Nagadoches)	Denies the KID the chance to pay for his own drink, explaining it has been paid for by the JUDGE.	8
Bathcat	A three-fingered member of the GLANTON GANG and a fugitive from Van Diemen's Land (Tasmania). A native Welshman. 'The necklace of human ears he wore looked like a string of dried black figs. He was big and raw-looking and one eyelid sagged where a knife had severed the small muscles there and he was furnished with gear of every class, the fine with the shoddy. He wore good boots and he carried a handsome rifle bound with german silver but the rifle was slung in a cutoff bootleg and his shirt was in tatters and his hat rancid.' (87) Later, one of the LOST SCOUTS found hanging from the tree (226–7).	86
Billy Carr	Member of the GLANTON GANG who accompanies the KID to one side of the ferry crossing to cut willowpoles.	263
Brassteeth also 'goldtoothed pervert' (74)	Overseer of the prisoners. Has a mouth of gold teeth. Probably killed by TOADVINE upon the return of the GLANTON GANG to Chihuaha City after the slaughtering of the GILENOS.	74
Brown brothers including David Brown or	Members of the GLANTON GANG who ride with JOHN GLANTON and the JUDGE to the hacienda of GENERAL ZULOAGA	89

Continued

Character	Notes	First appearance or mention (page)
'Davy' (126) and 'Charlie' (178)	(outside Correlitos).	
Buffalo hunter	Old hunter whom the MAN encounters on the plains. Relates to the man stories of the buffalo hunters and the extinction of the buffalo.	316
Caballo en Pelo	Leader of the Yumas. 'this old mogul wore a belted wool overcoat that would have served a far colder climate and beneath it a woman's blouse of embroidered silk and a pair of pantaloons of gray cassinette. He was small and wiry and had lost an eye to the Maricopas and he presented . . . a strange priapic leer that may have at one time been a smile.' (254)	254
Callaghan	Temporarily runs the ferry built then abandoned by GENERAL PATTERSON. Killed.	262
Candelario	One of the FILIBUSTERS. Presumably functions as an interpreter. Probably the Mexican guide.	49
Captain White *also* 'yon filibuster' (40)	Leader of the FILIBUSTERS. Ends up dead at the hands of Mexican thieves and his head pickled in a jar.	29
Casimero *also* 'grown boy' (89)	Boy with the MAGICIAN's troupe. Probably the magician's son. A juggler of dogs.	89
Charlie Brown	One of the BROWN BROTHERS. Member of the GLANTON GANG. Probably a lieutenant to JOHN GLANTON. Remains in Tucson after the Gang leaves.	89 (by name 178)
Child, Kid, Man *also* 'the boy' (31) 'Young Blasarius' (94) 'el joven' (93) 'el hombre mas joven' and 'el muchacho' (94)	The character around whom the events of the novel unfold. A native Tennessean who wanders west to Memphis before heading to St. Louis, New Orleans, and Texas. 'The child's face is curiously untouched behind the scars, the eyes oddly innocent.' (4) The child becomes the kid on or about page 4: 'Only now is the child divested of all he has been.' (4) Commissioned by CAPTAIN WHITE. Later joins the GLANTON GANG. Probably killed by the JUDGE in the Griffin saloon 'jakes' (outhouse).	'the child' (through page 4–5) 'the kid' (from page 4–5 to page 313–14; by name page 5) 'the man' (from page 313–14 to the end)

Appendixes

Character	Notes	First appearance or mention (page)
Child's father *also* 'his father' (3)	The CHILD's father. A former schoolmaster. A drunk. Given to quoting 'poets whose names are now lost.' (3) The second paragraph is his dialogue (3).	3
Chiricahua Apache	The tribe of Apache camped outside the Tucson walls. Led in whole or in part by MANGAS. Probably responsible for the deaths of the LOST SCOUTS.	204 (appear on 228)
Chiricahua deputation	Members of the Chiricahua tribe sent out to parley with the GLANTON GANG. 'They were Chiricahuas, twenty, twenty-five of them. Even with the sun up it was not above freezing and yet they sat the horses half-naked, naught but boots and breechclouts and the plumed hide helmets they wore, stoneage savages daubed with clay paints in obscure charges, greasy, stinking... They carried lances and bows and a few had muskets and they had long black hair and dead black eyes that cut among the riders studying their arms, the sclera bloodshot and opaque. None spoke even to another and they shouldered their horses through the party in a sort of ritual movement as if certain points of ground must be trod in a certain sequence.' (228)	228
Clark	FILIBUSTER who survives the COMANCHE WARRIOR attack only to be killed by the seven or eight Mexicans.	70
Clerk	Warns TOADVINE that SIDNEY will shoot him. Assaulted by Toadvine and the KID on their way out of the burning hotel.	12
Cloyce Bell *also* 'the owner' (233)	Brother of the 'idiot,' JAMES ROBERT BELL. Travels with the GLANTON GANG from Tucson as far as the Yuma ferry.	233 (by full name 256)
Colonel Corrasco	A Sonoran official, probably military, possibly political. Perhaps a governor.	34
Colonel Doniphan *also* 'Bill' (33)	Commander of the Missouri militia credited with victory over the Mexicans at Chihuahua City.	33
Comanche warriors *also*	Mount a surprise attack on the FILIBUSTERS. 'a fabled horde of mounted lancers and	52

Continued

Character	Notes	First appearance or mention (page)
'the savages' (52)	archers bearing shields bedight with bits of broken mirrorglass that cast a thousand unpieced suns against the eyes of their enemies. A legion of horribles, hundreds in number, half naked or clad in costumes attic or biblical or wardrobed out of a fevered dream with the skins of animals and silk finery and pieces of uniform still tracked with the blood of prior owners, coats of slain dragoons, frogged and braided cavalry jackets, one in a stovepipe hat and one with an umbrella and one in white stockings and a bloodstained weddingveil and some in headgear of cranefeathers or rawhide helmets that bore the horns of bull or buffalo and one in a pigeontailed coat worn backwards and otherwise naked and one in the armor of a spanish conquistador . . . and many with their braids spliced up with the hair of other beasts until they trailed upon the ground and their horses' ears and tails worked with bits of brightly colored cloth and one whose horse's whole head was painted crimson red and all the horsemen's faces gaudy and grotesque with daubings like a company of mounted clowns, death hilarious, all howling in a barbarous tongue and riding down upon them like a hoarde from a hell more horrible yet than the brimstone land of christian reckoning, screeching and yammering and clothed in smoke like those vaporous beings in regions beyond right knowing where the eye wanders and the lip jerks and drools.' (52–3)	
David Brown	One of the BROWN BROTHERS. Member of the GLANTON GANG. Holds a high place in 'rank' of the Glanton Gang, and is probably a lieutenant. Incarcerated briefly in San Diego. Eventually, he is hanged alongside TOADVINE in Los Angeles.	89 (by name 94)
Dead argonauts *also* 'those right pilgrims' (152)	Wagoneers killed by white murderers. Their deaths are disguised to be the work of the natives. 'nameless among the stones with their terrible wounds, the viscera spilled from their	152

Appendixes

Character	Notes	First appearance or mention (page)
	sides and the naked torsos bristling with arrowshafts. Some by their beards were men but yet wore strange menstrual wounds between their legs and no man's parts for these had been cut away and hung dark and strange from out their grinning mouths.' (152–3)	
Delawares (scouts)	Native Americans affiliated with the GLANTON GANG as scouts.	86
Dieguenos *also* 'indians' (300) 'halfnaked savages' (300) 'aborigines' (300)	Native Americans whose hospitality saves TOBIN and the KID from the desert. 'They would have died if the indians had not found them.' (300) One of the Dieguenos who shows interest in the kid's pistol and reaches to touch it. The kid puts the barrel to the Diegueno's head and cocks it to warn him off.	300
Doc Irving	Medic to the GLANTON GANG.	109
Dwarf whore	Selects the MAN as a customer in the anteroom of the Griffin saloon. After a dubious sexual encounter, she tells him he will be 'all right' once he has a drink.	332
Elrod (member of the party) *also* 'the one with the rifle' (320)	Fifteen-year-old member of the party. Probably the one who asks the MAN for tobacco and whiskey, and then inquires about whores. Calls the man a liar. RANDALL's brother. Echoes the KID when he says to the man and the party: 'Set there and talk about shootin somebody. They aint nobody done it yet.' (322) Killed by the man.	318 (by name 320)
Farrier (San Diego)	Gunstore owner threatened by DAVID BROWN when he will not cut down Brown's shotgun of English make.	265
Filibusters *also* 'men of the company' (30) 'the riders and wagons' (42) 'the scouts' (42) 'unhorsed Saxons' (54)	Men recruited by CAPTAIN WHITE to carry out the campaign against the Mexicans. 'the instruments of liberation in a dark and troubled land.' (34) They number forty-six men.	30
First man (Fort Griffin)	Warned by the THIRD MAN not to go into the jakes behind the Griffin saloon. Asks the	334

Continued

Character	Notes	First appearance or mention (page)
	third man twice if someone is in the jakes. Exclaims 'Good God almighty' (334) upon opening the jakes door.	
Frank Carroll	Runs the bodega in Jesus Maria. Later leaves Jesus Maria to join up with the GLANTON GANG. Reports on the black JOHN JACKSON to the JUDGE.	189
General Elias	Commander of the Sonoran cavalry sent in pursuit of the GLANTON GANG.	205
General Patterson	Leads the Company from Kentucky. Refuses to pay the fare JOHN GLANTON asks to use the ferry and builds his own.	262
General Worth	Leader of the U.S. army along the U.S./Mexico border.	40
General Zuloaga	Resident near the village of Correlitos. Hosts JOHN GLANTON, the JUDGE, and the BROWN BROTHERS.	89
Gilchrist	Member of the GLANTON GANG. One of the LOST SCOUTS.	227
Gilenos *also* 'the enemy' (154) 'a thousand souls' (155) 'victims' (156) 'dying' (156) 'those who knelt for mercy' (156) 'the heathen' (164)	A tribe of Apaches. Their village is marched upon by the GLANTON GANG in a surprise attack.	150
Glanton Gang *also* 'the killers' (79) 'the Americans' (84) 'the partisans' (86) 'the Texans' (88) 'los caballeros' (92) 'the adventurers' (94) 'fine caballeros' (103) 'the hunters' (117) 'the scalphunters'	Captain JOHN GLANTON's command. 'a pack of viciouslooking humans mounted on unshod indian ponies riding half drunk through the streets, bearded, barbarous, clad in the skins of animals stitched up with thews and armed with weapons of every description, revolvers of enormous weight and bowieknives the size of claymores and short twobarreled rifles with bores you could stick your thumbs in and the trappings of their horses fashioned out of human skin and their bridles woven up from human hair and decorated with human teeth and the riders	78

Appendixes

Character	Notes	First appearance or mention (page)
(119) 'the party' (154) 'the raiders' (155) 'horsemen' (156) 'these haggard butchers' (161) 'tattered campaigners' (166) 'mercenaries' (167) 'rough warriors' (168) 'insensate topers' (171) 'ordained agents' (172) 'spectre horsemen' (172) 'besotted bedlamites' (190) 'grimy visitants' (191) 'the body' (307)	wearing scapulars or necklaces of dried and blackened human ears and the horses rawlooking and wild in the eye and their teeth bared like feral dogs and riding also in the company a number of halfnaked savages reeling in the saddle, dangerous, filthy, brutal, the whole like a vistation from some heathen land where they and others like them fed on human flesh.' (78) 'one by one they began to divest themselves of their outer clothes, the hide slickers and raw wool serapes and vests, and one by one, they propagated about themselves a great crackling of sparks and each man was seen to wear a shroud of palest fire. Their arms aloft pulling at their clothes were luminous and each obscure soul was enveloped in audible shapes of light as if it had always been so. The mare at the far end of the stable snorted and shied at this luminosity in beings so endarkened.' (222)	
Governor Burnett	Governor of California at the time of CAPTAIN WHITE's expedition.	34
Governor of Sonora	Issues a contract to the GLANTON GANG for scalps. Probably dispatches GENERAL ELIAS and his Sonoran cavalry to apprehend the Glanton Gang shortly thereafter.	204
Governor Trias *also* 'Angel Trias' (168)	The Governor of the state of Chihuahua.	78 (by name 79; by full name 168)
Grandaddy (of Elrod and Randall)	According to the eldest member of the party, the grandfather was 'killed by a lunatic and buried in the woods like a dog.' (323)	323
Grannyrat Chambers *also* 'another Kentuckian' (76) 'the veteran' (77)	Takes the bed on one side of the KID. Member of COLONEL DONIPHAN's irregulars and a soldier in the sacking of Chihuahua City. Probably killed by the DELAWARES as a deserter from the GLANTON GANG.	75 (by name 77; by last name 104)
Grimley	Member of the GLANTON GANG. Stabbed by the drunk in the Nacori cantina.	178

Continued

Character	Notes	First appearance or mention (page)
Halfwitted killer from Missouri	A member of the GLANTON GANG who laughs at an interchange between the JUDGE and the black JOHN JACKSON.	85
Harlan *also* 'Tommy' (235)	Member of the GLANTON GANG elected to kill one of the wounded Delawares after the altercation with GENERAL ELIAS and his men.	205
Harnessmaker (in the judge's story)	Subject of a story told by the JUDGE. Dresses as a native in order to solicit alms from the passersby. Kills the young man (in the judge's story) and blames the death on robbers (in the judge's story). A figure with whom many of the members of the GLANTON GANG seem to be able to identify.	142
Harnessmaker's wife (in the judge's story)	Tends to the grave of the young man (in the judge's story) killed by the HARNESSMAKER.	142
Hayward	One of the FILIBUSTERS who prays for rain in the desert.	47
Henderson Smith	Member of the GLANTON GANG. Missourian. First through the door of the Nacori cantina and into the street when the funeral procession rocket goes off.	178
Hermit (San Jose de Tumacacori)	German hermit at the fallen church. Shot by JOHN PREWETT.	224
James Miller	Member of the GLANTON GANG. His horse is gored by a Spanish bull and he is thrown from it. Survives, and is unharmed, although disgusted.	224
James Robert Bell *also* 'the wild man' (233) 'imbecile' (233) 'the idiot' (233)	Mental defective caged up and marketed by CLOYCE BELL as an attraction, 'The idiot was small and misshapen and his face was smeared with feces and he sat peering at them with dull hostility silently chewing a turd.' (233)	233 (by name 256)
John Dorsey	Member of the GLANTON GANG. Missourian. First through the door of the Nacori cantina and into the street when the funeral procession rocket goes off.	178
John Glanton *also* 'El Jefe' (95) 'Cap' (98) 'Captain Glanton' (133)	Leader of the GLANTON GANG. 'a small blackhaired man' (79) 'He would live to look upon the western sea and he was equal to whatever might follow for he was complete at	79 (by name 79)

Appendixes 347

Character	Notes	First appearance or mention (page)
'John Joel Glanton' (275)	every hour.' (243)	
John Gunn	Member of the GLANTON GANG. Helps JOHN GLANTON secure the horses from the Jesus Maria stable to make the escape.	193
John Jackson (black) also 'the black' (92) 'dark querent' (92) 'Blackie' (93) 'Jackie' (93) 'the nigger' (196)	Member of the GLANTON GANG. Follower of the JUDGE. First man killed during the second Yuma attack on the ferry crossing.	81
John Jackson (white)	Member of the GLANTON GANG. Killed by the black JOHN JACKSON by decapitation with one swipe of a bowieknife.	81
John McGill	A member of the GLANTON GANG. The sole Mexican in the group.	98
John Prewett	Member of the GLANTON GANG. Shoots the German HERMIT at the church of San Jose de Tumacacori.	225
Judge (or Judge Holden) also 'sootysouled rascal' (124) 'cunning old malabarista' (246) 'great favorite' (335)	Appears at the tent revival in Nagadoches and accuses REVEREND GREEN of child molestation and bestiality. 'An enormous man dressed in an oilcloth slicker had entered the tent and removed his hat. He was bald as a stone and he had no trace of beard and he had no brows to his eyes nor lashes to them. He was close on to seven feet in height and he stood smoking a cigar even in this nomadic house of God and he seemed to have removed his hat only to chase the rain from it for now he put it on again.' (6) And 'His cheeks were ruddy and he was smiling and bowing to the ladies and doffing his filthy hat. The enormous dome of his head when he bared it was blinding white and perfectly circumscribed about so that it looked to have been painted.' (79) Keeps a ledger book wherein he keeps detailed notes of items he finds interesting. According to TOBIN, he has been seen in innumerable places, speaks several languages, and is an accomplished	6 (by title 8; by full name 82)

Continued

Character	Notes	First appearance or mention (page)
	dancer, among other things. Probably kills the KID in the Griffin saloon 'jakes' (outhouse).	
Kid	See the CHILD, KID, MAN.	5
Lieutenant Couts	Lieutenant in charge of the garrison stationed at Tucson. Attempts, and fails, to charge a GLANTON GANG member with the murder of OWENS.	231
Lincoln	Owner and operator of the ferry. A doctor. When his ferry is seized from him, he goes into hiding. Later killed and defiled by the YUMA warriors.	253
Little girl (Fort Griffin)	Cranks the organ to which the bear dances to in the Fort Griffin saloon. Ends up missing from the dance.	324
Little girl (Jesus Maria)	Girl who ends up missing from Jesus Maria.	191
Lost scouts	Forward patrol sent out by the GLANTON GANG while fleeing GENERAL ELIAS. They do not return. Later found hanging from a tree. 'They were skewered through the cords of their heels with sharpened shuttles of green wood and they hung gray and naked above the dead ashes of the coals where they'd been roasted until their heads had charred and the brains bubbled in the skulls and steam sang from their noseholes. Their tongues were drawn out and held with sharpened sticks thrust through them and they had been docked of their ears and their torsos were sliced open with flints until the entrails hung down on their chests. Some of the men . . . cut the bodies down' (226-7)	219-20
Magician (juggler)	Seeks passage with the GLANTON GANG as far as Janos for himself and his family. Assists in telling the fortunes of members of the Glanton Gang. A juggler.	89
Magician's wife	Seeks passage with the GLANTON GANG to Janos. Tells the fortunes of the Glanton Gang members. Described in relationship to the High Priestess card in the Tarot deck: 'like that blind interlocutrix between Boaz and	89

Appendixes

Character	Notes	First appearance or mention (page)
	Jachin inscribed upon the one card in the juggler's deck that they would not see come to light.' (94)	
Major Graham	Former commander of LIEUTENANT COUTS.	231
Maltese boatswain	Shoots the KID twice, once in the back, once below the heart, then flees.	4
Man	See the CHILD, KID, MAN.	314
Mangas Colorado	Leader of the CHIRICAHUAS, in whole or in part. Directly in charge of the eight or ten mounted warriors who come to the aide of the CHIRICAHUA DEPUTATION. 'a huge man with a huge head and he was dressed in overalls cut off at the knees to accommodate the leggingtops of his moccasins and he wore a checked shirt and a red scarf.' (229)	229
Maricopas	Mexican indians.	247
McCulloch	Captain of a military command in which TOBIN, TATE, and other members of the GLANTON GANG served.	95
Mennonite	Customer of the Bexar (San Antonio) saloon where the KID and the corporals go to drink. 'A thin man in a leather weskit, a black and straightbrim hat set square on his head, a thin rim of whiskers.' (39) Prophesies the demise of the FILIBUSTERS and eulogizes the fallen corporal with 'There is no such joy in the tavern as on the road thereto.' (41)	39
Mother (of CHILD/ KID/MAN)	The CHILD's mother. Dies giving birth to the child.	3
Mr. Riddle	Gun merchant for whom SPEYER is probably a negotiator, middleman, or spokesman. Co-owner of a hotel in Chihuahua City with STEPHENS. Serves as a kind of American consul to GOVERNOR TRIAS.	83 (appears on 171)
Old Hueco	Man who sat for a portrait by the JUDGE. He then later sought the judge's council on how best to keep it from the hands of his enemies.	141
Old man (botanist)	A botanist gathering herbs encountered on the trail by the GLANTON GANG. Questioned by JOHN GLANTON.	197

Continued

Character	Notes	First appearance or mention (page)
Old man (tyroler) *also* 'showman' (325)	Man in tyrolean, or German, outfit who solicits entertainment fees from the rabble in the Fort Griffin saloon. Owner of the dancing bear.	324
Oren	One of the herders. Tells the KID to tell Lonnie to 'get a piece for me.' (21)	21
Owens *also* 'tall thin man' (234)	Proprietor of the eatinghouse in Tucson. Shot dead by the black JOHN JACKSON.	234 (by name 235)
Pablo (Yuma)	One of CABALLO EN PELO's lieutenants. 'he was clad in a scarlet coat with tarnished braiding and tarnished epaulettes of silver wire. He was barefoot and bare of leg and he wore on his face a pair of round green goggles.' (254–5)	254
Pacheco	Stable helper who attends to the GLANTON GANG's horses. Also a smithy. Uses a meteorite for an anvil.	240
Penitents *also* 'troubled sect' (314) 'pilgrims' (314) 'company of penitents' (314)	Religious travelers in the wilderness. Killed in mysterious circumstances by unseen assailants. 'in the deep fastness of those rocks he met with men who seemed unable to abide the silence of the world.' (313) 'They were led by a pitero piping a reed and then in procession a clanging of tambourines and matracas and men naked to the waist in black capes and hoods who flailed themselves with whips of braided yucca and men who bore on their naked backs great loads of cholla and a man tied to a rope who was pulled this way and that by his companions and a hooded man in a white robe who bore a heavy wooden cross on his shoulders. They were all of them barefoot and they left a trail of blood across the rocks and they were followed by a rude carreta in which sat a carved wooden skeleton who rattled along stiffly holding before him a bow and arrow. He shared his cart with a load of stones and they went trundling over the rocks drawn by ropes tied to the heads and ankles of the bearers and accompanied by a deputation of women who carried small desert	313

Character	Notes	First appearance or mention (page)
	flowers in their folded hands or torches of sotol or primitive lanterns of pierced tin.' (314)	
Petit	Guards the San Diego jail where DAVID BROWN is incarcerated. Falls into Brown's scheme to liberate him from the cell. Shot by Brown.	269
Posthole Maker	Ambiguous figure who makes his way across the desert by means of a series of holes. 'He uses an implement with two handles and he chucks it into the hole and he enkindles the stone in the hole with his steel hole by hole striking the fire out of the rock which God has put there.' (337)	337
Preacher	Arkansas preacher who prays over JAMES ROBERT BELL in an attempt to cure him.	238
Priest (Jesus Maria)	Village pastor for Jesus Maria. Berates the GLANTON GANG. Drubbed by the Glanton Gang. Has coins flung at him by the Glanton Gang. 'When he rose he disdained to take up the coins until some small boys ran out to gather them and then he ordered them brought to him while the barbarians whooped and drank him a toast.' (190) Later leads the parade for Las Animas.	190
Randall (member of the party) *also* 'the youngest of them' (322) 'the orphan' (323)	ELROD's brother.	320 (by name 322)
Reverend Green	Preacher who has set up a revival in a tent in Nagadoches, Texas around the time of the KID's arrival there. Probably falsely accused of child molestation and bestiality by the JUDGE. Possibly killed by the posse of Nagadoches.	5
Sanford	American who rides out from Jesus Maria with FRANK CARROLL to join up with the GLANTON GANG.	194
Sarah Borginnis	Upbraids CLOYCE BELL for keeping his brother, JAMES ROBERT BELL, in a cage.	256

Continued

Character	Notes	First appearance or mention (page)
	Attempts to civilize (at least outwardly) James Robert, but it does not take.	
Scouts (Sonoran)	Forward company of GENERAL ELIAS' command. Stumble, literally, upon the sleeping KID and TATE. They number five men. They include a man shot by the kid, and a man who shoots (and misses) the kid.	211
Second man (Fort Griffin)	Warned by the THIRD MAN not to go into the jakes behind the Griffin saloon. Asks the FIRST MAN 'What is it?' (334)	334
Sergeant (San Diego)	Sergeant in charge of the San Diego garrison. Beaten senseless and stripped of his weapons by JOHN GLANTON and his men. Probably the SERGEANT OF THE GUARD.	272
Sergeant Aguillar	Commands the soldiers who investigate the gunfire after JOHN GLANTON tests the Whitneyville Colts outside Chihuahua City. Negotiated with by the JUDGE.	83 (by name 84)
Sergeant of the guard	Goes to the FARRIER's (San Diego) shop to investigate the incident involving DAVID BROWN and the threats made by him.	267
Sergeant Trammel *also* 'another rider' (28) 'the captain's man' (31)	Recruits the KID to join the company of FILIBUSTERS. Second in command of CAPTAIN WHITE's company. 'He was dressed in buckskin and he wore a plug hat of dusty black silk and he had a small Mexican cigar in the corner of his teeth.' (29)	28 (by name 35)
Shelby *also* 'Dick Shelby' (207)	Member of the GLANTON GANG sent by JOHN GLANTON for whores and drink in Ures, Sonora. Wounded in the altercation with GENERAL ELIAS' mounted troops. Left in the desert by the KID.	201
Shipman	A fellow inmate of the KID's when he is first jailed in the unnamed Mexican town. Probably another of the eight surviving members of the FILIBUSTERS.	71
Sidney, 'Old Sydney'	Man who TOADVINE seeks revenge against. Assaulted by Toadvine. Kicked in the mouth by the KID. Possibly the man with the shellaleigh. Possibly the owner of the hotel/ dramhouse in Nagadoches.	11
Sister to the CHILD	Sister to the CHILD before he runs away from home.	3

Appendixes

Character	Notes	First appearance or mention (page)
Sloat	Member of the GLANTON GANG recruited from Ures, Sonora. Dies shortly thereafter while fleeing GENERAL ELIAS and his Sonoran cavalry.	204
Soldier (Los Angeles)	Sells the KID DAVID BROWN's scapular of ears after Brown is hanged in Los Angeles.	312
Speyer	Gun merchant who sells JOHN GLANTON a box containing four dozen Whitneyville Colt revolvers.	82
Sproule	One of the FILIBUSTERS. Survives the attack by the COMANCHE WARRIORS. Wounded in the arm. Dies in the carreta on the way to an unnamed Mexican town.	56
Stephens	Part owner, with MR. RIDDLE, in the Riddle and Stephens hotel.	167
Strange dark child *also* 'Apache boy' (164)	Gileno child adopted, briefly, by the JUDGE.	160
Tate *also* 'Sam Tate' (158)	Member of the GLANTON GANG. A Kentuckian who fought with MCCULLOCH's Rangers with TOBIN and others of the Gang. Elected to kill the Mexican wounded in the altercation with GENERAL ELIAS and his Sonoran cavalry. Probably captured by General Elias' command.	95 (by full name 158)
Teamster	Converses briefly with the KID during REVEREND GREEN's sermon. Leads the kid out of the tent through a seam he cuts in it after the JUDGE makes his accusations.	6
Third man (Fort Griffin)	Discovers whatever catastrophe has occurred in the jakes behind the Griffin saloon. Urinates in the mud and warns the FIRST MAN and the SECOND MAN not to go into the jakes.	334
Tiguas *also* 'sons a bitches' (173)	Peaceful Native American tribe slaughtered by the GLANTON GANG.	173
Toadvine *also* 'Louis' (284)	Encounters the KID on the path to the jakes outside a saloon in Nagadoches. Tries to kill the kid first with a broken bottle, then an immense bowie knife. 'His head was strangely	8

Continued

Character	Notes	First appearance or mention (page)
	narrow and his hair was plastered up with mud in a bizarre and primitive coiffure. On his forehead were burned the letters H T and lower and almost between the eyes the letter F and these markings were splayed and garish as if the iron had been left too long. When he turned to look at the kid the kid could see that he had no ears.' (11) Later, the kid's partner in the assault against Old SIDNEY and the hotel burning. Rejoins the kid in the Chihuahua City jail. A member of the GLANTON GANG. Hanged in Los Angeles with DAVID BROWN.	
Tobin *also* 'the expriest' (93) 'the frockless one' (122) 'the cretin' (306)	Member of the GLANTON GANG. Fought with MCCULLOCH's Rangers with TATE and others of the Gang. Shoots the laggards in Nacori. Flees with the kid after the second attack on the ferry crossing. Loses the kid in San Diego.	93
Wilson	Member of the GLANTON GANG. Killed by the YUMAS during their attack on the ferry crossing.	274
Yumas	Members of the Yuma tribe of Native Americans. Present with the survivors (of the epidemic) when the GLANTON GANG passes through their campsite. 'The men wore their hair hacked to length with knives or plastered up in wigs of mud and they shambled about with heavy clubs dangling in their hands. Both they and the women were tattooed of face and the women were naked save for skirts of willowbark woven into string and many of them were lovely and many of them bore the marks of syphilis'. (253) Yuma warriors attack the ferry crossing when their treatment by the Glanton Gang becomes unbearable. Led by CABALLO EN PELO.	252

Appendix 6

All the Pretty Horses

List of characters

Character	Notes	First appearance or mention (page)
Abuela	LUISA's mother. 'who'd been on the ranch since before the turn of the century.' (18)	18 (by name 25)
Alcalde	Doctor at the Saltillo prison.	190
Alejandra Rocha	Daughter of DON HÉCTOR ROCHA. Lover of JOHN GRADY COLE. Confesses to her father her relationship with John Grady, and is therefore partially accountable for his and LACEY RAWLINS' imprisonment.	94 (by name 119)
Alejandra's maternal grandfather	Member of the Zaragoza Brigade under Raul Madero. Dies in the square in Zacatecas on June 23, 1913.	253
Antonio	One of the vaqueros. Brother of ARMANDO. Possibly the CAPORAL.	109
Armando	One of the vaqueros. Brother of ANTONIO. Possibly the GERENTE.	100
Arturo	Mexican worker on the Grady ranch. Probably LUISA's husband.	4
Baliff	Does not laugh when the JUDGE asks JOHN GRADY COLE to drop his pants to verify John Grady's story.	288
Barnett girl *also* 'Mary Catherine' (28)	Former girlfriend of JOHN GRADY COLE. Jilts him for another boy two years older who owns a car.	10 (by name 24; appears on 28)
Bautista brothers (including Faustino)	Two brothers imprisoned for killing a policeman. Befriend JOHN GRADY COLE in	190 (Faustino, by name 196)

Continued

Character	Notes	First appearance or mention (page)
	the Saltillo prison. Arrange for him to buy a knife.	
Betty Ward	Girl in a photo in LACEY RAWLINS' wallet. Possibly his girlfriend. The photo is ruined by JIMMY BLEVINS when he shoots Rawlins' wallet.	56
Blair	Referenced by LACEY RAWLINS. Probably a rancher in Texas.	91
Blevins' ancestors (including Blevins' paternal grandfather, uncle, and cousin; maternal great-uncle, cousin)	Relatives of JIMMY BLEVINS all killed by lightning strikes.	67–8
Blevins' father	Father of JIMMY BLEVINS. Killed in World War II.	64
Blevins' stepfather	Stepfather of JIMMY BLEVINS. Beats Blevins.	64
Booger Red	Legendary rider whom LACEY RAWLINS compares to JOHN GRADY COLE. Dead 'forever.' (58)	58
Bowling alley owner	Man for whom JIMMY BLEVINS works while in Ardmore, Oklahoma. Ships Blevins home after he is bitten by a bulldog.	63
Brother of the Dueña Alfonsa	Former owner of the Greener guns in the cabinet at the hacienda of La Purísma. A European traveler.	132
Buddy	Subject of one of JOHN GRADY COLE's father's anecdotes: 'Buddy when he come back from up in the panhandle told me one time it quit blowin up there and all the chickens fell over.' (8)	8
Caporal	Field leader of the vaqueros. Assistant, probably, to the GERENTE. Possibly ARMANDO or ANTONIO.	94
Captain *also* 'Raul' (262)	Law officer in Encantada. Arrests JIMMY BLEVINS. Later, interrogates LACEY RAWLINS and JOHN GRADY COLE. Facilitates the execution of BLEVINS. Later, kidnapped by JOHN GRADY and held hostage when he flees with RAWLINS' and Blevins' horses. Probably killed by the HOMBRES DEL PAIS.	157 (by title, 162; by name, 262)

Appendixes

Character	Notes	First appearance or mention (page)
Carlos	House hand at the hacienda of La Purísma.	112 (by name 128)
Carranza	A family of similar means as the Rochas and Maderos.	232
Clerk (courtroom) *also* 'Emil' (288)	Reads the charges in the ownership hearing between JOHN GRADY COLE and the plaintiffs to determine to whom JIMMY BLEVINS' horse belongs.	288
Clerk (San Antonio)	Clerk at the San Antonio hotel who informs JOHN GRADY COLE that there is no Mrs. Cole listed in the registry.	22
Clerk (Torreon)	Clerk at the hotel in Torreon who directs JOHN GRADY COLE to take his horse through the lobby and to the back.	244–5
Commandante	Man who releases JOHN GRADY COLE from the hospital and prison. Gives John Grady an envelope containing money sent by the DUEÑA ALFONSA.	206
Constable *also* 'Mr. Smith' (289)	Impounds JIMMY BLEVINS' horse when JOHN GRADY COLE returns it to the United States. Later charged with returning the horse to John Grady by the JUDGE.	287
Counter man	Directs JOHN GRADY COLE to Del Rio to try to find the REVEREND JIMMY BLEVINS.	294
Crawford Sykes	Name of a horse of some renown. Owned and/or bred by Billy Anson.	115
Crowds	Crowds of rebels led by VICTORIANO HUERTA against FRANCISCO and GUSTAVO MADERO. Kill Gustavo Madero in the town square.	238
Cuchillero	Knifeman who attempts to kill JOHN GRADY COLE at Saltillo prison. 'On the inside of his right forearm was a blue jaguar struggling in the coils of an anaconda. In the web of his left thumb the pachuco cross and the five marks. Nothing out of the ordinary.' (198) Killed by John Grady.	198
Cullen Cole	Owner of a shop in San Angelo that sells horse equipment. Possibly a cousin to JOHN GRADY COLE.	27
Díaz, Porfirio	Political dictator in pre-revolutionary Mexico. Forced to flee from Mexico by FRANCISCO MADERO.	145

Continued

Character	Notes	First appearance or mention (page)
Dirty showman	Man thrown in the Tyler, Texas, jail for having a dirty show. It is the same show that JIMMY BLEVINS saves his money for and travels to Ardmore, Oklahoma to see.	64
Doctor	Doctor who ministers to JOHN GRADY COLE during his recovery. Probably puts the stitches into John Grady's face and stomach.	205
Don Evaristo Madero	Father of FRANCISO and GUSTAVO MADERO. Godfather to DON HÉCTOR ROCHA. According to Don Héctor, 'Loyal to the regime of Díaz.' (145)	145
Don Héctor Rocha (Don Héctor Rocha y Villareal)	Owner of the Hacienda de Nuestra Señora de la Purísma Concepción. Father of ALEJANDRA ROCHA. Nephew of the DUEÑA ALFONSA. Wealthy breeder of horses, and knowledgeable on many aspects of the subject. A pilot. Befriends JOHN GRADY COLE and promotes him to a better position at La Purísma. Ultimately responsible for imprisoning John Grady Cole and LACEY RAWLINS after being informed of the former's relationship with his daughter.	96 (by full name 97)
Don Héctor Rocha's wife	Wife of DON HÉCTOR ROCHA and mother of ALEJANDRA ROCHA. Does not live at the hacienda, but instead lives in Mexico City.	97
Don Rafael	Owner of the hacienda where REDBO, JUNIOR, and JIMMY BLEVINS' horse is kept.	261
Dr. Brinkley	Man who investigates the REVEREND JIMMY BLEVINS' radio station.	297
Driver (Cuatro Cienagas)	Driver of the truck JOHN GRADY COLE gets on outside Cuatro Cienagas.	221
Driver (Texas)	Man who picks up JOHN GRADY COLE and gives him a lift back to the Grady ranch.	14
Dueña Alfonsa	Aunt of DON HÉCTOR ROCHA. Great aunt of ALEJANDRA ROCHA. Missing two fingers on her left hand. A chess player. A schoolteacher. Was at one time affiliated with the Maderos in their philanthropic (and later revolutionary) ideas. In love with GUSTAVO MADERO; possibly engaged to him. Engineers JOHN GRADY COLE's and LACEY RAWLINS'	132

Appendixes

Character	Notes	First appearance or mention (page)
	release from prison under the condition that Alejandra Rocha not see John Grady again.	
Dueña Alfonsa's great-grandfather	Subject of an oil painting in the hacienda of La Purísma.	132
Dueña Alfonsa's uncle	Travels with the DUEÑA ALFONSA to San Luis Potosi, where the Dueña has her shooting accident.	234
Earl	Runs the café in Langtry, Texas.	287
Ed Alison	Present at the burial of JOHN GRADY COLE's grandfather. Ambiguous as to whether he is a literal uncle of John Grady, or perhaps of John Grady's father.	7
Emilio Pérez *also* 'prisoner of means' (184) and 'papazote' (185)	A political prisoner who occupies his own private cell comprised of concrete blocks. Has a cook and bodyguard. Possibly conspires to murder JOHN GRADY COLE and LACEY RAWLINS or at least intimidate them into working for him, entertaining him, or at least paying him to get out of prison.	184 (by name 186)
Estéban *also* 'old groom'	Groomer of horses who lives in the barn. Occupies a room similar to JOHN GRADY COLE's when John Grady is promoted by DON HÉCTOR ROCHA.	117 (by name 139)
F W Axtell	Name of a company that either produces or advertises on windmills.	41
Forgeman	Person whose hammer and forge JOHN GRADY COLE hears from a distance.	279
Francisco Madero	Extremely progressive (radical) political figure. Educated in Europe and the United States. A philanthropist interested in helping the poverty-stricken population of Mexico. Leader of the revolution against the regime of DÍAZ. First (and only) elected president of Mexico. Brother of GUSTAVO MADERO. Assassinated by VICTORIANO HUERTA.	144
Francisco Madero's mother	Writes a telegram to President Taft asking for intervention in the case of FRANCISCO MADERO.	238
Franklin's assistant	Secretary who shows JOHN GRADY COLE into MR. FRANKLIN's office.	16

Continued

Character	Notes	First appearance or mention (page)
Gerente	Manager of the vaqueros. Responsible for hiring JOHN GRADY COLE and LACEY RAWLINS at La Purísma. Tells John Grady that he is 'full of shit. But in a nice way,' when John Grady claims to want to break the sixteen horses in four days. Probably ARMANDO.	94
Gustavo Madero	Extremely progressive (radical) political figure. Educated in Europe and the United States. Assists his brother FRANCISCO MADERO in helping the poverty-stricken population of Mexico. Participant in the revolution against the regime of DÍAZ. In love with the DUEÑA ALFONSA; possibly engaged to her. Shot to death by a mob in Mexico City.	145
Guzman	Author of a multi-volume study on horses loaned by DON HÉCTOR ROCHA to JOHN GRADY COLE.	143
Hamley	Producer of saddles.	14
Hombres del pais	Literally, 'men of the country.' Take custody of the CAPTAIN from JOHN GRADY COLE. One gives John Grady a serape to wear. They number three men.	280
Jimmy Blevins	A young fugitive from Texas who follows JOHN GRADY COLE and LACEY RAWLINS into Mexico. A probable horse thief. A marksman with a pistol. Loses his clothes, boots, horse, and pistol during a thunderstorm. Regains his horse by stealing it from a stable. Later shoots a Mexican officer and is imprisoned for it and it is for this murder that John Grady and Rawlins are ultimately charged as accomplices. Killed by the CAPTAIN.	38 (appears on 39; by name 44)
Joaquin Fernadez de Lizardi	'Mexican Thinker' (Pensador Mexicano).	253
John Grady Cole	Sixteen-year-old protagonist of the story. Descended on both sides from ranchers and horsemen. Father is a professional gambler; mother is an actress. Rides with LACEY RAWLINS into Mexico. Meets JIMMY BLEVINS on the road south through Mexico. Later works at the La Purísma ranch where he	3 (by name 7)

Appendixes

Character	Notes	First appearance or mention (page)
	meets and falls in love with ALEJANDRA. Jailed as a probable accomplice to Jimmy Blevins. Kills a prison assassin and kidnaps a Mexican CAPTAIN. Finally returns to the United States after rescuing the lost horses belonging to Lacey Rawlins and Jimmy Blevins.	
John Grady Cole's ancestors (including his great-grandfather and great-uncles, his grandfather's two brides)	Maternal ancestors of JOHN GRADY COLE. 'His grandfather was the oldest of eight boys and the only one to live past the age of twenty-five. They were drowned, shot, kicked by horses. They perished in fires. They seemed only to fear dying in bed. The last two were killed in Puerto Rico in eighteen ninety-eight and in that year he married.' (7)	6
John Grady Cole's father	Father of JOHN GRADY COLE. Professional gambler. Soldier in the Third Infantry during World War II. Suffers from some physical and/or psychological damage incurred in a POW camp called Goshee.	4
John Grady Cole's grandfather	Maternal grandfather of JOHN GRADY COLE and owner of the Grady ranch. First Grady to die in the ranch house.	3
Jose Chiquito *also* 'Little Joe'	Name of the sire horse out of which all of the horses at La Purísma come from.	101
Judge *also* 'Charles' (290)	Man who presides at the ownership hearing requested by JOHN GRADY COLE to determine who JIMMY BLEVINS' horse belongs to. Later advises John Grady about guilt.	288
Julius Ramsey	Anecdotal figure. Purportedly climbs into a tree with a stick to knock down a mountain lion for his hunting dogs to fight.	92
Junior	LACEY RAWLINS' horse.	87
Lacey Rawlins	Seventeen-year-old friend of JOHN GRADY COLE. Accompanies John Grady into Mexico. Works with John Grady at the La Purísma ranch. Later arrested with John Grady as a probable accomplice to JIMMY BLEVINS. Leaves Mexico shortly after he is released from prison.	9 (by first name 46)

Continued

Character	Notes	First appearance or mention (page)
Lamont	Anecdotal figure in LACEY RAWLINS' story about stealing feed and selling it to Mexicans.	215
Lawyer	Represents the plaintiffs against JOHN GRADY COLE. Claims mistaken identity when the JUDGE finds for John Grady.	289
Lucia	Friend of ALEJANDRA ROCHA. Alejandra mentions her to JOHN GRADY COLE as a possible 'date' for him.	124
Luis	A vaquero at La Puríma and a veteran of the Mexican revolution. Relates tales of the revolution and of the spiritual nature of horses.	110–11
Luisa	Mexican housewoman at the Grady ranch.	4 (by name 14)
Maid	Woman who cleans the CAPTAIN's office. Discovers JOHN GRADY COLE in the Captain's chair. Put in the town jail by John Grady so he might escape with the Captain.	258
Man who wishes to buy Blevins	One of the waxcampers. 'A thin man in a stained leather vest with embroidery on the front was watching John Grady with narrowed and speculative eyes.' (75) Offers to buy JIMMY BLEVINS from JOHN GRADY COLE.	75
Man with a knife	Knifeman who stabs LACEY RAWLINS.	189
Man with Blevins' pistol	Man in Encantada who has JIMMY BLEVINS' pistol in his back pocket. A civil servant of some kind. Later, shot by Blevins. Probably the brother of the Charro.	78
Maria	Cook at the hacienda of La Purísma.	112 (by name 112)
Matilde	Sister of the DUEÑA ALFONSA. Widowed twice by the age of twenty-one.	229
Matilde's husbands	Two husbands of MATILDE. Both shot as bigamists.	229
McCullogh	Ambiguous name of a place where JOHN GRADY COLE and his father unload their horses. Possibly a ranch or general store.	22
Meusebach survey of the Fisher-Miller grant	Names of the land grants of which the Grady ranch is a part. Named, presumably, for its original surveyors/owners.	6
Migrant traders	Traders on muleback travelling north. 'Brown and weathered men with burros three or four in tandem atotter with loads of candelilla or	66

Character	Notes	First appearance or mention (page)
	furs or goathides or coils of handmade rope fashioned out of lechugilla or the fermented drink called sotol decanted into drums and cans and strapped onto packframes made from treelimbs. They carried water in the skins of hogs or in canvas bags made waterproof with candelilla wax and children with them and they would shoulder the packanimals off into the brush and relinquish the road to the caballeros.' (65–6) They refuse to sell water to JOHN GRADY COLE, LACEY RAWLINS, and JIMMY BLEVINS. Instead, they sell sotol. Possibly confederates of the waxcampers.	
Minter	Subject of an analogy for ROCHA'S GRANDFATHER: a minter who takes a slug and makes it a coin and, from whose minting, all decisions made on the toss of a coin follow.	229–30
Morales	Vaquero at La Purísma. JOHN GRADY COLE mistakenly thinks Morales is glad to see him.	224
Morelos	Man whose statue GUSTAVO MADERO falls onto when he is attacked by the crowd. Almost certainly the historical figure Jose Maria Morelos y Pavon, the warrior/priest.	237
Mother of John Grady Cole	Sole beneficiary of the Grady ranch. An actress. Refuses to keep the ranch despite JOHN GRADY COLE's complaints. Recently divorced from John Grady's father. In the early pages of the novel, commonly referred to simply as 'she.'	4 (appears on 15)
Mr. Franklin	Lawyer who probably is the executor of JOHN GRADY COLE's grandfather's will. Probably processed the divorce of John Grady's parents.	16
Old man (Cuatro Cienagas)	Preacher who prays over the food the workers eat. 'he asked that the living here remember that the corn grows by the will of God and beyond that will there is neither corn nor growing nor light nor air nor rain nor anything at all save only darkness.' (221)	221
Old man (Torreon)	Explains to JOHN GRADY COLE that many things worse than a horse have gone through the lobby of the Torreon hotel.	245

Continued

Character	Notes	First appearance or mention (page)
Pérez's chamberlain	Attendant on EMILIO PÉREZ. Guards the door to Pérez's cell at Saltillo prison.	190
Pérez's cook	Personal chef for EMILIO PÉREZ.	184
Pérez's mistress	Subject of speculation for the prisoners when estimating EMILIO PÉREZ's influence.	190
Pérez's wife	Subject of speculation for the prisoners when estimating EMILIO PÉREZ's influence.	190
Pino Suárez	A fellow revolutionary with FRANCISCO and GUSTAVO MADERO. Arrested with the Maderos by VICTORIANO HUERTA. Shot.	237
Pollack	An Irish chess champion whose strategies the DUEÑA ALFONSA uses.	134
Priest	A priest who comes to make the chapel at the hacienda of La Purísma unsacred.	144
Proprietor (Eldorado)	Proprietor of the café just outside Eldorado.	33
Proprietor (Robert Lee)	Proprietor of a café in Robert Lee who calls JOHN GRADY COLE and his father by name.	23
Rafela Madero	Sister of FRANCISCO and GUSTAVO MADERO. Friend of the DUEÑA ALFONSA.	232
Raul Madero	Leader of the Zaragoza Brigade in Zacatecas.	253
Rawlins' parents	Parents of LACEY RAWLINS.	26
Redbo	JOHN GRADY COLE's horse.	14
Reverend Jimmy Blevins	Radio reverend heard all over the world and possibly on Mars. Hosts JOHN GRADY COLE to dinner when the latter tries to return JIMMY BLEVINS' horse. No relation to Blevins. Not the owner of Blevins' horse.	294
Robert Lee	Man for whom the town of Robert Lee is named. Robert Lee (the town) is in Coke county (neighboring Tom Green county).	23
Roberto	A boy from La Purísma who accompanies JOHN GRADY COLE and LACEY RAWLINS to the dance at La Vega.	122
Rocha's grandfather	Grandfather of DON HÉCTOR ROCHA. Father of the DUEÑA ALFONSA. Prevents the marriage between the Dueña and GUSTAVO MADERO.	
Rosco	One of the Grady ranch horses. Possibly JOHN GRADY COLE's father's horse.	9
Sheeran	Horse owner who sells DON HÉCTOR ROCHA stud rights to JOSE CHIQUITO.	101

Appendixes

Character	Notes	First appearance or mention (page)
Shooter	Man with a rifle at the hacienda of DON RAFAEL. Shoots JOHN GRADY COLE in the leg. Flees when John Grady returns fire. Possibly Don Rafael himself.	262
Steeldust	Ambiguous. Probably the name of a famous breeding horse.	16
Surgeon	Removes the stitches from JOHN GRADY COLE's face.	216
T-Bone Watts	Anecdotal figure for LACEY RAWLINS. Employee of Rawlins' father.	108
Thatcher Cole	Provides ARTURO with a job at the San Angelo school.	299
Uncle Billy Anson	Owner and/or breeder of CRAWFORD SYKES. Referred to by JOHN GRADY COLE as 'Uncle,' although probably not his literal uncle. Friend of John Grady's grandfather. Son of the Earl of Litchfield.	115
Vail	Owner of Three Bars. From Douglas, Arizona.	114
Vaqueros (employees of Blair)	Anecdotal figures for LACEY RAWLINS' story about boning out an animal.	91
Vaqueros (employees of Rocha)	Literally, 'cowboys.' First employees of the Hacienda de Nuestra Señora de la Purísma Concepción encountered by JOHN GRADY COLE and LACEY RAWLINS. Coworkers of John Grady and Rawlins at the ranch. Described as closer friends of Rawlins than John Grady (226).	93
Victoriano Huerta	Plotter who seizes control of the Mexican government from FRANCISCO MADERO after the fall of DÍAZ. According to LUIS, 'compared to Huerta Judas was himself but another Christ.' (110)	110
Wallace (author)	Author of *The American Horse*.	116
Wallace (employer)	Potential employer for JOHN GRADY COLE who might trade out labor in exchange for boarding a horse. Suggested by John Grady's father.	24
Woman (Blevins' house)	Woman at the REVEREND JIMMY BLEVINS' house. Fixes dinner for JOHN GRADY COLE. Almost certainly the Reverend's wife.	294

Appendix 7

The Crossing

List of characters

Character	Notes	First appearance or mention (page)
Aja	Person(s) responsible for the new hashknives operation.	349
Alfonso	Drunken man in the Janos bar with whom BILLY PARHAM gets in a debate and drinking showdown. Shot three times around his heart during the Mexican revolution.	358 (by name 358)
Alguacil	Law officer who discharges BILLY PARHAM after he is taken into custody. Later responsible for allowing Billy to leave the *feria* after Billy shoots THE WOLF. Possibly DON BETO.	97
Alguacil's entourage *also* 'the hunting party' (107)	Men who ride with the ALGUACIL for Morelos. 'garbed in the gaudy attire of the norteno and of the charro all spangled and trimmed with silver braid, the seams of their trousers done with silver shells. They rode saddles worked in silver with flat pommels the size of plates and some were drunk riding and doffed their hats in gestures of outlandish courtliness at women their horses had forced against buildings or into doorways.' (106)	106
Arrieros *also* 'pilgrims' (84)	Group of Mexicans who travel the landscape on burros. Encountered by BILLY PARHAM shortly after crossing the border into Mexico (first trip). Fear of THE WOLF sends the caravan into a panic.	84
Bandolero	Man who cuts up BILLY PARHAM's soogan full of bones and stabs NIÑO.	394

Appendixes

Character	Notes	First appearance or mention (page)
Billy Parham	Eldest son of WILL PARHAM. Brother of BOYD PARHAM. Captures and ties THE WOLF and takes it back into Mexico despite several questions about his sanity. After killing the wolf at the feria, returns to New Mexico to discover his family all dead except Boyd. Returns to Mexico to first to reclaim his family's horses, then the bones of his brother.	3 (by name 7)
Bird	BILLY PARHAM's horse.	13
Blind revolutionary	Soldier in the Mexican revolution. After the fall of Durango, he loses his eyes at the hands of WIRTZ. Wanders the countryside before finally finding the WOMAN (of the blind revolutionary).	274
Boyd Parham	Troublesome younger son of WILL PARHAM. Brother of BILLY PARHAM. In or near the house when Billy and Boyd's parents are killed. Rides with Billy into Mexico on the latter's second trip. Becomes involved with THE GIRL. Shot. Later killed and buried in Mexico. Reinterred in New Mexico after Billy retrieves his bones from Mexico.	3
Bruja	First nurse to BOYD PARHAM after he is shot. Gives him poultices of weeds and mud for his gunshot wounds.	300
Bud Langford	Notorious bachelor who tells people: 'It would take one hell of a wife to beat no wife at all.' (352)	352
Caborcan (man in the Priest's story)	Man from Caborca who figures most prominently in the PRIEST's story. Loses his son in the earthquake that destroys Bavispe. Abandons his wife. Travels first as a worker and messenger before returning to Caborca. There he takes up residence in the ruined church where the dome is suspended. Indicts God on many accounts and testifies, or bears witness, against God using passages from the Bible. Thought by most to be insane, yet influences the Priest with his arguments against God.	142

Continued

Character	Notes	First appearance or mention (page)
Carolyn Parham also 'Mama' (7)	Mrs. WILL PARHAM. Mother of BILLY and BOYD PARHAM. A Christian. Murdered.	7 (first appearance 13; by first name 338)
Casares	Enemy of the state. Takes in BOYD PARHAM after Boyd kills two men in Galeana.	385
Clerk (Silver City)	Informs BILLY PARHAM that it is not Sunday, but Friday and Christmas Day.	350
Corridero	Man who sings a corrido with some events that could come from BOYD PARHAM's life, others which do not.	375
Doctor	Doctor who ministers to BOYD PARHAM after he is shot in Boquilla y Anexas.	301
Doctor's *mozo*	Assitant or houseboy to the DOCTOR. Returns NIÑO to BILLY PARHAM after the doctor ministers to BOYD PARHAM.	300
Dog handlers	Men who bring in dogs to fight THE WOLF during the pit fight at the *feria*.	114
Don Arnulfo	A sickly old man who BILLY PARHAM seeks out to get advice on hunting wolves. Philosophizes on the nature of wolves, hunters, and men. Proclaims that none know what the wolf knows.	41 (appears on 42)
Don Beto	Man whom the two deputies work for. Probably either the HACENDADO or the ALGUACIL.	118
Gaspar	Man present with the stranded PRIMADONNA. Sits on the steps and smokes and listens to the conversation between the Primadonna and BILLY PARHAM. Possibly the father (or older relation) of GASPARITO. Later solicits Billy for money so he might eat.	227
Gasparito	Man who kills one of the OPERA COMPANY's mules with a machete. Probably the son (or younger relation) of GASPAR.	226
Gillian	Ganadero (livestock trader) in business with Soto. Agent by whom the KENO horse is acquired and sold to HAAS.	196
God's pilgrims (Billy's dream)	Figures in BILLY PARHAM's dream. 'God's pilgrims laboring upon a darkened verge in the last of the twilight of that day and they seemed to be returning from some deep	420–1

Appendixes

Character	Notes	First appearance or mention (page)
	enterprise that was not of war nor were they yet in flight but rather seemed coming from some labor to which perhaps these and all other thing stood subjugate.' (420–1)	
Guard 1	U.S. border guard present when BILLY and BOYD PARHAM ride into Mexico. Billy pays him the money he owes JOHN GILCHRIST.	178
Guard 2	Border guard at Columbus, New Mexico who informs BILLY PARHAM that World War II has begun.	333
Guard 3	Mexican border patrolman at his post when BILLY PARHAM crosses into Mexico the third time.	355
Gypsies out of Durango	Men with oxen in custody of an old plane which they convey along the road.	400
Haas (the German doctor)	Doctor in attendance at the funeral in Bacerac. Buys the KENO horse from Soto and GILLIAN. Shows BILLY PARHAM a *factura* for the horse.	183 (by name 197)
Hacendado (Morelos)	Hacendado suggested by the five men as the probable owner of THE WOLF. Present at the *feria*. Possibly DON BETO.	90
Hacendado's son	Confronts BILLY PARHAM in the *feria* pit when Billy tries to rescue THE WOLF. 'a young man who bore on the braided jacket he wore the scent of the women he'd so recently danced with.' (117)	117
Indian	Native American who scolds BILLY and BOYD PARHAM for spoiling his hunting stand. Gets them to bring him food; later murders their parents.	5
Jaime	Mexican who doctors up THE WOLF in the RANCHER's smokehouse.	70
Jaime *also* 'Punchinello' or the 'clown' (228)	Man to whom the PRIMADONNA asks BILLY PARHAM to convey a message of safety.	228
Jane Ellen *also* 'Mama' (66)	Wife of the RANCHER. Observes the doctoring of THE WOLF.	66 (appears on 67)

Continued

Character	Notes	First appearance or mention (page)
Jay Tom (and his son)	Man (and his son) who determine that two indians were responsible for killing the Parhams.	166
Jefe (La Babicora)	One-armed leader of the La Babicora vaqueros. An enemy of the people of the country. After he falls from his horse and breaks his back, BOYD PARHAM is heralded as a hero of the people, testimony to how much the Jefe is despised.	245
John Gilchrist	Border patrolman BILLY PARHAM encounters on his way back into the United States after his first trip into Mexico. Gives Billy fifty cents to eat on.	162
Keno	One of the Parham's horses. Sold by Soto and GILLIAN to HAAS.	181
Leader (of the gypsies)	One of the GYPSIES OUT OF DURANGO. Relates to BILLY PARHAM the story of the two planes, the dead pilots, and the efforts to retrieve the planes. Rescues NIÑO with a concoction like green tea.	400
Lena	One of the GYPSIES OUT OF DURANGO.	403
Leona *also* 'Sanders' granddaughter' (16)	Granddaughter and caretaker of MR. SANDERS' house. Later marriers a man who becomes a soldier in World War II and leaves the SK Bar.	16 (by name 164)
Louisa May Parham	Alias BILLY PARHAM uses for his mother's name on the U.S. Army enlistment forms.	338
Majordomo	Master of ceremonies for the OPERA COMPANY.	219
Mapmaker	Draws BILLY and BOYD PARHAM a map so they might find their way to Casas Grande. 'He sketched in the dust streams and promontories and pueblos and mountain ranges. He commenced to draw trees and houses. Clouds. A bird. He penciled in the horsemen themselves doubled upon their mount.' (184) Called insane by the disputants.	184
Margarita Evelyn Parham *also* 'sister' (3)	BOYD PARHAM's twin sister. Named for BILLY PARHAM and Boyd's maternal grandmother.	3 (by name 168)

Appendixes

Character	Notes	First appearance or mention (page)
Mennonites	Travellers carrying a sick girl to help. Encountered by BILLY PARHAM on his way to the mountains. They give him food.	91
Messenger	Figure in BILLY PARHAM's dream who brings a message, but of what, Billy does not know.	82
Moir (Army doctor 1)	First doctor to reject BILLY PARHAM from the U.S. Army.	340
Mr. Echols	Renowned tracker. Lives nearby MR. SANDERS. Never appears in the story, but his work and his possessions are described.	16
Mr. Sanders	Old rancher on the SK ranch who lives nearby MR. ECHOLS. 'His eyes were very blue and very beautiful half hid away in the leathery seams of his face. As if there were something there that the hardness of the country had not been able to touch.' (16) Lives with his granddaughter. Explains Echols' skills with trapping, hunting. Hosts BILLY PARHAM upon his return to the United States.	16
Muñoz family	Part of the contingent of ejiditarios. The matron of the family gives BILLY PARHAM a few coins in a rag when he departs. She also attends to BOYD PARHAM after he is shot after the altercation in Boquillas y Anexas.	217
Niño	Horse owned by WILL PARHAM.	168
Old hermit	First man BILLY PARHAM encounters after crossing the border into Mexico (first trip).	75
Old man (among the wild indians)	Perhaps a shaman. 'his clothes were embroidered with signs that had about them the geometric look of instructions, perhaps a game. He wore jewelry of jade and silver and his hair was long and blacker than his age would seem to warrant.' (134) Warns BILLY PARHAM that even though he is an orphan ('huerfano'), he should not make his life estranged from that of other men.	133–4
Old man in the Model A *also*	Man who stops to speak with BILLY PARHAM when he is out looking at the sets. A rancher whom Billy knows, but does not call by name.	37

Continued

Character	Notes	First appearance or mention (page)
'the old rancher' (58)	A hater of coyotes. Tells Billy a joke about a New Mexico lion and a Texas lion.	
Old *mozo*	Guards THE WOLF. Informs BILLY PARHAM that he cannot see the wolf without the HACENDADO's permission.	110–11
Old woman	Old woman among the ARRIEROS who stops while they pursue their runaway animals. Relates stories of the men and women of Mexico to BILLY PARHAM and summarizes the fate of the country: 'She said that the revolution had killed off all of the real men in the country and left only the tontos. She said moreover that fools beget their own kind and here was the proof of it and that as only foolish women would have them their progeny were twice doomed.' (86)	84
Oliver	Man who told WILL PARHAM that MR. ECHOLS could make trap sets without getting down from his horse.	23
Opera company	Performers who set up their traveling show outside the abandoned hacienda in San Diego. Includes several men and boys, a doorman to whom centavo admissions are paid, the muleteers or arrieros, etc. Later stopped on the road when GASPARITO kills a mule with a machete.	215–31
Pitchman (feria)	Man who sets up a tent and charges admission to see the captured WOLF.	104
Pitchman (sideshow)	Man at the fair offering free admittance to a sideshow to one whose card matches the card displayed on the wheel. BILLY PARHAM has the matching card, but refuses to enter.	375
Pitchman's assistant (feria)	Boy who sits in the tent and prods THE WOLF to make it seem more ferocious to paying customers.	105
Pitchman's assistant (sideshow)	Girl who assists the PITCHMAN.	375
Priest (Huisachepic)	Man who lives in the ruined church of Huisachepic with several cats. Hosts BILLY PARHAM to breakfast. Relates to Billy the story of the CABORCAN and the importance of the witness and the narrator.	137

Character	Notes	First appearance or mention (page)
Primadonna	Star of the OPERA COMPANY. Observed bathing by BILLY PARHAM. Warns that the road that Billy and BOYD PARHAM undertake is a difficult one for brothers to travel.	219
Quijada	Man who restores TOM, and NIÑO to BILLY and BOYD PARHAM. Writes them a note and signs it as a method of authentication. A Yaqui indian.	251 (by name 252)
Rafael	One of the GYPSIES OUT OF DURANGO.	403
Rancher	Owner of a ranch BILLY PARHAM passes on his way to the border. Feeds Billy and assists with the doctoring of THE WOLF. Husband of JANE ELLEN.	65
Rogelio	Man who attacks GASPARITO just after the death of the mule.	226
Ruiz	Stablehand for Mr. Chandler.	342
Sheriff	Tells BILLY PARHAM the results of the investigation into Billy's parents' deaths. Tells Billy that BOYD PARHAM is staying with the Websters. Gives Billy the papers on the horses owned by the Parhams.	165
The Girl	Mexican girl encountered in the road by BILLY and BOYD PARHAM. Later rescued from the two horsemen by Billy and Boyd.	203
The wolf	Pregnant she-wolf tracked by WILL and BILLY PARHAM. Eventually captured and taken back to Mexico by Billy. Shot by Billy at the *feria*.	24
The wolf's mate	Mate of THE WOLF. Caught in a trap. Bites at the wolf to get her to flee.	24
Tom	One of the Parham's horses.	241
Trooper	The Parham's dog.	7 (by name 239)
Will Parham *also* 'the old man' (7)	Father of BILLY and BOYD PARHAM. A rancher in New Mexico. Came out of Texas in 1919, but a native Missourian. Murdered.	11 (first appearance 13)
Wirtz	German mercenary who blinds the BLIND REVOLUTIONARY by sucking the eyes from the man's head.	276
Woman of the blind	Woman who lives with the BLIND	274

Continued

Character	Notes	First appearance or mention (page)
revolutionary	REVOLUTIONARY. Relates the blind revolutionary's tale to BILLY PARHAM.	
Young *mozo*	Young *mozo* who greets the two deputies at the office of the ALGUACIL.	97
Young woman of the campo	Woman who tells BILLY PARHAM that he will have trouble finding THE GIRL, and that it is untrue that the Girl was killed at Ignacio Zaragoza.	373

Appendix 8

Cities of the Plain

List of characters

Character	Notes	First appearance or mention (page)
Aldridge	Originator of the line of dogs in LUCY's lineage.	88
Archer	Hunter who pursues mountain lions with hunting dogs. Remembers episodes from the Mexican revolution and American involvement in it. Relates these and other stories to BILLY PARHAM and JOHN GRADY COLE. Participates in the hunt for the wild dogs.	87
Archer's parents	ARCHER's parents.	89
Army's recruiting doctors	Doctors who refuse BILLY PARHAM entrance into the United States Army in the early days of World War II. In the second book of the Border Trilogy, *The Crossing*, Billy is denied three times for a heart murmur.	265
Arturo	Longtime worker on JOHN GRADY COLE's GRANDFATHER's ranch in central Texas. Figures in the beginning and ending of the first book of the Border Trilogy, *All the Pretty Horses*.	204
Askins	One of the clientele at Maud's. Participates in a game of shuffleboard partnering with JESSIE versus the team of JC and TROY.	117
Babícora	Sprawling ranch owned by an American named Hearst. Its influence figures prominently in the second book of the Border Trilogy, *The Crossing*.	217

Continued

Character	Notes	First appearance or mention (page)
Betty	Sees to the aged BILLY PARHAM when he calls for Boyd in the night.	290 (by name 291)
Bill Reed	Subject of wonder for MR. JOHNSON. 'I think about old Bill Reed. Sometimes I'll say to myself, I'll say: I wonder whatever happened to old Bill Reed.' (187)	187
Billy Parham	Protagonist of the second novel in the Border Trilogy, *The Crossing*. Works on MAC's ranch with JOHN GRADY COLE and others. John Grady's partner on daily work. Later assists John Grady in his attempts to rescue MAGDALENA from the White Lake. After John Grady's death, takes to wandering the country looking for work well into the twenty-first century.	3
Billy Parham's brother *also* 'Boyd' (146)	Boyd Parham, brother of BILLY PARHAM. In the second book of the Border Trilogy, *The Crossing*, he is shot by a Mexican Jefe, but saved by a truckload of Mexican field laborers similar to the ones who appear on page 30.	36
Billy Parham's father	Will Parham. Father of BILLY PARHAM. Killed by unknown persons with a shotgun in the second book of the Border Trilogy, *The Crossing*.	219
Billy Parham's grandmother	BILLY PARHAM's dead grandmother. In the second book of the Border Trilogy, *The Crossing*, she is identified as a full-blooded Mexican woman named Margarita.	265
Billy Parham's sister	BILLY PARHAM's dead sister. Twin sister of Boyd Parham. In the second book of the Border Trilogy, she is identified as named Margaret, after her grandmother.	265
Billy Sanchez	Man for whom horses have an affinity. 'horses would follow Billy Sanchez to the outhouse and stand there and wait for him.' (15)	15
Bird	A horse on MAC's ranch. Possibly, but not necessarily, BILLY PARHAM's horse from the second book of the Border Trilogy, *The Crossing*.	38
Bloy	Runs an establishment where people go to meet. JOHNNY meets the WOMAN there and promises her he will quit drinking.	25

Appendixes

Character	Notes	First appearance or mention (page)
Boozer	Nighthorse in MR. JOHNSON's string when he was younger.	125
Cabdriver	Man who drives JOHN GRADY COLE around Juárez as he searches for MAGDALENA. Connects John Grady with MANOLO.	55
Cabman	Taxi driver who claims to be the cousin of RAMON GUTIÉRREZ. Drives MAGDALENA to her death.	223
Captain	Juárez police captain. A man of some moral character.	241
Carter	Famous producer of liver pills.	113
Chávez	Man who owned a horse resembling JOHN GRADY COLE's horse, according to CRAWFORD.	147
Client	Client at the White Lake who attempts to lie with MAGDALENA shortly before one of her epileptic seizures.	183
Clyde Stapp	Anecdotal figure. Man who works or worked with BILLY PARHAM, JOHN GRADY COLE and TROY. Taken to a whorehouse where he fell in love with an immense whore.	4
Colonel Fountain	Anecdotal figure inquired on by JOHN GRADY COLE to MR. JOHNSON. Dies in mysterious circumstances, possibly either at the hand or by the order of OLIVER LEE.	62
Cook	Cook at the Juárez café. Questioned by JOHN GRADY COLE the day after MAGDALENA's death as to Magdalena's whereabouts.	228
Crawford	Buys JOHN GRADY COLE's horse for three hundred dollars.	140
Criada (White Lake) also 'La Tuerta' (83)	Maid or attendant at the White Lake. Tends to the epileptic fits of MAGDALENA. Mother of TIBURCIO.	72
Davis	Man whose horses are shown at the auction attended by MAC, OREN, and JOHN GRADY COLE.	106
Delbert	Works on MAC's ranch with BILLY PARHAM, JOHN GRADY COLE, TROY, and others. Is	11

Continued

Character	Notes	First appearance or mention (page)
	let go for unknown reasons by Mac, giving John Grady a sense of guilt for taking his job.	
Doane	Man who operated a store that landmarks the start of Indian territory on the Red River when MR. JOHNSON was younger.	125
Doctor	Man who attends to JOHN GRADY COLE's injured foot.	15
Dreamer (stranger under the overpass in the Epilogue)	Encountered by the wandering BILLY PARHAM. Tells him the story of the map of his life and the dream of the TRAVELER and the serranos.	266
Driver	Man who picks up JOHN GRADY COLE and gives him a ride into El Paso on the night of the knifefight. Has a mare experiencing medical problems.	234
Eduardo	Operator of the White Lake whorehouse. A pimp. Possibly the 'owner' of MAGDALENA. Her frequent lover. In love with Magdalena. Later kills her. Dies in a knifefight with JOHN GRADY COLE.	72
Elton	Brother of TROY and JOHNNY. Relates the story of the WOMAN's reappearance at Bell's.	19 (appears on 23)
Elton's daughter	Daughter of ELTON and niece of TROY. Asks what's wrong with being called 'mam.' (24)	24
Fabens	Ranchowner or auctioneer who operates near MAC's ranch.	51
Family (Epilogue)	Family who takes in the wandering BILLY PARHAM in the later years of his life. Includes a man, his wife BETTY, a fourteen-year-old boy, and a twelve-year-old girl. They own a colt with which Billy helps them.	290
Funeral party	Funeral party that passes in the street in front of MAGDALENA. 'The musicians who appeared were old men in suits of dusty black. Behind them came the pallbearers carrying upon their shoulders a flowerstrewn pallet. Wreathed among those flowers the pale face of a young man newly dead. His hands lay at his sides and he jostled woodenly on his coolingboard there astride the shoulders of his bearers and the wild notes from the dented	207

Appendixes 379

Character	Notes	First appearance or mention (page)
	gypsy horns carried back from the glass of the storefronts they passed and back from the old mud or stuccoed facades and a clutch of women in black rebozos passed weeping and children and men in black or with black armbands and among them led by the girl the blind maestro shuffling with his small steps and look of pained wonder.' (207)	
Gene Edmonds	Anecdotal figure. Man of a reckless reputation in the Oldsmobile with TROY when he runs over the jackrabbits.	21
Girl	Waitress at the Juárez café. Questioned by JOHN GRADY COLE the day after MAGDALENA's death as to Magdalena's whereabouts.	228
Girl (Hacendado's daughter)	Alejandra Rocha. Daughter of the HACENDADO, Don Héctor Rocha. Lover of JOHN GRADY COLE. Figures prominently in the first book of the Border Trilogy, *All the Pretty Horses*.	205
Government trapper	Man who poisons wolves and hangs their carcasses on a fencewire.	126
Hacendado	Don Héctor Rocha y Villareal. Owner of the hacienda at La Purísma. Figures prominently in the first book of the Border Trilogy, *All the Pretty Horses*. Responsible for the jailing of JOHN GRADY COLE in the prison at Janos.	205
Hector	Ranchhand at MAC's ranch. Helps JOHN GRADY COLE with clean-up of the cabin/house.	199
Hostess	Woman who comes to the door when JOHN GRADY COLE arrives at the White Lake searching for MAGDALENA.	65
JC	Works on MAC's ranch with BILLY PARHAM, JOHN GRADY COLE, TROY, and others. Participates in the hunt for the wild dogs.	5
Jessie	One of the clientele at Maud's. Participates in a game of shuffleboard partnering with ASKINS versus the team of JC and TROY.	117
Joaquín	Works on MAC's ranch with BILLY PARHAM, JOHN GRADY COLE, TROY, and others. Participates in the hunt for the wild dogs.	13

Continued

Character	Notes	First appearance or mention (page)
John Grady Cole	Protagonist of the first novel in the Border Trilogy, *All the Pretty Horses*. Works on MAC's ranch with BILLY PARHAM and others. Billy's partner on daily work. An expert rider and horse-breaker. Nearly breaks his foot when he falls from a horse. Source of some unrest at the ranch. Falls in love with the whore MAGDALENA. Dies in the street after a knifefight with EDUARDO.	3
John Grady Cole's father	JOHN GRADY COLE's father. A professional poker player. Veteran of World War II and participant in the Bataan Death March. Dies near the end of the first book of the Border Trilogy, *All the Pretty Horses*.	204
John Grady Cole's grandfather	JOHN GRADY COLE's maternal grandfather. Owner of a ranch in central Texas. In the first book of the Border Trilogy, *All the Pretty Horses*, his death presages the selling of the ranch and John Grady's leaving for Mexico.	203
John Grady Cole's mother	JOHN GRADY COLE's mother. Heir to the ranch left by John Grady's maternal grandfather. An actress. Figures in the beginning of the first book of the Border Trilogy, *All the Pretty Horses*.	205
John Prather	Landowner whose ranch is near MAC's.	62
Johnny	TROY and ELTON's brother. Becomes involved with the WOMAN and is ruined by her. Dies in unspoken circumstances. Possibly a suicide.	26
Jones	Man who owns a horse that produced one of ELTON's foals.	26
Josefina	Whore at the White Lake. Observes while the CRIADA makes up MAGDALENA.	99
Junior	Accompanies CRAWFORD on his visit to MAC's ranch to buy JOHN GRADY COLE's horse.	147
Lee Brothers	Famous breeders of dogs. Bred the ALDRIDGE line of dogs, out of which LUCY comes.	
Louis	Assistant to the TALL MAN.	44
Lucy	One of ARCHER's and TRAVIS' hunting dogs. Of a line of dogs bred by the LEE BROTHERS	88

Appendixes 381

Character	Notes	First appearance or mention (page)
	for ALDRIDGE. 'They just forgot to build in the quit.' (88)	
Mac (McGovern)	Owns/runs the ranch where BILLY PARHAM, JOHN GRADY COLE, TROY, and others work. A widower. Holds John Grady in high esteem, almost like an adopted son.	11
Maestro (the blind pianist)	Musician employed by the White Lake. Supporter and adviser of JOHN GRADY COLE. Tells him MAGDALENA is not meant to be 'among us.' (81) Relates to John Grady the story of the patron and the ward. Refuses to become Magdalena's patron.	80
Maestro's daughter *also* 'Maria' (189)	Girl at the White Lake who reads to the blind pianist as he plays.	80
Magdalena	Seventeen-year-old whore with whom JOHN GRADY COLE falls in love. An epileptic. 'Owned' by the pimp EDUARDO.	6 (by name 67)
Maggie (Fountain)	Daughter of COLONEL FOUNTAIN who insists that her eight-year-old son ride with Colonel Fountain on the day of his murder.	62
Maggie (Fountain)'s son	Dies with COLONEL FOUNTAIN.	62
Maggie (Mac's wife, also Margaret)	Wife of MAC. Daughter of MR. JOHNSON. Held in high esteem by both and BILLY PARHAM. Dead.	12 (by name 62)
Manolo	Informant paid by JOHN GRADY COLE for information regarding MAGDALENA's whereabouts.	56
Maud	Owner (or at least the person for whom it is named) of Maud's, a bar where the cowboys from MAC's ranch go to drink beer and play shuffleboard.	117
McKinney	Man whose horses are shown at the auction attended by MAC, OREN, and JOHN GRADY COLE.	110
McNew	Owns a ranch near MAC's ranch.	38
Mexican laborers	Mexican laborers in a truck bound for Sanderson, Texas. BILLY PARHAM comes to their aid when they get a flat tire.	30

Continued

Character	Notes	First appearance or mention (page)
Mr. Johnson	Old man on MAC's ranch. Father of Mac's dead wife, Margaret. 'He'd been born in east Texas in eighteen sixty-seven and come out to this country as a young man. In his time the country had gone from the oil lamp and the horse and buggy to jet planes and the atomic bomb but that wasn't what confused him. It was the fact that his daughter was dead that he couldn't get the hang of.' (106)	9
Musicians	Questioned by JOHN GRADY COLE the day after MAGDALENA's death as to Magdalena's whereabouts.	228
Oliver Lee	Man of dubious reputation. Comes to New Mexico on the promise of being left alone. Possibly involved in the murder of COLONEL FOUNTAIN and his grandson.	61
Orderly	Orderly at the Juárez morgue. Takes JOHN GRADY COLE to MAGDALENA's corpse. Verifies her identity.	229
Oren	Works on MAC's ranch with BILLY PARHAM, JOHN GRADY COLE, TROY, and others. 'He'd not always been a cowboy. He'd been a miner in northern Mexico and he'd fought in wars and revolutions and he'd been an oilfield roustabout in the Permian Basin and a mariner under three different flags. He'd even been married once.' (152)	8
Oren's father-in-law	Father of OREN's wife. When he dies, Oren's mother-in-law moves in with Oren and his wife. They are divorced shortly thereafter.	202
Oren's mother-in-law	Mother of OREN's wife. Cause of the divorce of OREN and his wife. 'The mother was just a goddamned awful woman.' (202)	202
Oren's wife	OREN's wife, to whom he is married for three years before the mother-in-law moves in, causing the break-up of the marriage.	202
Pawnshop broker	Man who gives JOHN GRADY COLE thirty dollars for John Grady's grandfather's pistol and holster. Explains that all the weapons in his case were someone's grandfather's.	94
Pilgrims	Those who have passed the table rock in the DREAMER's dream.	270

Appendixes

Character	Notes	First appearance or mention (page)
Rachel	ELTON's wife. Cooks dinner for the visiting BILLY PARHAM and TROY. Does not like to be called 'mam.' (23) Encounters the WOMAN at a store and receives a cool reception.	19 (appears on 23)
Ramon Gutiérrez	Mexican cabdriver with whom JOHN GRADY COLE makes arrangements to bring MAGDALENA to the United States.	205
Red	Man whose horses are shown at the auction attended by MAC, OREN, and JOHN GRADY COLE.	109
Rep	Man who harasses the herd MR. JOHNSON works as a younger man. Throws a flaming cat into a herd and causes a stampede.	125
Rider	Encountered by JOHN GRADY COLE shortly after MAGDALENA's death. Presumes that Magdalena has quit John Grady.	230
Roscoe	Dog of high repute commented on by ARCHER and TRAVIS. 'People thought he was part bluetick but he was full leopard cur with a glass eye and he did love to fight.' (88)	88
Schoolchildren and schoolteacher	Schoolchildren and a schoolteacher crossing the road near the crate where JOHN GRADY COLE dies. 'The Sabbath had passed and in the gray Monday dawn a procession of schoolchildren dressed in blue uniforms all alike were being led along the gritty walkway. The woman had stepped from the curb to take them across at the intersection when she saw the man coming up the street all dark with blood bearing in his arms the dead body of his friend.' (261)	261
Shineboy	Fourteen-year-old shoe shiner who advises JOHN GRADY COLE on the ways of women. Longs to be an airplane pilot.	94
Shoeman	Repairs BILLY PARHAM's worn boots at no charge.	265
Socorro	Cook at MAC's ranch.	8
Spurlocks	Ranch or ranchowners for whom TRAVIS and/or ARCHER worked.	90

Continued

Character	Notes	First appearance or mention (page)
Tall man	Man in charge of the delivery and receipt of the lame filly. Unsuccessfully tries to bribe JOHN GRADY COLE to take the lame filly.	44
Thatcher Cole	JOHN GRADY COLE's cousin. Picks up John Grady's body for conduct back to San Angelo.	263
Tiburcio (alcahuete at the White Lake)	Assistant to EDUARDO. Takes money from the patrons at the White Lake. Later fights with BILLY PARHAM and is quickly disarmed and disabled.	69
Traveler	Man in the DREAMER's dream who sleeps on the table rock and dreams of the serranos.	270
Travis	Hunter who pursues mountain lions with hunting dogs. Remembers episodes from the Mexican revolution and American involvement in it. Participates in the hunt for the wild dogs.	88
Troy	Works with BILLY PARHAM and JOHN GRADY COLE on MAC's ranch. Goes with them on excursions to the whorehouses of Juárez. Participates in the hunt for the wild dogs.	3
Troy's father	Father of TROY. Gets in a fistfight with JOHNNY.	28
Uncle Pless	ARCHER's mother's uncle. Made new firing pins for Mexican rebel artillery in his shop on Alameda street.	89
Walter Deveraux	One of the waddies who worked with the younger MR. JOHNSON. Hears the screaming, flaming cat hurled by the REP.	125
Ward	Owner of a stud horse bred to one of MAC's mares.	73
Watson	Owner of a horse JOHN GRADY COLE rides when he goes to look for troubled cattle.	51
Wendell Williams	Man who rides with MR. JOHNSON into Mexico in order to recover seventy head of stolen horses. Fights alongside Mr. Johnson after the recovery.	63
Wolfenbarger	Man who buys a filly (that may or may not be lame when he purchases it) for his wife and wishes to have it trained on MAC's	43 (by name 60)

Appendixes 385

Character	Notes	First appearance or mention (page)
	ranch. Appears at the horseauction and is out-hustled by Mac.	
Wolfenbarger's wife	Recipient of WOLFENBARGER's filly.	43
Woman (Juárez)	Woman who extends an offer to MAGDALENA to come and live with her and her children shortly after Magdalena leaves the hospital. Magdalena is unknown to her.	210
Yardman	Sells JOHN GRADY COLE various items from his junkyard, including window sashes, panes of glass, and an old Mennonite table.	178
Young boy	Goes through JOHN GRADY COLE's pockets after the knifefight with EDUARDO. Responsible for bringing BILLY PARHAM to the dying John Grady.	255

Bibliography

For an extensive and continuously updated multilingual critical bibliography on Cormac McCarthy, please see the Cormac McCarthy Society home page on the World Wide Web at www.cormacmccarthy.com.

Abbey, Edward. *Desert Solitaire, A Season in the Wilderness.* New York: McGraw-Hill, 1968.
Aldridge, John W. 'Cormac McCarthy's Bizarre Genius.' *Atlantic Monthly* (August 1994): 89–96.
Althusser, Louis. *For Marx.* London: Verso, 1996.
Arnold, Edwin T. 'The Last of the Trilogy: First Thoughts on *Cities of the Plain.*' *Perspectives on Cormac McCarthy.* Ed. Arnold and Luce. 221–47.
——. 'Naming, Knowing and Nothingness: McCarthy's Moral Parables.' *Southern Quarterly* 30.4 (1992): 31–50.
——. 'The Mosaic of McCarthy's Fiction.' *Sacred Violence.* Ed. Hall and Wallach. 17–23.
Arnold, Edwin T. and Dianne C. Luce, eds *Perspectives on Cormac McCarthy.* Rev. edn. Jackson: University Press of Mississippi, 1999.
Austin, J. L. *How to Do Things with Words.* New York: Oxford University Press, 1962.
Bailey, Charles. '"Doomed Enterprises" and Faith: The Structure of Cormac McCarthy's *The Crossing.*' *Southwestern American Literature* 20.1 (Fall 1994): 57–67.
——. 'The Last Stage of the Hero's Evolution: Cormac McCarthy's *Cities of the Plain.*' *Southwestern American Literature* 25.1 (Fall 1999): 74–82.
Baker, Carlos. *Hemingway: The Writer As Artist.* 4th edn. Princeton University Press, 1972.
Balfour, Graham. *The Life of Robert Louis Stevenson*, vol. II. New York: Scribner's, 1901.
Barthes, Roland. 'Authors and Writers.' *A Barthes Reader.* Ed. Susan Sontag. New York: Hill and Wang, 1982. 185–93.
——. *Camera Lucida: Reflections on Photography,* trans. Richard Howard. New York: Noonday, 1981.
——. 'L'Effet de réel', *Littérature et réalité.* Paris: Points Seuil, 1982.
——. *Mythologies,* trans. Annette Lavers. St Albans: Paladin, 1973; revised 1976.
Bateman, James A. *Animal Traps and Trapping.* Harrisburg, PA: Stackpole Books, 1988.
Bell, Vereen M. *The Achievement of Cormac McCarthy.* Baton Rouge: Louisiana State University Press, 1988.
——. 'The Ambiguous Nihilism of Cormac McCarthy.' *Southern Literary Journal* 15 (1983): 31–41.

———. 'Between the Wish and the Thing the World Lies Waiting.' *Southern Review* 28.4 (1992): 920–7.
Benjamin, W. *Illuminations*. London: Fontana Press, 1992.
Berman, Art. *From the New Criticism to Deconstruction: The Reception of Structuralism and Post-Structuralism*. Urbana: University of Illinois Press, 1988.
Birkirts, Sven. 'The Lone Soul State.' *New Republic* 211.2 (July 11, 1994): 38–41.
Bleikasten, Andre. 'Fathers in Faulkner.' *The Fictional Father*. Ed. Robert Con Davis. Boston: University of Massachusetts Press, 1981.
Bogue, Ronald. 'Gilles Deleuze: Postmodern Philosopher?' *The Ends of Theory*. Ed. Jerry Herron et al. Detroit: Wayne State University Press, 1996. 166–82.
Borch-Jacobsen, Mikkel. *Lacan: The Absolute Master*, trans. Douglas Brick. Stanford: Stanford University Press, 1991.
Bowie, Malcolm. *Freud, Proust and Lacan*. Cambridge: Cambridge University Press, 1987.
Brown, David E., ed. *The Wolf in the Southwest: The Making of an Endangered Species*. Fourth printing. Tucson: University of Arizona Press, 1992.
———. Telephone interview. August 30, 1998.
Brown, Vinson. *Voices of Earth and Sky: Vision Search of the Native Americans*. Happy Camp, CA: Naturegraph, 1976.
Burroughs, William. *The Western Lands*. London: Picador, 1988.
Busby, Mark. Review of *The Crossing. Southwestern American Literature* 19.2 (1994): 80–1.
Butterworth, D. S. 'Pearls as Swine: Recentering the Marginal in Cormac McCarthy's *Suttree*.' *Sacred Violence*. Ed. Hall and Wallach. 96–101.
Camus, Albert. *The Myth of Sisyphus and Other Essays*. 1942. Trans. Justin O'Brien. New York: Knopf, 1958.
Caputo, John D. *Radical Hermeneutics: Repetition, Deconstruction, and the Hermeneutic Project*. Bloomington: Indiana University Press, 1987.
Carlson, Oliver and Ernest Sutherland Bates. *Hearst: Lord of San Simeon*. New York: Viking, 1937.
Carman, Michael D. *United States Customs and the Maders Revolution*. El Paso: Texas Western Press, 1976.
Castaneda, Carlos. *Journey to Ixtlan: The Lessons of Don Juan*. New York: Pocket Books, 1972.
Coleridge, Samuel Taylor. *Biographia Literaria: The Collected Works of Samuel Taylor Coleridge*. Ed. James Engell and W. Jackson Bate. Vol. VII. Princeton University Press, 1990.
'Contributors'. *The Phoenix* [University of Tennessee *Orange and White* Literary Supplement] October 1959: 12.
Cruickshank, John. *Albert Camus and the Literature of Revolt*. New York: Oxford University Press, 1960.
Cuddon, J. A. *The Penguin Dictionary of Literary Terms and Literary Theory*. London: Penguin, 1992.
Daugherty, Leo. 'Gravers False and True: *Blood Meridian* as Gnostic Tragedy.' *Perspectives on Cormac McCarthy*. Ed. Arnold and Luce. 157–72.
Davie, Donald. *Articulate Energy*. London: Routledge & Kegan Paul, 1955.
Davies, Sir John. *A Discovery of the True Causes Why Ireland Was Never Entirely Subdued [And] Brought Under Obedience of the Crown of England Until the Beginning of His Majesty's Happy Reign*. 1612. Ed. James P. Myers, Jr. Washington, D.C.: Catholic University Press, 1988.

Deleuze, Gilles. *Difference and Repetition*, trans. Paul Patton. New York: Columbia University Press, 1994.
Donoghue, Denis. Personal interview. December 5, 1995.
Eagleton, Terry. *Marxism and Literary Criticism*. London: Routledge, 1976.
Eliot, T. S. 'Ulysses, Order, and Myth.' *Selected Prose of T. S. Eliot*. Frank Kermode, ed. Ny: Harcourt Brace, 1975. 175–8.
Ellis, Albert. *The American Sexual Tragedy*. New York: Twayne Publishers, 1954.
Emerson, Ralph Waldo. 'The American Scholar.' *Selected Essays*. New York: Penguin, 1982.
Eron, Leonard D. 'Introduction' to *Aggressive Behavior: Current Perspectives*. Ed. L. Rowell Huesmann. New York: Plenum Press, 1994.
Evenson, Brian. 'McCarthy's Wanderers: Nomadology, Violence, and Open Country.' *Sacred Violence*. Ed. Hall and Wallach. 41–8.
Faulkner, William. *Absalom, Absalom!* New York: Vintage International, 1990.
———. Unattributed quotation from *A Sound Portrait of William Faulkner*. A Question of Place series, Part 8. National Public Radio: 1980.
Fiedler, Leslie. *The Return of the Vanishing American*. St Albans: Paladin, 1968.
Florescano, Enrique. *Memory, Myth, and Time in Mexico: From the Aztecs to Independence*. Austin: University of Texas Press, 1994.
Foster, R. F. *Modern Ireland: 1600–1972*. New York: Penguin, 1989.
Fraser, J. T. *Time, the Familiar Stranger*. Amherst: University of Massachusetts Press, 1987.
Fukuyama, Francis. *The End of History and the Last Man*. London: Hamish Hamilton, 1992.
"Gardner's [sic] Son' on PBS This Week, Written by Louisvillian.' *News-Sentinel* [Knoxville, TN] (January 2, 1977): G7.
Gass, William. *Habitations of the Word*. New York: Simon & Shuster, 1985.
Goncourt, Edmund and Jules de. *Pages from the Goncourt Journal*. Ed. and trans. Robert Baldick. New York: Penguin, 1984.
Gordon, George, Lord Byron. From *Childe Harold's Pilgrimage, a Romaunt*. Ed. Kermode and Hollander. 293–307.
Grammer, John M. 'A Thing Against Which Time Will Not Prevail: Pastoral and History in Cormac McCarthy's South.' *Southern Quarterly* 30 (1992): 19–30.
Gray, I. Thord. *Gringo Rebel*. Coral Gables, Florida: University of Miami Press, 1960.
Gregory, Lady Isabella. *Cuchulain of Muirthemne: The Story of the Men of the Red Branch of Ulster. A Treasury of Irish Myth, Legend, and Folklore*. Ed. Claire Booss. New York: Crown Press, 1986. 327–704.
———. From *Don Juan*. Ed. Kermode and Hollander. 315–72.
———. From *Lara*. Ed. Kermode and Hollander. 290–2.
Hall, Wade and Rick Wallach, eds *Sacred Violence: A Reader's Companion to Cormac McCarthy*. El Paso: Texas Western Press, 1995.
Hamon, Philippe. *Du descriptif*. Paris: Hachette, 1993.
Hanrahan, Gene Z. *The Bad Yankee El Peligro Yankee: Documents of the Mexican Revolution*, vol. 1. Chapel Hill, NC: Documentary Publications, 1985.
Hart, John Mason. *Revolutionary Mexico: The Coming and Process of the Mexican Revolution*. Berkeley: University of California Press, 1987.
Harvey, David. *The Condition of Postmodernity*. Cambridge: Blackwell, 1990.
Hass, Robert. 'Travels with a She-Wolf.' *The New York Times Book Review* (June 1994): 1, 38–40.
Heaney, Seamus. 'The Act of Union.' *North*. London: Faber, 1975. 49–50.
Heidegger, Martin. *Being and Time*, trans. John Macquarrie and Edward Robinson. New York: Harper & Row, 1962.

Bibliography

Hemingway, Ernest. *Selected Letters: 1917–1961*. Ed. Carlos Baker. New York: Scribner's, 1981.
Hesse, Herman. *Siddhartha*, trans. Hilda Rosner. New York: New Directions, 1951.
Hite, Molly. *Ideas of Order in the Novels of Thomas Pynchon*. Columbus: Ohio State University Press, 1983.
Holman, C. Hugh. *A Handbook to Literature*. Indianapolis: Bobbs-Merrill Educational Publishing, 1980.
Hunt, Alex. 'Right and False Suns: Cormac McCarthy's *The Crossing* and the Advent of the Atomic Age.' *Southwestern American Literature* 32.2 (Spring 1998): 31–7.
Irwin, John T. *Doubling and Incest/Repetition and Revenge: A Speculative Reading of Faulkner*. Baltimore: Johns Hopkins University Press, 1975.
James, Henry. 'Preface to the New York Edition of *The Portrait of a Lady*.' *The Portrait of a Lady*. Ed. Robert D. Bamberg. New York: Norton, 1975. 3–15.
Jameson, Fredric. *Postmodernism, or The Cultural Logic of Late Capitalism*. London: Verso, 1991.
———. *The Ideologies of Theory. Essays 1971–1986. Volume 1: Situations of Theory*. Minneapolis: University of Minnesota Press, 1988.
———. *The Ideologies of Theory. Essays 1971–1986. Volume 2: Syntax of History*. Minneapolis: University of Minnesota Press, 1988.
———. *The Political Unconscious: Narrative as a Socially Symbolic Act*. London: Routledge, 1989.
Jarrett, Robert L. *Cormac McCarthy*. London: Twayne, 1997.
Jenkins, Keith. 'Introduction: On Being Open About Our Closures.' *The Postmodern History Reader*. Ed. Keith Jenkins. London: Routledge, 1997. 1–30.
Jordan, Richard. '"Just Write" Says Successful Author.' *Daily Beacon* [University of Tennessee] January 28, 1969: 6.
Joyce, James. *A Portrait of the Artist As A Young Man*. New York: Viking, 1964.
———. *Ulysses*. London: Penguin Books, 1986.
Joyce, P. W. 'The Druids: Their Function and Powers.' *The Druid Source Book: From the Earliest Times to the Present Day*. Ed. John Matthews. London: Blandford Press, 1997. 42–54.
Kartiganer, Donald. 'Faulkner's Art of Repetition.' *Faulkner and the Craft of Fiction: Faulkner and Yoknapatawpha*. 1987. Ed. Ann Abadie and Doreen Fowler. Jackson: University Press of Mississippi, 1989. 21–47.
Kayser, Wolfgang. *The Grotesque in Art and Literature*. 1957. Trans. Ulrich Weisstein. Bloomington: Indiana University Press, 1963.
Kermode, Frank and John Hollander, gen. eds *The Oxford Anthology of English Literature*, vol. II. New York: Oxford University Press, 1973.
Kierkegaard, Søren. *Fear and Trembling/Repetition*, trans. and ed. Howard V. Hong and Edna H. Hong. Princeton University Press, 1983.
Kreml, Nancy. 'Stylistic Variation and Cognitive Constraint in *All the Pretty Horses*'. *Sacred Violence*. Ed. Hall and Wallach. 137–48.
Kristeva, Julia. *Desire in Language: A Semiotic Approach to Literature and Linguistics*. New York: Columbia University Press, 1980.
———. *Powers of Horror: An Essay on Abjection*, trans. Leon S. Roudiez. New York: Columbia University Press, 1982.
———. 'Women's Time.' *The Kristeva Reader*. Ed. Toril Moi. New York: Columbia University Press 1986. 188–213.
———. 'Word Dialogue and Novel.' *The Kristeva Reader*. Ed. Moi. 34–61.

Lacan, Jacques. *Écrits: A Selection*, trans. Alan Sheridan. New York: W. W. Norton & Co., 1977.

———. *Four Fundamental Concepts of Psycho-Analysis*, trans. Alan Sheridan. New York: Norton, 1981.

Langer, Susanne K. *Philosophy in a New Key*. New York: The New American Library, 1955.

Lauter, Paul et al. Introduction to 'Colonial Period' in *The Heath Anthology of American Literature*, vol. 1. Lexington, MA: Heath, 1990.

Lawrence, D. H. *Studies in Classic American Literature*. Harmondsworth: Penguin, 1971.

Lechte, John. *Julia Kristeva*. London: Routledge, 1990.

Limerick, Patricia Nelson. *The Legacy of Conquest: The Unbroken Past of the American West*. New York: Norton, 1988.

Link, Mike and Kate Crowley. *Following the Pack: The World of Wolf Research*. Stillwater, MN: Voyageur Press, 1994.

Longhurst, Derek, ed. *Gender Genre and Narrative Pleasure*. London: Unwin Hyman, 1989.

Lonigan, Paul R. *The Druids: Priests of the Ancient Celts*. Westport: Greenwood Press, 1996.

Luce, Dianne C. 'Cormac McCarthy's First Screenplay: *The Gardener's Son*.' *Perspectives on Cormac McCarthy*. Ed. Arnold and Luce. 69–94.

———. 'The Murderers Behind *Child of God*.' Cormac McCarthy International Colloquy. El Paso, Texas. October 16, 1998.

———. 'The Road and the Matrix: The World as Tale in *The Crossing*.' *Perspectives on Cormac McCarthy*. Ed. Arnold and Luce. 195–219.

———. '"When You Wake": John Grady Cole's Heroism in *All the Pretty Horses*.' *Sacred Violence*. Ed. Hall and Wallach. 155–67.

Lundberg, Ferdinand. *Imperial Hearst: A Social Biography*. 1936. Westport Connecticut: Greenwood Press, 1970.

Mandel, Ernest. *An Introduction to Marxist Economic Theory*. New York: Pathfinder, 1973.

———. *Late Capitalism*. London: Verso, 1978.

Mann, Thomas. *Tonio Kröger*. From *Death in Venice and Other Stories*, trans. David Luke. New York: Bantam Books, 1988.

Marcuse, Herbert. *Eros and Civilization: A Philosophical Inquiry into Freud*. London: Ark, 1987.

Markdale, Jean. *The Celts: Uncovering the Mythic and Historic Origins of Western Culture*. Rochester: Inner Traditions Press, 1993.

Marx, Karl. *Capital: A Critique of Political Economy Volume 3*. London: Penguin, 1991.

———. *Grundrisse: Foundations of the Critique of Political Economy*. London: Penguin, 1993.

Marx, Karl, and Engels, Frederick. *The Communist Manifesto*. Toronto: Canadian Scholar's Press, 1987.

———. *The German Ideology*. London: Lawrence and Wishart, 1974.

McBride, Roy T. 'Status of the Gray Wolf (*Canis lupus baileyi*) in Mexico: A Progress Report to the U.S. Fish and Wildlife Service,' 1978.

McCarthy, C. J. [Cormac]. 'A Drowning Incident.' *The Phoenix* [University of Tennessee *Orange and White* Literary Supplement] March 1960: 3–4.

McCarthy, C. J., Jr. [Cormac]. 'Wake for Susan.' *The Phoenix* [University of Tennessee *Orange and White* Literary Supplement] October 1959: 3–6.

McCarthy, Cormac. *All the Pretty Horses*. New York: Vintage, 1993.

———. *Blood Meridian or the Evening Redness in the West.* London: Picador, 1990.
———. *Child of God.* New York: Vintage, 1973.
———. *Cities of the Plain.* New York: Alfred A. Knopf, 1998. Vol. 3 of the Border Trilogy. 3 vols. 1993–98.
———. *The Crossing.* New York: Alfred A. Knopf, 1994. Vol. 2 of the Border Trilogy. 3 vols. 1993–98.
———. *The Gardener's Son: A Screenplay.* Hopewell, NJ: Ecco, 1996.
———. Shooting script of *The Gardener's Son*, ts. Richard Inman Pearce Collection. South Caroliniana Library. University of South Carolina.
———. *The Orchard Keeper.* 1965. New York: Vintage, 1993.
———. *Outer Dark.* 1968. New York: Vintage, 1993.
———. *The Stonemason: A Play in Five Acts.* Hopewell, NJ: Ecco Press, 1994.
———. *Suttree.* New York: Vintage, 1986.
———. 'The Wolf Trapper.' *Esquire* 120:1 (July 1993): 95–104.
McElroy, Bernard. *Fiction of the Modern Grotesque.* New York: St. Martin's Press, 1989.
McHale, Brian. *Postmodernist Fiction.* London: Routledge, 1987.
McIntyre, Rick, ed. *War Against the Wolf: America's Campaign to Exterminate the Wolf.* Stillwater, MN: Voyageur Press, 1995.
Melville, Herman. *Moby Dick.* Harmondsworth: Penguin, 1972.
———. *Pierre or, The Ambiguities; Israel Potter: His Fifty Years of Exile; The Piazza Tales; The Confidence-Man: His Masquerade; Uncollected Prose; Billy Budd, Sailor (An Inside Narrative).* New York: Library of America, 1984.
Messent, P. 'All The Pretty Horses: Cormac McCarthy's Mexican Western.' *Borderlines* 2:2 (December 1994).
Meyer, Michael C. Introduction. *The Border and the Revolution.* By Charles H. Harris III and Louis Sadler. Las Cruces, New Mexico: New Mexico State University, 1988.
Miller, Arthur. *Death of A Salesman* in *The Portable Arthur Miller.* Ed. Harold Clurman. New York: Viking, 1971. Reprint. New York: Penguin Books, 1977.
Miller, Henry. *Aller Retour New York.* New York: New Directions, 1991.
Miller, J. Hillis. *Fiction and Repetition: Seven English Novels.* Cambridge, MA: Harvard University Press, 1982.
Milner, C. A., ed. *Major Problems in American Western History.* Lexington: D. C. Heath, 1989.
Minh-Ha, Trinh. T. *Framer Framed.* New York: Routledge, 1991.
Morrison, Gail Moore. 'All the Pretty Horses: John Grady Cole's Expulsion from Paradise.' *Perspectives on Cormac McCarthy.* Ed. Arnold and Luce. 175–94.
Mottram, Eric. *Blood on the Nash Ambassador.* London: Radius, 1989.
Muller, Gilbert H. *Nightmares and Visions: Flannery O'Connor and the Catholic Grotesque.* Athens: University of Georgia Press, 1972.
Naef, Weston J. *Era of Exploration: The Rise of Landscape Photography in the American West, 1860–1885.* Buffalo: Albright Knox Art Gallery, 1975.
Neumann, Erich. *The Great Mother: An Analysis of the Archetype,* trans. Ralph Manheim. New York: Princeton University Press, 1972.
Nicholls, Kenneth. *Gaelic and Gaelicised Ireland in the Middle Ages.* Dublin: Gill and MacMillan, 1972.
Nietzsche, Friedrich. 'On Truth and Lies in a Nonmoral Sense.' *The Rhetorical Tradition: Readings from Classical Times to the Present.* Ed. Patricia Bizzell and Bruce Herzberg. Boston: Bedford Books, 1990. 888–96.

———. *Thus Spoke Zarathustra*, trans. R. J. Hollingdale. London: Penguin Books, 1961.
O'Connot, Flannery. *Mystery and Manners*. Ed. Sally and Robert Fitzgerald. New York: Farrar, Straus & Giroux, 1969.
Palmer, Bryan D. *Descent into Discourse: The Reification of Language and the Writing of Social History*. Philadelphia: Temple University Press, 1990.
Parrish, Tim. 'The Killer Wears the Halo: Cormac McCarthy, Flannery O'Connor, and the American Religion.' *Sacred Violence*. Ed. Hall and Wallach. 25–39.
Paster, Gail Kern. *The Body Embarrassed: Drama and the Disciplines of Shame in Early Modern England*. Ithaca: Cornell University Press, 1993.
Pattison, Felicia S. 'Incest.' April 14, 1999. Online posting. The Cormac McCarthy Forum. July 23, 1999. <http://www.discussionontheweb.com/cormacmccarthy/getthread.asp/>
Pearce, Richard Inman. 'Foreword.' *The Gardener's Son*. Hopewell, NJ: Ecco, 1996: v–vi.
———. Research newsletter [c. April 7, 1975]. Richard Inman Pearce Collection. South Caroliniana Library. University of South Carolina.
———. Research newsletter, October 8, 1975. Richard Inman Pearce Collection. South Caroliniana Library. University of South Carolina.
Phillips, Dana. 'History and the Ugly Facts of Cormac McCarthy's *Blood Meridian*'. *American Literature* 68(2) (June 1996): 433–60.
Pilkington, Tom. 'Fate and Free Will on the American Frontier: Cormac McCarthy's Western Fiction.' *Western American Literature* 27.4 (1993): 311–22.
———. *My Blood's Country*. Fort Worth: Texas Christian University Press, 1973.
———. *State of Mind: Texas Literature and Culture*. College Station: Texas A&M University Press, 1998.
Plimpton, George, ed. *Writers at Work: The Paris Review Interviews*. New York: Penguin, 1977.
Poe, Edgar Allan. 'The Fall of the House of Usher.' *'The Fall of the House of Usher' and Other Writings*. New York: Penguin, 1986. 138–57.
Poirier, Richard. 'Humans, Review of Slow Learner by Thomas Pynchon.' *London Review of Books* 24 (January 1985): 18.
Poland, Tim. 'And the Word Becomes Horseflesh: The Unheard Discourse of Cormac McCarthy's *All the Pretty Horses*.' *Southwestern American Literature* 20.1 (Fall 1994): 45–56.
Pughe, Thomas. 'Revision and Vision: Cormac McCarthy's *Blood Meridian*'. *Revue Française D'Etudes Americaines* 17/62 (1994): 371–82.
Puttenham, George. 'The Art of English Poesy.' *The Renaissance in England: Non-dramatic Prose and Verse of the Sixteenth Century*. Ed. Hyder E. Rollins and Herschel Baker. Prospect Heights: Waveland Press Inc., 1992.
Rabelais, François. *The Portable Rabelais*. Ed. Samuel Putnam. New York: Viking, 1946.
Ragan, David P. 'Values and Structure in *The Orchard Keeper*.' *Southern Quarterly* 30 (1992): 10–18.
Ricks, Christopher. 'Robert Lowell: "The War of Words."' *The Force of Poetry*. Oxford: Clarendon Press, 1995.
Riding, Alan. *Distant Neighbors*. New York: Vintage Books, 1989.
Rilke, Rainer Maria. *The Notebooks of Malte Laurids Brigge*, trans. Stephen Mitchell. New York: Vintage Books, 1983.
Robinson, James Oliver. *American Myth American Reality*. New York: Hill and Wang, 1980.
Ross, Marc H. 'Social Structure, Psychocultural Dispositions, and Violent Conflict: Extensions from a Cross-cultural Study.' *Aggression and Peacefulness in Humans and*

Other Primates. Ed. James Silverberg and J. Patrick Gray. New York: Oxford University Press, 1992. 272–99.

Said, Edward. *Culture and Imperialism*. London: Vintage, 1994.

Schopen, Bernard A. '"They Rode On": *Blood Meridian* and the Art of Narrative'. *Western American Literature*, 30.2 (1995): 179–94.

Schor, Naomi. *Lectures du detail*. Paris: Nathan 1994 (French translation of *Reading in Detail: Aesthetics and the Feminine*. London: Methuen, 1987).

Scoones, Jacqueline. 'McCarthy's "Girls" and the Ethics of Dwelling in *The Border Trilogy*.' American Literature Association Conference. Baltimore, Maryland. 28 May 1999.

Scott, Sir Walter. 'Proud Maisie.' *The Norton Anthology of English Literature, Vol II*. Sixth Edition. Eds M. H. Abrams et al. New York: Norton, 1993. 322–3.

Sepich, John. *Notes on Blood Meridian*. Louisville: Bellarmine CP, 1993.

Shakespeare, William. *The Life of King Henry the Fifth* in *The Complete Works of Shakespeare*. Edited by David Bevington. Glenview: Scott, 1980.

———. *The Tragedy of Hamlet* in *The Complete Works of Shakespeare*. Edited by David Bevington. Glenview: Scott, 1980.

Shapiro, James. *Shakespeare and the Jews*. New York: Columbia University Press, 1996.

Shaviro, Steven. '"The Very Life of the Darkness": A Reading of *Blood Meridian*.' *Perspectives on Cormac McCarthy*. Ed. Arnold and Luce. 143–56.

Simpson, Lewis. *Dispossessed Garden: Pastoral and History in Southern Literature*. Ann Arbor: Books on Demand, 1983.

———. 'Southern Fiction.' *The Harvard Guide to Contemporary American Writing*. Ed. Daniel Hoffman. Cambridge, MA: Belknap Press of Harvard University Press, 1979.

Slotkin, Richard. *Gunfighter Nation: The Myth of the Frontier in Twentieth Century America*. New York: Harper Perennial, 1992.

———. *The Fatal Environment: The Myth of the Frontier in the Age of Industrialization, 1800–1890*. New York: Atheneum, 1985.

Solnit, Rebecca. 'Scapeland.' *Crimes and Splendors: The Desert Cantos of Richard Misrach*. Boston: Bullfinch / Little, Brown, in association with The Museum of Fine Arts, Houston, 1996: 40.

Spencer, William C. 'Altered States of Consciousness in *Suttree*.' *Southern Quarterly* 35.2 (1997): 87–92.

Spenser, Edmund. *The Faerie Queene: Books I to III*. Ed. Douglas Brooks-Davies. Introduction and other critical apparatus. J. M. Dent. London: Everyman Library, 1993.

Stephanson, Anders. 'Regarding Postmodernism: A Conversation with Fredric Jameson.' *Postmodernism, Jameson, Critique*. Ed. Douglas Kellner. Washington: Maisonneuve Press, 1989. 43–74.

Sullivan, Nell. 'Cormac McCarthy and the Text of *Jouissance*.' *Sacred Violence*. Ed. Hall and Wallach. 115–23.

Sullivan, Walter. *A Requiem for the Renascence: The State of Fiction in the Modern South*. Athens: University of Georgia Press, 1976.

Swanberg, W. A. *Citizen Hearst*. New York: Scribner, 1961.

Tate, Allen. 'The Profession of Letters in the South.' *Essays of Four Decades*. Chicago: Swallow Press, 1968.

Thoreau, Henry David. 'From Walden, or Life in the Woods.' *The Norton Anthology of American Literature*. 3rd edn. Eds Nana Baym et al. New York: W. W. Norton & Co, 1989. 728–826.

———. *The Journal of Henry David Thoreau: Volume I: 1837–1846*. Ed. Bradford Torrey and Francis H. Allen. Salt Lake City: Smith, 1984.
———. *Walden*, in *The Portable Thoreau*. Ed. Carl Bede. New York: Viking, 1947.
Thurber, James. *Selected Letters of James Thurber*. Ed. Helen Thurber and Edward Weeks. New York: Little, Brown, 1981.
Toch, Hans. *Violent Men*. Rev. edn. Cambridge, MA: Schenkman Publishing Co., 1984.
Tompkins, Jane. *West of Everything: The Inner Life of Westerns*. Oxford: Oxford University Press, 1992.
Trachtenberg, Alan. *The Incorporation of America*. New York: Hill & Wang, 1982.
Trollope, Anthony. *Dr. Thorne*. London: The Zodiac Press, 1951.
Truettner, W., ed. *The West as America*. Washington: Smithsonian Institute Press, 1991.
Turner, Frederick Jackson. *The Frontier in American History*. Ed. Ray Billington. New York: Holt, Rinehart and Winston, 1962.
———. 'The Significance of the Frontier in American History.' *Major Problems in the History of the American West*. Ed. Clyde A Milner II. Lexington: Heath, 1989. 2–21.
United States Government Printing Office. 'Control of Predatory Animals.' House Doc. #496, 70th Congress, 2d session. Committee on Agriculture. January 3, 1929.
United States Government Printing Office. 'Predatory and Other Wild Animal Control.' House Rept. #2396, 71st Congress, 3d session. January 27, 1931.
Uruburu, Paula. *The Gruesome Doorway: An Analysis of the American Grotesque*. New York: Peter Lang, 1987.
Valzelli, Luigi. *Psychobiology of Aggression and Violence*. New York: Raven Press, 1981.
Vanderwood, Paul J. and Frank N. Samponaro. *Border Fury: A Picture Postcard Record of Mexico's Revolution and U.S. War Preparedness 1910–1917*. Albuquerque: University of New Mexico Press, 1988.
Virgil. *The Aeneid*, trans. Robert Fitzgerald. New York: Random House, 1983.
Voltaire. *Candide*, in *The Portable Voltaire*. Ed. Ben Ray Redman. New York: The Viking Press, 1968.
Wallach, Rick. 'Judge Holden, *Blood Meridian*'s Evil Archon.' *Sacred Violence*. Ed. Hall and Wallach. 125–36.
Walter, Jacob. *The Diary of A Napoleonic Foot Soldier*. New York: Penguin, 1993.
Wegner, John. 'Whose Story is it?: History and Fiction in Cormac McCarthy's *All the Pretty Horses*'. *Southern Quarterly* 36.2 (Winter 1998): 103–10.
Witek, Terri. 'Reeds and Hides: Cormac McCarthy's Domestic Spaces.' *Southern Review* 30.1 (1994): 136–42.
Woodson, Linda Townley. 'Deceiving the Will to Truth: The Semiotic Foundation of *All the Pretty Horses*.' *Sacred Violence*. Ed. Hall and Wallach. 149–54.
Woodward, Richard B. 'Venomous Fiction.' *The New York Times Magazine* (April 19, 1992), natl. edn, sec. 6: 28+.
Young, Thomas Daniel. *Tennessee Writers*. Knoxville: University of Tennessee Press, 1981.
Young, Thomas D. Jr. 'The Imprisonment of Sensibility: *Suttree*.' *Perspectives on Cormac McCarthy*. Ed. Arnold and Luce. 95–120.

Index

Note: 'n' after a page reference indicates a note number on that page.

Abbey, Edward 93
absurdity 37, 38, 41, 47, 49, 53
Alderson, Tom 2
Aldridge, John 100
All the Pretty Horses 8–9, 125, 131, 142, 203, 213, 220, 245, 256, 258; border crossings in 227, 231–6, 237, 244; chess in 269, 270–1; female characters 259–60, 261, 262, 279–80, 281; Mexican Revolution 188–9, 250; myths of the West 225; repetition in 272–84; as romance 245, 294–5; violence in 263
American Dream 171, 173, 225
American literary tradition, youthful heroes in 233, 245, 274
animals 43–4, 237, 266; *see also* horses; wolves
anti-heroism 9, 51, 293, 294, 296, 299, 300, 301
Appalachian novels xv, 16, 17
Arena Stage 141, 144, 145, 149, 150–1
Arnold, Edwin T. 115n, 198n, 241, 247, 273
atavistic vision 108–15
atomic tests 243
authorship 190
Aztec history 230

Bailey, Charles 236, 242
Balfour, Graham 119
barbarism 217
barter 172

Barthes, Roland 91, 207, 212, 214, 219
Bell, Vereen 46, 56, 66, 114, 197, 257
Benedict, Pinckney 5–6
Benjamin, Walter 217
Bildungsroman 17, 257, 274, 283
Birkirts, Sven 241
Blood Meridian 8, 10, 35, 90, 98n, 215, 257, 282, 283; chess in 269; compared with *All the Pretty Horses* 273; dead children in 19; history of the West in 217–25; language in 84–5, 91, 191, 192, 194–5, 197, 201–3; narrative voice in 25; readings of 187; resurrection scene 180–1; revisionism 192, 195–6, 218, 220, 221, 222–5
Bloom, Harold 293
Bogue, Ronald 268
Borch-Jacobson, Mikkel 283
border crossings 227, 229, 231, 234, 236–7, 246
Border Trilogy xv, 8–10, 227; ideology of representation in 185–97; language in 201–8; *see also All the Pretty Horses; Cities of the Plain; The Crossing*
Bowie, Malcolm 278
boyhood 39; initiation 231, 233, 244, 245, 295; youthful heroes 233, 245, 274
Boyle, Richard 66
Brown, Larry, *Father and Son* 6
Brown, Vinson 100, 101, 102, 103, 104, 105, 106–7

Burroughs, William 225
Byron, Lord George 293–4, 299

Camus, Albert 37, 38, 40, 41, 43, 52, 53
capitalism 175, 187–8, 195–6, 198n
Cardenas, Lazaro 251
Castaneda, Carlos 101, 105
characters 83–4, 85, 86, 108; in *The Stonemason* 127–8
chess 269–71, 297
Child of God 17, 22, 83–4, 90, 108, 109, 139; dead girlfriend motif 73, 74–6, 77
Cities of the Plain 19, 149, 190–1, 227, 228, 256–7; border crossings in 244–8; chess scenes 271; epilogue 188, 189, 190, 192, 194, 196, 206, 215, 230, 247; female characters 70, 77, 261–2; hero in 293, 294, 295–7, 298; and Mexico 250, 253; violence in 264
Cold Mountain (Frazier) 6–7
Coleridge, S. T. 78
colonization, resistance to 55–6, 58
commas 166–9
commodification 189, 196
community values 61, 62–3
compassion 267
cowboys, disappearance of 298, 301
crafts 16, 17, 143, 152
creative imagination 21, 22, 23
Crossing, The 35, 77, 121, 188, 194, 208, 210, 228, 258; border crossings in 227, 231, 236–43; female characters 260–1, 262; Mexican Revolution in 250–3; Native American culture 101; photographs in 90, 91, 212–14; relationship between world and reality 203–5; trapping in 288–92; violence in 264, 265
Cruickshank, John 53
Cuchulain 55, 59–60, 63
culture 187, 189; imposition of 56, 57–8, 65

Daugherty, Leo 187
Davie, Donald 81
Davies, Sir John 57, 64
daydreams 16
dead children 19, 83, 85, 223

dead girlfriend motif; in *Child of God* 74–7; in *Outer Dark* 68–73
death 40–1, 108, 112, 232; in *Blood Meridian* 201, 206, 220; female sexuality and 68, 73, 74–6; and the grotesque 41–2, 45, 48; photographs and 214
deconstruction 189; in *Blood Meridian* 193, 194, 195, 196
Deleuze, Gilles 257–8, 268
deserts 210, 211
details 89, 90, 92, 93–4, 95–6, 97
determinism 280, 281, 282, 283–4
dialect 4, 244
dialogue 86–7, 204, 244, 245
Díaz, Porfiro 231, 251
Dr Thorne (Trollope), stonemason in 125–6
dreams 129–30, 131, 189, 207; of horses 235
'Drowning Incident, A' 15, 18–20
druidic religion 61–3
Dumas, Alexandre 120

Ecco Press 142
Echols, W. C. 289, 290
educated diction 4–5, 78, 79–80, 80–1, 86
Eron, Leonard D. 263
Erskine, Albert 3–4, 8, 144
Esquire, proposed profile of McCarthy 3–4
estrangement 37, 38, 90, 273–4, 276; in *The Orchard Keeper* 40, 42, 44, 47, 50, 51, 52
evil 128–9, 201, 234, 240–1, 243
existentiality 42, 43–4, 47, 52, 53

father–son relationships; in *Blood Meridian* 202–3, 224; in *Cities of the Plain* 295–6; in *The Stonemason* 130, 153; in *Suttree* 177–8
Faulkner, William 4–5, 10, 109, 228, 284n
female body 69–70, 74
female characters 70, 73, 74–5, 297–8; in the Border Trilogy 258–63
female sexuality, death and 68, 73, 74–6
Fiedler, Leslie 220
Florescano, Enrique 248n

Index

Foster, R. F. 56, 66
fosterage 59–60, 61
freedom 272; repetition as 281–4
frontier 219–20, 221, 222, 228, 229, 276
futility 110–11

Gaelic society 58–60, 63–4
Gaelic tradition 55–6, 57–8, 65–6
Gardener's Son, The 21, 25, 26, 29–34, 77, 121, 134, 141
Gass, William 89, 93
Gauss, Karl F. 121
God 239–40; in *The Stonemason* 124, 129–30
Grammer, John 57, 109
grotesque 37–8, 41–2, 45; in *The Orchard Keeper* 40, 41, 43

hallucinations 102–3; and recollection 26, 27–8, 29, 31–2, 40, 41, 45
Hamlet (Shakespeare) 139, 295
Hausam, Wiley 143–4, 145, 146, 147, 148, 149, 150, 151
Hearst family 251–2
Heidegger, Martin 284
Hemingway, Ernest 4, 136, 244–5
heroes 9, 293–4, 298, 299, 300, 301; knightly 294, 297; tragic man as 295–6
Hesse, Herman, *Siddhartha* 126
historical artifacts 21–36, 213, 250
history 176, 220, 254–5, 281; literature and 186–7, 190, 196, 218; Marxism and 199n; photography and 212, 213; *see also* past
Hite, Molly 267
Holman, C. H. 256
horses 277, 278–9, 285–7n; dreams of 235
hospitality 63–4
Huckleberry Finn 69, 257
Huerta, Victoriana 250
human beings, dark view of 108, 109, 110
human relationships 43, 266, 267
human responsibility 45, 245–6, 247
Hunt, Alex 243

illusions 232
imagination 39, 40, 53; creative 21, 22, 23

initiation 231, 233, 244, 245, 295
Ireland, English conquest 57–8, 65–6

James, Henry 70–1
Jameson, Fredric 190, 197
Jarrett, Robert 70, 193, 217
Joyce, James 201
Juárez (Mexico) 253–4

Kayser, Wolfgang 37–8, 40
kinship 58–9
Kristeva, Julia 76, 204

Lacan, Jacques 68, 71, 276, 278, 283
landscape 210, 246–7, 261–2
language 188, 189, 191, 197, 207, 278, 283; in *Blood Meridian* 191, 194–5; and reality 201–2, 205–6, 208; and representation 192, 196; storytellers and 189–90
Lauter, Paul 105
Ligon, J. S. 289
Limerick, Patricia N. 210, 218, 285n
literalization 94–5
literary fiction, historical processes in 186–7, 190, 196, 218
literary style 78, 79–80, 243
loss 96–7, 272, 273, 276–9, 283
Luce, Dianne 77n, 248n

McBride, Roy T. 291
McCarthy, Cormac 2–3, 4, 35–6n, 145; assumed to be black 144, 145; early short stories 15–20; influence of 5–7; influence of Faulkner on 4–5, 10, 244; modern or postmodern writer 109, 111–12, 115; opus of 7–10; pen name 55; and *The Stonemason* 145, 147–8, 149–50, 151; style of 4–5, 7, 268
McElroy, Bernard 37, 43, 45
McHale, Brian 109
McMurty, Larry 242
Madero, Francisco I., President of Mexico 231, 250, 252
male psyche 263, 264–5, 266, 267
manifest destiny 193, 202, 219, 221, 222
Mann, Thomas 181
Markdale, Jean 58, 63, 66

Marxism 124–5, 190
Maslon, Larry 145, 146, 147, 148, 150, 151
masonry 126–7, 128, 138, 142–3, 152
meaning 190, 191, 192, 193, 194, 195, 196, 268
Melville, Herman 32, 34, 221, 274, 275
memory 21, 22, 26, 228
Mexican Revolution 231, 249, 250, 251, 253, 254, 280
Mexico 191, 230, 232–3; anti-American sentiment 252–3, 254
Miller, Henry 134
Minh-Ha, T. T. 218
misogyny 68–9, 74, 75, 76–7
modernism 90, 109, 188, 197; and postmodernism 109–10, 111, 115
monologues, in *The Stonemason* 123, 146, 147, 153
Morrison, Gail Moore 232, 234–5, 274, 281
Mottram, Eric 221
Muger, Henri 120
Muller, Gilbert H. 41
mythopoeia 111
myths of the West 218, 219, 223, 225, 229

narration 61–5; in *The Orchard Keeper* 38–40, 42, 43, 46, 201
narrative voice 23, 25, 26–7, 31–2, 87–8
narrative structure 114, 152
Native American mythology 102, 105
Naturalism 265–6
nature 24, 91, 93, 101–2, 237, 247, 275; abuse of 63; human alienation from 243, 246; violence of 44
New Western History 218
Nietzsche, Friedrich 182, 203, 204, 205, 206
nihilism 56, 66, 112, 121
Norris, Frank 168
nostalgia xv, 15, 16, 246
novelistic universe 37, 41, 43, 51–2
novelists, as playwrights 119–20, 149

O'Connor, Flannery 7, 9, 240
Oedipal drama 15, 17, 276, 278–9, 295–6
Old West, code of 273–5

Orchard Keeper, The 16, 17, 18, 21, 22–9, 82–3, 108; imposition and resistance in 55–67; narration in 38–54
order, quest for 111–12, 113, 114
O'Sullivan, Timothy 209–10
Outer Dark 19, 68–73, 76–7, 83, 94–5, 108, 109, 114

parataxis 91–3
Paris, reading *The Stonemason* in 131–4, 135–8
past 111, 211, 212–13, 214, 222, 223, 240, 243; search for 29–30; *see also* history
Paster, Gail K. 69
Pattison, Felicia 70
Pearce, Richard 29, 30, 31, 121, 141, 143
Penn, William 289
Phoenix, The, short stories published in 15, 21
photographs 90, 212–14
photography, information about the West 209–10, 212
Pilkington, Tom 229, 233, 272–3
plays 119–20
plots, of the Border Trilogy 256, 257–8, 262
Poe, Edgar Allan 69, 73
Poirier, Richard 267
possession/dispossession 232–3, 240
postmodernism 190, 191, 208, 218; language and 207; modernism and 109–10, 111, 115
prodigality 15, 17, 171, 177–8
Pulitzer Prize 142
punctuation, lack of 201, 244
Pynchon, Thomas 267

race, in *The Stonemason* 153
racial insensitivity 148–9, 153
racial stereotypes 148–9
Ragan, David P. 48–9, 54, 56, 57, 62
realism 89, 91, 93–4, 96
reality effect 91, 99n
religious faith 61–3
repetition 272, 279–84
representation 188, 192; in *Blood Meridian* 193–4, 196; in the Border Trilogy 193, 194, 215–16

Index

revenge, as history 280–4
revisionism 195–6, 212, 217, 218, 29
rhyme 81–2, 84, 85, 87
rhythmic repetition 81, 82–3, 84, 85, 87, 96
rhythm 201
Richards, Lloyd 143, 146
Ricks, Christopher 94
Riding, Alan 229, 230–1
romance 245, 294–5
Ross, Marc H. 263
rustic diction 4, 78, 79, 86–7

sacrifice 230
Schopen, Bernard 25
Scott, Sir Walter, 'Proud Maisie' 68, 73
Sepich, John 269, 288
Shapiro, James 136
Shaviro, Steven 187, 191
short stories 15–20
Silko, Leslie 243
Simpson, Lewis 228
Slotkin, Richard 219
socialism 124
southern fiction 108–10, 228
southwestern novels xv, 18, 177, 218, 227
Speake, J. W. 30
spirit animals 104–5
Stein, Gertrude 120
Stevenson, R. L. 119
stone 124, 126–7, 131–2, 138, 141
Stonemason, The 119, 120–31, 136–7, 141–3; cancellation of 150–1; discussions on staging 143–4, 145–6; revision of 151–2; stage directions 121–2, 151; workshop format 146–8, 150
stories 204, 205, 207, 211, 227, 239, 242
storytellers/storytelling 189–90, 207, 208, 211, 239, 247
Sullivan, Walter 108–9
Suttree 1–2, 7–8, 54, 77, 78–9, 80, 172; atavistic vision of 110–14; details in 89–99; Gothinburg chapter 92, 96–7; rhythmic repetition 82, 85, 87; vision quest 100–7
syntax 81

temporality 168–9
Thompson, Tazewell 146
Thoreau, Henry 132, 275
Thurber, James 120
Toch, Hans 263
Tompkins, Jane 285–6n
traditional values 47–8, 49, 50, 56, 64, 65
transcoding 197
trappers 289–91
trickster figure 105
Trilling, Lionel 293
Turner, Frederick Jackson 217, 218–19, 219–20, 222, 225
Twain, Mark 257, 274

Urban, Amanda 144
Uruburu, Paula 37, 42

values 49–50, 51; *see also* traditional values
Valzelli, Luigi 265
vernacular style 78, 79, 86–7
violence 48, 230, 263, 265; in the Border Trilogy 263–5; and the grotesque 41–2, 43
vision quest 100–7

Wager, Douglas 144, 145, 147, 150
'Wake for Susan' 15–17, 17–18, 21–5, 68, 73
Wallach, Rick 187, 191, 201–2
Walter, Jacob 127
Welty, Eudora 111
West 220–1, 222, 225, 298; codes of 273, 274–5; history of 273–4; revisionist history 217–25
Westerns 274–5, 283, 299
Winchell, Mark R. 57
wolves 288, 289, 291–2, 298–9
women: in *Child of God* 74–7; in *Outer Dark* 68–73; portrayal of 68; *see also* female characters
Woodson, Linda 285n
Woodward, Richard B. 141
words 81, 82, 86, 87, 89, 90, 93, 94, 95, 96–7, 187
Wordsworth, William 78
writing 187, 188, 208

EU authorised representative for GPSR:
Easy Access System Europe, Mustamäe tee 50,
10621 Tallinn, Estonia
gpsr.requests@easproject.com

www.ingramcontent.com/pod-product-compliance
Ingram Content Group UK Ltd.
Pitfield, Milton Keynes, MK11 3LW, UK
UKHW021837140426
5217IPUK00021B/1492